# Law of Internet Speech

# Law of Internet Speech

Madeleine Schachter

CAROLINA ACADEMIC PRESS
Durham, North Carolina

ISBN 0-89089-944-4
LCCN 00-109581

CAROLINA ACADEMIC PRESS
700 Kent Street
Durham, North Carolina 27701
Telephone (919) 489-7486
Fax (919) 493-5668
www.cap-press.com

Printed in the United States of America

*for*

*David Stagliano,*
*Mark and Emily*

# Contents

# Preface

Free speech has long been recognized as critical to a free society. First Amendment jurisprudence evinces a clear and strident commitment to promoting unencumbered discourse, while seeking to accommodate interests that vie for protection. Thus, under certain circumstances, one may be held culpable for false and defamatory speech. Likewise, privacy interests sometimes yield to free expression. Similarly, the constitutionally-rooted proprietary interests in expressive content may be protected from unbridled reproduction.

Recent technological advances have made both the acquisition and the dissemination of information possible in unprecedented fashion. Access to information is now readily available virtually instantaneously, on a global basis. The distribution of content, both by the originator and by others, similarly transcends geographic boundaries and covers topics of unprecedented scope.

Are emerging technologies to be governed by a separate framework, imposed through newly-devised judicial constructs and legislative mandate? Are cyberspace[1] communications to be evaluated by application of existing principles, adapted to accommodate qualitative differences of speed and expanse? Under what circumstances, and under what rationales, do on-line communications warrant different treatment from that afforded to more "traditional" content dissemination?

The materials included in this book intermingle discussion of the inter-disciplinary jurisprudence on "traditional" media cases with the emerging jurisprudence on Internet media in order to promote foundational and contextual analysis. The author is an in-house attorney at Time Warner Trade Publishing Inc., which is part of Time Warner Inc. In January 2000, America Online, Inc. and Time Warner Inc. announced an agreement to merge. The materials included in this book, which contain divergent viewpoints, are intended to serve as an intellectual catalyst to provoke discussion and thought. But to the extent views are inferred, nothing herein should be construed as necessarily expressing the views of anyone other than the author.

This book examines the fundamental principles of free speech, the nature of the Internet, and the analytical framework for application of traditional First Amendment analyses to digital media. The evolving caselaw concerning the scope of permissible regulatory intervention by government is also covered. Reputational, privacy, and propri-

---

1. The term "cyberspace" has been used in this book as it is colloquially, to refer to computer communications generally; the term "Internet" is broader than the "World Wide Web," *see infra* at 7–10. "Traditional media" as used herein refers to such media as print and broadcast; of course, the rapid entrenchment of the Internet as a means of communications refutes any inference that it, too, has not become a conventional and customary vehicle for speech.

etary interests are then explored insofar as they impinge on electronic communications. A glossary of Internet terms is included to assist the reader.

In light of the extraordinary fluidity and growth of on-line communications, materials included in this work[2] no doubt will deserve updating even before the book goes to press in mid-2000. The work therefore is intended to serve as a foundation for courses on Internet speech, and may be supplemented as appropriate by other materials or by links and cites to sources for legal developments.

---

2. Footnotes, headings, and citations to case records have been selectively omitted, and other stylistic modifications have been made to court decisions, statutes, and secondary sources, in order to promote consistency and facilitate review. Footnotes within cases, to the extent they have been included herein, correspond to the footnote numbers in the published reports.

# Acknowledgments

This book came together because of the extraordinary efforts of many people, to whom I am extremely grateful.

The content of the book was editorially reviewed by Paul D. Connuck of Kramer Levin Naftalis & Frankel; Kevin W. Goering of Coudert Brothers; Bruce E.H. Johnson of Davis Wright Tremaine; Bruce P. Keller of Debevoise & Plimpton; Robert P. LoBue and Stephanie B. Glaser of Patterson Belknap Webb & Tyler; Jeffrey D. Neuburger of Brown Raysman Millstein Felder & Steiner; Robert Penchina of Clifford Chance Rogers & Wells; Dean Ringel of Cahill Gordon & Reindel; David A. Schulz of Clifford Chance Rogers & Wells and also an Adjunct Associate Professor at Fordham Law School; and Peter J. Spiro, Professor of Law at Hofstra University. They generously gave their time and extensive expertise to provide insightful and thoughtful comments.

Fordham Law School students Melissa P. Gellert, Daphna Bar-Zuri, and Edina Ghazarossian ably and enthusiastically provided editorial review and cite-checking assistance, and Fordham Law School students Thomas Maeglin and Todd Higgins kindly spent considerable time checking citations. I also thank Fordham Law School, and in particular John D. Feerick, Michael M. Martin, C. Lincoln Brown, and Kenneth Pokrowski, for their kind support.

Time Warner Trade Publishing's General Counsel, Carol Fein Ross, has been extremely gracious and supportive of this project. My assistant, Diana Gonzalez, cheerfully provided enormous help with numerous administrative tasks.

Carolina Academic Press' Keith Sipe, Glenn Perkins, Tim Colton, and Robert Conrow have been exceedingly helpful with the production aspects of this book.

I value the support and devotion of my families (and I especially thank Gina Anderson for her words of encouragement).

Most of all, I am, as ever, profoundly grateful for the love and support of my husband, David Stagliano, and our children, Mark and Emily.

The author gratefully acknowledges the following authors and copyright holders who permitted works (or excerpts of works) to be included in this book:

Kevin W. Goering, *Defining Newsworthiness: Separating Matters of Legitimate Public Interest from Matters Which Simply Interest the Public*, reprinted by permission

Bruce E.H. Johnson, *Technology Shapes 21st Century Newsgathering: Reflections from the Last Millennium and Its Last Month*, Davis Wright Tremaine First Amendment Law Letter (Winter 2000), © Bruce E.H. Johnson, reprinted by permission

Cynthia L. Kahn, Robert Penchina, Srinandan R. Kasi, Clifford Chance Rogers & Wells LLP (and Madeleine Schachter), *Glossary of Internet Terms*

Bruce P. Keller and Madeleine Schachter, *Intellectual Property and Advertising Law for the Corporate Lawyer*, Corporate Legal Departments (3d ed. 2000)

Mark A. Lemley and Eugene Volokh, *Freedom of Speech and Injunctions in Intellectual Property Cases*, 48 Duke L.J. 147 (1998), © 1998 Mark A. Lemley and Eugene Volokh, reprinted by permission

Lawrence Lessig, *The Law of the Horse: What Cyberlaw Might Teach*, 113 Harv. L. Rev. 501 (1999), © 1999 The Harvard Law Review Association, reprinted by permission

Allison Roarty, *Link Liability: The Argument for Inline Links and Frames as Infringements of the Copyright Display Right*, 68 Fordham L. Rev. 1011 (1999), © Fordham Law Review, reprinted by permission

Paul M. Schwartz, *Privacy and Democracy in Cyberspace*, 52 Vand. L. Rev. 1609 (1999), © Vanderbilt Law Review, Vanderbilt School of Law and Paul M. Schwartz, reprinted by permission

# Law of Internet Speech

# Chapter I

# Fundamental Principles of Free Speech and the Nature of the Internet

## Values Served by the First Amendment

> Congress shall make no law...abridging the freedom of speech, or of the press; or the right of the people peaceably to assemble, and to petition the Government for redress of grievances.

U.S. Const. amend. I.

"The phrase 'Congress shall make no law' is composed of plain words, easily understood." Hugo L. Black, *The Bill of Rights*, 35 N.Y.U.L. Rev. 865, 874 (1960). And yet, the First Amendment has spawned a considerable body of interpretative jurisprudence, virtually unparalleled in the level of staunch eloquence protecting sacrosanct rights of freedom of expression.

The First Amendment has its historical roots in a deep conviction that freedom of speech propels liberty. The laudable objectives of protecting free speech and a free press are multi-faceted, and have been variously prioritized. Application of First Amendment jurisprudence (such as libel and privacy), and of fundamental principles relating to proprietary interests (such as copyright and trademark law), to communications conducted over the Internet compel a foundational understanding of the analytical framework underlying the Amendment's policies and values.

What then, are the fundamental purposes of the First Amendment? Distilled to its essence, the constitutional amendment's succinct protection facilitates an enlightened citizenry, imbued with capabilities for self-determination, endowed with the capacity for self-government, unencumbered by fear of official reprisal for critical speech.

> Those who won our independence believed that the final end of the state was to make men free to develop their faculties; and that in its government the deliberative forces should prevail over the arbitrary. They valued liberty both as an end and as a means. They believed liberty to be the secret of happiness and courage to be the secret of liberty. They believed that freedom to think as you will and to speak as you think are means indispensable to the discovery and spread of political truth; that without free speech and assembly discussion would be futile; that with them, discussion affords ordinarily adequate protec-

3

tion against the dissemination of noxious doctrine; that the greatest menace to freedom is an inert people; that public discussion is a political duty; and that this should be a fundamental principle of the American government. They recognized the risks to which all human institutions are subject. But they knew that order cannot be secured merely through fear of punishment for its infraction; that it is hazardous to discourage thought, hope and imagination; that fear breeds repression; that repression breeds hate; that hate menaces stable government; that the path of safety lies in the opportunity to discuss freely supposed grievances and proposed remedies; and that the fitting remedy for evil counsels is good ones. Believing in the power of reason as applied through public discussion, they eschewed silence coerced by law—the argument of force in its worst form. Recognizing the occasional tyrannies of governing majorities, they amended the Constitution so that free speech and assembly should be guaranteed.

*Whitney v. California*, 274 U.S. 357, 375–76 (1927) (Brandeis, J., concurring) (footnote omitted).

As Thomas Emerson observed, "freedom of expression is essential as a means of assuring individual self-fulfillment." Thomas I. Emerson, *The System of Free Expression* 6 (1970). Suppression of opinion is antithetical to a free mind, and hence at odds with an enlightened society. The First Amendment is "an integral part of the development of ideas and a sense of identity...[underlying] the individual's worth and dignity." *Procunier v. Martinez*, 416 U.S. 396, 427 (1974) (Marshall, J., concurring). "A free press stands as one of the great interpreters between the government and the people. To allow it to be fettered is to fetter ourselves." *Grosjean v. American Press Co.*, 297 U.S. 233, 250 (1936). At bottom, protection of freedom of expression is the requirement for "individual dignity and choice upon which our political system rests." *Cohen v. California*, 403 U.S. 15, 24 (1971).

A corollary to this principle is the notion that knowledge and truth emerge from informed discourse and robust debate. "It is the function of speech to free men from the bondage of irrational fears." *Whitney v. California*, 274 U.S. at 376 (Brandeis, J., concurring).

[W]hen men have realized that time has upset many fighting faiths, they may come to believe even more than they believe the very foundations of their own conduct that the ultimate good desired is better reached by free trade in ideas—that the best test of truth is the power of the thought to get itself accepted in the competition of the market, and that truth is the only ground upon which their wishes safely can be carried out. That at any rate is the theory of our Constitution.

*Abrams v. United States*, 250 U.S. 616, 630 (1919) (Holmes, J., dissenting). "[T]he basis of the First Amendment is the hypothesis that speech can rebut speech, propaganda will answer propaganda, free debate of ideas will result in the wisest governmental policies. It is for this reason that th[e Supreme] Court has recognized the inherent value of free discourse." *Dennis v. United States*, 341 U.S. 494, 503 (1951). We depend, then, upon the "marketplace of ideas" for correction of pernicious views. "[R]ight conclusions are more likely to be gathered out of a multitude of tongues, than through any kind of authoritative selection. To many this is, and always will be folly; but we have staked upon it our all." *United States v. Associated Press*, 52 F. Supp. 362, 372 (S.D.N.Y. 1943), *aff'd*, 326 U.S. 1 (1945).

While the viability of a marketplace metaphor has generated scholarly debate, *see, e.g.*, John H. Wigmore, Abrams v. United States: *Freedom of Speech and Freedom of*

*Thuggery in War-Time and Peace-Time,* 14 Ill. L. Rev. 539, 550–51 (1920), the concept has become enmeshed even in Internet jurisprudence. "It is no exaggeration to conclude that the Internet has achieved, and continues to achieve, the most participatory marketplace of mass speech that this country—and indeed the world—has yet seen." *American Civil Liberties Union v. Reno,* 929 F. Supp. 824, 881 (E.D. Pa. 1996), *aff'd,* 521 U.S. 844 (1997).

Whether conceptualized as a critical purpose of the First Amendment or as ancillary to the objective of promoting self-enlightenment, it is clear that the protection of free expression also serves a self-governance function, such that order is not to be exalted at the cost of liberty. "Whatever differences may exist about interpretations of the First Amendment, there is practically universal agreement that a major purpose of that Amendment was to protect the free discussion of governmental affairs." *Mills v. Alabama,* 384 U.S. 214, 218 (1966).

As well, the First Amendment presupposes that both freedom of expression and an unfettered press propel effective government by the people, thereby dissuading and deterring tyrannical reign unconcerned about the popular good. Hence, freedom of expression serves as a vital check on governmental abuses of power. The expression of political views, including those critical of the incumbent regime, must be permitted to be advanced without fear of reprisal. The press, specifically referenced in the First Amendment, functions as an additional check on governmental abuse by serving as the public's surrogate to scrutinize and monitor the workings of those in power. "[P]aramount among the responsibilities of a free press is the duty to prevent any part of the government from deceiving the people...." *New York Times Co. v. United States,* 403 U.S. 713, 717 (1971) (Black, J., concurring).

As a consequence of these vital protections, the potentially detrimental effects of political unrest are curtailed and contained. Because the citizenry has a viable and acceptable means of expressing its dissent through speech, the community is rendered more stable. "[L]usty speech provides a useful safety valve for the tensions which often accompany...controversies." *Linn v. United Plant Guard Workers,* 383 U.S. 53, 73 (1966) (Fortas, J., dissenting).

---

# The Nature of the Internet

With the inexorable march of time has come an age of technology of previously unimagined dimensions. Methods for news delivery have advanced apace with general scientific achievements. While town criers had for centuries informed the local citizenry, general circulation newspapers eventually made criers superfluous. Early in this century, news, transmitted by radio and telephone, became available to subscribers through dedicated news tickers and to the public by "extra" editions of newspapers. Widely available radio and television made news known to the public within minutes of its occurrence. In the last few years, instantaneous news has become available to subscribers with access to a microcomputer and a telephone, even at home.

*Daniel v. Dow Jones & Co., Inc.,* 520 N.Y.S.2d 334, 335, 137 Misc.2d 94, 94–95 (N.Y. Civ. Ct. 1987). Technological advances have been the source of wonder and amazement for generations. The *Daniel* court made its pronouncement well over a decade ago about a news service that can be accessed from subscribers' computers. Since then, the availability of Internet functionality has proliferated dramatically. Even the *Daniel* court's prescient statement could scarcely portend the technological advancements in communications, which have been unparalleled in scope and proportion.

The number of computers and users connected to the Internet has increased exponentially in recent years. Numerous surveys endeavor to grasp the extent to which the Internet has become a common mode of communication, but reliable estimation is an inherently difficult task in light of the constant and prolific expansion of the Internet. In 1996, approximately 40 million people used the Internet. *See Reno v. American Civil Liberties Union*, 521 U.S. 844, 850 (1997). In 1999, the Internet was believed to connect more than 159 countries and over 109 million users. *See American Civil Liberties Union v. Johnson*, 194 F.3d 1149, 1153 (10th Cir. 1999). Nua Internet Surveys issued an "educated guess" that, as of June 2000, more than 332 million engaged in on-line communication. *See* Nua Internet Surveys, <http://www.nua.ie/surveys/how_many_online/index.htm>.

The Internet is a profoundly global medium. The United States Department of Commerce expects that as the millennium gets underway, the United States and Canada will account for less than 50 percent of the global on-line population. U.S. Dep't of Commerce, *Economics and Statistics Administration* at v–vi (June 2000) <http://www.esa.doc.gov/de2000.pdf>. The amount of information available on-line reportedly has increased ten-fold from 1997 to 2000, to an aggregate of more than one billion discrete pages. *See* U.S. Dep't of Commerce, *Economics and Statistics Administration* at v–vi (June 2000) <http://www.esa.doc.gov/de2000.pdf>. Traffic on the Internet has been estimated to double every 100 days. *See Building Out the Internet*, <http://www.ecommerce.gov/building.htm>.

Findings reported in mid-2000 revealed that approximately 81 percent of home offices were on-line by the end of 1999, compared with 26 percent in 1996. *See* IDC Research, reporting on "Home Offices on the Internet: Forecast and Analysis, 1999–2004," <http://www.nua.ie/surveys/?f=VS&art_id=905355944&rel=tru>. Approximately one in four American consumers acquires news on-line at least four days a week, according to a survey conducted by the Radio and Television News Directors Foundation and the personalized news service Zatso. *See* Nua Internet Surveys <http://www.nua.ie/surveys/?f=VS&art_id=905355713&rel=tru>.

Each minute, an estimated five million e-mail messages are sent around the world. *See* Carleton Fiorina, *The Communications Revolution*, Commonwealth Club of Cal. Monthly Newsl. (July 19, 1999) <http://www.commonwealthclub.org>. Although the first 700 million telephone lines were installed over the course of a century, the next 15 years likely will see the installation of 700 million more. *See id.*

The dramatic effects wrought by pervasive usage of interactive computer services often have been analogized to the social and cultural transformations that resulted from the invention of the printing press. Arguably the expansive and virtually boundless potential of cyberspace exponentially exceeds the impact of any other technological revolution to date.

"The Internet is not a physical or tangible entity, but rather a giant network which interconnects innumerable smaller groups of linked computer networks. It is thus a network of networks." *American Civil Liberties Union v. Reno*, 929 F. Supp. 824, 830 (E.D. Pa. 1996), *aff'd*, 521 U.S. 844 (1997). The Internet is a "unique and wholly new medium of worldwide human communication." 929 F. Supp. at 844.

"Cyberspace" has become a familiar figurative term for the exchange of communications and information and the conducting of transactions that do not occur in any physical space. The judiciary seems particularly enamored of metaphorical references to the Internet. For example, the Internet has been described as an informational highway, comprised of streets leading to sources of information. *See Edias Software International, L.L.C. v. Basis International Ltd.*, 947 F. Supp. 413, 419 & n. 7 (D. Ariz. 1996). "The highway metaphor highlights the expansiveness of the Internet—the ability for a user to reach another person or database instantly despite great physical distances." *Id.* at 419.

The Internet also has been envisaged as a supermarket or a shopping mall, in which users can shop for goods, services, and even information. *See id.* at 419 & n. 8. "The shopping mall metaphor reveals the newly developed commercial feature of the Internet as a place to go to purchase needed items or services." *Id.* at 419.

Additionally, cyberspace has been conceptualized as a telephone system for computers by which databases of information can be downloaded to the user, as though all the information existed perpetually in the computer's hard drive. *See id.* at 419 & n. 9. "The structure of the Internet [also] bears a striking resemblance to a railroad, highway, or other means of interstate transportation." *American Civil Liberties Union v. Johnson*, 194 F.3d at 1162 (quoting Kenneth D. Bassinger, *Dormant Commerce Clause Limits on State Regulation of the Internet: The Transportation Analogy*, 32 Ga. L. Rev. 889, 904 (1998)).

One intellectual property specialist has opined that "although it may be colorful, it is not analytically useful to think of the Internet as a transportation vehicle in which one makes 'virtual' voyages. To the contrary, the Internet is an earthbound network of interconnected computes, each with a specific physical location, connected by a physical telecommunications backbone. One no more makes a 'virtual visit' when using the Internet than when telephoning long distance." Bruce P. Keller, *The Game's the Same: Why Gambling in Cyberspace Violates Federal Law*, 108 Yale L.J. 1569, 1572 (May 1999).

As a system, the Internet is extraordinarily elegant, resilient, and multi-functional. The Internet serves as a valuable and regular avenue of communication for corporate communication and social interaction; it serves the needs of students and faculty engaged in research; and it provides an impressive resource for commercial transactions. The Internet also provides a means of storing and transmitting personal data, financial information, corporate databases, governmental records. It affords ample means for dialogue exchanged between two individuals intimately known to one another, or among multiple persons whose encounters have been achieved exclusively through digital media.

Professor Ethan Katsh regards cyberspace not simply as a location, but as a cultural environment with embedded norms and values. Cyberspace consists of "an environment where one's informational activities are not limited by many of the temporal or spatial constraints of the physical environment. This leads to an expansion of economic and creative interactions, a largely beneficial consequence of an electronic environment, and, inevitably, an expansion of disputes involving the acquisition, use, possession, processing and communication of information." M. Ethan Katsh, *Symposium: Dispute Resolution in Cyberspace*, 28 Conn. L. Rev. 953, 956 (1996).

Originating in 1969 as an experimental project of the Advanced Research Project Agency, the network of linked computers and computer networks was first designed to service the military, defense contractors, and university laboratories conducting defense-related research. *See American Civil Liberties Union v. Reno*, 929 F. Supp. at 831.

The system evolved to encompass universities, corporations, and people around the world. *See id.*

From its inception, the Internet was designed as a decentralized, self-maintaining series of redundant links between computers and computer networks, intended to rapidly transmit communications without direct human involvement or control. *See id.; see also* Barry M. Leiner, *et al., A Brief History of the Internet* (last modified Apr. 14, 2000) <http://www.isoc.org/internet-history/brief.html.> The Internet is a global electronic network, consisting of smaller, inter-connected networks, that allows millions of computers to exchange information over telephone wires, dedicated data cables, and wireless links. The Internet links personal computers by means of servers, which run specialized operating systems and applications designed for servicing a network environment. *See United States v. Microsoft Corp.,* 84 F. Supp. 2d 9, 13 (D.D.C. 1999), *judgment entered by* 97 F. Supp. 2d 59 (D.D.C. 2000).

Access to the Internet generally is physically achieved through the use of a computer terminal, or through a modem connected over a telephone line to a computer network, that is directly connected to a computer network that is itself directly or indirectly connected to the Internet. Businesses, academicians, public libraries, community-based services, and commercial on-line providers are among those that routinely provide access to the Internet. *See American Civil Liberties Union v. Reno,* 929 F. Supp. at 832–33.

A distinguishing characteristic of the Internet is its enhanced interactive capability. "Far from the mass-media of newspapers and broadcasting, with their limited interactive responses through letters to the editor and talk television, computer-mediated communication offers open access to uploading messages (speech) and open access to downloading information (also speech). ... This makes the Networld an attractive conduit for democratic discourse." Anne Wells Branscomb, *Anonymity, Autonomy, and Accountability: Challenges to the First Amendment in Cyberspace,* 104 Yale L.J. 1639, 1670 (1995).

On-line speech is conducted in a variety of forms. One-to-one messaging, such as electronic mail ("e-mail"), occurs from one person to one or more others. One-to-many messaging, commonly referred to as "listservs" or "mail exploders," allows communications about particular subjects of interest to a group of people.

Distributed message databases, such as USENET newsgroups, are exemplified by user-sponsored newsgroups. They consist of open discussions and exchanges on particular topics. Sometimes such newsgroups are "moderated," which means that the content is screened for purposes of relevance or propriety. Real-time communication networks, commonly known as "chat rooms," allow communication to appear almost immediately on remote computers.

A central feature of the Internet is the "World Wide Web," known colloquially as the "Web." The Web originally was developed at CERN Laboratory (the Centre European pour la Recherche Nucleaire), the European Particle Physics Laboratory, and was initially used to allow information sharing within internationally dispersed teams of researchers and engineers. The CERN computer system has been described as "labryrinthine," because data was dispersed over various computers that did not necessarily interact. *See* Shahrooz Feizabadi, *www: Beyond the Basics* <http://ei.cs.vt.edu/www.btb/book/chap1/web_hist.html>. The Internet "all began when Tim Berners-Lee, a graduate of Oxford University, got frustrated with the fact that his daily schedule planner, his list of phone numbers, and his documents were stored in different databases on different machines thus making it difficult to access them simultaneously. He set out to fix this problem." *Id.* Lee developed a program to take advantage of the capabilities of "hypertext," which allows links to documents located on CERN machines. Use of the Web has extended well beyond the scientific and academic community to which it was initially targeted to include communications by individuals, non-profit organizations, and businesses. *American Civil Liberties Union v. Reno*, 929 F. Supp. at 836.

Essentially, the Web is a massive collection of digital information resources stored on servers throughout the Internet. The Web utilizes a formatting language called "hypertext markup language" ("HTML"). Hypertext documents, commonly referred to as "Web pages," may incorporate various combinations of text, graphics, audio and video content, software programs, and other data. A "web-site" is a collection of Web pages. The web-site's "home page" is the first point of access to the site.

Each web-site is connected to the Internet by means of protocols that permit "the information to become part of a single body of knowledge accessible by all Web visitors." *American Libraries Ass'n v. Pataki*, 969 F. Supp. 160, 166 (S.D.N.Y. 1997). Programs that "browse" the Web can display HTML documents. An essential element of the Web is that every document has an address, and can "link" or be "linked" to other documents. Such documents can include links to other types of information or resources, so that while viewing an HTML document, users can, with a computer mouse, "click" on the resource and be connected immediately to the resource itself. This process, known as "hyperlinking," allows information to be accessed and organized in very flexible ways, and allows people to locate and efficiently view related information, even when the information is stored on multiple computers in various countries. *See American Civil Liberties Union v. Reno*, 929 F. Supp. at 836. Hyperlinks function as cross-references within a single document, between documents on the same site, or between documents on different sites. *See United States v. Microsoft Corp.*, 84 F. Supp. 2d at 14. Therefore, although information on the Web is contained in individual computers, the fact that each of these computers is connected to the Internet through a series of protocols allows all of the information to become part of a single body of knowledge. *See American Civil Liberties Union v. Reno*, 929 F. Supp. at 836.

The Web's organization is recursive, because Web pages contain links to other pages that in turn link to additional pages or back to the original linking site. Ultimately, the World Wide Web serves as a platform for a global, on-line repository of knowledge, which contains information from a diversity of sources and is routinely accessible to Internet users around the world.

Additionally, the "Web exists fundamentally as a platform through which people and organizations can communicate through shared information." *Id.* at 837. Web-sites can be made open to the general universe of Internet users; or closed, which means that the information is accessible only to those with advance authorization. *See id.* at 837. Restrictions on access may be accomplished by assigning specific user names and passwords as a prerequisite to access to the site, or, in the case of web-sites maintained for internal use by a single organization, access can be restricted to other computers within that organization's local network. *See id.* at 837.

A variety of systems that allow users of the World Wide Web to search for particular data among the public sites that are part of the Web have developed. Services known as "search engines" allow users to search for web-sites that contain certain categories of information, or to search for keywords. Search engines operate through "spiders" that "crawl" the Web to seek out and harvest embedded codes containing keywords that are responsive to the search. These coded bits of data, known as "metatags," help the search engine build an index of sites for review by the user. The resultant index also serves to function as a series of links to those sites. As the user reviews references to the sites retrieved, he can access particular links, browsing through the information on each site, until the desired material is located.

A key advantage of the Web is that it utilizes basic standards to allow communication and the exchange of information. Despite the fact that many types of computers are used to access, display, and exchange information on the Web, and despite the fact that many of these computers are otherwise incompatible with one another, basic technical protocols enable those who publish information on the Web to communicate effectively with those who seek to access information.

> No single entity—academic, corporate, governmental, or non-profit— administers the Internet. It exists and functions as a result of the fact that hundreds of thousands of separate operators of computers and computer networks independently decided to use common data transfer protocols to exchange communications and information with other computers (which in turn exchange communications and information with still other computers). There is no centralized storage location, control point, or communications channel for the Internet, and it would not be technically feasible for a single entity to control all of the information conveyed on the Internet.

*Id.* at 832.

The nature of the Internet "is such that it is very difficult, if not impossible, to determine its size at a given moment." *Id.* at 831. Because the Internet exists without geographical boundaries, the World Wide Web is accessible to Internet users worldwide. "[V]irtually all Internet speech is...available everywhere." *Cyberspace Communications, Inc. v. Engler,* 55 F. Supp. 2d 737, 751 (E.D. Mich. 1999). The revolutionary effects of the Internet are attributable, at least in part, to the formation of a virtual community. The Internet effectively

> negates geometry...it is fundamentally and profoundly anti-spatial. You cannot say where it is or describe its memorable shape and proportions or tell a stranger how to get there. But you can find things in it without knowing where they are. The [Internet] is ambient—nowhere in particular and everywhere at once.

*American Civil Liberties Union v. Reno,* 217 F.3d 162, 169 (3d Cir. 2000) (citation omitted).

---

# Janet RENO v. AMERICAN CIVIL LIBERTIES UNION

## No. 96-511, 521 U.S. 844
### Supreme Court of the United States
### June 26, 1997

Stevens, J., delivered the opinion of the Court, in which Scalia, Kennedy, Souter, Thomas, Ginsburg, and Breyer, JJ., joined. O'Connor, J., filed an opinion concurring in the judgment in part and dissenting in part, in which Rehnquist, C.J., joined.

At issue is the constitutionality of two statutory provisions enacted to protect minors from "indecent" and "patently offensive" communications on the Internet. Notwithstanding the legitimacy and importance of the congressional goal of protecting children from harmful materials, we agree with the three-judge District Court that the statute abridges "the freedom of speech" protected by the First Amendment....

The Internet is an international network of interconnected computers. It is the outgrowth of what began in 1969 as a military program called "ARPANET,"[3] which was designed to enable computers operated by the military, defense contractors, and universities conducting defense-related research to communicate with one another by redundant channels even if some portions of the network were damaged in a war. While the ARPANET no longer exists, it provided an example for the development of a number of civilian networks that, eventually linking with each other, now enable tens of millions of people to communicate with one another and to access vast amounts of information from around the world. The Internet is "a unique and wholly new medium of worldwide human communication."

The Internet has experienced "extraordinary growth." The number of "host" computers—those that store information and relay communications—increased from about 300 in 1981 to approximately 9,400,000 by the time of the trial in 1996. Roughly 60% of these hosts are located in the United States. About 40 million people used the Internet at the time of trial, a number that is expected to mushroom to 200 million by 1999.

Individuals can obtain access to the Internet from many different sources, generally hosts themselves or entities with a host affiliation. Most colleges and universities provide access for their students and faculty; many corporations provide their employees with access through an office network; many communities and local libraries provide free access; and an increasing number of storefront "computer coffee shops" provide access for a small hourly fee. Several major national "online services" such as America Online, CompuServe, the Microsoft Network, and Prodigy offer access to their own extensive proprietary networks as well as a link to the much larger resources of the Internet. These commercial online services had almost 12 million individual subscribers at the time of trial.

Anyone with access to the Internet may take advantage of a wide variety of communication and information retrieval methods. These methods are constantly evolving and difficult to categorize precisely. But, as presently constituted, those most relevant to this case are electronic mail (e-mail), automatic mailing list services ("mail exploders," sometimes referred to as "listservs"), "newsgroups," "chat rooms," and the "World Wide Web." All of these methods can be used to transmit text; most can transmit sound, pictures, and moving video images. Taken together, these tools constitute a unique medium—known to its users as "cyberspace"—located in no particular geographical location but available to anyone, anywhere in the world, with access to the Internet.

E-mail enables an individual to send an electronic message—generally akin to a note or letter—to another individual or to a group of addressees. The message is generally stored electronically, sometimes waiting for the recipient to check her "mailbox" and sometimes making its receipt known through some type of prompt. A mail exploder is a sort of e-mail group. Subscribers can send messages to a common e-mail address, which then forwards the message to the group's other subscribers. Newsgroups also serve groups of regular participants, but these postings may be read by others as well. There are thousands of such groups, each serving to foster an exchange of information or opinion on a particular topic running the gamut from, say, the music of Wagner to Balkan politics to AIDS prevention to the Chicago Bulls. About 100,000 new messages

---

3. An acronym for the network developed by the Advanced Research Project Agency.

are posted everyday. In most newsgroups, postings are automatically purged at regular intervals. In addition to posting a message that can be read later, two or more individuals wishing to communicate more immediately can enter a chat room to engage in real-time dialogue—in other words, by typing messages to one another that appear almost immediately on the others' computer screens. The District Court found that at any given time "tens of thousands of users are engaging in conversations on a huge range of subjects." It is "no exaggeration to conclude that the content on the Internet is as diverse as human thought."

The best known category of communication over the Internet is the World Wide Web, which allows users to search for and retrieve information stored in remote computers, as well as, in some cases, to communicate back to designated sites. In concrete terms, the Web consists of a vast number of documents stored in different computers all over the world. Some of these documents are simply files containing information. However, more elaborate documents, commonly known as Web "pages," are also prevalent. Each has its own address —"rather like a telephone number." Web pages frequently contain information and sometimes allow the viewer to communicate with the page's (or "site's") author. They generally also contain "links" to other documents created by that site's author or to other (generally) related sites. Typically, the links are either blue or underlined text—sometimes images.

Navigating the Web is relatively straightforward. A user may either type the address of a known page or enter one or more keywords into a commercial "search engine" in an effort to locate sites on a subject of interest. A particular Web page may contain the information sought by the "surfer," or, through its links, it may be an avenue to other documents located anywhere on the Internet. Users generally explore a given Web page, or move to another, by clicking a computer "mouse" on one of the page's icons or links. Access to most Web pages is freely available, but some allow access only to those who have purchased the right from a commercial provider. The Web is thus comparable, from the readers' viewpoint, to both a vast library including millions of readily available and indexed publications and a sprawling mall offering goods and services.

From the publishers' point of view, it constitutes a vast platform from which to address and hear from a worldwide audience of millions of readers, viewers, researchers, and buyers. Any person or organization with a computer connected to the Internet can "publish" information. Publishers include government agencies, educational institutions, commercial entities, advocacy groups, and individuals.[9] Publishers may either make their material available to the entire pool of Internet users, or confine access to a selected group, such as those willing to pay for the privilege. "No single organization controls any membership in the Web, nor is there any single centralized point from which individual Web sites or services can be blocked from the Web." ...

--------

9. "Web publishing is simple enough that thousands of individual users and small community organizations are using the Web to publish their own personal 'home pages,' the equivalent of individualized newsletters about that person or organization, which are available to everyone on the Web."

# Technology Shapes 21st Century Newsgathering: Reflections From the Last Millennium and Its Last Month

## Bruce E.H. Johnson*

Will the Internet change the gathering of news, and how? How will American institutions, including legal rules governing the media, be transformed by an interconnected world? As 1999 has clicked over into 2000, several recent events offer hints of profound change and remarkable continuity, suggesting ways that the 21st century media will be affected by new technologies.

This is not a new process. Technology shapes our lives in strange and unexpected ways, bringing changes that can overwhelm existing civic and political institutions. In past centuries, transforming the forms of communication and news led to the transformation or destruction of competing social systems.

Highlights of the last millennium in the United States—and in particular the last month of 1999—may offer some useful guidance about past technologies, how they changed the newsgathering process and the law, and where new media may be headed.

### Printing

Printing and democracy were a combustible mixture. The American Revolution, for example, was the direct product of the invention of printing—ignited when 18th century chat-room participants and letter-writers suddenly decided to share their opinions with the public. The new technology appropriated the old: the letter, the dominant form of communication, was transformed into a newsgathering and opinion-shaping tool.

From 1763 to 1775, the number of newspapers in the Colonies doubled. These newspapers were said to be infected by a "nearly epidemic degree of seditious libel" with "press criticism of government policies and politicians" raging "contemptuously and scorchingly. When riots broke out in Boston in 1765, the Royal Governor, Thomas Bernard, blamed the *Boston Gazette*, and accused the newspaper of "raising that flame in America which has given so much trouble." Two years later, Lord Grenville tried to persuade Parliament to censure "certain papers, published at Boston," as "libelous and treasonable," but was talked out of the effort, because "it was below the dignity of Parliament to pay any regard to angry newspaper writers."

By 1774 and 1775, royal authority had collapsed in the Colonies and "new authorities, committees and congresses began putting together new popular structures of authority from the bottom up. Legally speaking, these were informal associations; politically speaking, they were conspiracies, providing (to adopt the Web analogy) links to one another's viewpoints. These Committees of Correspondence communicated with one another; but they also communicated with members of the public and shaped public opinion. These "correspondents" were not just letter writers; they also helped create news and became, in effect, newspaper correspondents. Some also promoted revolution.

As with today's Internet, the latest technology made this revolution a worldwide event. For example, in April 1775, the Massachusetts Committee of Safety learned that the British Army General Thomas Gage was preparing an official report on the battles

---

* © Bruce E.H. Johnson.

of Lexington and Concord, collected 100 depositions and letters from battle participants, and enlisted the owner and sailing master of a fast American schooner to transmit their evidence to London readers. Speed worked in their favor, as did the British
commander's view that information should be entrusted to "others in proportion to
their rank." Although the American ship had left Boston four days after General Gage's,
its accounts reached the London press two weeks before Gage's and immediately shaped
English public opinion in the Americans' favor.

Another well-known example was Thomas Paine's influential *Common Sense*, one of
400 pamphlets produced by American printers in 1776. Paine originally had intended a
series of letters but instead decided to write an anonymous pamphlet ridiculing monar-
chy and advocating American independence. It was published in Philadelphia in January
1776. Several printers immediately battled for the copyright, and unauthorized editions
began pouring from colonial printing presses. One month later, a German translation
appeared in Pennsylvania and Common Sense was published in New York. By April, a
Boston edition appeared and Paine estimated that 120,000 copies had been published.
Editions soon appeared in Salem, Newport, Hartford, Lancaster, Newburyport, Nor-
wich, Albany, and Providence. By May, *Common Sense* was circulating in Quebec and
Warsaw's *Gazeta Warszawska* was publishing excerpts. Later that year, editions appeared
in London, Edinburgh, and Newcastle; a French translation was published in Rotterdam.

## Telegraphs, Railroads, and Telephones

Two 19th century innovations, the railroad and the telegraph, led to such varied results as the demise of the British aristocracy, the rise of Impressionism, the settlement
of the American West, the creation of a global stock market, the abolition of slavery,
and the replacement of local time by an international girdle of time zones. In the
United States, the private press expanded its powers as it exploited new technologies.
Through these technological shifts, newsgathering moved from individual to association and to corporate consolidation, which empowered an extensive system of private
media that challenged serious governmental controls.

The invention of the telegraph coincided with an era of American law that reflected
the "release" of private entrepreneurial "energy." New technology immediately broke
down barriers of time and distance, states simplified their incorporation procedures to
allow more businesses to take new risks without undue liability burdens, and, as the
"penny press" expanded the reading public, these technological and legal changes drove
a new profit motive: "Increasingly, news was worth money." Financier James Roth-
schild, whose family fortune was based on exclusive control of access to financial information, complained that, with the telegraph, "anyone can get the news."

The telegraph was efficient for delivering news to newspaper offices, but it was not
suitable for distributing news directly to readers. Thus, newspapers immediately utilized the new modes of communication by associating with other newspapers across the
United States. Because speed was important, the press no longer relied on the efforts of
individual correspondents writing sporadic letters from distant cities. The Associated
Press, one of these "news agencies," established "cozy relationships with the telegraph
companies and was soon able to dominate the business of selling news to newspapers."
Among AP members, news stories were shared, much like current Web links.

The French observer Alexis de Tocqueville, when he visited America in 1831, remarked on the "spirit of association" and how "that freedom of association favors the
welfare and even the tranquillity of the citizens." De Tocqueville also saw a powerful

press, capable of resisting governmental power. The "hallmark of the American journalist," he noted, "is a direct and coarse attack, without any subtleties, on the passions of his readers; he disregards principles to seize on people, following them into their private lives and laying bare their weaknesses and their vices." Yet, nothing was "rarer than to see judicial proceedings taken against" the media, because Americans believed the people, not the government, were sovereign and that courts were "powerless" against the press. After the Civil War, the explosion of investment in railroads (financed, ironically, by government grants) led to the Gilded Age and to the consolidation of vast corporate structures, as private capital became newly energized and powerful, dwarfing existing governmental institutions. Such consolidation was typical, as well, within the telegraph industry; by 1880, one company (Western Union) handled 80 percent of America's message traffic.

Meanwhile, courts creatively applied and adapted the Constitution and the common law to encourage use of the new technologies, allowing the spread of wires without unnecessary legal risks. Because railroads and telegraphs operated in interstate commerce, the United States Supreme Court prevented states from regulating them. Recognizing that immunity to transmit libelous messages "must be broad enough" to enable the telegraph company to render its public service efficiently and with dispatch, and "that speed is the essence of the service," federal and state courts also devised new common law privileges to avoid hamstringing the new technologies with libel judgments. The courts even extended this conduit immunity to the newspapers' news associations, developing the so-called "wire service" defense, which created the doctrinal base for the *New York Times v. Sullivan* "actual malice" rule.

Adapting to these new technologies, the American media also consolidated, with Hearst, Pulitzer, and other chains dominating national discourse and retaining reporters as corporate employees (a relationship typified by Hearst's classic telegram to artist Frederic Remington, "You furnish the pictures and I'll furnish the war.") Yellow journalism was powerful enough to press the buttons of government; when America jumped into war with Spain in 1898, it was "the Journal's war." Meanwhile, laissez faire government became somewhat irrelevant to the new media empires, requiring few court decisions on press rights and producing the so-called "forgotten years" for freedoms of speech and press. Indeed, the 19th century "produced some important issues for individual civil liberties, but showed no impressive record of grappling with them."

### Radio, Television, and Cable

Government firmly took control of two 20th century news technologies, radio and television. Interestingly, the broadcast regulatory system, a product of the Progressive Era, was in fact an accident the consequence of a stray iceberg in North Atlantic shipping lanes.

Between 1906 and 1912, America experienced its first radio boom. As with today's Internet, the broadcast spectrum was largely unregulated and controlled by amateurs. Hundreds of "schoolboys" across the United States built radio sets and sent messages to one another. These amateurs behaved like "kids"—indeed, some amateurs "deliberately sent false or obscene messages, especially to the navy," which began mounting a campaign (largely unsuccessful, at first) to curb their activities.

In April 1912, the Titanic sank, accompanied by "ceaseless interference, cruel rumors, and misleading messages that filled the air from unknown sources during the disaster." The press unanimously denounced radio amateurs after the Titanic disaster "for interfering with 'legitimate' message handling. What caused the amateurs to lose their freedom to roam the ether at will was not so much that the government would no longer tolerate that freedom, but that a very influential business, the press, found their activities a disruptive encroachment on its turf." The disaster led to a public demand for increased government regulation of the wireless spectrum. As a result of the Titanic, "the United States government seized control of the airwaves."

The Radio Act of 1912 began federal control of the American radio spectrum. Later, prodded by Secretary of Commerce Herbert Hoover, Congress enacted the Radio Act of 1927 which expressly rejected any private ownership of the airwaves, developed an emphasis on the "broadcast" rather than point-to-point format, and adopted a public utility model for license allocation and distribution.

This licensing model meant the removal of minority viewpoints from broadcasting in favor of the "general public interest." Thus, the Federal Radio Commission, created by the 1927 law, immediately attacked "propaganda stations," warned a New York Socialist station that it must "operate with due regard for the opinions of others," announced that there was no "room in the broadcast band for every school of thoughts each to have its separate broadcasting stations, its mouth-piece in the ether," and removed the licenses of KGEF in Los Angeles because of the "sensational" attacks on public officials and corruption by "Fighting Bob" Shuler, and of KFKB in Kansas City because of the efforts by the "goat-gland doctor," John R. Brinkley, to promote his peculiar theories of rejuvenating middle-aged male sexuality.

The Communications Act of 1934, with its emphasis on administrative expertise, continued this trend. By that time, the dominant European-based political ideologies, including Fascism, Socialism, and Communism, together with the American New Deal, were premised on theories of major government control over the private market. Moreover, in contrast to the legal system that had shaped the news media's use of 19th century technologies and encouraged association and consolidation, broadcast licensees' efforts to associate and combine were subject to strict government controls. While none of the federal regulatory statutes had expressly dealt with broadcast networks, the Federal Communications Commission extended its controls over networks with its "chain broadcasting rules," and was upheld by the Supreme Court in 1943.

These regulations, which imposed major barriers to entry, nurtured large media broadcast entities that were subject to significant federal controls and protections. By the 1960s, an American industrial structure built on large companies such as the Big Three automakers was mirrored by a media system comprised of three large television networks. These national broadcast networks were devoted to a large public, providing undifferentiated national news to everyone.

In 1964, in a case involving a major national newspaper, the United States Supreme Court granted the news media major First Amendment protection against local governmental authorities that had sought to use state libel laws to stop coverage of civil rights protests that undermined Southern élites.[29] But, for broadcasters, the federal licensing system devised in the *Titanic's* wake brought a noteworthy erosion of First Amendment rights. Based on the rationale that the broadcast spectrum was a uniquely scarce public resource (a theory that has been severely criticized), government regulations, such as

---

29. *New York Times v. Sullivan,* 376 U.S. 254 (1964).

right-of-reply requirements[31] and content controls[32] were routinely upheld by the federal courts. Frequently, the major networks found themselves battling directly with United States senators or the Executive Branch—for example, Edward R. Murrow and Senator McCarthy—to defend First Amendment values. By the 1970s, the government's control of this licensing structure was the springboard for the Nixon Administration's "assault on the networks," a campaign that was finally aborted by Watergate.

In recent years, telecasting has moved beyond broadcast technology. With the development of cable news systems, neither dependent on broadcast licenses nor entangled with a "scarcity" theory mandating government involvement, the courts have allowed more First Amendment protections for television. For example, they developed a doctrine called "intermediate scrutiny" that permits cable news companies to escape some (but not all) of the limitations of the federal television licensing system and allows fewer content controls than regular broadcasting. For the electronic media, however, use of new technology has been accompanied by new liabilities, as some courts have begun expanding privacy definitions and penalizing routine electronic newsgathering techniques.[35]

*Internet Trends*

By the beginning of 2000, with America Online poised to purchase Time Warner, the Internet has now become a major player among national and international news media. But, at least in the United States, its technology and politics are very different from print, broadcast, or cable. Several events from the last month of 1999 show, moreover, that the Web is already blazing a new trail in newsgathering, which recalls the informal but revolutionary links between 18th-century printers and correspondents, the entrepreneurial strengths of the 19th century, and the governmental battles faced by 20th-century media.

Web news certainly has broken with the broadcast news model launched at the beginning of the 20th century with the sinking of the Titanic. This is because, despite Vice-President Gore's recent claims of paternity,[36] the Internet is really the libertarian child of Reaganism and Thatcherism. Proponents of greater government involvement and control over the Web, such as Harvard's Lawrence Lessig,[37] are thus the exception rather than the rule. In *Reno v. ACLU*, the Supreme Court decisively rejected a broadcasting analogy and endorsed the conclusion that the Internet, as "the most participatory form of mass speech ever developed," is entitled to "the highest protection from government intrusion."

---

31. *Red Lion Broadcasting v. FCC*, 395 U.S. 367 (1969).

32. *Pacifica Foundation v. FCC*, 438 U.S. 726 (1978).

35. For example, interviewing the subject of a news story is what reporters ordinarily do and asking questions is a "routine" reporting technique protected by the First Amendment. *See Nicholson v. McClatchy Newspapers*, 177 Cal. App. 3d 509 (1986). If the reporter is a member of the electronic media and uses a microphone and tape recorder rather than a pencil to record the interview, however, he or she now risks invasion of privacy liability to the interviewee merely because, as some courts have suggested, "a person may reasonably expect privacy against the electronic recording of a communication, even though he or she had no reasonable expectation as to confidentiality of the communication's contents." *Alpha Therapeutic Corp. v. Nippon Hoso Kyokai*, 1999 U.S. App. LEXIS 33928 (9th Cir. 1999) (quoting *Sanders v. ABC*, 20 Cal. 4th 907, 915 (1999)); *contra Deteresa v. ABC, Inc.*, 121 F.3d 460 (9th Cir. 1997).

36. The claims are not entirely unjustified. The ARPANet, which later became the Internet, was originally developed by the federal government and nurtured while Gore was in the United States Senate.

37. *See* Lawrence Lessig, *Code and Other Laws of Cyberspace* (1999).

With its libertarian impetus intact after *Reno v. ACLU*, Net newsgathering has returned American media to its Revolutionary roots, with everyone in the world a potential correspondent. One of the most stunning demonstrations of this new medium occurred from November 30 to December 3, 1999, when the World Trade Organization's ministerial conference met in Seattle. The WTO meeting was overshadowed by (in the words of local news anchor Jean Enersen) "the first post-modern riot, the first riot to be organized on the Internet," with thousands of anti-trade protesters demonstrating against the WTO, blocking and attacking WTO delegates, and vandalizing downtown Seattle. In the following days, joined by the National Guard, the Seattle police switched tactics, took control of a major section of the city center, and began arresting and battling demonstrators and local civilians.

Anti-WTO activists dissatisfied with coverage of trade issues by "the mainstream press" organized the Seattle Independent Media Center, rented a storefront location near the epicenter of the riots and protests, persuaded local technology firms to donate equipment and services, and created a news website (www.indymedia.org) devoted exclusively to anti-WTO information and activities.

During the WTO meeting and the accompanying protests and riots, the Independent Media Center encouraged members of the public opposed to free trade policies (even the Buchanan for President campaign) to post their own information and commentary on their website without prior editorial intervention or scrutiny. During the disturbances, protesters brought film to the Center for immediate processing and posting on the Web. The Indymedia website also invited contributors to "[p]ublish your text article, audio segment, video footage, or picture" by clicking and transmitting this information for immediate uploading to the Web. Thus, viewers across the world could click on the page and see current photographs of altercations between Seattle police and protesters and receive live streaming video and audio.

Facilitating this democratic viewpoint of Web journalism is a growing body of case law that firmly rejects defamation and privacy liability by third parties such as websites and Internet service providers. Courts have recognized that, to facilitate freedom of speech, the Internet must be shielded from major liabilities. Thus, like their 19th century predecessors who nursed the growth of telegraphy, some courts have protected the Internet as an organ of interstate and international commerce and have refused state regulatory schemes.[39] Also, beginning with *Zeran v. AOL* in 1997, courts have consistently applied Section 230 of the Communications Decency Act[41] in dismissing defamation and similar state law claims against ISPs and others.

On December 2, 1999, while police and anti-trade demonstrators were fighting in Seattle, the New York Court of Appeals extended the *Zeran* principle when it refused to hold Prodigy Services Company liable for negligence or defamation resulting from some vulgar email messages and bulletin board postings by an unknown imposter using the plaintiff's name.[42] Citing telegraph and telephone legal cases, the court rejected such liability as a matter of common law doctrine and extended to this Internet "conduit" the same "common-law qualified privilege accorded to telephone and telegraph companies." Like its predecessors grappling with the "wire service" defense, the New York

---

39. *See, e.g., ACLU v. Johnson*, 194 F.3d 1149 (10th Cir. 1999). Some courts have attempted to impose more local government controls over the Internet. *See, e.g., AT&T Corp. v. City of Portland*, 43 F. Supp. 2d 1146 (D. Or. 1999).

41. 47 U.S.C. §230.

42. *Lunney v. Prodigy Services Co.*, 1999 WL 1082126 (N.Y. 1999).

court freely admitted that its choice was motivated by public policy; its view that the "public would not be well served by compelling an ISP to examine and screen millions of e-mail communications, on pain of liability for defamation."

But the legal battles between government and the media, which typified much of 20th century press law, are not over. With the rise of the Internet, it appears that "privacy" is the newest argument against press freedom. On December 14, 1999, the Committee on Financial Disclosure of the Judicial Conference of the United States refused the request of an internet news service, APBNews.com,[43] for a copy of certain public records that listed the 1998 financial disclosures by members of the federal judiciary. The Committee was opposed to APBNews.com's request because it intended to post the financial data on its website so that individual readers could make use of the information. These same documents had been routinely released to reporters in the past, resulting in major news articles about the judges' conflicts of interest that were published in the *Kansas City Star* and the *Washington Post*.

Aided by a temporary restraining order that was quickly issued by a Florida federal judge a few days earlier, the Committee ruled that these public records were not public records as far as the Internet is concerned and decided to change the rules because they feared real publicity; *i.e.*, ready accessibility online. To justify its decision, the Committee adopted what a *Washington Post* editorial characterized as a "laughable" interpretation of the Ethics in Government Act and ruled that they must be kept from Internet users. Simultaneously, the Committee permitted other media to obtain the same financial records.

The Committee's decision to brand the Web taboo, of course, illegally discriminates against one form of journalism in favor of others. More tellingly, it also illustrates a familiar attitude that has surfaced repeatedly during the last millennium of American history, the distrust of democracy, and recalls British General Gage's policy to share useful information with "others in proportion to their rank."

On December 22, 1999, as the 1900's drew to a close, APBNews.com filed suit in federal court in New York City. "This is a fight to gain access to public records for all Internet users," said Mark Sauter, chief operating officer of APB Online Inc., the parent company of APBnews.com. "The Internet is not just a legitimate but a superior means to disseminate these documents to the public."

----

# Is There a Dichotomy Between Freedom of Speech and Freedom of the Press?

"Through the use of chat rooms, any person with a phone line can become a town crier with a voice that resonates farther than it could from any soapbox. Through the use of Web pages, mail exploders, and newsgroups, the same individual can become a pamphleteer." *Reno v. American Civil Liberties Union*, 521 U.S. 844, 870 (1997). Much of the appeal of the Internet lies in its "relatively unlimited, low cost capacity for commu-

----

43. Members of the New York office of Davis Wright Tremaine LLP [of which the author is a member in the firm's Seattle office] represented APBNews.com in connection with this dispute.

nication of all kinds." *Id.* This feature enables "individual citizens of limited means [to] speak to a worldwide audience on issues of concern to them. Federalists and Anti-Federalists may debate the structure of their government nightly, but these debates occur in newsgroups or chat rooms rather than in pamphlets." *American Civil Liberties Union v. Reno*, 929 F. Supp. 824, 881 (E.D. Pa. 1996), *aff'd*, 521 U.S. 844 (1997).

The "press" has been afforded special protections, many of which are constitutionally-rooted. For example, because journalists have been regarded as having a unique role as surrogates for the public in gaining access to information, the press has been shielded under certain circumstances from compelled disclosure of the identity of their sources and the substance of their newsgathering materials. This enables the press to investigate and report on a wide range of issues more effectively and more comprehensively.

---

## Paul M. BRANZBURG v. John P. HAYES
### Supreme Court of the United States
### Nos. 70-85, 70-94, 70-57, 408 U.S. 665
### June 29, 1972

[Three cases were consolidated. One related to judgments of the Kentucky Court of Appeals involving petitioner Paul M. Branzburg, who was a staff reporter for the *Courier-Journal*, a daily newspaper published in Louisville, Kentucky. On November 15, 1969, the newspaper carried a story under Branzburg's by-line, describing in detail his observations of two young residents of Jefferson County synthesizing hashish from marihuana. The article stated that Branzburg had promised not to reveal their identity. He was subpoenaed by the Jefferson County grand jury; he appeared but refused to identify the two individuals.

Another action involving petitioner Branzburg arose out of a subsequent story, published on January 10, 1971, in which he described in detail the use of drugs in Frankfort, Kentucky. The article reported that in order to provide a comprehensive survey of the "drug scene" in Frankfort, Branzburg had "spent two weeks interviewing several dozen drug users in the capital city" and had seen some of them smoking marihuana. Branzburg was subpoenaed to appear before a Franklin County grand jury to testify in the matter of violation of statutes concerning the use and sale of drugs. His motion to quash the summons was denied; although an order was issued protecting Branzburg from revealing "confidential associations, sources or information," he nonetheless was required to "answer any questions which concern or pertain to any criminal act, the commission of which was actually observed by [him.]"

A second petitioner, Paul Pappas, a television newsman-photographer, went to New Bedford, Massachusetts to report on civil disorders that involved fires and other "turmoil." On July 30, 1970, he recorded and photographed a prepared statement read by a Black Panther leader, and was admitted to the Panther headquarters on the condition that he agree not to disclose anything he saw or heard inside the store, with the exception of an anticipated police raid. The police raid did not happen, and Pappas did not write a story about what did occur. Two months later, he was summoned before the Bristol County Grand Jury; he appeared but refused to answer questions about what had taken place inside the Panther headquarters while he was there. His motion to quash a second summons was denied.

Earl Caldwell was a reporter for *The New York Times*, assigned to cover the Black Panther Party and other black militant groups. He was served with a subpoena *duces tecum* on February 2, 1970, ordering him to appear before a grand jury to testify and bring notes and tape recordings of interviews with the Black Panther Party concerning its purposes and activities. A second subpoena, served the following month, ordered him to appear to testify before the grand jury. The motion to quash brought by Caldwell and *The New York Times* was denied. A subsequent subpoena *ad testificandum* was issued, Caldwell's motion to quash was denied, and Caldwell refused to appear before the grand jury. He ultimately was ordered committed for contempt until such time as he complied with the court's order or until the expiration of the term of the grand jury. On appeal, the Court of Appeals reversed the contempt order.

In November 1969, an officer of the Black Panther Party reportedly had made a publicly televised speech in which he had declared that "[w]e will kill Richard Nixon." Caldwell had written about the Black Panther Party that "[i]n their role as the vanguard in a revolutionary struggle the Panthers have picked up guns." He quoted the Chief of Staff of the Party as declaring that "We advocate the very direct overthrow of the Government by way of force and violence. By picking up guns and moving against it because we recognize it as being oppressive and in recognizing that we know that the only solution to it is armed struggle [sic]."]

Opinion of the Court by Mr. Justice WHITE, announced by THE CHIEF JUSTICE.

The issue in these cases is whether requiring newsmen to appear and testify before state or federal grand juries abridges the freedom of speech and press guaranteed by the First Amendment. We hold that it does not....

## II

Petitioners Branzburg and Pappas and respondent Caldwell press First Amendment claims that may be simply put: that to gather news it is often necessary to agree either not to identify the source of information published or to publish only part of the facts revealed, or both; that if the reporter is nevertheless forced to reveal these confidences to a grand jury, the source so identified and other confidential sources of other reporters will be measurably deterred from furnishing publishable information, all to the detriment of the free flow of information protected by the First Amendment. Although the newsmen in these cases do not claim an absolute privilege against official interrogation in all circumstances, they assert that the reporter should not be forced either to appear or to testify before a grand jury or at trial until and unless sufficient grounds are shown for believing that the reporter possesses information relevant to a crime the grand jury is investigating, that the information the reporter has is unavailable from other sources, and that the need for the information is sufficiently compelling to override the claimed invasion of First Amendment interests occasioned by the disclosure.... The heart of the claim is that the burden on news gathering resulting from compelling reporters to disclose confidential information outweighs any public interest in obtaining the information.

We do not question the significance of free speech, press, or assembly to the country's welfare. Nor is it suggested that news gathering does not quality for First Amendment protection; without some protection for seeking out the news, freedom of the press could be eviscerated. But these cases involve no intrusions upon speech or assembly, no prior restraint or restriction on what the press may publish, and no express or implied command that the press publish what it prefers to withhold. No exaction or tax for the privilege of publishing, and no penalty, civil or criminal, related to the content of published material is at issue here. The use of confidential sources by the press is not forbidden or restricted; reporters remain free to seek news from any source by means within the law. No attempt is made to require the press to publish its sources of information or indiscriminately to disclose them on request.

The sole issue before us is the obligation of reporters to respond to grand jury subpoenas as other citizens do and to answer questions relevant to an investigation into the commission of crime. Citizens generally are not constitutionally immune from grand jury subpoenas; and neither the First Amendment nor any other constitutional provision protects the average citizen from disclosing to a grand jury information that he has received in confidence.[21] The claim is, however, that reporters are exempt from these obligations because if forced to respond to subpoenas and identify their sources or disclose other confidences, their informants will refuse or be reluctant to furnish newsworthy information in the future. This asserted burden on news gathering is said to make compelled testimony from newsmen constitutionally suspect and to require a privileged position for them.

It is clear that the First Amendment does not invalidate every incidental burdening of the press that may result from the enforcement of civil or criminal statutes of general applicability. Under prior cases, otherwise valid laws serving substantial public interests may be enforced against the press as against others, despite the possible burden that may be imposed. The Court has emphasized that "[t]he publisher of a newspaper has no special immunity from the application of general laws. He has no special privilege to invade the rights and liberties of others." *Associated Press v. NLRB*, 301 U.S. 103, 132–133, 57 S.Ct. 650, 656, 81 L.Ed. 953 (1937). It was there held that the Associated Press, a news-gathering and disseminating organization, was not exempt from the requirements of the National Labor Relations Act. The holding was reaffirmed in *Oklahoma Press Publishing Co. v. Walling*, 327 U.S. 186, 192–193, 66 S.Ct. 494, 497–498, 90 L.Ed. 614 (1946), where the Court rejected the claim that applying the Fair Labor Standards Act to a newspaper publishing business would abridge the freedom of press guaranteed by the First Amendment. *See also Mabee v. White Plains Publishing Co.*, 327 U.S. 178, 66 S.Ct. 511, 90 L.Ed. 607 (1946). *Associated Press v. United States*, 326 U.S. 1, 65 S.Ct. 1416, 89 L.Ed. 2013 (1945), similarly overruled assertions that the First Amendment precluded application of the Sherman Act to a news-gathering and disseminating organization. *Cf. Indiana Farmer's Guide Publishing Co. v. Prairie Farmer Publishing Co.*, 293 U.S. 268, 276, 55 S.Ct. 182, 184, 79 L.Ed. 356 (1934); *Citizen Publishing Co. v. United States*, 394 U.S. 131, 139, 89 S.Ct. 927, 931, 22 L.Ed.2d 148 (1969); *Lorain Journal Co. v. United States*, 342 U.S. 143, 155–156, 72 S.Ct. 181, 187–188, 96 L.Ed. 162 (1951). Likewise, a newspaper may be subjected to nondiscriminatory forms of general taxation. *Grosjean v. American Press Co.*, 297 U.S. 233, 250, 56 S.Ct. 444, 449, 80 L.Ed. 660 (1936); *Murdock v. Pennsylvania*, 319 U.S. 105, 112, 63 S.Ct. 870, 874, 87 L.Ed. 1292 (1943).

---

21. "In general, then, the mere fact that a communication was made in express confidence, or in the implied confidence of a confidential relation, does not create a privilege...No pledge of privacy nor oath of secrecy can avail against demand for the truth in a court of justice." 8 J. Wigmore, *Evidence* §2286 (McNaughton rev. 1961). This was not always the rule at common law, however. In 17th century England, the obligations of honor among gentlemen were occasionally recognized as privileging from compulsory disclosure information obtained in exchange for a promise of confidence. *See Bulstrod v. Letchmere*, 2 Freem. 6, 22 Eng. Rep. 1019 (1676); *Lord Grey's Trial*, 9 How. St. Tr. 127 (1682).

The prevailing view is that the press is not free to publish with impunity everything and anything it desires to publish. Although it may deter or regulate what is said or published, the press may not circulate knowing or reckless falsehoods damaging to private reputation without subjecting itself to liability for damages, including punitive damages, or even criminal prosecution. *See New York Times Co. v. Sullivan*, 376 U.S. 254, 279–280, 84 S.Ct. 710, 725–726, 11 L.Ed.2d 686 (1964); *Garrison v. Louisiana*, 379 U.S. 64, 74, 85 S.Ct. 209, 215, 13 L.Ed.2d 125 (1964); *Curtis Publishing Co. v. Butts*, 388 U.S. 130, 147, 87 S.Ct. 1975, 1987, 18 L.Ed.2d 1094 (1967) (opinion of Harlan, J.,); *Monitor Patriot Co. v. Roy*, 401 U.S. 265, 277, 91 S.Ct. 621, 628, 28 L.Ed.2d 35 (1971). A newspaper or a journalist may also be punished for contempt of court, in appropriate circumstances. *Craig v. Harney*, 331 U.S. 367, 377–378, 67 S.Ct. 1249, 1255–1256, 91 L.Ed. 1546 (1947).

It has generally been held that the First Amendment does not guarantee the press a constitutional right of special access to information not available to the public generally. *Zemel v. Rusk*, 381 U.S. 1, 16–17, 85 S.Ct. 1271, 1280–1281, 14 L.Ed.2d 179 (1965); *New York Times Co. v. United States*, 403 U.S. 713, 728–730, 91 S.Ct. 2140, 2148–2149, 29 L.Ed.2d 822 (1971) (Stewart, J., concurring); *Tribune Review Publishing Co. v. Thomas*, 254 F.2d 883, 885 (CA3 1958); *In the Matter of United Press Assns. v. Valente*, 308 N.Y. 71, 77, 123 N.E.2d 777, 778 (1954). In *Zemel v. Rusk, supra*, for example, the Court sustained the Government's refusal to validate passports to Cuba even though that restriction "render[ed] less than wholly free the flow of information concerning that country." 381 U.S. at 16, 85 S.Ct. at 1281. The ban on travel was held constitutional, for "[t]he right to speak and publish does not carry with it the unrestrained right to gather information." *Id*. at 17, 85 S.Ct. at 1281.[22]

Despite the fact that news gathering may be hampered, the press is regularly excluded from grand jury proceedings, our own conferences, the meetings of other official bodies gathered in executive session, and the meetings of private organizations. Newsmen have no constitutional right of access to the scenes of crime or disaster when the general public is excluded, and they may be prohibited from attending or publishing information about trials if such restrictions are necessary to assure a defendant a fair trial before an impartial tribunal. In *Sheppard v. Maxwell*, 384 U.S. 333, 86 S.Ct. 1507, 16 L.Ed.2d 600 (1966), for example, the Court reversed a state court conviction where the trial court failed to adopt "stricter rules governing the use of the courtroom by newsmen, as Sheppard's counsel requested," neglected to insulate witnesses from the press, and made no "effort to control the release of leads, information, and gossip to the press by police officers, witnesses, and the counsel for both sides." *Id*. at 358, 359, 86 S.Ct. at 1520. "[T]he trial court might well have proscribed extrajudicial statements by any lawyer, party, witness, or court official which divulged prejudicial matters." *Id*. at 361, 86 S.Ct. at 1521. *See also Estes v. Texas*, 381 U.S. 532, 539–540, 85 S.Ct. 1628, 1631–1632, 14 L.Ed.2d 543 (1965); *Rideau v. Louisiana*, 373 U.S. 723, 726, 83 S.Ct. 1417, 1419, 10 L.Ed.2d 663 (1963).

It is thus not surprising that the great weight of authority is that newsmen are not exempt from the normal duty of appearing before a grand jury and answering questions

---

22. "There are few restrictions on action which could not be clothed by ingenious argument in the garb of decreased data flow. For example, the prohibition of unauthorized entry into the White House diminishes the citizen's opportunities to gather information he might find relevant to his opinion of the way the country is being run, but that does not make entry into the White House a First Amendment right." 381 U.S. at 16–17, 85 S.Ct. at 1281.

relevant to a criminal investigation. At common law, courts consistently refused to recognize the existence of any privilege authorizing a newsman to refuse to reveal confidential information to a grand jury....

The prevailing constitutional view of the newsman's privilege is very much rooted in the ancient role of the grand jury that has the dual function of determining if there is probable cause to believe that a crime has been committed and of protecting citizens against unfounded criminal prosecutions.[23] Grand jury proceedings are constitutionally mandated for the institution of federal criminal prosecutions for capital or other serious crimes, and "its constitutional prerogatives are rooted in long centuries of Anglo-American history." *Hannah v. Larche*, 363 U.S. 420, 489–490, 80 S.Ct. 1502, 1544, 4 L.Ed.2d 1307 (1960). (Frankfurter, J., concurring in result). The Fifth Amendment provides that "[n]o person shall be held to answer for a capital, or otherwise infamous crime, unless on a presentment or indictment of a Grand Jury."[24] The adoption of the grand jury "in our Constitution as the sole method for preferring charges in serious criminal cases shows the high place it held as an instrument of justice." *Costello v. United States*, 350 U.S. 359, 362, 76 S.Ct. 406, 408, 100 L.Ed. 397 (1956). Although state systems of criminal procedure differ greatly among themselves, the grand jury is similarly guaranteed by many state constitutions and plays an important role in fair and effective law enforcement in the overwhelming majority of the States. Because its task is to inquire into the Existence of possible criminal conduct and to return only well-founded indictments, its investigative powers are necessarily broad. "It is a grand inquest, a body with powers of investigation and inquisition, the scope of whose inquiries is not to be limited narrowly by questions of propriety or forecasts of the probable result of the investigation, or by doubts whether any particular individual will be found properly subject to an accusation of crime." *Blair v. United States*, 250 U.S. 273, 282, 39 S.Ct. 468, 471, 63 L.Ed. 979 (1919). Hence, the grand jury's authority to subpoena witnesses is not only historic, *id.* at 279–281, 39 S.Ct. at 470–471, but essential to its task. Although the powers of the grand jury are not unlimited and are subject to the supervision of a judge, the longstanding principle that "the public...has a right to every man's evidence," except for those persons protected by a constitutional, common-law, or statutory privilege, *United States v. Bryan*, 339 U.S. 323, 331, 70 S.Ct. 724, 730, 94 L.Ed. 884 (1950); *Blackmer v. United States*, 284 U.S. 421, 438, 52 S.Ct. 252, 255, 76 L.Ed. 375 (1932); 8 J. Wigmore, *Evidence* § 2192 (McNaughton rev. 1961), is particularly applicable to grand jury proceedings.[26]

---

23. "Historically, [the grand jury] has been regarded as a primary security to the innocent against hasty, malicious and oppressive persecution; it serves the invaluable function in our society of standing between the accuser and the accused...to determine whether a charge is founded upon reason or was dictated by an intimidating power or by malice and personal ill will." *Wood v. Georgia*, 370 U.S. 375, 390, 82 S.Ct. 1364, 1373, 8 L.Ed.2d 569 (1962) (footnote omitted).

24. It has been held that "infamous" punishments include confinement at hard labor, *United States v. Moreland*, 258 U.S. 433, 42 S.Ct. 368, 66 L.Ed. 700 (1922); incarceration in a penitentiary, *Mackin v. United States*, 117 U.S. 348, 6 S.Ct. 777, 29 L.Ed. 909 (1886); and imprisonment for more than a year, *Barkman v. Sanford*, 162 F.2d 592 (CA5), *cert. denied*, 332 U.S. 816, 68 S.Ct. 155, 92 L.Ed. 393 (1947)....

26. ...

Are men of the first rank and consideration—are men high in office— men whose time is not less valuable to the public than to themselves—are such men to be forced to quit their business, their functions, and what is more than all, their pleasure, at the beck of every idle or malicious adversary, to dance attendance upon every petty cause? Yes, as far as it is necessary, they and everybody....Were the Prince of Wales, the Archbishop of Canterbury, and the Lord High Chancellor, to be passing by in the same coach, while a chim-

A number of States have provided newsmen a statutory privilege of varying breadth,[27] but the majority have not done so, and none has been provided by federal statute. Until now the only testimonial privilege for unofficial witnesses that is rooted in the Federal Constitution is the Fifth Amendment privilege against compelled self-incrimination. We are asked to create another by interpreting the First Amendment to grant newsmen a testimonial privilege that other citizens do not enjoy. This we decline to do.[29] Fair and effective law enforcement aimed at providing security for the person and property of the individual is a fundamental function of government, and the grand jury plays an important, constitutionally mandated role in this process. On the records now before us, we perceive no basis for holding that the public interest in law enforcement and in ensuring effective grand jury proceedings is insufficient to override the consequential, but uncertain, burden on news gathering that is said to result from insisting that reporters, like other citizens, respond to relevant questions put to them in the course of a valid grand jury investigation or criminal trial.

This conclusion itself involves no restraint on what newspapers may publish or on the type or quality of information reporters may seek to acquire, nor does it threaten the vast bulk of confidential relationships between reporters and their sources. Grand juries address themselves to the issues of whether crimes have been committed and who committed them. Only where news sources themselves are implicated in crime or possess information relevant to the grand jury's task need they or the reporter be concerned about grand jury subpoenas. Nothing before us indicates that a large number or percentage of all confidential news sources falls into either category and would in any way be deterred by our holding that the Constitution does not, as it never has, exempt the newsman from performing the citizen's normal duty of appearing and furnishing information relevant to the grand jury's task.

The preference for anonymity of those confidential informants involved in actual criminal conduct is presumably a product of their desire to escape criminal prosecu-

---

ney-sweeper and a barrow-woman were in dispute about a halfpennyworth of apples, and the chimney-sweeper or the barrow-woman were to think proper to call upon them for their evidence, could they refuse it? No, most certainly.

4 *The Works of Jeremy Bentham* 320–321 (J. Bowring ed. 1843).

In *United States v. Burr*, 25 Fed. Cas. pp. 30, 34 (No. 14,692d) (C.C. Va. 1807), Chief Justice Marshall, sitting on Circuit, opined that in proper circumstances a subpoena could be issued to the President of the United States.

27. Thus far, 17 States have provided some type of statutory protection to a newsman's confidential sources: Ala.Code, Tit. 7, §370 (1960); Alaska Stat. §09.25.150 (Supp.1971); Ariz.Rev.Stat.Ann. §12-2337 (Supp.1971–1972); Ark.Stat.Ann. §43-917 (1964); Cal.Evid.Code §1070 (Supp.1972); Ind. Ann.Stat. §2-1733 (1968), IC 1971, 34-3-5-1; Ky.Rev.Stat. §421.100 (1962); La.Rev.Stat.Ann. §§45: 1451–45:1454 (Supp.1972); Md.Ann.Code, art. 35, §2 (1971); Mich.Comp.Laws §767.5a (Supp. 1956), Mich.Stat.Ann. §28.945(1) (1954); Mont.Rev.Codes Ann. §93-601-2 (1964); Nev.Rev.Stat. §49.275 (1971); N.J.Rev.Stat. §§2A:84A-21, 2A:84A-29 (Supp.1972–1973); N.M.Stat.Ann. §20-1-12.1 (1970); N.Y.Civil Rights Laws, McKinney's Consol.Laws, c. 6, §79-h (Supp.1971–1972); Ohio Rev.Code Ann. §2739.12 (1954); Pa.Stat.Ann., Tit. 28, §330 (Supp.1972–1973).

29. The creation of new testimonial privileges has been met with disfavor by commentators since such privileges obstruct the search for truth. Wigmore condemns such privileges as "so many derogations from a positive general rule (that everyone is obligated to testify when properly summoned)" and as "obstacle(s) to the administration of justice." 8 J. Wigmore, *Evidence* §2192 (McNaughton rev. 1961). His criticism that "all privileges of exemption from this duty are exceptional, and are therefore to be discountenanced," *id.* at §2192, p. 73, has been frequently echoed.... Neither the ALI's Model Code of Evidence (1942), the Uniform Rules of Evidence of the National Conference of Commissioners on Uniform State Laws (1953), nor the Proposed Rules of Evidence for the United States Courts and Magistrates (rev. ed. 1971), has included a newsman's privilege.

tion, and this preference, while understandable, is hardly deserving of constitutional protection. It would be frivolous to assert—and no one does in these cases—that the First Amendment, in the interest of securing news or otherwise, confers a license on either the reporter or his news sources to violate valid criminal laws. Although stealing documents or private wiretapping could provide newsworthy information, neither reporter nor source is immune from conviction for such conduct, whatever the impact on the flow of news. Neither is immune, on First Amendment grounds, from testifying against the other, before the grand jury or at a criminal trial. The Amendment does not reach so far as to override the interest of the public in ensuring that neither reporter nor source is invading the rights of other citizens through reprehensible conduct forbidden to all other persons. To assert the contrary proposition

> [i]s to answer it, since it involves in its very statement the contention that the freedom of the press is the freedom to do wrong with impunity and implies the right to frustrate and defeat the discharge of those governmental duties upon the performance of which the freedom of all, including that of the press, depends.... It suffices to say that however complete is the right of the press to state public things and discuss them, that right, as every other right enjoyed in human society, is subject to the restraints which separate right from wrongdoing.

*Toledo Newspaper Co. v. United States*, 247 U.S. 402, 419–420, 38 S.Ct. 560, 564, 62 L.Ed. 1186 (1918).

Thus, we cannot seriously entertain the notion that the First Amendment protects a newsman's agreement to conceal the criminal conduct of his source, or evidence thereof, on the theory that it is better to write about crime than to do something about it. Insofar as any reporter in these cases undertook not to reveal or testify about the crime he witnessed, his claim of privilege under the First Amendment presents no substantial question. The crimes of news sources are no less reprehensible and threatening to the public interest when witnessed by a reporter than when they are not.

There remain those situations where a source is not engaged in criminal conduct but has information suggesting illegal conduct by others. Newsmen frequently receive information from such sources pursuant to a tacit or express agreement to withhold the source's name and suppress any information that the source wishes not published. Such informants presumably desire anonymity in order to avoid being entangled as a witness in a criminal trial or grand jury investigation. They may fear that disclosure will threaten their job security or personal safety or that it will simply result in dishonor or embarrassment.

The argument that the flow of news will be diminished by compelling reporters to aid the grand jury in a criminal investigation is not irrational, nor are the records before us silent on the matter. But we remain unclear how often and to what extent informers are actually deterred from furnishing information when newsmen are forced to testify before a grand jury. The available data indicate that some newsmen rely a great deal on confidential sources and that some informants are particularly sensitive to the threat of exposure and may be silenced if it is held by this Court that, ordinarily, newsmen must testify pursuant to subpoenas, but the evidence fails to demonstrate that there would be a significant construction of the flow of news to the public if this Court reaffirms the prior common-law and constitutional rule regarding the testimonial obligations of newsmen. Estimates of the inhibiting effect of such subpoenas on the willingness of informants to make disclosures to newsmen are widely divergent and to a great extent speculative. It would be difficult to canvass the views of the informants themselves; surveys of reporters on this topic are chiefly opinions of predicted informant behavior and must be viewed in the light of the professional self-interest of the interviewees. Reliance by the press on confidential informants does not mean that all such sources will in fact dry up because of the later possible appearance of the newsman before a grand jury. The reporter may never be called and if he objects to testifying, the prosecution may not insist. Also, the relationship of many informants to the press is a symbiotic one which is unlikely to be greatly inhibited by the threat of subpoena: quite often, such informants are members of a minority political or cultural group that relies heavily on the media to propagate its views, publicize its aims, and magnify its exposure to the public. Moreover, grand juries characteristically conduct secret proceedings, and law enforcement officers are themselves experienced in dealing with informers, and have their own methods for protecting them without interference with the effective administration of justice. There is little before us indicating that informants whose interest in avoiding exposure is that it may threaten job security, personal safety, or peace of mind, would in fact be in a worse position, or would think they would be, if they risked placing their trust in public officials as well as reporters. We doubt if the informer who prefers anonymity but is sincerely interested in furnishing evidence of crime will always or very often be deterred by the prospect of dealing with those public authorities characteristically charged with the duty to protect the public interest as well as his.

Accepting the fact, however, that an undetermined number of informants not themselves implicated in crime will nevertheless, for whatever reason, refuse to talk to newsmen if they fear identification by a reporter in an official investigation, we cannot accept the argument that the public interest in possible future news about crime from undisclosed, unverified sources must take precedence over the public interest in pursuing and prosecuting those crimes reported to the press by informants and in thus deterring the commission of such crimes in the future.

We note first that the privilege claimed is that of the reporter, not the informant, and that if the authorities independently identify the informant, neither his own reluctance to testify nor the objection of the newsman would shield him from grand jury inquiry, whatever the impact on the flow of news or on his future usefulness as a secret source of information. More important, it is obvious that agreements to conceal information relevant to commission of crime have very little to recommend them from the standpoint of public policy. Historically, the common law recognized a duty to raise the "hue and cry" and report felonies to the authorities. Misprision of a felony—that is, the concealment of a felony "which a man knows, but never assented to...(so as to become) either principal or accessory," 4 W. Blackstone, *Commentaries*, was often said to be a common-law crime. The first Congress passed a statute, 1 Stat. 113, §6, as amended, 35 Stat. 1114, §146, 62 Stat. 684, which is still in effect, defining a federal crime of misprision:

> Whoever, having knowledge of the actual commission of a felony cognizable by a court of the United States, conceals and does not as soon as possible make known the same to some judge or other person in civil or military authority under the United States, shall be [guilty of misprision].

18 U.S.C. §4.

It is apparent from this statute, as well as from our history and that of England, that concealment of crime and agreements to do so are not looked upon with favor. Such conduct deserves no encomium, and we decline now to afford it First Amendment protection by denigrating the duty of a citizen, whether reporter or informer, to respond to grand jury subpoena and answer relevant questions put to him.

Of course, the press has the right to abide by its agreement not to publish all the information it has, but the right to withhold news is not equivalent to a First Amendment exemption from the ordinary duty of all other citizens to furnish relevant information to a grand jury performing an important public function. Private restraints on the flow of information are not so favored by the First Amendment that they override all other public interests. As Mr. Justice Black declared in another context, "[f]reedom of the press from governmental interference under the First Amendment does not sanction repression of that freedom by private interests." *Associated Press v. United States*, 326 U.S. at 20, 65 S.Ct. at 1425.

Neither are we now convinced that a virtually impenetrable constitutional shield, beyond legislative or judicial control, should be forged to protect a private system of informers operated by the press to report on criminal conduct, a system that would be unaccountable to the public, would pose a threat to the citizen's justifiable expectations of privacy, and would equally protect well-intentioned informants and those who for pay or otherwise betray their trust to their employer or associates. The public through its elected and appointed law enforcement officers regularly utilizes informers, and in proper circumstances may assert a privilege against disclosing the identity of these informers. But

> [t]he purpose of the privilege is the furtherance and protection of the public interest in effective law enforcement. The privilege recognizes the obligation of citizens to communicate their knowledge of the commission of crimes to law-enforcement officials and, by preserving their anonymity, encourages them to perform that obligation.

*Roviaro v. United States*, 353 U.S. 53, 59, 77 S.Ct. 623, 627, 1 L.Ed.2d 639 (1957).

Such informers enjoy no constitutional protection. Their testimony is available to the public when desired by grand juries or at criminal trials; their identity cannot be concealed from the defendant when it is critical to his case. *Roviaro v. United States, supra,* at 60–61, 62, 77 S.Ct. at 627–628, 629; *McCray v. Illinois*, 386 U.S. 300, 310, 87 S.Ct. 1056, 1062, 18 L.Ed.2d 62 (1967); *Smith v. Illinois*, 390 U.S. 129, 131, 88 S.Ct. 748, 749, 19 L.Ed.2d 956 (1968); *Alford v. United States*, 282 U.S. 687, 693, 51 S.Ct. 218, 220, 75 L.Ed. 624 (1931). Clearly, this system is not impervious to control by the judiciary and the decision whether to unmask an informer or to continue to profit by his anonymity is in public, not private, hands. We think that it should remain there and that public authorities should retain the options of either insisting on the informer's testimony relevant to the prosecution of crime or of seeking the benefit of further information that his exposure might prevent.

We are admonished that refusal to provide a First Amendment reporter's privilege will undermine the freedom of the press to collect and disseminate news. But this is not the lesson history teaches us. As noted previously, the common law recognized no such privilege, and the constitutional argument was not even asserted until 1958. From the beginning of our country the press has operated without constitutional protection for press informants, and the press has flourished. The existing constitutional rules have not been a serious obstacle to either the development or retention of confidential news sources by the press.

It is said that currently press subpoenas have multiplied, that mutual distrust and tension between press and officialdom have increased, that reporting styles have changed, and that there is now more need for confidential sources, particularly where the press seeks news about minority cultural and political groups or dissident organizations suspicious of the law and public officials. These developments, even if true, are treacherous grounds for a far-reaching interpretation of the First Amendment fastening a nationwide rule on courts, grand juries, and prosecuting officials everywhere. The obligation to testify in response to grand jury subpoenas will not threaten these sources not involved with criminal conduct and without information relevant to grand jury investigations, and we cannot hold that the Constitution places the sources in these two categories either above the law or beyond its reach....

The requirements of those cases, which hold that a State's interest must be "compelling" or "paramount" to justify even an indirect burden on First Amendment rights, are...met here. As we have indicated, the investigation of crime by the grand jury implements a fundamental governmental role of securing the safety of the person and property of the citizen, and it appears to us that calling reporters to give testimony in the manner and for the reasons that other citizens are called "bears a reasonable relationship to the achievement of the governmental purpose asserted as its justification." *Bates v. Little Rock, supra,* 361 U.S. at 525, 80 S.Ct. at 417. If the test is that the government "convincingly show a substantial relation between the information sought and a subject of overriding and compelling state interest," *Gibson v. Florida Legislative Investigation Committee,* 372 U.S. 539, 546, 83 S.Ct. 889, 894, 9 L.Ed.2d 929 (1963), it is quite apparent (1) that the State has the necessary interest in extirpating the traffic in illegal drugs, in forestalling assassination attempts on the President, and in preventing the community from being disrupted by violent disorders endangering both persons and property; and (2) that, based on the stories Branzburg and Caldwell wrote and Pappas' admitted conduct, the grand jury called these reporters as they would others—because it was likely that they could supply information to help the government determine whether illegal conduct had occurred and, if it had, whether there was sufficient evidence to return an indictment.

Similar considerations dispose of the reporters' claims that preliminary to requiring their grand jury appearance, the State must show that a crime has been committed and that they possess relevant information not available from other sources, for only the grand jury itself can make this determination. The role of the grand jury as an important instrument of effective law enforcement necessarily includes an investigatory function with respect to determining whether a crime has been committed and who committed it. To this end it must call witnesses, in the manner best suited to perform its task. "When the grand jury is performing its investigatory function into a general problem area...society's interest is best served by a thorough and extensive investigation." *Wood v. Georgia,* 370 U.S. 375, 392, 82 S.Ct. 1364, 1374, 8 L.Ed.2d 569 (1962). A grand jury investigation "is not fully carried out until every available clue has been run down and all witnesses examined in every proper way to find if a crime has been committed." *United States v. Stone,* 249 F.2d 138, 140 (C.A.2 1970). Such an investigation may be triggered by tips, rumors, evidence proffered by the prosecutor, or the personal knowledge of the grand jurors. *Costello v. United States,* 350 U.S. at 362, 76 S.Ct. at 408. It is only after the grand jury has examined the evidence that a determination of whether the proceeding will result in an indictment can be made.... We see no reason to hold that these reporters, any more than other citizens, should be excused from furnishing information that may help the grand jury in arriving at its initial determinations.

The privilege claimed here is conditional, not absolute; given the suggested preliminary showings and compelling need, the reporter would be required to testify. Presumably, such a rule would reduce the instances in which reporters could be required to appear, but predicting in advance when and in what circumstances they could be compelled to do so would be difficult. Such a rule would also have implications for the issuance of compulsory process to reporters at civil and criminal trials and at legislative hearings. If newsmen's confidential sources are as sensitive as they are claimed to be, the prospect of being unmasked whenever a judge determines the situation justifies it is hardly a satisfactory solution to the problem. For them, it would appear that only an absolute privilege would suffice.

We are unwilling to embark the judiciary on a long and difficult journey to such an uncertain destination. The administration of a constitutional newsman's privilege would present practical and conceptual difficulties of a high order. Sooner or later, it would be necessary to define those categories of newsmen who qualified for the privilege, a questionable procedure in light of the traditional doctrine that liberty of the press is the right of the lonely pamphleteer who uses carbon paper or a mimeograph just as much as of the large metropolitan publisher who utilizes the latest photocomposition methods. *Cf. In re Grand Jury Witnesses*, 322 F. Supp. 573, 574 (N.D. Cal. 1970). Freedom of the press is a "fundamental personal right" which "is not confined to newspapers and periodicals. It necessarily embraces pamphlets and leaflets.... The press in its historic connotation comprehends every sort of publication which affords a vehicle of information and opinion." *Lovell v. City of Griffin*, 303 U.S. 444, 450, 452, 58 S.Ct. 666, 669, 82 L.Ed. 949 (1938). *See also Mills v. Alabama*, 384 U.S. 214, 219, 86 S.Ct. 1434, 1437, 16 L.Ed.2d 484 (1966); *Murdock v. Pennsylvania*, 319 U.S. 105, 111, 63 S.Ct. 870, 874, 87 L.Ed. 1292 (1943). The informative function asserted by representatives of the organized press in the present cases is also performed by lecturers, political pollsters, novelists, academic researchers, and dramatists. Almost any author may quite accurately assert that he is contributing to the flow of information to the public, that he relies on confidential sources of information, and that these sources will be silenced if he is forced to make disclosures before a grand jury.[40]

In each instance where a reporter is subpoenaed to testify, the courts would also be embroiled in preliminary factual and legal determinations with respect to whether the proper predicate had been laid for the reporter's appearance: Is there probable cause to believe a crime has been committed? Is it likely that the reporter has useful information gained in confidence? Could the grand jury obtain the information elsewhere? Is the official interest sufficient to outweigh the claimed privilege?

Thus, in the end, by considering whether enforcement of a particular law served a "compelling" governmental interest, the courts would be inextricably involved in distinguishing between the value of enforcing different criminal laws. By requiring testimony from a reporter in investigations involving some crimes but not in others, they would

---

40. Such a privilege might be claimed by groups that set up newspapers in order to engage in criminal activity and to therefore be insulated from grand jury inquiry, regardless of Fifth Amendment grants of immunity. It might appear that such "sham" newspapers would be easily distinguishable, yet the First Amendment ordinarily prohibits courts from inquiring into the content of expression, except in cases of obscenity or libel, and protects speech and publications regardless of their motivation, orthodoxy, truthfulness, timeliness, or taste. *New York Times Co. v. Sullivan*, 376 U.S. 254, at 269–270, 84 S.Ct. 710, at 720–721, 11 L.Ed.2d 686; *Kingsley International Pictures Corp. v. Regents*, 360 U.S. 684, 689, 79 S.Ct. 1362, 1365, 3 L.Ed.2d 1512 (1959); *Winters v. New York*, 333 U.S. 507, 510, 68 S.Ct. 665, 667, 92 L.Ed. 840 (1948); *Thomas v. Collins*, 323 U.S. 516, at 537, 65 S.Ct. 315, at 326, 89 L.Ed. 430. By affording a privilege to some organs of communication but not to others, courts would inevitably be discriminating on the basis of content.

be making a value judgment that a legislature had declined to make, since in each case the criminal law involved would represent a considered legislative judgment, not constitutionally suspect, of what conduct is liable to criminal prosecution. The task of judges, like other officials outside the legislative branch, is not to make the law but to uphold it in accordance with their oaths.

At the federal level, Congress has freedom to determine whether a statutory newsman's privilege is necessary and desirable and to fashion standards and rules as narrow or broad as deemed necessary to deal with the evil discerned and, equally important, to refashion those rules as experience from time to time may dictate. There is also merit in leaving state legislatures free, within First Amendment limits, to fashion their own standards in light of the conditions and problems with respect to the relations between law enforcement officials and press in their own areas....

In addition, there is much force in the pragmatic view that the press has at its disposal powerful mechanisms of communication and is far from helpless to protect itself from harassment or substantial harm. Furthermore, if what the newsmen urged in these cases is true—that law enforcement cannot hope to gain and may suffer from subpoenaing newsmen before grand juries—prosecutors will be loath to risk so much for so little. Thus, at the federal level the Attorney General has already fashioned a set of rules for federal officials in connection with subpoenaing members of the press to testify before grand juries or at criminal trials.[41] These rules are a major step in the direction the reporters herein desire to move. They may prove wholly sufficient to resolve the bulk of disagreements and controversies between press and federal officials.

Finally, as we have earlier indicated, news gathering is not without its First Amendment protections, and grand jury investigations if instituted or conducted other than in good faith, would pose wholly different issues for resolution under the First Amendment.[42] Official harassment of the press undertaken not for purposes of law enforcement but to disrupt a reporter's relationship with his news sources would have no justification. Grand juries are subject to judicial control and subpoenas to motions to quash. We do not expect courts will forget that grand juries must operate within the limits of the First Amendment as well as the Fifth.

---

41. The Guidelines for Subpoenas to the News Media were first announced in a speech by the Attorney General on August 10, 1970, and then were expressed in Department of Justice Memo. No. 692 (Sept. 2, 1970), which was sent to all United States Attorneys by the Assistant Attorney General in charge of the Criminal Division. The Guidelines state that: "The Department of Justice recognizes that compulsory process in some circumstances may have a limiting effect on the exercise of First Amendment rights. In determining whether to request issuance of a subpoena to the press, the approach in every case must be to weigh that limiting effect against the public interest to be served in the fair administration of justice" and that: "The Department of Justice does not consider the press "an investigative arm of the government." Therefore, all reasonable attempts should be made to obtain information from non-press sources before there is any consideration of subpoenaing the press. The Guidelines provide for negotiations with the press and require the express authorization of the Attorney General for such subpoenas. The principles to be applied in authorizing such subpoenas are stated to be whether there is "sufficient reason to believe that the information sought (from the journalist) is essential to a successful investigation," and whether the Government has unsuccessfully attempted to obtain the information from alternative non-press sources. The Guidelines provide, however, that in "emergencies and other unusual situations," subpoenas may be issued which do not exactly conform to the Guidelines.

42. Cf. *Younger v. Harris*, 401 U.S. 37, 49, 53–54, 91 S.Ct. 746, 753, 754–755, 27 L.Ed.2d 669 (1971).

## III

We turn, therefore, to the disposition of the cases before us. From what we have said, it necessarily follows that the decision in *United States v. Caldwell*, No. 70-57, must be reversed. If there is no First Amendment privilege to refuse to answer the relevant and material questions asked during a good-faith grand jury investigation, then it is *a fortiori* true that there is no privilege to refuse to appear before such a grand jury until the Government demonstrates some "compelling need" for a newsman's testimony. Other issues were urged upon us, but since they were not passed upon by the Court of Appeals, we decline to address them in the first instance.

The decisions in No. 70-85, *Branzburg v. Hayes* and *Branzburg v. Meigs*, must be affirmed. Here, petitioner refused to answer questions that directly related to criminal conduct that he had observed and written about. The Kentucky Court of Appeals noted that marihuana is defined as a narcotic drug by statute, Ky. Rev. Stat. §218.010(14) (1962), and that unlicensed possession or compounding of it is a felony punishable by both fine and imprisonment. Ky. Rev. Stat. §218.210 (1962). It held that petitioner "saw the commission of the statutory felonies of unlawful possession of marijuana and the unlawful conversion of it into hashish," in *Branzburg v. Pound*, 461 S.W.2d at 346. Petitioner may be presumed to have observed similar violations of the state narcotics laws during the research he did for the story that forms the basis of the subpoena in *Branzburg v. Meigs*. In both cases, if what petitioner wrote was true, he had direct information to provide the grand jury concerning the omission of serious crimes.

The only question presented at the present time in *In re Pappas*, No. 70-94, is whether petitioner Pappas must appear before the grand jury to testify pursuant to subpoena. The Massachusetts Supreme Judicial Court characterized the record in this case as "meager," and it is not clear what petitioner will be asked by the grand jury. It is not even clear that he will be asked to divulge information received in confidence. We affirm the decision of the Massachusetts Supreme Judicial Court and hold that petitioner must appear before the grand jury to answer the questions put to him, subject, of course, to the supervision of the presiding judge as to "the propriety, purposes, and scope of the grand jury inquiry and the pertinence of the probable testimony." 358 Mass. at 614, 266 N.E.2d at 303–304.

So ordered.

Mr. Justice POWELL, concurring.

I add this brief statement to emphasize what seems to me to be the limited nature of the Court's holding. The Court does not hold that newsmen, subpoenaed to testify before a grand jury, are without constitutional rights with respect to the gathering of news or in safeguarding their sources. Certainly, we do not hold, as suggested in Mr. Justice Stewart's dissenting opinion, that state and federal authorities are free to "annex" the news media as "an investigative arm of government." The solicitude repeatedly shown by this Court for First Amendment freedoms should be sufficient assurance against any such effort, even if one seriously believed that the media—properly free and untrammeled in the fullest sense of these terms—were not able to protect themselves.

As indicated in the concluding portion of the opinion, the Court states that no harassment of newsmen will be tolerated. If a newsman believes that the grand jury investigation is not being conducted in good faith he is not without remedy. Indeed, if the newsman is called upon to give information bearing only a remote and tenuous relationship to the subject of the investigation, or if he has some other reason to believe that his testimony implicates confidential source relationship without a legitimate need of law enforcement, he will have access to the court on a motion to quash and an appropriate protective order may be entered. The asserted claim to privilege should be judged on its facts by the striking of a proper balance between freedom of the press and the obligation of all citizens to give relevant testimony with respect to criminal conduct. The balance of these vital constitutional and societal interests on a case-by-case basis accords with the tried and traditional way of adjudicating such questions.*

In short, the courts will be available to newsmen under circumstances where legitimate First Amendment interests require protection.

Mr. Justice STEWART, with whom Mr. Justice BRENNAN and Mr. Justice MARSHALL join, dissenting.

The Court's crabbed view of the First Amendment reflects a disturbing insensitivity to the critical role of an independent press in our society. The question whether a reporter has a constitutional right to a confidential relationship with his source is of first impression here, but the principles that should guide our decision are as basic as any to be found in the Constitution. While Mr. Justice Powell's enigmatic concurring opinion gives some hope of a more flexible view in the future, the Court in these cases holds that a newsman has no First Amendment right to protect his sources when called before a grand jury. The Court thus invites state and federal authorities to undermine the historic independence of the press by attempting to annex the journalistic profession as an investigative arm of government. Not only will this decision impair performance of the press' constitutionally protected functions, but it will, I am convinced, in the long run, harm rather than help the administration of justice.

I respectfully dissent.

I

The reporter's constitutional right to a confidential relationship with his source stems from the broad societal interest in a full and free flow of information to the public. It is this basic concern that underlies the Constitution's protection of a free press, *Grosjean v. American Press Co.*, 297 U.S. 233, 250, 56 S.Ct. 444, 449, 80 L.Ed. 660; *New York Times Co. v. Sullivan*, 376 U.S. 254, 269, 84 S.Ct. 710, 720, 11 L.Ed.2d 686,[1] be-

---

* It is to be remembered that Caldwell asserts a constitutional privilege not even to appear before the grand jury unless a court decides that the Government has made a showing that meets the three preconditions specified in the dissenting opinion of Mr. Justice Stewart. To be sure, this would require a "balancing" of interests by the court, but under circumstances and constraints significantly different from the balancing that will be appropriate under the court's decision. The newsman witness, like all other witnesses, will have to appear; he will not be in a position to litigate at the threshold the State's very authority to subpoena him. Moreover, absent the constitutional preconditions that Caldwell and that dissenting opinion would impose as heavy burdens of proof to be carried by the State, the court—when called upon to protect a newsman from improper or prejudicial questioning—would be free to balance the competing interests on their merits in the particular case. The new constitutional rule endorsed by that dissenting opinion would, as a practical matter, defeat such a fair balancing and the essential societal interest in the detection and prosecution of crime would be heavily subordinated.

1. We have often described the process of informing the public as the core purpose of the constitutional guarantee of free speech and a free press. *See, e.g., Stromberg v. California*, 283 U.S. 359, 369, 51 S.Ct. 532, 535, 75 L.Ed. 1117; *De Jonge v. Oregon*, 299 U.S. 353, 365, 57 S.Ct. 255, 260, 81 L.Ed. 278; *Smith v. California*, 361 U.S. 147, 153, 80 S.Ct. 215, 218, 4 L.Ed.2d 205.

cause the guarantee is "not for the benefit of the press so much as for the benefit of all of us." *Time, Inc. v. Hill*, 385 U.S. 374, 389, 87 S.Ct. 534, 543, 17 L.Ed.2d 456.[2]

Enlightened choice by an informed citizenry is the basic ideal upon which an open society is premised, and a free press is thus indispensable to a free society. Not only does the press enhance personal self-fulfillment by providing the people with the widest possible range of fact and opinion, but it also is an incontestable precondition of self-government. The press "has been a mighty catalyst in awakening public interest in governmental affairs, exposing corruption among public officers and employees and generally informing the citizenry of public events and occurrences...." *Estes v. Texas*, 381 U.S. 532, 539, 85 S.Ct. 1628, 1631, 14 L.Ed.2d 543; *Mills v. Alabama*, 384 U.S. 214, 219, 86 S.Ct. 1434, 1437, 16 L.Ed.2d 484; *Grosjean, supra*, 297 U.S. at 250, 56 S.Ct. at 449. As private and public aggregations of power burgeon in size and the pressures for conformity necessarily mount, there is obviously a continuing need for an independent press to disseminate a robust variety of information and opinion through reportage, investigation, and criticism, if we are to preserve our constitutional tradition of maximizing freedom of choice by encouraging diversity of expression.

## A

In keeping with this tradition, we have held that the right to publish is central to the First Amendment and basic to the existence of constitutional democracy. *Grosjean, supra*, at 250, 56 S.Ct. at 449; *New York Times, supra*, 376 U.S. at 270, 84 S.Ct. at 720.

A corollary of the right to publish must be the right to gather news. The full flow of information to the public protected by the free-press guarantee would be severely curtailed if no protection whatever were afforded to the process by which news is assembled and disseminated. We have, therefore, recognized that there is a right to publish without prior governmental approval, *Near v. Minnesota*, 283 U.S. 697, 51 S.Ct. 625, 75 L.Ed. 1357; *New York Times Co. v. United States*, 403 U.S. 713, 91 S.Ct. 2140, 29 L.Ed.2d 822, a right to distribute information, *see, e.g., Lovell v. Griffin*, 303 U.S. 444, 452, 58 S.Ct. 666, 669, 82 L.Ed. 949; *Marsh v. Alabama*, 326 U.S. 501, 66 S.Ct. 276, 90 L.Ed. 265; *Martin v. City of Struthers*, 319 U.S. 141, 63 S.Ct. 862, 87 L.Ed. 1313; *Grosjean, supra*, and a right to receive printed matter, *Lamont v. Postmaster General*, 381 U.S. 301, 85 S.Ct. 1493, 14 L.Ed.2d 398.

No less important to the news dissemination process is the gathering of information. News must not be unnecessarily cut off at its source, for without freedom to acquire in-

---

2. As I see it, a reporter's right to protect his source is bottomed on the constitutional guarantee of a full flow of information to the public. A newsman's personal First Amendment rights or the associational rights of the newsman and the source are subsumed under that broad societal interest protected by the First Amendment. Obviously, we are not here concerned with the parochial personal concerns of particular newsmen or informants.

The newsman-informer relationship is different from...other relationships whose confidentiality is protected by statute, such as the attorney-client and physician-patient relationship. In the case of other statutory privileges, the right of nondisclosure is granted to the person making the communication in order that he will be encouraged by strong assurances of confidentiality to seek such relationships which contribute to his personal well-being. The judgment is made that the interests of society will be served when individuals consult physicians and lawyers; the public interest is thus advanced by creating a zone of privacy that the individual can control. However, in the case of the reporter-informer relationship, society's interest is not in the welfare of the informant per se, but rather in creating conditions in which information possessed by news sources can reach public attention.

Note, 80 Yale L.J. 317, 343 (1970) (footnotes omitted) (hereinafter Yale Note).

formation the right to publish would be impermissibly compromised. Accordingly, a right to gather news, of some dimensions, must exist. *Zemel v. Rusk*, 381 U.S. 1, 85 S.Ct. 1271, 14 L.Ed.2d 179.[4] Note, The *Right of the Press to Gather Information*, 71 Col. L. Rev. 838 (1971). As Madison wrote: "A popular Government, without popular information, or the means of acquiring it, is but a Prologue to a Farce or a Tragedy; or perhaps both." 9 *Writings of James Madison* 103 (G. Hunt ed. 1910).

B

The right to gather news implies, in turn, a right to a confidential relationship between a reporter and his source. This proposition follows as a matter of simple logic once three factual predicates are recognized: (1) newsmen require informants to gather news; (2) confidentiality—the promise or understanding that names or certain aspects of communications will be kept off the record—is essential to the creation and maintenance of a news-gathering relationship with informants; and (3) an unbridled subpoena power—the absence of a constitutional right protecting, in any way, a confidential relationship from compulsory process—will either deter sources from divulging information or deter reporters from gathering and publishing information.

It is obvious that informants are necessary to the news-gathering process as we know it today.... It is equally obvious that the promise of confidentiality may be a necessary prerequisite to a productive relationship between a newsman and his informants. An officeholder may fear his superior; a member of the bureaucracy, his associates; a dissident, the scorn of majority opinion. All may have information valuable to the public discourse, yet each may be willing to relate that information only in confidence to a reporter whom he trusts, either because of excessive caution or because of a reasonable fear of reprisals or censure for unorthodox views. The First Amendment concern must not be with the motives of any particular news source, but rather with the conditions in which informants of all shades of the spectrum may make information available through the press to the public. *Cf. Talley v. California*, 362 U.S. 60, 65, 80 S.Ct. 536, 539, 4 L.Ed.2d 559; *Bates v. City of Little Rock*, 361 U.S. 516, 80 S.Ct. 412, 4 L.Ed.2d 480; *NAACP v. Alabama*, 357 U.S. 449, 78 S.Ct. 1163, 2 L.Ed.2d 1488.... Commentators and individual reporters have repeatedly noted the importance of confidentiality.[8] And surveys among reporters and editors indicate that the promise of nondisclosure is necessary for many types of news gathering.

Finally, and most important, when governmental officials possess an unchecked power to compel newsmen to disclose information received in confidence, sources will clearly be deterred from giving information, and reporters will clearly be deterred from publishing it, because uncertainty about exercise of the power will lead to "self-censorship." *Smith v. California*, 361 U.S. 147, 149–154, 80 S.Ct. 215, 216–219, 4 L.Ed.2d 205; *New York Times Co. v. Sullivan*, 376 U.S. at 279, 84 S.Ct. at 725. The uncertainty arises,

---

4. In *Zemel v. Rusk*, 381 U.S. 1, 85 S.Ct. 1271, 14 L.Ed.2d 179, we held that the Secretary of State's denial of a passport for travel to Cuba did not violate a citizen's First Amendment rights. The rule was justified by the "weightiest considerations of national security" and we concluded that the "right to speak and publish does not carry with it the unrestrained right to gather information." *Id.* at 16–17, 85 S.Ct. at 1281. The necessary implication is that some right to gather information does exist.

8. ... As Walter Cronkite, a network television reporter, said in an affidavit in *Caldwell*: "In doing my work, I (and those who assist me) depend constantly on information, ideas, leads and opinions received in confidence. Such material is essential in digging out newsworthy facts and, equally important, in assessing the importance and analyzing the significance of public events."

of course, because the judiciary has traditionally imposed virtually no limitations on the grand jury's broad investigatory powers. *See* Antell, *The Modern Grand Jury: Benighted Supergovernment*, 51 A.B.A.J. 153 (1965).

After today's decision, the potential informant can never be sure that his identity or off-the-record communications will not subsequently be revealed through the compelled testimony of a newsman. A public-spirited person inside government, who is not implicated in any crime, will now be fearful of revealing corruption or other governmental wrongdoing, because he will now know he can subsequently be identified by use of compulsory process. The potential source must, therefore, choose between risking exposure by giving information or avoiding the risk by remaining silent.

The reporter must speculate about whether contact with a controversial source or publication of controversial material will lead to a subpoena. In the event of a subpoena, under today's decision, the newsman will know that he must choose between being punished for contempt if he refuses to testify, or violating his profession's ethics[10] and impairing his resourcefulness as a reporter if he discloses confidential information.[11] ...

The impairment of the flow of news cannot, of course, be proved with scientific precision, as the Court seems to demand. Obviously, not every news-gathering relationship requires confidentiality. And it is difficult to pinpoint precisely how many relationship do require a promise or understanding of nondisclosure. But we have never before demanded that First Amendment rights rest on elaborate empirical studies demonstrating beyond any conceivable doubt that deterrent effects exist; we have never before required proof of the exact number of people potentially affected by governmental action, who would actually be dissuaded from engaging in First Amendment activity.

Rather, on the basis of common sense and available information, we have asked, often implicitly, (1) whether there was a rational connection between the cause (the governmental action) and the effect (the deterrence or impairment of First Amendment activity), and (2) whether the effect would occur with some regularity, i.e., would not be de minimis. *See, e.g., Grosjean v. American Press Co.*, 297 U.S. at 244–245, 56 S.Ct. at 446–447; *Burstyn, Inc. v. Wilson*, 343 U.S. 495, 503, 72 S.Ct. 777, 781, 96 L.Ed. 1098; *Sweezy v. New Hampshire*, 354 U.S. 234, 248, 77 S.Ct. 1203, 1210, 1 L.Ed.2d 1311 (plurality opinion); *NAACP v. Alabama*, 357 U.S. at 461–466, 78 S.Ct. at 1171–1174; *Smith v. California*, 361 U.S. at 150–154, 80 S.Ct. at 217–219; *Bates v. City of Little Rock*, 361 U.S. at 523–524, 80 S.Ct. at 416–417; *Talley v. California*, 362 U.S. at 64–65, 80 S.Ct. at 538–539; *Shelton v. Tucker*, 364 U.S. 479, 485–486, 81 S.Ct. 247, 250–251, 5 L.Ed.2d 231; *Cramp v. Board of Public Instructions*, 368 U.S. 278, 286, 82 S.Ct. 275, 280, 7 L.Ed.2d 285; *NAACP v. Button*, 371 U.S. 415, 431–438, 83 S.Ct. 328, 337–341, 9 L.Ed.2d 405; *Gibson v. Florida Legislation Investigation Committee*, 372 U.S. 539, 555–557, 83 S.Ct. 889, 898–899, 9 L.Ed.2d 929; *New York Times Co. v. Sullivan*, 376 U.S. at 277–278, 84 S.Ct. at 724–725; *Freedman v. Maryland*, 380 U.S. 51, 59, 85 S.Ct. 734, 739, 13

---

10. The American Newspaper Guild has adopted the following rule as part of the newsman's code of ethics: "[N]ewspapermen shall refuse to reveal confidences or disclose sources of confidential information in court or before other judicial or investigating bodies." G. Bird & F. Merwin, *The Press and Society* 592 (1971).

11. Obviously, if a newsman does not honor a confidence he will have difficulty establishing other confidential relationships necessary for obtaining information in the future. *See* Siebert & Ryniker, *Press Winning Fight to Guard Sources*, Editor & Publisher, Sept. 1, 1934, pp. 9, 36–37.

L.Ed.2d 649; *DeGregory v. Attorney General of New Hampshire*, 383 U.S. 825, 86 S.Ct. 1148, 16 L.Ed.2d 292; *Elfbrandt v. Russell*, 384 U.S. 11, 16–19, 86 S.Ct. 1238, 1240–1242, 16 L.Ed.2d 321. And, in making this determination, we have shown a special solicitude towards the "indispensable liberties" protected by the First Amendment, *NAACP v. Alabama, supra*, 357 U.S. at 461, 78 S.Ct. at 1171; *Bantam Books, inc. v. Sullivan*, 372 U.S. 58, 66, 83 S.Ct. 631, 637, 9 L.Ed.2d 584, for "[f]reedoms such as these are protected not only against heavy-handed frontal attack, but also from being stifled by more subtle governmental interference." *Bates, supra*, 361 U.S. at 523, 80 S.Ct. at 416. Once this threshold inquiry has been satisfied, we have then examined the competing interests in determining whether there is an unconstitutional infringement of First Amendment freedoms....

To require any greater burden of proof is to shirk our duty to protect values securely embedded in the Constitution. We cannot await an unequivocal—and therefore unattainable—imprimatur from empirical studies. We can and must accept the evidence developed in the record, and elsewhere, that overwhelmingly supports the premise that deterrence will occur with regularity in important types of news-gathering relationships.

Thus, we cannot escape the conclusion that when neither the reporter nor his source can rely on the shield of confidentiality against unrestrained use of the grand jury's subpoena power, valuable information will not be published and the public dialogue will inevitably be impoverished.

## II

Posed against the First Amendment's protection of the newsman's confidential relationships in these cases is society's interest in the use of the grand jury to administer justice fairly and effectively. The grand jury serves two important functions: "to examine into the commission of crimes" and "to stand between the prosecutor and the accused, and to determine whether the charge was founded upon credible testimony or was dictated by malice or personal ill will." *Hale v. Henkel*, 201 U.S. 43, 59, 26 S.Ct. 370, 373, 50 L.Ed. 652. And to perform these functions the grand jury must have available to it every man's relevant evidence. *See Blair v. United States*, 250 U.S 273, 281, 39 S.Ct. 468, 471, 63 L.Ed. 979; *Blackmer v. United States*, 284 U.S. 421, 438, 52 S.Ct. 252, 255, 76 L.Ed. 375.

Yet the longstanding rule making every person's evidence available to the grand jury is not absolute. The rule has been limited by the Fifth Amendment, the Fourth Amendment, and the evidentiary privileges of the common law. So it was that in *Blair, supra*, after recognizing that the right against compulsory self-incrimination prohibited certain inquiries, the Court noted that "some confidential matters are shielded from considerations of policy, and perhaps in other cases for special reasons a witness may be excused from telling all that he knows." *Id.* 250 U.S. at 281, 39 S.Ct. at 471. And in *United States v. Bryan*, 339 U.S. 323, 70 S.Ct. 724, 94 L.Ed. 844, the Court observed that any exemption from the duty to testify before the grand jury "presupposes a very real interest to be protected." *Id.* at 332, 70 S.Ct. at 731.

Such an interest... functions to insure nothing less than democratic decisionmaking through the free flow of information to the public, and it serves, thereby, to honor the "profound national commitment to the principle that debate on public issues should be uninhibited, robust, and wide-open." *New York Times Co. v. Sullivan*, 376 U.S. at 270, 84 S.Ct. at 721...

[W]hen a reporter is asked to appear before a grand jury and reveal confidences, I would hold that the government must (1) show that there is probable cause to believe that the newsman has information that is clearly relevant to a specific probable viola-tion of law; (2) demonstrate that the information sought cannot be obtained by alter-native means less destructive of First Amendment rights; and (3) demonstrate a com-pelling and overriding interest in the information.

This is not to say that a grand jury could not issue a subpoena until such a showing were made, and it is not to say that a newsman would be in any way privileged to ig-nore any subpoena that was issued. Obviously, before the government's burden to make such a showing were triggered, the reporter would have to move to quash the sub-poena, asserting the basis on which he considered the particular relationship a confi-dential one.

The crux of the Court's rejection of any newsman's privilege is its observation that only "where news sources themselves are implicated in crime or possess information rel-evant to the grand jury's task need they or the reporter be concerned about grand jury subpoenas." See ante, at 2661. But this is a most misleading construct. For it is obviously not true that the only persons about whom reporters will be forced to testify will be those "confidential informants involved in actual criminal conduct" and those having "information suggesting illegal conduct by others." See ante, at 2661, 2662. As noted above, given the grand jury's extraordinarily broad investigative powers and the weak standards of relevance and materiality that apply during such inquiries, reporters, if they have no testimonial privilege, will be called to give information about informants who have neither committed crimes nor have information about crime. It is to avoid de-terrence of such sources and thus to prevent needless injury to First Amendment values that I think the government must be required to show probable cause that the newsman has information that is clearly relevant to a specific probable violation of criminal law.[34]

Similarly, a reporter may have information from a confidential source that is "re-lated" to the commission of crime, but the government may be able to obtain an indict-ment or otherwise achieve its purposes by subpoenaing persons other than the reporter. It is an obvious but important truism that when government aims have been fully served, there can be no legitimate reason to disrupt a confidential relationship between a reporter and his source. To do so would not aid the administration of justice and would only impair the flow of information to the public. Thus, it is to avoid deterrence of such sources that I think the government must show that there are no alternative means for the grand jury to obtain the information sought.

Both the "probable cause" and "alternative means" requirements would thus serve the vital function of mediating between the public interest in the administration of jus-

---

34. If this requirement is not met, then the government will basically be allowed to undertake a "fishing expedition" at the expense of the press. Such general, exploratory investigations will be most damaging to confidential news-gathering relationships, since they will create great uncertainty in both reporters and their sources. The Court sanctions such explorations, by refusing to apply a meaningful "probable cause" requirement. See ante, at 2666–2667. As the Court states, a grand jury investigation "may be triggered by tips, rumors, evidence proffered by the prosecutor, or the per-sonal knowledge of the grand jurors." Ante, at 2666. It thereby invites government to try to annex the press as an investigative arm, since any time government wants to probe the relationships be-tween the newsman and his source, it can, on virtually any pretext, convene a grand jury and com-pel the journalist to testify.

The Court fails to recognize that under the guise of "investigating crime" vindictive prosecutors can, using the broad powers of the grand jury which are, in effect, immune from judicial supervi-sion, explore the newsman's sources at will, with no serious law enforcement purpose. The secrecy of grand jury proceedings, affords little consolation to a news source; the prosecutor obviously will, in most cases, have knowledge of testimony given by grand jury witnesses.

tice and the constitutional protection of the full flow of information. These requirements would avoid a direct conflict between these competing concerns, and they would generally provide adequate protection for newsmen. *See* Part III, *infra.*[35] No doubt the courts would be required to make some delicate judgments in working out this accommodation. But that, after all, is the function of courts of law. Better such judgments, however difficult, than the simplistic and stultifying absolutism adopted by the Court in denying any force to the First Amendment in these cases....

### III

...On the record before us the United States has not met the burden that I think the appropriate newsman's privilege should require.

In affidavits before the District Court, the United States said it was investigating possible violations of 18 U.S.C. §871 (threats against the President), 18 U.S.C. §1751 (assassination, attempts to assassinate, conspiracy to assassinate the President), 18 U.S.C. §231 (civil disorders), 18 U.S.C. §2101 (interstate travel to incite a riot), 18 U.S.C. §1341 (mail fraud and swindles) and other crimes that were not specified. But, with one exception, there has been no factual showing in this case of the probable commission of, or of attempts to commit, any crimes. The single exception relates to the allegation that a Black Panther Party leader, David Hilliard, violated 18 U.S.C. §871 during the course of a speech in November 1969. But Caldwell was subpoenaed two months after an indictment was returned against Hilliard, and that charge could not, subsequent to the indictment, be investigated by a grand jury. *See In re National Window Glass Workers, D.C.* 287 F. 219; *United States v. Dardi,* 2 Cir., 330 F.2d 316, 336. Furthermore, the record before us does not show that Caldwell probably had any information about the violation of any other federal criminal laws, or that alternative means of obtaining the desired information were pursued....

Accordingly, I would affirm the judgment of the Court of Appeals in No. 70-57, *United States v. Caldwell.* In the other two cases before us, No. 70-85, *Branzburg v. Hayes and Meigs,* and No. 70-94, *In re Pappas,* I would vacate the judgments and remand the cases for further proceedings not inconsistent with the views I have expressed in this opinion.

---

## Notes and Questions

1. Paradoxically, Justice Stewart's dissenting opinion in *Branzburg v. Hayes,* 408 U.S. 665, has served as a framework to analyze reporters' efforts to resist compelled disclosure confidential information or the identity of confidential sources. To what extent does his formulation of a test for the application of the privilege facilitate an analytical construct for litigants and judges?

2. Might a journalist's reliance on an anonymous World Wide Web source serve to so attenuate his relationship with the source that ultimately he may be unable to identify the source?

3. If a reporter does rely on an anonymous Web source, how will efforts to compel disclosure by the Internet service provider of the anonymous poster affect the journalistic privilege? May the Internet service provider assert the privilege, which rests

---

35. We need not, therefore, reach the question of whether government's interest in these cases is "overriding and compelling." I do not, however, believe, as the Court does, that all grand jury investigations automatically would override the newsman's testimonial privilege.

with the newsperson, on behalf of the anonymous poster or at the behest of the newsperson? Is the provider's ability to assert such a privilege affected if the reporter is not a subscriber to the provider's service?

---

A threshold inquiry, particularly in the Internet speech context, requires identification of "the press." In other words, who is entitled to claim the privilege? Decades before the *Branzburg v. Hayes* decision, the Supreme Court had observed that "[t]he liberty of the press is not confined to newspapers and periodicals.... The press in its historic connotation comprehends every sort of publication which affords a vehicle of information and opinion." *Lovell v. City of Griffin*, 303 U.S. 444, 452 (1935). The *Branzburg v. Hayes* court specifically acknowledged that "[t]he informative function asserted by representatives of the organized press... is also performed by lecturers, political pollsters, novelists, academic researchers and dramatists." 408 U.S. at 705.

Determination of the issue may be affected by the applicable state statute. Yet courts have eschewed rigid construction of shield statutes that would exclude putative journalists. Shield law protection has been extended to such entities as a tabloid publication that was distributed without cost, even though the applicable statute referred to a "newspaper" as a publication with a paid circulation. *See In re Avila*, 206 N.J. Super. 61, 501 A.2d 1018 (N.J. Super. 1985). The court's decision evinces "sensitiv[ity] to the legislative momentum that has steadily expanded the scope of the statutory newsperson's privilege since its first enactment.... [The New Jersey Supreme Court] has declared that the scope of its present protection is 'the greatest extent permitted by the Constitution of the United States and that of the State of New Jersey.'" *Id.* at 1019 (citation omitted).

In *Blum v. Schlegel*, 150 F.R.D. 42, 43 (W.D.N.Y. 1993), a law student was served with a subpoena, seeking production of a tape recording of an interview with the school's associate dean that was used to prepare an article for the school newspaper. The plaintiff argued that the New York Shield Law was inapposite to the student because he did not qualify as a "professional journalist" working "for gain or livelihood." *See* N.Y. Civ. Rights Law § 79-h(a)(6). The court rejected the argument, ruling that "whether a person is a professional journalist is irrelevant. The question is how the person asserting the privilege intended to use the information gathered. Therefore, "'although prior experience as a professional journalist may be persuasive evidence of present intent to gather for the purpose of dissemination, it is not the *sine qua non*. The burden indeed may be sustained by one who is a novice in the field.'" *Blum v. Schlegel*, 150 F.R.D. at 45 (quoting *von Bulow by Auersperg v. von Bulow*, 811 F.2d 136, 144 (2d Cir.), *cert. denied*, 481 U.S. 1015 (1987)).

Courts have probed the purposes for which the information in issue was created and disseminated. Materials that relate to matters of public concern are more likely to come within the protective ambit of the privilege, perhaps based on implicit conceptualization of the press' function to inform the citizenry.

In *von Bulow by Auersperg v. von Bulow*, 811 F.2d 136, a companion of the defendant, Claus von Bulow, who had been sued by the children of his former wife in connection with an alleged scheme to kill or incapacitate her, claimed that she was a member of the class entitled to assert the journalist's privilege. The Second Circuit considered whether she had intended to use the material to disseminate information to the public and whether such intent existed at the inception of the newsgathering process. *See id.* at 144. After scrutinizing the salient facts, the court rejected her argument. The fact that she had obtained investigative reports primarily in connection with efforts to vindicate von Bulow, that she initially had described her notes as "worthless doodles," and that negotiations for an agreement to publish the work had not reached fruition, belied her assertions that she had been meaningfully engaged in the gathering and dissemination of news. *See id.* at 145.

In *Silkwood v. Kerr-McKee Corp.*, 563 F.2d 433 (10th Cir. 1977), the Tenth Circuit similarly considered the purposes for which the material had been gathered, but allowed a documentary filmmaker to invoke the privilege. The filmmaker had been a freelance reporter who thereafter learned of allegations that Karen Silkwood had been willfully contaminated with toxic plutonium radiation. *Id.* at 435. The filmmaker had advised the witnesses whom he had interviewed that he was endeavoring to make a factually accurate portrayal of events, and had extended assurances to those who demanded confidentiality.

The court noted that while he had been acting as a filmmaker, rather than as a newspaper reporter, "[h]is mission in this case was to carry out investigative reporting for use in the preparation of a documentary film. He is shown to have spent considerable time and effort in obtaining facts and information of the subject matter in this lawsuit, but it cannot be disputed that his intention, at least, was to make use of this in preparation of the film." *Id.* at 436–37. It also struck the court as "somewhat anomalous that [those requesting the material] would argue that [the filmmaker] is not a genuine reporter entitled to the privilege, implying a lack of ability, while at the same time they are making a major legal effort to get hold of his material. *Id.* at 437.

In another case, discovery was sought from a bi-monthly publication that discussed the properties, efficacy, and adverse effects of various pharmaceuticals. Information relating to the author of a preliminary draft and the names of consultant physicians was sought from the publication, *The Medical Letter*. The publication, which had a circulation of 70,000, was regarded as performing "a public and professional service by providing information on various drugs. Free communication in the vital area of health, just as in politics, should be encouraged." *Apicella v. McNeil Laboratories, Inc.*, 66 F.R.D. 78, 85 (E.D.N.Y. 1975).

Under a similar rationale, the privilege also has been available to a financial rating service. *See In re Pan Am Corp. v. Delta Air Lines*, 161 Bankr. 577, 584 (S.D.N.Y. 1993). Standard & Poor's made its own analysis and retained editorial control over the form and content of its publications, which are designed not merely for the personal use of rated companies but for the benefit of all who might read its publication. Consequently, it was eligible to invoke the privilege. *In re Scott Paper Co. Sec. Litig.*, 145 F.R.D. 366, 370 (E.D. Pa. 1992). Likewise, the privilege has been held applicable to an investment analyst who researched and wrote a report about a company and distributed the report to potential investors, on the theory that the analyst had engaged in the dissemination of the report to the business community. *See Summit Technology, Inc. v. Healthcare Capital Group, Inc.*, 141 F.R.D. 381, 384 (D. Mass. 1992).[2]

---

2. Those who perform ancillary roles in the newsgathering process also have been held worthy of protection. In *Solargen Electrical Motor Car Corp. v. American Motors Corp.*, 506 F. Supp. 546, 552 (N.D.N.Y. 1981), for example, the court stated that "[i]nsofar as camerapersons in fact gather news, albeit with electric equipment, as well as disseminate information, such individuals reasonably should share the same privilege enjoyed by traditional journalists."

# IN RE: Michael A. CUSUMANO and David B. YOFFIE [UNITED STATES of AMERICA v. MICROSOFT CORPORATION]

United States Court of Appeals, First Circuit
No. 98-2133, 162 F.3d 708
December 15, 1998

Before Selya, Circuit Judge, Coffin and Bownes, Senior Circuit Judges.

OPINION BY: SELYA

In this appeal, petitioner-appellant Microsoft Corporation (Microsoft) invites us to reverse the district court's denial of its motion to compel production of research materials compiled by two academic investigators. Microsoft wants to use the subpoenaed materials in defending a civil antitrust case, *United States v. Microsoft Corp.*, presently being tried in the United States District Court for the District of Columbia. Mindful that important First Amendment values are at stake, we decline Microsoft's invitation....

On May 18, 1998, the United States Department of Justice (DOJ) and several state attorneys general brought suit in the United States District Court for the District of Columbia, charging Microsoft with various antitrust violations. The complaint's main allegations center around Microsoft's accretion of market share for its Internet Explorer product. DOJ asserts that Microsoft, mindful that browsers potentially can be used as platforms on which to run software and thus replace, or at least compete with, operating systems, set out to increase its share of the browser market in a no-holds-barred campaign to safeguard its hegemony in the operating systems market....

In the course of pretrial discovery in the antitrust case, Microsoft learned about a forthcoming book entitled *Competing on Internet Time: Lessons from Netscape and the Battle with Microsoft* (*Lessons*) and obtained a copy of the manuscript. As its title implies, *Lessons* deals extensively with the "browser war" waged between Microsoft and Netscape. Its authors (respondents-appellees here) are distinguished academicians: Michael A. Cusumano, a tenured full professor at Massachusetts Institute of Technology's Sloan School of Management, and David B. Yoffie, a tenured full professor at Harvard Business School.

As part of their research for *Lessons*, the respondents interviewed over 40 current and former Netscape employees. Their interview protocol dealt with confidentiality on two levels. First, the respondents signed a nondisclosure agreement with Netscape, in which they agreed not to disclose proprietary information conveyed to them in the course of their investigation except upon court order, and then only after giving Netscape notice and an opportunity to oppose disclosure. Second, the respondents requested and received permission from interview subjects to record their discussions, and, in return, promised that each interviewee would be shown any quotes attributed to him upon completion of the manuscript, so that he would have a chance to correct any errors or to object to quotations selected by the authors for publication.

On September 18, 1998, believing that certain statements from Netscape employees reported in *Lessons* offered succor for its defense, Microsoft subpoenaed the professors' notes, tape recordings and transcripts of interviews, and correspondence with interview subjects. *See* Fed. R. Civ. P. 45. The respondents produced some correspondence, but declined to surrender the notes, tapes, or transcripts. Microsoft moved to compel the production of these items on October 1, 1998....

Initially, we must determine whether the respondents' academic research is protected in a manner similar to the work product of journalists. This inquiry entails[, among other aspects, an analysis as to] whether the respondents' positions warrant conferral of any special consideration....

Who Is Protected? Microsoft acknowledges that the law supplies a measure of protection for materials compiled by journalists. See *Bruno & Stillman, Inc. v. Globe Newspaper Co.*, 633 F.2d 583, 595–98 (1st Cir. 1980). The respondents, however, are academic researchers and commentators, not professional newsmen. We do not think that this makes a dispositive difference in whether special protection vests. Academicians engaged in pre-publication research should be accorded protection commensurate to that which the law provides for journalists.

Courts afford journalists a measure of protection from discovery initiatives in order not to undermine their ability to gather and disseminate information. See *United States v. LaRouche Campaign*, 841 F.2d 1176, 1181 (1st Cir. 1988). Journalists are the personification of a free press, and to withhold such protection would invite a "chilling effect on speech," *id.*, and thus destabilize the First Amendment. The same concerns suggest that courts ought to offer similar protection to academicians engaged in scholarly research. After all, scholars too are information gatherers and disseminators. If their research materials were freely subject to subpoena, their sources likely would refuse to confide in them. As with reporters, a drying-up of sources would sharply curtail the information available to academic researchers and thus would restrict their output. Just as a journalist, stripped of sources, would write fewer, less incisive articles, an academician, stripped of sources, would be able to provide fewer, less cogent analyses. Such similarities of concern and function militate in favor of a similar level of protection for journalists and academic researchers.

Given this mise-en-scene, it is unsurprising that several of our sister circuits have held that the medium an individual uses to provide his investigative reporting to the public does not make a dispositive difference in the degree of protection accorded to his work. See *In re Madden*, 151 F.3d 125, 128–31 (3d Cir. 1998); *Shoen v. Shoen*, 5 F.3d 1289, 1293–94 (9th Cir. 1993); *von Bulow v. von Bulow*, 811 F.2d 136, 142–44 (2d Cir. 1987). Whether the creator of the materials is a member of the media or of the academy, the courts will make a measure of protection available to him as long as he intended "at the inception of the newsgathering process" to use the fruits of his research "to disseminate information to the public." *von Bulow*, 811 F.2d at 144.

This case fits neatly into the architecture of these precedents. The sole purpose of the respondents' interviews of Netscape personnel was to gather data so that they could compile, analyze, and report their findings anent management practices in the internet technology industry. Thus, the respondents are within a group whose pre-publication research merits a modicum of protection....

---

Are protections accorded to the press derived from general constitutional free speech norms or from the specific reference to freedom of the press in the First Amendment? Justice Stewart, in his famous "Or of the Press" address, *see* 26 Hastings L.J. 631 (1975), opined that the "free press" clause of the First Amendment was devised to imbue the institutional press with rights more expansive than those provided to the citizenry through the "free speech" clause, and the press generally has been treated more favorably in certain circumstances. Reporters have been the beneficiaries of greater protection from compulsory disclosure of their confidential sources, for instance, than has the general public. Will these protections be extended to everyone who "publishes" newsworthy information on the Internet? As the law relating to Internet speech evolves, courts and legislatures will need to grapple with the level of protection available to a wide range of disparate Internet publishers. Will there be gradations of privileges and protections extended to a spectrum of Web publishers? Will a definition of the "press" as an institution evolve?

"Defining 'press,' of course, is a matter that the Supreme Court has studiously, even adamantly avoided." Randall P. Bezanson, *The Developing Law of Editorial Judgment*, 78 Neb. L. Rev. 754, 755 (1999). Considerable scholarly debate has focused on this issue. *See, e.g., id.* & n. 4; C. Edwin Baker, *Press Rights and Government Power to Structure the Press*, 34 U. Miami L. Rev. 819 (1980); Vincent Blasi, *The Checking Value in First Amendment Theory*, 1977 Am. B. Found. Res. J. 521. One theory is that the press' claim to freedom is most profoundly asserted when its speech is the product of independently exercised editorial judgment, "audience oriented, and grounded in a reasoned effort to publish information (typically current or currently relevant) judged useful and important for the maintenance of freedom is a self-governing society." *See* Randall P. Bezanson, *The Developing Law of Editorial Judgment*, 78 Neb. L. Rev. at 760. An essential function of the press—and a concomitant attribute of the press—is its exercise of editorial judgment.

"A newspaper is more than a passive receptacle or conduit for news, comment, and advertising. The choice of material to go into a newspaper, and the decisions made as to limitations on the size and content of the paper, and treatment of public issues and public officials—whether fair or unfair—constitute the exercise of editorial control and judgment." *Miami Herald Publ'g Co. v. Tornillo*, 418 U.S. 241, 258 (1974) (footnote omitted). Arguably publishers of content on the World Wide Web are similarly exercising such judgments.

The Reporter's Committee for Freedom of the Press has reported that a self-described "amateur reporter" challenged a decision by city and county officials to restrict his ability to attend and report on court proceedings. Robert Corn-Revere, *"Amateur Reporter," Appeals Case Over Courthouse Access*, Reporter's Committee Freedom Press (Mar. 29, 2000) <http://www.rcfp.org/news/2000/0329humins.htm>. Scott Huminski asserted that he had been "investigating and reporting on Court proceedings and law enforcement" in Vermont for the previous three years, publishing his findings on placards that he posted on his house and his van. *Id.* The dispute arose in connection with a notice of trespass served on Huminski, who was ordered to leave the courthouse after he had displayed a poster critical of one of the judges. *Id.; see Huminski v. Rutland City Police Dep't*, 2000 WL 1005609 at *1 (2d Cir. July 20, 2000) (dismissing the appeal for lack of appellate jurisdiction). Is Huminski entitled to the protections traditionally extended to journalists? If he published his investigative findings on the Web instead of on placards, would that change the analysis?

In another case, major movie studios have objected to links by a Web publisher to sites carrying a software program, known as DeCSS, that circumvents a security system on DVD movie disks. *See Universal City Studios, Inc. v. Reimerdes*, No. 00 Civ. 0277, 2000 U.S. Dist. LEXIS 11696 (S.D.N.Y. Aug. 17, 2000). The defendants argued that the "[p]laintiffs seek to punish defendants for engaging in exactly the same linking acts as other media entities like *The New York Times, San Jose Mercury News*, the AP website, and numerous universities and academics." Brief Submitted By Media Defendant 2600 Enterprises, Inc. and Eric Corley a/k/a "Emmanuel Goldstein" in Opposition to Plaintiffs' Motion to Modify the Preliminary Injunction and in Support of Defendants' Cross-

Motion to Vacate the Preliminary Injunction, dated May 3, 2000, at 2; *see also* Carl S. Kaplan, *First Amendment Lawyer Takes on Movie Studios in DVD Case*, Cyber L.J. (Apr. 28, 2000) <http://www.nytimes.com/library/tech/yr/mo/cyber/cyberlaw/28law.html>. Do linking practices support an inference that the linking site was engaged in journalism or news reporting?

A 16-year-old boy in Utah was arrested, and the County Attorney reportedly considered bringing criminal defamation charges, a class B misdemeanor. Joe Baird, *Teen's Exile Over Web Site Growing Into First Amendment Battle*, Salt Lake Trib. (June 16, 2000) <http://www.sltrib.com/106162000/nation_w/nation_w.htm>. Evidently teased at school, the boy responded with "a profanity-laced home page" that insulted classmates and a school official. *See id.* The boy reportedly had first researched defamation law and stated that he had endeavored to reduce the identifiability of the subjects of his statements. The student spent seven nights in a juvenile detention facility. *See id.* Thereafter, he pleaded not guilty to the criminal charge in a misdemeanor juvenile hearing, and an accompanying slander charge was dismissed by the prosecutor. *See* John Magrisso, *Student Charged With Criminal Libel Over Web Site Content*, Reporters' Committee Freedom Press (June 22, 2000) <http://www.rcfp.org/news/2000/0622utahvl.htm>. Is the web-site tantamount to a journalistic publication, subject to the same standards as any other press report?

In *Blumenthal v. Drudge*, 992 F. Supp. 44 (D.D.C. 1998), the district court judge refused to dismiss a defamation claim against one of the defendants, Matt Drudge, author of the on-line "Drudge Report."* Drudge had stated that, according to an unnamed source, White House Aide Sidney Blumenthal had abused his wife. (The Drudge Report also referenced a denial of the charge's plausibility, by another unnamed source.)

The federal district court scoffed at Drudge's efforts to portray himself as a journalist. "Drudge is not a reporter, a journalist or a newsgatherer," said the court. *Id.* at 57 n. 18. "He is, as he himself admits, simply a purveyor of gossip. His argument that he should benefit from the 'news gathering exception' to . . . the long-arm statute merits no serious consideration." *Id.*

In applying the provisions of a state pre-suit notification statute, one court discussed the distinction between "media" and "non-media" entities. The latter were characterized as "'third parties who are not engaged in the dissemination of news and information through the news and broadcast media from those who are so engaged.'" *Zelinka v. Americare Healthscan, Inc.*, No. 99-3030, 2000 Fla. App. LEXIS 500 at *7–8 (Fla. App. Jan. 26, 2000) (quoting *Mancini v. Personalized Air Conditioning & Heating, Inc.*, 702 So. 2d 1376 (Fla. App. 1997)). Thus, the notice requirement has been held applicable to a newspaper columnist who made allegedly defamatory statements in her column, and to the newspaper, but not to "private individuals." The *Zelinka* court concluded, "based on overwhelming authority," that the notice requirement does not apply to a private individual who posts a message on a computer service that is owned and operated by someone else. *Zelinka v. Americare Healthscan, Inc.*, No. 99-3030, 2000 Fla. App. LEXIS 500 at *8. Stating that "[i]t may well be that someone who maintains a web site and regularly publishes internet 'magazines' on that site might be considered a 'media defendant' who would be entitled to notice," the court ruled that the defendant "does not fall into that category; he is a private individual who merely made statements on a web site

---

* The plaintiffs also sued America Online, the service provider on which the Drudge Report appeared. That claim was dismissed. *See id.*

owned and maintained by someone else." *Id.* The court's holding implies that "regular" dissemination might transmute a private individual into a member of the media. The court's dicta illustrates the difficulty of fashioning a definition of the press, as application of a standard based on "regular" dissemination would not accommodate the novice—or the unsuccessful—journalist.

Can standards for determining whether a person or entity is engaged in press functions be articulated consistent with constitutional norms? Would such a definitional exercise that operated on an exclusionary basis be constitutionally suspect as tantamount to imposing a licensing system? *See, e.g., Branzburg v. Hayes,* 408 U.S. at 704; *cf.* Jane E. Kirtley, *The EU Data Protection Directive and the First Amendment: Why a "Press Exemption" Won't Work,* 80 Iowa L. Rev. 639, 648 (1995) (expressing similar concerns in the context of data collection practices). Even if it were legally permissible to delineate a test to determine whether an individual or entity that publishes content on the Web is a member of the "press," is it necessary or desirable to do so in order to assess whether privileges traditionally afforded to the press may be invoked?

Internet fora—vast, democratic, and readily accessible—present a paradox: an elegantly structured catalyst for diverse and robust dialogue and an eroding of a finite, discrete structure of the press as an institution. First Amendment expert Floyd Abrams recently expressed qualms about the notion that low entry barriers suggest that everyone is a publisher, stating, "it would be disturbingly ironic if the 'everyone is a publisher' feature of the Internet ultimately leads to all publishers having less in the way of First Amendment rights." Floyd Abrams, *A Transcript Featuring the 1999–2000 Oliver Wendell Holmes Lecturer—Floyd Abrams,* 51 Mercer L. Rev. 833, 847 (2000); *see also* Theodore Y. Blumoff, *1999–2000 Oliver Wendell Holmes Devise Symposium: The Marketplace of Ideas in Cyberpsace,* 51 Mercer L. Rev. 817, 822 (2000). Will courts and legislatures be recalcitrant in according the press special privileges, lest they confront the dilemma of determining who qualifies as a member of the press?

---

## "Or of the Press"\* †
### Potter Stewart
#### 26 Hastings L.J. 631 (1975)

I turn this morning to an inquiry into an aspect of constitutional law that has only recently begun to engage the attention of the Supreme Court. Specifically, I shall discuss the role of the organized press—of the daily newspapers and other established news media—in the system of government created by our Constitution.

It was less than a decade ago—during the Vietnam years—that the people of our country began to become aware of the twin phenomena on a national scale of so-called investigative reporting and an adversary press—that is, a press adversary to the Executive Branch of the Federal Government. And only in the two short years that culmi-

---

\* This article was first published in 26 HASTINGS L. J. 631 (1975)....

† Excerpted from an address on November 2, 1974, at the Yale Law School Sesquicentennial Convocation, New Haven, Connecticut. The Hastings Law Journal holds no copyright in this material.

nated last summer in the resignation of a President did we fully realize the enormous power that an investigative and adversary press can exert.

The public opinion polls that I have seen indicate that some Americans firmly believe that the former Vice President and former President of the United States were hounded out of office by an arrogant and irresponsible press that had outrageously usurped dictatorial power. And it seems clear that many more Americans, while appreciating and even applauding the service performed by the press in exposing official wrongdoing at the highest levels of our national government, are nonetheless deeply disturbed by what they consider to be the illegitimate power of the organized press in the political structure of our society. It is my thesis this morning that, on the contrary, the established American press in the past ten years, and particularly in the past two years, has performed precisely the function it was intended to perform by those who wrote the First Amendment of our Constitution. I further submit that this thesis is supported by the relevant decisions of the Supreme Court.

Surprisingly, despite the importance of newspapers in the political and social life of our country the Supreme Court has not until very recently been called upon to delineate their constitutional role in our structure of government.

Our history is filled with struggles over the rights and prerogatives of the press, but these disputes rarely found their way to the Supreme Court. The early years of the Republic witnessed controversy over the constitutional validity of the short-lived Alien and Sedition Act, but the controversy never reached the Court. In the next half century there was nationwide turmoil over the right of the organized press to advocate the then subversive view that slavery should be abolished. In Illinois a publisher was killed for publishing abolitionist views. But none of this history made First Amendment law because the Court had earlier held that the Bill of Rights applied only against the Federal Government, not against the individual states.

With the passage of the Fourteenth Amendment, the constitutional framework was modified, and by the 1920's the Court had established that the protections of the First Amendment extend against all government—federal, state, and local.

The next fifty years witnessed a great outpouring of First Amendment litigation, all of which inspired books and articles beyond number. But, with few exceptions, neither these First Amendment cases nor their commentators squarely considered the Constitution's guarantee of a Free Press. Instead, the focus was on its guarantee of free speech. The Court's decisions dealt with the rights of isolated individuals, or of unpopular minority groups, to stand up against governmental power representing an angry or frightened majority. The cases that came to the Court during those years involved the rights of the soapbox orator, the nonconformist pamphleteer, the religious evangelist. The Court was seldom asked to define the rights and privileges, or the responsibilities, of the organized press.

In very recent years cases involving the established press finally have begun to reach the Supreme Court, and they have presented a variety of problems, sometimes arising in complicated factual settings.

In a series of cases, the Court has been called upon to consider the limits imposed by the free press guarantee upon a state's common or statutory law of libel. As a result of those cases, a public figure cannot successfully sue a publisher for libel unless he can show that the publisher maliciously printed a damaging untruth.[1]

---

1. *See Rosenbloom v. Metromedia, Inc.*, 403 U.S. 29 (1971); *Curtis Publ'g Co. v. Butts*, 388 U.S. 130 (1967); *New York Times Co. v. Sullivan*, 376 U.S. 254 (1964).

The Court has also been called upon to decide whether a newspaper reporter has a First Amendment privilege to refuse to disclose his confidential sources to a grand jury. By a divided vote, the Court found no such privilege to exist in the circumstances of the cases before it.[2]

In another noteworthy case, the Court was asked by the Justice Department to restrain publication by the *New York Times* and other newspapers of the so-called Pentagon Papers. The Court declined to do so.[3]

In yet another case, the question to be decided was whether political groups have a First Amendment or statutory right of access to the federally regulated broadcast channels of radio and television. The Court held there was no such right of access.[4]

Last Term the Court confronted a Florida statute that required newspapers to grant a "right of reply" to political candidates they had criticized. The Court unanimously held this statute to be inconsistent with the guarantees of a free press.[5]

It seems to me that the Court's approach to all these cases has uniformly reflected its understanding that the Free Press guarantee is, in essence, a *structural* provision of the Constitution. Most of the other provisions in the Bill of Rights protect specific liberties or specific rights of individuals: freedom of speech, freedom of worship, the right to counsel, the privilege against compulsory self-incrimination, to name a few. In contrast, the Free Press Clause extends protection to an institution. The publishing business is, in short, the only organized private business that is given explicit constitutional protection.

This basic understanding is essential, I think, to avoid an elementary error of constitutional law. It is tempting to suggest that freedom of the press means only that newspaper publishers are guaranteed freedom of expression. They *are* guaranteed that freedom, to be sure, but so are we all, because of the Free Speech Clause. If the Free Press guarantee meant no more than freedom of expression, it would be a constitutional redundancy. Between 1776 and the drafting of our Constitution, many of the state constitutions contained clauses protecting freedom of the press while at the same time recognizing no general freedom of speech. By including both guarantees in the First Amendment, the Founders quite clearly recognized the distinction between the two.

It is also a mistake to suppose that the only purpose of the constitutional guarantee of a free press is to insure that a newspaper will serve as a neutral forum for debate, a "market place for ideas," a kind of Hyde Park corner for the community. A related theory sees the press as a neutral conduit of information between the people and their elected leaders. These theories, in my view, again give insufficient weight to the institutional autonomy of the press that it was the purpose of the Constitution to guarantee.

In setting up the three branches of the Federal Government, the Founders deliberately created an internally competitive system. As Mr. Justice Brandeis once wrote:[6]

> The [Founders'] purpose was, not to avoid friction, but, by means of the inevitable friction incident to the distribution of the governmental powers among three departments, to save the people from autocracy.

2. *Branzburg v. Hayes*, 408 U.S. 665 (1972).
3. *New York Times Co. v. United States*, 403 U.S. 713 (1971).
4. *Columbia Broadcasting Sys., Inc. v. Democratic Nat'l Comm.*, 412 U.S. 94 (1973).
5. *Miami Herald Publ'g Co. v. Tornillo*, 98 S.Ct. 2831 (1974).
6. *Myers v. United States*, 272 U.S. 52, 293 (1926) (dissenting opinion).

The primary purpose of the constitutional guarantee of a free press was a similar one: to create a fourth institution outside the Government as an additional check on the three official branches. Consider the opening words of the Free Press Clause of the Massachusetts Constitution, drafted by John Adams:

> The liberty of the press is essential to the security of the state.

The relevant metaphor, I think, is the metaphor of the Fourth Estate. What Thomas Carlyle wrote about the British Government a century ago has a curiously contemporary ring:

> Burke said there were Three Estates in Parliament; but, in the Reporters' Gallery yonder, there sat a Fourth Estate more important far than they all. It is not a figure of speech or witty saying; it is a literal fact—very momentus to us in these times.

For centuries before our Revolution, the press in England had been licensed, censored, and bedeviled by prosecutions for seditious libel. The British Crown knew that a free press was not just a neutral vehicle for the balanced discussion of diverse ideas. Instead, the free press meant organized, expert scrutiny of government. The press was a conspiracy of the intellect, with the courage of numbers. This formidable check on official power was what the British Crown had feared—and what the American Founders decided to risk.

It is this constitutional understanding, I think, that provides the unifying principle underlying the Supreme Court's recent decisions dealing with the organized press.

Consider first the libel cases. Officials within the three governmental branches are, for all practical purposes, immune from libel and slander suits for statements that they make in the line of duty.[7] This immunity, which has both constitutional and common law origins, aims to insure bold and vigorous prosecution of the public's business. The same basic reasoning applies to the press. By contrast, the Court has never suggested that the constitutional right of free *speech* gives an *individual* any immunity from liability for either libel or slander.

In the cases involving the newspaper reporters' claims that they had a constitutional privilege not to disclose their confidential news sources to a grand jury, the Court rejected the claims by a vote of five to four, or, considering Mr. Justice Powell's concurring opinion, perhaps by a vote of four and a half to four and a half. But if freedom of the press means simply freedom of speech for reporters, this question of a reporter's asserted right to withhold information would have answered itself. None of us—as individuals—has a "free speech" right to refuse to tell a grand jury the identity of someone who has given us information relevant to the grand jury's legitimate inquiry. Only if a reporter is a representative of a protected *institution* does the question become a different one. The members of the Court disagreed in answering the question, but the question did not answer itself.

The cases involving the so-called "right of access" to the press raised the issue whether the First Amendment allows government, or indeed *requires* government, to regulate the press so as to make it a genuinely fair and open "market place for ideas." The Court's answer was "no" to both questions. If a newspaper wants to serve as a neutral market place for debate, that is an objective which it is free to choose. And, within

---

7. *See Barr v. Matteo*, 360 U.S. 564 (1959).

limits, that choice is probably necessary to commercially successful journalism. But it is a choice that government cannot constitutionally impose.

Finally the Pentagon Papers case involved the line between secrecy and openness in the affairs of Government. The question, or at least one question, was whether that line is drawn by the Constitution itself. The Justice Department asked the Court to find in the Constitution a basis for prohibiting the publication of allegedly stolen government documents. The Court could find no such prohibition. So far as the Constitution goes, the autonomous press may publish what it knows, and may seek to learn what it can.

But this autonomy cuts both ways. The press is free to do battle against secrecy and deception in government. But the press cannot expect from the Constitution any guarantee that it will succeed. There is no constitutional right to have access to particular government information, or to require openness from the bureaucracy.[8] The public's interest in knowing about its government is protected by the guarantee of a Free Press, but the protection is indirect. The Constitution itself is neither a Freedom of Information Act nor an Official Secrets Act.

The Constitution, in other words, establishes the contest, not its resolution. Congress may provide a resolution, at least in some instances, through carefully drawn legislation. For the rest, we must rely, as so often in our system we must, on the tug and pull of the political forces in American society.

Newspapers, television networks, and magazines have sometimes been outrageously abusive, untruthful, arrogant, and hypocritical. But it hardly follows that elimination of a strong and independent press is the way to eliminate abusiveness, untruth, arrogance, or hypocrisy from government itself.

It is quite possible to conceive of the survival of our Republic without an autonomous press. For openness and honesty in government, for an adequate flow of information between the people and their representatives, for a sufficient check on autocracy and despotism, the traditional competition between the three branches of government, supplemented by vigorous political activity, might be enough.

The press could be relegated to the status of a public utility. The guarantee of free speech would presumably put some limitation on the regulation to which the press could be subjected. But if there were no guarantee of a free press, government could convert the communications media into a neutral "market place of ideas." Newspapers and television networks could then be required to promote contemporary government policy or current notions of social justice.[9]

Such a constitution is possible; it might work reasonably well. But it is not the Constitution the Founders wrote. It is not the Constitution that has carried us through nearly two centuries of national life. Perhaps our liberties might survive without an independent established press. But the Founders doubted it, and, in the year 1974, I think we can all be thankful for their doubts.

---

8. *Cf. Pell v. Procunier*, 94 S. Ct. 2800 (1974); *Saxbe v. Washington Post Co.*, 94 S.Ct. 2811 (1974).

9. *Cf. Pittsburgh Press Co. v. Pittsburgh Comm'n on Human Relations*, 413 U.S. 366 (1973).

# FIRST NATIONAL BANK of BOSTON v.
# Francis X. BELLOTTI

Supreme Court of the United States
No. 76-1172, 435 U.S. 765
April 26, 1978

Mr. Justice POWELL delivered the opinion of the Court.

In sustaining a state criminal statute that forbids certain expenditures by banks and business corporations for the purpose of influencing the vote on referendum proposals, the Massachusetts Supreme Judicial Court held that the First Amendment rights of a corporation are limited to issues that materially affect its business, property, or assets. The court rejected appellants' claim that the statute abridges freedom of speech in violation of the First and Fourteenth Amendments. The issue presented in this context is one of first impression in this Court.... We now reverse.

The statute at issue, Mass. Gen. Laws Ann., ch. 55, § 8 (West Supp. 1977), prohibits appellants, two national banking associations and three business corporations,[1] from making contributions or expenditures "for the purpose of... influencing or affecting the vote on any question submitted to the voters, other than one materially affecting any of the property, business or assets of the corporation." The statute further specifies that "[n]o question submitted to the voters solely concerning the taxation of the income, property or transactions of individuals shall be deemed materially to affect the property, business or assets of the corporation." A corporation that violates § 8 may receive a maximum fine of $50,000; a corporate officer, director, or agent who violates the section may receive a maximum fine of $10,000 or imprisonment for up to one year, or both.

Appellants wanted to spend money to publicize their views on a proposed constitutional amendment that was to be submitted to the voters as a ballot question at a general election on November 2, 1976. The amendment would have permitted the legislature to impose a graduated tax on the income of individuals. After appellee, the Attorney General of Massachusetts, informed appellants that he intended to enforce § 8 against them, they brought this action seeking to have the statute declared unconstitutional....

The court below framed the principal question in this case as whether and to what extent corporations have First Amendment rights. We believe that the court posed the wrong question. The Constitution often protects interests broader than those of the party seeking their vindication. The First Amendment, in particular, serves significant societal interests. The proper question therefore is not whether corporations "have" First Amendment rights and, if so, whether they are coextensive with those of natural persons. Instead, the question must be whether § 8 abridges expression that the First Amendment was meant to protect. We hold that it does.

The speech proposed by appellants is at the heart of the First Amendment's protection.

The freedom of speech and of the press guaranteed by the Constitution embraces at the least the liberty to discuss publicly and truthfully all matters of

---

1. Appellants are the First National Bank of Boston, New England Merchants National Bank, the Gillette Co., Digital Equipment Corp., and Wyman-Gordon Co.

public concern without previous restraint or fear of subsequent punishment.... Freedom of discussion, if it would fulfill its historic function in this
nation, must embrace all issues about which information is needed or appropriate to enable the members of society to cope with the exigencies of
their period.

*Thornhill v. Alabama,* 310 U.S. 88, 101–102, 60 S.Ct. 736, 744, 84 L.Ed. 1093 (1940).

The referendum issue that appellants wish to address falls squarely within this description. In appellants' view, the enactment of a graduated personal income tax, as
proposed to be authorized by constitutional amendment, would have a seriously adverse effect on the economy of the State. The importance of the referendum issue to the
people and government of Massachusetts is not disputed. Its merits, however, are the
subject of sharp disagreement.

As the Court said in *Mills v. Alabama,* 384 U.S. 214, 218, 86 S.Ct. 1434, 1437, 16
L.Ed.2d 484 (1966), "there is practically universal agreement that a major purpose of
[the First] Amendment was to protect the free discussion of governmental affairs." If the
speakers here were not corporations, no one would suggest that the State could silence
their proposed speech. It is the type of speech indispensable to decisionmaking in a
democracy,[11] and this is no less true because the speech comes from a corporation
rather than an individual.[12] The inherent worth of the speech in terms of its capacity for
informing the public does not depend upon the identity of its source, whether corporation, association, union, or individual.

The court below nevertheless held that corporate speech is protected by the First
Amendment only when it pertains directly to the corporation's business interests. In deciding whether this novel and restrictive gloss on the First Amendment comports with
the Constitution and the precedents of this Court, we need not survey the outer boundaries of the Amendment's protection of corporate speech, or address the abstract question whether corporations have the full measure of rights that individuals enjoy under
the First Amendment.[13] The question in this case, simply put, is whether the corporate
identity of the speaker deprives this proposed speech of what otherwise would be its
clear entitlement to protection....

"In a series of decisions beginning with *Gitlow v. New York,* 268 U.S. 652, 45 S.Ct.
625, 69 L.Ed. 1138 (1925), this Court held that the liberty of speech and of the press
which the First Amendment guarantees against abridgment by the federal government

---

11. Freedom of expression has particular significance with respect to government because "[i]t
is here that the state has a special incentive to repress opposition and often wields a more effective
power of suppression." T. Emerson, *Toward a General Theory of the First Amendment* 9 (1966). *See
also* A. Meiklejohn, *Free Speech and Its Relation to Self-Government* 24–26 (1948).

12. The individual's interest in self-expression is a concern of the First Amendment separate
from the concern for open and informed discussion, although the two often converge. *See* G. Gun-
ther, *Cases and Materials on Constitutional Law* 1044 (9th ed. 1975); T. Emerson, *The System of Freedom of Expression* 6 (1970). The Court has declared, however, that "speech concerning public affairs
is more than self-expression; it is the essence of self-government." *Garrison v. Louisiana,* 379 U.S. 64,
74–75, 85 S.Ct. 209, 216, 13 L.Ed.2d 125 (1964). And self-government suffers when those in power
suppress competing views on public issues "from diverse and antagonistic sources." *Associated Press
v. United States,* 326 U.S. 1, 20, 65 S.Ct. 1416, 1424, 89 L.Ed. 2013 (1945), quoted in *New York Times
Co. v. Sullivan,* 376 U.S. 254, 266, 84 S.Ct. 710, 718, 11 L.Ed.2d 686 (1964).

13. Nor is there any occasion to consider in this case whether, under different circumstances, a
justification for a restriction on speech that would be inadequate as applied to individuals might
suffice to sustain the same restriction as applied to corporations, unions, or like entities.

is within the liberty safeguarded by the Due Process Clause of the Fourteenth Amendment from invasion by state action. That principle has been followed and reaffirmed to the present day." *Joseph Burstyn, Inc. v. Wilson*, 343 U.S. 495, 500–501, 72 S.Ct. 777, 780, 96 L.Ed. 1098 (1952) (footnote omitted).

Freedom of speech and the other freedoms encompassed by the First Amendment always have been viewed as fundamental components of the liberty safeguarded by the Due Process Clause, *see Gitlow v. New York*, 268 U.S. 652, 666, 45 S.Ct. 625, 629, 69 L.Ed. 1138 (1925); *id.* at 672, 45 S.Ct. at 632 (Holmes, J., dissenting); *NAACP v. Alabama ex rel. Patterson*, 357 U.S. 449, 460, 78 S.Ct. 1163, 1170, 2 L.Ed.2d 1488 (1958); *Stromberg v. California*, 283 U.S. 359, 368, 51 S.Ct. 532, 535, 75 L.Ed. 1117 (1931); *De Jonge v. Oregon*, 299 U.S. 353, 364, 57 S.Ct. 255, 259, 81 L.Ed. 278 (1937); Warren, *The New Liberty Under the Fourteenth Amendment*, 39 Harv. L. Rev. 431 (1926), and the Court has not identified a separate source for the right when it has been asserted by corporations. *See, e. g., Times Film Corp. v. City of Chicago*, 365 U.S. 43, 47, 81 S.Ct. 391, 393, 5 L.Ed.2d 403 (1961); *Kingsley Int'l Pictures Corp. v. Regents*, 360 U.S. 684, 688, 79 S.Ct. 1362, 1365, 3 L.Ed.2d 1512 (1959); *Joseph Burstyn, supra.* In *Grosjean v. American Press Co.*, 297 U.S. 233, 244, 56 S.Ct. 444, 446, 80 L.Ed. 660 (1936), the Court rejected the very reasoning adopted by the Supreme Judicial Court and did not rely on the corporation's property rights under the Fourteenth Amendment in sustaining its freedom of speech.

Yet appellee suggests that First Amendment rights generally have been afforded only to corporations engaged in the communications business or through which individuals express themselves, and the court below apparently accepted the "materially affecting" theory as the conceptual common denominator between appellee's position and the precedents of this Court. It is true that the "materially affecting" requirement would have been satisfied in the Court's decisions affording protection to the speech of media corporations and corporations otherwise in the business of communication or entertainment, and to the commercial speech of business corporations. In such cases, the speech would be connected to the corporation's business almost by definition. But the effect on the business of the corporation was not the governing rationale in any of these decisions. None of them mentions, let alone attributes significance to, the fact that the subject of the challenged communication materially affected the corporation's business.

The press cases emphasize the special and constitutionally recognized role of that institution in informing and educating the public, offering criticism, and providing a forum for discussion and debate.[17] *Mills v. Alabama*, 384 U.S. at 219, 86 S.Ct. at 1437; *see Saxbe v. Washington Post Co.*, 417 U.S. 843, 863–864, 94 S.Ct. 2811, 2821–2822, 41 L.Ed.2d 514 (1974) (Powell, J., dissenting). But the press does not have a monopoly on either the First Amendment or the ability to enlighten.[18] *Cf. Buckley v. Valeo*, 424

---

17. By its terms, §8 would seem to apply to corporate members of the press. The court below noted, however, that no one "has...asserted that [§8] bars the press, corporate, institutional or otherwise, from engaging in discussion or debate on the referendum question." 371 Mass. at 785 n. 13, 359 N.E.2d at 1270 n. 13. Because none of the appellants claimed to be part of the institutional press, the court did not "venture an opinion on such matters." *Ibid.*

The observation of Mr. Justice White, *post*, at 1432 n. 8, that media corporations cannot be "immunize[d]" from restrictions on electoral expenditures, ignores the fact that those corporations need not make separately identifiable expenditures to communicate their views. They accomplish the same objective each day within the framework of their usual protected communications.

18. If we were to adopt appellee's suggestion that communication by corporate members of the institutional press is entitled to greater constitutional protection than the same communication by appellants, the result would not be responsive to the informational purpose of the First Amend-

U.S. at 51 n. 56, 96 S.Ct. at 650; *Red Lion Broadcasting Co. v. FCC*, 395 U.S. 367, 389–390, 89 S.Ct. 1794, 1806–1807, 23 L.Ed.2d 371 (1969); *New York Times Co. v. Sullivan*, 376 U.S. 254, 266, 84 S.Ct. 710, 718, 11 L.Ed.2d 686 (1964); *Associated Press v. United States*, 326 U.S. 1, 20, 65 S.Ct. 1416, 1424, 89 L.Ed. 2013 (1945). Similarly, the Court's decisions involving corporations in the business of communication or entertainment are based not only on the role of the First Amendment in fostering individual self-expression but also on its role in affording the public access to discussion, debate, and the dissemination of information and ideas.[19] *See Red Lion Broadcasting Co. v. FCC, supra; Stanley v. Georgia*, 394 U.S. 557, 564, 89 S.Ct. 1243, 1247, 22 L.Ed.2d 542 (1969); *Time, Inc. v. Hill, supra*, 385 U.S. 374, 389, 87 S.Ct. 534, 542, 17 L.Ed.2d 456 (1967). Even decisions seemingly based exclusively on the individual's right to express himself acknowledge that the expression may contribute to society's edification. *Winters v. New York*, 333 U.S. 507, 510, 68 S.Ct. 665, 667, 92 L.Ed. 840 (1948).

Nor do our recent commercial speech cases lend support to appellee's business interest theory. They illustrate that the First Amendment goes beyond protection of the press and the self-expression of individuals to prohibit government from limiting the stock of information from which members of the public may draw. A commercial advertisement is constitutionally protected not so much because it pertains to the seller's business as because it furthers the societal interest in the "free flow of commercial information." *Virginia State Bd. of Pharmacy v. Virginia Citizens Consumer Council, Inc.*, 425 U.S. 748, 764, 96 S.Ct. 1817, 1827, 48 L.Ed.2d 346 (1976); *see Linmark Associates, Inc. v. Township of Willingboro*, 431 U.S. 85, 95, 97 S.Ct. 1614, 1619, 52 L.Ed.2d 155 (1977).

We thus find no support in the First or Fourteenth Amendment, or in the decisions of this Court, for the proposition that speech that otherwise would be within the protection of the First Amendment loses that protection simply because its source is a corporation that cannot prove, to the satisfaction of a court, a material effect on its business or prop-

---

ment. Certainly there are voters in Massachusetts, concerned with such economic issues as the tax rate, employment opportunities, and the ability to attract new business into the State and to prevent established businesses from leaving, who would be as interested in hearing appellants' views on a graduated tax as the views of media corporations that might be less knowledgeable on the subject. "[P]ublic debate must not only be unfettered; it must also be informed." *Saxbe v. Washington Post Co.*, 417 U.S. 843, 862–863, 94 S.Ct. 2811, 2821, 41 L.Ed.2d 514 (1974) (Powell, J., dissenting).

Mr. Justice White's dissenting view would empower a State to restrict corporate speech far more narrowly than would the opinion of the Massachusetts court or the statute under consideration. This case involves speech in connection with a referendum. Mr. Justice White's rationale would allow a State to proscribe the expenditure of corporate funds at any time for the purpose of expressing views on "political [or] social questions" or in connection with undefined "ideological crusades," unless the expenditures were shown to be "integrally related to corporate business operations." *Post*, at 1430, 1431, 1436, 1438, 1439. Thus corporate activities that are widely viewed as educational and socially constructive could be prohibited. Corporations no longer would be able safely to support—by contributions or public service advertising—educational, charitable, cultural, or even human rights causes. Similarly, informational advertising on such subjects of national interest as inflation and the worldwide energy problem could be prohibited. Many of these "causes" and subjects could be viewed as "social," "political," or "ideological." No prudent corporate management would incur the risk of criminal penalties, such as those in the Massachusetts Act, that would follow from a failure to prove the materiality to the corporation's "business, property or assets" of such contributions or advertisements. *See* n. 21, *infra*.

19. The suggestion in Mr. Justice White's dissent, *post* at 1432, that the First Amendment affords less protection to ideas that are not the product of "individual choice" would seem to apply to newspaper editorials and every other form of speech created under the auspices of a corporate body. No decision of this Court lends support to such a restrictive notion.

erty. The "materially affecting" requirement is not an identification of the boundaries of corporate speech etched by the Constitution itself. Rather, it amounts to an impermissible legislative prohibition of speech based on the identity of the interests that spokesmen may represent in public debate over controversial issues and a requirement that the speaker have a sufficiently great interest in the subject to justify communication.

Section 8 permits a corporation to communicate to the public its views on certain referendum subjects—those materially affecting its business—but not others. It also singles out one kind of ballot question—individual taxation—as a subject about which corporations may never make their ideas public. The legislature has drawn the line between permissible and impermissible speech according to whether there is a sufficient nexus, as defined by the legislature, between the issue presented to the voters and the business interests of the speaker.

In the realm of protected speech, the legislature is constitutionally disqualified from dictating the subjects about which persons may speak and the speakers who may address a public issue. *Police Dept. of Chicago v. Mosley*, 408 U.S. 92, 96, 92 S.Ct. 2286, 2290, 33 L.Ed.2d 212 (1972). If a legislature may direct business corporations to "stick to business," it also may limit other corporations—religious, charitable, or civic—to their respective "business" when addressing the public. Such power in government to channel the expression of views is unacceptable under the First Amendment.[21] Especially where, as here, the legislature's suppression of speech suggests an attempt to give one side of a debatable public question an advantage in expressing its views to the people, the First Amendment is plainly offended....

The constitutionality of § 8's prohibition of the "exposition of ideas" by corporations turns on whether it can survive the exacting scrutiny necessitated by a state-imposed restriction of freedom of speech. Especially where, as here, a prohibition is directed at speech itself, and the speech is intimately related to the process of governing, "the State may prevail only upon showing a subordinating interest which is compelling," *Bates v. City of Little Rock*, 361 U.S. 516, 524, 80 S.Ct. 412, 417, 4 L.Ed.2d 480 (1960); *see NAACP v. Button*, 371 U.S. 415, 438–439, 83 S.Ct. 328, 340–341, 9 L.Ed.2d 405 (1963); *NAACP v. Alabama ex rel. Patterson*, 357 U.S. at 463, 78 S.Ct. at 1172; *Thomas v. Collins*, 323 U.S. 516, 530, 65 S.Ct. 315, 322, 89 L.Ed. 430 (1945), "and the burden is on the Government to show the existence of such an interest." *Elrod v. Burns*, 427 U.S. 347, 362, 96 S.Ct. 2673, 49 L.Ed.2d 547 (1976). Even then, the State must employ means "closely drawn to avoid unnecessary abridgment...." *Buckley v. Valeo*, 424 U.S., at 25, 96 S.Ct. at 638; *see NAACP v. Button, supra*, 371 U.S. at 438, 83

---

21. Even assuming that the rationale behind the "materially affecting" requirement itself were unobjectionable, the limitation in § 8 would have an impermissibly restraining effect on protected speech. Much valuable information which a corporation might be able to provide would remain unpublished because corporate management would not be willing to risk the substantial criminal penalties—personal as well as corporate—provided for in § 8. *New York Times Co. v. Sullivan*, 376 U.S. at 279, 84 S.Ct. at 725; *Smith v. California*, 361 U.S. 147, 151, 80 S.Ct. 215, 217, 4 L.Ed.2d 205 (1959); *Speiser v. Randall*, 357 U.S. 513, 526, 78 S.Ct. 1332, 1342, 2 L.Ed.2d 1460 (1958). As the facts in this case illustrate, management never could be sure whether a court would disagree with its judgment as to the effect upon the corporation's business of a particular referendum issue. In addition, the burden and expense of litigating the issue—especially when what must be established is a complex and amorphous economic relationship—would unduly impinge on the exercise of the constitutional right. "[T]he free dissemination of ideas [might] be the loser." *Smith v. California, supra*, 361 U.S., at 151, 80 S.Ct. at 218; *see Freedman v. Maryland*, 380 U.S. 51, 59–60, 85 S.Ct. 734, 739–740, 13 L.Ed.2d 649 (1965).

S.Ct. at 340; *Shelton v. Tucker*, 364 U.S. 479, 488, 81 S.Ct. 247, 252, 5 L.Ed.2d 231 (1960).

The Supreme Judicial Court did not subject §8 to "the critical scrutiny demanded under accepted First Amendment and equal protection principles," *Buckley, supra*, 424 U.S. at 11, 96 S.Ct. at 631, because of its view that the First Amendment does not apply to appellants' proposed speech....

Finally, appellee argues that §8 protects corporate shareholders, an interest that is both legitimate and traditionally within the province of state law. *Cort v. Ash*, 422 U.S. 66, 82–84, 95 S.Ct. 2080, 2089–2091, 45 L.Ed.2d 26 (1975). The statute is said to serve this interest by preventing the use of corporate resources in furtherance of views with which some shareholders may disagree. This purpose is belied, however, by the provisions of the statute, which are both underinclusive and overinclusive....

Mr. Chief Justice BURGER, concurring.

I join the opinion and judgment of the Court but write separately to raise some questions likely to arise in this area in the future.

A disquieting aspect of Massachusetts' position is that it may carry the risk of impinging on the First Amendment rights of those who employ the corporate form—as most do—to carry on the business of mass communications, particularly the large media conglomerates. This is so because of the difficulty, and perhaps impossibility, of distinguishing, either as a matter of fact or constitutional law, media corporations from corporations such as the appellants in this case.

Making traditional use of the corporate form, some media enterprises have amassed vast wealth and power and conduct many activities, some directly related—and some not—to their publishing and broadcasting activities. *See Miami Herald Publishing Co. v. Tornillo*, 418 U.S. 241, 248–254, 94 S.Ct. 2831, 2835–2838, 41 L.Ed.2d 730 (1974). Today, a corporation might own the dominant newspaper in one or more large metropolitan centers, television and radio stations in those same centers and others, a newspaper chain, news magazines with nationwide circulation, national or worldwide wire news services, and substantial interests in book publishing and distribution enterprises. Corporate ownership may extend, vertically, to pulp mills and pulp timberlands to insure an adequate, continuing supply of newsprint and to trucking and steamship lines for the purpose of transporting the newsprint to the presses. Such activities would be logical economic auxiliaries to a publishing conglomerate. Ownership also may extend beyond to business activities unrelated to the task of publishing newspapers and magazines or broadcasting radio and television programs. Obviously, such far-reaching ownership would not be possible without the state-provided corporate form and its "special rules relating to such matters as limited liability, perpetual life, and the accumulation, distribution, and taxation of assets...." *Post*, at 1433 (White, J., dissenting).

In terms of "unfair advantage in the political process" and "corporate domination of the electoral process," *post*, at 1433, it could be argued that such media conglomerates as I describe pose a much more realistic threat to valid interests than do appellants and similar entities not regularly concerned with shaping popular opinion on public issues. *See Miami Herald Publishing Co. v. Tornillo, supra; ante*, at 1423 n. 29. In *Tornillo*, for example, we noted the serious contentions advanced that a result of the growth of modern media empires "has been to place in a few hands the power to inform the American people and shape public opinion." 418 U.S. at 250, 94 S.Ct. at 2836.

In terms of Massachusetts' other concern, the interests of minority shareholders, I perceive no basis for saying that the managers and directors of the media conglomerates are more or less sensitive to the views and desires of minority shareholders than are corporate officers generally.[1] Nor can it be said, even if relevant to First Amendment analysis—which it is not—that the former are more virtuous, wise, or restrained in the exercise of corporate power than are the latter. *Cf. Columbia Broadcasting System v. Democratic National Committee*, 412 U.S. 94, 124–125, 93 S.Ct. 2080, 2097–2098, 36 L.Ed.2d 772 (1973); 14 *The Writings of Thomas Jefferson* 46 (A. Libscomb ed. 1904) (letter to Dr. Walter Jones, Jan. 2, 1814). Thus, no factual distinction has been identified as yet that would justify government restraints on the right of appellants to express their views without, at the same time, opening the door to similar restraints on media conglomerates with their vastly greater influence.

Despite these factual similarities between media and nonmedia corporations, those who view the Press Clause as somehow conferring special and extraordinary privileges or status on the "institutional press"—which are not extended to those who wish to express ideas other than by publishing a newspaper—might perceive no danger to institutional media corporations flowing from the position asserted by Massachusetts. Under this narrow reading of the Press Clause, government could perhaps impose on nonmedia corporations restrictions not permissible with respect to "media" enterprises. *Cf.* Bezanson, *The New Free Press Guarantee*, 63 Va. L. Rev. 731, 767–770 (1977).[2] The Court has not yet squarely resolved whether the Press Clause confers upon the "institutional press" any freedom from government restraint not enjoyed by all others.[3]

I perceive two fundamental difficulties with a narrow reading of the Press Clause. First, although certainty on this point is not possible, the history of the Clause does not suggest that the authors contemplated a "special" or "institutional" privilege. *See* Lange, *The Speech and Press Clauses*, 23 UCLA L. Rev. 77, 88–99 (1975). The common 18th century understanding of freedom of the press is suggested by Andrew Bradford, a colonial American newspaperman. In defining the nature of the liberty, he did not limit it to a particular group:

> But, by the Freedom of the Press, I mean a Liberty, within the Bounds of Law, for any Man to communicate to the Public, his Sentiments on the Important Points of Religion and Government; of proposing any Laws, which he appre-

---

1. It may be that a nonmedia corporation, because of its nature, is subject to more limitations on political expression than a media corporation whose very existence is aimed at political expression. For example, the charter of a nonmedia corporation may be so framed as to render such activity or expression *ultra vires*; or its shareholders may be much less inclined to permit expenditure for corporate speech. Moreover, a nonmedia corporation may find it more difficult to characterize its expenditures as ordinary and necessary business expenses for tax purposes.

2. It is open to question whether limitations can be placed on the free expression rights of some without undermining the guarantees of all. Experience with statutory limitations on campaign expenditures on behalf of candidates or parties may shed some light on this issue. *Cf. Buckley v. Valeo*, 424 U.S. 1, 96 S.Ct. 612, 46 L.Ed.2d 659 (1976).

3. Language in some cases perhaps may be read as assuming or suggesting no independent scope to the Press Clause, *see Pell v. Procunier*, 417 U.S. 817, 834, 94 S.Ct. 2800, 2810, 41 L.Ed.2d 495 (1974), or the contrary, *see Bigelow v. Virginia*, 421 U.S. 809, 828, 95 S.Ct. 2222, 2235, 44 L.Ed.2d 600 (1975). The Court, however, has not yet focused on the issue. *See* Lange, *The Speech and Press Clauses*, 23 UCLA L. Rev. 77 (1975); Nimmer, *Introduction—Is Freedom of the Press a Redundancy: What Does It Add to Freedom of Speech?*, 26 Hastings L.J. 639 (1975); *cf.* Bezanson, *The New Free Press Guarantee*, 63 Va. L. Rev. 731 (1977).

hends may be for the Good of his Country, and of applying for the Repeal of such, as he Judges pernicious....

This is the Liberty of the Press, the great Palladium of all our other Liberties, which I hope the good People of this Province, will forever enjoy....

A. Bradford, *Sentiments on the Liberty of the Press*, in L. Levy, *Freedom of the Press from Zenger to Jefferson* 41–42 (1966) (emphasis deleted) (first published in Bradford's *The American Weekly Mercury*, a Philadelphia newspaper, Apr. 25, 1734).

Indeed most pre-First Amendment commentators "who employed the term 'freedom of speech' with great frequency, used it synonymously with freedom of the press." L. Levy, *Legacy of Suppression: Freedom of Speech and Press in Early American History* 174 (1960).

Those interpreting the Press Clause as extending protection only to, or creating a special role for, the "institutional press" must either (a) assert such an intention on the part of the Framers for which no supporting evidence is available, *cf. Lange, supra*, at 89–91; (b) argue that events after 1791 somehow operated to "constitutionalize" this interpretation, *see* Bezanson, *supra* n. 3, at 788; or (c) candidly acknowledging the absence of historical support, suggest that the intent of the Framers is not important today. *See* Nimmer, *supra* n. 3, at 640–641.

To conclude that the Framers did not intend to limit the freedom of the press to one select group is not necessarily to suggest that the Press Clause is redundant. The Speech Clause standing alone may be viewed as a protection of the liberty to express ideas and beliefs,[4] while the Press Clause focuses specifically on the liberty to disseminate expression broadly and "comprehends every sort of publication which affords a vehicle of information and opinion." *Lovell v. Griffin*, 303 U.S. 444, 452, 58 S.Ct. 666, 669, 82 L.Ed. 949 (1938).[5] Yet there is no fundamental distinction between expression and dissemination. The liberty encompassed by the Press Clause, although complementary to and a

---

4. The simplest explanation of the Speech and Press Clauses might be that the former protects oral communications; the latter, written. But the historical evidence does not strongly support this explanation. The first draft of what became the free expression provisions of the First Amendment, one proposed by Madison on June 8, 1789, as an addition to Art. 1, §9, read:

> The people shall not be deprived or abridged of their right to speak, to write, or to publish their sentiments; and the freedom of the press, as one of the great bulwarks of liberty, shall be inviolable.

1 Annals of Cong. 434 (1789).

The language was changed to its current form, "freedom of speech, or of the press," by the Committee of Eleven to which Madison's amendments were referred. (There is no explanation for the change and the language was not altered thereafter.) It seems likely that the Committee shortened Madison's language preceding the semicolon in his draft to "freedom of speech" without intending to diminish the scope of protection contemplated by Madison's phrase; in short, it was a stylistic change. *Cf. Kilbourn v. Thompson*, 103 U.S. 168, 26 L.Ed. 377 (1881); *Doe v. McMillan*, 412 U.S. 306, 93 S.Ct. 2018, 36 L.Ed.2d 912 (1973) (Speech or Debate Clause extends to both spoken and written expressions within the legislative function).

5. It is not strange that "press," the word for what was then the sole means of broad dissemination of ideas and news, would be used to describe the freedom to communicate with a large, unseen audience.

Changes wrought by 20th century technology, of course, have rendered the printing press as it existed in 1791 as obsolete as Watt's copying or letter press. It is the core meaning of "press" as used in the constitutional text which must govern.

natural extension of Speech Clause liberty, merited special mention simply because it had been more often the object of official restraints. Soon after the invention of the printing press, English and continental monarchs, fearful of the power implicit in its use and the threat to Establishment thought and order—political and religious—devised restraints, such as licensing, censors, indices of prohibited books, and prosecutions for seditious libel, which generally were unknown in the pre-printing press era. Official restrictions were the official response to the new, disquieting idea that this invention would provide a means for mass communication.

The second fundamental difficulty with interpreting the Press Clause as conferring special status on a limited group is one of definition. *See Lange, supra,* at 100–107. The very task of including some entities within the "institutional press" while excluding others, whether undertaken by legislature, court, or administrative agency, is reminiscent of the abhorred licensing system of Tudor and Stuart England—a system the First Amendment was intended to ban from this country. *Lovell v. Griffin, supra,* 303 U.S. at 451–452, 58 S.Ct. at 668–669. Further, the officials undertaking that task would be required to distinguish the protected from the unprotected on the basis of such variables as content of expression, frequency or fervor of expression, or ownership of the technological means of dissemination. Yet nothing in this Court's opinions supports such a confining approach to the scope of Press Clause protection. Indeed, the Court has plainly intimated the contrary view:

> Freedom of the press is a "fundamental personal right" which "is not confined to newspapers and periodicals. It necessarily embraces pamphlets and leaflets.... The press in its historic connotation comprehends every sort of publication which affords a vehicle of information and opinion."... The informative function asserted by representatives of the organized press...is also performed by lecturers, political pollsters, novelists, academic researchers, and dramatists. Almost any author may quite accurately assert that he is contributing to the flow of information to the public....

*Branzburg v. Hayes,* 408 U.S. 665, 704–705, 92 S.Ct. 2646, 2668, 33 L.Ed.2d 626 (1972), quoting *Lovell v. Griffin, supra,* 303 U.S. at 450, 452, 58 S.Ct. at 668, 669.

The meaning of the Press Clause, as a provision separate and apart from the Speech Clause, is implicated only indirectly by this case. Yet Massachusetts' position poses serious questions. The evolution of traditional newspapers into modern corporate conglomerates in which the daily dissemination of news by print is no longer the major part of the whole enterprise suggests the need for caution in limiting the First Amendment rights of corporations as such. Thus, the tentative probings of this brief inquiry are wholly consistent, I think, with the Court's refusal to sustain §8's serious and potentially dangerous restriction on the freedom of political speech.

Because the First Amendment was meant to guarantee freedom to express and communicate ideas, I can see no difference between the right of those who seek to disseminate ideas by way of a newspaper and those who give lectures or speeches and seek to enlarge the audience by publication and wide dissemination. "[T]he purpose of the Constitution was not to erect the press into a privileged institution but to protect all persons in their right to print what they will as well as to utter it. '....the liberty of the press is no greater and no less....' than the liberty of every citizen of the Republic." *Pennekamp v. Florida,* 328 U.S. 331, 364, 66 S.Ct. 1029, 1046, 90 L.Ed. 1295 (1946) (Frankfurter, J., concurring).

In short, the First Amendment does not "belong" to any definable category of persons or entities: It belongs to all who exercise its freedoms....

Mr. Justice REHNQUIST, dissenting....

The question presented today, whether business corporations have a constitutionally protected liberty to engage in political activities, has never been squarely addressed by any previous decision of this Court.[1] However, the General Court of the Commonwealth of Massachusetts, the Congress of the United States, and the legislatures of 30 other States of this Republic have considered the matter, and have concluded that restrictions upon the political activity of business corporations are both politically desirable and constitutionally permissible. The judgment of such a broad consensus of governmental bodies expressed over a period of many decades is entitled to considerable deference from this Court. I think it quite probable that their judgment may properly be reconciled with our controlling precedents, but I am certain that under my views of the limited application of the First Amendment to the States, which I share with the two immediately preceding occupants of my seat on the Court, but not with my present colleagues, the judgment of the Supreme Judicial Court of Massachusetts should be affirmed....

The appellants herein either were created by the Commonwealth or were admitted into the Commonwealth only for the limited purposes described in their charters and regulated by state law. Since it cannot be disputed that the mere creation of a corporation does not invest it with all the liberties enjoyed by natural persons, *United States v. White*, 322 U.S. 694, 698–701, 64 S.Ct. 1248, 1251–1252, 88 L.Ed. 1542 (1944) (corporations do not enjoy the privilege against self-incrimination), our inquiry must seek to determine which constitutional protections are "incidental to its very existence." *Dartmouth College, supra*, 4 Wheat. [518,] 636 [(1819)]....

I can see no basis for concluding that the liberty of a corporation to engage in political activity with regard to matters having no material effect on its business is necessarily incidental to the purposes for which the Commonwealth permitted these corporations to be organized or admitted within its boundaries. Nor can I disagree with the Supreme Judicial Court's factual finding that no such effect has been shown by these appellants. Because the statute as construed provides at least as much protection as the Fourteenth Amendment requires, I believe it is constitutionally valid.

It is true, as the Court points out, that recent decisions of this Court have emphasized the interest of the public in receiving the information offered by the speaker seeking protection. The free flow of information is in no way diminished by the Commonwealth's decision to permit the operation of business corporations with limited rights of political expression. All natural persons, who owe their existence to a higher sovereign than the Commonwealth, remain as free as before to engage in political activity. *Cf. Maher v. Roe*, 432 U.S. 464, 474, 97 S.Ct. 2376, 2382, 53 L.Ed.2d 484 (1977).

I would affirm the judgment of the Supreme Judicial Court.

---

1. Our prior cases, mostly of recent vintage, have discussed the boundaries of protected speech without distinguishing between artificial and natural persons. *See, e. g., Linmark Associates, Inc. v. Township of Willingboro*, 431 U.S. 85, 97 S.Ct. 1614, 52 L.Ed.2d 155 (1977); *Buckley v. Valeo*, 424 U.S. 1, 96 S.Ct. 612, 46 L.Ed.2d 659 (1976). Nevertheless, the Court today affirms that the failure of those cases to draw distinctions between artificial and natural persons does not mean that no such distinctions may be drawn. The Court explicitly states that corporations may not enjoy all the political liberties of natural persons, although it fails to articulate the basis of its suggested distinction. *Ante*, at 1416 n. 13.

## Notes and Questions

1.  To what degree is Chief Justice Burger's concurring opinion in *First National Bank v. Bellotti*, 435 U.S. 765, 797–802 (1978) (Burger, C.J., concurring), a response to Justice Stewart's address at Yale Law School, Potter Stewart, *"Or of the Press,"* 26 Hastings L.J. 631 (1975)?

2.  One professor has opined that

    > [a]ffording non-media defendants less first amendment protection than media defendants would deter non-media contributions to the democratic dialogue (and thus would waken the media's contribution), would favor those with greater capacity to cause damage and with greater ability to compensate for that damage (by spreading the risk), would require difficult determinations as to which communications would and would not merit the label "press" or "media," would strain basic principles of first amendment equality, and would diminish respect for the democratic process.

    Steven Shiffrin, *Defamatory Non-Media Speech and First Amendment Methodology*, 25 UCLA L. Rev. 915, 934–45 (1978).

3.  Consider *Putnam Pit, Inc. v. City of Cookeville*, No. 98-6438, 2000 WL 992229 (6th Cir. July 19, 2000), in which the publisher of a free tabloid and Internet Web page, edited by plaintiff Geoffrey Davidian, asserted a claim pursuant to 42 U.S.C.A. § 1983. The plaintiffs alleged that the City of Cookeville violated their freedom of the press rights by denying them access to city parking ticket records in electronic form. The Sixth Circuit stated that:

    > The collection of information is an important aspect of First Amendment freedoms. *See Branzburg v. Hayes*, 408 U.S. 665, 728, 92 S.Ct. 2646, 33 L.Ed.2d 626 (1972) (stating that "without freedom to acquire information the right to publish would be impermissibly compromised"). This ability to collect information is not absolute, however. Although the First Amendment protects information gathering, it does not provide blanket access to information within the government's control. *See Houchins v. KQED, Inc.*, 438 U.S. 1, 8, 98 S.Ct. 2588, 57 L.Ed.2d 553 (1978).
    >
    > First, "[t]he First Amendment does not guarantee the press a constitutional right of special access to information not available to the public generally." *Branzburg*, 408 U.S. at 684. Although some circumstances may dictate distinguishing journalists from the general public, the difficulty of this court's determining who may be considered "press" is obvious. *See Branzburg*, 408 U.S. at 704; *see also Smith v. Plati*, 56 F. Supp. 2d 1195, 1203 (D. Colo. 1999) (rejecting claim of a publisher of an Internet Web site on University of Colorado athletics who alleged, among other things, that he had been denied press privileges by a university media liaison). In this case, Davidian, by publishing The Putnam Pit, is akin to a twenty-first century "lonely pamphleteer," *Branzburg*, 408 U.S. at 704, whose access to information must be equal to that granted to members of the public. There is no indication in the record that access to parking ticket records in electronic form had ever been allowed by the city. Davidian has no greater right to this in-

formation than the general public; accordingly, the city does not have an affirmative duty to provide this information to him. *See Pell v. Procunier*, 417 U.S. 817, 834–35, 94 S.Ct. 2800, 41 L.Ed.2d 495 (1974).

*Id.* at *2 (footnote omitted).

4. How is society's notion of the press as an institution affected by the extraordinary increase in available topics and viewpoints via the Internet?

> As listeners get more control over the topics and viewpoints they see, they may choose to focus on a much narrower mix of information. They may subscribe only to articles on topics in which they're interested, or to commentators with whose opinions they already agree....

> Listeners will no longer be a captive audience to the selection that the intermediaries—publishers and broadcasters—want to feed them. Will listeners do a better job of informing themselves than the intermediaries have been doing?

Eugene Volokh, *Symposium— Emerging Media Technology and the First Amendment: Cheap Speech and What It Will Do*, 104 Yale L.J. 1805, 1849 (1995). Historically, press entities have decided such issues as which matters merit attention, and the priority of reporting on such issues. Will users of the Internet engage in editorial functions that traditionally have been within the sole province of the press?

5. The U.S. Department of Justice has promulgated guidelines relating to the issuance of subpoenas to "members of the news media." 28 C.F.R. § 50.10 (1999). The regulations are notable for their implicit recognition that law enforcement investigations may be subordinate to protection of the press from compelled disclosure of information. Who are "members of the news media" in Internet publications and thus within the purview of the guidelines?

6. Reporting on newsworthy matters necessitates access to information. How should governmental agencies determine who is a member of the press for purposes of issuing press credentials to admit reporters to such restricted areas as crime scenes? Does the dissemination of news content on the Internet, as opposed to via newspapers, magazines, television, or radio, suggest any reason why the issuing authority may apply different standards?

---

# UNITED STATES of AMERICA v. Lawrence Charles MATTHEWS

United States District Court, District of Maryland
Criminal Action No. AW-97-270, 11 F. Supp. 2d 656
June 29, 1998

Williams, Jr., District Judge.

[Defendant, a seasoned journalist, was indicted for receiving and transporting, via computer, visual depictions of minors engaged in sexually explicit conduct, production of which involved use of minors engaged in sexually explicit conduct. While working as a business reporter for WTOP radio in Washington, D.C., he]...became aware of the availability of child pornography over the Internet, and...[he] reported to the Federal

Bureau of Investigation ("F.B.I.") that he had been in contact with a person who offered her two children for prostitution. Defendant spoke with an agent about the person, and also claims to have had further contacts with the agent regarding the availability of child pornography on the Internet....

After leaving WTOP to become a freelance journalist, Defendant claims to have continued to investigate child pornography on the Internet, specifically concerning the role of law enforcement agents. It is this alleged further investigation that led to the present indictment....

On December 11, 1996, the F.B.I. executed a search warrant, searched Defendant's home, and seized certain materials. The subsequent grand jury indictment, dated July 28, 1997, charges Defendant with eleven counts of receiving and four counts of transporting, via computer, visual depictions of minors engaged in sexually explicit conduct, the production of which involved the use of minors engaged in sexually explicit conduct....

## Analysis

...The Defendant...moves to dismiss the complaint on the grounds that it is unconstitutional as applied to a journalist's news gathering activities. The Government has stated clearly that it does not believe that Defendant's activities were part of his work as a reporter, and argues that it has evidence to support its contention. Because of the Government's position, a jury would have to decide the reason why the Defendant might have committed these acts. However, the Government also argues that the First Amendment provides no defense to the charges even if the Defendant was acting as a journalist. Accordingly, the Government has filed a motion in limine, asking the Court to exclude any evidence, testimony, or argument concerning Defendant's alleged journalistic motive. The question for the Court, therefore, is whether Defendant enjoys a First Amendment defense that can be presented to the jury.

The Court's analysis begins with *New York v. Ferber,* 458 U.S. 747, 102 S.Ct. 3348, 73 L.Ed.2d 1113 (1982). In *Ferber,* the Supreme Court upheld the constitutionality of a New York statute which banned distribution of non-obscene child pornography. The Court found that the state's interest in safeguarding minors not only is a sufficiently compelling state interest, but that it is of "surpassing importance." *See id.* at 756–57, 102 S.Ct. 3348. The legislative judgment that children are seriously harmed when used pornographic subjects "easily passes muster under the First Amendment." *Id.* at 758, 102 S.Ct. 3348. The Court also found that the distribution of child pornography is "intrinsically related" to the sexual abuse targeted by the legislature. *See id.* at 759, 102 S.Ct. 3348. The image itself is a "permanent record" of the child's participation in the act, and the harm to the child is exacerbated as the image is circulated. *Id.* In addition, the Court recognized that the imposition of severe sentences on those who distribute child pornography may be the only way to curtail the industry in light of the difficulty in reaching the clandestine producers themselves. *Id.* at 759–60, 102 S.Ct. 3348.

Defendant's "as applied" challenge in this case arises from the manner in which the *Ferber* Court considered whether the New York law was unconstitutionally overbroad. The New York Court of Appeals had found the statute unconstitutional, in part, because it could reach "some protected expression, ranging from medical textbooks to pictorials in the National Geographic." *See id.* at 773, 102 S.Ct. 3348. The Supreme Court rejected the overbreadth attack, doubting that "these arguably impermissible applications of the statute amount to more than a tiny fraction of the materials within the statute's reach." *Id.* The Court instructed that potentially unconstitutional applications of the law should be addressed on a " 'case-by-case' " basis. *See id.* at 773–74, 102 S.Ct. 3348 (quoting *Broadrick v. Oklahoma,* 413 U.S. 601, 615–16, 93 S.Ct. 2908, 37 L.Ed.2d 830 (1973)).

*Ferber* does not explain exactly which applications of the child pornography law would implicate speech protected by the First Amendment. Justice White's reference to pictures in "medical textbooks" and "pictorials in the National Geographic" suggests that the content of the pictures themselves, and perhaps the context in which they are displayed, determines whether they are protected by the First Amendment. Justice O'Connor, concurring, expressed a concern about the same types of material, mentioning "clinical pictures of adolescent sexuality, such as those that might appear in medical textbooks" and "pictures of children engaged in rites widely approved by their cultures, such as those that might appear in issues of the National Geographic." *See id.* at 775, 102 S.Ct. 3348 (O'Connor, J., concurring). Justice Brennan, with whom Justice Marshall joined, also seems to have been concerned about pictures whose content classifies them as protected speech. Justice Brennan expressed his view that any application of the statute to "depictions of children that in themselves do have serious literary, artistic, scientific, or medical value, would violate the First Amendment." *See id.* at 776, 102 S.Ct. 3348 (Brennan, J., concurring in the judgment). The opinion providing Defendant with the most support is that of Justice Stevens, who wrote that there may be constitutionally protected uses of child pornography. *See id.* at 778, 102 S.Ct. 3348 (Stevens, J., concurring in the judgment). Justice Stevens suggested that a viewing of the film before a legislative committee or before a group of research scientists could not constitute a criminal act. *See id.*

Defendant does not principally rely on the First Amendment's protection of speech, and Defendant has not argued that he intended to use the pictures in a context that would give them serious literary, artistic, scientific, or medical value. Instead, Defendant argues that his use of the pictures is protected by the First Amendment's protection of the press. The only manner in which Defendant's argument implicates free speech is that the public's ability to express themselves depends on the press's ability to inform. Defendant has relied not on free speech cases, but on cases concerning the First Amendment's protection of news gathering activities....

The First Amendment protects the public's right to a free press charged with the responsibility of informing the community of matters of public importance. *See Branzburg v. Hayes,* 408 U.S. 665, 726–27, 92 S.Ct. 2646, 33 L.Ed.2d 626 (1972) (Stewart, J., dissenting); *New York Times Co. v. United States,* 403 U.S. 713, 717, 91 S.Ct. 2140, 29 L.Ed.2d 822 (1971) (Black, J., concurring); *Thornhill v. Alabama,* 310 U.S. 88, 95, 101–02, 60 S.Ct. 736, 84 L.Ed. 1093 (1940). Because the right to a free press would be worthless without some protection for the press's ability to seek out the news, the Supreme Court has recognized that the First Amendment also protects news gathering activities. *See Branzburg,* 408 U.S. at 681, 92 S.Ct. 2646.

But the First Amendment's protection of the press is far from unlimited. It is well-settled that the First Amendment does not grant the press automatic relief from laws of general application. *See Cohen v. Cowles Media Co.,* 501 U.S. 663, 669–70, 111 S.Ct. 2513, 115 L.Ed.2d 586 (1991); *Zacchini v. Scripps-Howard Broadcasting Co.,* 433 U.S. 562, 576–79, 97 S.Ct. 2849, 53 L.Ed.2d 965 (1977) (press must obey copyright laws); *Branzburg,* 408 U.S. at 682–83, 92 S.Ct. 2646 (citing decisions refusing to exempt news organizations from National Labor Relations Act, Fair Labor Standards Act, Sherman Act, and laws of general taxation). Most relevant to this case, the First Amendment's protection of news gathering activity does not guarantee the press special access to information not available to the general public, *see Branzburg*, 408 U.S. at 684, 92 S.Ct. 2646 (citing cases), nor does it grant the press a right to travel to restricted locations in the search for news, *see Zemel v. Rusk*, 381 U.S. 1, 16–17, 85 S.Ct. 1271, 14 L.Ed.2d 179 (1965) ("The right to speak and publish does not carry with it the unrestrained right to gather information."), nor does it grant the press a right to break and enter a home or office in a search for news. *See Cohen v. Cowles Media. Co.*, 501 U.S. at 669, 111 S.Ct. 2513.

18 U.S.C. § 2252 prohibits any member of the general public from knowingly receiving or transporting child pornography in interstate commerce. In this regard, it is a law that limits the public's access to specific material, and the question posed is whether the First Amendment requires that the Defendant be granted relief from this general prohibition if he violated the law during news gathering activity.

Supreme Court precedent demonstrates that the Court must balance the competing interests involved in this particular case. In *Branzburg*, the Supreme Court declined to create a testimonial privilege protecting reporters from having to testify before a grand jury. *See* [408 U.S. 665,] 690, 92 S.Ct. 2646. The Court examined both the expected burden on news gathering and the important role of the grand jury in effective law enforcement, and concluded that the public's interest in law enforcement was sufficient to override the burden imposed. *See id.* at 690–91, 695, 92 S.Ct. 2646; *see also id.* at 710, 92 S.Ct. 2646 (Powell, J., concurring) (discussing balance between freedom of the press and obligation of citizens to give relevant testimony about criminal conduct); *id.* at 734–35, 92 S.Ct. 2646 (Stewart, J., dissenting) (must examine competing interests in determining whether there is an unconstitutional infringement). In *Cohen v. Cowles Media Co.*, 501 U.S. at 671–72, 111 S.Ct. 2513, the Supreme Court reasoned that while allowing a newspaper to be sued for breach of contract/breach of promise might inhibited the press in its quest to publish newsworthy information, such inhibition would be "incidental" and "constitutionally insignificant." ...

Defendant argues that the balance must be struck in favor of the press because of his overriding need to access child pornography on the Internet. Defendant first relies on his contention that he was investigating the role of law enforcement officials on the Internet. Amici support Defendant's contention by arguing that law enforcement agencies historically have misunderstood the Internet and are usually either indifferent or overzealous in their prosecutions. Although the Court agrees that the press cannot rely on the government to disclose its own wrongdoing, it fails to see how this leads to the conclusion that the Defendant has a compelling need to transmit and receive child pornography. If law enforcement officials are doing something improper in their investigations, the Court does not understand how Defendant would uncover that malfeasance by receiving and disseminating the material himself.

Defendant also suggests that the public has a right to know whether the government is doing enough to curtail the availability of child pornography on the Internet. Again, the Defendant has not explained how his own transportation of the material would further this investigation. Surely there are other ways of determining the amount of child pornography available on the Internet and whether the images are easy to obtain. While the Court is hesitant to give news gathering tips, the Court agrees with the Government that other, legal avenues of investigation are available. For example, a reporter could study the number of prosecutions brought by the government and examine the public records in those cases. A reporter could develop sources, including victims of child pornography and people already convicted of violations. Finally, a reporter could examine reports to public interest groups that track incidents of child pornography distribution. The Court is sure that a seasoned reporter could think of other resources that would not require that the reporter depend on the government for information. Even if these resources did not provide the entire picture, they would give at least as much insight into the scope of the problem as the reporter's own transactions on his home computer.

Even assuming that Defendant's "exploration" would in some way advance his investigation, the degree to which a reporter gains knowledge about the general subject matter by committing his own violations is insignificant compared to the government's interest in preventing the exploitation of children. One must keep in mind that the Defendant's receipt and dissemination of the pornography is the exact harm identified in *Ferber* as contributing to the sexual exploitation of children. *See Ferber*, 458 U.S. at 759–60, 102 S.Ct. 3348. In comparison, Defendant's minimal interests in obtaining his own child pornography does not strike the Court as being nearly as important as the journalist's interest in confidential sources considered in *Branzburg*. And the magnitude of the government's interest in this case is truly striking when compared to the less compelling interest justifying a restriction on a reporter's foreign travel. *See Zemel*, 381 U.S. at 14–17, 85 S.Ct. 1271....

Finally, Amici point to the anonymous nature of on-line communication, and argue that a reporter cannot "take the word of someone in a chat room that he or she has child pornography to sell or trade." The Court does not believe that the only way a reporter can confirm that pornography is available on the Internet is to obtain and distribute the images himself. Any person, reporter or otherwise, who wants to know whether child pornography is available on the Internet is free to come to federal court and observe a prosecution for a § 2252 violation. That person will quickly learn that there are people trading child pornography over the Internet.

Defendant is justified in noting that Congress may never have passed this very law had journalists not exposed the widespread availability of child pornography. But the Court does not believe that a reporter must traffic in child pornography to reveal its availability to the public. The Court understands that the availability of the material over the Internet may not be an easy matter to explore. However, it does not seem substantially different from other means of distribution, such as mail received from overseas providers. There must be other, admittedly more labor-intensive means of reporting this story. In sum, the Court does not agree that its ruling will prevent journalists from informing the public about the existence of child pornography on the Internet....

[T]he Court will deny Defendant's motion to dismiss and will grant the Government's motion in limine.

## Conclusion

Defendant has argued that he should be allowed to receive and distribute child pornography in order to gather news for a future story. However, the law is clear that a press pass is not a license to break the law. Because of the government's surpassing interest in protecting children from the harm caused by the spread of child pornography, and because of the Defendant's minimal interests in obtaining and transmitting the images himself, the Court will deny both motions to dismiss and will grant the Government's motion in limine....

## Notes and Questions

1.  Matthews ultimately pled guilty, while preserving his constitutional defense for appeal. He was sentenced to 18 months in prison, three years' probation, and a fine of $4,000.00. In the spring of 2000, the Fourth Circuit rejected Matthews' First Amendment defense and affirmed his conviction. *United States v. Matthews*, 209 F.3d 338 (4th Cir. 2000). The appellate court framed the issue as one of first impression in its circuit: "does the First Amendment permit a *bona fide* reporter to trade in child pornography to 'create a work of journalism?'" *Id.* at 342. The Fourth Circuit deemed the government to have a compelling interest in preventing the sexual exploitation and abuse of minors at the time pornography is created.

    > Indeed, by its careful explanation of the pernicious and lasting damage caused to children by the distribution of child pornography, the Court made a compelling case for upholding—without exception—the constitutionality of broad restrictive legislation criminalizing that activity. Although, as Matthews points out, the *Ferber* Court did note that there were "limits on the category of child pornography...unprotected by the First Amendment," [*New York v. Ferber*, 458 U.S. 747,] 764, 102 S.Ct. 3348, those limits do nothing to assist Matthews either. The Court's strictures do not establish a "legitimate" value exception to legislative prohibitions on the distribution of child pornography, but rather emphasize the need for clarity in statutory language imposing such prohibitions.

    *Id.* at 343. In sum, the appellate court concluded that "Matthews' asserted First Amendment defense simply enjoys no support in the law." *Id.* at 350.

    The Fourth Circuit also declined to review Matthews' sentence, pointing out that the district court had found that he had not shown by a preponderance of the evidence that the sole purpose for receipt and transmission of the pornographic material was journalistic. *Id.* at 352-53.

2.  In *United States v. Morris*, 928 F.2d 504 (2d Cir. 1991), the defendant, Robert Morris, was charged under the Computer Fraud and Abuse Act, 18 U.S.C. § 1030,* with having released a "worm" into the Internet. Extensive malfunctioning at various educational and governmental web-sites ensued, although the court determined that the defendant did not intend to cause damage to the sites. *Id.* Morris challenged his conviction, arguing that the statute requires a showing that he intentionally accessed the computers and intentionally caused the resultant damage. *Id.* Morris maintained that his intention was not to cause damage, but merely to highlight the lack of computer security. *Id.* The Second Circuit rejected the defense on the ground that the intentional component of the statute related only to unauthorized access, and not to the causing of damage. *Id.*

3.  How might a journalist protect himself if he wanted to engage in research on the Internet to assess whether potentially criminal activity could readily be conducted?

4.  Child pornography has long been considered inimical to the public welfare. Distribution of child pornography has been deemed to abuse children by creating a permanent record of their participation in sexual activities that exacerbates the harm to the child every time the material is circulated. *See, e.g., New York v. Ferber*, 458 U.S. 747, 759 (1982). The damage caused to children by the distribution of child

---

\* This Act was modified in 1996 by the National Information Infrastructure Protection Act.

pornography has been considered so detrimental, with lasting effects so pernicious, that comprehensive legislation criminalizing the activity has been constitutionally upheld. Note that the Fourth Circuit in *United States v. Matthews* chastised Matthews for "miss[ing] the fundamental distinction between child pornography and adult pornography.... The government has an interest in prohibiting the dissemination of both. But the government's interest in prohibiting the distribution of adult pornography—to protect 'the sensibilities of unwilling recipients,' pales in comparison to its interest in prohibiting the dissemination of child pornography—to prevent 'sexual exploitation and abuse of children.'" 209 F.3d at 345 (citations omitted).

5.   In *Ferber v. New York*, 458 U.S. 747, Justice Stevens wrote a separate opinion, arguing that exhibition of child pornography "before a legislative committee studying a proposed amendment to a state law, or before a group of research scientists studying human behavior...." should be exempted from penal sanction. 458 U.S. at 778 (Stevens, J., concurring). The Fourth Circuit eschewed application of this argument to the defense in *United States v. Matthews,* noting that while Justice Stevens' "observation has intuitive appeal, its doctrinal roots are unclear;" and that the Supreme Court's decisions on child pornography issues focused on the depictions themselves, rather than on their use. *United States v. Matthews,* 209 F.3d at 348.

6.   *Compare United States v. Hilton,* 167 F.3d 61 (1st Cir. 1999) (holding that the Child Pornography Prevention Act survives facial constitutional challenge), *cert. denied,* 120 S.Ct. 115 (1999) *and United States v. Acheson,* 195 F.3d 645 (11th Cir. 1999) (same) *with Free Speech Coalition v. Reno,* 198 F.3d 1083 (9th Cir. 1999) (holding that the First Amendment prohibits the imposition of penal sanctions for the generation of images of fictitious children engaged in imaginary but explicit sexual conduct), *reh'g en banc denied,* No. 97-16536, 2000 WL 1010063 (9th Cir. July 24, 2000).

7.   The Supreme Court has stated that "[t]he extraordinary protections afforded by the First Amendment carry with them something in the nature of a fiduciary duty to exercise the protected rights responsibly[,] a duty widely acknowledged but not always observed by editors and publishers." *Nebraska Press Ass'n v. Stuart,* 427 U.S. 539, 560 (1976). What is the scope of such a "duty"? How does this apply to Web publishers and to information providers? Does a claim to a preferred position under the First Amendment subject the press to regulation as a public fiduciary, susceptible to prescribed standards of care? *See* William W. Van Alstyne, *The Hazards to the Press of Claiming a "Preferred Position,"* 28 Hastings L.J. 761 (1977).

8.   Consider *Associated Press v. United States,* 326 U.S. 1 (1945), which upheld the enforcement of antitrust laws against a news service. The Supreme Court stated that the First Amendment "rests on the assumption that the widest possible dissemination of information from diverse and antagonistic sources is essential to the welfare of the public." *Id.* at 20.

9.   The press also has protections from compulsory publication. Even when a newspaper would incur no additional cost to comply with a compulsory access law or be forced to forgo publication of news or opinion by the inclusion of material, there must be no impermissible intrusion on the publisher's editorial function. *See Miami Herald Publ'g Co. v. Tornillo,* 418 U.S. 241 (1974); *see also PruneYard Shopping Center v. Robbins,* 447 U.S. 74, 82 (1980) ("the State cannot tell a newspaper what it must print"). "The power of a privately owned newspaper to advance its

own political, social, and economic views is bounded by only two factors: first, the acceptance of a sufficient number of readers—and hence advertisers—to assure financial success; and, second, the journalistic integrity of its editors and publishers." *Columbia Broadcasting Sys., Inc. v. Democratic Nat'l Committee*, 412 U.S. 94, 117 (1973). How do these two factors apply to Web publishers, who may launch and maintain web-sites without significant capital expenditure and independently of editorial review?

---

# Theodore M. SMITH v. David PLATI

United States District Court, District of Colorado
Civ. A. No. 99-K-491, 56 F. Supp. 2d 1195
July 22, 1999

KANE, Senior District Judge.

The Plaintiff, Theodore M. Smith,...is a lawyer appearing *pro se*. He operates an Internet website known as "Netbuffs.com," which supplies information about University of Colorado varsity athletic programs to the general public. The website began operating on September 2, 1997. Defendant David Plati (Plati) is Assistant Athletic Director for Media Relations at the University of Colorado at Boulder. The University of Colorado, a state higher education entity, is governed by the Regents of the University of Colorado (together, the University).

Smith claims (1) Plati, in his individual and official capacities, arbitrarily and capriciously denied him and Netbuffs.com "media" status at the University of Colorado and seeks an order under Colorado Rules of Civil Procedure Rule 106 declaring that he be recognized as "media" and "press" by Plati and the University; (2) Plati, individually and officially, and the University denied him records that are subject to disclosure under the Colorado Open Records Act, Colo.Rev.Stat. § 24-72-201, *et seq.* (1998) and seeks a mandatory injunction requiring the University to provide him with certain records and documents; and (3) Plati, individually and officially, deprived him of "rights and privileges and enjoyment in retaliation for Smith's publication on the Internet," and seeks compensatory and exemplary damages against Plati, as well as injunctive relief....

## I. Factual Allegations.

The dispute between Smith and Plati centers on whether the Office of Athletic Media Relations for the University of Colorado must allow Smith access to information about its varsity sports programs so he can effectively operate his website.

According to Smith, from the time of the inception of his website until approximately August 1998, the University provided him with the same access and privileges afforded to members of the press. This allowed him ample opportunity to take photographs, interview players and coaches, and copy documents which he could then post on his Internet website. Starting in August 1998, however, Plati purportedly began a course of conduct designed to limit Smith's access to publishable information. Specifically, Smith avers, Plati (1) denied him resources and documents routinely given to members of the press; (2) required payment for schedules, press releases, and photographs ordinarily given freely to other members of the public; (3) prevented the distribution of notices advertising Netbuffs.com; (4) threatened to copyright basic information such as varsity sports schedules; and (5) attempted to dissuade his attorney from defending him in a related criminal action....

[I]t seems Smith is arguing (1) Plati, in his individual capacity, is obligated to recognize Smith as "media" or "press" and afford him all benefits of such status; or (2) Smith has a legally enforceable right or entitlement to be recognized as "media" or "press."

On the first assertion, it is important to emphasize this discussion addresses this claim insofar as it is asserted against Plati in his individual capacity. There is no law or legal precedent which would place a duty on Plati to recognize Smith as "media" or "press" just because Smith operates an Internet Website. Even if Plati did concede Smith was qualified for treatment as "media" or "press," in his individual capacity, he would have no authority to provide him any benefits of such status. His ability to provide "media" and "press" entities with special access to information regarding University of Colorado athletic programs stems directly from his position as the Assistant Athletic Director of Media Relations. Thus, only in his official capacity could Plati provide Smith with the relief he desires. In this sense, Smith's Rule 106 claim against Plati, in his individual capacity, fails.

Secondly, as a general rule, the Constitution does not require government officials "to make available to journalists sources of information not available to members of the public generally." *Pell v. Procunier,* 417 U.S. 817, 834, 94 S.Ct. 2800, 41 L.Ed.2d 495 (1974). More fundamental, however, is the question of who is entitled to recognition as "press" in the first place. One commentator suggests the Supreme Court has denied members of the press special privileges under the First Amendment because "according the press special rights presents the insolvable problem of determining who qualifies as 'the press.'" *The Supreme Court, 1977 Term,* 92 Harv. L.Rev. 174, 179 (1978).

Furthermore, "[a]ny meaningful definition of the press would involve the state in choosing among media representatives in a potentially unconstitutional manner." *Id.* This sentiment was expressed in *Branzburg v. Hayes,* 408 U.S. 665, 704, 92 S.Ct. 2646, 33 L.Ed.2d 626 (1972), where the Court recognized, if special press rights were afforded, it would "be necessary to define those categories of newsmen who qualified for the privilege, a questionable procedure in light of the traditional doctrine that liberty of the press is the right of the lonely pamphleteer who uses carbon paper or a mimeograph just as much as of the large metropolitan publisher who utilizes the latest photocomposition methods." Accordingly, for Smith to claim he has a legally enforceable right to be recognized as "media" or "press," and afforded special treatment as such, is flatly incomprehensible.

For the forgoing reasons, I dismiss Smith's Rule 106 claim against Plati in his individual capacity....

Smith cites *Patrick v. Miller,* 953 F.2d 1240, 1247 (10th Cir. 1992), to support the proposition that speech related to "any matter of political, social or other concern to the community" is protected by the First Amendment. He also cites *Pickering v. Board of Education,* 391 U.S. 563, 568, 88 S.Ct. 1731, 20 L.Ed.2d 811 (1968), to support his argument that a public employee may openly criticize policies of public agencies and facilities without being subjected to retribution. Curiously, Smith is not a public employee and his reliance on *Pickering* is perplexing at best.

Under *Patrick,* Smith has a right to speak freely about "any matter of political, social or other concern to the community," including athletic programs at the University of Colorado. Likewise, under *Pickering,* he claims a right to criticize the University of Colorado without punishment.

Smith's argument runs into problems, however, in proving he was actually censored, or targeted for retribution, by Plati's actions. Censorship is "review of publications, movies, plays, and the like for the purpose of prohibiting the publication, distribution, or production of material deemed objectionable...." *Black's Law Dictionary* 224 (6th ed. 1992). There are no allegations that Plati reviewed information Smith intended to post on his website with the purpose of prohibiting its publication. Smith continues to possess the ability to publish anything any citizen could by opening a privately operated website. Smith cites several instances where Plati undertook a course of action which made it difficult for him to gain access to information ordinarily provided to the press. However, the First Amendment does not ensure anyone, even the press, access to special information or treatment: "the First Amendment does not guarantee the press a constitutional right of special access to information not available to the public generally." *Branzburg*, 408 U.S. at 684, 92 S.Ct. 2646. At all times, Smith retained, and still retains, the ability to speak freely about any political, social or other concern related to the University of Colorado athletic programs.

Likewise, retribution involves a relationship in which an employee is discharged or disciplined for expressing personal opinions which are contrary to those of the employer. Indeed, this is the situation which existed in *Pickering* where a high school teacher was discharged for publicly criticizing his school board's allocation of money throughout the district. The *Pickering* Court held it was a violation of the First Amendment to subject an employee to serious penalty or censure for publicly expressing personal opinions. *Pickering*, 391 U.S. at 568, 88 S.Ct. 1731. The *Pickering* rule has no application to the present circumstances. Smith does not, nor did he at any time relevant to this controversy, work for the University of Colorado at Boulder; therefore, he was not disciplined for his actions as the plaintiff was in *Pickering*. Plati and the University were entitled to exclude private individuals from access to information or privileges designated specifically for the press or media. *Branzburg*, 408 U.S. at 684, 92 S.Ct. 2646. In sum, Plati and the University are "doing business" when they provide access to information or special privileges to some and not to others. They are not required to "do business" with Smith. Thus Smith has not alleged the deprivation of an actual First Amendment constitutional right based on censorship and retribution....

## IV. Conclusion.

For the aforesaid reasons, I grant the motions to dismiss....

---

# Analytical Frameworks for Internet Speech

The First Amendment "rests on the assumption that the widest possible dissemination of information from diverse and antagonistic sources is essential to the welfare of the public, that a free press is a condition of a free society.... Freedom to publish means freedom for all and not for some." *Associated Press v. United States*, 326 U.S. 1, 20 (1945). The Supreme Court has cast the doctrinal underpinnings of the right to free expression as "a profound national commitment to the principle that debate on public issues should be uninhibited, robust, and wide-open." *New York Times Co. v. Sullivan*, 376 U.S. 254, 270 (1964).

When the First Amendment was ratified in 1791 as part of the Bill of Rights, "[e]ntry into publishing was inexpensive; pamphlets and books provided meaningful alternatives to the organized press for the expression of unpopular ideas and often treated events and expressed views not covered by conventional newspapers. A true marketplace of ideas existed in which there was relatively easy access to the channels of communication." *Miami Herald Publishing Co. v. Tornillo*, 418 U.S. 241, 248 (1974) (footnote omitted).

Cyberspace has been characterized as

> our new arena for public and private activities. It reveals information technology's great promise: to form new links between people and to marshal these connections to increase collaboration in political and other activities that promote democratic community. In particular, cyberspace has a tremendous potential to revitalize democratic self-governance at a time when a declining level of participation in communal life endangers civil society in the United States.

Paul M. Schwartz, *Privacy and Democracy in Cyberspace*, 52 Vand. L. Rev. 1607, 1610 (1999).

Are regulatory schemes imposed on Internet communications subject to the same analyses as those designed for other types of speech? Should claims that arise from communicative speech in the Internet context be subject to identical analyses as those advanced based on other media? Are electronic communications simply effected on a more expeditious, more global basis, albeit imbued with the same protections afforded to print, broadcast, and other media? Do the new information technologies consist essentially of communicative mechanisms that enhance existing means of dialogue, or are they fundamentally components of an entirely new and radically distinct cultural medium? One court observed that we have embarked upon "a brave new world of free speech." *Blumenthal v. Drudge*, 992 F. Supp. 44, 48 n. 7 (D.D.C. 1998). Do the same normative analytical constructs apply to digital media?

The argument has been made that the Internet differs fundamentally from traditional forms of mass communication because the former is capable of maintaining an unlimited array of information and exists without institutionalized editorial constraint. "The genius of the Internet is that it is distributed, without any central location to serve as the main repository of information or through which all electronic traffic must flow." William S. Byassee, *Jurisdiction of Cyberspace: Applying Real World Precedent to the Virtual Community*, 30 Wake Forest L. Rev. 197, 200 (1995).

One way the Internet differs from traditional media is that it provides users with an ability to interact with other users. *American Civil Liberties Union v. Reno*, 929 F. Supp. 824, 843–44 (E.D. Pa. 1996), *aff'd*, 521 U.S. 844 (1997). Such reciprocal exchanges are undertaken deliberately; communication conducted over the Internet has been distinguished from communication on radio or television on the theory that Internet communications do not "invade" an individual's home or appear on one's computer screen unbidden. *See* 929 F. Supp. at 844. Rather, the receipt of information on the Internet "requires a series of affirmative steps more deliberate and directed than merely turning a dial." *Reno v. American Civil Liberties Union*, 521 U.S. at 854 (quoting *American Civil Liberties Union v. Reno*, 929 F. Supp. at 845).

Does speech take on a different complexion when it occurs via the Internet instead of via print or broadcast media? Is the most efficacious and principled approach one that focuses primarily on the underlying activity in question, without undue emphasis on the medium through which the activity occurs, in order to assess the policy underlying the formation of the legal conventions that governed the conduct in the first place?

Historically, to some degree, each medium of expression has been "assessed for First Amendment purposes by standards suited to it, for each may present its own problems." *Southeastern Promotions, Ltd. v. Conrad*, 420 U.S. 546, 557 (1975). "Each method of communicating is 'a law unto itself' and that law must reflect the different natures, values, abuses, and dangers" of each such method. *Metromedia, Inc. v. City of San Diego*, 453 U.S. 490, 501 (1981).

Certain types of media have been functionally distinguished, leading to disparate judicial appraisals of attendant rights. When broadcast radio networks challenged rules promulgated by the Federal Communications Commission that restricted the time affiliated stations could air programming, the Supreme Court distinguished the networks from other mass media. A license to broadcast was ruled a privilege, because such "facilities are limited; they are not available to all who may wish to use them...." *National Broadcasting Co. v. United States*, 319 U.S. 190, 213 (1943); *see also FCC v. Pacifica Foundation*, 438 U.S. 726 (1978); *Red Lion Broadcasting Co. v. FCC*, 395 U.S. 367 (1969). Hence, spectrum scarcity provided the legal justification for certain broadcast regulation.

The Supreme Court stated:

> Although broadcasting is clearly a medium afforded First Amendment interest, differences in the characteristics of new media justify differences in the First Amendment standards applied to them...
>
> Where there are substantially more individuals who want to broadcast than there are frequencies to allocate, it is idle to posit an unabridgeable First Amendment right to broadcast comparable to the right of every individual to speak, write or publish....
>
> [T]he people as a whole retain their interest in free speech by radio and their collective right to have the medium function consistently with the ends and purposes of the First Amendment. It is the right of the viewers and listeners, not the rights of the broadcasters, which is paramount.

*Id.* at 386–90 (footnotes and citations omitted). Requests for deregulation ensued, premised in part on arguments that the proliferation of cablecasters, direct broadcast satellites, and other electronic media rendered outlets for content less scarce. Justice Brennan commented that "[t]he prevailing rationale for broadcast regulation based upon spectrum scarcity has come under increasing criticism in recent years. Critics... charge that with the advent of cable and satellite technology, communities now have access to such a wide variety of stations that the scarcity doctrine is obsolete." *FCC v. League of Women Voters of California*, 468 U.S. 364, 376 n. 11 (1984) (citation omitted).

> New technologies create interesting challenges to long established legal concepts. Thus, just as when the telephone gained nationwide use and acceptance, when automobiles became the established mode of transportation, and when cellular telephones came into widespread use, now personal computers, hooked up to large networks, are so widely used that the scope of Fourth Amendment core concepts of "privacy" as applied to them must be reexamined.

*United States v. Maxwell*, 45 M.J. 406, 410 (C.A.A.F. 1996).

Yet unlike the conditions that existed when Congress initially authorized regulation of the broadcast spectrum, "the Internet can hardly be considered a 'scarce' expressive commodity. It provides relatively unlimited, low-cost capacity for communication of all kinds." *Reno v. American Civil Liberties Union*, 521 U.S. at 870. Much of the Internet jurisprudence that has evolved thus far evinces clear judicial commitment to extend the same level of First Amendment solicitude accorded to other forms of communication to speech conducted on-line. As one court noted, "[w]hat achieved success was the very chaos that the Internet is. The strength of the Internet is that chaos. Just as the strength of the Internet is chaos, so the strength of our liberty depends upon the chaos and cacophony of the unfettered speech the First Amendment protects." *American Civil Liberties Union v. Reno*, 929 F. Supp. at 883 (footnote omitted). "It is no exaggeration to conclude that the Internet has achieved, and continues to achieve, the most participatory marketplace of mass speech that this country—and indeed the world—has yet seen." *Id.* at 881. Lest there be any doubt about the protection merited by the Internet, the Supreme Court proclaimed that there is "no basis for qualifying the level of First Amendment scrutiny that should be applied to this medium." *Reno v. American Civil Liberties Union*, 521 U.S. at 870.

Nevertheless, courts are also grappling with conceptualization of the new technologies. In *United States v. Mohrbacher*, 182 F.3d 1041 (9th Cir. 1999), for example, the defendant was charged with transporting visual depictions of minors engaged in sexually explicit conduct and with possession of items containing such depictions. Pivotal to his defense was an argument that downloading is properly characterized as the *receipt*—rather than the *transport or shipping*—of such images by computer. *See id.* at 1047. *Compare* 18 U.S.C. §2252(a)(1) (knowingly transports or ships) *with* 18 U.S.C. §2252(a)(2) (knowingly receives or distributes).

In *Brookfield Communications, Inc. v. West Coast Entertainment Corp.*, 174 F.3d 1036 (9th Cir. 1999), a federal appellate court expressly observed that adjudication of cases involving digital media requires a flexible approach. *Id.* at 1054; *see also Playboy Enterprises, Inc. v. Welles*, 7 F. Supp. 2d 1098, 1103 (S.D. Cal.) (stating that the multi-factor trademark likelihood of confusion test is merely a guideline; "this is not a standard trademark case"), *aff'd*, 162 F.3d 1169 (9th Cir. 1998); *Playboy Enterprises, Inc. v. Netscape Communications Corp.*, 55 F. Supp. 2d 1070, 1073 (C.D. Cal.) (noting "the difficulty of applying well-established doctrines to what can only be described as an amorphous situs of information, anonymous messenger of communications, and seemingly endless stream of commerce"), *aff'd*, 202 F.3d 278 (9th Cir. 1999).

In considering " 'the unique factors that affect communication in the new and technology-laden medium of the Web,' " the Third Circuit was persuaded that there "are crucial differences between a 'brick and mortar outlet' and the online Web that dramatically affect a First Amendment analysis" of statutes regulating obscene material." *American Civil Liberties Union v. Reno*, 217 F.3d 162, 174–75 (3d Cir. 2000) (quoting *United States v. Playboy Entertainment, Group, Inc.*, — U.S. —, —, 120 S.Ct. 1878, 2000 WL 646196 at *8 (May 22, 2000)). One professor has questioned such an approach, suggesting that "[s]ome cyberspace issues seem wholly unremarkable: it is evident to any legal eye that they are readily governed by the same rules applicable to other forms of communication." I. Trotter Hardy, *The Proper Legal Regime For "Cyberspace,"* 55 U. Pitt. L. Rev. 993, 989–99 (1994). To a large degree, courts presuppose that existing frameworks of equitable and legal principles are sufficiently elastic to accommodate disputes generated by the use of emerging technologies.

But is it possible that a statute may be struck down as "unconstitutional today, or was unconstitutional two years ago, but will be constitutional next week?...Or next year or in two years?" Justice Scalia posed this question during an oral argument in a challenge to a statute regulating obscene and indecent communications on the Internet. Transcript of Oral Argument, *Reno v. American Civil Liberties Union*, 521 U.S. 844, *available in* 1997 WL 136253 at *49 (Mar. 19, 1997). Judicial opinions are replete with presumptions and factual findings about the state of the world, implicitly predicting the impact that the rulings likely will have on future events.

Professor Stuart Minor Benjamin explores a number of options for judicial evaluation of disputes that arise in rapidly changing realms such as cyberspace. *See* Stuart Minor Benjamin, *Stepping Into the Same River Twice: Rapidly Changing Facts and the Appellate Process*, 78 Tex. L. Rev. 269 (1999).[3] Legislatures could refrain from enacting statutes; courts could delay adjudication until the facts stabilize; appellate courts could remand the case to the original fact-finder to update its factual findings or could retain jurisdiction and determine the new facts. Another solution may be to streamline the judicial process in order to avoid the time lapse between the initial finding and the final appellate ruling.

Justice Kennedy opined that the courts' "application of the First Amendment has adjusted to meet new threats to speech." *Alexander v. United States*, 509 U.S. 544, 565 (1993) (Kennedy, J., dissenting) (analyzing forfeiture as a prior restraint). To what extent should courts endeavor to articulate principles that are sufficiently elastic to transcend factual changes and technological developments? How do dramatic developments affect traditional *stare decisis* precepts and the predictability they afford? Benajmin concludes that "in light of the centrality of facts to adjudication, rapidly changing facts require that courts be willing to reconsider earlier opinions the factual basis of which has shifted....[J]udicial opinions can only be as permanent as the facts on which they rest....Ultimately, whether we like it or not, judicial opinions are written in sand." Stuart Minor Benjamin, *Stepping Into the Same River Twice: Rapidly Changing Facts and the Appellate Process*, 78 Tex. L. Rev. at 366–67.

Scholarly debate has centered on the appropriate means to structure normative conduct for Internet communications. Is the adjudication of rights in particular disputes as they arise the most suitable approach? Does this approach allow the law, confronted with new technological devices, to develop gradually, making incremental modifications to established principles? Does judicial reticence to formulate new legal precepts impede the process or reflect appropriate deference to the legislature?

As an example, *Sony Corp. v. Universal City Studios, Inc.*, 464 U.S. 417 (1984), dealt with videocassette recorders as a new technology. The Supreme Court observed, "[s]ound policy, as well as history, supports our consistent deference to Congress when major technological innovations alter the market for copyrighted materials. Congress has the constitutional authority and the institutional ability to accommodate fully the varied permutations of competing interests that are inevitably implicated by such new technology. In a case...in which Congress has not plainly marked our course, we must be circumspect in construing the scope of rights created by a legislative enactment which never contemplated such a calculus of interests." *Id.* at 431.

---

3. The clever title of Benjamin's article comes from the philosopher Heraclitus' proposition that one can never step in the same river twice, because everything is in a constant state of flux, even when it seems stable on the surface. Because water flows constantly, the water in which the first footstep falls has moved downstream by the time the second step is taken. *Id.* at 269 n.

Is regulation through legislative pronouncement sensible, so as to consider the generalized application of rules, formulated by elected officials ostensibly representing constituent views? To what extent is Congress equipped to timely promulgate rules relating to "Net architecture"? Do the courts provide a reasonable means of resolution in the interim? *Cf. id.* at 457 (Blackmun, J., dissenting) ("I would hope that [the questions with which the Court is faced today]...ultimately will be considered seriously and in depth by the Congress and be resolved there, despite the fact that the Court's decision today provides little incentive for congressional action. Our task in the meantime, however, is to resolve these issues as best we can in the light of ill-fitting existing copyright law.").

The invention of the printing press, which made possible a new form of copying, served as the impetus for copyright protection. The development and marketing of player pianos and perforated rolls of music preceded the enactment of the Copyright Act of 1909; innovations in copying techniques gave rise to the statutory exemption for library copying, 17 U.S.C.A. § 108 (West 1995); the development of the technology that made it possible to re-transmit television programs via cable or microwave systems prompted enactment of additional statutory provisions, 17 U.S.C.A. §§ 111(d)(2)(B), 111(d)(5). In the cyberspace environment, a vivid illustration of Congressional action —and a response to judicial decision, see *Stratton Oakmont, Inc. v. Prodigy Services, Co.,* 63 U.S.L.W. 2765, 1995 WL 343710, 23 Media L. Rptr. (BNA) 1794 (N.Y. Sup. May 24, 1995); 141 Cong. Rec. H8460-01, H84-1 (daily ed. Aug. 4, 1995),—may be found in the Communications Decency Act, 47 U.S.C. § 230 (West Supp. 2000), which provides immunities to service providers. *See* discussion *infra* at 203.

Is the commercial marketplace the most appropriate arena to establish policies, and to develop technological solutions to objectionable digital practices? Absent pronouncement of legal precepts by which behavior should be governed, how are industry and individuals able to make reasonable predictions about lawful conduct?

Ultimately, the judicial system, legislative regulation, and the development of technological innovations in the marketplace likely will function as they always have—synergistically, independently, compatibly, and inconsistently—resulting in evolving principles of normative conduct, redressing wrongful conduct through the adjudication of civil claims and the imposition of penal sanctions, and developing the technical means to accommodate new technological uses.

---

# The Law of the Horse: What Cyberlaw Might Teach
## Lawrence Lessig[*]
### 113 Harv. L. Rev. 501 (1999)[†]

A few years ago, at a conference on the "Law of Cyberspace" held at the University of Chicago, Judge Frank Easterbrook told the assembled listeners, a room packed with "cyberlaw" devotees (and worse), that there was no more a "law of cyberspace" than there

---

* Jack N. and Lillian R. Berkman Professor for Entrepreneurial Legal Studies, Harvard Law School. [The author has since become a Professor of Law at Stanford University.] An earlier draft of this article was posted at the Stanford Technology Law Review, <http://stlr.stanford.edu>. This draft is a substantial revision of that earlier version....I expand many of the arguments developed here in a book..., *Code and Other Laws of Cyberspace* (1999).

† © 1999 by The Harvard Law Review Association.

was a "Law of the Horse;"[1] that the effort to speak as if there were such a law would just muddle rather than clarify; and that legal academics ("dilettantes") should just stand aside as judges and lawyers and technologists worked through the quotidian problems that this souped-up telephone would present. "Go home," in effect, was Judge Easterbrook's welcome.

As is often the case when my then-colleague speaks, the intervention, though brilliant, produced an awkward silence, some polite applause, and then quick passage to the next speaker. It was an interesting thought — that this conference was as significant as a conference on the law of the horse. (An anxious student sitting behind me whispered that he had never heard of the 'law of the horse.') But it did not seem a very helpful thought, two hours into this day-long conference. So marked as unhelpful, it was quickly put away. Talk shifted in the balance of the day, and in the balance of the contributions, to the idea that either the law of the horse was significant after all, or the law of cyberspace was something more. Some of us, however, could not leave the question behind. I am one of that some. I confess that I've spent too much time thinking about just what it is that a law of cyberspace could teach. This essay is an introduction to an answer.

Easterbrook's concern is a fair one. Courses in law school, Easterbrook argued, "should be limited to subjects that could illuminate the entire law." "[T]he best way to learn the law applicable to specialized endeavors," he argued, "is to study general rules." This "the law of cyberspace," conceived of as torts in cyberspace, contracts in cyberspace property in cyberspace, etc., was not.

My claim is to the contrary. I agree that our aim should be courses that "illuminate the entire law," but unlike Easterbrook, I believe that there is an important general point that comes from thinking in particular about how law and cyberspace connect.

This general point is about the limits on law as a regulator and about the techniques for escaping those limits. This escape, both in real space and in cyberspace,[5] comes from recognizing the collection of tools that a society has at hand for affecting constraints upon behavior. Law in its traditional sense — an order backed by a threat directed at primary behavior — is just one of these tools. The general point is that law can affect these other tools — that they constrain behavior themselves, and can function as tools of the law. The choice among tools obviously depends upon their efficacy. But importantly, the choice will also raise a question about values. By working through these examples of law interacting with cyberspace, we will throw into relief a set of general questions about law's regulation outside of cyberspace.

I do not argue that any specialized area of law would produce the same insight. I am not defending the law of the horse. My claim is specific to cyberspace. We see something when we think about the regulation of cyberspace that other areas would not show us. . . .

---

1. See Frank H. Easterbrook, *Cyberspace and the Law of the Horse*, 1996 U. Chi. Legal F. 207. The reference is to an argument by Gerhard Casper, who, when he was dean of the University of Chicago Law School, boasted that the law school did not offer a course in "The Law of the Horse." *Id.* at 207 (internal quotation marks omitted). The phrase originally comes from Karl Llewellyn, who contrasted the U.C.C. with the "rules for idiosyncratic transactions between amateurs." *Id.* at 214.

5. I have discussed in considerable detail the idea that one is always in real space while in cyberspace or, alternatively, that cyberspace is not a separate place. *See* Lawrence Lessig, *The Zones of Cyberspace*, 48 Stan. L. Rev. 1403, 1403 (1996).

I. Regulatory Spaces, Real and "Cyber"

Consider two cyber-spaces, and the problems that each creates for two different so-cial goals. Both spaces have different problems of "information"—in the first, there is not enough; in the second, too much. Both problems come from a fact about code—about the software and hardware that make each cyber-space the way it is. As I argue more fully in the sections below, the central regulatory challenge in the context of cy-berspace is how to make sense of this effect of code.

A. Two Problems in Zoned Speech

1. Zoning Speech.—Porn in real space is zoned from kids. Whether because of laws (banning the sale of porn to minors), or norms (telling us to shun those who do sell porn to minors), or the market (porn costs money), it is hard in real space for kids to buy porn. In the main, not everywhere; hard, not impossible. But on balance the regu-lations of real space have an effect. That effect keeps kids from porn.

These real-space regulations depend upon certain features in the "design" of real space. It is hard in real space to hide that you are a kid. Age in real space is a self-au-thenticating fact. Sure—a kid may try to disguise that he is a kid; he may don a mus-tache or walk on stilts. But costumes are expensive, and not terribly effective. And it is hard to walk on stilts. Ordinarily a kid transmits that he is a kid; ordinarily, the seller of porn knows a kid is a kid, and so the seller of porn, either because of laws or norms, can at least identify underage customers. Self-authentication makes zoning in real space easy.

In cyberspace, age is not similarly self-authenticating. Even if the same laws and norms did apply in cyberspace, and even if the constraints of the market were the same (as they are not), any effort to zone porn in cyberspace would face a very difficult prob-lem. Age is extremely hard to certify. To a website accepting traffic, all requests are equal. There is no simple way for a website to distinguish adults from kids, and, like-wise, no easy way for an adult to establish that he is an adult. This feature of the space makes zoning speech there costly—so costly, the Supreme Court concluded in *Reno v. ACLU*,[8] that the Constitution may prohibit it.

2. Protected Privacy.—If you walked into a store, and the guard at the store recorded your name; if cameras tracked your every step, noting what items you looked at and what items you ignored; if an employee followed you around, calculating the time you spent in any given aisle; if before you could purchase an item you selected, the cashier demanded that you reveal who you were—if any or all of these things happened in real space, you would notice. You would notice and could then make a choice about whether you wanted to shop in such a store. Perhaps the vain enjoy the attention; perhaps the thrifty are attracted by the resulting lower prices. They might have no problem with this data collection regime. But at least you would know. Whatever the reason, whatever the consequent choice, you would know enough in real space to know to make a choice.

In cyberspace, you would not. You would not notice such monitoring because such tracking in cyberspace is not similarly visible. As Jerry Kang aptly describes,[10] when you

---

8. 521 U.S. 844 (1997).

10. *See* Jerry Kang, *Information Privacy in Cyberspace Transactions*, 50 Stan. L. Rev. 1193, 1198–99 (1998); *cf. Developments in the Law—The Law of Cyberspace*, 112 Harv. L. Rev. 1574, 1643 (1999) [hereinafter Developments] (suggesting that upstream filtering's invisibility is one potential problem of a proposed solution to children's access to pornography).

enter a store in cyberspace, the store can record who you are; click monitors (watching what you choose with your mouse) will track where you browse, how long you view a particular page; an "employee" (if only a bot[11]) can follow you around, and when you make a purchase, it can record who you are and from where you came. All this happens in cyberspace—invisibly. Data is collected, but without your knowledge. Thus you cannot (at least not as easily) choose whether you will participate in or consent to this surveillance. In cyberspace, surveillance is not self-authenticating. Nothing reveals whether you are being watched,[12] so there is no real basis upon which to consent.

These examples mirror each other, and present a common pattern. In each, some bit of data is missing, which means that in each, some end cannot be pursued. In the first case, that end is collective (zoning porn); in the second, it is individual (choosing privacy). But in both, it is a feature of cyberspace that interferes with the particular end. And hence in both, law faces a choice—whether to regulate to change this architectural feature, or to leave cyberspace alone and disable this collective or individual goal. Should the law change in response to these differences? Or should the law try to change the features of cyberspace, to make them conform to the law? And if the latter, then what constraints should there be on the law's effort to change cyberspace's "nature"? What principles should govern the law's mucking about with this space? Or, again, how should law *regulate*?

* * *

To many this question will seem very odd. Many believe that cyberspace simply cannot be regulated. Behavior in cyberspace, this meme insists, is beyond government's reach. The anonymity and multi-jurisdictionality of cyberspace makes control by government in cyberspace impossible. The nature of the space makes behavior there *unregulable*.

This belief about cyberspace is wrong, but wrong in an interesting way. It assumes either that the nature of cyberspace is fixed—that its architecture, and the control it enables, cannot be changed—or that government cannot take steps to change this architecture.

Neither assumption is correct. Cyberspace has no nature; it has no particular architecture that cannot be changed.[14] Its architecture is a function of its design—or, as I will describe it in the section that follows, its code.[15] This code can change, either be-

---

11. A "bot" is a computer program that acts as an agent for a user and performs a task, usually remotely, in response to a request.

12. *See* Federal Trade Comm'n, *Privacy Online: A Report to Congress* 3 & n. 9 (1998) [hereinafter Privacy Online].

14. *See Developments, supra* note 10, at 1635 ("The fundamental difference between [real space and cyberspace] is that the architecture of cyberspace is open and malleable. Anyone who understands how to read and write code is capable of rewriting the instructions that define the possible.").

15. As I define the term, *code* refers to the software and hardware that constitute cyberspace as it is—or, more accurately, the rules and instructions embedded in the software and hardware that together constitute cyberspace as it is. Obviously there is a lot of "code" that meets this description, and obviously the nature of this "code" varies dramatically depending upon the context. Some of this code is within the Internet Protocol (IP) layer, where protocols for exchanging data on the Internet (including TCP/IP) operate. Some of this code is above this IP layer, or in Jerome H. Saltzer's terms, at its "end":

> For the case of the data communication system, this range includes encryption, duplicate message detection, message sequencing, guaranteed message delivery, detecting host crashes, and delivery receipts. In a broader context, the argument seems to apply to many other functions of a computer operating system, including its file system.

Jerome H. Saltzer, David P. Reed & David D. Clark, *End-to-End Arguments in System Design, in Innovations in Internetworking* 195, 196 (Craig Partridge ed., 1988). More generally, this second layer would include any applications that might interact with the network (browsers, e-mail programs,

cause it evolves in a different way, or because government or business pushes it to evolve in a particular way. And while particular versions of cyberspace do resist effective regulation, it does not follow that every version of cyberspace does so as well. Or alternatively, there are versions of cyberspace where behavior can be regulated, and the government can take steps to increase this regulability.

To see just how, we should think more broadly about the question of regulation. What does it mean to say that someone is "regulated"? How is that regulation achieved? What are its modalities?

### B. Modalities of Regulation

1. Four Modalities of Regulation in Real Space and Cyberspace.—Behavior, we might say, is regulated by four kinds of constraints. Law is just one of those constraints. Law (in at least one of its aspects) orders people to behave in certain ways; it threatens punishment if they do not obey. The law tells me not to buy certain drugs, not to sell cigarettes without a license, and not to trade across international borders without first filing a customs form. It promises strict punishments if these orders are not followed. In this way, we say that law regulates.

But not only law regulates in this sense. Social norms do as well. Norms control where I can smoke; they affect how I behave with members of the opposite sex; they limit what I may wear; they influence whether I will pay my taxes. Like law, norms regulate by threatening punishment ex post. But unlike law, the punishments of norms are not centralized. Norms are enforced (if at all) by a community, not by a government. In this way, norms constrain, and therefore regulate.

Markets, too, regulate. They regulate by price. The price of gasoline limits the amount one drives—more so in Europe than in the United States. The price of subway tickets affects the use of public transportation—more so in Europe than in the United States. Of course the market is able to constrain in this manner only because of other constraints of law and social norms: property and contract law govern markets; markets operate within the domain permitted by social norms. But given these norms, and given this law, the market presents another set of constraints on individual and collective behavior.

And finally, there is a fourth feature of real space that regulates behavior—"architecture." By "architecture" I mean the physical world as we find it, even if "*as we find it*" is simply *how it has already been made*. That a highway divides two neighborhoods limits the extent to which the neighborhoods integrate. That a town has a square, easily accessible with a diversity of shops, increases the integration of residents in that town. That Paris has large boulevards limits the ability of revolutionaries to protest.[18] That the Con-

---

file-transfer clients) as well as operating system platforms upon which these applications might run.

In the analysis that follows, the most important "layer" for my purposes will be the layer above the IP layer. The most sophisticated regulations will occur at this level, given the Net's adoption of Saltzer's end-to-end design.... [C]f. Timothy Wu, *Application-Centered Internet Analysis*, 85 Va. L. Rev. 1163, 1164 (1999) (arguing that a legal analysis of the Internet that focuses on the user must necessarily focus on this layer).

Finally, when I say that cyberspace "has no nature," I mean that any number of possible designs or architectures may affect the functionality we now associate with cyberspace. I do not mean that, given its present architecture, no features exist that together constitute its nature.

18. In 1853, Louis Napoleon III changed the layout of Paris, broadening the streets in order to minimize the opportunity for revolt. *See* Alain Plessis, *The Rise and Fall of the Second Empire*, 1852–1871, at 121 (Jonathan Mandelbaum trans., 1985) (1979); Haussmann, George-Eugene Baron, 5 *Encyclopaedia Britannica* 753 (15th ed. 1993).

stitutional Court in Germany is in Karlsruhe, while the capital is in Berlin, limits the influence of one branch of government over the other. These constraints function in a way that shapes behavior. In this way, they too regulate.

These four modalities regulate together. The "net regulation" of any particular policy is the sum of the regulatory effects of the four modalities together. A policy trades off among these four regulatory tools. It selects its tool depending upon what works best.

So understood, this model describes the regulation of cyberspace as well. There, too, we can describe four modalities of constraint.

Law regulates behavior in cyberspace—copyright, defamation, and obscenity law all continue to threaten ex post sanctions for violations. How efficiently law regulates behavior in cyberspace is a separate question— in some cases it does so more efficiently, in others not. Better or not, law continues to threaten an expected return. Legislatures enact, prosecutors threaten, courts convict.

Norms regulate behavior in cyberspace as well: talk about democratic politics in the alt.knittingnewsgroup, and you open yourself up to "flaming" (an angry, text-based response). "Spoof" another's identity in a "MUD" (a text-based virtual reality), and you may find yourself "toaded" your character removed).[22] Talk too much on a discussion list, and you are likely to wind up on a common "bozo" filter (blocking messages from you). In each case norms constrain behavior, and, as in real space, the threat of ex post (but decentralized) sanctions enforce these norms.

Markets regulate behavior in cyberspace too. Prices structures often constrain access, and if they do not, then busy signals do. (America Online (AOL) learned this lesson when it shifted from an hourly to a flat-rate pricing plan). Some sites on the web charge for access, as on-line services like AOL have for some time. Advertisers reward popular sites; on-line services drop unpopular forums. These behaviors are all a function of market constraints and market opportunity, and they all reflect the regulatory role of the market.

And finally the architecture of cyberspace, or its *code*, regulates behavior in cyberspace. The code, or the software and hardware that make cyberspace the way it is, constitutes a set of constraints on how one can behave.[24] The substance of these constraints varies—cyberspace is not one place. But what distinguishes the architectural constraints from other constraints is how they are experienced. As with the constraints of architecture in real space—railroad tracks that divide neighborhoods, bridges that block the access of buses, constitutional courts located miles from the seat of the government—they are experienced as conditions on one's access to areas of cyberspace. The conditions, however,

---

22. *See* Julian Dibbell, *A Rape in Cyberspace or How an Evil Clown, a Haitian Trickster Spirit, Two Wizards, and a Cast of Dozens Turned a Database Into a Society,* 2 Ann. Surv. Am. L. 471, 477–78 (1995).

24. *Cf. Developments, supra* note 10, at 1635 (suggesting that alterations in code can be used to solve the problems of cyberspace). By "code" in this essay, I do not mean the basic protocols of the Internet—for example, TCP/IP. *See generally* Craig Hunt, *TCP/IP Network Administration* 1–22 (2d ed. 1998) (explaining how TCP/IP works); Ed Krol, *The Whole Internet: User's Guide & Catalog* 23–25 (2d ed. 1992) (same); Pete Loshin, *TCP/IP Clearly Explained* 3–83 (2d ed. 1997) (same); Ben Segal, *A Short History of Internet Protocols at CERN* (visited Aug. 14, 1999) <http://wwwinfo.cern.ch/pdp/ns/ben/TCPHIST.html> (describing the history of Internet protocols generally, including the TCP/IP protocol). Rather, I mean "application space" code—that is, the code of applications that operates on top of the basic protocols of the Internet. As Tim Wu describes, TCP/IP can be usefully thought of as the electric grid of the Internet; applications "plug into" the Internet. *See* Wu, *supra* note 15, at 1191–92 (1999). As I use the term "code" here, I am describing the applications that plug into the Internet.

are different. In some places, one must enter a password before one gains access;[25] in other places, one can enter whether identified or not.[26] In some places, the transactions that one engages in produce traces, or "mouse droppings," that link the transactions back to the individual; in other places, this link is achieved only if the individual consents. In some places, one can elect to speak a language that only the recipient can understand (through encryption); in other places, encryption is not an option. Code sets these features; they are features selected by code writers; they constrain some behavior (for example, electronic eavesdropping) by making other behavior possible (encryption). They embed certain values, or they make the realization of certain values impossible. In this sense, these features of cyberspace also regulate, just as architecture in real space regulates.

These four constraints—both in real space and in cyberspace—operate together. For any given policy, their interaction may be cooperative, or competitive.[32] Thus, to understand how a regulation might succeed, we must view these four modalities as acting on the same field, and understand how they interact.

The two problems from the beginning of this section are a simple example of this point:

(a) Zoning Speech. — If there is a problem zoning speech in cyberspace, it is a problem traceable (at least in part) to a difference in the architecture of that place. In real space, age is (relatively) self-authenticating. In cyberspace, it is not. The basic architecture of cyberspace permits users' attributes to remain invisible. So norms, or laws, that turn upon a consumer's age are more difficult to enforce in cyberspace. Law and norms are disabled by this different architecture.

(b) Protecting Privacy. — A similar story can be told about the "problem" of privacy in cyberspace. Real-space architecture makes surveillance generally self-authenticating. Ordinarily, we can notice if we are being followed, or if data from an identity card is being collected. Knowing this enables us to decline giving information if we do not want that information known. Thus, real space interferes with non-consensual collection of data. Hiding that one is spying is relatively hard.

The architecture of cyberspace does not similarly flush out the spy. We wander through cyberspace, unaware of the technologies that gather and track our behavior. We cannot function in life if we assume that everywhere we go such information is collected. Collection practices differ, depending on the site and its objectives. To consent to being tracked, we must know that data is being collected. But the architecture disables (relative to real space) our ability to know when we are being monitored, and to take steps to limit that monitoring.

In both cases, the difference in the possibility of regulation—the difference in the regulability (both collective and individual) of the space—turns on differences in the modalities of constraint. Thus, as a first step to understanding why a given behavior in cyberspace might be different from one in real space, we should understand these differences in the modalities of constraint.

---

25. An example of such a place is an online service like America Online (AOL).

26. For example, USENET postings can be anonymous. *See Answers to Frequently Asked Questions about Usenet* (visited Oct. 5, 1999) <http:// www.faqs.org/faqs/usenet/faq/part1/>.

32. Of course, the way they regulate differs. Law regulates (in this narrow sense) through the threat of punishments ex post; norms regulate (if they regulate effectively) through ex post punishment, as well as ex ante internalization; markets and architecture regulate by a present constraint— no ex ante constraint or ex post punishment is necessary to keep a person from walking through a brick wall.

## C. How Modalities Interact

1. Direct and Indirect Effects.—Though I have described these four modalities as distinct, obviously they do not operate independently. In obvious ways they interact. Norms will affect which objects get traded in the market (norms against selling blood); the market will affect the plasticity, or malleability, of architecture (cheaper building materials create more plasticity in design); architectures will affect what norms are likely to develop (common rooms affect privacy); all three will influence what laws are possible.

Thus a complete description of the interaction among the four modalities would trace the influences of each upon the others. But in the account that follows, I focus on just two. One is the effect of law on the market, norms, and architecture; the other is the effect of architecture on law, market, and norms.

I isolate these two modalities for different reasons. I focus on law because it is the most obvious *self-conscious* agent of regulation. I focus on architecture because, in cyberspace, it will be the most pervasive agent. Architecture will be the regulator of choice, yet as the balance of this essay will argue, our intuitions for thinking about a world regulated by architecture are undeveloped. We notice things about a world regulated by architecture (cyberspace) that go unnoticed when we think about a world regulated by law (real space).

With each modality, there are two distinct effects. One is the effect of each modality on the individual being regulated. (How does law, for example, directly constrain an individual? How does architecture directly constrain an individual?) The other is the effect of a given modality of regulation upon a second modality of regulation, an effect that in turn changes the effect of the second modality on the individual. (How does law affect architecture, which in turn affects the constraints on an individual? How does architecture affect law, which in turn affects the constraints on an individual?) The first effect is direct; the second is *indirect*.

A regulator uses both direct and indirect effects to bring about a given behavior. When the regulator acts indirectly, we can say that it uses or co-opts the second modality of constraint to bring about its regulatory end. So for example, when the law directs that architecture be changed, it does so to use architecture to bring about a regulatory end. Architecture becomes the tool of law when the direct action of the law alone would not be as effective....

[T]he most effective way to regulate behavior in cyberspace will be through the regulation of code—direct regulation either of the code of cyberspace itself, or of the institutions (code writers) that produce that code. Subject to an increasingly important qualification,[42] we should therefore expect regulators to focus more upon this code as time passes....

---

42. [I have made an important simplifying assumption in this analysis, which I do not make in other writings. *See* Lawrence Lessig, *The Limits in Open Code: Regulatory Standards and the Future of the Net*, 14 Berkeley Tech. L.J. 759 (1999). My assumption is that these code writers—the targets of this regulation by the state—are writing closed, as opposed to open, code. Closed code is code that does not travel with its source code, and it is not easily modified. If a standard or protocol is built into this closed code, it is unlikely that users, or adopters of that code, can undo that standard. Open code is different. If the government mandated a given standard or protocol within an open code software design, users or adopters would always be free to accept or reject the government's portion of the design. Thus, if application space is primarily open-source software, the government's regulatory power is diminished.]

## Conclusion

At the center of any lesson about cyberspace is an understanding of the role of law. We must make a choice about life in cyberspace—about whether the values embedded there will be the values we want. The code of cyberspace constitutes those values; it can be made to constitute values that resonate with our tradition, just as it can be made to reflect values inconsistent with our tradition.

As the Net grows, as its regulatory power increases, as its power as a source of values becomes established, the values of real-space sovereigns will at first lose out. In many cases, no doubt, that is a very good thing. But there is no reason to believe that it will be a good thing generally or indefinitely. There is nothing to guarantee that the regime of values constituted by code will be a liberal regime; and little reason to expect that an invisible hand of code writers will push it in that direction. Indeed, to the extent that code writers respond to the wishes of commerce, a power to control may well be the tilt that this code begins to take. Understanding this tilt will be a continuing project of the "law of cyberspace."

Nevertheless, Judge Easterbrook argued that there was no reason to teach the "law of cyberspace," any more than there was reason to teach the "law of the horse," because neither, he suggested, would "illuminate the entire law." This essay has been a respectful disagreement. The threats to values implicit in the law—threats raised by changes in the architecture of code—are just particular examples of a more general point: that more than law alone enables legal values, and law alone cannot guarantee them. If our objective is a world constituted by these values, then it is as much these other regulators—code, but also norms and the market—that must be addressed. Cyberspace makes plain not just how this interaction takes place, but also the urgency of understanding how to affect it.

---

The formation of analytical analogues to be used in connection with issues relating to speech conducted in cyberspace are particularly relevant to the scope of permissible governmental action and individuals' fundamental rights in four primary contexts. The study of the law of Internet speech is inherently inter-disciplinary.

First, free speech constructs exist for application to the governance and regulation of Internet content. Illustrations of the tension between free speech rights and governmental interests may be found in discussion of the acceptable constraints on substantive communication relating to hate speech and speech that promotes violence; speech relating to matters of national security; and obscene and indecent speech. *See infra* at Chapter II.

Second, issues of on-line defamation have garnered a fair share of judicial attention. Who may be held accountable for the electronic display of defamatory content? Is the identity of an anonymous or pseudonymous speaker of defamatory statements worthy of protection from compelled disclosure by the aggrieved subject of the statements? Under what circumstances is the subject of opprobrium a public, as opposed to a private, figure? Which subjects discussed via the Internet constitute matters of "public concern?" *See infra* at Chapter III.

Third, the Internet is not without intrusive capacity. Absent the implementation of countervailing mechanisms, technical devices can monitor and track users' Internet activity, and such data is vulnerable to perpetuated manipulation by others. To what extent are traditional privacy law constructs applicable to the digital environment? *See infra* at Chapter IV.

Fourth, copyright and trademark laws generally have accommodated technological innovation. The Internet concomitantly facilitates lawful dissemination of material and dissemination of unauthorized, seamlessly reproduced copies. Are intellectual property principles sufficiently elastic to accommodate digital displays and transmissions? *See infra* at Chapter V.

One commentator has observed that:

> The law developed because of the capabilities of print, and...benefited from the inherent limitations of print. [It] reveals a desire both to control information and to achieve an accommodation among First Amendment concerns, property interests, and social or moral values. The definition of each legal doctrine implies a particular balance among these competing interests, and it is this balance that is currently vulnerable.... Whether the information was unavailable because of legal restrictions or limitations of prior modes of communication, the ultimate effect of the new communications environment will be a new kind of accommodation, a new balance, and a new meaning.

M. Ethan Katsh, *The Electronic Media and the Transformation of Law* 171 (1989).

---

# Jurisdiction as an Illustration

Illustrative of the applications of existing principles to electronic communication is the caselaw relating to jurisdiction. Due process principles protect the individual's liberty interest from binding judgments of a forum with which he has established no meaningful contacts, ties, or relations. Therefore, courts may require a non-resident defendant to defend against claims only when he has "certain minimum contacts with [the forum] such that the maintenance of the suit does not offend 'traditional notions of fair play and substantial justice.'" *International Shoe Co. v. Washington*, 326 U.S. 310, 316 (1945) (quoting *Milliken v. Meyer*, 311 U.S. 457, 463 (1940)).

Personal jurisdiction may be exercised over non-resident defendants via either general or specific jurisdiction. *See, e.g., Helicopteros Nacionales de Colombia, S. A. v. Hall*, 466 U.S. 408 (1984). General jurisdiction may be asserted if the non-resident defendant is either present in the forum or maintains sufficient continuous and systematic contacts with the state. *See, e.g., id.* at 414–15; *see also Perkins v. Benguet Consolidated Mining Co.*, 342 U.S. 437, 445 (1952). Specific jurisdiction arises when an out-of-state defendant who has not consented to suit in the forum has purposefully directed activities toward the forum state, from which the litigation arises or to which it relates. The constitutional touchstone for the jurisdictional inquiry is whether the defendant purposefully established minimum contacts with the forum state such that he should reasonably anticipate being brought into court there. This purposeful availment requirement ensures that a defendant will not be haled into a jurisdiction solely as a result of random, fortuitous, or attenuated contacts, or as a result of the unilateral activity of another.

Courts have been called upon repeatedly to apply these principles in the context of publication of traditional media products. As technology evolves to transcend traditional geographic boundaries, questions relating to jurisdiction inevitably arise, and courts increasingly are being asked to apply these principles to disputes over allegedly defamatory communications. Nearly half a century ago, the Supreme Court observed that "[a]s technological progress has increased the flow of commerce between States, the need for jurisdiction over nonresidents has undergone a similar increase." *Hanson v.*

*Denckla*, 357 U.S. 235, 250–51 (1958). Even before the advent of widespread Internet usage, the Supreme Court recognized that "it is an inescapable fact of modern commercial life that a substantial amount of business is transacted solely by mail and wire communications across state lines, thus obviating the need for physical presence within a State in which business is conducted." *Burger King Corp. v. Rudzewicz*, 471 U.S. 462, 476 (1985).

At what point does the cyberspace conduct in issue cross state lines? In *United States v. Kammersell*, 7 F. Supp. 2d 1196 (D. Utah 1998), *aff'd*, 196 F.3d 1137 (10th Cir. 1999), *cert. denied*, 120 S.Ct. 2664 (2000), the defendant was indicted on a charge of making a threatening communication, in violation of 18 U.S.C. §875(c). The criminal statute prohibits transmissions in interstate or foreign commerce of ransom demands for kidnapped persons. *Id.* The defendant was a Utah resident who allegedly had sent a threat via e-mail to another Utah resident. *United States v. Kammersell*, 7 F. Supp. 2d at 1997. The government took the position that the statute was appropriately invoked on the ground that the defendant had electronically transmitted the message through an Internet service provider. *Id.* at 1198. The defendant countered that interstate jurisdiction was not established even if the message traveled from one part of Utah, outside of Utah, and then back into Utah. *Id.* The court rejected the defense, stating that the statutory requirement that the threat be "'[t]ransmit[ted]...in interstate commerce' is not ambiguous.... Its plain meaning encompasses the conduct in this case." *Id.* at 1199–1200 (citations omitted).

Jurisdiction is driven by inherent notions of territoriality; the Internet, however, has as its basic feature a capacity to transcend boundaries and to do so instantaneously. The distinguishing characteristic of the Internet for purposes of jurisdictional analysis is not that it represents a new territorial structure; the concept of the Internet as its own, ethereal jurisdiction is, as one intellectual property lawyer said, "fanciful." Bruce P. Keller, *The Game's the Same: Why Gambling in Cyberspace Violates Federal Law*, 108 Yale L.J. 1569, 1572 (May 1999). Cyberspace, "[f]or all of its unique attributes,...'exists' as a separate jurisdiction only in the sense that Never-Never Land does." *Id.* The point of logical inquiry begins not by envisaging the Internet as a distinct and independent jurisdiction, but rather by focusing on the activity conducted to evaluate whether the non-resident defendant may, consistent with due process norms, be haled before the forum state's court.

What happens when a plaintiff wants to take advantage of a particular state's substantive or procedural law by initiating suit in that forum against an entity whose ties to the jurisdiction exist by virtue of the geographically indiscriminate accessibility of the World Wide Web? The ostensibly ephemeral nature of electronic communications may lull those who transmit messages into false complacency about the availability for redress by subjects aggrieved by the contents. The proximity of the vast quantity of data available on the Internet, and the technical, albeit invisible, means by which it is conveyed, may erroneously suggest that all communications occur within the state where the user is located.

Analytical models relating to the exercise of jurisdiction in connection with Internet disputes have focused largely on: (1) the totality of the defendant's contacts with the forum state, including the nature of the defendant's web-site; (2) the location of the effect of the defendant's conduct and the harm alleged to have been suffered; and (3) whether the non-resident defendant continuously and deliberately disseminated content into the forum state.

In considering the totality of the defendant's contacts with the forum state, one issue that commonly arises is whether the nature of a non-resident defendant's web-site is an adequate basis upon which to invoke personal jurisdiction in the state where the site was accessed. As a general matter, courts look to gradations of interactivity by the site; the more interactive the site, the more likely jurisdiction will be exercised, and, conversely, the more passive the site, the less likely the forum will entertain the claim.

The leading case to articulate these principles is *Zippo Mfg. Co. v. Zippo Dot Com, Inc.*, 952 F. Supp. 1119 (W.D. Pa. 1997). There, a manufacturer asserted trademark infringement, dilution, and false designation claims, challenging a computer news service's domain names. The plaintiff manufactured a product called "Zippo" lighters; the defendant operated a web-site that included the word "Zippo" in its domain name. *Id.* at 1120. The defendant's contacts with the forum state were almost exclusively conducted via the Internet. *Id.*

In order to decide the question of whether personal jurisdiction could be constitutionally exercised over the defendant, the court looked to the "nature and quality of commercial activity that an entity conducts over the Internet." *Id.* at 1124. The district court conceptualized the issue as one involving a spectrum; at one end is a defendant who clearly does business over the Internet, by entering into contracts with residents of a foreign jurisdiction that involve the knowing and repeated transmission of computer files over the Internet. Under such circumstances, the court reasoned that personal jurisdiction is proper. *See id.* The other end of the spectrum includes situations where a defendant simply posts information on an Internet web-site that is accessible to users in foreign jurisdictions. Such a "passive" web-site is one that does "little more than make information available to those who are interested," and generally does not provide a basis for the exercise of personal jurisdiction. *Id.* The "middle" ground is occupied by "interactive web-sites where a user can exchange information with the host computer." *Id.* (citations omitted). Hence, key factors for the determination as to whether jurisdiction may be invoked are the level of interactivity and the nature of the exchange that occurs on the web-site. *Id.*

Subsequent cases have approached the issue similarly, reasoning that when an entity intentionally reaches beyond its boundaries to conduct business with foreign residents, the exercise of jurisdiction generally is appropriate. Thus, a defendant who has ongoing Internet relationships, evidenced, for instance, by having "enter[ed] into contracts with residents...that involve the knowing and repeated transmission of computer files over the Internet," may be subject to jurisdiction. *Millennium Enterprises, Inc. v. Millennium Music, LP*, 33 F. Supp. 2d 907, 920 (D. Or. 1999) (quoting *Zippo Mfg. Co. v. Zippo Dot Com, Inc.*, 952 F. Supp. at 1124). *Compare Mink v. AAAA Development, LLC*, 190 F.3d 333, 337 & n. 1 (5th Cir. 1999) (dismissing claim grounded in conspiracy to copy the plaintiff's software system for financial gain on the ground that the defendant conducted no business in the forum state, even though it provided contact information on its site; "the mere existence of an e-mail link, without more, would not change th[e] Court's conclusion that there is no personal jurisdiction") *with Panavision International L.P. v. Toeppen*, 141 F.3d 1316 (9th Cir. 1998) (challenging defendant's registration of trademark owner's marks as cyberpiracy; defendant held subject to personal jurisdiction on ground that registration of marks in Internet domain names constituted a commercial use).*

---

* In *Archdoicese of St. Louis v. Internet Entertainment Group, Inc.*, 34 F. Supp. 2d 1145 (E.D. Mo. 1999), the district court sustained jurisdiction when the Archdiocese of St. Louis claimed that its trademark was infringed by the defendant, who had registered the domain names "papalvisit.com" and "papalvisit1999.com." *Id.* at 1146. To what extent was the court influenced by the fact that the defendant's web-sites were "sexually explicit" and associated the plaintiffs' family of trademarks "with adult entertainment venues that are inconsistent with the positive and spiritual uplifting

Mere creation of a web-site has been rejected as a basis for the exercise of jurisdiction. *See, e.g., Bensusan Restaurant Corp. v. King*, 937 F. Supp. 295, 301 (S.D.N.Y. 1996), *aff'd*, 126 F.3d 25 (2d Cir. 1997) (declining to exercise jurisdiction over an out-of-state jazz club on the basis of its alleged use of the trademarked phrase "The Blue Note" in its web-site and its creation of a hyperlink to the plaintiff's club in New York). "Creating a site, like placing a product into the stream of commerce, may be felt nationwide—or even worldwide—but without more, it is not an act purposefully directed toward the forum state." *Id.* at 301. Other courts likewise have declined to assert jurisdiction based solely on advertising conducted by the web-site operator. *See, e.g., Graphic Controls Corp. v. Utah Medical Products*, No. 96-CV-0459ECF, 1997 WL 276232 (W.D.N.Y. May 21, 1997), *aff'd*, 149 F.3d 1382 (Fed. Cir. 1998).

Similarly, in *Barrett v. Catacombs Press*, 44 F. Supp. 2d 717 (E.D. Pa. 1999), the court deemed allegedly defamatory discussion group postings insufficient to confer jurisdiction. "Not unlike the maintenance of a 'passive' Web site, anyone who is interested could become a member of such listservs or USENET groups, and we cannot see how from that fact alone, it can be inferred that the Defendant directed its efforts toward Pennsylvania's residents." *Id.* at 728 (citations omitted). *But compare Bochan v. La Fontaine*, 68 F. Supp. 2d 692 (E.D. Va. 1999) (posting of allegedly defamatory messages to a Usenet group held sufficient to subject the defendant to jurisdiction because he had solicited business in the forum state by promoting and advertising his company through the web-site). In *Lamb v. Turbine Designs, Inc.*, 207 F.3d 1259 (11th Cir. 2000), the Eleventh Circuit took another approach. The court felt that the question of whether the defendant had disclosed trade secrets to a federal agency in Georgia was an adequate basis upon which to invoke the Georgia long-arm statute, was an "issue of state law [that] is both unsettled and pivotal to the resolution of this case." *Id.* at 1262. The Eleventh Circuit was "reluctant to guess on an issue which so greatly impacts on the basic jurisdiction of the Georgia courts," and so certified the question to the Georgia Supreme Court. *Id.*

In determining whether an aggrieved individual can invoke long-arm jurisdictional statutes on the basis of allegedly defamatory postings, courts may also find purposeful availment by the defendant when the claim involves an intentional tort allegedly committed over the Internet, such that the defendant intentionally directed his tortious activities at the forum state. *See generally Millennium Enterprises, Inc. v. Millennium Music, LP*, 33 F. Supp. 2d at 916 and cases cited therein. This approach is generally based on the "effects test" articulated in *Calder v. Jones*, 465 U.S. 783, 788–90 (1984), where personal jurisdiction was sustained over a defendant who published allegedly defamatory material that was directed at the plaintiff resident of the forum state. Under this theory, jurisdiction in the forum state is countenanced on the ground that the state "is the focal point both of the story and the harm suffered." *Id.* at 789.

The U.S. District Court for the District of Arizona, for instance, has held that a libel defendant had purposefully availed itself of the protections and benefits of Arizona, and thus its allegedly defamatory e-mail messages and other postings satisfied the "effects test" for the exercise of jurisdiction. *Edias Software International v. Basis International Ltd.*, 947 F. Supp. 413, 421 (D. Ariz. 1996). Note that the court focused not only on the

---

image plaintiffs have striven to create and maintain in connection with the Pope's upcoming visit to St. Louis"? *Id.* at 1146.

defendant's allegedly defamatory postings on its web-site, but also on the defendant's non-Internet connections to the forum state, such as the fact that it had entered into a contract with an Arizona entity, contacted the plaintiff's employees by telephone and facsimile, and had dispatched employees into Arizona. *See id.*

In *Copperfield v. Cogedipresse*, 26 Media L. Rptr. (BNA) 1185 (C.D. Cal. Nov. 3, 1997), magician David Copperfield claimed that he had been defamed by an issue of *Paris Match* magazine, which described his relationship with model Claudia Schiffer. Among other things, Copperfield pointed to the magazine's web-site as a basis for jurisdiction in California. The court declined to invoke general jurisdiction, however, finding that "a web site on the Internet is a presence only in the jurisdiction or jurisdictions where the web site is created and where it is maintained or placed on a host computer.... To find otherwise is in conflict with existing technology, with which producers of web sites can not selectively choose who will receive their material." *Id.* at 1187 (citation omitted). In addition to concluding that the site's interactivity was limited, consisting almost entirely of advertising, the federal court also declined to exercise jurisdiction based on a *Calder* effects analysis. "The alleged defamation was contained in an article published in France in a French magazine, written in the French language, investigated by French reporters, and with a circulation primarily to readers in France." *Id.* at 1189.

Continuous and deliberate circulation of a publication in the forum state suggests that the defendant should have reasonably foreseen that it would be haled into the foreign state's court to account for the publication's content. *See Keeton v. Hustler Magazine, Inc.*, 465 U.S. 770 (1984). Under what circumstances does the posting of a defamatory publication on the World Wide Web give rise to a similar inference? To what degree do courts focus on non-Internet connections with the forum state when the non-resident defendant's electronic connections are relatively tenuous?

---

# Sidney BLUMENTHAL and Jacqueline Jordan Blumenthal v. Matt DRUDGE and America Online, Inc.

United States District Court for the District of Columbia
No. CIV.A. 97-1968 PLF, 992 F. Supp. 44
April 22, 1998

PAUL L. FRIEDMAN, District Judge.

This is a defamation case revolving around a statement published on the Internet by defendant Matt Drudge.... [For the background of this case, *see infra* at 214.]

Defendant Drudge has moved, pursuant to Rule 12(b)(2) of the Federal Rules of Civil Procedure, for an order dismissing this action for lack of personal jurisdiction or, alternatively, to transfer it to the United States District Court for the Central District of California. In order for this Court to maintain personal jurisdiction over a non-resident defendant, jurisdiction must be proper under the District of Columbia long-arm statute and consistent with the demands of due process. *United States v. Ferrara*, 54 F.3d 825, 828 (D.C. Cir. 1995); *Crane v. Carr*, 814 F.2d 758, 762 (D.C. Cir. 1987). Plaintiffs have the burden of establishing that this Court has personal jurisdiction over defendant Drudge and alleging specific facts upon which personal jurisdiction may be based. *See Cellutech Inc. v. Centennial Cellular Corp.*, 871 F. Supp. 46, 48 (D.D.C. 1994).

A. D.C. Long-Arm Statute

The only provision of the District of Columbia long-arm statute that is relevant to this case is Section 13-423(a)(4), which provides:

> A District of Columbia court may exercise personal jurisdiction over a person, who acts directly or by an agent, as to a claim for relief arising from the person's...causing tortious injury in the District of Columbia by an act or omission outside the District of Columbia if he regularly does or solicits business, engages in any other persistent course of conduct, or derives substantial revenue from goods used or consumed or services rendered, in the District of Columbia.

D.C. Code § 13-423(a)(4). In order to establish personal jurisdiction under this provision a plaintiff must make a prima facie showing that (1) plaintiff suffered a tortious injury in the District of Columbia; (2) the injury was caused by the defendant's act or omission outside of the District of Columbia; and (3) defendants had one of three enumerated contacts with the District of Columbia. *Trager v. Berrie*, 593 F. Supp. 223, 225 (D.D.C. 1984); *Akbar v. New York Magazine Co.*, 490 F. Supp. 60, 63 (D.D.C. 1980). Plaintiffs must satisfy all three requirements and also establish minimum contacts within the confines of due process before the Court can exercise personal jurisdiction over defendant Drudge.

It is undisputed that the Drudge Report transmission in question was written, published and transmitted by defendant Drudge from his computer located in Los Angeles, California. It is also undisputed that the tortious injury caused by defendant Drudge's act of transmitting the report was suffered by the Blumenthals in the District of Columbia. The only question before this Court therefore is whether defendant Drudge (1) regularly does or solicits business in the District of Columbia, or (2) derives substantial revenue from goods used or consumed or services rendered in the District, or (3) engages in any other persistent course of conduct here. *See* D.C. Code § 13-423(a)(4).

Justice Ginsburg in *Crane v. Carr* has described these as the "plus factors," factors that demonstrate some "reasonable connection" between the jurisdiction in which the court sits "separate from and in addition to" injury caused in the jurisdiction. *Crane v. Carr*, 814 F.2d at 762. The "plus factor" or factors need not be related to the act that caused the injury; all that is required is "some other reasonable connection between the defendant and the forum." *Id.* at 762–63. The "plus factor" does not itself provide the basis for jurisdiction (the injury does) "but it does serve to filter out cases in which the in forum impact is an isolated event and the defendant otherwise has no, or scant, affiliation with the forum." *Id.* at 763. The question here is whether plaintiffs have shown a "persistent course of conduct" by defendant Drudge in the District of Columbia or other reasonable connections between the District and Drudge besides the alleged defamatory statement and the alleged injury.

Plaintiffs point out that the Drudge Report has been regularly transmitted over the Internet to Drudge's subscribers and repeatedly posted on Drudge's web site, where it has been available 24 hours a day to District residents; that Drudge personally maintains a list of e-mail addresses, which enables him to distribute the Drudge Report to anyone who requests it, including e-mail addresses in the District of Columbia; and that he has solicited contributions and collected money from persons in the District of Columbia who read the Drudge Report. In addition, they state that Drudge has traveled to the District of Columbia twice, including once for a C-SPAN interview that was for the express purpose of promoting the Drudge Report. Plaintiffs also note, and defendant Drudge admits, that Drudge has been in contact (via e-mail, telephone and the U.S. mail) with District residents who supply him with gossip.

Defendant Drudge argues that he has not specifically targeted persons in the District of Columbia for readership, largely because of the non-geographic nature of communicating via the Internet. For example, while it is true that subscribers to the Drudge Report include District residents, generally the only information about those subscribers available to Drudge is an e-mail address—an address that, unlike a postal address or even a telephone number, typically provides no geographic information. For instance, if Jane Doe from the District of Columbia subscribes to the Drudge Report, it is most likely sent to an e-mail address such as "janedoe@aol.com," and Drudge has no idea where Jane Doe lives or receives the Report. The same is true for on-line browsers who read the Drudge Report, since screen names used to browse the web also are not generally identified by geographic location. Defendant Drudge also claims that he has never advertised the Drudge Report column or web site in physical locations or in local newspapers in the District of Columbia.

Defendant Drudge also argues that his travel to Washington, D.C. is not sufficient to establish a persistent course of conduct in the District of Columbia because his contacts have been so infrequent and sporadic that they are simply not enough to be viewed as "persistent." As for his solicitation of contributions in the District of Columbia, Drudge claims that his solicitation was directed to all readers of the Drudge Report and not specifically aimed at the District. Furthermore, from that appeal Drudge received only approximately $250 from fewer than fifteen persons in the District of Columbia. The Court concludes that plaintiffs have the better of the argument; defendant Drudge has had sufficient contacts with the District of Columbia to warrant the exercise of personal jurisdiction.

The legal questions surrounding the exercise of personal jurisdiction in "cyberspace" are relatively new, and different courts have reached different conclusions as to how far their jurisdiction extends in cases involving the Internet. Generally, the debate over jurisdiction in cyberspace has revolved around two issues: passive web sites versus interactive web sites, and whether a defendant's Internet-related contacts with the forum combined with other non-Internet related contacts are sufficient to establish a persistent course of conduct....

In *Heroes, Inc. v. Heroes Foundation,* Judge Flannery found that he did not need to decide whether the defendant's home page by itself subjected the defendant to personal jurisdiction in the District of Columbia because the defendant had substantial non-Internet related contacts with the District that were sufficient under the D.C. long-arm statute. The defendant's home page solicited contributions and provided a toll-free number which browsers used to donate money; the solicitation also appeared in advertisements in the *Washington Post.* Judge Flannery concluded that these non-Internet related contacts with the District of Columbia, together with the maintenance of a web site constantly available to D.C. residents, constituted a persistent course of conduct that reasonably connected the defendant to the forum. *Heroes, Inc. v. Heroes Foundation,* 958 F. Supp. 1, 4–5 (D.D.C. 1996); *see also Telco Communications v. An Apple A Day,* 977 F. Supp. 404, 407 (E.D. Va. 1997) (posting of web site advertisement solicitation over the Internet, which could be accessed by Virginia residents 24 hours a day, is a persistent course of conduct; two or three press releases rise to the level of regularly doing or soliciting business); *Digital Equipment Corp. v. Altavista Technology, Inc.,* 960 F. Supp. [456, 467 (D. Mass. 1997)] (maintenance of web site that can be accessed by Massachusetts citizens 24 hours a day coupled with other contacts is persistent course of conduct sufficient to confer personal jurisdiction). The courts in each of these cases required only a relatively tenuous electronic connection between the creator of a web site and the forum to effect personal jurisdiction, so long as there were sufficient other non-Internet connections.

As noted, many courts have focused on the level of interactivity of a web site in determining whether there was personal jurisdiction. In *Cybersell, Inc. v. Cybersell, Inc.*, the court noted that an interactive web site allows users to "exchange information with the host computer" and concluded that courts must look at the "level of interactivity and [the] commercial nature of the exchange of information that occurs on the Web site to determine if sufficient contacts exist to warrant the exercise of jurisdiction." *Cybersell, Inc. v. Cybersell Inc.*, 130 F.3d 414, 418 (9th Cir. 1997) (internal quotation marks omitted). *Compare Maritz, Inc. v. Cybergold, Inc.*, 947 F. Supp. 1328, 1332–33 (E.D. Mo. 1996) (exercise of jurisdiction warranted where defendant's interactive web site encouraged browsers to add their address to mailing list that subscribed the user to the service), *and Zippo Mfg. Co. v. Zippo Dot Com, Inc.*, 952 F. Supp. [1119, 1122-25 (W.D. Pa. 1997)] (interactive web site where defendants contracted with 3,000 individuals and seven Internet providers in forum state conferred personal jurisdiction), *with Bensusan Restaurant Corp. v. King*, 937 F. Supp. 295, 299–300 (S.D.N.Y. 1996), *aff'd*, 126 F.3d 25 (2d Cir. 1997) (passive web site which only posted information for interested persons who may have accessed the web site not sufficient for exercise of jurisdiction), and *Hearst Corporation v. Goldberger*, No. 96 Civ. 3620(PKL)(AJP), 1997 WL 97097, at *15 (S.D.N.Y. Feb. 26, 1997) (no persistent course of conduct because defendant's passive web site only provided information regarding future services).

Under the analysis adopted by these courts, the exercise of personal jurisdiction is contingent upon the web site involving more than just the maintenance of a home page; it must also allow browsers to interact directly with the web site on some level. In addition, there must also be some other non-Internet related contacts between the defendant and the forum state in order for the court to exercise personal jurisdiction. Because the Court finds that defendant Drudge has an interactive web site that is accessible to and used by District of Columbia residents and, in addition, that he has had sufficient non-Internet related contacts with the District of Columbia, the Court concludes that Drudge has engaged in a persistent course of conduct in the District. The exercise of personal jurisdiction over defendant Drudge by this Court therefore is warranted.[17]

---

17. Defendant Drudge's reliance on this Court's decision in *Mallinckrodt v. Sonus Pharmaceuticals, Inc.* is misplaced. In *Mallinckrodt*, this Court held that an "A transmission from Seattle to Virginia, which was subsequently posted on an AOL electronic bulletin board and may have been accessed by AOL subscribers in the District of Columbia, cannot be construed as 'transacting business' in the District of Columbia" under subsection (a)(1) of the long-arm statute, D.C. Code § 13-423(a)(1). *Mallinckrodt v. Sonus Pharmaceuticals, Inc.*, 989 F. Supp. 265, 271 (D.D.C. 1998). The defendant posted a message that was not sent to or from the District, the content of the message did not concern persons residing in the District or incorporated in the District, neither plaintiffs nor defendants worked or lived in the District, and the defendant's electronic bulletin board was in no way interactive, as is the case with the Drudge Report. This Court, therefore found that the defendant had no reasonable connection to the District, even though a person from the District may have read the message, because it had not engaged in "an act purposefully or foreseeably aimed at the District of Columbia." *Id.* The defendant's electronic bulletin board message therefore did not "constitute transacting business within the District of Columbia for purposes of [subsection (a)(1)] of the long-arm statute." *Id.* (internal quotations omitted).

With respect to subsection (a)(4) of the long-arm statute, the Court in *Mallinckrodt* concluded that plaintiffs fared no better, primarily because plaintiffs did not live or work in the District of Columbia and therefore did not "suffer[ ] any injury in the District of Columbia that they could not have suffered or did not suffer in any state in the nation where someone may have read the [AOL] message and reacted negatively toward plaintiffs." *Mallinckrodt v. Sonus Pharmaceuticals, Inc.*, 989 F. Supp. 265, 1998 WL 6546 at *8. The Blumenthals, by contrast, do live and work in the District of Columbia and suffered injury in the District. Furthermore, in contrast to the facts in *Mallinckrodt,*

Despite the attempts of Drudge and his counsel to label the Drudge Report as a "passive" web site, the Court finds this characterization inapt. The Drudge Report's web site allows browsers, including District of Columbia residents, to directly e-mail defendant Drudge, thus allowing an exchange of information between the browser's computer and Drudge's host computer. [S]ee *Zippo Mfg. Co. v. Zippo Dot Com, Inc.,* 952 F. Supp. at 1124. In addition, browsers who access the web site may request subscriptions to the Drudge Report, again by directly e-mailing their requests to Drudge's host computer. In turn, as each new edition of the Drudge Report is created, it is then sent by Drudge to every e-mail address on his subscription mailing list, which includes the e-mail addresses of all browsers who have requested subscriptions by directly e-mailing Drudge through his web site. The constant exchange of information and direct communication that District of Columbia Internet users are able to have with Drudge's host computer via his web site is the epitome of web site interactivity.

Not only is defendant Drudge's web site interactive, the subject matter of the Drudge Report primarily concerns political gossip and rumor in Washington, D.C. Defendant Drudge characterizes himself as the "Thomas Paine of the Internet,... who is circulating information for the citizenry reporting on [federal] governmental abuses....and...at the White House." Even though Drudge may not advertise in physical locations or local newspapers in Washington, D.C., the subject matter of the Drudge Report is directly related to the political world of the Nation's capital and is quintessentially "inside the Beltway" gossip and rumor. Drudge specifically targets readers in the District of Columbia by virtue of the subjects he covers and even solicits gossip from District residents and government officials who work here. By targeting the Blumenthals who work in the White House and live in the District of Columbia, Drudge knew that "the primary and most devastating effects of the [statements he made] would be felt" in the District of Columbia. *Telco Communications v. An Apple A Day,* 977 F. Supp. at 407. He should have had no illusions that he was immune from suit here.

In addition, defendant Drudge also solicited contributions from District residents via the Drudge Report's homepage. While during the time period relevant to this case, defendant Drudge may have received only $250 from fifteen District of Columbia residents from that advertised solicitation, the Drudge Report was always accessible in the District, via AOL and through Drudge's world wide web site, making the advertised solicitation was repeatedly available to District residents.

Defendant Drudge also has had a number of non-Internet related contacts with the District. He sat for an interview with C-SPAN in Washington, D.C. and visited the District of Columbia on at least one other occasion. He also contacts District of Columbia residents via telephone and the U.S. mail in order to collect gossip for the Drudge Report. These non-Internet related contacts with the District of Columbia, coupled with the interactive nature of Drudge's web site, which particularly focuses on Washington gossip, are contacts that together are sufficient to establish that defendant Drudge engaged in a persistent course of conduct in the District of Columbia.

In sum, the Court concludes that the circumstances presented by this case warrant the exercise of personal jurisdiction under subsection (a)(4) of the District of Columbia long-arm statute because of: (1) the interactivity of the web site between the defendant Drudge and District residents; (2) the regular distribution of the Drudge Report via AOL, e-mail and the world wide web to District residents; (3) Drudge's solicitation and

---

the Court finds that in this case defendant has engaged in a persistent course of conduct in the District of Columbia.

receipt of contributions from District residents; (4) the availability of the web site to District residents 24 hours a day; (5) defendant Drudge's interview with C-SPAN; and (6) defendant Drudge's contacts with District residents who provide gossip for the Drudge Report. The requirements of subsection (a)(4) of the District of Columbia long-arm statute have been satisfied.

## B. Due Process

Traditionally, in order to exercise personal jurisdiction over an out-of-state defendant, a court must determine whether the defendant has sufficient minimum contacts with the jurisdiction in which the court sits such that maintenance of a suit does not offend "traditional notions of fair play and substantial justice." *International Shoe Co. v. Washington*, 326 U.S. 310, 316, 66 S.Ct. 154, 90 L.Ed. 95 (1945). While in the Internet context there must be "something more" than an Internet advertisement alone "to indicate that the defendant purposefully (albeit electronically) directed his activity in a substantial way to the forum state," *Cybersell, Inc. v. Cybersell, Inc.*, 130 F.3d at 414, such that he should "reasonably anticipate being haled into court" there, *Burger King Corp. v. Rudzewicz*, 471 U.S. 462, 474–75, 105 S.Ct. 2174, 85 L.Ed.2d 528 (1985), that test is easily met here. *See, e.g., Digital Equipment Corp. v. Altavista Technology, Inc.*, 960 F. Supp. at 469–70. Because subsection (a)(4) of the long-arm statute does not reach the outer limits of due process, *Crane v. Carr*, 814 F.2d at 762, and the Court has concluded that there are sufficient "plus factors" to meet the requisites of subsection (a)(4), it follows that there are also sufficient minimum contacts to satisfy due process. Drudge's motion to dismiss or transfer for want of personal jurisdiction therefore will be denied.

---

# PEOPLE SOLUTIONS, INC. v. PEOPLE SOLUTIONS, INC.

United States District Court, Northern District of Texas, Dallas Division
CIVIL ACTION NO. 3:99-CV-2339-L, 2000 U.S. Dist. LEXIS 10444
Decided July 25, 2000

Opinion by: SAM A. LINDSAY

### ...I. Factual and Procedural Background

Plaintiff People Solutions, Inc. is a Texas corporation that provides human resources management, consulting, outsourcing, and executive search services. Plaintiff uses the mark "PEOPLE SOLUTIONS" in its business, and has been granted federal registration of the mark by the United States Patent and Trademark Office.

Defendant People Solutions, Inc. is a California corporation that has its principal place of business in Pleasant Hill, California. Defendant is a research and consulting company that offers human resources related products and services to other organizations. Defendant maintains an internet website using the "PEOPLE SOLUTIONS" name. Defendant's web site provides detailed descriptions and interactive pages regarding the products and services it offers. The web site also contains interactive pages that allow customers to test Defendant's products, download product demos, obtain product brochures and information, and order products online.

Plaintiff has sued Defendant over Defendant's alleged use of the "PEOPLE SOLUTIONS" trademark in its business. Plaintiff contends that it is the owner of the "PEOPLE SOLUTIONS" trademark and that Defendant should cease using it. Plaintiff filed its Complaint on October 13, 1999, asserting claims for federal trademark infringement, common law trademark infringement, unfair competition, state trademark infringement, and injury to business reputation. Defendant now moves to dismiss this action under Fed. R. Civ. P. 12(b)(3), contending that venue is improper in the Northern District of Texas....

A. Personal Jurisdiction

A determination of personal jurisdiction over a nonresident defendant consists of two elements. First, the court must determine whether the nonresident is subject to jurisdiction under the law of the state in which it sits, and secondly, it must determine whether the exercise of jurisdiction over the defendant comports with the due process requirements of the United States Constitution. *Stuart v. Spademan,* 772 F.2d 1185, 1189 (5th Cir. 1985); *CD Solutions, Inc. v. Tooker,* 965 F. Supp. 17, 19 (N.D. Tex. 1997). Plaintiff contends that the exercise of personal jurisdiction over Defendant is appropriate in this case pursuant to the Texas long-arm statute. The Texas long-arm statute has been interpreted to extend as far as the limits of constitutional due process permit. *Stuart,* 772 F.2d at 1189. Therefore, the court is only required to consider whether an exercise of jurisdiction over Defendant satisfies constitutional due process. *Stuart,* 772 F.2d at 1189; *CD Solutions,* 965 F. Supp. at 19.

The due process inquiry is further divided into two parts. First, it must be established that the nonresident has "minimum contacts" with the forum resulting from an affirmative act on its part, and second, if minimum contacts are established, the exercise of jurisdiction must be fair and reasonable to the defendant. *Id.* The "minimum contacts" required can be established either through contacts sufficient to support specific jurisdiction, or contacts that adequately support general jurisdiction. *Alpine View Co. Ltd. v. Atlas Copco AB,* 205 F.3d 208, 215 (5th Cir. 2000); *Wilson v. Belin,* 20 F.3d 644, 647 (5th Cir.), *cert. denied,* 513 U.S. 930, 130 L. Ed. 2d 282, 115 S. Ct. 322 (1994). Specific jurisdiction arises when the Defendant has purposefully directed activities toward the forum state, from which the litigation arises or to which it relates. *Burger King Corp. v. Rudzewicz,* 471 U.S. 462, 472, 85 L. Ed. 2d 528, 105 S. Ct. 2174 (1985); *Alpine View,* 205 F.3d at 215. General jurisdiction will attach where the Defendant's contacts with the forum state are not related to the Plaintiff's cause of action, but are continuous and systematic. *Helicopteros Nacionales de Colombia, S.A. v. Hall,* 466 U.S. 408, 415–16, 80 L. Ed. 2d 404, 104 S. Ct. 1868 (1984); *Alpine View,* 205 F.3d at 215.

Defendant claims that this case should be dismissed because it is not subject to personal jurisdiction in Texas. Defendant is a California corporation with its principal place of business in Pleasant Hill, California. It is undisputed that Defendant has no offices in Texas, no employees in Texas, owns no property in Texas and has no registered agent for service in Texas. Defendant therefore argues that it does not have the "minimum contacts" with this forum that are required for personal jurisdiction. Plaintiff contends that the following contacts with Texas show that Defendant is subject to personal jurisdiction here: Defendant has a web site which can be accessed and viewed by Texas residents; and Plaintiff has a client located in Farmers Branch, Texas. The court will examine each of these contacts to determine whether they provide a basis for personal jurisdiction over Defendant, either alone or in combination.

1. Defendant's Web Site

Plaintiff contends that specific jurisdiction over Defendant is present because it uses the "PEOPLE SOLUTIONS" name on its web site. The Fifth Circuit has recently addressed the impact of an Internet website that is accessible to Texas residents on the customary personal jurisdiction analysis. *See Mink v. AAAA Development, LLC*, 190 F.3d 333 (5th Cir. 1999). Prior to the *Mink* decision, many courts faced with this issue, including this one, used the analysis presented in *Zippo Mfg. Co. v. Zippo Dot Com, Inc.*, 952 F. Supp. 1119, 1124 (W.D. Pa. 1997). *See, e.g., Fix My PC, LLC v. N.F.N. Associates, Inc.*, 48 F. Supp.2d 640, 643 (N.D. Tex. 1999); *Thompson v. Handa-Lopez, Inc.*, 998 F. Supp. 738, 742–43 (W.D. Tex. 1998); *Mieczkowski v Masco Corp.*, 997 F. Supp. 782, 786 (E.D. Tex. 1998). In *Mink*, the Fifth Circuit embraced the use of the *Zippo* analysis when evaluating minimum contacts which may be established by a Defendant's Internet activities. 190 F.3d at 336.

The *Zippo* decision instructs courts to look to the "nature and quality of commercial activity that an entity conducts over the Internet." 952 F. Supp. at 1124; *see also Mink*, 190 F.3d at 336. This test examines a Defendant's Internet activities in relation to a spectrum of three areas. *Mink*, 190 F.3d at 336. At one end of the spectrum are defendants who are conducting their businesses over the Internet, entering into contracts with residents of other states involving the "knowing and repeated" transmission of computer files over the Internet. *Id.* "Passive" web sites are at the other end of the scale. *Mink*, 190 F.3d at 336; *Thompson*, 998 F. Supp. at 743. These web sites do nothing more than provide information and advertising to those who access the site. *Mink*, 190 F.3d at 336; *Fix My PC*, 48 F. Supp. 2d at 643. Passive web sites, on their own, do not provide for personal jurisdiction over the owner of the site. *Mink*, 190 F.3d at 336; *Fix My PC*, 48 F. Supp. 2d at 643. Interactive web sites that allow Internet users to communicate and exchange information with the organization sponsoring the site are in the middle of the spectrum. *Mink*, 190 F.3d at 336; *Fix My PC*, 48 F. Supp. 2d at 643; *Thompson*, 998 F. Supp at 743. In this "middle ground," the exercise of jurisdiction depends upon "the level of interactivity and commercial nature of the exchange of information" conducted on the defendant's web site. *Mink*, 190 F.3d at 336, quoting *Zippo*, 952 F. Supp. at 1124.

The facts related to Defendant's web site in this case are as follows: the web site contains several interactive pages which allow customers to take and score performance tests, download product demos, and order products online. The web site also provides a registration form whereby customers may obtain product brochures, test demonstration diskettes, or answers to questions. Defendant has sold no products exclusively through its web site. It further has sold no products or contracted for services with anyone in Texas through the web site or as a result of any Texan's interaction with the web site.

Defendant attempts to argue that these facts render its web site "passive" and thus not a basis for personal jurisdiction. Based upon the facts set forth above, the court disagrees with Defendant. The court does not believe, however, that the evidence supports a finding that Defendant has, through its web site, repeatedly contracted with Texas residents over the Internet, as described in *Zippo*, 952 F. Supp. at 1124 and *Mink*, 190 F.3d at 336. Therefore, the court finds that Defendant's web site is of the type that falls into the "middle ground" identified in *Zippo* and adopted by the Fifth Circuit in *Mink*, 190 F.3d at 336. Despite this categorization of Defendant's web site, the court finds that in this case, the relevant facts do not support a finding of personal jurisdiction over Defendant. Although Defendant appears to have the potential to interact with, sell products to, and contract with Texas residents on its web site, the evidence does not support a finding that this level of activity has taken place. Personal jurisdiction should not be premised on the mere possibility, with nothing more, that Defendant may be able to do business with Texans over its web site; rather, Plaintiff must show that Defendant has "purposefully availed itself" of the benefits of the forum state and its laws. Defendant's web site alone does not subject it to personal jurisdiction here; therefore the court must consider any additional contacts Defendant has with the forum.

### 2. Defendant's Texas Client

Plaintiff contends that its argument for personal jurisdiction is reinforced by the fact that Defendant has a client located in Farmers Branch, Texas. According to Plaintiff, when this fact is considered in combination with Defendant's web site, personal jurisdiction over Defendant is established. The court disagrees. The record reflects that Defendant's contacts with this client are made through the client's Menlo Park, California and Chicago, Illinois offices. At the client's behest, Defendant sends invoices to this client's branch office in Texas. These attenuated contacts do not sufficiently establish a basis for personal jurisdiction over Defendant. *See Burger King*, 471 U.S. at 475; *Guardian Royal Exchange, Ltd. v. English China Clays, P.L.C.*, 815 S.W.2d 223, 226 (Tex. 1991). Furthermore, the combination of Defendant's web site with its contacts related to its Farmers Branch, Texas client does not sufficiently satisfy the "purposeful availment" requirement for personal jurisdiction.

For the reasons stated herein, this court has no personal jurisdiction over Defendant. Defendant's Motion to Dismiss is granted, and this action must be dismissed....

### III. Conclusion

The court has considered the parties' briefing on this matter, the record evidence, and the applicable case law. For the reasons stated herein, Defendant's web site and other contacts with Texas do not, alone or in combination, establish that the court may exercise personal jurisdiction over Defendant. This action is hereby dismissed without prejudice because the court does not have personal jurisdiction over Defendant....

---

## Notes and Questions

1. May the parties determine for themselves whether they can be haled into a foreign jurisdiction? In *Decker v. Circus Circus Hotel*, 49 F. Supp. 2d 743 (D.N.J. 1999), the defendant hotel maintained a web-site to facilitate reservations. The site included a jurisdictional clause, stating that disputes would be resolved in the state and federal courts of Nevada. Notwithstanding the commercial nature of the defendant's site, the district court enforced the defendant's forum selection clause. *Id.* at 743.

2. For a discussion of in rem jurisdiction relating to domain names, *see Lucent Technologies, Inc. v. Lucentsucks.com*, 95 F. Supp. 2d 528 (E.D. Va. 2000).

3. The Supreme Court has observed that "because 'modern transportation and communications have made it much less burdensome for a party sued to defend himself in a State where he engages in economic activity,' it usually will not be unfair to subject [the out-of-state defendant] to the burdens of litigation in another forum for disputes relating to such activity." *Burger King Corp. v. Rudzewicz*, 471 U.S. at 473 (citation omitted). How do recent technological innovations, such as the availability of electronic court filings, affect this principle?

4. A guiding principle of the due process implications of jurisdiction is the requirement that individuals have fair warning that a particular activity may subject them

to the jurisdiction of a foreign sovereign, so as to give a degree of predictability to the legal system that allows potential defendants to structure their conduct with some minimum assurance as to where that conduct will and will not render them susceptible to suit. *See Burger King Corp. v. Rudzewicz,* 471 U.S. at 472; *see also Shaffer v. Heitner,* 433 U.S. 186, 218 (1977). Does the fact that normative conduct and business relations over the Internet are still evolving diminish such predictability?

5.  How does the transnational dimension of the Internet affect jurisdictional issues? In *Berezovsky v. Michaels and Another,* [2000] 1 WLR 1004 (May 11, 2000), *Forbes,* an American magazine, published an article alleging that a prominent Russian businessman and governmental official had been involved in organized crime and corruption in Russia. Sales of the issue of the magazine were predominantly in the United States and Canada; 785,000 were sold in those countries, compared with 1,900 in England and Wales and 13 in Russia. In sustaining jurisdiction over the libel claims in England, the High Court noted that the magazine was available on the Internet. Juxtaposed with this observation was Lord Steyn's comment that "[t]he readers of *Forbes* are predominantly people involved in business. Typically, many of its readers would have come from those working in corporate finance departments of banks and financial institutions." *Id.* To what extent might the court have been influenced by an impression that readers of the magazine may be cybersavvy?

# Chapter II

# Regulation of Internet Content

## First Amendment
## Analytical Frameworks

The solicitude afforded to speech is reflected in the jurisprudence on "prior restraints," which consist of an official restriction upon speech prior to its publication. *See, e.g., Forbes v. City of Seattle*, 113 Wash.2d 929, 935–36, 785 P.2d 431 (1990). First Amendment jurisprudence, as espoused by the Supreme Court, is clear that "prior restraints" of expression are presumptively unconstitutional and that a "heavy burden" rests with the party who seeks such relief. *See, e.g., Bantam Books, Inc. v. Sullivan*, 372 U.S. 58, 70 (1963); *Nebraska Press Ass'n v. Stuart*, 427 U.S. 539, 561 (1976) (cautioning that "it is...clear that the barriers to prior restraint remain high...."); *cf. id.* at 571 (Powell, J., concurring) (issuing a prior restraint is proper only when it is shown to be necessary to prevent the dissemination of prejudicial publicity that otherwise poses a high likelihood of preventing, directly, and irreparably a jury's impartiality); *id.* at 572 (Brennan, J., concurring) (resorting to a prior restraint on the press' freedom is a constitutionally impermissible method for enforcing even the right to a fair trial by a jury of one's peers, which is one of the "most precious and sacred safeguards enshrined in the Bill of Rights."). *But cf. Cable News Network, Inc. v. Noriega*, 498 U.S. 976 (1990) (declining to overrule or review a temporary restraining order barring broadcast of tape recordings of conversations between former Panamanian leader Manual Noriega and members of his defense team).

"The thread running through [such] cases is that prior restraints on speech and publication are the most serious and the least tolerable infringement on First Amendment rights." *Nebraska Press Ass'n v. Stuart*, 427 U.S. at 559. "If it can be said that a threat of criminal or civil sanctions after publication 'chills' speech, prior restraint 'freezes' it at least for the time." *Id.* (footnote omitted).

Under what circumstances may speech legitimately be regulated by the government? In discussing governmental regulation in another context, Professor Burt Neuborne eloquently stated:

> In any liberal democracy, the consummate act of political statesmanship is drawing the line between a public sphere that is subject to a degree of government regulation, and a private sphere that is reserved for individual choice. In a democracy like ours, blessed with a written Bill of Rights, and an independent judiciary vested with power to enforce it, the line between the public and

private spheres is often drawn by judges as they construe the delphic constitutional text. Text, history, and precedent obviously play significant roles in giving precise definition to the judicially-drawn line. In many settings, though, judges have a choice about precisely where to draw the public-private line. That choice is, I believe, deeply affected by two forces pulling in opposite directions that reflect the American political culture's love-hate relationship with the very idea of government. On one hand, we fear government. We rightly understand that even democratically elected majorities can be tyrannical. We rightly understand that government power can be inefficient, cumbersome and, all too often, selfishly and unfairly deployed. On the other hand, we need government. We recoil from the consequences of unconstrained private power.

Burt Neuborne, *The Supreme Court and Free Speech: Love and a Question*, 42 St. Louis U.L.J. 789, 791 (1998) (footnotes omitted).

The First Amendment protects communicative expression, but it is another matter to "establish[ ] a test for determining at what point conduct becomes so intertwined with expression that it becomes necessary to weigh the State's interest in proscribing conduct against the constitutionally protected interest in freedom of expression." *Cowgill v. California*, 396 U.S. 371, 372 (1970) (Harlan, J., concurring). The first question, then, is what, in essence, is speech? That is, where is the demarcation between speech and conduct?

While the First Amendment literally forbids only the abridgement of "speech," it is well-established that the protection extended by the Amendment is not confined to written or spoken words. "Symbolic speech" is exemplified by conduct designed to convey a point of view. Such "conduct" is countenanced by the First Amendment when: (1) there is an intent to convey a message via the conduct; (2) the conduct could be perceived as communication because of the use of recognizable symbols; and (3) the intended message is understandable in context. *See, e.g., Spence v. Washington*, 418 U.S. 405, 410–411 (1974) (per curiam). Desecration of an American flag in the context of a political protest has been sustained, for example, as "conduct 'sufficiently imbued with elements of communication'…to implicate the First Amendment." *Texas v. Johnson*, 491 U.S. 397, 404 (1989) (quoting *Spence v. Washington*, 418 U.S. at 409). Even silence may be protected under certain circumstances; the Constitution protects "both the right to speak freely and the right to refrain from speaking at all." *Wooley v. Maynard*, 430 U.S. 705, 714 (1977).

If the expressive element is determined to constitute speech, under what circumstances may it be regulated? When is the government's interest in curtailing communicative expression sufficiently important to merit a diminution of constitutional protection to speech? The standard of review applicable to regulatory schemes that impinge on free expression generally requires a determination as to whether such regulations are "content-neutral" or "content-based."

Content-neutral regulations are not necessarily or specifically directed to the communicative or substantive impact of speech, but they nonetheless effectively burden its expression. The government is prohibited from regulating speech based on hostility or favoritism towards the underlying message expressed. *See R.A.V. v. St. Paul*, 505 U.S. 377, 386 (1992). Thus, the principal test for content neutrality is whether the government has adopted a regulation of speech because it agrees or disagrees with the message it conveys; or, conversely, whether the government has adopted a regulation of speech "without reference to the content of the regulated speech." *Ward v. Rock Against Racism*, 491 U.S. 781, 791 (1989) (citation omitted).

Relative to content-based restrictions, content-neutral restrictions are measured against a less penetrating standard; the inquiry focuses on whether the challenged provisions burden speech no more than is necessary to serve a significant governmental interest. *See, e.g., Madsen v. Women's Health Center, Inc.,* 512 U.S. 753, 765 (1994). To survive constitutional scrutiny, such regulations must serve an important or substantial governmental interest, and incidentally restrict First Amendment freedoms no more than is essential to the furtherance of that interest.

Content-based regulations, by contrast, are directed to the communicative impact of the expression itself. "If there is a bedrock principle underlying the First Amendment, it is that the government may not prohibit the expression of an idea simply because society finds the idea itself offensive or disagreeable." *Texas v. Johnson,* 491 U.S. at 414. If a statute regulates speech based on its content, it must be narrowly tailored to promote a compelling governmental interest. *See, e.g., Sable Communications of Cal., Inc. v. FCC,* 492 U.S. 115, 126 (1989). The least restrictive means to further the government's purpose must be chosen. *See, e.g., Reno v. American Civil Liberties Union,* 521 U.S. 844, 874 (1997) (stating that the burden of the indecency provisions of the Communications Decency Act "on adult speech is unacceptable if less restrictive alternatives would be at least as effective in achieving the legitimate purpose that the statute was enacted to serve"). The Supreme Court has emphasized that "[t]o do otherwise would be to restrict speech without an adequate justification, a course the First Amendment does not permit." *United States v. Playboy Entertainment Group, Inc.,* — U.S. —, —, 120 S.Ct. 1878, 1886 (2000). Thus, content-based restrictions on speech are subjected to strict scrutiny, unless the speech is deemed worthy of little or no constitutional protection.

Certain categories of speech have been deemed to be outside the ambit of full First Amendment protection. This "categorical approach" to First Amendment analysis was summarized by the Supreme Court in *Chaplinsky v. New Hampshire:*

> There are certain well-defined and narrowly limited classes of speech, the prevention and punishment of which have never been thought to raise any Constitutional problem. These include the lewd and obscene, the profane, the libelous, and the insulting or "fighting" words—those which by their very utterance inflict injury or tend to incite an immediate breach of the peace. It has been well observed that such utterances are no essential part of any exposition of ideas, and are of such slight social value as a step to truth that any benefit that may be derived from them is clearly outweighed by the social interest in order and morality.

315 U.S. 568, 571–72 (1942) (footnotes omitted).

Historically, one justification for reduced protection for speech was that the expressive content presented "a clear and present danger." This test was first enunciated in *Schenck v. United States,* 249 U.S. 47 (1919), in which the defendants were accused of attempting to obstruct the draft during World War I through espionage. Justice Oliver Wendell Holmes, writing for a unanimous Supreme Court, stated:

> The question in every case is whether the words used are used in such circumstances and are of such a nature as to create a clear and present danger that they will bring about the substantive evils that Congress has a right to prevent. It is a question of proximity and degree. When a nation is at war many things that might be said in time of peace are such a hindrance to its effort that their utterance will not be endured so long as men fight and that no court could regard them as protected by any constitutional right.

*Id.* at 52.

The Supreme Court has since reformulated the analytical test for proscriptions on advocacy of the use of force or legal violation. Essentially, such advocacy cannot be punished consistent with constitutional norms unless the advocacy is "directed to inciting or producing imminent lawless action and is likely to incite or produce such action." *Brandenburg v. Ohio*, 395 U.S. 444, 447 (1969) (footnote omitted). "[T]he mere abstract teaching of…the moral propriety or even moral necessity for a resort to force and violence is not the same as preparing a group for violent action and steeling it to such action." *Noto v. United States*, 367 U.S. 290, 297–98 (1961). Statutes that fail to draw the distinction impermissibly "sweep[ ] within [their] condemnation speech which our Constitution has immunized from governmental control." *Brandenburg v. Ohio*, 395 U.S. at 448.

Regulatory schemes may encompass speech and non-speech elements. In such hybrid situations, a sufficiently important governmental interest in regulating the non-speech elements may justify incidental limitations on First Amendment freedoms. "The critical point is that nonspeech elements may create hazards for society above and beyond the speech elements. They are subject to regulation in appropriate circumstances because the government has an interest in dealing with the potential hazards of the nonspeech elements despite the fact that they are joined with expressive elements.… [T]he presence of expression in some broader mosaic does not result in the entire mosaic being treated as 'speech.' " *Universal City Studios, Inc. v. Reimerdes*, No. 00 CV 0277, 2000 U.S. Dist. LEXIS 11696 at *87 & n. 192 (Aug. 17, 2000).

The computer age has demanded increased focus on the demarcation between speech and non-speech elements. With respect to computer code, for example, "[t]he path from idea to human language to source code to object code is a continuum. As one moves from one to the other, the levels of precision and, arguably, abstraction increase, as does the level of training necessary to discern the idea from the expression." *Id.* at *81. Such codes as decryption devices therefore implicate free speech interests.

Encryption and security devices have been the subject of governmental regulation, as have technological devices designed to circumvent such measures.

> Society increasingly depends upon technological means of controlling access to digital files and systems, whether they are military computers, bank records, academic records, copyrighted works or something else entirely. There are far too many who, given any opportunity, will bypass those security measures, some for the sheer joy of doing it, some for innocuous reasons, and others for more malevolent purposes. Given the virtually instantaneous and worldwide dissemination widely available via the Internet, the only rational assumption is that once a computer program capable of bypassing such an access control system is disseminated, it will be used.

*Id.* at *98.

In *Junger v. Daley*, 209 F.3d 481 (6th Cir. 2000), the plaintiff challenged regulations prohibiting the export of encryption software, contending that they violated his free speech rights because the software was expressive. The Sixth Circuit recognized that computer code is expressive and thus fell within the ambit of First Amendment protection. The code's inclusion of certain functional capabilities also affected analysis of the government's interest in regulating the code. *Id.* at 485. Under the intermediate scrutiny standard applied by the court, the regulation of speech "is valid, in part, if 'it furthers an important or substantial governmental interest.' " *Id.* (citations omitted). Even where the asserted governmental interest is important, the government must defend the restriction on speech by doing more than simply "'posit the existence of the disease sought to be cured.'...The government 'must demonstrate that the recited harms are real, not merely conjectural, and that the regulation will in fact alleviate these harms in a direct and material way.'" *Id.* (citations omitted). Because the court found that the case record did not resolve the question of whether the exercise of presidential power in furtherance of national security interests should overrule the interests in allowing the free exchange of encryption source code, the case was remanded for consideration of the constitutional challenge to the regulations.

Regulatory schemes that prohibit—or even burden—speech are vulnerable to invalidation under other doctrinal challenges. For instance, such regulations will not be sustained if they are overbroad; that is, if they encompass protected speech within the prohibition. Challenges based on overbreadth are exempted from ordinary standing conventions, because they may be advanced even by a person to whom the statute may be constitutionally applied on the ground that the statute conceivably may be applied unconstitutionally to others who are not before the court. When statutes regulate speech, "the transcendent value to all society of constitutionally protected expression is deemed to justify 'attacks on overly broad statutes with no requirement that the person making the attack demonstrate that his own conduct could not be regulated by a statute drawn with the requisite narrow specificity.'" *Gooding v. Wilson*, 405 U.S. 518, 520–21 (1972) (quoting *Dombrowski v. Pfister*, 380 U.S. 479, 486 (1965)). The principle accommodates timorous third parties who might not exercise their rights for fear that they will trigger application of the statute's sanctions.

Facial overbreadth adjudication is an exception to traditional rules, however, and its function attenuates as the otherwise unprotected behavior that it forbids the state to sanction moves from "pure speech" toward conduct that is otherwise valid. The general rule reflects principles of the "personal nature of constitutional rights and the prudential limitations on constitutional adjudication." *Los Angeles Police Department v. United Reporting Publ'g Corp.*, 528 U.S. 32 (1999) (quoting *New York v. Ferber*, 458 U.S. 747, 769 (1982)).

In *Universal City Studios, Inc. v. Reimerdes,* No. 00 CV 0277, 2000 U.S. Dist. LEXIS 11696, the U.S. District Court for the Southern District of New York evaluated an overbreadth challenge to the Digital Millennium Copyright Act, Pub. L. No. 105–304, 112 Stat. 2860 (1998) (codified as amended at 17 U.S.C.A. §§1201–05 (West Supp. 2000)); *see* discussion *infra* at 402, which proscribes the circumvention of encryption devices. The court rejected the defendants' overbreadth challenge, acknowledging that while some persons not before the court may have lawful purposes for circumventing the encryption device, the defendants were alleged to have circumvented in violation of the Act. The court stated that the question as to whether the statutory regime

> substantially affects rights, much less constitutionally protected rights, of members of the "fair use community" cannot be decided *in bloc*, without consideration of the circumstances of each member or similarly situated groups of members. Thus, the prudential concern with ensuring that constitutional questions be decided only when the facts before the Court so require counsels against permitting defendants to mount an overbreadth challenge here.

*Universal City Studios, Inc. v. Reimerdes,* No. 00 CV 0277, 2000 U.S. Dist. LEXIS 11696 at *121. Further, the court noted that there was no basis to presume that prospective fair users would be deterred from asserting their rights. The court also was influenced by the fact that the controversy in issue did not deal with pure speech, but rather with the dissemination of technology that principally is functional in nature. *Id.* at *121–23.

Restrictions also may be rendered void for vagueness, as when they are so lacking in definitional precision that their scope is not readily apparent. In *Universal City Studios, Inc. v. Reimerdes,* the court rejected the defendants' vagueness challenge, however, on the ground that "[t]here can be no serious doubt that posting a computer program the sole purpose for which is to defeat an encryption system controlling access to plaintiff's copyrighted movies constituted an 'offer to the public' of 'technology [or a] product' that was 'primarily designed for the purpose of circumventing' plaintiffs' access control system. Defendants thus engaged in conduct clearly proscribed by the [statute] and will not be heard to complain of any vagueness as applied to others." *Id.* at *124–25 (footnote omitted).

Judges and legislators alike have sought to delimit the parameters of cherished freedoms of expression bestowed by the First Amendment. For the most part, the analyses have been applied to so-called conventional speech, such as speeches, books, periodicals, and broadcast presentations. Are these frameworks suitable for analysis of communications in the electronic environment?

Analysis of claims arising from on-line communications necessitates, of course, a foundational understanding of the operative functionalities of the technologies involved. Judicial decisions that adjudicate such claims routinely begin with a background discussion about the nature and workings of the Internet itself. *See, e.g., Reno v. American Civil Liberties Union,* 521 U.S. at 849–57 (discussing the nature and functioning of the Internet); *Bernstein v. United States Dep't of Justice,* 176 F.3d 1132, 1141 (9th Cir.) (discussing the capabilities and purposes of encryption and decryption software), *reh'g en banc granted, opinion withdrawn,* 192 F.3d 1308 (9th Cir. 1999); *Panavision International, L.P. v. Toeppen,* 141 F.3d 1316, 1318–19 (9th Cir. 1998) (discussing domain names); *Playboy Enterprises, Inc. v. Netscape Communications Corp.,* 55 F. Supp. 2d 1070, 1077–79 (C.D. Cal. 1999) (discussing banner advertisements), *aff'd,* 202 F.3d 278 (9th Cir. 1999); *Mainstream Loudoun v. Board of Trustees of the Loudoun County Library,* 24 F. Supp. 2d 552, 556 (E.D. Va. 1998) (discussing filtering technology); *American Civil Liberties Union v. Reno,* 929 F. Supp. 824, 830–49 (E.D. Pa. 1996) (discussing the nature and functioning of the Internet, filtering devices, and age verification methodologies), *aff'd,* 521 U.S. 844 (1997); *United States v. Maxwell,* 45 M.J. 406, 411–12 (C.A.A.F. 1996) (discussing instant messaging, chat rooms, and electronic messages); *Steve Jackson Games v. United States Secret Service,* 36 F.3d 457, 460–62 (5th Cir. 1994) (discussing the seizure of a computer, used to operate an electronic bulletin board system and containing private e-mail messages). Courts then endeavor to determine the most suitable analogy or analytical rationale for the particular factual dispute with which they are confronted.

Under what circumstances may speech be regulated, consistent with constitutional norms? Justice Homes eloquently admonished, "if there is any principle of the Constitution that more imperatively calls for attachment than any other it is the principle of free thought—not free thought for those who agree with us but freedom for the thought that we hate." *United States v. Schwimmer,* 279 U.S. 644, 653 (1929) (Holmes, J., dissenting). With respect to the press, "[w]e have learned, and continue to learn, from what we view as the unhappy experiences of other nations where government has been allowed to meddle in the internal editorial affairs of newspapers. Regardless of how beneficent-sounding the purposes of controlling the press might be, we...remain intensely skeptical about those measures that would allow government to insinuate itself into the editorial rooms of this Nation's press." *Miami Herald Publishing Co. v. Tornillo,* 418 U.S. 241, 259 (1974) (White, J., concurring) (quoted in *Nebraska Press Ass'n v. Stu-*

*art*, 427 U.S. at 560–61); *see also Columbia Broadcasting Sys., Inc. v. Democratic Nat'l Comm.*, 412 U.S. 94 (1973). Are regulatory schemes for Internet speech—whether formulated as to the press or as to individuals—susceptible to any less perilous results? Three illustrations of on-line content that have been the subject of regulatory regimes are examined to assess the nature and scope of digital content regulation: (1) hate speech and speech that promotes harm, *see* discussion *infra* at 106; (2) speech pertaining to matters of national security, *see* discussion *infra* at 130; and (3) obscene and indecent content, *see* discussion *infra* at 158.

## Notes and Questions

1. To what degree will the courts probe the legislative motives for a regulation that impinges on free expression? *See United States v. O'Brien*, 391 U.S. 367 (1968).

2. How effective are efforts to delineate between political advocacy and speech that is likely to incite? Justice Holmes, dissenting in *Gitlow v. New York*, 268 U.S. 652, 673 (1925), observed:

   > Every idea is an incitement. It offers itself for belief and if believed it is acted on unless some other belief outweighs it or some failure of energy stifles the movement at its birth. The only difference between the expression of an opinion and an incitement in the narrower sense is the speaker's enthusiasm for the result. Eloquence may set fire to reason. But whatever may be thought of the redundant discourse [contained in the documents discussing Communism that were the subject of judicial scrutiny in the *Gitlow* case,] it had no chance of starting a present conflagration. If in the long run the beliefs expressed in proletarian dictatorship are destined to be accepted by the dominant forces of the community, the only meaning of free speech is that they should be given their chance and have their way.

3. Does the prevailing political climate appear to influence legislative enactments, prosecutorial decisions, and judicial rulings in determinations as to whether speech is inimical to social values? *Compare Schenck v. United States*, 249 U.S. 47 (1919) (charging defendant with attempts to cause insubordination in the military and obstruction of enlistment during World War I) *with Texas v. Johnson*, 491 U.S. 397 (1989) (desecration of an American flag to protest the Vietnam War implicates First Amendment interests) *and Tinker v. Des Moines Independent Community School Dist.*, 393 U.S. 503, 505 (1969) (recognizing expressive nature of students' black armbands to protest American military involvement in Vietnam). *But see United States v. O'Brien*, 391 U.S. 367 (sustaining conviction for burning draft card during time of Vietnam War because it frustrated the government's substantial interest in assuring card's continued availability).

4. Justice Holmes famously offered an exemption to free speech protection: "The most stringent protection of free speech would not protect a man in falsely shouting fire in a theater and causing a panic." *Schenck v. United States*, 249 U.S. at 52. Justice William Douglas, a staunch supporter of free speech rights, stated that "[o]ne's beliefs have long been thought to be sanctuaries which government could not invade." *Brandenburg v. Ohio*, 395 U.S. at 456 (Douglas, J., concurring). He distinguished the example of penalizing one who falsely shouts fire and causes a panic as "a classic case where speech is brigaded with action." *Id.*

# Hate Speech and Speech
# That Promotes Harm

Among the types of expressive content that have proliferated on the Internet is speech that promotes hate, racism, and violence. The FBI documented nearly 8,000 "hate crimes" in 1995, reported by more than 9,500 governmental agencies across the country. *See* Rachel Weintraub-Reiter, *Hate Speech Over the Internet: A Traditional Constitutional Analysis Or a New Cyber Constitution?* 8 B.U. Pub. Int. L.J. 145, 148 n. 16 (1998) (citing Debbie N. Kaminer, *Hate Crime Laws* (Anti-Defamation League, New York, NY 1997)). A recent study by the software-filtering industry estimated that of the 40,000 to 60,000 new web-sites launched each week, approximately 180 are sites devoted to hate or discrimination issues; 400 are dedicated to violence; 1,250 are dedicated to weapons, and 50 relate to murder and/or suicide. *See* Richard Raysman and Peter Brown, *Extreme Speech on the Internet*, N.Y.L.J. (June 8, 1999) at 3, 7. Ideas laden with hateful sentiments may be espoused in disparate Internet fora, such as on web-sites launched by the sentiments' proponents, in chat rooms, and in e-mail messages. Statements that threaten and encourage violence likewise have proliferated.

First Amendment interests are implicated when such speech is the subject of prosecution, because threats must be distinguished from permissible speech. *See, e.g., Watts v. United States*, 394 U.S. 705, 707 (1969). One commentator remarked that "distinguishing between hate crimes and hate speech is a crucial aspect of a constitutional analysis. Hate crimes are criminal activity that receive enhanced punishment, while hate speech is permissible speech unrestricted by the First Amendment." Rachel Weintraub-Teiter, *Hate Speech Over the Internet: a Traditional Constitutional Analysis or a New Cyber Constitution?* 8 B.U. Pub. Int. L.J. at 147. Well over a century ago, one court observed that, while such speech offends,

> it is not the policy of the law to punish those unsuccessful threats which it is not presumed would terrify ordinary persons excessively; and there is so much opportunity for magnifying or misunderstanding undefined menaces that probably as much mischief would be caused by letting them be prosecuted as by refraining from it.

*People v. Jones*, 62 Mich. 304, 306, 28 N.W. 839, 840 (Mich. 1886). Coercive or extortionate threats are paradigmatic subjects of prosecution, as are threats that are intimately entwined with proscribed conduct. *See, e.g., United States v. Kelner*, 534 F.2d 1020 (2d Cir.), *cert. denied*, 429 U.S. 1022 (1976). "Although it may offend our sensibilities, a communication objectively indicating a serious expression of an intention to inflict bodily harm cannot constitute a threat unless the communication also is conveyed for the purpose of furthering some goal through the use of intimidation." *United States v. Alkhabaz*, 104 F.3d 1492, 1495 (6th Cir. 1997).

In *Planned Parenthood of the Columbia/Williamette, Inc. v. American Coalition of Life Activists*, 23 F. Supp. 2d 1182 (D. Or. 1998), several doctors sued anti-abortion advocates, alleging, among other claims, violations of the Freedom of Access to Clinic Entrances Act. The plaintiffs-physicians objected to the on-line posting of what were called the "Nuremberg files," which identified physicians who performed abortions. *Id.* at 1187. The web-site purported to list the names so that "we may be able to hold them on trial for crimes against humanity." *Id.* Included on the site were photographs, addresses, telephone numbers, and license plate numbers of health-care providers, as well as the names of spouses and children. *Id.* at 1887–88. The names of certain health-care providers who had been killed had been visibly crossed-out on the site; others, who had been wounded, were shaded in gray. *Planned Parenthood of the Columbia/Williamette, Inc. v. American Coalition of Life Activists,* 41 F. Supp. 2d 1130, 1133 (D. Or. 1999).

Defendants' arguments that the speech was protected by the First Amendment were unavailing. *Planned Parenthood of the Columbia/Williamette, Inc. v. American Coalition of Life Activists,* 23 F. Supp. 2d at 1191–94. The court stated that what may properly be considered a threat is to be governed by an objective standard; that is, "whether a reasonable person would foresee that the statement would be interpreted by those to whom the maker communicates the statement as a serious expression of intent to harm or assault." *Id.* at 1189 (quoting *United States v. Orozco-Santillan,* 903 F.2d 1262 (9th Cir. 1990)). Thereafter, a jury awarded the plaintiffs more than $100 million in punitive damages. *See* Richard Raysman and Peter Brown, *Extreme Speech on the Internet,* N.Y.L.J. (June 8, 1999) at 7. The court entered a permanent injunction, prohibiting the defendants from "publishing, republishing, reproducing and/or distributing in print or electronic form the personally identifying information about plaintiffs contained in... the Nuremberg Files...with a specific intent to threaten." *Parenthood of the Columbia/Williamette, Inc. v. American Coalition of Life Activists,* 41 F. Supp. 2d at 1156.

---

# UNITED STATES of AMERICA v. Abraham Jacob ALKHABAZ, also known as Jake Baker

United States Court of Appeals, Sixth Circuit
No. 95-1797, 104 F.3d 1492
January 29, 1997

Before: MARTIN, Chief Judge, and KRUPANSKY and DAUGHTREY, Circuit Judges. MARTIN, C.J., delivered the opinion of the court, in which DAUGHTREY, J., joined. KRUPANSKY, J, delivered a separate dissenting opinion.

Claiming that the district court erred in determining that certain electronic mail messages between Abraham Jacob Alkhabaz, a.k.a. Jake Baker, and Arthur Gonda did not constitute "true threats," the government appeals the dismissal of the indictment charging Baker with violations of 18 U.S.C. § 875(c).

From November 1994 until approximately January 1995, Baker and Gonda exchanged e-mail messages over the Internet, the content of which expressed a sexual interest in violence against women and girls. Baker sent and received messages through a computer in Ann Arbor, Michigan, while Gonda—whose true identity and whereabouts are still unknown—used a computer in Ontario, Canada.

Prior to this time, Baker had posted a number of fictional stories to "alt.sex.stories," a popular interactive Usenet news group. Using such shorthand references as "B & D," "snuff," "pedo," "mf," and "nc," Baker's fictional stories generally involved the abduction, rape, torture, mutilation, and murder of women and young girls. On January 9,

Baker posted a story describing the torture, rape, and murder of a young woman who shared the name of one of Baker's classmates at the University of Michigan.

On February 9, Baker was arrested and appeared before a United States Magistrate Judge on a criminal complaint alleging violations of 18 U.S.C. §875(c), which prohibits interstate communications containing threats to kidnap or injure another person.... [Baker was ordered detained as a danger to the community.] Upon Baker's motion to be released on bond, this Court ordered a psychological evaluation. When the evaluation concluded that Baker posed no threat to the community, this Court ordered Baker's release.

On February 14, a federal grand jury returned a one-count indictment charging Baker with a violation of 18 U.S.C. §875(c). On March 15, 1995, citing several e-mail messages between Gonda and Baker, a federal grand jury returned a superseding indictment, charging Baker and Gonda with five counts of violations of 18 U.S.C. §875(c). The e-mail messages supporting the superseding indictment were not available in any publicly accessible portion of the Internet.... The government argues that the district court erred in dismissing the indictment because the communications between Gonda and Baker do constitute "true threats" and, as such, do not implicate First Amendment free speech protections....

[I]n determining the sufficiency of the indictment against Baker, we must consider the elements of the offense that Congress intended to prohibit when it created Section 875(c). Because Congress's intent is essentially a question of statutory interpretation, we review the district court's decision *de novo. United States v. Spinelle*, 41 F.3d 1056, 1057 (6th Cir. 1994); *United States v. Brown*, 915 F.2d 219, 223 (6th Cir. 1990).

Title 18, United States Code, Section 875(c) states:

> Whoever transmits in interstate or foreign commerce any communication containing any threat to kidnap any person or any threat to injure the person of another, shall be fined under this title or imprisoned not more than five years, or both.

The government must allege and prove three elements to support a conviction under Section 875(c): "(1) a transmission in interstate [or foreign] commerce; (2) a communication containing a threat; and (3) the threat must be a threat to injure [or kidnap] the person of another." [*United States v. DeAndino*, 958 F.2d 146, 148 (6th Cir. 1992)]. In this case, the first and third elements cannot be seriously challenged by the defendant. However, the second element raises several issues that this Court must address.... Our law does not punish bad purpose standing alone, however; instead we require that mens rea accompany the actus reus specifically proscribed by statute." *Id.* As the Supreme Court has recognized, William Shakespeare's lines here illustrate sound legal doctrine.

> His acts did not o'ertake his bad intent;
> And must be buried but as an intent
> That perish'd by the way: thoughts are no subjects,
> Intents but merely thoughts.

*United States v. Apfelbaum*, 445 U.S. 115, 131 n. 13, 100 S.Ct. 948, 957 n. 13, 63 L.Ed.2d 250 (1980) (quoting William Shakespeare's Measure for Measure, Act V, Scene 1; G. Williams, *Criminal Law, The General Part* 1 (2d ed. 1961)).

Although its language does not specifically contain a mens rea element, this Court has interpreted Section 875(c) as requiring only general intent. *DeAndino*, 958 F.2d at 148–50. Accordingly, Section 875(c) requires proof that a reasonable person would have taken the defendant's statement as "a serious expression of an intention to inflict bodily harm." *Id.* at 148 (citing *United States v. Lincoln*, 462 F.2d 1368, 1369 (6th Cir. 1972))....

To determine what type of action Congress intended to prohibit, it is necessary to consider the nature of a threat. At their core, threats are tools that are employed when one wishes to have some effect, or achieve some goal, through intimidation. This is true regardless of whether the goal is highly reprehensible or seemingly innocuous.

For example, the goal may be extortionate or coercive. In *United States v. Cox*, 957 F.2d 264 (6th Cir. 1992), a bank repossessed the defendant's vehicle, including several personal items. The defendant then telephoned the bank and threatened to "hurt people" at the bank, unless the bank returned his property. Similarly, in *United States v. Schroeder*, 902 F.2d 1469 (10th Cir.), *cert. denied*, 498 U.S. 867, 111 S.Ct. 181, 112 L.Ed.2d 145 (1990), the defendant informed an Assistant United States Attorney that "people would get hurt" if the government did not give him money. In both cases, the defendant used a threat in an attempt to extort property from the threatened party.

Additionally, the goal, although not rising to the level of extortion, may be the furtherance of a political objective. For example, in *United States v. Kelner*, 534 F.2d 1020 (2d Cir. 1976), the defendant threatened to assassinate Yasser Arafat, leader of the Palestine Liberation Organization (PLO), during a news conference. Kelner claimed that his sole purpose in issuing the threat was to inform the PLO that "we (as Jews) would defend ourselves and protect ourselves." *Id.* at 1021–22. Although Kelner's threat was not extortionate, he apparently sought to further the political objectives of his organization by intimidating the PLO with warnings of violence.

Finally, a threat may be communicated for a seemingly innocuous purpose. For example, one may communicate a bomb threat, even if the bomb does not exist, for the sole purpose of creating a prank. However, such a communication would still constitute a threat because the threatening party is attempting to create levity (at least in his or her own mind) through the use of intimidation.

The above examples illustrate threats because they demonstrate a combination of the mens rea with the actus reus. Although it may offend our sensibilities, a communication objectively indicating a serious expression of an intention to inflict bodily harm cannot constitute a threat unless the communication also is conveyed for the purpose of furthering some goal through the use of intimidation.

Accordingly, to achieve the intent of Congress, we hold that, to constitute "a communication containing a threat" under Section 875(c), a communication must be such that a reasonable person (1) would take the statement as a serious expression of an intention to inflict bodily harm (the mens rea), and (2) would perceive such expression as being communicated to effect some change or achieve some goal through intimidation (the actus reus).

... [T]he actus reus element of a Section 875(c) violation must be determined objectively, from the perspective of the receiver.

Our interpretation of the actus reus requirement of Section 875(c) conforms not only to the nature of a threat, but also to the purpose of prohibiting threats. Several other circuits have recognized that statutes prohibiting threats are designed to protect the recipient's sense of personal safety and well being. *United States v. Aman*, 31 F.3d 550 (7th Cir. 1994); *United States v. Bellrichard*, 994 F.2d 1318 (8th Cir. 1993); *see, e.g., R. A. V. v. St. Paul*, 505 U.S. 377, 112 S.Ct. 2538, 120 L.Ed.2d 305 (1992) (threats of violence are proscribable because of the fear caused by the threat, the disruption engendered by such fear, and the possibility that the threat of violence will occur). If an otherwise threatening communication is not, from an objective standpoint, transmitted for the purpose of intimidation, then it is unlikely that the recipient will be intimidated or that the recipient's peace of mind will be disturbed....

Applying our interpretation of the statute to the facts before us, we conclude that the communications between Baker and Gonda do not constitute "communication[s] containing a threat" under Section 875(c). Even if a reasonable person would take the communications between Baker and Gonda as serious expressions of an intention to inflict bodily harm, no reasonable person would perceive such communications as being conveyed to effect some change or achieve some goal through intimidation. Quite the opposite, Baker and Gonda apparently sent e-mail messages to each other in an attempt to foster a friendship based on shared sexual fantasies.

Ultimately, the indictment against Baker fails to "set forth...all the elements necessary to constitute the offense intended to be punished" and must be dismissed as a matter of law. *DeAndino*, 958 F.2d at 146 (quoting *Hamling v. United States*, 418 U.S. 87, 117, 94 S.Ct. 2887, 2907, 41 L.Ed.2d 590 (1974)). We agree with the district court, that "[w]hatever Baker's faults, and he is to be faulted, he did not violate 18 U.S.C. § 875(c)." *United States v. Baker*, 890 F. Supp. at 1390, 1391.

For the foregoing reasons, the judgment of the district court is affirmed.

————————

Speech relating to violence has permeated even the virtual fantasy world. For example, in April 1993, an on-line character called "Mr. Bungle" was programmed on a multi-user dungeon to create a virtual "voodoo doll," which allowed characters to be manipulated on screen without the authorization or knowledge of their creators. The software, "LamdaMoo," was utilized to attribute to several members a variety of explicit acts, including sexual assault. Despite protests by the participants, the proponent of the virtual attacks persisted until he effectively was "eliminated" through "toading" (i.e., having his user's account cancelled). *See* Julian Dibbell, *A Rape in Cyberspace,* The Village Voice, Dec. 21, 1993 at 38; *see also* <http://www.websteruniv.edu/philosphy/~umbaugh/courses/frosh/produce/dan.htm>. One commentator stated:

> Mr. Bungle's conduct resulted in an outpouring of anger and vituperation against him, both from the victims and from other members of LambdaMOO, including calls for a virtual death penalty—permanent elimination both of the character and of the member's account on the system....The discussion...indicates that the community recognizes that real-world laws do not govern the conduct at issue and that the remedy should come from within the virtual community itself.

William S. Byassee, *Jurisdiction of Cyberspace: Applying Real World Precedent to the Virtual Community,* 30 Wake Forest L. Rev. 197, 218 (1995) (footnotes omitted).

Public concern about speech promoting violence has heightened after the bombing of a federal office building in Oklahoma City in 1995 and the shootings at Columbine High School in Colorado in 1999. In May 1995, for example, the Senate Judiciary Committee Sub-Committee on Terrorism, Technology, and Government Information held hearings on "The Availability of Bomb Making Information on the Internet." Testimony at the hearings included references to web-sites that displayed "recipes" for building bombs. The Department of Justice stated that information about the construction of bombs is "freely available on the Internet" and on "computer bulletin boards." *See The*

*Availability of Bomb Making Information on the Internet, Hearings Before the Subcom. on Terrorism, Technology, and Government Information of the Senate Judiciary Committee,* 104th Cong. (1995) (statement of Robert S. Litt, Deputy Assistant Attorney General, Criminal Division, United States Department of Justice). The Justice Department concluded that "acts of violence like the Oklahoma City bombing are facilitated by the free flow of information on how to construct destructive weapons." *Id.* Senator Edward Kennedy expressed concern that his staff was able to download the "Terrorist's Handbook," which recited instructions for building different types of bombs. *See* Brock N. Meeks, *Will the Net Be the Next Bomb "Victim?"* Interactive Week (1995) at 42.

Recent Congressional attention to the subject of hate-laden and threatening speech also includes the Violent and Repeat Juvenile Offender Accountability and Rehabilitation Act of 1999, S. 254, 106th Cong. Amendments to the Act already have been proposed. For example, the Provision of Internet Filtering Or Screening Software By Certain Internet Service Providers requires Internet service providers to furnish to residential customers, at no cost, computer software or other filtering or blocking systems that allow the customers to prevent the access of certain on-line material to minors. S. 5178, 106th Cong. (1999). Another amendment proposes to make it a crime to teach or demonstrate the making of explosives, weapons, or other destructive devices. Yet another legislative initiative, the Internet Gun Trafficking Act of 1999, S. 637, 106th Cong. (1999), criminalizes certain operations of web-sites that evince "a clear purpose" of offering ten or more firearms for sale or exchange at one time.

Noted First Amendment attorney Dean Ringel has observed that:

> [w]hile to some, the beauty of the Internet lies in the freedom of speech it fosters, to others it is instead a refuge for fringe speakers and societal outcasts who take advantage of the Internet to spew messages of hate, lies, and violence. Prior to the development of the Internet, such speakers were likely marginalized in their communities. With the Internet, however, many of these speakers have banded together with others from around the country and the world to create a more visible and disturbing presence to the world community at large.

Dean Ringel, *et al., The Law of Cyberspace "A Brave New World of Free Speech?"* (Aug. 19, 1999) at 15.

Guides to committing violent conduct existed before the Internet, of course. Does the accessibility of the Internet change the analysis of the First Amendment implications of regulation in this area? Because the Internet presents extremely low entry barriers to publishers and distributors of information, it is an especially attractive means of diverse discourse. Electronic access to such content facilitates communication, including on an anonymous basis. Yet "shouting fire in cyberspace is actually far less threatening, and thus less deserving of censure, than the equivalent act in the physical world." *The Availability of Bomb Making Information on the Internet, Hearings Before the Sub-Committee on Terrorism, Technology, and Government Information, Senate Judiciary Committee,* 104th Cong. (1995) (statement of Jerry Berman, Executive Director, Center for Democracy and Technology) (emphasis omitted). Is regulation of the speech via electronic dissemination the appropriate remedy? Perhaps "[i]f we are concerned with a particular item being communicated, in addition to the purpose of the communication, we ought to focus on what it is that is being communicated, rather than the form of [the] communication." *See id.* (statement of Frank Tuerkheimer, University of Wisconsin Law School).

How may society's concerns about potentially harmful conduct be reconciled with the nation's clear commitment to freedom of expression? The Department of Justice has stated that the promulgation of prohibitions on dissemination of information about the building of a bomb, absent a showing of intent to cause harm or imminent risk that violence will occur, would be constitutionally suspect. *See* U.S. Dep't of Justice, *Report on the Availability of Bombmaking Information* (1997) at 49–50. May the legal system permissibly restrict the both the potential dissemination and the receipt of such information?

---

# R. A. V. v. CITY of ST. PAUL, Minnesota

Supreme Court of the United States
No. 90-7675, 505 U.S. 377
June 22, 1992.

Justice SCALIA delivered the opinion of the Court.

In the predawn hours of June 21, 1990, petitioner and several other teenagers allegedly assembled a crudely made cross by taping together broken chair legs. They then allegedly burned the cross inside the fenced yard of a black family that lived across the street from the house where petitioner was staying. Although this conduct could have been punished under any of a number of laws, one of the two provisions under which respondent city of St. Paul chose to charge petitioner (then a juvenile) was the St. Paul Bias-Motivated Crime Ordinance, St. Paul, Minn., Legis. Code § 292.02 (1990), which provides:

> Whoever places on public or private property a symbol, object, appellation, characterization or graffiti, including, but not limited to, a burning cross or Nazi swastika, which one knows or has reasonable grounds to know arouses anger, alarm or resentment in others on the basis of race, color, creed, religion or gender commits disorderly conduct and shall be guilty of a misdemeanor.

Petitioner moved to dismiss this count on the ground that the St. Paul ordinance was substantially overbroad and impermissibly content based and therefore facially invalid under the First Amendment....

The First Amendment generally prevents government from proscribing speech, *see, e.g., Cantwell v. Connecticut,* 310 U.S. 296, 309–311, 60 S.Ct. 900, 905–906, 84 L.Ed. 1213 (1940), or even expressive conduct, *see, e.g., Texas v. Johnson,* 491 U.S. 397, 406, 109 S.Ct. 2533, 2540, 105 L.Ed.2d 342 (1989), because of disapproval of the ideas expressed. Content-based regulations are presumptively invalid. *Simon & Schuster, Inc. v. Members of N.Y. State Crime Victims Bd.,* 502 U.S. 105, 115, 112 S.Ct. 501, 508, 116 L.Ed.2d 476 (1991). *Id.* at 124, 112 S.Ct. at 512–513 (KENNEDY, J., concurring in judgment); *Consolidated Edison Co. of N.Y. v. Public Serv. Comm'n of N.Y.,* 447 U.S. 530, 536, 100 S.Ct. 2326, 2332–2333, 65 L.Ed.2d 319 (1980); *Police Dept. of Chicago v. Mosley,* 408 U.S. 92, 95, 92 S.Ct. 2286, 2289–2290, 33 L.Ed.2d 212 (1972). From 1791 to the present, however, our society, like other free but civilized societies, has permitted restrictions upon the content of speech in a few limited areas, which are "of such slight social value as a step to truth that any benefit that may be derived from them is clearly outweighed by the social interest in order and morality." *Chaplinsky* [*v. New Hampshire,* 315 U.S. 568, 572, (1942)]. We have recognized that "the freedom of speech" referred to by the First Amendment does not include a freedom to disregard these traditional limitations. *See, e.g., Roth v. United States,* 354 U.S. 476, 77 S.Ct. 1304, 1 L.Ed.2d 1498 (1957) (obscenity); *Beauharnais v. Illinois,* 343 U.S. 250, 72 S.Ct. 725, 96 L.Ed. 919 (1952) (defamation*); Chaplinsky v. New Hampshire, supra* ("'fighting' words"); *see generally Simon & Schuster, supra*, 502 U.S. at 124, 112 S.Ct. at 513–514 (KENNEDY, J., concurring in judgment). Our decisions since the 1960's have narrowed the scope of the traditional categorical exceptions for defamation, *see New York Times Co. v. Sullivan*, 376 U.S. 254, 84 S.Ct. 710, 11 L.Ed.2d 686 (1964*); Gertz v. Robert Welch, Inc.*, 418 U.S. 323, 94 S.Ct. 2997, 41 L.Ed.2d 789 (1974*); see generally Milkovich v. Lorain Journal Co.*, 497 U.S. 1, 13–17, 110 S.Ct. 2695, 2702–2705, 111 L.Ed.2d 1 (1990), and for obscenity, *see Miller v. California*, 413 U.S. 15, 93 S.Ct. 2607, 37 L.Ed.2d 419 (1973), but a limited categorical approach has remained an important part of our First Amendment jurisprudence.

We have sometimes said that these categories of expression are "not within the area of constitutionally protected speech," *Roth, supra*, 354 U.S. at 483, 77 S.Ct. at 1308; *Beauharnais, supra*, 343 U.S. at 266, 72 S.Ct. at 735; *Chaplinsky, supra*, 315 U.S. at 571–572, 62 S.Ct. at 768–769; or that the "protection of the First Amendment does not extend" to them, *Bose Corp. v. Consumers Union of United States, Inc.*, 466 U.S. 485, 504, 104 S.Ct. 1949, 1961, 80 L.Ed.2d 502 (1984); *Sable Communications of Cal., Inc. v. FCC*, 492 U.S. 115, 124, 109 S.Ct. 2829, 2835, 106 L.Ed.2d 93 (1989). Such statements must be taken in context, however, and are no more literally true than is the occasionally repeated shorthand characterizing obscenity "as not being speech at all," Sunstein, *Pornography and the First Amendment*, 1986 Duke L.J. 589, 615, n. 146. What they mean is that these areas of speech can, consistently with the First Amendment, be regulated because of their constitutionally proscribable content (obscenity, defamation, etc.)—not that they are categories of speech entirely invisible to the Constitution, so that they may be made the vehicles for content discrimination unrelated to their distinctively proscribable content. Thus, the government may proscribe libel; but it may not make the further content discrimination of proscribing only libel critical of the government. We recently acknowledged this distinction in [*New York v. Ferber*, 458 U.S. 747, 763 (1982)], where, in upholding New York's child pornography law, we expressly recognized that there was no "question here of censoring a particular literary theme...." *See also id.* at 775, 102 S.Ct. at 3364 (O'CONNOR, J., concurring) ("As drafted, New York's statute does not attempt to suppress the communication of particular ideas").

Our cases surely do not establish the proposition that the First Amendment imposes no obstacle whatsoever to regulation of particular instances of such proscribable expression, so that the government "may regulate [them] freely," *post*, at 2552 (WHITE, J., concurring in judgment). That would mean that a city council could enact an ordinance prohibiting only those legally obscene works that contain criticism of the city government or, indeed, that do not include endorsement of the city government. Such a simplistic, all-or-nothing-at-all approach to First Amendment protection is at odds with common sense and with our jurisprudence as well. It is not true that "fighting words" have at most a "de minimis" expressive content, *ibid.*, or that their content is in all respects "worthless and undeserving of constitutional protection," *post*, at 2553; sometimes they are quite expressive indeed. We have not said that they constitute "no part of the expression of ideas," but only that they constitute "no essential part of any exposition of ideas." *Chaplinsky, supra*, 315 U.S. at 572, 62 S.Ct. at 769.

The proposition that a particular instance of speech can be proscribable on the basis of one feature (e.g., obscenity) but not on the basis of another (e.g., opposition to the city government) is commonplace and has found application in many contexts. We have long held, for example, that nonverbal expressive activity can be banned because of the action it entails, but not because of the ideas it expresses—so that burning a flag in violation of an ordinance against outdoor fires could be punishable, whereas burning a flag in violation of an ordinance against dishonoring the flag is not. *See Johnson*, 491

U.S. at 406–407, 109 S.Ct. at 2540–2541. *See also Barnes v. Glen Theatre, Inc.*, 501 U.S. 560, 569–570, 111 S.Ct. 2456, 2462, 115 L.Ed.2d 504 (1991) (plurality opinion); *id.* at 573–574, 111 S.Ct. at 2464–2465 (SCALIA, J., concurring in judgment); *id*, at 581–582, 111 S.Ct. at 2468–2469 (SOUTER, J., concurring in judgment); *United States v. O'Brien*, 391 U.S. 367, 376–377, 88 S.Ct. 1673, 1678–1679, 20 L.Ed.2d 672 (1968). Similarly, we have upheld reasonable "time, place, or manner" restrictions, but only if they are "justified without reference to the content of the regulated speech." *Ward v. Rock Against Racism*, 491 U.S. 781, 791, 109 S.Ct. 2746, 2753–2754, 105 L.Ed.2d 661 (1989) (internal quotation marks omitted); *see also Clark v. Community for Creative Non-Violence*, 468 U.S. 288, 298, 104 S.Ct. 3065, 3071, 82 L.Ed.2d 221 (1984) (noting that the *O'Brien* test differs little from the standard applied to time, place, or manner restrictions). And just as the power to proscribe particular speech on the basis of a noncontent element (e.g., noise) does not entail the power to proscribe the same speech on the basis of a content element; so also, the power to proscribe it on the basis of one content element (e.g., obscenity) does not entail the power to proscribe it on the basis of other content elements.

In other words, the exclusion of "fighting words" from the scope of the First Amendment simply means that, for purposes of that Amendment, the unprotected features of the words are, despite their verbal character, essentially a "nonspeech" element of communication. Fighting words are thus analogous to a noisy sound truck: Each is, as Justice Frankfurter recognized, a "mode of speech," *Niemotko v. Maryland*, 340 U.S. 268, 282, 71 S.Ct. 325, 333, 95 L.Ed. 267 (1951) (opinion concurring in result); both can be used to convey an idea; but neither has, in and of itself, a claim upon the First Amendment. As with the sound truck, however, so also with fighting words: The government may not regulate use based on hostility—or favoritism—towards the underlying message expressed. *Compare Frisby v. Schultz*, 487 U.S. 474, 108 S.Ct. 2495, 101 L.Ed.2d 420 (1988) (upholding, against facial challenge, a content-neutral ban on targeted residential picketing), *with Carey v. Brown*, 447 U.S. 455, 100 S.Ct. 2286, 65 L.Ed.2d 263 (1980) (invalidating a ban on residential picketing that exempted labor picketing)....

Even the prohibition against content discrimination that we assert the First Amendment requires is not absolute. It applies differently in the context of proscribable speech than in the area of fully protected speech. The rationale of the general prohibition, after all, is that content discrimination "raises the specter that the Government may effectively drive certain ideas or viewpoints from the marketplace," *Simon & Schuster*, 502 U.S. at 116, 112 S.Ct. at 508; *Leathers v. Medlock*, 499 U.S. 439, 448, 111 S.Ct. 1438, 1444, 113 L.Ed.2d 494 (1991); *FCC v. League of Women Voters of Cal.*, 468 U.S. 364, 383–384, 104 S.Ct. 3106, 3119–3120, 82 L.Ed.2d 278 (1984); *Consolidated Edison Co.*, 447 U.S. at 536, 100 S.Ct. at 2333; *Police Dept. of Chicago v. Mosley*, 408 U.S. at 95–98, 92 S.Ct. at 2289–2292. But content discrimination among various instances of a class of proscribable speech often does not pose this threat.

When the basis for the content discrimination consists entirely of the very reason the entire class of speech at issue is proscribable, no significant danger of idea or viewpoint discrimination exists. Such a reason, having been adjudged neutral enough to support exclusion of the entire class of speech from First Amendment protection, is also neutral enough to form the basis of distinction within the class. To illustrate: A State might choose to prohibit only that obscenity which is the most patently offensive in its prurience—i.e., that which involves the most lascivious displays of sexual activity. But it may not prohibit, for example, only that obscenity which includes offensive political messages. *See Kucharek v. Hanaway*, 902 F.2d 513, 517 (CA7 1990), *cert. de-*

*nied*, 498 U.S. 1041, 111 S.Ct. 713, 112 L.Ed.2d 702 (1991). And the Federal Government can criminalize only those threats of violence that are directed against the President, *see* 18 U.S.C. § 871 — since the reasons why threats of violence are outside the First Amendment (protecting individuals from the fear of violence, from the disruption that fear engenders, and from the possibility that the threatened violence will occur) have special force when applied to the person of the President. *See Watts v. United States*, 394 U.S. 705, 707, 89 S.Ct. 1399, 1401, 22 L.Ed.2d 664 (1969) (upholding the facial validity of § 871 because of the "overwhelmin[g] interest in protecting the safety of [the] Chief Executive and in allowing him to perform his duties without interference from threats of physical violence"). But the Federal Government may not criminalize only those threats against the President that mention his policy on aid to inner cities....

Another valid basis for according differential treatment to even a content-defined subclass of proscribable speech is that the subclass happens to be associated with particular "secondary effects" of the speech, so that the regulation is "justified without reference to the content of the...speech," *Renton v. Playtime Theatres, Inc.*, 475 U.S. 41, 48, 106 S.Ct. 925, 929, 89 L.Ed.2d 29 (1986) (quoting *Virginia State Bd. of Pharmacy, supra*, 425 U.S. at 771, 96 S.Ct. at 1830); *see also Young v. American Mini Theatres, Inc.*, 427 U.S. 50, 71, n. 34, 96 S.Ct. 2440, 2453, n. 34, 49 L.Ed.2d 310 (1976) (plurality opinion); *Id.* at 80–82, 96 S.Ct. at 2457–2458 (Powell, J., concurring); *Barnes*, 501 U.S. at 586, 111 S.Ct. at 2470–2471 (SOUTER, J., concurring in judgment). A State could, for example, permit all obscene live performances except those involving minors.... Where the government does not target conduct on the basis of its expressive content, acts are not shielded from regulation merely because they express a discriminatory idea or philosophy.

These bases for distinction refute the proposition that the selectivity of the restriction is "even arguably 'conditioned upon the sovereign's agreement with what a speaker may intend to say.'" *Metromedia, Inc. v. San Diego*, 453 U.S. 490, 555, 101S.Ct. 2882, 2917, 69 L.Ed.2d 800 (1981) (STEVENS, J., dissenting in part) (citation omitted). There may be other such bases as well. Indeed, to validate such selectivity (where totally proscribable speech is at issue) it may not even be necessary to identify any particular "neutral" basis, so long as the nature of the content discrimination is such that there is no realistic possibility that official suppression of ideas is afoot.... Save for that limitation, the regulation of "fighting words," like the regulation of noisy speech, may address some offensive instances and leave other, equally offensive, instances alone. *See Posadas de Puerto Rico*, 478 U.S. at 342–343, 106 S.Ct. at 2977–2978.

Applying these principles to the St. Paul ordinance, we conclude that, even as narrowly construed by the Minnesota Supreme Court, the ordinance is facially unconstitutional. Although the phrase in the ordinance, "arouses anger, alarm or resentment in others," has been limited by the Minnesota Supreme Court's construction to reach only those symbols or displays that amount to "fighting words," the remaining, unmodified terms make clear that the ordinance applies only to "fighting words" that insult, or provoke violence, "on the basis of race, color, creed, religion or gender." Displays containing abusive invective, no matter how vicious or severe, are permissible unless they are addressed to one of the specified disfavored topics. Those who wish to use "fighting words" in connection with other ideas — to express hostility, for example, on the basis of political affiliation, union membership, or homosexuality — are not covered. The First Amendment does not permit St. Paul to impose special prohibitions on those speakers who express views on disfavored subjects. *See Simon & Schuster*, 502 U.S. at 116, 112 S.Ct. at 508; *Arkansas Writers' Project, Inc. v. Ragland*, 481 U.S. 221, 229–230, 107 S.Ct. 1722, 1727–1728, 95 L.Ed.2d 209 (1987).

In its practical operation, moreover, the ordinance goes even beyond mere content discrimination, to actual viewpoint discrimination. Displays containing some words—odious racial epithets, for example—would be prohibited to proponents of all views. But "fighting words" that do not themselves invoke race, color, creed, religion, or gender—aspersions upon a person's mother, for example—would seemingly be usable *ad libitum* in the placards of those arguing in favor of racial, color, etc., tolerance and equality, but could not be used by those speakers' opponents. One could hold up a sign saying, for example, that all "anti-Catholic bigots" are misbegotten; but not that all "papists" are, for that would insult and provoke violence "on the basis of religion." St. Paul has no such authority to license one side of a debate to fight freestyle, while requiring the other to follow Marquis of Queensberry rules.

What we have here, it must be emphasized, is not a prohibition of fighting words that are directed at certain persons or groups (which would be facially valid if it met the requirements of the Equal Protection Clause); but rather, a prohibition of fighting words that contain (as the Minnesota Supreme Court repeatedly emphasized) messages of "bias-motivated" hatred and in particular, as applied to this case, messages "based on virulent notions of racial supremacy." 64 N.W.2d at 508, 511. One must wholeheartedly agree with the Minnesota Supreme Court that "[i]t is the responsibility, even the obligation, of diverse communities to confront such notions in whatever form they appear," *id.* at 508, but the manner of that confrontation cannot consist of selective limitations upon speech. St. Paul's brief asserts that a general "fighting words" law would not meet the city's needs because only a content-specific measure can communicate to minority groups that the "group hatred" aspect of such speech "is not condoned by the majority." The point of the First Amendment is that majority preferences must be expressed in some fashion other than silencing speech on the basis of its content....

The content-based discrimination reflected in the St. Paul ordinance comes within neither any of the specific exceptions to the First Amendment prohibition we discussed earlier nor a more general exception for content discrimination that does not threaten censorship of ideas. It assuredly does not fall within the exception for content discrimination based on the very reasons why the particular class of speech at issue (here, fighting words) is proscribable....St. Paul has not singled out an especially offensive mode of expression—it has not, for example, selected for prohibition only those fighting words that communicate ideas in a threatening (as opposed to a merely obnoxious) manner. Rather, it has proscribed fighting words of whatever manner that communicate messages of racial, gender, or religious intolerance. Selectivity of this sort creates the possibility that the city is seeking to handicap the expression of particular ideas....

Finally, St. Paul and its amici defend the conclusion of the Minnesota Supreme Court that, even if the ordinance regulates expression based on hostility towards its protected ideological content, this discrimination is nonetheless justified because it is narrowly tailored to serve compelling state interests. Specifically, they assert that the ordinance helps to ensure the basic human rights of members of groups that have historically been subjected to discrimination, including the right of such group members to live in peace where they wish. We do not doubt that these interests are compelling, and that the ordinance can be said to promote them. But the "danger of censorship" presented by a facially content-based statute, *Leathers v. Medlock*, 499 U.S. at 448, 111 S.Ct. at 1444, requires that that weapon be employed only where it is "necessary to serve the asserted [compelling] interest," *Burson v. Freeman*, 504 U.S. 191, 199, 112 S.Ct. 1846, 1852, 119 L.Ed.2d 5 (1992) (plurality opinion); *Perry Ed. Assn. v. Perry Local Educators' Assn.*, 460 U.S. 37, 45, 103 S.Ct. 948, 954–955, 74 L.Ed.2d 794 (1983). The existence of adequate content-neutral alternatives thus "undercut[s] significantly" any defense of such a statute, *Boos v. Barry, supra*, 485 U.S. at 329, 108 S.Ct. at 1168, casting considerable doubt on the government's protestations that "the asserted justification is in fact an accurate description of the purpose and effect of the law," *Burson, supra*, 504 U.S. at 213, 112 S.Ct. at 1859 (KENNEDY, J., concurring). *See Boos, supra*, 485 U.S. at 324–329, 108 S.Ct. at 1165–1168; *cf. Minneapolis Star & Tribune Co. v. Minnesota Comm'r of Revenue*, 460 U.S. 575, 586–587, 103 S.Ct. 1365, 1372–1373, 75 L.Ed.2d 295 (1983). The dispositive question in this case, therefore, is whether content discrimination is reasonably necessary to achieve St. Paul's compelling interests; it plainly is not. An ordinance not limited to the favored topics, for example, would have precisely the same beneficial effect. In fact the only interest distinctively served by the content limitation is that of displaying the city council's special hostility towards the particular biases thus singled out. That is precisely what the First Amendment forbids. The politicians of St. Paul are entitled to express that hostility—but not through the means of imposing unique limitations upon speakers who (however benightedly) disagree.

Let there be no mistake about our belief that burning a cross in someone's front yard is reprehensible. But St. Paul has sufficient means at its disposal to prevent such behavior without adding the First Amendment to the fire.

The judgment of the Minnesota Supreme Court is reversed, and the case is remanded for proceedings not inconsistent with this opinion....

---

## Vivian RICE v. THE PALADIN ENTERPRISES, INCORPORATED, a/k/a The Paladin Press
No. 96-2412, 128 F.3d 233
United States Court of Appeals, Fourth Circuit.
November 10, 1997

LUTTIG, Circuit Judge:

> To Those Who Think,
> To Those Who Do,
> To Those Who Succeed.
> Success is nothing more than taking advantage of an opportunity.

A woman recently asked how I could, in good conscience, write an instruction book on murder.

"How can you live with yourself if someone uses what you write to go out and take a human life?" she whined.

I am afraid she was quite offended by my answer.

It is my opinion that the professional hit man fills a need in society and is, at times, the only alternative for "personal" justice. Moreover, if my advice and the proven methods in this book are followed, certainly no one will ever know....

[W]ithin the pages of this book you will learn one of the most successful methods of operation used by an independent contractor. You will follow the procedures of a man who works alone, without backing of organized crime or on a personal vendetta. Step by step you will be taken from research to equipment selection to job preparation to successful job completion. You will learn where to find employment, how much to charge, and what you can, and cannot, do with the money you earn....

[When you go to commit the murder, you will need] several (at least four or five pairs) of flesh-tone, tight-fitting surgical gloves. If these are not available, rubber gloves can be purchased at a reasonable price in the prescription department of most drug stores in boxes of 100. You will wear the gloves when you assemble and disassemble your weapons as well as on the actual job. Because the metal gun parts cause the rubber to wear quickly, it is a good practice to change and dispose of worn gloves several times during each operation.

[The bag you take to the kill also] should contain a few pairs of cheap handcuffs, usually available at pawn shops or army surplus stores.

Dress, as well as disguises, should be coordinated according to the job setting.

Black, dark brown or olive green clothes do not stand out and will probably appear at first glance to be a mechanic or delivery driver's uniform....And underneath, you can wear your street clothes for a quick change after the job is completed....

Although several shots fired in succession offer quick and relatively humane death to the victim, there are instances when other methods of extermination are called for. The employer may want you to gather certain information from the mark before you do away with him. At other times, the assignment may call for torture or disfigurement as a "lesson" for the survivors....

Then, some day, when you've done and seen it all; when there doesn't seem to be any challenge left or any new frontier left to conquer, you might just feel cocky enough to write a book about it.

Selected passages from *Hit Man: A Technical Manual for Independent Contractors*. [The court cited several additional passages from the book as representative, both in substance and presentation, of the instructions it contains. The court also stated that it "even felt it necessary to omit portions of these few illustrative passages in order to minimize the danger to the public from their repetition herein."]...

On the night of March 3, 1993, readied by these instructions and steeled by these seductive adjurations from *Hit Man: A Technical Manual for Independent Contractors*, a copy of which was subsequently found in his apartment, James Perry brutally murdered Mildred Horn, her eight-year-old quadriplegic son Trevor, and Trevor's nurse, Janice Saunders, by shooting Mildred Horn and Saunders through the eyes and by strangling Trevor Horn. Perry's despicable crime was not one of vengeance; he did not know any of his victims. Nor did he commit the murders in the course of another offense. Perry acted instead as a contract killer, a "hit man," hired by Mildred Horn's ex-husband, Lawrence Horn, to murder Horn's family so that Horn would receive the $2 million that his eight-year-old son had received in settlement for injuries that had previously left him paralyzed for life. At the time of the murders, this money was held in trust for the benefit of Trevor, and, under the terms of the trust instrument, the trust money was to be distributed tax-free to Lawrence in the event of Mildred's and Trevor's deaths.

In soliciting, preparing for, and committing these murders, Perry meticulously followed countless of *Hit Man*'s 130 pages of detailed factual instructions on how to murder and to become a professional killer....

[T]he parties stipulate: "The parties agree that the sole issue to be decided by the Court...is whether the First Amendment is a complete defense, as a matter of law, to the civil action set forth in the plaintiffs' Complaint. All other issues of law and fact are specifically reserved for subsequent proceedings."

Paladin, for example, has stipulated for purposes of summary judgment that Perry followed the above-enumerated instructions from *Hit Man*, as well as instructions from another Paladin publication, *How to Make a Disposable Silencer, Vol. II*, in planning, executing, and attempting to cover up the murders of Mildred and Trevor Horn and Janice Saunders. Paladin has stipulated not only that, in marketing Hit Man, Paladin "intended to attract and assist criminals and would-be criminals who desire information and instructions on how to commit crimes," but also that it "intended and had knowledge" that *Hit Man* actually "would be used, upon receipt, by criminals and would-be criminals to plan and execute the crime of murder for hire." Indeed, the publisher has even stipulated that, through publishing and selling *Hit Man*, it assisted Perry in particular in the perpetration of the very murders for which the victims' families now attempt to hold Paladin civilly liable.[2]...

In the seminal case of *Brandenburg v. Ohio*, 395 U.S. 444, 89 S.Ct. 1827, 23 L.Ed.2d 430 (1969), the Supreme Court held that abstract advocacy of lawlessness is protected speech under the First Amendment. Although the Court provided little explanation for this holding in its brief per curiam opinion, it is evident the Court recognized from our own history that such a right to advocate lawlessness is, almost paradoxically, one of the ultimate safeguards of liberty. Even in a society of laws, one of the most indispensable freedoms is that to express in the most impassioned terms the most passionate disagreement with the laws themselves, the institutions of, and created by, law, and the individual officials with whom the laws and institutions are entrusted. Without the freedom to criticize that which constrains, there is no freedom at all.

However, while even speech advocating lawlessness has long enjoyed protections under the First Amendment, it is equally well established that speech which, in its effect, is tantamount to legitimately proscribable nonexpressive conduct may itself be legitimately proscribed, punished, or regulated incidentally to the constitutional enforcement of generally applicable statutes. *Cf. Cohen v. Cowles Media Co.*, 501 U.S. 663, 669,

---

2. The...fact stipulation[s] of the parties read[ in pertinent part]:...

  (4) Defendants concede, for purposes of this motion, and for no other purposes, that:

    a. [D]efendants engaged in a marketing strategy intended to attract and assist criminals and would-be criminals who desire information and instructions on how to commit crimes; and

    b. [I]n publishing, marketing, advertising and distributing *Hit Man* and *Silencers*, defendants intended and had knowledge that their publications would be used, upon receipt, by criminals and would-be criminals to plan and execute the crime of murder for hire, in the manner set forth in the publications.

    c. The conditional factual concessions made in this ¶ 4 relate only to the defendants' state of mind, and do not preclude defendants from contending that defendants' published words, in and of themselves, were neither directed at causing imminent unlawful action nor likely to produce such action, for purposes of the doctrine of *Brandenburg v. Ohio*, 395 U.S. 444, 89 S.Ct. 1827, 23 L.Ed.2d 430 (1969)....

  (7) Defendants concede, for the purpose of this motion and for no other purposes, that in publishing, distributing and selling *Hit Man* and *Silencers* to Perry, defendants assisted him in the subsequent perpetration of the murders which are the subject of this litigation, [as alleged in the complaint].

111 S.Ct. 2513, 2518, 115 L.Ed.2d 586 (1991) (noting "well-established line of decisions holding that generally applicable laws do not offend the First Amendment simply because their enforcement against the press has incidental effects on its ability to gather and report the news"). As no less a First Amendment absolutist than Justice Black wrote for the Supreme Court almost fifty years ago in *Giboney v. Empire Storage & Ice Co.*, in rejecting a First Amendment challenge to an injunction forbidding unionized distributors from picketing to force an illegal business arrangement:

> It rarely has been suggested that the constitutional freedom for speech and press extends its immunity to speech or writing used as an integral part of conduct in violation of a valid criminal statute. We reject the contention now....It is true that the agreements and course of conduct here were as in most instances brought about through speaking or writing. But it has never been deemed an abridgment of freedom of speech or press to make a course of conduct illegal merely because the conduct was in part initiated, evidenced, or carried out by means of language, either spoken, written, or printed. Such an expansive interpretation of the constitutional guaranties of speech and press would make it practically impossible ever to enforce laws against agreements in restraint of trade as well as many other agreements and conspiracies deemed injurious to society.

336 U.S. 490, 498, 502, 69 S.Ct. 684, 688–89, 691, 93 L.Ed. 834 (1949) (citations omitted). And as the Court more recently reaffirmed:

> Although agreements to engage in illegal conduct undoubtedly possess some element of association, the State may ban such illegal agreements without trenching on any right of association protected by the First Amendment. The fact that such an agreement necessarily takes the form of words does not confer upon it, or upon the underlying conduct, the constitutional immunities that the First Amendment extends to speech. [W]hile a solicitation to enter into an agreement arguably crosses the sometimes hazy line distinguishing conduct from pure speech, such a solicitation, even though it may have an impact in the political arena, remains in essence an invitation to engage in an illegal exchange for private profit, and may properly be prohibited.

*Brown v. Hartlage*, 456 U.S. 45, 55, 102 S.Ct. 1523, 1529–30, 71 L.Ed.2d 732 (1982); *see also Osborne v. Ohio*, 495 U.S. 103, 110, 110 S.Ct. 1691, 1696–97, 109 L.Ed.2d 98 (1990) (quoting *Giboney*, 336 U.S. at 498, 69 S.Ct. at 688–89); *New York v. Ferber*, 458 U.S. 747, 761–62, 102 S.Ct. 3348, 3356–57, 73 L.Ed.2d 1113 (1982) (same*); Ohralik v. Ohio State Bar Ass'n*, 436 U.S. 447, 456, 98 S.Ct. 1912, 1918–19, 56 L.Ed.2d 444 (1978) (quoting *Giboney*, 336 U.S. at 502, 69 S.Ct. at 690–91); *National Organization for Women v. Operation Rescue*, 37 F.3d 646, 656 (D.C. Cir. 1994) ("That 'aiding and abetting' of an illegal act may be carried out through speech is no bar to its illegality."); *United States v. Varani*, 435 F.2d 758, 762 (6th Cir. 1970) ("[S]peech is not protected by the First Amendment when it is the very vehicle of the crime itself."); Laurence H. Tribe, *American Constitutional Law* 837 (2d ed. 1988) ("[T]he law need not treat differently the crime of one man who sells a bomb to terrorists and that of another who publishes an instructional manual for terrorists on how to build their own bombs out of old Volkswagen parts.").

Were the First Amendment to bar or to limit government regulation of such "speech brigaded with action," *Brandenburg*, 395 U.S. at 456, 89 S.Ct. at 1834 (Douglas, J., concurring), the government would be powerless to protect the public from countless of even the most pernicious criminal acts and civil wrongs. *See, e.g.,* Model Penal Code § 223.4 (extortion or blackmail); *id.* § 240.2 (threats and other improper influences in official and political matters); *id.* § 241 (perjury and various cognate crimes); *id.* § 5.02 and § 2.06(3)(a)(i) (criminal solicitation); 18 U.S.C. § 871 (threatening the life of the President); Model Penal Code § 5.03 (conspiracy); *id.* § 250.4 (harassment); *id.* § 224.1 (forgery); *id.* § 210.5(2) (successfully soliciting another to commit suicide); *id.* § 250.3 (false public alarms); and the like....

In particular as it concerns the instant case, the speech-act doctrine has long been invoked to sustain convictions for aiding and abetting the commission of criminal offenses. Indeed, every court that has addressed the issue, including this court, has held that the First Amendment does not necessarily pose a bar to liability for aiding and abetting a crime, even when such aiding and abetting takes the form of the spoken or written word.

Thus, in a case indistinguishable in principle from that before us, the Ninth Circuit expressly held in *United States v. Barnett*, 667 F.2d 835 (9th Cir. 1982), that the First Amendment does not provide publishers a defense as a matter of law to charges of aiding and abetting a crime through the publication and distribution of instructions on how to make illegal drugs. In rejecting the publisher's argument that there could be no probable cause to believe that a crime had been committed because its actions were shielded by the First Amendment, and thus *a fortiori* there was no probable cause to support the search pursuant to which the drug manufacturing instructions were found, the Court of Appeals explicitly foreclosed a First Amendment defense not only to the search itself, but also to a later prosecution:

> To the extent... that Barnett appears to contend that he is immune from search or prosecution because he uses the printed word in encouraging and counseling others in the commission of a crime, we hold expressly that the first amendment does not provide a defense as a matter of law to such conduct.

*Id.* at 843; *see also id.* at 842 ("The first amendment does not provide a defense to a criminal charge simply because the actor uses words to carry out his illegal purpose. Crimes, including that of aiding and abetting, frequently involve the use of speech as part of the criminal transaction."). The Ninth Circuit derided as a "specious syllogism" with "no support in the law" the publisher's argument that the First Amendment protected his sale of the instruction manual simply because the First Amendment protects the written word. *Id.* at 842....

The principle of *Barnett*, that the provision of instructions that aid and abet another in the commission of a criminal offense is unprotected by the First Amendment, has been uniformly accepted, and the principle has been applied to the aiding and abetting of innumerable crimes.

Notably, then-Judge Kennedy, in express reliance upon *Barnett*, invoked the principle in *United States v. Freeman* to sustain convictions for the aiding and abetting of tax fraud. 761 F.2d 549, 552–53 (9th Cir. 1985), *cert. denied*, 476 U.S. 1120, 106 S.Ct. 1982, 90 L.Ed.2d 664 (1986). In *Freeman*, the Ninth Circuit concluded that the defendant could be held criminally liable for counseling tax evasion at seminars held in protest of the tax laws, even though the speech that served as the predicate for the conviction "spr[ang] from the anterior motive to effect political or social change." 761 F.2d at 551. Said the court:

> [T]he First Amendment is quite irrelevant if the intent of the actor and the objective meaning of the words used are so close in time and purpose to a substantive evil as to become part of the ultimate crime itself. In those instances,

where speech becomes an integral part of the crime, a First Amendment defense is foreclosed even if the prosecution rests on words alone.

*Id.* at 552 (citations omitted). Thus, the court held that a First Amendment instruction was required only for those counts as to which there was evidence that the speaker "directed his comments at the unfairness of the tax laws generally, without soliciting or counseling a violation of the law in an immediate sense [and] made statements that, at least arguably, were of abstract generality, remote from advice to commit a specific criminal act." *Id.* at 551–52. For those counts as to which the defendant, through his speech, directly assisted in the preparation and review of false tax returns, the court held that the defendant was not entitled to a First Amendment instruction at all. *Id.* at 552. *See also United States v. Mendelsohn*, 896 F.2d 1183, 1186 (9th Cir. 1990) (holding *Brandenburg* inapplicable to a conviction for conspiring to transport and aiding and abetting the interstate transportation of wagering paraphernalia, where defendants disseminated a computer program that assisted others to record and analyze bets on sporting events; program was "too instrumental in and intertwined with the performance of criminal activity to retain first amendment protection")....

> The cloak of the First Amendment envelops critical, but abstract, discussions of existing laws, but lends no protection to speech which urges the listeners to commit violations of current law. *Brandenburg v. Ohio*, 395 U.S. 444, 89 S.Ct. 1827, 23 L.Ed.2d 430; *United States v. Buttorff*, 572 F.2d 619 (8th Cir. 1978). It was no theoretical discussion of non-compliance with laws; action was urged; the advice was heeded, and false forms were filed.

*Kelley*, 769 F.2d at 217. Analogously, we held in *United States v. Fleschner*, 98 F.3d 155 (4th Cir. 1996), *cert. denied*, — U.S. —, 117 S.Ct. 2484, 138 L.Ed.2d 992 (1997), that defendants who instructed and advised meeting attendees to file unlawful tax returns were not entitled to a First Amendment jury instruction on the charge of conspiracy to defraud the United States of income tax revenue because "[t]he defendants' words and acts were not remote from the commission of the criminal acts." 98 F.3d at 158–59.

Indeed, as the Department of Justice recently advised Congress, the law is now well established that the First Amendment, and *Brandenburg*'s "imminence" requirement in particular, generally poses little obstacle to the punishment of speech that constitutes criminal aiding and abetting, because "culpability in such cases is premised, not on defendants' 'advocacy' of criminal conduct, but on defendants' successful efforts to assist others by detailing to them the means of accomplishing the crimes." Department of Justice, "Report on the Availability of Bombmaking Information, the Extent to Which Its Dissemination is Controlled by Federal Law, and the Extent to Which Such Dissemination May Be Subject to Regulation Consistent with the First Amendment to the United States Constitution" 37 (April 1997) (footnote omitted) [hereinafter "DOJ Report"]; *see also id.* ("[T]he question of whether criminal conduct is 'imminent' is relevant for constitutional purposes only where, as in *Brandenburg* itself, the government attempts to restrict advocacy, as such.").[3] And, while there is considerably less authority on the sub-

---

3. Congress, in the Antiterrorism and Effective Death Penalty Act of 1996 ["the AEDPA"], Pub.L. No. 104-132, 110 Stat. 1214, 1297, required the Attorney General to conduct a study concerning, *inter alia*, the extent to which there is available public access to materials instructing on "how to make bombs, destructive devices, or weapons of mass destruction;" the application of then-existing federal laws to such materials; and the extent to which the First Amendment protects such materials and their private and commercial distribution. The statutory mandate to the Attorney General was prompted by legislation proposed by Senators Feinstein and Biden in the aftermath of the Oklahoma City bombing, which would criminalize the teaching or demonstration of the

ject, we assume that those speech acts which the government may criminally prosecute with little or no concern for the First Amendment, the government may likewise subject to civil penalty or make subject to private causes of action. *Compare Garrison v. Louisiana*, 379 U.S. 64, 85 S.Ct. 209, 13 L.Ed.2d 125 (1964) (applying the same "actual malice" standard to both criminal libel prosecutions and private defamation actions) *with New York Times Co. v. Sullivan*, 376 U.S. 254, 84 S.Ct. 710, 11 L.Ed.2d 686 (1964). *Cf. Cohen*, 501 U.S. 663, 111 S.Ct. 2513, 115 L.Ed.2d 586 (finding in civil promissory estoppel case that First Amendment does not bar liability for newspaper's publication of confidential source's name); *Zacchini v. Scripps-Howard Broadcasting Co.*, 433 U.S. 562, 97 S.Ct. 2849, 53 L.Ed.2d 965 (1977) (First Amendment does not bar liability for common law tort of unlawful appropriation of "right to publicity" where television station broadcast "human cannonball" act in its entirety without plaintiff's authorization*); Harper & Row, Publishers, Inc. v. Nation Enterprises*, 471 U.S. 539, 105 S.Ct. 2218, 85 L.Ed.2d 588 (1985) (rejecting First Amendment defense to copyright infringement action against magazine for printing unauthorized presidential memoir excerpts). Even if this is not universally so, we believe it must be true at least where the government's interest in preventing the particular conduct at issue is incontrovertibly compelling....

Here, it is alleged, and a jury could reasonably find, that Paladin aided and abetted the murders at issue through the quintessential speech act of providing step-by-step instructions for murder (replete with photographs, diagrams, and narration) so comprehensive and detailed that it is as if the instructor were literally present with the would-be murderer not only in the preparation and planning, but in the actual commission of, and follow-up to, the murder; here is not even a hint that the aid was provided in the form of speech that might constitute abstract advocacy. As the district court itself concluded, *Hit Man* "merely teaches what must be done to implement a professional hit." Moreover, although we do not believe such would be necessary, we are satisfied a jury could readily find that the provided instructions not only have no, or virtually no, non-instructional communicative value, but also that their only instructional communicative "value" is the indisputably illegitimate one of training persons how to murder and to engage in the business of murder for hire. *See id.; see also id.* at 221 ("This Court,

---

manufacture of explosive materials "if the person intends or knows that such explosive materials or information will likely be used for, or in furtherance of" specified criminal offenses.

The AEDPA required the Attorney General to submit to the Congress a report on these subjects and to make that report available to the public. Recognizing that the exhaustive legal analysis set forth in that report was directly relevant to the issues pending before us, the parties jointly moved for, and we granted them, permission to file the report with the court. The decision we reach today, which, as noted, was urged upon us by Attorney General Reno and the Department of Justice, follows from the principal conclusion reached by the Attorney General and the Department in that report:

> The First Amendment would impose substantial constraints on any attempt to proscribe indiscriminately the dissemination of bombmaking information. The government generally may not, except in rare circumstances, punish persons either for advocating lawless action or for disseminating truthful information—including information that would be dangerous if used—that such persons have obtained lawfully. However, the constitutional analysis is quite different where the government punishes speech that is an integral part of a transaction involving conduct the government otherwise is empowered to prohibit; such "speech acts"—for instance, many cases of inchoate crimes such as aiding and abetting and conspiracy—may be proscribed without much, if any, concern about the First Amendment, since it is merely incidental that such "conduct" takes the form of speech.

DOJ Report at 2.

quite candidly, personally finds *Hit Man* to be reprehensible and devoid of any significant redeeming social value").

Aid and assistance in the form of this kind of speech bears no resemblance to the
"theoretical advocacy," *Scales v. United States*, 367 U.S. 203, 235, 81 S.Ct. 1469, 1489, 6
L.Ed.2d 782 (1961), the advocacy of "principles divorced from action," *Yates v. United
States*, 354 U.S. 298, 320, 77 S.Ct. 1064, 1077, 1 L.Ed.2d 1356 (1957), *overruled on other
grounds, Burks v. United States*, 437 U.S. 1, 98 S.Ct. 2141, 57 L.Ed.2d 1 (1978), the "doctrinal justification," *id.* at 321, 77 S.Ct. at 1078, "the mere abstract teaching [of] the
moral propriety or even moral necessity for a resort to force and violence," *Brandenburg*, 395 U.S. at 448, 89 S.Ct. at 1830 (quoting *Noto v. United States*, 367 U.S. 290,
297–98, 81 S.Ct. 1517, 1520–22, 6 L.Ed.2d 836 (1961)), or any of the other forms of
discourse critical of government, its policies, and its leaders, which have always animated, and to this day continue to animate, the First Amendment. Indeed, this detailed,
focused instructional assistance to those contemplating or in the throes of planning
murder is the antithesis of speech protected under *Brandenburg*. It is the teaching of the
"techniques" of violence, *Scales*, 367 U.S. at 233, 81 S.Ct. at 1488, the "advocacy and
teaching of concrete action," *Yates*, 354 U.S. at 320, 77 S.Ct. at 1077, the
"prepar[ation]...for violent action and [the] steeling...to such action," *Brandenburg*,
395 U.S. at 448, 89 S.Ct. at 1830 (quoting *Noto*, 367 U.S. at 297–98, 81 S.Ct. at
1520–21). It is the instruction in the methods of terror of which Justice Douglas spoke
in *Dennis v. United States*, when he said, "If this were a case where those who claimed
protection under the First Amendment were teaching the techniques of sabotage...I
would have no doubts. The freedom to speak is not absolute; the teaching of methods
of terror...should be beyond the pale...." 341 U.S. 494, 581, 71 S.Ct. 857, 903, 95 L.Ed.
1137 (1951) (Douglas, J., dissenting). As such, the murder instructions in *Hit Man* are,
collectively, a textbook example of the type of speech that the Supreme Court has quite
purposely left unprotected, and the prosecution of which, criminally or civilly, has historically been thought subject to few, if any, First Amendment constraints. Accordingly,
we hold that the First Amendment does not pose a bar to the plaintiffs' civil aiding and
abetting cause of action against Paladin Press. If, as precedent uniformly confirms, the
states have the power to regulate speech that aids and abets crime, then certainly they
have the power to regulate the speech at issue here....

[A] reasonable jury clearly could conclude from the stipulations of the parties, and,
apart from the stipulations, from the text of *Hit Man* itself and the other facts of record,
that Paladin aided and abetted in Perry's triple murder by providing detailed instructions on the techniques of murder and murder for hire with the specific intent of aiding
and abetting the commission of these violent crimes....

Indeed, Paladin's protests notwithstanding, this book constitutes the archetypal example of speech which, because it methodically and comprehensively prepares and steels
its audience to specific criminal conduct through exhaustively detailed instructions on
the planning, commission, and concealment of criminal conduct, finds no preserve in
the First Amendment. To the extent that confirmation of this is even needed, given the
book's content and declared purpose to be "an instruction book on murder," *Hit Man* at
ix, that confirmation is found in the stark contrast between this assassination manual
and the speech heretofore held to be deserving of constitutional protection....

At the risk of belaboring the obvious, but in order to appreciate the encyclopedic
character of *Hit Man*'s instructions, one need only consider the following chapter-by-
chapter synopsis.

Chapter One of Hit Man, entitled "The Beginning—Mental and Physical Preparation," starts by outlining the "essential" steps to becoming a professional killer....

Chapter Two of the book, entitled "Equipment—Selection and Purpose," imparts a wealth of information on the "basic equipment" the "beginner" will need as tools of his trade, *id.* at 21, and provides detailed instructions as to the equipment's use....

Chapter Three, entitled "The Disposable Silencer—A Poor Man's Access to a Rich Man's Toy," teaches the reader, with step-by-step instructions and accompanying photographic illustration, how to construct a "whisper-quiet," "inexpensive," and "effective" disposable silencer that is "reusable for over four hundred rounds." These directions are designed to allow the "amateur" to construct disposable silencers, which, the book explains, are "one of the most important tools a professional will ever have." As the book explains, these "same directions can be followed successfully to construct a silencer for any weapon, with only the size of the drill rod used for alignment changed...." *Id.* at 39.

*Hit Man*'s Chapter Four, entitled "More Than One Way To Kill a Rabbit—The Direct Hit is Not Your Only Alternative," includes discursive instructions on numerous additional methods of killing and torture....

The next chapter, entitled "Homework and Surveillance—Mapping a Plan and Checking It for Accuracy," instructs on how to obtain information about the victim from the client. It explains the importance of finding out information such as whether the victim has a dog or other pet that might provide a warning of the impending assassination, the layout of the victim's residence, and whether the victim has roommates or neighbors. The chapter includes a lengthy "sample information sheet" that may be used in planning a first kill.

Chapter Six, entitled "Opportunity Knocks—Finding Employment, What to Charge, What to Avoid," teaches readers how to find someone who will hire their services as professional killers. The chapter explains where to find potential employers, what to look for in such persons, and what to charge for each murder....

In the following chapter, titled "Getting the Job Done Right—Why the Described Hit Went Down the Way It Did," *Hit Man* provides instructions for reaching the victim's location, transporting tools, preparing to commit the murder, and cleaning up the crime scene and escaping after the killing....

Chapter 8, entitled "Danger: Ego, Women, and Partners—Controlling Your Situation" instructs the reader on how, as a professional killer, to use money, women, and partners....

The final chapter of *Hit Man*, entitled "Legally Illegal," includes various sections instructing the reader on how and where to purchase false identification, how to make false identification, how to launder illegal money, and how to act in encounters with law enforcement officers. For example, the book instructs on how to "launder" "illegal money" through the use of a tax haven in the Cayman Islands....

Indeed, one finds in *Hit Man* little, if anything, even remotely characterizable as the abstract criticism that *Brandenburg* jealously protects. *Hit Man* 's detailed, concrete instructions and adjurations to murder stand in stark contrast to the vague, rhetorical threats of politically or socially motivated violence that have historically been considered part and parcel of the impassioned criticism of laws, policies, and government indispensable in a free society and rightly protected under *Brandenburg*. The speech of *Hit Man* defies even comparison with the Klansman's chilling, but protected, statement in *Brandenburg* itself that, "[the Ku Klux Klan is] not a revengent organization, but if our President, our Congress, our Supreme Court, continues to suppress the white, Caucasian race, it's possible that there might have to be some revengeance taken," 395 U.S. at 446, 89 S.Ct. at 1829; the protestor's inciteful, but protected, chant in *Hess v. Indiana*, 414 U.S. 105, 108, 94 S.Ct. 326, 328–29, 38 L.Ed.2d 303 (1973), that "[w]e'll take the fucking street again;" the NAACP speaker's threat, rhetorical in its context, to boycott violators that "[i]f we catch any of you going in any of them racist stores, we're gonna break your damn neck," which was held to be protected in *NAACP v. Claiborne Hardware Co.*, 458 U.S. 886, 902, 102 S.Ct. 3409, 3420, 73 L.Ed.2d 1215 (1982); or the draft protestor's crude, but protected, blustering in Watts that "[i]f they ever make me carry a rifle the first man I want to get in my sights is L.B.J," *Watts v. United States*, 394 U.S. 705, 706, 89 S.Ct. 1399, 1401, 22 L.Ed.2d 664 (1969).

Plaintiffs observed in their submissions before the district court that,

> *Hit Man* is not political manifesto, not revolutionary diatribe, not propaganda, advocacy, or protest, not an outpouring of conscience or credo.... It contains no discussion of ideas, no argument, no information about politics, religion, science, art, or culture...it offers no agenda for self-governance, no insight into the issues of the day....

And, this is apt observation. *Hit Man* is none of this. Ideas simply are neither the focus nor the burden of the book. To the extent that there are any passages within *Hit Man's* pages that arguably are in the nature of ideas or abstract advocacy, those sentences are so very few in number and isolated as to be legally of no significance whatsoever. *Cf. Kois v. Wisconsin*, 408 U.S. 229, 231, 92 S.Ct. 2245, 2246, 33 L.Ed.2d 312 (1972) ("A quotation from Voltaire in the flyleaf of a book will not constitutionally redeem an otherwise obscene publication."); *see also Miller*, 413 U.S. at 24, 93 S.Ct. at 2614–15; *Penthouse International, Ltd. v. McAuliffe*, 610 F.2d 1353 (5th Cir. 1980), *cert. dismissed*, 447 U.S. 931, 100 S.Ct. 3031, 65 L.Ed.2d 1131 (1980). *Hit Man* is, pure and simple, a step-by-step murder manual, a training book for assassins. There is nothing even arguably tentative or recondite in the book's promotion of, and instruction in, murder.[10] To the contrary, the book directly and unmistakably urges concrete violations of the laws against murder and murder for hire and coldly instructs on the commission of these crimes. The Supreme Court has never protected as abstract advocacy speech so explicit in its palpable entreaties to violent crime....

Paladin, joined by a spate of media amici, including many of the major networks, newspapers, and publishers, contends that any decision recognizing even a potential cause of action against Paladin will have far-reaching chilling effects on the rights of free speech and press....Paladin and amici insist that recognizing the existence of a cause of action against Paladin predicated on aiding and abetting will subject broadcasters and publishers to liability whenever someone imitates or "copies" conduct that is either described or depicted in their broadcasts, publications, or movies. This is simply not true. In the "copycat" context, it will presumably never be the case that the broadcaster or publisher actually intends, through its description or depiction, to assist another or others in the commission of violent crime; rather, the information for the dissemina-

---

10. The several brief "disclaimers" and "warnings" in *Hit Man's* advertisement description and on its cover, that the book's instructions are "for informational purposes only!" and "for academic study only!," and that "[n]either the author nor the publisher assumes responsibility for the use or misuse of the information contained in this book," are plainly insufficient in themselves to alter the objective understanding of the hundreds of thousands of words that follow, which, in purely factual and technical terms, tutor the book's readers in the methods and techniques of killing. These "disclaimers" and "warnings" obviously were affixed in order to titillate, rather than "to dissuade readers from engaging in the activity [the book] describes," as the district court suggested they might be understood.

tion of which liability is sought to be imposed will actually have been misused vis-à-vis the use intended, not, as here, used precisely as intended. It would be difficult to overstate the significance of this difference insofar as the potential liability to which the media might be exposed by our decision herein is concerned.

And, perhaps most importantly, there will almost never be evidence proffered from which a jury even could reasonably conclude that the producer or publisher possessed the actual intent to assist criminal activity. In only the rarest case, as here where the publisher has stipulated in almost taunting defiance that it intended to assist murderers and other criminals, will there be evidence extraneous to the speech itself which would support a finding of the requisite intent; surely few will, as Paladin has, "stand up and proclaim to the world that because they are publishers they have a unique constitutional right to aid and abet murder." Moreover, in contrast to the case before us, in virtually every "copycat" case, there will be lacking in the speech itself any basis for a permissible inference that the "speaker" intended to assist and facilitate the criminal conduct described or depicted. Of course, with few, if any, exceptions, the speech which gives rise to the copycat crime will not directly and affirmatively promote the criminal conduct, even if, in some circumstances, it incidentally glamorizes and thereby indirectly promotes such conduct.

Additionally, not only will a political, informational, educational, entertainment, or other wholly legitimate purpose for the description or depiction be demonstrably apparent; but the description or depiction of the criminality will be of such a character that an inference of impermissible intent on the part of the producer or publisher would be unwarranted as a matter of law. So, for example, for almost any broadcast, book, movie, or song that one can imagine, an inference of unlawful motive from the description or depiction of particular criminal conduct therein would almost never be reasonable, for not only will there be (and demonstrably so) a legitimate and lawful purpose for these communications, but the contexts in which the descriptions or depictions appear will themselves negate a purpose on the part of the producer or publisher to assist others in their undertaking of the described or depicted conduct. *Compare Miller,* 413 U.S. 15, 93 S.Ct. 2607.

Paladin contends that exposing it to liability under the circumstances presented here will necessarily expose broadcasters and publishers of the news, in particular, to liability when persons mimic activity either reported on or captured on film footage and disseminated in the form of broadcast news. This contention, as well, is categorically wrong. News reporting, we can assume, no matter how explicit it is in its description or depiction of criminal activity, could never serve as a basis for aiding and abetting liability consistent with the First Amendment. It will be self-evident in the context of news reporting, if nowhere else, that neither the intent of the reporter nor the purpose of the report is to facilitate repetition of the crime or other conduct reported upon, but, rather, merely to report on the particular event, and thereby to inform the public.

A decision that Paladin may be liable under the circumstances of this case is not even tantamount to a holding that all publishers of instructional manuals may be liable for the misconduct that ensues when one follows the instructions which appear in those manuals. Admittedly, a holding that Paladin is not entitled to an absolute defense to the plaintiffs' claims here may not bode well for those publishers, if any, of factually detailed instructional books, similar to *Hit Man,* which are devoted exclusively to teaching the techniques of violent activities that are criminal *per se.* But, in holding that a defense to liability may not inure to publishers for their dissemination of such manuals of criminal conduct, we do not address ourselves to the potential liability of a publisher for the criminal use of published instructions on activity that is either entirely lawful, or lawful or not depending upon the circumstances of its occurrence. Assuming, as we do, that liability could not be imposed in these circumstances on a finding of mere foresee-ability or knowledge that the instructions might be misused for a criminal purpose, the chances that claims arising from the publication of instructional manuals like these can withstand motions for summary judgment directed to the issue of intent seem to us re-mote indeed, at least absent some substantial confirmation of specific intent like that that exists in this case.

Thus, while the "horribles" paraded before us by Paladin and amici have quite prop-erly prompted us to examine and reexamine the established authorities on which plain-tiffs' case firmly rests, we regard them ultimately as but anticipatory of cases wholly un-like the one we must decide today.

Paladin Press in this case has stipulated that it specifically targeted the market of murderers, would-be murderers, and other criminals for sale of its murder manual. Pal-adin has stipulated both that it had knowledge and that it intended that *Hit Man* would immediately be used by criminals and would-be criminals in the solicitation, planning, and commission of murder and murder for hire. And Paladin has stipulated that, through publishing and selling *Hit Man*, it "assisted" Perry in particular in the perpe-tration of the brutal triple murders for which plaintiffs now seek to hold the publisher liable. Beyond these startling stipulations, it is alleged, and the record would support, that Paladin assisted Perry through the quintessential speech act of providing Perry with detailed factual instructions on how to prepare for, commit, and cover up his murders, instructions which themselves embody not so much as a hint of the theoretical advo-cacy of principles divorced from action that is the hallmark of protected speech. And it is alleged, and a jury could find, that Paladin's assistance assumed the form of speech with little, if any, purpose beyond the unlawful one of facilitating murder.

Paladin's astonishing stipulations, coupled with the extraordinary comprehensiveness, detail, and clarity of *Hit Man*'s instructions for criminal activity and murder in particular, the boldness of its palpable exhortation to murder, the alarming power and effectiveness of its peculiar form of instruction, the notable absence from its text of the kind of ideas for the protection of which the First Amendment exists, and the book's evident lack of any even arguably legitimate purpose beyond the promotion and teaching of murder, render this case unique in the law. In at least these circumstances, we are confident that the First Amendment does not erect the absolute bar to the imposition of civil liability for which Paladin Press and amici contend. Indeed, to hold that the First Amendment for-bids liability in such circumstances as a matter of law would fly in the face of all precedent of which we are aware, not only from the courts of appeals but from the Supreme Court of the United States itself. *Hit Man* is, we are convinced, the speech that even Justice Dou-glas, with his unrivaled devotion to the First Amendment, counseled without any equivo-cation "should be beyond the pale" under a Constitution that reserves to the people the ultimate and necessary authority to adjudge some conduct—and even some speech—fundamentally incompatible with the liberties they have secured unto themselves.

The judgment of the district court is hereby reversed, and the case remanded for trial.

---

The parties settled their dispute in May 2000. Paladin Press reportedly agreed to make a multi-million dollar payment and to refrain from selling additional copies of the book. *See, e.g.,* 60 Minutes (CBS Television Broadcast, Sept. 15, 1999).

The text of the book *Hit Man* has been available on the World Wide Web, however. As of February 2000, the number of times it was downloaded "was swiftly approaching the number of sales of the paper-and-ink version during its 13-year life." Mike Godwin, *The Net Effect*, Am. Law. (Feb. 2000) at 47. The *American Lawyer Magazine* published the web-site where the text could be found, and suggested that the availability of the book on-line "makes it possible to evaluate the First Amendment arguments in a clearer light." *Id.* at 48.

Other titles published by Paladin Press include: *Be Your Own Undertaker: How to Dispose of a Dead Body* and *Guerrilla's Arsenal: Advanced Techniques for Making Explosives and Time-Delay Bombs*. Paladin Press has maintained that the company was "purveying information," and sold books to such readers as physicians, lawyers, and law enforcement agencies. *See* 60 Minutes (CBS Television Broadcast, Sept. 15, 1999).

---

## Notes and Questions

1.  Recall the discussion on the free speech and the free press clauses of the First Amendment. *See* discussion *supra* at 19. Would different considerations apply if, rather than *American Lawyer Magazine*, a non-media person or entity linked to the text of *Hit Man*?

2.  French authorities are seeking to force Yahoo Inc. to restrict French citizens from gaining access to Nazi artifacts that appear on its auction web-site. The artifacts included Nazi flags, belt buckles, and medals.

    Previously, in May 2000, the Superior Court of Paris had ordered Yahoo! to "dissuade and render impossible" the ability of Web surfers in France to gain access to sales of Nazi-related memorabilia on the auction service Yahoo.com hosts. The court's decision deemed the display of the objects "an offense against the collective memory of a country profoundly wounded by the atrocities committed by and in the home of the Nazi criminal enterprise." *See* Carl S. Kaplan, *French Nazi Memorabilia Case Presents Jurisdiction Dilemma*, N.Y. Times (Aug. 11, 2000) at B10. One journalist crafted the issue as: "Should Yahoo Inc. bow to a French law condemning the trivialization of the Nazi era, or should France yield to Yahoo's rights of freedom of expression as embodied in the United States Constitution?" *Id.*

    In the summer of 2000, the French court enlisted the assistance of three experts to examine mechanisms for blocking content from web-sites originating from the United States. *See* Jim Hu and Evan Hansen, *Yahoo Auction Case May Reveal Borders of Cyberspace*, CNETNews.com (Aug. 11, 2000) <http://news.net.com/news/0-1005-200-2495751.htm>. If Yahoo! cannot technologically block access to the on-line exposition of the artifacts by French visitors exclusively, may the French court require Yahoo to remove the display entirely? May the French court compel Yahoo! to post a statement on the site, dissuading French surfers from accessing the display?

3.  To what degree are judicially devised principles relating to hate speech effective in the Internet context? Are "fighting words" more likely to incite reaction when they are uttered in a digital environment, rather than in a face-to-face confrontation where an emotive and violent response may be more proximate and immediate?

4.  International efforts to deal with speech promoting racism and violence are ongoing. Singapore, for example, has established a policy to restrict content that could undermine morality, political stability, and religious harmony, and China has implemented a policy of prohibiting the flow of what it regards as "detrimental infor-

mation." *See* Michael L. Siegel, *Hate Speech, Civil Rights, and the Internet: The Juris-dictional and Human Rights Nightmare*, 9 Alb. L.J. Sci. & Tech. 375, 394 & n. 141 (1999). Systematically addressing the issue by means of an international treaty might, at first blush, appear to promote a global and consistent approach to the issue. Even if cohesive standardization were feasible, however, enactment of such a treaty doubtlessly could not adequately accommodate free speech interests.

Proposals to address the proliferation of cyberspace communications promoting hate, racism, and violence include technological filtering. "However there are critics who suggest that using filtering software to block the offensive content is similar to averting your eyes without dealing with the underlying issues." *Id.* Additionally, software that blocks some offensive speech also may eliminate acceptable material or render the remainder of the text inaccurate or unintelligible.

"Attempts at censorship will meet...resistance from Internet users and from those who are more skilled at evading censorship techniques." *Id.* at 397. Such organizations as the Anti-Defamation league, the Simon Weisenthal Center, the Southern Law Poverty Center, and the National Association for the Advancement of Colored People have addressed issues relating to hate-laden speech on their websites. Ultimately, the most efficacious proposals appear to be those designed to counteract hate speech with discussion of the causes of such sentiments and responses to them.

---

# Speech Relating to Matters of National Security

More than eighty years ago, Justice Holmes wrote the Supreme Court's decision that upheld the convictions of several men who had circulated among conscripts a pamphlet opposing the draft as violative of the constitutional prohibition on slavery. *Schenck v. United States*, 249 U.S. 47 (1919). Justice Holmes produced the oft-quoted exemption from free speech protection that "the most stringent protection of free speech would not protect a man in falsely shouting 'fire' in a theater and causing a panic." *Id.* at 52.

As discussed previously, *see* discussion *supra* at 106, the on-line availability of information relating to bomb devices has generated significant public concern and legislative attention. Under what circumstances may the government permissibly quell speech that may allegedly jeopardize the preservation of national security?

---

# UNITED STATES of AMERICA v.
# The PROGRESSIVE, INC.

United States District Court, Western District of Wisconsin
No. 79-C-98, 467 F. Supp. 990
March 26, 1979

WARREN, District Judge.

On March 9, 1979, this Court, at the request of the government, but after hearing from both parties, issued a temporary restraining order enjoining defendants, their employees, and agents from publishing or otherwise communicating or disclosing in any manner any restricted data contained in the article: "The H-Bomb Secret: How We Got It, Why We're Telling It."...

Under the facts here alleged, the question before this Court involves a clash between allegedly vital security interests of the United States and the competing constitutional doctrine against prior restraint in publication.

In its argument and briefs, plaintiff relies on national security, as enunciated by Congress in The Atomic Energy Act of 1954, as the basis for classification of certain documents. Plaintiff contends that, in certain areas, national preservation and self-interest permit the retention and classification of government secrets. The government argues that its national security interest also permits it to impress classification and censorship upon information originating in the public domain, if when drawn together, synthesized and collated, such information acquires the character of presenting immediate, direct and irreparable harm to the interests of the United States.

Defendants argue that freedom of expression as embodied in the First Amendment is so central to the heart of liberty that prior restraint in any form becomes anathema. They contend that this is particularly true when a nation is not at war and where the prior restraint is based on surmise or conjecture. While acknowledging that freedom of the press is not absolute, they maintain that the publication of the projected article does not rise to the level of immediate, direct and irreparable harm which could justify incursion into First Amendment freedoms....

From the founding days of this nation, the rights to freedom of speech and of the press have held an honored place in our constitutional scheme. The establishment and nurturing of these rights is one of the true achievements of our form of government.

Because of the importance of these rights, any prior restraint on publication comes into court under a heavy presumption against its constitutional validity. *New York Times v. United States,* 403 U.S. 713, 91 S.Ct. 2140, 29 L.Ed.2d 822 (1971).

However, First Amendment rights are not absolute. They are not boundless.

Justice Frankfurter dissenting in *Bridges v. California,* 314 U.S. 252, 282, 62 S.Ct. 190, 203, 86 L.Ed. 192 (1941), stated it in this fashion: "Free speech is not so absolute or irrational a conception as to imply paralysis of the means for effective protection of all the freedoms secured by the Bill of Rights." In the *Schenck* case, Justice Holmes recognized: "The character of every act depends upon the circumstances in which it is done." *Schenck v. United States,* 249 U.S. 47, 52, 39 S.Ct. 247, 249, 63 L.Ed. 470 (1931).

In *Near v. Minnesota,* 283 U.S. 697, 51 S.Ct. 625, 75 L.Ed. 1357 (1931), the Supreme Court specifically recognized an extremely narrow area, involving national security, in which interference with First Amendment rights might be tolerated and a prior restraint on publication might be appropriate. The Court stated:

> "When a nation is at war many things that might be said in time of peace are such a hindrance to its effort that their utterance will not be endured so long as men fight and that no Court could regard them as protected by any constitutional right." No one would question but that a government might prevent actual obstruction to its recruiting service or the publication of the sailing dates of transports or the number and location of troops.

*Id.* at 716, 51 S.Ct. at 631 (citation omitted). Thus, it is clear that few things, save grave national security concerns, are sufficient to override First Amendment interests. A court is well admonished to approach any requested prior restraint with a great deal of skepticism.

Juxtaposed against the right to freedom of expression is the government's contention that the national security of this country could be jeopardized by publication of the article.

The Court is convinced that the government has a right to classify certain sensitive documents to protect its national security. The problem is with the scope of the classification system.

Defendants contend that the projected article merely contains data already in the public domain and readily available to any diligent seeker. They say other nations already have the same information or the opportunity to obtain it. How then, they argue, can they be in violation of 42 U.S.C. §§ 2274(b) and 2280 which purport to authorize injunctive relief against one who would disclose restricted data "with reason to believe such data will be utilized to injure the United States or to secure an advantage to any foreign nation…"?

Although the government states that some of the information is in the public domain, it contends that much of the data is not, and that the Morland article contains a core of information that has never before been published.

Furthermore, the government's position is that whether or not specific information is "in the public domain" or has been "declassified" at some point is not determinative. The government states that a court must look at the nature and context of prior disclosures and analyze what the practical impact of the prior disclosures are as contrasted to that of the present revelation.

The government feels that the mere fact that the author, Howard Morland, could prepare an article explaining the technical processes of thermonuclear weapons does not mean that those processes are available to everyone. They lay heavy emphasis on the argument that the danger lies in the exposition of certain concepts never heretofore disclosed in conjunction with one another….

[T]he Court finds concepts within the article that it does not find in the public realm concepts that are vital to the operation of the hydrogen bomb.

Even if some of the information is in the public domain, due recognition must be given to the human skills and expertise involved in writing this article. The author needed sufficient expertise to recognize relevant, as opposed to irrelevant, information and to assimilate the information obtained. The right questions had to be asked or the correct educated guesses had to be made….

Does the article provide a "do-it yourself" guide for the hydrogen bomb? Probably not. A number of affidavits make quite clear that a *sine qua non* to thermonuclear capability is a large, sophisticated industrial capability coupled with a coterie of imaginative, resourceful scientists and technicians. One does not build a hydrogen bomb in the basement. However, the article could possibly provide sufficient information to allow a medium size nation to move faster in developing a hydrogen weapon. It could provide a ticket to by-pass blind alleys.

The Morland piece could accelerate the membership of a candidate nation in the thermonuclear club. Pursuit of blind alleys or failure to grasp seemingly basic concepts have been the cause of many inventive failures.

For example, in one of the articles submitted to the Court, the author described how, in the late 1930's, physicists in various countries were simultaneously, but independently, working on the idea of a nuclear chain reaction. The French physicists in their equation neglected to take full account of the fact that the neutrons produced by fission could go on to provoke further fissions in a many-step process which is the essence of a chain reaction. Even though this idea seems so elementary, the concept of neutron multiplication was so novel that no nuclear physicists saw through the French team's oversight for about a year.

Thus, once basic concepts are learned, the remainder of the process may easily follow.

Although the defendants state that the information contained in the article is relatively easy to obtain, only five countries now have a hydrogen bomb. Yet the United States first successfully exploded the hydrogen bomb some twenty-six years ago.

The point has also been made that it is only a question of time before other countries will have the hydrogen bomb. That may be true. However, there are times in the course of human history when time itself may be very important. This time factor becomes critical when considering mass annihilation weaponry witness the failure of Hitler to get his V-1 and V-2 bombs operational quickly enough to materially affect the outcome of World War II.

Defendants have stated that publication of the article will alert the people of this country to the false illusion of security created by the government's futile efforts at secrecy. They believe publication will provide the people with needed information to make informed decisions on an urgent issue of public concern.

However, this Court can find no plausible reason why the public needs to know the technical details about hydrogen bomb construction to carry on an informed debate on this issue. Furthermore, the Court believes that the defendants' position in favor of nuclear non-proliferation would be harmed, not aided, by the publication of this article.... A ... most vital difference between [New York Times Co. v. United States, 403 U.S. 713 (1971), and this case ... ] is the fact that a specific statute is involved here. Section 2274 of The Atomic Energy Act prohibits anyone from communicating, transmitting or disclosing any restricted data to any person "with reason to believe such data will be utilized to injure the United States or to secure an advantage to any foreign nation."

Section 2014 of the Act defines restricted data. " 'Restricted Data' means all data concerning 1) design, manufacture, or utilization of atomic weapons; 2) the production of special nuclear material; or 3) the use of special nuclear material in the production of energy, but shall not include data declassified or removed from the Restricted Data category pursuant to section 2162 of this title."

As applied to this case, the Court finds that the statute in question is not vague or overbroad. The Court is convinced that the terms used in the statute "communicates, transmits or discloses" include publishing in a magazine.

The Court is of the opinion that the government has shown that the defendants had reason to believe that the data in the article, if published, would injure the United States or give an advantage to a foreign nation. Extensive reading and studying of the documents on file lead to the conclusion that not all the data is available in the public realm in the same fashion, if it is available at all.

What is involved here is information dealing with the most destructive weapon in the history of mankind, information of sufficient destructive potential to nullify the right to free speech and to endanger the right to life itself.

Stripped to its essence then, the question before the Court is a basic confrontation between the First Amendment right to freedom of the press and national security.

Our Founding Fathers believed, as we do, that one is born with certain inalienable rights which, as the Declaration of Independence intones, include the right to life, liberty and the pursuit of happiness. The Constitution, including the Bill of Rights, was enacted to make those rights operable in everyday life.

The Court believes that each of us is born seized of a panoply of basic rights, that we institute governments to secure these rights and that there is a hierarchy of values attached to these rights which is helpful in deciding the clash now before us.

Certain of these rights have an aspect of imperativeness or centrality that make them transcend other rights. Somehow it does not seem that the right to life and the right to not have soldiers quartered in your home can be of equal import in the grand scheme of things. While it may be true in the long-run, as Patrick Henry instructs us, that one would prefer death to life without liberty, nonetheless, in the short-run, one cannot enjoy freedom of speech, freedom to worship or freedom of the press unless one first enjoys the freedom to live.

Faced with a stark choice between upholding the right to continued life and the right to freedom of the press, most jurists would have no difficulty in opting for the chance to continue to breathe and function as they work to achieve perfect freedom of expression.

Is the choice here so stark? Only time can give us a definitive answer. But considering another aspect of this panoply of rights we all have is helpful in answering the question now before us. This aspect is the disparity of the risk involved.

The destruction of various human rights can come about in differing ways and at varying speeds. Freedom of the press can be obliterated overnight by some dictator's imposition of censorship or by the slow nibbling away at a free press through successive bits of repressive legislation enacted by a nation's lawmakers. Yet, even in the most drastic of such situations, it is always possible for a dictator to be overthrown, for a bad law to be repealed or for a judge's error to be subsequently rectified. Only when human life is at stake are such corrections impossible.

The case at bar is so difficult precisely because the consequences of error involve human life itself and on such an awesome scale.

The Secretary of State states that publication will increase thermonuclear proliferation and that this would "irreparably impair the national security of the United States." The Secretary of Defense says that dissemination of the Morland paper will mean a substantial increase in the risk of thermonuclear proliferation and lead to use or threats that would "adversely affect the national security of the United States."

Howard Morland asserts that "if the information in my article were not in the public domain, it should be put there . . . so that ordinary citizens may have informed opinions about nuclear weapons."

Erwin Knoll, the editor of *The Progressive*, states he is "totally convinced that publication of the article will be of substantial benefit to the United States because it will demonstrate that this country's security does not lie in an oppressive and ineffective system of secrecy and classification but in open, honest, and informed public debate about issues which the people must decide."

The Court is faced with the difficult task of weighing and resolving these divergent views.

A mistake in ruling against *The Progressive* will seriously infringe cherished First Amendment rights. If a preliminary injunction is issued, it will constitute the first instance of prior restraint against a publication in this fashion in the history of this country, to this Court's knowledge. Such notoriety is not to be sought. It will curtail defendants' First Amendment rights in a drastic and substantial fashion. It will infringe upon our right to know and to be informed as well.

A mistake in ruling against the United States could pave the way for thermonuclear annihilation for us all. In that event, our right to life is extinguished and the right to publish becomes moot....

[T]his Court concludes that publication of the technical information on the hydrogen bomb contained in the article is analogous to publication of troop movements or locations in time of war and falls within the extremely narrow exception to the rule against prior restraint.

Because of this "disparity of risk," because the government has met its heavy burden of showing justification for the imposition of a prior restraint on publication of the objected-to technical portions of the Morland article, and because the Court is unconvinced that suppression of the objected-to technical portions of the Morland article would in any plausible fashion impede the defendants in their laudable crusade to stimulate public knowledge of nuclear armament and bring about enlightened debate on national policy questions, the Court finds that the objected-to portions of the article fall within the narrow area recognized by the Court in *Near v. Minnesota* in which a prior restraint on publication is appropriate....

## Notes and Questions

1. The Court's empathy for both arguments was palpable. At the conclusion of its decision, the Court adjourned the proceedings and invited the parties to submit to a panel of five mediators to be appointed by the Court. The parties declined.

2. Ultimately, the parties' dispute was rendered moot. While *The Progressive*'s appeal was pending, a Wisconsin newspaper published a letter containing the information that had been enjoined from publication.

3. Application of the "collateral bar rule" precludes one charged with contempt for disobeying an injunction from defending on the ground that the injunction was unconstitutional. The rule is designed to preserve the integrity of judicial authority and the orderly resolution of disputes. An exception to the rule exists when the injunction that is ignored is transparently invalid, such as when there is no statutory authority for the injunction, the putative interests implicated are an insufficient basis to issue a prior restraint, and dissemination of the information sought to be suppressed is available elsewhere. *See, e.g., In re Providence Journal Co.*, 820 F.2d

1342 (1st Cir. 1986), *modified by reh'g en banc,* 820 F.2d 1354 (1st Cir. 1987) (en banc), *cert. dismissed,* 444 U.S. 814 (1988). Courts have acknowledged "the difficulties of imposing upon a publisher the requirement of pursuing the normal appeal process. Not only would such entail time and expense, but the right sought to be vindicated could be forfeited or the value of the embargoed information considerably cheapened." 820 F.2d at 1354 (per curiam) (expecting the publisher, even when it believes that it is the subject of a transparently unconstitutional order of prior restraint, to make a good faith effort to seek emergency relief from the appellate court; if timely access is not available or timely decision is not forthcoming, the publisher may proceed to publish and challenge the constitutionality of the order in contempt proceedings). Does the pace of digital media affect this analysis, by encumbering or delaying the posting of the publication? Alternatively, does the analysis accommodate the Internet's inherent expediency within the construct of the timeliness factor?

---

# NEW YORK TIMES COMPANY v. UNITED STATES

Supreme Court of the United States
Nos. 1873, 1885, 403 U.S. 713
June 30, 1971

## PER CURIAM

We granted certiorari . . . in these cases in which the United States seeks to enjoin the *New York Times* and the *Washington Post* from publishing the contents of a classified study entitled "History of U.S. Decision-Making Process on Viet Nam Policy."

"Any system of prior restraints of expression comes to this Court bearing a heavy presumption against its constitutional validity." *Bantam Books, Inc. v. Sullivan,* 372 U.S. 58, 70, 83 S.Ct. 631, 639, 9 L.Ed.2d 584 (1963); *see also Near v. Minnesota ex rel. Olson,* 283 U.S. 697, 51 S.Ct. 625, 75 L.Ed. 1357 (1931). The Government "thus carries a heavy burden of showing justification for the imposition of such a restraint." *Organization for a Better Austin v. Keefe,* 402 U.S. 415, 419, 91 S.Ct. 1575, 1578, 29 L.Ed.2d 1 (1971). The District Court for the Southern District of New York in the *New York Times* case, 328 F. Supp. 324, and the District Court for the District of Columbia and the Court of Appeals for the District of Columbia Circuit, 446 F.2d 1327, in the *Washington Post* case held that the Government had not met that burden. We agree.

The judgment of the Court of Appeals for the District of Columbia Circuit is therefore affirmed. The order of the Court of Appeals for the Second Circuit is reversed, 444 F.2d 544, and the case is remanded with directions to enter a judgment affirming the judgment of the District Court for the Southern District of New York. The stays entered June 25, 1971, by the Court are vacated. The judgments shall issue forthwith.

So ordered.

Judgment of the Court of Appeals for the District of Columbia Circuit affirmed; order of the Court of Appeals for the Second Circuit reversed and case remanded with directions.

Mr. Justice BLACK, with whom Mr. Justice DOUGLAS joins, concurring.

I adhere to the view that the Government's case against the *Washington Post* should have been dismissed and that the injunction against the *New York Times* should have been vacated without oral argument when the cases were first presented to this Court. I believe that every moment's continuance of the injunctions against these newspapers amounts to a flagrant, indefensible, and continuing violation of the First Amendment. Furthermore, after oral argument, I agree completely that we must affirm the judgment of the Court of Appeals for the District of Columbia Circuit and reverse the judgment of the Court of Appeals for the Second Circuit for the reasons stated by my Brothers Douglas and Brennan. In my view it is unfortunate that some of my Brethren are apparently willing to hold that the publication of news may sometimes be enjoined. Such a holding would make a shambles of the First Amendment.

Our Government was launched in 1789 with the adoption of the Constitution. The Bill of Rights, including the First Amendment, followed in 1791. Now, for the first time in the 182 years since the founding of the Republic, the federal courts are asked to hold that the First Amendment does not mean what it says, but rather means that the Government can halt the publication of current news of vital importance to the people of this country.

In seeking injunctions against these newspapers and in its presentation to the Court, the Executive Branch seems to have forgotten the essential purpose and history of the First Amendment. When the Constitution was adopted, many people strongly opposed it because the document contained no Bill of Rights to safeguard certain basic freedoms.[1] They especially feared that the new powers granted to a central government might be interpreted to permit the government to curtail freedom of religion, press, assembly, and speech. In response to an overwhelming public clamor, James Madison offered a series of amendments to satisfy citizens that these great liberties would remain safe and beyond the power of government to abridge. Madison proposed what later became the First Amendment in three parts, two of which are set out below, and one of which proclaimed: "The people shall not be deprived or abridged of their right to speak, to write, or to publish their sentiments; and the freedom of the press, as one of the great bulwarks of liberty, shall be inviolable." The amendments were offered to curtail and restrict the general powers granted to the Executive, Legislative, and Judicial Branches two years before in the original Constitution. The Bill of Rights changed the original Constitution into a new charter under which no branch of government could abridge the people's freedoms of press, speech, religion, and assembly. Yet the Solicitor General argues and some members of the Court appear to agree that the general powers of the Government adopted in the original Constitution should be interpreted to limit and restrict the specific and emphatic guarantees of the Bill of Rights adopted later. I can imagine no greater perversion of history. Madison and the other Framers of the First Amendment, able men that they were, wrote in language they earnestly believed could never be misunderstood: "Congress shall make no law...abridging the freedom...of the press...." Both the history and language of the First Amendment support the view that the press must be left free to publish news, whatever the source, without censorship, injunctions, or prior restraints.

In the First Amendment the Founding Fathers gave the free press the protection it must have to fulfill its essential role in our democracy. The press was to serve the gov-

---

1. In introducing the Bill of Rights in the House of Representatives, Madison said: "[B]ut I believe that the great mass of the people who opposed [the Constitution], disliked it because it did not contain effectual provisions against the encroachments on particular rights...." 1 Annals of Cong. 433. Congressman Goodhue added: "[I]t is the wish of many of our constituents, that something should be added to the Constitution, to secure in a stronger manner their liberties from the inroads of power." *Id.* at 426.

erned, not the governors. The Government's power to censor the press was abolished so that the press would remain forever free to censure the Government. The press was protected so that it could bare the secrets of government and inform the people. Only a free and unrestrained press can effectively expose deception in government. And paramount among the responsibilities of a free press is the duty to prevent any part of the government from deceiving the people and sending them off to distant lands to die of foreign fevers and foreign shot and shell. In my view, far from deserving condemnation for their courageous reporting, the *New York Times*, the *Washington Post*, and other newspapers should be commended for serving the purpose that the Founding Fathers saw so clearly. In revealing the workings of government that led to the Vietnam war, the newspapers nobly did precisely that which the Founders hoped and trusted they would do.

The Government's case here is based on premises entirely different from those that guided the Framers of the First Amendment. The Solicitor General has carefully and emphatically stated:

> Now, Mr. Justice [Black], your construction of...[the First Amendment] is well known, and I certainly respect it. You say that no law means no law, and that should be obvious. I can only say, Mr. Justice, that to me it is equally obvious that "no law" does not mean "no law," and I would seek to persuade the Court that that is true.....[T]here are other parts of the Constitution that grant powers and responsibilities to the Executive, and...the First Amendment was not intended to make it impossible for the Executive to function or to protect the security of the United States.

And the Government argues in its brief that in spite of the First Amendment, "[t]he authority of the Executive Department to protect the nation against publication of information whose disclosure would endanger the national security stems from two interrelated sources: the constitutional power of the President over the conduct of foreign affairs and his authority as Commander-in-Chief."

In other words, we are asked to hold that despite the First Amendment's emphatic command, the Executive Branch, the Congress, and the Judiciary can make laws enjoining publication of current news and abridging freedom of the press in the name of "national security." The Government does not even attempt to rely on any act of Congress. Instead it makes the bold and dangerously far-reaching contention that the courts should take it upon themselves to "make" a law abridging freedom of the press in the name of equity, presidential power and national security, even when the representatives of the people in Congress have adhered to the command of the First Amendment and refused to make such a law.[5] *See* concurring opinion of Mr. Justice Douglas, *post,* at 2145. To find that the President has "inherent power" to halt the publication of news by resort to the courts would wipe out the First Amendment and destroy the fundamental liberty and security of the very people the Government hopes to make "secure." No one can read the history of the adoption of the First Amendment without being convinced

---

5. Compare the views of the Solicitor General with those of James Madison, the author of the First Amendment. When speaking of the Bill of Rights in the House of Representatives, Madison said: "If they (the first ten amendments) are incorporated into the Constitution, independent tribunals of justice will consider themselves in a peculiar manner the guardians of those rights; they will be an impenetrable bulwark against every assumption of power in the Legislative or Executive; they will be naturally led to resist every encroachment upon rights expressly stipulated for in the Constitution by the declaration of rights." 1 Annals of Cong. 439.

beyond any doubt that it was injunctions like those sought here that Madison and his collaborators intended to outlaw in this Nation for all time.

The word "security" is a broad, vague generality whose contours should not be invoked to abrogate the fundamental law embodied in the First Amendment. The guarding of military and diplomatic secrets at the expense of informed representative government provides no real security for our Republic. The Framers of the First Amendment, fully aware of both the need to defend a new nation and the abuses of the English and Colonial Governments, sought to give this new society strength and security by providing that freedom of speech, press, religion, and assembly should not be abridged. This thought was eloquently expressed in 1937 by Mr. Chief Justice Hughes—great man and great Chief Justice that he was—when the Court held a man could not be punished for attending a meeting run by Communists.

> The greater the importance of safeguarding the community from incitements to the overthrow of our institutions by force and violence, the more imperative is the need to preserve inviolate the constitutional rights of free speech, free press and free assembly in order to maintain the opportunity for free political discussion, to the end that government may be responsive to the will of the people and that changes, if desired, may be obtained by peaceful means. Therein lies the security of the Republic, the very foundation of constitutional government.

Mr. Justice DOUGLAS, with whom Mr. Justice BLACK joins, concurring.

While I join the opinion of the Court I believe it necessary to express my views more fully.

It should be noted at the outset that the First Amendment provides that "Congress shall make no law...abridging the freedom of speech, or of the press." That leaves, in my view, no room for governmental restraint on the press.

There is, moreover, no statute barring the publication by the press of the material which the *Times* and the *Post* seek to use....

These disclosures[3] may have a serious impact. But that is no basis for sanctioning a previous restraint on the press. As stated by Chief Justice Hughes in *Near v. Minnesota ex rel. Olson,* 283 U.S. 697, 719–720, 51 S.Ct. 625, 632, 75 L.Ed. 1357:

> While reckless assaults upon public men, and efforts to bring obloquy upon those who are endeavoring faithfully to discharge official duties, exert a baleful influence and deserve the severest condemnation in public opinion, it cannot be said that this abuse is greater, and it is believed to be less, than that which characterized the period in which our institutions took shape. Meanwhile, the administration of government has become more complex, the opportunities for malfeasance and corruption have multiplied, crime has grown to most serious proportions, and the danger of its protection by unfaithful officials and of the impairment of the fundamental security of life and property by criminal alliances and official neglect, emphasizes the primary need of a vigilant and

---

3. There are numerous sets of this material in existence and they apparently are not under any controlled custody. Moreover, the President has sent a set to the Congress. We start then with a case where there already is rather wide distribution of the material that is destined for publicity, not secrecy. I have gone over the material listed in the in camera brief of the United States. It is all history, not future events. None of it is more recent than 1968.

courageous press, especially in great cities. The fact that the liberty of the press may be abused by miscreant purveyors of scandal does not make any the less necessary the immunity of the press from previous restraint in dealing with official misconduct.

As we stated only the other day in *Organization for a Better Austin v. Keefe*, 402 U.S. 415, 419, 91 S.Ct. 1575, 1578, 29 L.Ed.2d 1, "[a]ny prior restraint on expression comes to this Court with a 'heavy presumption' against its constitutional validity."

The Government says that it has inherent powers to go into court and obtain an injunction to protect the national interest, which in this case is alleged to be national security.

*Near v. Minnesota ex rel. Olson*, 283 U.S. 697, 51 S.Ct. 625, 75 L.Ed. 1357, repudiated that expansive doctrine in no uncertain terms.

The dominant purpose of the First Amendment was to prohibit the widespread practice of governmental suppression of embarrassing information. It is common knowledge that the First Amendment was adopted against the widespread use of the common law of seditious libel to punish the dissemination of material that is embarrassing to the powers-that-be. *See* T. Emerson, *The System of Freedom of Expression*, c. V (1970); Z. Chafee, *Free Speech in the United States*, c. XIII (1941). The present cases will, I think, go down in history as the most dramatic illustration of that principle. A debate of large proportions goes on in the Nation over our posture in Vietnam. That debate antedated the disclosure of the contents of the present documents. The latter are highly relevant to the debate in progress.

Secrecy in government is fundamentally anti-democratic, perpetuating bureaucratic errors. Open debate and discussion of public issues are vital to our national health. On public questions there should be "uninhibited, robust, and wide-open" debate. *New York Times Co. v. Sullivan*, 376 U.S. 254, 269–270, 84 S.Ct. 710, 720–721, 11 L.Ed.2d 686.

I would affirm the judgment of the Court of Appeals in the Post case, vacate the stay of the Court of Appeals in the Times case and direct that it affirm the District Court.

The stays is these cases that have been in effect for more than a week constitute a flouting of the principles of the First Amendment as interpreted in *Near v. Minnesota ex rel. Olson*.

Mr. Justice BRENNAN, concurring.

I write separately in these cases only to emphasize what should be apparent: that our judgments in the present cases may not be taken to indicate the propriety, in the future, of issuing temporary stays and restraining orders to block the publication of material sought to be suppressed by the Government. So far as I can determine, never before has the United States sought to enjoin a newspaper from publishing information in its possession. The relative novelty of the questions presented, the necessary haste with which decisions were reached, the magnitude of the interests asserted, and the fact that all the parties have concentrated their arguments upon the question whether permanent restraints were proper may have justified at least some of the restraints heretofore imposed in these cases. Certainly it is difficult to fault the several courts below for seeking to assure that the issues here involved were preserved for ultimate review by this Court. But even if it be assumed that some of the interim restraints were proper in the two cases before us, that assumption has no bearing upon the propriety of similar judicial action in the future. To begin with, there has now been ample time for reflection and judgment; whatever values there may be in the preservation of novel questions for appellate review may not support any restraints in the future. More important, the First Amendment stands as an absolute bar to the imposition of judicial restraints in circumstances of the kind presented by these cases.

The error that has pervaded these cases from the outset was the granting of any injunctive relief whatsoever, interim or otherwise. The entire thrust of the Government's claim throughout these cases has been that publication of the material sought to be enjoined "could," or "might," or "may" prejudice the national interest in various ways. But the First Amendment tolerates absolutely no prior judicial restraints of the press predicated upon surmise or conjecture that untoward consequences may result.* Our cases, it is true, have indicated that there is a single, extremely narrow class of cases in which the First Amendment's ban on prior judicial restraint may be overridden. Our cases have thus far indicated that such cases may arise only when the Nation "is at war," *Schenck v. United States*, 249 U.S. 47, 52, 39 S.Ct. 247, 249, 63 L.Ed. 470 (1919), during which times "[n]o one would question but that a government might prevent actual obstruction to its recruiting service or the publication of the sailing dates of transports or the number and location of troops." *Near v. Minnesota ex rel. Olson*, 283 U.S. 697, 716, 51 S.Ct. 625, 631, 75 L.Ed. 1357 (1931). Even if the present world situation were assumed to be tantamount to a time of war, or if the power of presently available armaments would justify even in peacetime the suppression of information that would set in motion a nuclear holocaust, in neither of these actions has the Government presented or even alleged that publication of items from or based upon the material at issue would cause the happening of an event of that nature. "[T]he chief purpose of [the First Amendment's] guaranty [is] to prevent previous restraints upon publication." *Near v. Minnesota ex rel. Olson, supra*, at 713, 51 S.Ct. at 630. Thus, only governmental allegation and proof that publication must inevitably, directly, and immediately cause the occurrence of an event kindred to imperiling the safety of a transport already at sea can support even the issuance of an interim restraining order. In no event may mere conclusions be sufficient: for if the Executive Branch seeks judicial aid in preventing publication, it must inevitably submit the basis upon which that aid is sought to scrutiny by the judiciary. And therefore, every restraint issued in this case, whatever its form, has violated the First Amendment—and not less so because that restraint was justified as necessary to afford the courts an opportunity to examine the claim more thoroughly. Unless and until the Government has clearly made out its case, the First Amendment commands that no injunction may issue.

Mr. Justice STEWART, with whom Mr. Justice WHITE joins, concurring.

In the governmental structure created by our Constitution, the Executive is endowed with enormous power in the two related areas of national defense and international relations. This power, largely unchecked by the Legislative[1] and Judicial branches, has

---

* *Freedman v. Maryland*, 380 U.S. 51, 85 S.Ct. 734, 13 L.Ed.2d 649 (1965), and similar cases regarding temporary restraints of allegedly obscene materials are not in point. For those cases rest upon the proposition that "obscenity is not protected by the freedoms of speech and press." *Roth v. United States*, 354 U.S. 476, 481, 77 S.Ct. 1304, 1307, 1 L.Ed.2d 1498 (1957). Here there is no question but that the material sought to be suppressed is within the protection of the First Amendment; the only question is whether, notwithstanding that fact, its publication may be enjoined for a time because of the presence of an overwhelming national interest. Similarly, copyright cases have no pertinence here: the Government is not asserting an interest in the particular form of words chosen in the documents, but is seeking to suppress the ideas expressed therein. And the copyright laws, of course, protect only the form of expression and not the ideas expressed.

1. The President's power to make treaties and to appoint ambassadors is, of course, limited by the requirement of Art. II, §2, of the Constitution that he obtain the advice and consent of the Sen-

been pressed to the very hilt since the advent of the nuclear missile age. For better or for worse, the simple fact is that a President of the United States possesses vastly greater constitutional independence in these two vital areas of power than does, say, a prime minister of a country with a parliamentary form of government.

In the absence of the governmental checks and balances present in other areas of our national life, the only effective restraint upon executive policy and power in the areas of national defense and international affairs may lie in an enlightened citizenry—in an informed and critical public opinion which alone can here protect the values of democratic government. For this reason, it is perhaps here that a press that is alert, aware, and free most vitally serves the basic purpose of the First Amendment. For without an informed and free press there cannot be an enlightened people.

Yet it is elementary that the successful conduct of international diplomacy and the maintenance of an effective national defense require both confidentiality and secrecy. Other nations can hardly deal with this Nation in an atmosphere of mutual trust unless they can be assured that their confidences will be kept. And within our own executive departments, the development of considered and intelligent international policies would be impossible if those charged with their formulation could not communicate with each other freely, frankly, and in confidence. In the area of basic national defense the frequent need for absolute secrecy is, of course, self-evident.

I think there can be but one answer to this dilemma, if dilemma it be. The responsibility must be where the power is.[3] If the Constitution gives the Executive a large degree of unshared power in the conduct of foreign affairs and the maintenance of our national defense, then under the Constitution the Executive must have the largely unshared duty to determine and preserve the degree of internal security necessary to exercise that power successfully. It is an awesome responsibility, requiring judgment and wisdom of a high order. I should suppose that moral, political, and practical considerations would dictate that a very first principle of that wisdom would be an insistence upon avoiding secrecy for its own sake. For when everything is classified, then nothing is classified, and the system becomes one to be disregarded by the cynical or the careless, and to be manipulated by those intent on self-protection or self-promotion. I should suppose, in short, that the hallmark of a truly effective internal security system would be the maximum possible disclosure, recognizing that secrecy can best be preserved

---

ate. Article I, § 8, empowers Congress to "raise and support Armies," and "provide and maintain a Navy." And, of course, Congress alone can declare war. This power was last exercised almost 30 years ago at the inception of World War II. Since the end of that war in 1945, the Armed Forces of the United States have suffered approximately half a million casualties in various parts of the world.

3. "It is quite apparent that if, in the maintenance of our international relations, embarrassment—perhaps serious embarrassment—is to be avoided and success for our aims achieved, congressional legislation which is to be made effective through negotiation and inquiry within the international field must often accord to the President a degree of discretion and freedom from statutory restriction which would not be admissible were domestic affairs alone involved. Moreover, he, not Congress, has the better opportunity of knowing the conditions which prevail in foreign countries, and especially is this true in time of war. He has his confidential sources of information. He has his agents in the form of diplomatic, consular and other officials. Secrecy in respect of information gathered by them may be highly necessary, and the premature disclosure of it productive of harmful results. Indeed, so clearly is this true that the first President refused to accede to a request to lay before the House of Representatives the instructions, correspondence and documents relating to the negotiation of the Jay Treaty—a refusal the wisdom of which was recognized by the House itself and has never since been doubted...." *United States v. Curtiss-Wright Export Corp.*, 299 U.S. 304, 320, 57 S.Ct. 216, 221, 81 L.Ed. 255.

only when credibility is truly maintained. But be that as it may, it is clear to me that it is the constitutional duty of the Executive—as a matter of sovereign prerogative and not as a matter of law as the courts know law—through the promulgation and enforcement of executive regulations, to protect the confidentiality necessary to carry out its responsibilities in the fields of international relations and national defense.

This is not to say that Congress and the courts have no role to play. Undoubtedly Congress has the power to enact specific and appropriate criminal laws to protect government property and preserve government secrets. Congress has passed such laws, and several of them are of very colorable relevance to the apparent circumstances of these cases. And if a criminal prosecution is instituted, it will be the responsibility of the courts to decide the applicability of the criminal law under which the charge is brought. Moreover, if Congress should pass a specific law authorizing civil proceedings in this field, the courts would likewise have the duty to decide the constitutionality of such a law as well as its applicability to the facts proved.

But in the cases before us we are asked neither to construe specific regulations nor to apply specific laws. We are asked, instead, to perform a function that the Constitution gave to the Executive, not the Judiciary. We are asked, quite simply, to prevent the publication by two newspapers of material that the Executive Branch insists should not, in the national interest, be published. I am convinced that the Executive is correct with respect to some of the documents involved. But I cannot say that disclosure of any of them will surely result in direct, immediate, and irreparable damage to our Nation or its people. That being so, there can under the First Amendment be but one judicial resolution of the issues before us. I join the judgments of the Court.

Mr. Justice WHITE, with whom Mr. Justice STEWART joins, concurring.

I concur in today's judgments, but only because of the concededly extraordinary protection against prior restraints enjoyed by the press under our constitutional system. I do not say that in no circumstances would the First Amendment permit an injunction against publishing information about government plans or operations.[1] Nor, after examining the materials the Government characterizes as the most sensitive and destructive, can I deny that revelation of these documents will do substantial damage to public interests. Indeed, I am confident that their disclosure will have that result. But I nevertheless agree that the United States has not satisfied the very heavy burden that it must

---

1. The Congress has authorized a strain of prior restraints against private parties in certain instances. The National Labor Relations Board routinely issues cease-and-desist orders against employers who it finds have threatened or coerced employees in the exercise of protected rights. See 29 U.S.C. § 160(c). Similarly, the Federal Trade Commission is empowered to impose cease-and-desist orders against unfair methods of competition. 15 U.S.C. § 45(b). Such orders can, and quite often do, restrict what may be spoken or written under certain circumstances. See, e.g., NLRB v. Gissel Packing Co., 395 U.S. 575, 616–620, 89 S.Ct. 1918, 1941–1943, 23 L.Ed.2d 547 (1969). Article I, § 8, of the Constitution authorizes Congress to secure the "exclusive right" of authors to their writings, and no one denies that a newspaper can properly be enjoined from publishing the copyrighted works of another. See L. A. Westermann Co. v. Dispatch Printing Co., 249 U.S. 100, 39 S.Ct. 194, 63 L.Ed. 499 (1919). Newspapers do themselves rely from time to time on the copyright as a means of protecting their accounts of important events. However, those enjoined under the statutes relating to the National Labor Relations Board and the Federal Trade Commission are private parties, not the press; and when the press is enjoined under the copyright laws the complainant is a private copyright holder enforcing a private right. These situations are quite distinct from the Government's request for an injunction against publishing information about the affairs of government, a request admittedly not based on any statute.

meet to warrant an injunction against publication in these cases, at least in the absence of express and appropriately limited congressional authorization for prior restraints in circumstances such as these.

The Government's position is simply stated: The responsibility of the Executive for the conduct of the foreign affairs and for the security of the Nation is so basic that the President is entitled to an injunction against publication of a newspaper story whenever he can convince a court that the information to be revealed threatens "grave and irreparable" injury to the public interest;[2] and the injunction should issue whether or not the material to be published is classified, whether or not publication would be lawful under relevant criminal statutes enacted by Congress, and regardless of the circumstances by which the newspaper came into possession of the information.

At least in the absence of legislation by Congress, based on its own investigations and findings, I am quite unable to agree that the inherent powers of the Executive and the courts reach so far as to authorize remedies having such sweeping potential for inhibiting publications by the press. Much of the difficulty inheres in the "grave and irreparable danger" standard suggested by the United States. If the United States were to have judgment under such a standard in these cases, our decision would be of little guidance to other courts in other cases, for the material at issue here would not be available from the Court's opinion or from public records, nor would it be published by the press. Indeed, even today where we hold that the United States has not met its burden, the material remains sealed in court records and it is properly not discussed in today's opinions. Moreover, because the material poses substantial dangers to national interests and because of the hazards of criminal sanctions, a responsible press may choose never to publish the more sensitive materials. To sustain the Government in these cases would start the courts down a long and hazardous road that I am not willing to travel, at least without congressional guidance and direction.

It is not easy to reject the proposition urged by the United States and to deny relief on its good-faith claims in these cases that publication will work serious damage to the country. But that discomfiture is considerably dispelled by the infrequency of prior-restraint cases. Normally, publication will occur and the damage be done before the Government has either opportunity or grounds for suppression. So here, publication has already begun and a substantial part of the threatened damage has already occurred. The fact of a massive breakdown in security is known, access to the documents by many unauthorized people is undeniable, and the efficacy of equitable relief against these or other newspapers to avert anticipated damage is doubtful at best.

What is more, terminating the ban on publication of the relatively few sensitive documents the Government now seeks to suppress does not mean that the law either requires or invites newspapers or others to publish them or that they will be immune from criminal action if they do. Prior restraints require an unusually heavy justification under the First Amendment; but failure by the Government to justify prior restraints does not measure its constitutional entitlement to a conviction for criminal publication. That the Government mistakenly chose to proceed by injunction does not mean that it could not successfully proceed in another way.

---

2. The "grave and irreparable danger" standard is that asserted by the Government in this Court. In remanding to Judge Gurfein for further hearings in the *Times* litigation, five members of the Court of Appeals for the Second Circuit directed him to determine whether disclosure of certain items specified with particularity by the Government would "pose such grave and immediate danger to the security of the United States as to warrant their publication being enjoined."

When the Espionage Act was under consideration in 1917, Congress eliminated from the bill a provision that would have given the President broad powers in time of war to proscribe, under threat of criminal penalty, the publication of various categories of information related to the national defense. Congress at that time was unwilling to clothe the President with such far-reaching powers to monitor the press, and those opposed to this part of the legislation assumed that a necessary concomitant of such power was the power to "filter out the news to the people through some man." 55 Cong.Rec. 2008 (remarks of Sen. Ashurst). However, these same members of Congress appeared to have little doubt that newspapers would be subject to criminal prosecution if they insisted on publishing information of the type Congress had itself determined should not be revealed....

The Criminal Code contains numerous provisions potentially relevant to these cases. Section 797 makes it a crime to publish certain photographs or drawings of military installations. Section 798, also in precise language, proscribes knowing and willful publication of any classified information concerning the cryptographic systems or communication intelligence activities of the United States as well as any information obtained from communication intelligence operations. If any of the material here at issue is of this nature, the newspapers are presumably now on full notice of the position of the United States and must face the consequences if they publish. I would have no difficulty in sustaining convictions under these sections on facts that would not justify the intervention of equity and the imposition of a prior restraint.

The same would be true under those sections of the Criminal Code casting a wider net to protect the national defense. Section 793(e) makes it a criminal act for any unauthorized possessor of a document "relating to the national defense" either (1) willfully to communicate or cause to be communicated that document to any person not entitled to receive it or (2) willfully to retain the document and fail to deliver it to an officer of the United States entitled to receive it.... Of course, in the cases before us, the unpublished documents have been demanded by the United States and their import has been made known at least to counsel for the newspapers involved. In *Gorin v. United States*, 312 U.S. 19, 28, 61 S.Ct. 429, 434, 85 L.Ed. 488 (1941), the words "national defense" as used in a predecessor of § 793 were held by a unanimous Court to have "a well understood connotation"—a "generic concept of broad connotations, referring to the military and naval establishments and the related activities of national preparedness"—and to be "sufficiently definite to apprise the public of prohibited activities" and to be consonant with due process. 312 U.S. at 28, 61 S.Ct. at 434. Also, as construed by the Court in *Gorin*, information "connected with the national defense" is obviously not limited to that threatening "grave and irreparable" injury to the United States.

It is thus clear that Congress has addressed itself to the problems of protecting the security of the country and the national defense from unauthorized disclosure of potentially damaging information. *Cf. Youngstown Sheet & Tube Co. v. Sawyer*, 343 U.S. 579, 585–586, 72 S.Ct. 863, 865–866, 96 L.Ed. 1153 (1953); *see also id.* at 593–628, 72 S.Ct. at 888–928 (Frankfurter, J., concurring). It has not, however, authorized the injunctive remedy against threatened publication. It has apparently been satisfied to rely on criminal sanctions and their deterrent effect on the responsible as well as the irresponsible press. I am not, of course, saying that either of these newspapers has yet committed a crime or that either would commit a crime if it published all the material now in its possession. That matter must await resolution in the context of a criminal proceeding if one is instituted by the United States. In that event, the issue of guilt or innocence would be determined by procedures and standards quite different from those that have purported to govern these injunctive proceedings.

Mr. Justice MARSHALL, concurring.

The Government contends that the only issue in these cases is whether in a suit by the United States, 'the First Amendment bars a court from prohibiting a newspaper from publishing material whose disclosure would pose a 'grave and immediate danger to the security of the United States." With all due respect, I believe the ultimate issue in this case is even more basic than the one posed by the Solicitor General. The issue is whether this Court or the Congress has the power to make law.

In these cases there is no problem concerning the President's power to classify information as "secret" or "top secret." Congress has specifically recognized Presidential authority, which has been formally exercised in Exec. Order 10501 (1953), to classify documents and information. *See, e.g.,* 18 U.S.C. §798; 50 U.S.C. §783. Nor is there any issue here regarding the President's power as Chief Executive and Commander in Chief to protect national security by disciplining employees who disclose information and by taking precautions to prevent leaks.

The problem here is whether in these particular cases the Executive Branch has authority to invoke the equity jurisdiction of the courts to protect what it believes to be the national interest. *See In re Debs,* 158 U.S. 564, 584, 15 S.Ct. 900, 906, 39 L.Ed. 1092 (1895). The Government argues that in addition to the inherent power of any government to protect itself, the President's power to conduct foreign affairs and his position as Commander in Chief give him authority to impose censorship on the press to protect his ability to deal effectively with foreign nations and to conduct the military affairs of the country. Of course, it is beyond cavil that the President has broad powers by virtue of his primary responsibility for the conduct of our foreign affairs and his position as Commander in Chief. *Chicago & Southern Air Lines v. Waterman S.S. Corp.,* 333 U.S. 103, 68 S.Ct. 431, 92 L.Ed. 568 (1948); *Kiyoshi Hirabayashi v. United States,* 320 U.S. 81, 93, 63 S.Ct. 1375, 1382, 87 L.Ed. 1774 (1943); *United States v. Curtiss-Wright Export Corp.,* 299 U.S. 304, 57 S.Ct. 216, 81 L.Ed. 255 (1936). And in some situations it may be that under whatever inherent powers the Government may have, as well as the implicit authority derived from the President's mandate to conduct foreign affairs and to act as Commander in Chief, there is a basis for the invocation of the equity jurisdiction of this Court as an aid to prevent the publication of material damaging to "national security," however that term may be defined.

It would, however, be utterly inconsistent with the concept of separation of powers for this Court to use its power of contempt to prevent behavior that Congress has specifically declined to prohibit. There would be a similar damage to the basic concept of these co-equal branches of Government if when the Executive Branch has adequate authority granted by Congress to protect "national security" it can choose instead to invoke the contempt power of a court to enjoin the threatened conduct. The Constitution provides that Congress shall make laws, the President execute laws, and courts interpret laws. *Youngstown Sheet & Tube Co. v. Sawyer,* 343 U.S. 579, 72 S.Ct. 863, 96 L.Ed. 1153 (1952). It did not provide for government by injunction in which the courts and the Executive Branch can "make law" without regard to the action of Congress. It may be more convenient for the Executive Branch if it need only convince a judge to prohibit conduct rather than ask the Congress to pass a law, and it may be more convenient to enforce a contempt order than to seek a criminal conviction in a jury trial. Moreover, it may be considered politically wise to get a court to share the responsibility for arresting those who the Executive Branch has probable cause to believe are violating the law. But convenience and political considerations of the moment do not justify a basic departure from the principles of our system of government.

In these cases we are not faced with a situation where Congress has failed to provide the Executive with broad power to protect the Nation from disclosure of damaging state secrets. Congress has on several occasions given extensive consideration to the problem of protecting the military and strategic secrets of the United States. This consideration has resulted in the enactment of statutes making it a crime to receive, disclose, communicate, withhold, and publish certain documents, photographs, instruments, appliances, and information. The bulk of these statutes is found in chapter 37 of U.S.C., Title 18, entitled Espionage and Censorship. In that chapter, Congress has provided penalties ranging from a $10,000 fine to death for violating the various statutes....

Thus it would seem that in order for this Court to issue an injunction it would require a showing that such an injunction would enhance the already existing power of the Government to act. *See People ex rel. Bennett v. Laman,* 277 N.Y. 368, 14 N.E.2d 439 (1938). It is a traditional axiom of equity that a court of equity will not do a useless thing just as it is a traditional axiom that equity will not enjoin the commission of a crime. *See* Z. Chafee & E. Re, *Equity* 935–954 (5th ed. 1967); 1 H. Joyce, *Injunctions* §§ 58–60a (1909). Here there has been no attempt to make such a showing. The Solicitor General does not even mention in his brief whether the Government considers that there is probable cause to believe a crime has been committed or whether there is a conspiracy to commit future crimes.

If the Government had attempted to show that there was no effective remedy under traditional criminal law, it would have had to show that there is no arguably applicable statute. Of course, at this stage this Court could not and cannot determine whether there has been a violation of a particular statute or decide the constitutionality of any statute. Whether a good-faith prosecution could have been instituted under any statute could, however, be determined.

At least one of the many statutes in this area seems relevant to these cases. Congress has provided in 18 U.S.C. § 793(e) that whoever "having unauthorized possession of, access to, or control over any document, writing, code book, signal book...or note relating to the national defense, or information relating to the national defense which information the possessor has reason to believe could be used to the injury of the United States or to the advantage of any foreign nation, willfully "communicates, delivers, transmits...the same to any person not entitled to receive it, or willfully retains the same and fails to deliver it to the officer or employee of the United States entitled to receive it...[s]hall be fined not more than $10,000 or imprisoned not more than ten years, or both." Congress has also made it a crime to conspire to commit any of the offenses listed in 18 U.S.C. § 793(e).

It is true that Judge Gurfein found that Congress had not made it a crime to publish the items and material specified in § 793(e). He found that the words "communicates, delivers, transmits...did not refer to publication of newspaper stories." And that view has some support in the legislative history and conforms with the past practice of using the statute only to prosecute those charged with ordinary espionage. *But see* 103 Cong. Rec. 10449 (remarks of Sen. Humphrey). Judge Gurfein's view of the Statute is not, however, the only plausible construction that could be given. *See* my Brother White's concurring opinion.

Even if it is determined that the Government could not in good faith bring criminal prosecutions against the *New York Times* and the *Washington Post*, it is clear that Congress has specifically rejected passing legislation that would have clearly given the President the power he seeks here and made the current activity of the newspapers unlawful. When Congress specifically declines to make conduct unlawful it is not for this Court to redecide those issues—to overrule Congress. *See Youngtown Sheet & Tube Co. v. Sawyer*, 343 U.S. 579, 72 S.Ct. 863, 96 L.Ed. 1153 (1952).

On at least two occasions Congress has refused to enact legislation that would have made the conduct engaged in here unlawful and given the President the power that he seeks in this case. In 1917 during the debate over the original Espionage Act, still the basic provisions of §793, Congress rejected a proposal to give the President in time of war or threat of war authority to directly prohibit by proclamation the publication of information relating to national defense that might be useful to the enemy.... The Executive Branch has not gone to Congress and requested that the decision to provide such power be reconsidered. Instead, the Executive Branch comes to this Court and asks that it be granted the power Congress refused to give.

...[The United States Commission on Government Security] proposed that "Congress enact legislation making it a crime for any person willfully to disclose without proper authorization, for any purpose whatever, information classified 'secret' or 'top secret,' knowing, or having reasonable grounds to believe, such information to have been so classified." Report of Commission on Government Security 619–620 (1957). After substantial floor discussion on the proposal, it was rejected. *See* 103 Cong.Rec. 10447–10450. If the proposal that Sen. Cotton championed on the floor had been enacted, the publication of the documents involved here would certainly have been a crime. Congress refused, however, to make it a crime. The Government is here asking this Court to remake that decision. This Court has no such power.

Either the Government has the power under statutory grant to use traditional criminal law to protect the country or, if there is no basis for arguing that Congress has made the activity a crime, it is plain that Congress has specifically refused to grant the authority the Government seeks from this Court. In either case this Court does not have authority to grant the requested relief. It is not for this Court to fling itself into every breach perceived by some Government official nor is it for this Court to take on itself the burden of enacting law, especially a law that Congress has refused to pass.

I believe that the judgment of the United States Court of Appeals for the District of Columbia Circuit should be affirmed and the judgment of the United States Court of Appeals for the Second Circuit should be reversed insofar as it remands the case for further hearings.

Mr. Chief Justice BURGER, dissenting.

So clear are the constitutional limitations on prior restraint against expression, that from the time of *Near v. Minnesota ex rel. Olson*, 283 U.S. 697, 51 S.Ct. 625, 75 L.Ed. 1357 (1931), until recently in *Organization for a Better Austin v. Keefe*, 402 U.S. 415, 91 S.Ct. 1575, 29 L.Ed.2d 1 (1971), we have had little occasion to be concerned with cases involving prior restraints against news reporting on matters of public interest. There is, therefore, little variation among the members of the Court in terms of resistance to prior restraints against publication. Adherence to this basic constitutional principle, however, does not make these cases simple ones. In these cases, the imperative of a free and unfettered press comes into collision with another imperative, the effective functioning of a complex modern government and specifically the effective exercise of certain constitutional powers of the Executive. Only those who view the First Amendment as an absolute in all circumstances — a view I respect, but reject — can find such cases as these to be simple or easy.

These cases are not simple for another and more immediate reason. We do not know the facts of the cases. No District Judge knew all the facts. No Court of Appeals Judge knew all the facts. No member of this Court knows all the facts.

Why are we in this posture, in which only those judges to whom the First Amendment is absolute and permits of no restraint in any circumstances or for any reason, are really in a position to act?

I suggest we are in this posture because these cases have been conducted in unseemly haste. Mr. Justice Harlan covers the chronology of events demonstrating the hectic pressures under which these cases have been processed and I need not restate them. The prompt settling of these cases reflects our universal abhorrence of prior restraint. But prompt judicial action does not mean unjudicial haste.

Here, moreover, the frenetic haste is due in large part to the manner in which the *Times* proceeded from the date it obtained the purloined documents. It seems reasonably clear now that the haste precluded reasonable and deliberate judicial treatment of these cases and was not warranted. The precipitate action of this Court aborting trials not yet completed is not the kind of judicial conduct that ought to attend the disposition of a great issue.

The newspapers make a derivative claim under the First Amendment; they denominate this right as the public "right to know;" by implication, the *Times* asserts a sole trusteeship of that right by virtue of its journalistic "scoop." The right is asserted as an absolute. Of course, the First Amendment right itself is not an absolute, as Justice Holmes so long ago pointed out in his aphorism concerning the right to shout 'fire' in a crowded theater if there was no fire. There are other exceptions, some of which Chief Justice Hughes mentioned by way of example *in Near v. Minnesota ex rel. Olson.* There are no doubt other exceptions no one has had occasion to describe or discuss. Conceivably such exceptions may be lurking in these cases and would have been flushed had they been properly considered in the trial courts, free from unwarranted deadlines and frenetic pressures. An issue of this importance should be tried and heard in a judicial atmosphere conducive to thoughtful, reflective deliberation, especially when haste, in terms of hours, is unwarranted in light of the long period the *Times*, by its own choice, deferred publication.[1]

It is not disputed that the *Times* has had unauthorized possession of the documents for three to four months, during which it has had its expert analysts studying them, presumably digesting them and preparing the material for publication. During all of this time, the *Times*, presumably in its capacity as trustee of the public's "right to know," has held up publication for purposes it considered proper and thus public knowledge was delayed. No doubt this was for a good reason; the analysis of 7,000 pages of complex material drawn from a vastly greater volume of material would inevitably take time

---

1. As noted elsewhere the *Times* conducted its analysis of the 47 volumes of Government documents over a period of several months and did so with a degree of security that a government might envy. Such security was essential, of course, to protect the enterprise from others. Meanwhile the *Times* has copyrighted its material and there were strong intimations in the oral argument that the Times contemplated enjoining its use by any other publisher in violation of its copyright. Paradoxically this would afford it a protection, analogous to prior restraint, against all others — a protection the *Times* denies the Government of the United States.

and the writing of good news stories takes time. But why should the United States Government, from whom this information was illegally acquired by someone, along with all the counsel, trial judges, and appellate judges be placed under needless pressure? After these months of deferral, the alleged "right to know" has somehow and suddenly become a right that must be vindicated instanter.

Would it have been unreasonable, since the newspaper could anticipate the Government's objections to release of secret material, to give the Government an opportunity to review the entire collection and determine whether agreement could be reached on publication? Stolen or not, if security was not in fact jeopardized, much of the material could not doubt have been declassified, since it spans a period ending in 1968. With such an approach—one that great newspapers have in the past practiced and stated editorially to be the duty of an honorable press—the newspapers and Government might well have narrowed the area of disagreement as to what was and was not publishable, leaving the remainder to be resolved in orderly litigation, if necessary. To me it is hardly believable that a newspaper long regarded as a great institution in American life would fail to perform one of the basic and simple duties of every citizen with respect to the discovery or possession of stolen property or secret government documents. That duty, I had thought—perhaps naively—was to report forthwith, to responsible public officers. This duty rests on taxi drivers, Justices, and the *New York Times*. The course followed by the *Times*, whether so calculated or not, removed any possibility of orderly litigation of the issues. If the action of the judges up to now has been correct, that result is sheer happenstance.[2]

Our grant of the writ of certiorari before final judgment in the *Times* case aborted the trial in the District Court before it had made a complete record pursuant to the mandate of the Court of Appeals for the Second Circuit.

The consequence of all this melancholy series of events is that we literally do not know what we are acting on. As I see it, we have been forced to deal with litigation concerning rights of great magnitude without an adequate record, and surely without time for adequate treatment either in the prior proceedings or in this Court. It is interesting to note that counsel, on both sides, in oral argument before this Court, were frequently unable to respond to questions on factual points. Not surprisingly they pointed out that they had been working literally "around the clock" and simply were unable to review the documents that give rise to these cases and were not familiar with them. This Court is in no better posture. I agree generally with Mr. Justice Harlan and Mr. Justice Blackmun but I am not prepared to reach the merits.[3]

I would affirm the Court of Appeals for the Second Circuit and allow the District Court to complete the trial aborted by our grant of *certiorari*, meanwhile preserving the status quo in the post case. I would direct that the District Court on remand give prior-

---

2. Interestingly the *Times* explained its refusal to allow the Government to examine its own purloined documents by saying in substance this might compromise its sources and informants! The *Times* thus asserts a right to guard the secrecy of its sources while denying that the Government of the United States has that power.

3. With respect to the question of inherent power of the Executive to classify papers, records, and documents as secret, or otherwise unavailable for public exposure, and to secure aid of the courts for enforcement, there may be an analogy with respect to this Court. No statute gives this Court express power to establish and enforce the utmost security measures for the secrecy of our deliberations and records. Yet I have little doubt as to the inherent power of the Court to protect the confidentiality of its internal operations by whatever judicial measures may be required.

ity to the *Times* case to the exclusion of all other business of that court but I would not set arbitrary deadlines.

I should add that I am in general agreement with much of what Mr. Justice White has expressed with respect to penal sanctions concerning communication or retention of documents or information relating to the national defense.

We all crave speedier judicial processes but when judges are pressured as in these cases the result is a parody of the judicial function.

Mr. Justice HARLAN, with whom THE CHIEF JUSTICE and Mr. Justice BLACKMUN join, dissenting.

These cases forcefully call to mind the wise admonition of Mr. Justice Holmes, dissenting in *Northern Securities Co. v. United States*, 193 U.S. 197, 400–401, 24 S.Ct. 436, 468, 48 L.Ed. 679 (1904):

> Great cases, like hard cases, make bad law. For great cases are called great, not by reason of their real importance in shaping the law of the future, but because of some accident of immediate overwhelming interest which appeals to the feelings and distorts the judgment. These immediate interests exercise a kind of hydraulic pressure which makes what previously was clear seem doubtful, and before which even well settled principles of law will bend.

With all respect, I consider that the Court has been almost irresponsibly feverish in dealing with these cases.

Both the Court of Appeals for the Second Circuit and the Court of Appeals for the District of Columbia Circuit rendered judgment on June 23. *The New York Times'* petition for certiorari, its motion for accelerated consideration thereof, and its application for interim relief were filed in this Court on June 24 at about 11 a.m. The application of the United States for interim relief in the *Post* case was also filed here on June 24 at about 7:15 p.m. This Court's order setting a hearing before us on June 26 at 11 a.m., a course which I joined only to avoid the possibility of even more peremptory action by the Court, was issued less than 24 hours before. The record in the *Post* case was filed with the Clerk shortly before 1 p.m. on June 25; the record in the *Times* case did not arrive until 7 or 8 o'clock that same night. The briefs of the parties were received less than two hours before argument on June 26.

This frenzied train of events took place in the name of the presumption against prior restraints created by the First Amendment. Due regard for the extraordinarily important and difficult questions involved in these litigations should have led the Court to shun such a precipitate timetable. In order to decide the merits of these cases properly, some or all of the following questions should have been faced:

1. Whether the Attorney General is authorized to bring these suits in the name of the United States. *Compare In re Debs*, 158 U.S. 564, 15 S.Ct. 900, 39 L.Ed. 1092 (1895), *with Youngstown Sheet & Tube Co. v. Sawyer*, 343 U.S. 579, 72 S.Ct. 863, 96 L.Ed. 1153 (1952). This question involves as well the construction and validity of a singularly opaque statute—the Espionage Act, 18 U.S.C. § 793(e).

2. Whether the First Amendment permits the federal courts to enjoin publication of stories which would present a serious threat to national security. *See Near v. Minnesota, ex rel. Olson*, 283 U.S. 697, 716, 51 S.Ct. 625, 631, 75 L.Ed. 1357 (1931) (dictum).

3. Whether the threat to publish highly secret documents is of itself a sufficient implication of national security to justify an injunction on the theory that regardless

of the contents of the documents harm enough results simply from the demonstration of such a breach of secrecy.

4. Whether the unauthorized disclosure of any of these particular documents would seriously impair the national security.

5. What weight should be given to the opinion of high officers in the Executive Branch of the Government with respect to questions 3 and 4.

6. Whether the newspapers are entitled to retain and use the documents notwithstanding the seemingly uncontested facts that the documents, or the originals of which they are duplicates, were purloined from the Government's possession and that the newspapers received them with knowledge that they had been feloniously acquired. *Cf. Liberty Lobby, Inc. v. Pearson,* 129 U.S.App.D.C. 74, 390 F.2d 489 (1967, amended 1968).

7. Whether the threatened harm to the national security or the Government's possessory interest in the documents justifies the issuance of an injunction against publication in light of—

     a. The strong First Amendment policy against prior restraints on publication;

     b. The doctrine against enjoining conduct in violation of criminal statutes; and

     c. The extent to which the materials at issue have apparently already been otherwise disseminated.

These are difficult questions of fact, of law, and of judgment; the potential consequences of erroneous decision are enormous. The time which has been available to us, to the lower courts, and to the parties has been wholly inadequate for giving these cases the kind of consideration they deserve. It is a reflection on the stability of the judicial process that these great issues—as important as any that have arisen during my time on the Court— should have been decided under the pressures engendered by the torrent of publicity that has attended these litigations from their inception.

Forced as I am to reach the merits of these cases, I dissent from the opinion and judgments of the Court. Within the severe limitations imposed by the time constraints under which I have been required to operate, I can only state my reasons in telescoped form, even though in different circumstances I would have felt constrained to deal with the cases in the fuller sweep indicated above.

It is a sufficient basis for affirming the Court of Appeals for the Second Circuit in the *Times* litigation to observe that its order must rest on the conclusion that because of the time elements the Government had not been given an adequate opportunity to present its case to the District Court. At the least this conclusion was not an abuse of discretion.

In the *Post* litigation the Government had more time to prepare; this was apparently the basis for the refusal of the Court of Appeals for the District of Columbia Circuit on rehearing to conform its judgment to that of the Second Circuit. But I think there is another and more fundamental reason why this judgment cannot stand—a reason which also furnishes an additional ground for not reinstating the judgment of the District Court in the *Times* litigation, set aside by the Court of Appeals. It is plain to me that the scope of the judicial function in passing upon the activities of the Executive Branch of the Government in the field of foreign affairs is very narrowly restricted. This view is, I think, dictated by the concept of separation of powers upon which our constitutional system rests.

In a speech on the floor of the House of Representatives, Chief Justice John Marshall, then a member of that body, stated: "The President is the sole organ of the nation in its external relations, and its sole representative with foreign nations." 10 Annals of Cong. 613.

From that time, shortly after the founding of the Nation, to this, there has been no substantial challenge to this description of the scope of executive power. *See United States v. Curtiss-Wright Export Corp.,* 299 U.S. 304, 319–321, 57 S.Ct. 216, 220–221, 81 L.Ed. 255 (1936), collecting authorities.

From this constitutional primacy in the field of foreign affairs, it seems to me that certain conclusions necessarily follow. Some of these were stated concisely by President Washington, declining the request of the House of Representatives for the papers leading up to the negotiation of the Jay Treaty:

> The nature of foreign negotiations requires caution, and their success must often depend on secrecy, and even when brought to a conclusion a full disclosure of all the measures, demands, or eventual concessions which may have been proposed or contemplated would be extremely impolitic; for this might have a pernicious influence on future negotiations, or produce immediate inconveniences, perhaps danger and mischief, in relation to other powers.

1 J. Richardson, *Messages and Papers of the Presidents* 194–195 (1896).

The power to evaluate the "pernicious influence" premature disclosure is not, however, lodged in the Executive alone. I agree that, in performance of its duty to protect the values of the First Amendment against political pressures, the judiciary must review the initial Executive determination to the point of satisfying itself that the subject matter of the dispute does lie within the proper compass of the President's foreign relations power. Constitutional considerations forbid "a complete abandonment of judicial control." *Cf. United States v. Reynolds,* 345 U.S. 1, 8, 73 S.Ct. 528, 532, 97 L.Ed. 727 (1953). Moreover the judiciary may properly insist that the determination that disclosure of the subject matter would irreparably impair the national security be made by the head of the Executive Department concerned—here the Secretary of State or the Secretary of Defense—after actual personal consideration by that officer. This safeguard is required in the analogous area of executive claims of privilege for secrets of state. *See id.* at 8 and n. 20, 73 S.Ct. at 532; *Duncan v. Cammell, Laird & Co.,* (1942) A.C. 624, 638 (House of Lords).

But in my judgment the judiciary may not properly go beyond these two inquiries and redetermine for itself the probable impact of disclosure on the national security.

> [T]he very nature of executive decisions as to foreign policy is political, not judicial. Such decisions are wholly confided by our Constitution to the political departments of the government, Executive and Legislative. They are delicate, complex, and involve large elements of prophecy. They are and should be undertaken only by those directly responsible to the people whose welfare they advance or imperil. They are decisions of a kind for which the Judiciary has neither aptitude, facilities nor responsibility and have long been held to belong in the domain of political power not subject to judicial intrusion or inquiry.

*Chicago & Southern Air Lines, Inc. v. Waterman Steamship Corp.,* 333 U.S. 103, 111, 68 S.Ct. 431, 436, 92 L.Ed. 568 (1948) (Jackson J.).

Even if there is some room for the judiciary to override the executive determination, it is plain that the scope of review must be exceedingly narrow. I can see no indication in the opinions of either the District Court or the Court of Appeals in the *Post* litigation that the conclusions of the Executive were given even the deference owing to an administrative agency, much less that owing to a co-equal branch of the Government operating within the field of its constitutional prerogative.

Accordingly, I would vacate the judgment of the Court of Appeals for the District of Columbia Circuit on this ground and remand the case for further proceedings in the District Court. Before the commencement of such further proceedings, due opportunity should be afforded the Government for procuring from the Secretary of State or the Secretary of Defense or both an expression of their views on the issue of national security. The ensuing review by the District Court should be in accordance with the views expressed in this opinion. And for the reasons stated above I would affirm the judgment of the Court of Appeals for the Second Circuit.

Pending further hearings in each case conducted under the appropriate ground rules, I would continue the restraints on publication. I cannot believe that the doctrine prohibiting prior restraints reaches to the point of preventing courts from maintaining the status quo long enough to act responsibly in matters of such national importance as those involved here.

Mr. Justice BLACKMUN, dissenting.

I join Mr. Justice HARLAN in his dissent. I also am in substantial accord with much that Mr. Justice WHITE says, by way of admonition, in the latter part of his opinion.

At this point the focus is on only the comparatively few documents specified by the Government as critical. So far as the other material—vast in amount—is concerned, let it be published and published forthwith if the newspapers, once the strain is gone and the sensationalism is eased, still feel the urge so to do.

But we are concerned here with the few documents specified from the 47 volumes....

The present cases, if not great, are at least unusual in their posture and implications, and the Holmes observation [referenced in Mr. Justice Harlan's dissent] certainly has pertinent application.

The *New York Times* clandestinely devoted a period of three months to examining the 47 volumes that came into its unauthorized possession. Once it had begun publication of material from those volumes, the New York case now before us emerged. It immediately assumed, and ever since has maintained, a frenetic pace and character. Seemingly once publication started, the material could not be made public fast enough. Seemingly, from then on, every deferral or delay, by restraint or otherwise, was abhorrent and was to be deemed violative of the First Amendment and of the public's "right immediately to know." Yet that newspaper stood before us at oral argument and professed criticism of the Government for not lodging its protest earlier than by a Monday telegram following the initial Sunday publication.

The District of Columbia case is much the same.

Two federal district courts, two United States courts of appeals, and this Court—within a period of less than three weeks from inception until today—have been pressed into hurried decision of profound constitutional issues on inadequately developed and largely assumed facts without the careful deliberation that, one would hope, should characterize the American judicial process. There has been much writing about the law and little knowledge and less digestion of the facts. In the New York case the judges, both trial and appellate, had not yet examined the basic material when the case was brought here. In the District of Columbia case, little more was done, and what was accomplished in this respect was only on required remand, with the *Washington Post,* on the excuse that it was trying to protect its source of information, initially refusing to reveal what material it actually possessed, and with the District Court forced to make assumptions as to that possession.

With such respect as may be due to the contrary view, this, in my opinion, is not the way to try a lawsuit of this magnitude and asserted importance. It is not the way for federal courts to adjudicate, and to be required to adjudicate, issues that allegedly concern the Nation's vital welfare. The country would be none the worse off were the cases tried quickly, to be sure, but in the customary and properly deliberative manner. The most recent of the material, it is said, dates no later than 1968, already about three years ago, and the *Times* itself took three months to formulate its plan of procedure and, thus, deprived its public for that period.

The First Amendment, after all, is only one part of an entire Constitution. Article II of the great document vests in the Executive Branch primary power over the conduct of foreign affairs and places in that branch the responsibility for the Nation's safety. Each provision of the Constitution is important, and I cannot subscribe to a doctrine of unlimited absolutism for the First Amendment at the cost of downgrading other provisions. First Amendment absolutism has never commanded a majority of this Court. *See,* for example, *Near v. Minnesota, ex rel. Olson,* 283 U.S. 697, 708, 51 S.Ct. 625, 628, 75 L.Ed. 1357 (1931), and *Schenck v. United States,* 249 U.S. 47, 52, 39 S.Ct. 247, 249, 63 L.Ed. 470 (1919). What is needed here is a weighing, upon properly developed standards, of the broad right of the press to print and of the very narrow right of the Government to prevent. Such standards are not yet developed. The parties here are in disagreement as to what those standards should be. But even the newspapers concede that there are situations where restraint is in order and is constitutional. Mr. Justice Holmes gave us a suggestion when he said in *Schenck,*

> It is a question of proximity and degree. When a nation is at war many things that might be said in time of peace are such a hindrance to its effort that their utterance will not be endured so long as men fight and that no Court could regard them as protected by any constitutional right.

249 U.S. at 52, 39 S.Ct. at 249.

I therefore would remand these cases to be developed expeditiously, of course, but on a schedule permitting the orderly presentation of evidence from both sides, with the use of discovery, if necessary, as authorized by the rules, and with the preparation of briefs, oral argument, and court opinions of a quality better than has been seen to this point. In making this last statement, I criticize no lawyer or judge. I know from past personal experience the agony of time pressure in the preparation of litigation. But these cases and the issues involved and the courts, including this one, deserve better than has been produced thus far.

It may well be that if these cases were allowed to develop as they should be developed, and to be tried as lawyers should try them and as courts should hear them, free of pressure and panic and sensationalism, other light would be shed on the situation and contrary considerations, for me, might prevail. But that is not the present posture of the litigation.

The Court, however, decides the cases today the other way. I therefore add one final comment.

I strongly urge, and sincerely hope, that these two newspapers will be fully aware of their ultimate responsibilities to the United States of America. Judge Wilkey, dissenting in the District of Columbia case, after a review of only the affidavits before his court (the basic papers had not then been made available by either party), concluded that there were a number of examples of documents that, if in the possession of the Post, and if published, "could clearly result in great harm to the nation," and he defined "harm" to mean "the death of soldiers, the destruction of alliances, the greatly increased difficulty of negotiation with our enemies, the inability of our diplomats to negotiate....." I, for one, have now been able to give at least some cursory study not only to the affidavits, but to the material itself. I regret to say that from this examination I fear that Judge Wilkey's statements have possible foundation. I therefore share his concern. I hope that damage has not already been done. If, however, damage has been done, and if, with the Court's action today, these newspapers proceed to publish the critical documents and there results therefrom "the death of soldiers, the destruction of alliances, the greatly increased difficulty of negotiation with our enemies, the inability of our diplomats to negotiate," to which list I might add the factors of prolongation of the war and of further delay in the freeing of United States prisoners, then the Nation's people will know where the responsibility for these sad consequences rests.

## Notes and Questions

1.  *New York Times Co. v. United States*, 403 U.S. 713 (1971), became known as "the Pentagon Papers case." No criminal charges were brought against the newspapers in connection with their publication of the Pentagon Papers.

2.  William Glendon, who argued the Pentagon Papers case in the Supreme Court on behalf of *The Washington Post*, recounted that during the argument, Chief Justice Burger alluded to the fact that the newspapers, to protect their sources, had refused to produce the Pentagon Papers they held. "He pointed out that those coming into a court of equity must do equity. To which I replied, we had not come into a court of equity, we 'were brought in kicking and screaming.' While hardly a legalistic or even equitable answer, it seemed to do the job, since we passed on to another subject." William R. Glendon, *Fifteen Days In June That Shook the First Amendment: A First Person Account of the Pentagon Papers Case*, 65 N.Y. State Bar J. 24, 26 (Nov. 1993).

3.  "A responsible press has always been regarded as the handmaiden of effective judicial administration, especially in the criminal field. Its function in this regard is documented by an impressive record of service over several centuries. The press does not simply publish information about trials but guards against the miscarriage of justice by subjecting the police, prosecutors, and judicial processes to extensive public scrutiny and criticism." *Sheppard v. Maxwell*, 384 U.S. 333, 350 (1966). Further, "[a] responsible press is an undoubtedly desirable goal, but press responsibility is not mandated by the Constitution and like many other virtues it cannot be legislated." *Miami Herald Pub'g Co. v. Tornillo*, 418 U.S. 241, 256 (1974).

4.  A review of "accepted jurisprudence" reveals that "the First Amendment erects a virtually insurmountable barrier between government and the print media so far as government tampering in advance of publication, with news and editorial content is concerned." *Id.* at 259 (White, J., concurring) (citing *New York Times Co. v. United States*, 403 U.S. 713).

5.  With respect to national security interests in the context of exporting encryption source code, *see* discussion *infra* at 372.

Note the concerns expressed by Justices Burger and Harlan that the proceedings in the Pentagon Papers case were conducted "frenetic[ally]" and in "in unseemly haste." Today's era offers wordprocessing, laser printers, facsimile transmission, computerized research databases, rapid duplicating equipment, and speedy and diverse travel options. In addition, American courts have been experimenting for several years with electronic court filings, ranging from the Advanced Court Engineering project launched in Albuquerque, New Mexico, to an out-sourced electronic filing project in Colorado. *See* Evan Hansen, *E-Filing Aims to Reduce Courts' Dependence on Paper*, CNETNews.com (Aug. 6, 2000) <http://news.cnet.com/news/0-100S-200-2451274.htm>. Would these devices and resources likely have alleviated the judges' concern or exacerbated it?

More significantly, how does the immediacy with which content can be disseminated over the Internet impact on the analysis? First Amendment expert Floyd Abrams has mused, "I wonder, if that individual wanted to leak such information today, if, instead of giving it or making available to *The New York Times*, it would just be posted on the Internet." Floyd Abrams, *First Amendment Postcards From the Edge of Cyberspace*, 11 St. John's J. Legal Cmt. 693, 698–99 (1996). Would efforts to secure a prior restraint through judicial imprimatur be rendered moot by the facile ease of digital transmission capabilities?

On June 23, 2000, the Associated Press reported that a web-site posted a secret Central Intelligence Agency briefing by an individual who allegedly had received it from an anonymous source in Japan. Reportedly included in the posting was information on staffing for the National Foreign Intelligence Program and the home telephone number of a CIA official. Information about a Japanese law enforcement agency also evidently was displayed. *See* The Associated Press, *Web-Site Posts Secret CIA Papers* (July 23, 2000) <http://news.cnet.com/news/0-1005-200-2326930.htm>. From a pragmatic standpoint, what options are available to a governmental entity that seeks to prevent such speech?

Consider the impact of "mirroring" technology on these issues. Mirroring is the copying of substantially all of the contents of a server to a remote server. Documents can then be accessed at the remote site by the user. What are the ramifications for a web-site that utilizes mirroring technology when its content is the subject of efforts to secure a prior restraint?

In a different context, the plaintiff alleged that the defendants had misappropriated trade secrets and posted the information on their web-sites. *DVD Copy Control Association, Inc. v. McLaughlin*, No. CV 786804, 2000 WL 48512 (Cal. Super. Jan. 21, 2000). The court enjoined the postings by the defendants, but pointed out that it was "mindful of the many enforcement problems. However, a possibility or even a likelihood that an order may be disobeyed or not enforced in other jurisdictions is not a reason to deny the relief sought." *Id.* at *3.

In *Universal City Studios, Inc. v. Reimerdes*, No. 00 Civ. 0277, 2000 U.S. Dist. LEXIS 11696 at *143 (S.D.N.Y. Aug. 17, 2000), the court remarked:

> If a plaintiff seeks to enjoin a defendant from burning a pasture, it is no answer that there is a wild fire burning in its direction. If the defendant itself threatens the plaintiff with irreparable harm, then equity will enjoin the defendant from carrying out the threat even if other threats abound and even if part of the pasture already is burned.

A city council in Britain had objected to postings on the Web by British journalists of a government report that analyzed an official response to Nottinghamshire County officials to claims of Satanism and child abuse. The city council sought an injunction against the journalists who had posted the report, premising the right to such relief on a charge of copyright infringement. The journalists then reportedly posted links to mirror sites, so that the substance of the report was available from other sites whose operators previously had downloaded and re-posted the report. The Internet effectively confounded the city council's efforts to quell disclosure of the report on-line. "By the time the document was removed from British sites, it had already zinged its way around the globe." Ashley Craddock, *Little Pig, I'll Blow Your Site Down*, Wired News (June 13, 1997) <http://www.wired.con/news/politics/0,1283,4418,00.html>.

---

# Obscenity and Indecency

The nature of the speech in issue has had an impact on the scope of protection extended. Political speech, such as speech pertaining to elections or the government, has been characterized as "close to the core" of the First Amendment, and thus deserving of enhanced protection. "Categorization is used not only to deny protection altogether, but to single out certain kinds of speech for more or less protection. As a result, categorization today is almost always linked with balancing, with the choice of category determining the level of scrutiny to be used when balancing the competing interests in restricting the expression and protecting free speech." Marc A. Franklin, *et al., Mass Media Law* 79 (6th ed. 2000).

Obscene speech has been characterized as "[t]he most conspicuous categorical exception to the First Amendment." *Id.* at 78. However, "[d]espite the [Supreme] Court's continued adherence to the categorical approach, there is much about the law of obscenity that does not seem categorical at all. Even obscene material receives some First Amendment protection." *Id.* Ultimately, as Justice Kennedy has stated, "[t]he First Amendment is a rule of substantive protection, not an artifice of categories." *Alexander v. United States*, 509 U.S. 544, 565 (1993) (Kennedy, J., dissenting).

In *Miller v. California*, 413 U.S. 15 (1973), the Supreme Court articulated the test for regulating obscenity: (1) whether the average person, applying contemporary community standards, would find that the work, taken as a whole, appeals to the prurient interest; (2) whether the work depicts or describes in a patently offensive way sexual conduct specifically defined by the applicable state law; and (3) whether the work, taken as a whole, lacks serious literary, artistic, political, or scientific value. *Id.* at 24 (citations omitted). By incorporating a standard of contemporary community standards, the *Miller* test offers both flexibility and uncertainty, as the reviewing court may take into consideration changing values, morals, and perspectives.

The Supreme Court later refined the test for obscene expression insofar as it pertained to child pornography. *See New York v. Ferber*, 458 U.S. 747, 764 (1982). Heightened concerns about the deleterious effects of pornography when children were exploited led the Court to delineate a separate test from that enunciated in *Miller*. Unlike the *Miller* formulation, the trier of fact need not find that the material in issue appeals to the prurient interest of the average person or that the sexual conduct was portrayed in a patently offensive manner. Nor must the material at issue be considered as a whole. *New York v. Ferber*, 458 U.S. at 764.

Obscene and indecent materials are among the types of content distributed over the Internet. Significant attention has been focused on the parameters for legislatively-imposed constraints on obscene expression. Congress' initial approach to the issue, reflected in the Communications Decency Act of 1996, 47 U.S.C.A. § 223 (West 1991 & Supp. 2000), was struck down as unconstitutional:

_____

# Janet RENO v. AMERICAN CIVIL LIBERTIES UNION
### Supreme Court of the United States
### No. 96-511, 521 U.S. 844
### June 26, 1997

Justice STEVENS delivered the opinion of the Court.

At issue is the constitutionality of two statutory provisions enacted to protect minors from "indecent" and "patently offensive" communications on the Internet. Notwithstanding the legitimacy and importance of the congressional goal of protecting children from harmful materials, we agree with the three-judge District Court that the statute abridges "the freedom of speech" protected by the First Amendment....

The Telecommunications Act of 1996, Pub. L. 104-104, 110 Stat. 56, was an unusually important legislative enactment. As stated on the first of its 103 pages, its primary purpose was to reduce regulation and encourage "the rapid deployment of new telecommunications technologies." The major components of the statute have nothing to do with the Internet; they were designed to promote competition in the local telephone service market, the multichannel video market, and the market for over-the-air broadcasting.... Title V [is] known as the "Communications Decency Act of 1996" (CDA)....[One provision,] 47 U.S.C. §223(a) (Supp. 1997), prohibits the knowing transmission of obscene or indecent messages to any recipient under 18 years of age.... [Another] provision, §223(d), prohibits the knowing sending or displaying of patently offensive messages in a manner that is available to a person under 18 years of age....

The breadth of these prohibitions is qualified by two affirmative defenses. *See* §223(e)(5). One covers those who take "good faith, reasonable, effective, and appropriate actions" to restrict access by minors to the prohibited communications. §223(e)(5)(A). The other covers those who restrict access to covered material by requiring certain designated forms of age proof, such as a verified credit card or an adult identification number or code. §223(e)(5)(B)....

In arguing for reversal, the Government contends that the CDA is plainly constitutional under three of our prior decisions: (1) *Ginsberg v. New York*, 390 U.S. 629, 88 S.Ct. 1274, 20 L.Ed.2d 195 (1968); (2) *FCC v. Pacifica Foundation*, 438 U.S. 726, 98 S.Ct. 3026, 57 L.Ed.2d 1073 (1978); and (3) *Renton v. Playtime Theatres, Inc.*, 475 U.S. 41, 106 S.Ct. 925, 89 L.Ed.2d 29 (1986). A close look at these cases, however, raises—rather than relieves—doubts concerning the constitutionality of the CDA.

In *Ginsberg*, we upheld the constitutionality of a New York statute that prohibited selling to minors under 17 years of age material that was considered obscene as to them even if not obscene as to adults. We rejected the defendant's broad submission that "the scope of the constitutional freedom of expression secured to a citizen to read or see material concerned with sex cannot be made to depend on whether the citizen is an adult or a minor." 390 U.S. at 636, 88 S.Ct. at 1279. In rejecting that contention, we relied not only on the State's independent interest in the well-being of its youth, but also on our consistent recognition of the principle that "the parents' claim to authority in their own household to direct the rearing of their children is basic in the structure of our society." In four important respects, the statute upheld in *Ginsberg* was narrower than the CDA. First, we noted in *Ginsberg* that "the prohibition against sales to minors does not bar parents who so desire from purchasing the magazines for their children." *Id.* at 639, 88 S.Ct. at 1280. Under the CDA, by contrast, neither the parents' consent—nor even their participation—in the communication would avoid the application of the statute. Second, the New York statute applied only to commercial transactions, *id.* at 647, 88 S.Ct. at 1284–1285, whereas the CDA contains no such limitation. Third, the New York statute cabined its definition of material that is harmful to minors with the requirement that it be "utterly without redeeming social importance for minors." *Id.* at 646, 88 S.Ct. at 1284. The CDA fails to provide us with any definition of the term "indecent" as used in §223(a)(1) and, importantly, omits any requirement that the "patently offensive" material covered by §223(d) lack serious literary, artistic, political, or scientific value. Fourth, the New York statute defined a minor as a person under the age of 17, whereas the CDA, in applying to all those under 18 years, includes an additional year of those nearest majority.

In *Pacifica,* we upheld a declaratory order of the Federal Communications Commission, holding that the broadcast of a recording of a 12-minute monologue entitled "Filthy Words" that had previously been delivered to a live audience "could have been the subject of administrative sanctions." 438 U.S. at 730, 98 S.Ct. at 3030 (internal quotation marks omitted). The Commission had found that the repetitive use of certain words referring to excretory or sexual activities or organs "in an afternoon broadcast when children are in the audience was patently offensive" and concluded that the monologue was indecent "as broadcast." *Id.* at 735, 98 S.Ct. at 3033. The respondent did not quarrel with the finding that the afternoon broadcast was patently offensive, but contended that it was not "indecent" within the meaning of the relevant statutes because it contained no prurient appeal....

In the portion of the lead opinion not joined by Justices Powell and Blackmun, the plurality stated that the First Amendment does not prohibit all governmental regulation that depends on the content of speech. *Id.* at 742–743, 98 S.Ct. at 3036–3037. Accordingly, the availability of constitutional protection for a vulgar and offensive monologue that was not obscene depended on the context of the broadcast. *Id.* at 744–748, 98 S.Ct. at 3037–3040. Relying on the premise that "of all forms of communication" broadcasting had received the most limited First Amendment protection, *id.* at 748–749, 98 S.Ct. at 3039–3040, the Court concluded that the ease with which children may obtain access to broadcasts, "coupled with the concerns recognized in *Ginsberg*," justified special treatment of indecent broadcasting. *Id.* at 749–750, 98 S.Ct. at 3040–3041.

As with the New York statute at issue in *Ginsberg*, there are significant differences between the order upheld in *Pacifica* and the CDA. First, the order in *Pacifica*, issued by an agency that had been regulating radio stations for decades, targeted a specific broadcast that represented a rather dramatic departure from traditional program content in order to designate when—rather than whether—it would be permissible to air such a program in that particular medium. The CDA's broad categorical prohibitions are not limited to particular times and are not dependent on any evaluation by an agency familiar with the unique characteristics of the Internet. Second, unlike the CDA, the Commission's declaratory order was not punitive; we expressly refused to decide whether the indecent broadcast "would justify a criminal prosecution." 438 U.S. at 750, 98 S.Ct. at 3041. Finally, the Commission's order applied to a medium which as a matter of history had "received the most limited First Amendment protection," *id.* at 748,

98 S.Ct. at 3040, in large part because warnings could not adequately protect the listener from unexpected program content. The Internet, however, has no comparable history. Moreover, the District Court found that the risk of encountering indecent material by accident is remote because a series of affirmative steps is required to access specific material.

In *Renton*, we upheld a zoning ordinance that kept adult movie theaters out of residential neighborhoods. The ordinance was aimed, not at the content of the films shown in the theaters, but rather at the "secondary effects"—such as crime and deteriorating property values—that these theaters fostered: "'It is th[e] secondary effect which these zoning ordinances attempt to avoid, not the dissemination of "offensive" speech.'" 475 U.S. at 49, 106 S.Ct. at 930 (quoting *Young v. American Mini Theatres, Inc.*, 427 U.S. 50, 71, n. 34, 96 S.Ct. 2440, 2453, n. 34, 49 L.Ed.2d 310 (1976)). According to the Government, the CDA is constitutional because it constitutes a sort of "cyberzoning" on the Internet. But the CDA applies broadly to the entire universe of cyberspace. And the purpose of the CDA is to protect children from the primary effects of "indecent" and "patently offensive" speech, rather than any "secondary" effect of such speech. Thus, the CDA is a content-based blanket restriction on speech, and, as such, cannot be "properly analyzed as a form of time, place, and manner regulation." 475 U.S. at 46, 106 S.Ct. at 928. *See also Boos v. Barry*, 485 U.S. 312, 321, 108 S.Ct. 1157, 1163, 99 L.Ed.2d 333 (1988) ("Regulations that focus on the direct impact of speech on its audience" are not properly analyzed under *Renton*); *Forsyth County v. Nationalist Movement*, 505 U.S. 123, 134, 112 S.Ct. 2395, 2403, 120 L.Ed.2d 101 (1992) ("Listeners' reaction to speech is not a content-neutral basis for regulation").

These precedents, then, surely do not require us to uphold the CDA and are fully consistent with the application of the most stringent review of its provisions.

In *Southeastern Promotions, Ltd. v. Conrad*, 420 U.S. 546, 557, 95 S.Ct. 1239, 1245–1246, 43 L.Ed.2d 448 (1975), we observed that "[e]ach medium of expression... may present its own problems." Thus, some of our cases have recognized special justifications for regulation of the broadcast media that are not applicable to other speakers, *see Red Lion Broadcasting Co. v. FCC*, 395 U.S. 367, 89 S.Ct. 1794, 23 L.Ed.2d 371 (1969); *FCC v. Pacifica Foundation*, 438 U.S. 726, 98 S.Ct. 3026, 57 L.Ed.2d 1073 (1978). In these cases, the Court relied on the history of extensive Government regulation of the broadcast medium, *see, e.g., Red Lion*, 395 U.S. at 399–400, 89 S.Ct. at 1811–1812; the scarcity of available frequencies at its inception, *see, e.g., Turner Broadcasting System, Inc. v. FCC*, 512 U.S. 622, 637–638, 114 S.Ct. 2445, 2456–2457, 129 L.Ed.2d 497 (1994); and its "invasive" nature, *see Sable Communications of Cal., Inc. v. FCC*, 492 U.S. 115, 128, 109 S.Ct. 2829, 2837–2838, 106 L.Ed.2d 93 (1989).

Those factors are not present in cyberspace. Neither before nor after the enactment of the CDA have the vast democratic forums of the Internet been subject to the type of government supervision and regulation that has attended the broadcast industry. Moreover, the Internet is not as "invasive" as radio or television. The District Court specifically found that "[c]ommunications over the Internet do not 'invade' an individual's home or appear on one's computer screen unbidden. Users seldom encounter content 'by accident.'" 929 F. Supp. at 844....

Finally, unlike the conditions that prevailed when Congress first authorized regulation of the broadcast spectrum, the Internet can hardly be considered a "scarce" expressive commodity. It provides relatively unlimited, low-cost capacity for communication of all kinds. The Government estimates that "[a]s many as 40 million people use the Internet today, and that figure is expected to grow to 200 million by 1999." This dynamic, multifaceted category of communication includes not only traditional print and news services, but also audio, video, and still images, as well as interactive, real-time dialogue. Through the use of chat rooms, any person with a phone line can become a town crier with a voice that resonates farther than it could from any soapbox. Through the use of Web pages, mail exploders, and newsgroups, the same individual can become a pamphleteer. As the District Court found, "the content on the Internet is as diverse as human thought." 929 F. Supp. at 842 (finding 74). We agree with its conclusion that our cases provide no basis for qualifying the level of First Amendment scrutiny that should be applied to this medium.

Regardless of whether the CDA is so vague that it violates the Fifth Amendment, the many ambiguities concerning the scope of its coverage render it problematic for purposes of the First Amendment. For instance, each of the two parts of the CDA uses a different linguistic form. The first uses the word "indecent," 47 U.S.C. §223(a) (1994 ed., Supp. II), while the second speaks of material that "in context, depicts or describes, in terms patently offensive as measured by contemporary community standards, sexual or excretory activities or organs," §223(d). Given the absence of a definition of either term, this difference in language will provoke uncertainty among speakers about how the two standards relate to each other and just what they mean. Could a speaker confidently assume that a serious discussion about birth control practices, homosexuality, the First Amendment issues raised by the Appendix to our *Pacifica* opinion, or the consequences of prison rape would not violate the CDA? This uncertainty undermines the likelihood that the CDA has been carefully tailored to the congressional goal of protecting minors from potentially harmful materials.

The vagueness of the CDA is a matter of special concern for two reasons. First, the CDA is a content-based regulation of speech. The vagueness of such a regulation raises special First Amendment concerns because of its obvious chilling effect on free speech. *See, e.g., Gentile v. State Bar of Nev.,* 501 U.S. 1030, 1048–1051, 111 S.Ct. 2720, 2731–2733, 115 L.Ed.2d 888 (1991). Second, the CDA is a criminal statute. In addition to the opprobrium and stigma of a criminal conviction, the CDA threatens violators with penalties including up to two years in prison for each act of violation. The severity of criminal sanctions may well cause speakers to remain silent rather than communicate even arguably unlawful words, ideas, and images. *See, e.g., Dombrowski v. Pfister,* 380 U.S. 479, 494, 85 S.Ct. 1116, 1125, 14 L.Ed.2d 22 (1965). As a practical matter, this increased deterrent effect, coupled with the "risk of discriminatory enforcement" of vague regulations, poses greater First Amendment concerns than those implicated by the civil regulation reviewed in *Denver Area Ed. Telecommunications Consortium, Inc. v. FCC,* 518 U.S. 727, 116 S.Ct. 2374, 135 L.Ed.2d 888 (1996)....

In contrast to *Miller* and our other previous cases, the CDA thus presents a greater threat of censoring speech that, in fact, falls outside the statute's scope. Given the vague contours of the coverage of the statute, it unquestionably silences some speakers whose messages would be entitled to constitutional protection. That danger provides further reason for insisting that the statute not be overly broad. The CDA's burden on protected speech cannot be justified if it could be avoided by a more carefully drafted statute.

We are persuaded that the CDA lacks the precision that the First Amendment requires when a statute regulates the content of speech. In order to deny minors access to potentially harmful speech, the CDA effectively suppresses a large amount of speech that adults have a constitutional right to receive and to address to one another. That burden on adult speech is unacceptable if less restrictive alternatives would be at least as effective in achieving the legitimate purpose that the statute was enacted to serve....

The breadth of the CDA's coverage is wholly unprecedented. Unlike the regulations upheld in *Ginsberg* and *Pacifica*, the scope of the CDA is not limited to commercial speech or commercial entities. Its open-ended prohibitions embrace all nonprofit entities and individuals posting indecent messages or displaying them on their own computers in the presence of minors. The general, undefined terms "indecent" and "patently offensive" cover large amounts of nonpornographic material with serious educational or other value. Moreover, the "community standards" criterion as applied to the Internet means that any communication to a nation wide audience will be judged by the standards of the community most likely to be offended by the message. The regulated subject matter includes any of the seven "dirty words" used in the *Pacifica* monologue, the use of which the Government's expert acknowledged could constitute a felony. It may also extend to discussions about prison rape or safe sexual practices, artistic images that include nude subjects, and arguably the card catalog of the Carnegie Library....

The breadth of this content-based restriction of speech imposes an especially heavy burden on the Government to explain why a less restrictive provision would not be as effective as the CDA. It has not done so. The arguments in this Court have referred to possible alternatives such as requiring that indecent material be "tagged" in a way that facilitates parental control of material coming into their homes, making exceptions for messages with artistic or educational value, providing some tolerance for parental choice, and regulating some portions of the Internet—such as commercial Web sites—differently from others, such as chat rooms. Particularly in the light of the absence of any detailed findings by the Congress, or even hearings addressing the special problems of the CDA, we are persuaded that the CDA is not narrowly tailored if that requirement has any meaning at all....

In this Court, though not in the District Court, the Government asserts that—in addition to its interest in protecting children—its "[e]qually significant" interest in fostering the growth of the Internet provides an independent basis for upholding the constitutionality of the CDA. The Government apparently assumes that the unregulated availability of "indecent" and "patently offensive" material on the Internet is driving countless citizens away from the medium because of the risk of exposing themselves or their children to harmful material.

We find this argument singularly unpersuasive. The dramatic expansion of this new marketplace of ideas contradicts the factual basis of this contention. The record demonstrates that the growth of the Internet has been and continues to be phenomenal. As a matter of constitutional tradition, in the absence of evidence to the contrary, we presume that governmental regulation of the content of speech is more likely to interfere with the free exchange of ideas than to encourage it. The interest in encouraging freedom of expression in a democratic society outweighs any theoretical but unproven benefit of censorship.

For the foregoing reasons, the judgment of the District Court is affirmed.

———

The second Congressional effort to legislate in this area, representing the Child On-Line Protection Act, 47 U.S.C. § 201, *et seq.* ("COPA"), likewise was preliminarily enjoined by the U.S. District Court for the Eastern District of Pennsylvania. *American Civil Liberties Union v. Reno*, 31 F. Supp. 2d 473 (E.D. Pa. 1999). The government appealed the decision to the Third Circuit:

———

# AMERICAN CIVIL LIBERTIES UNION v. Janet RENO
United States Court of Appeals, Third Circuit
No. 99-1324, 217 F.3d 162
June 22, 2000

GARTH, Circuit Judge:

This appeal "presents a conflict between one of society's most cherished rights—freedom of expression—and one of the government's most profound obligations—the protection of minors." *American Booksellers v. Webb*, 919 F.2d 1493, 1495 (11th Cir. 1990). The government challenges the District Court's issuance of a preliminary injunction which prevents the enforcement of the Child Online Protection Act, Pub. L. No. 105-277, 112 Stat. 2681 (1998) (codified at 47 U.S.C. §231) ("COPA"), enacted in October of 1998. At issue is COPA's constitutionality, a statute designed to protect minors from "harmful material" measured by "contemporary community standards" knowingly posted on the World Wide Web ("Web") for commercial purposes.

We will affirm the District Court's grant of a preliminary injunction because we are confident that the ACLU's attack on COPA's constitutionality is likely to succeed on the merits. Because material posted on the Web is accessible by all Internet users worldwide, and because current technology does not permit a Web publisher to restrict access to its site based on the geographic locale of each particular Internet user, COPA essentially requires that every Web publisher subject to the statute abide by the most restrictive and conservative state's community standards in order to avoid criminal liability. Thus, because the standard by which COPA gauges whether material is "harmful to minors" is based on identifying "contemporary community standards" the inability of Web publishers to restrict access to their Web sites based on the geographic locale of the site visitor, in and of itself, imposes an impermissible burden on constitutionally protected First Amendment speech.

In affirming the District Court, we are forced to recognize that, at present, due to technological limitations, there may be no other means by which harmful material on the Web may be constitutionally restricted, although, in light of rapidly developing technological advances, what may now be impossible to regulate constitutionally may, in the not-too-distant future, become feasible.

## I. BACKGROUND

COPA was enacted into law on October 21, 1998. Commercial Web publishers subject to the statute that distribute material that is harmful to minors are required under COPA to ensure that minors do not access the harmful material on their Web site. COPA is Congress's second attempt to regulate the dissemination to minors of indecent material on the Web/Internet. The Supreme Court had earlier, on First Amendment grounds, struck down Congress's first endeavor, the Communications Decency Act, ("CDA") which it passed as part of the Telecommunications Act of 1996. *See ACLU v. Reno*, 521 U.S. 844, 117 S.Ct. 2329, 138 L.Ed.2d 874 (1997) ("*Reno II*")....

The CDA prohibited Internet users from using the Internet to communicate material that, under contemporary community standards, would be deemed patently offensive to minors under the age of eighteen. *See Reno II*, 521 U.S. at 859–60. In so restricting Internet users, the CDA provided two affirmative defenses to prosecution; (1) the use of a credit card or other age verification system, and (2) any good faith effort to restrict access by minors. *See id.* at 860. In holding that the CDA violated the First Amendment, the Supreme Court explained that without defining key terms the statute was unconstitutionally vague. Moreover, the Court noted that the breadth of the CDA was "wholly unprecedented" in that, for example, it was "not limited to commercial speech or commercial entities...[but rather its] open-ended prohibitions embrace all nonprofit entities and individuals posting indecent messages or displaying them on their own computers." *Id.* at 877.

Further, the Court explained that, as applied to the Internet, a community standards criterion would effectively mean that because all Internet communication is made available to a worldwide audience, the content of the conveyed message will be judged by the standards of the community most likely to be offended by the content. *See id.* at 877–78. Finally, with respect to the affirmative defenses authorized by the CDA, the Court concluded that such defenses would not be economically feasible for most noncommercial Web publishers, and that even with respect to commercial publishers, the technology had yet to be proven effective in shielding minors from harmful material. *See id.* at 881. As a result, the Court held that the CDA was not tailored so narrowly as to achieve the government's compelling interest in protecting minors, and that it lacked the precision that the First Amendment requires when a statute regulates the content of speech. *See id.* at 874. *See also United States v. Playboy Entertainment Group, Inc.,* — U.S. —, 120 S.Ct. 1878, — L.Ed.2d —, 2000 WL 646196 (U.S. May 22, 2000).

COPA, the present statute, attempts to "address[ ] the specific concerns raised by the Supreme Court" in invalidating the CDA. H.R. Rep. No. 105-775 at 12 (1998); *see* S.R. Rep. No. 05-225, at 2 (1998). COPA prohibits an individual or entity from:

> knowingly and with knowledge of the character of the material, in interstate or foreign commerce by means of the World Wide Web, mak[ing] any communication for commercial purposes that is available to any minor and that includes any material that is harmful to minors.

47 U.S.C. §231(a)(1). As part of its attempt to cure the constitutional defects found in the CDA, Congress sought to define most of COPA's key terms. COPA attempts, for example, to restrict its scope to material on the Web rather than on the Internet as a whole; to target only those Web communications made for "commercial purposes;" and to limit its scope to only that material deemed "harmful to minors."

Under COPA, whether material published on the Web is "harmful to minors" is governed by a three-part test, each of which must be found before liability can attach:

> (A) the average person, applying contemporary community standards, would find, taking the material as a whole and with respect to minors, is designed to appeal to, or is designed to pander to, the prurient interest;

> (B) depicts, describes, or represents, in a manner patently offensive with respect to minors, an actual or simulated sexual act or sexual contact, an actual or simulated normal or perverted sexual act, or a lewd exhibition of the genitals or post-pubescent female breast; and

> (C) taken as a whole, lacks serious, literary, artistic, political, or scientific value for minors.

47 U.S.C. §231(e)(6). The parties conceded at oral argument that this "contemporary community standards" test applies to those communities within the United States, and not to foreign communities. Therefore, the more liberal community standards of Amsterdam or the more restrictive community standards of Tehran would not impact upon the analysis of whether material is "harmful to minors" under COPA.

COPA also provides Web publishers subject to the statute with affirmative defenses. If a Web publisher "has restricted access by minors to material that is harmful to minors" through the use of a "credit card, debit account, adult access code, or adult personal identification number...a digital certificate that verifies age...or by any other reasonable measures that are feasible under available technology," then no liability will attach to the Web publisher even if a minor should nevertheless gain access to restricted material under COPA. 47 U.S.C. §231(c)(1). COPA violators face both criminal (maximum fines of $50,000 and a maximum prison term of six months, or both) and civil (fines of up to $50,000 for each day of violation) penalties....

## II. ANALYSIS

...A. Reasonable probability of success on the merits

We begin our analysis by considering what, for this case, is the most significant prong of the preliminary injunction test—whether the ACLU met its burden of establishing a reasonable probability of succeeding on the merits in proving that COPA trenches upon the First Amendment to the United States Constitution. Initially, we note that the District Court correctly determined that as a content-based restriction on speech, COPA is "both presumptively invalid and subject to strict scrutiny analysis." See [*American Civil Liberties Union v. Reno*, 31 F. Supp. 2d 473, 493 (E.D. Pa 1999) ("*Reno III*")]. As in all areas of constitutional strict scrutiny jurisprudence, the government must establish that the challenged statute is narrowly tailored to meet a compelling state interest, and that it seeks to protect its interest in a manner that is the least restrictive of protected speech. See, e.g., *Schaumberg v. Citizens for a Better Environment*, 444 U.S. 620, 637, 100 S.Ct. 826, 63 L.Ed.2d 73 (1980); *Sable Comm of Calif. v. FCC*, 492 U.S. 115, 126 (1989). These principles have been emphasized again in the Supreme Court's most recent opinion, *United States v. Playboy Entertainment Group, Inc.*, — U.S. —, 120 S.Ct. 1878, — L.Ed.2d ——, 2000 WL 646196 (U.S. May 22, 2000), where the Court, concerned with the "bleeding" of cable transmissions, held §505 of the Telecommunications Act of 1996 unconstitutional as violative of the First Amendment.

It is undisputed that the government has a compelling interest in protecting children from material that is harmful to them, even if not obscene by adult standards. See *Reno III*, 31 F. Supp. 2d at 495 (citing *Sable*, 492 U.S. at 126 (1989); *Ginsberg v. New York*, 390 U.S. 629, 639–40, 88 S.Ct. 1274, 20 L.Ed.2d 195 (1968)). At issue is whether, in achieving this compelling objective, Congress has articulated a constitutionally permissible means to achieve its objective without curtailing the protected free speech rights of adults. See *Reno III*, 31 F. Supp. 2d at 492 (citing *Sable*, 492 U.S. at 127; *Butler v. Michigan*, 352 U.S. 380, 383, 77 S.Ct. 524, 1 L.Ed.2d 412 (1957)). As we have observed, the District Court found that it had not—holding that COPA was not likely to succeed in surviving strict scrutiny analysis.

We base our particular determination of COPA's likely unconstitutionality, however, on COPA's reliance on "contemporary community standards" in the context of the electronic medium of the Web to identify material that is harmful to minors. The overbreadth of COPA's definition of "harmful to minors" applying a "contemporary community standards" clause—although virtually ignored by the parties and the amicus in their respective briefs but raised by us at oral argument—so concerns us that we are persuaded that this aspect of COPA, without reference to its other provisions, must lead inexorably to a holding of a likelihood of unconstitutionality of the entire COPA statute. Hence we base our opinion entirely on the basis of the likely unconstitutionality of this clause, even though the District Court relied on numerous other grounds.

As previously noted, in passing COPA, Congress attempted to resolve all of the problems raised by the Supreme Court in striking down the CDA as unconstitutional. One concern noted by the Supreme Court was that, as a part of the wholly unprecedented broad coverage of the CDA, "the 'community standards' criterion as applied to the Internet means that any communication available to a nationwide audience will be judged by the standards of the community most likely to be offended by the message." *Reno II*, 521 U.S. at 877–78. We are not persuaded that the Supreme Court's concern with respect to the "community standards" criterion has been sufficiently remedied by Congress in COPA.

Previously, in addressing the mailing of unsolicited sexually explicit material in violation of a California obscenity statute, the Supreme Court held that the fact-finder must determine whether " 'the average person, applying contemporary community standards' would find the work taken as a whole, [to appeal] to the prurient interest." *Miller v. California*, 413 U.S. 15, 24, 93 S.Ct. 2607, 37 L.Ed.2d 419 (1973) (quoting *Kois v. Wisconsin*, 408 U.S. 229, 230, 92 S.Ct. 2245, 33 L.Ed.2d 312 (1972)). In response to the Supreme Court's criticism of the CDA, Congress incorporated into COPA this *Miller* test, explaining that in so doing COPA now "conforms to the standards identified in *Ginsberg*, as modified by the Supreme Court in *Miller v. California*, 413 U.S. 15, 93 S.Ct. 2607, 37 L.Ed.2d 419 (1973)." H.R. Rep. No. 105-775 at 13 (1998); 47 U.S.C. §231(e)(6)(A). Even in so doing, Congress remained cognizant of the fact that "the application of community standards in the context of the Web is controversial." H.R. Rep. No. 107-775 at 28. Nevertheless, in defending the constitutionality of COPA's use of the *Miller* test, the government insists that "there is nothing dispositive about the fact that [in COPA] commercial distribution of such [harmful] materials occurs through an online, rather than a brick and mortar outlet."

Despite the government's assertion, "[e]ach medium of expression 'must be assessed for First Amendment purposes by standards suited to it, for each may present its own problems.'" *Reno III*, 31 F. Supp. 2d at 495 (quoting *Southeastern Promotions, Ltd. v. Conrad*, 420 U.S. 546, 557, 95 S.Ct. 1239, 43 L.Ed.2d 448 (1975)). *See also United States v. Playboy Entertainment Group, Inc.*, — U.S. —, —, 120 S.Ct. 1878, — L.Ed.2d —, at —, 2000 WL 646196, at *8 (U.S. May 22, 2000). In considering "the unique factors that affect communication in the new and technology-laden medium of the Web," we are convinced that there are crucial differences between a "brick and mortar outlet" and the online Web that dramatically affect a First Amendment analysis. *Id.*

Unlike a "brick and mortar outlet" with a specific geographic locale, and unlike the voluntary physical mailing of material from one geographic location to another, as in *Miller*, the uncontroverted facts indicate that the Web is not geographically constrained. *See Reno III*, 31 F. Supp. 2d at 482–92; *American Libraries*, 969 F. Supp. at 169 ("geography, however, is a virtually meaningless construct on the Internet"). Indeed, and of extreme significance, is the fact, as found by the District Court, that Web publishers are without any means to limit access to their sites based on the geographic location of particular Internet users. As soon as information is published on a Web site, it is accessible to all other Web visitors. *See American Libraries*, 969 F. Supp. at 166; *Reno III*, 31 F. Supp. 2d at 483. Current technology prevents Web publishers from circumventing particular jurisdictions or limiting their site's content "from entering any [specific] geographic community." *Reno III*, 31 F. Supp. 2d at 484. This key difference necessarily affects our analysis in attempting to define what contemporary community standards should or could mean in a medium without geographic boundaries.

In expressing its concern over the wholly unprecedented broad coverage of the CDA's scope, the Supreme Court has already noted that because of the peculiar geography-free nature of cyberspace, a "community standards" test would essentially require every Web communication to abide by the most restrictive community's standards. *See Reno II*, 521 U.S. at 877–78. Similarly, to avoid liability under COPA, affected Web publishers would either need to severely censor their publications or implement an age or credit card verification system whereby any material that might be deemed harmful by the most puritan of communities in any state is shielded behind such a verification system. Shielding such vast amounts of material behind verification systems would prevent access to protected material by any adult seventeen or over without the necessary age verification credentials. Moreover, it would completely bar access to those materials to all minors under seventeen—even if the material would not otherwise have been deemed "harmful" to them in their respective geographic communities.

The government argues that subjecting Web publishers to varying community standards is not constitutionally problematic or, for that matter, unusual. The government notes that there are numerous cases in which the courts have already subjected the same conduct to varying community standards, depending on the community in which the conduct occurred. For example, the Supreme Court has stated that "distributors of allegedly obscene materials may be subjected to varying community standards in the various federal judicial districts into which they transmit the material [but that] does not render a federal statute unconstitutional because of the failure of the application of uniform national standards of obscenity." *Hamling v. United States*, 418 U.S. 87, 106, 94 S.Ct. 2887, 41 L.Ed.2d 590 (1974). Similarly, the government cites to the "dial-a-porn" cases in which the Supreme Court has held that even if the "audience is comprised of different communities with different local standards" the company providing the obscene material "ultimately bears the burden of complying with the prohibition on obscene messages" under each community's respective standard. *Sable Comm. of California v. F.C.C.*, 492 U.S. 115, 125–26, 109 S.Ct. 2829, 106 L.Ed.2d 93 (1989).

These cases, however, are easily distinguished from the present case. In each of those cases, the defendants had the ability to control the distribution of controversial material with respect to the geographic communities into which they released it. Therefore, the defendants could limit their exposure to liability by avoiding those communities with particularly restrictive standards, while continuing to provide the controversial material in more liberal-minded communities. For example, the pornographer in *Hamling* could have chosen not to mail unsolicited sexually explicit material to certain communities while continuing to mail them to others. Similarly, the telephone pornographers ("dial-a-porn") in *Sable* could have screened their incoming calls and then only accepted a call if its point of origination was from a community with standards of decency that were not offended by the content of their pornographic telephone messages.

By contrast, Web publishers have no such comparable control. Web publishers cannot restrict access to their site based on the geographic locale of the Internet user visiting their site. In fact, "an Internet user cannot foreclose access to...work from certain states or send differing versions of...communication[s] to different jurisdictions...The Internet user has no ability to bypass any particular state." *American Libraries Ass'n v. Pataki*, 969 F. Supp. 160 (S.D.N.Y. 1997). As a result, unlike telephone or postal mail pornographers, Web publishers of material that may be harmful to minors must "comply with the regulation imposed by the State with the most stringent standard or [entirely] forego Internet communication of the message that might or might not subject [the publisher] to prosecution." *Id*. . . .

Our concern with COPA's adoption of *Miller*'s "contemporary community standards" test by which to determine whether material is harmful to minors is with respect to its overbreadth in the context of the Web medium. Because no technology currently exists by which Web publishers may avoid liability, such publishers would necessarily be compelled to abide by the "standards of the community most likely to be offended by the message" *Reno II*, 521 U.S. at 877–78, even if the same material would not have been deemed harmful to minors in all other communities. Moreover, by restricting their publications to meet the more stringent standards of less liberal communities, adults whose constitutional rights permit them to view such materials would be unconstitutionally deprived of those rights. Thus, this result imposes an overreaching burden and restriction on constitutionally protected speech.

We recognize that invalidating a statute because it is overbroad is "strong medicine." *Broadrick v. Oklahoma*, 413 U.S. 601, 613, 93 S.Ct. 2908, 37 L.Ed.2d 830 (1972). As such, before concluding that a statute is unconstitutionally overbroad, we seek to determine if the statute is "'readily susceptible' to a narrowing construction that would make it constitutional…[because courts] will not rewrite a…law to conform it to constitutional requirements." *Virginia v. American Booksellers' Ass'n*, 484 U.S. 383, 397, 108 S.Ct. 636, 98 L.Ed.2d 782 (1988) (quoting *Erznoznik v. City of Jacksonville*, 422 U.S. 205, 95 S.Ct. 2268, 45 L.Ed.2d 125 (1975)). *See also Broadrick*, 413 U.S. at 613; *Forsyth County v. Nationalist Movement*, 505 U.S. 123, 130, 112 S.Ct. 2395, 120 L.Ed.2d 101 (1992); *Shea*, 930 F. Supp. at 939.

Two possible ways to limit the interpretation of COPA are (a) assigning a narrow meaning to the language of the statute itself, or (b) deleting that portion of the statute that is unconstitutional, while preserving the remainder of the statute intact. *See, e.g., Brockett v. Spokane Arcades, Inc.*, 472 U.S. 491, 502, 105 S.Ct. 2794, 86 L.Ed.2d 394 (1985); *Shea*, 930 F. Supp. at 939.…

Despite the government's effort to salvage this clause of COPA from unconstitutionality, we have before us no evidence to suggest that adults everywhere in America would share the same standards for determining what is harmful to minors. To the contrary, it is significant to us that throughout case law, community standards have always been interpreted as a geographic standard without uniformity. *See, e.g., American Libraries Ass'n v. Pataki*, 969 F. Supp. 160, 182–83 (S.D.N.Y. 1997) ("Courts have long recognized, however, that there is no single 'prevailing community standard' in the United States. Thus, even were all 50 states to enact laws that were verbatim copies of the New York [obscenity] Act, Internet users would still be subject to discordant responsibilities.").

In fact, *Miller,* the very case from which the government derives its "community standards" concept, has made clear that community standards are to be construed in a localized geographic context. "People in different States vary in their tastes and attitudes and this diversity is not to be strangled by the absolutism of imposed uniformity." *Miller,* 413 U.S. at 33. Even more directly, the Supreme Court stated in *Miller* that "our nation is simply too big and too diverse for this Court to reasonably expect that such standards [of what is patently offensive] could be articulated for all 50 states in a single formulation.…To require a State to structure obscenity proceedings around evidence of a national 'community standard' would be an exercise in futility." *Id.* at 30. We therefore conclude that the interpretation of "contemporary community standards" is not "readily susceptible" to a narrowing construction of "adult" rather than "geographic" standard.

With respect to the second salvaging mechanism, it is an "'elementary principle that the same statute may be in part constitutional and in part unconstitutional, and that if the parts are wholly independent of each other, that which is constitutional may stand while that which is unconstitutional will be rejected.'" *Brockett v. Spokane Arcades, Inc.*, 472 U.S. 491, 502, 105 S.Ct. 2794, 86 L.Ed.2d 394 (1985) (quoting *Allen v. Louisiana*, 103 U.S. 80, 83–84, 26 L.Ed. 318 (1881))....Here, however, striking "contemporary community standards" from COPA is not likely to succeed in salvaging COPA's constitutionality as this standard is an integral part of the statute, permeating and influencing the whole of the statute. We see no means by which to excise those "unconstitutional" elements of the statute from those that are constitutional (assuming for the moment, without deciding, that the remaining clauses of COPA are held to be constitutional). This is particularly so in a preliminary injunction context when we are convinced that the very test or standard that COPA has established to determine what is harmful to minors is more likely than not to be held unconstitutional. *See Brockett*, 472 U.S. at 504–05.

Our foregoing discussion that under either approach—of narrowing construction or deleting an unconstitutional element—COPA is not "readily susceptible" to a construction that would make it constitutional. We agree with the Second Circuit that "[t]he State may not regulate at all if it turns out that even the least restrictive means of regulation is still unreasonable when its limitations on freedom of speech are balanced against the benefits gained from those limitations." *Carlin Communications, Inc. v. FCC*, 837 F.2d 546, 555 (2d Cir. 1988). As regulation under existing technology is unreasonable here, we conclude that with respect to this first prong of our preliminary injunction analysis, it is more likely than not that COPA will be found unconstitutional on the merits.

Our holding in no way ignores or questions the general applicability of the holding in *Miller* with respect to "contemporary community standards." We remain satisfied that *Miller*'s "community standards" test continues to be a useful and viable tool in contexts other than the Internet and the Web under present technology. *Miller* itself was designed to address the mailing of unsolicited sexually explicit material in violation of California law, where a publisher could control the community receiving the publication. *Miller*, however, has no applicability to the Internet and the Web, where Web publishers are currently without the ability to control the geographic scope of the recipients of their communications. *See Reno II*, 521 U.S. at 889 (O'Connor, J., concurring in judgment in part and dissenting in part) (noting that the "twin characteristics of geography and identity" differentiate the world of *Ginsberg* [and *Miller*] from that of the Internet.).

### B. Irreparable Harm by Denial of Relief

The second prong of our preliminary injunction analysis requires us to consider "whether the movant will be irreparably harmed by denial of the relief." *Allegheny Energy, Inc. v. DQE, Inc.*, 171 F.3d 153, 158 (3d Cir. 1999). Generally, "[i]n a First Amendment challenge, a plaintiff who meets the first prong of the test for a preliminary injunction will almost certainly meet the second, since irreparable injury normally arises out of the deprivation of speech rights." *Reno I*, 929 F. Supp. 824, 866. This case is no exception.

If a preliminary injunction were not to issue, COPA-affected Web publishers would most assuredly suffer irreparable harm—the curtailment of their constitutionally protected right to free speech. As the Supreme Court has clearly stated, "the loss of First Amendment freedoms, for even minimal periods of time, unquestionably constitutes irreparable injury." *Elrod v. Burns*, 427 U.S. 347, 373, 96 S.Ct. 2673, 49 L.Ed.2d 547

(1976). We, therefore, conclude that this element of our preliminary injunction analysis has been satisfied.

## C. Injury Outweighs Harm

The third prong of our preliminary injunction analysis requires us to consider "whether granting preliminary relief will result in even greater harm to the nonmoving party." *Allegeny Inc. v. DQE, Inc.,* 171 F.3d 153, 158 (3d Cir. 1999). We are convinced that in balancing the parties' respective interests, COPA's threatened constraint on constitutionally protected free speech far outweighs the damage that would be imposed by our failure to affirm this preliminary injunction. We are also aware that without a preliminary injunction, Web publishers subject to COPA would immediately be required to censor constitutionally protected speech for adults, or incur substantial financial costs to implement COPA's affirmative defenses. Therefore, we affirm the District Court's holding that plaintiffs sufficiently met their burden in establishing this third prong of the preliminary injunction analysis.

## D. Public Interest

As the fourth and final element of our preliminary injunction analysis, we consider "whether granting the preliminary relief will be in the public interest." *Allegeny Inc. v. DQE, Inc.,* 171 F.3d 153, 158 (3d Cir. 1999). Curtailing constitutionally protected speech will not advance the public interest, and "neither the Government nor the public generally can claim an interest in the enforcement of an unconstitutional law." *Reno I,* 929 F. Supp. at 866. Having met this final element of our preliminary injunction analysis, the District Court properly granted the ACLU's petition for a preliminary injunction.

## III. CONCLUSION

Due to current technological limitations, COPA—Congress' laudatory attempt to achieve its compelling objective of protecting minors from harmful material on the World Wide Web—is more likely than not to be found unconstitutional as overbroad on the merits. Because the ACLU has met its burden in establishing all four of the necessary elements to obtain a preliminary injunction, and the District Court properly exercised its discretion in issuing the preliminary injunction, we will affirm the District Court's order....

---

Invalidation of the obscenity laws enacted by Congress has been justified in part on the judiciary's assessment that Congress inappropriately included a "community standards" criterion, *see Reno v. American Civil Liberties Union,* 521 U.S. at 877–78, and then failed to remedy the concern adequately, *see American Civil Liberties Union v. Reno,* 217 F.3d 162. Obscenity is determined by the standards of the community where the trial takes place. *See Miller v. California,* 413 U.S. at 15, 30–34. Interstate distributors therefore may be subject to varying community standards. *See, e.g., Hamling v. United States,* 418 U.S. 87, 106 (1974). For purposes of federal obscenity prosecutions, the applicable "community" whose standards are to be examined are those of any district in which such offense was begun, continued, or completed. *See* 18 U.S.C.A. §3237 (West 2000). Potentially, then, individuals in a community to which material has been sent may be prosecuted under that community's standards, even though the community from which the material originated would tolerate its circulation.

When obscene content is disseminated electronically over the Internet, where is the relevant "community"? Note that when it enacted COPA, Congress was mindful that "application of community standards in the context of the Web is controversial." H.R. Rep. No. 107-775 at 28 (1998). The Third Circuit was "convinced that there are crucial differences between a 'brick and mortar outlet' and the online Web that dramatically affect a First Amendment analysis." *Id.* (quoting *United States v. Playboy Entertainment Group, Inc.*, — U.S. —, —, 120 S.Ct. 1878, 2000 WL 646196, at *8 (U.S. May 22, 2000)). The current technology precluding Web publishers from avoiding publication of content in prescribed locales was held to constitute a "key difference [that] necessarily affect[ed the court's] analysis in attempting to define what contemporary community standards should or could mean in a medium without geographic boundaries." *American Civil Liberties Union v. Reno,* 217 F.3d at 175.

In *United States v. Thomas,* 74 F.3d 701 (6th Cir. 1996), *cert. denied,* 519 U.S. 820 (1996), the Sixth Circuit was unconvinced that disparate standards in the communities in which the material was received furnished an adequate basis for invalidating the statute. In that case, the defendants had argued that their operation of a computer bulletin board system mandated a new definition of community,

> one that is based on the broad-ranging connections among people in cyberspace rather than the geographic locale of the federal judicial district of the criminal trial. Without a more flexible definition, [the Defendants] argue, there will be an impermissible chill on protected speech because [bulletin board system ("BBS")] operators cannot select who gets the materials they make available on their bulletin boards. Therefore, [the Defendants] contend, BBS operators like Defendants will be forced to censor their materials so as not to run afoul of the standards of the community with the most restrictive standards.

*Id.* at 711.

The Sixth Circuit rejected the argument, distinguishing the case from situations in which the bulletin board operator had no knowledge or control over the jurisdictions where materials were distributed for downloading or printing. Access to the defendants' bulletin board system was limited to members whose applications were screened. As a result, defendants had in place methods to limit user access in jurisdictions where there were greater risks that the material would be deemed obscene. "If Defendants did not wish to subject themselves to liability in jurisdictions with less tolerant standards for determining obscenity, they could have refused to give passwords to members in those districts, thus precluding the risk of liability." *Id.*

The Sixth Circuit felt fortified in its conclusion by the Supreme Court's decision in *Sable Communications of Cal., Inc. v. F.C.C.,* 492 U.S. 115, 125–26 (1989), in which the defendant had argued that it should not be compelled to tailor its dial-a-porn messages to the standards of the least tolerant community. *See United States v. Thomas,* 74 F.3d at 711-12. The Supreme Court in *Sable* had recognized that distributors of allegedly obscene material may be subjected to the standards of the varying communities when they transmit their material, but noted that the distributors are "free to tailor [their] messages, on a selective basis, if [they] so choose[ ], to the communities [they] choose[ ] to serve." *Sable Communications of Cal., Inc. v. F.C.C.,* 492 U.S. at 125. The Supreme Court also found that the fact that a distributor would be forced to incur costs to develop and implement a method for screening a customer's location and providing messages compatible with community standards did not constitute a constitutional impediment. *Id.*

The Third Circuit acknowledged the apparent inconsistency between its holding and that of the Sixth Circuit, and reaffirmed its respect for the general applicability and continued viability of the contemporary community standards test enunciated in *Miller v. California*, 413 U.S. 15. The Third Circuit felt that its holding nonetheless could be reconciled with that rendered by the Sixth Circuit, because in *Thomas*, the defendants were able to geographically restrict user access. *See American Civil Liberties Union v. Reno*, 217 F.3d at 176.

The virtuality of cyberspace arguably "erodes the rationale for applying local community standards as the definitive touchstone for whether the materials are, in fact, obscene." William S. Byassee, *Jurisdiction of Cyberspace: Applying Real World Precedent to the Virtual Community*, 30 Wake Forest L. Rev. 197, 204 (1995). Further, statutory schemes may be invalidated when they subject use of the Internet to inconsistent regulation. "The unique nature of the Internet highlights the likelihood that a single actor might be subject to haphazard, uncoordinated, and even outright inconsistent regulation by states that the actor never intended to reach and possibly was unaware were being accessed. Typically, states' jurisdictional limits are related to geography; geography, however, is a virtually meaningless construct on the Internet." *American Libraries Ass'n v. Pataki*, 969 F. Supp. 160, 168–69 (S.D.N.Y. 1997).

Is the defect in the obscenity provisions of the Communications Decency Act susceptible to cure if a "community standards" reference is incorporated within the legislation? The Third Circuit observed, that as of June 2000 when it issued its decision, "no federal court [had] yet ruled on whether the Web/Internet may be constitutionally regulated in light of differing community standards." *American Civil Liberties Union v. Reno*, 217 F.3d at 166.

---

## Notes and Questions

1.  How would technological changes that enable Web publishers to circumvent particular jurisdictions or geographically limit access to their sites affect the analysis? In *Reno v. American Civil Liberties Union*, 521 U.S. 844, the Supreme Court relied on evidentiary hearings that had been conducted by the district court approximately a year before the Supreme Court heard oral argument. There were technological developments between the district court's ruling and the Supreme Court's decision, however. Among the technological issues on which the ensuing decision was premised were the findings that age verification systems were not technically possible for certain non-Web Internet systems (such as USENET newsgroups, listservs, and chat rooms), and that the Internet did not appear unbidden on a user's computer. Professor Stuart Minor Benjamin points out that the government had argued that age verification in the relevant systems had become feasible. Further, "push" technology (i.e., where material is "pushed" by the provider onto computers, rather than having specific content "pulled" by users) was employed to allow the delivery of content directly to users without requests by the users. Stuart Minor Benjamin, *Stepping Into the Same River Twice: Rapidly Changing Facts and the Appellate Process*, 78 Tex. L. Rev. 269, 291–93 (1999). Thereafter, ironically, "[t]he confident assumption that push would become the dominant paradigm has yet to materialize, and now many think it never will (but, of course, that could change, too)." *Id.* at 294.

2.  *Compare Reno v. American Civil Liberties Union*, 521 U.S. 844 *with ApolloMedia Corp. v. Reno*, 19 F. Supp. 2d 1081 (N.D. Cal. 1998), *aff'd*, 526 U.S. 1061 (1999)

(upholding section 223(a)(1)(A) of the Communications Decency Act, which subjects to prosecution those who use telecommunications devices to knowingly initiate the transmission of obscene proposals and images).

3. Note the judiciary's recognition of the government's interest in protecting minors from electronic display of obscene matter, juxtaposed with its solicitude for free speech rights:

> Despite the Court's personal regret that th[e] preliminary injunction [enjoining enforcement of the Child On-Line Protection Act, 47 U.S.C. § 201, *et seq.*,] will delay once again the careful protection of our children, I without hesitation acknowledge the duty imposed on the Court and the greater good such duty serves. Indeed, perhaps we do the minors of this country harm if First Amendment protections, which they will with age inherit fully, are chipped away in the name of their protection.

*American Civil Liberties Union v. Reno*, 31 F. Supp. 2d 473, 498 (E.D. Pa. 1999), *aff'd*, 217 F.3d 162 (3d Cir. 2000). The Third Circuit "approvingly reiterated" these sentiments and expressed "confidence and firm conviction that developing technology will soon render the 'community standards' challenge moot, thereby making congressional regulation to protect minors from harmful material on the Web constitutionally practicable." *American Civil Liberties Union v. Reno*, 217 F.3d at 181.

4. Six professors employed at various public colleges and universities in Virginia challenged the constitutionality of a Virginia statute, Va. Code Ann. §§ 2.1-804–806, which restricted state employees from accessing sexually explicit material on computers that are owned or leased by the state. The district court granted summary judgment in favor of the professors, ruling that the statute unconstitutionally infringed on the First Amendment rights of state employees. *Urofsky v. Allen*, 995 F. Supp. 634 (E.D. Va. 1998). The Fourth Circuit reversed the decision, reasoning that the restriction on state employees' access to sexually explicit material under the circumstances specified in the legislation is constitutional because the Act regulates only state employees' speech in their capacity as state employees; the employees' speech was not constrained in their capacity as citizens addressing matters of public concern. *Urofsky v. Gilmore*, 216 F.3d 401 (4th Cir. 1999) (en banc).

5. *Compare United States v. Simons*, 29 F. Supp. 2d 324 (E.D. Va. 1998) (accusing defendant of inappropriately accessing child pornography from his workstation), *aff'd on other grounds*, 206 F.3d 392 (4th Cir. 2000) *with United States v. Maxwell*, 45 MJ. 406 (C.A.A.F. 1996) (discussing a limited expectation of privacy in e-mail messages transmitted and received by army personnel).

---

Regulatory schemes relating to on-line dissemination of content that is harmful to minors also have been challenged on the ground that they impermissibly burden interstate commerce. "The negative or dormant implication of the Commerce Clause prohibits state…regulation…that discriminates against or unduly burdens interstate commerce and thereby 'imped[es] free private trade in the national marketplace.'" *General Motors Corp. v. Tracy*, 519 U.S. 278, 287 (1997) (quoting *Reeves, Inc. v. Stake*, 447 U.S. 429, 437 (1980)) (citations omitted). Because "virtually all Internet speech is…available everywhere," *Cyberspace Communications, Inc. v. Engler*, 55 F. Supp. 2d 737, 751 (E.D. Mich. 1999), legislation may be constitutionally infirm because it cannot effectively be limited to purely intrastate communications over the Internet.

# AMERICAN CIVIL LIBERTIES UNION v. Gary JOHNSON
United States Court of Appeals, Tenth Circuit
No. 98-2199, 194 F.3d 1149
November 2, 1999

STEPHEN H. ANDERSON, Circuit Judge.

Defendants appeal from the grant of a preliminary injunction enjoining the enforcement of a New Mexico statute, N.M. Stat. Ann. § 30-37-3.2(A), which criminalizes the dissemination by computer of material that is harmful to minors. The... plaintiffs, the American Civil Liberties Union ("ACLU") and various organizations and entities which communicate on the Internet,... [seek injunctive relief, claiming that] section 30-37-3.2(A) violated the First Amendment and the Commerce Clause of the United States Constitution....

## BACKGROUND

In its 1998 session, the New Mexico Legislature enacted section 30-37-3.2(A), which provides as follows:

30-37-3.2 Dissemination of material that is harmful to a minor by computer

A. Dissemination of material that is harmful to a minor by computer consists of the use of a computer communications system that allows the input, output, examination or transfer of computer data or computer programs from one computer to another, to knowingly and intentionally initiate or engage in communication with a person under eighteen years of age when such communication in whole or in part depicts actual or simulated nudity, sexual intercourse or any other sexual conduct. Whoever commits dissemination of material that is harmful to a minor by computer is guilty of a misdemeanor.

The statute provides the following defenses:

In a prosecution for dissemination of material that is harmful to a minor by computer, it is a defense that the defendant has:

(1) in good faith taken reasonable, effective and appropriate actions under the circumstances to restrict or prevent access by minors to indecent materials on computer, including any method that is feasible with available technology;

(2) restricted access to indecent materials by requiring the use of a verified credit card, debit account, adult access code or adult personal identification number; or

(3) in good faith established a mechanism such as labeling, segregation or other means that enables indecent material to be automatically blocked or screened by software or other capability reasonably available to persons who wish to effect such blocking or screening and the defendant has not otherwise solicited a minor not subject to such screening or blocking capabilities to access the indecent material or to circumvent screening or blocking.

N.M. Stat. Ann. § 30-37-3.2(C). The statute became effective July 1, 1998....

## DISCUSSION

...The district court found that plaintiffs had satisfied all four conditions for the issuance of a preliminary injunction. We agree.... [The court addressed First and Fourteenth Amendment challenges to the statute, and then discussed in dicta an alleged Commerce Clause violation.]

The district court...held that plaintiffs in this case demonstrated a likelihood of success on their argument that section 30-37-3.2(A) violated the Commerce Clause....

The "dormant implication of the Commerce Clause prohibits state...regulation... that discriminates against or unduly burdens interstate commerce and thereby 'imped[es] free private trade in the national marketplace.'" *General Motors Corp. v. Tracy*, 519 U.S. 278, 287, 117 S.Ct. 811, 136 L.Ed.2d 761 (1997) (quoting *Reeves, Inc. v. Stake*, 447 U.S. 429, 437, 100 S.Ct. 2271, 65 L.Ed.2d 244 (1980)) (citations omitted). Moreover, the Supreme Court has long recognized that certain types of commerce are uniquely suited to national, as opposed to state, regulation. *See, e.g., Wabash, St. L. & P.R. Co. v. Illinois*, 118 U.S. 557, 7 S.Ct. 4, 30 L.Ed. 244 (1886) (holding states cannot regulate railroad rates).

The district court held that section 30-37-3.2(A) violated the Commerce Clause in three ways: (1) it regulates conduct occurring wholly outside of the state of New Mexico; (2) it constitutes an unreasonable and undue burden on interstate and foreign commerce; and (3) it subjects interstate use of the Internet to inconsistent state regulation. The court below largely relied upon the detailed Commerce Clause analysis in *American Libraries Ass'n v. Pataki*, 969 F. Supp. 160, 168–83 (S.D.N.Y. 1997). We agree with that analysis. As the *Pataki* court observed:

> The unique nature of the Internet highlights the likelihood that a single actor might be subject to haphazard, uncoordinated, and even outright inconsistent regulation by states that the actor never intended to reach and possibly was unaware were being accessed. Typically, states' jurisdictional limits are related to geography; geography, however, is a virtually meaningless construct on the Internet.

*Id.* at 168–69.

### a. Regulation of conduct outside New Mexico

Defendants argue that section 30-37-3.2(A), properly construed, only addresses intrastate conduct. As the *Pataki* court stated in rejecting that same argument, that analysis "is unsupportable in light of the text of the statute itself...and the reality of Internet communications." *Pataki*, 969 F. Supp. at 169. Section 30-37-3.2(A) contains no express limitation confining it to communications which occur wholly within its borders. Rather, it "applies to any communication, intrastate or interstate, that fits within the prohibition and over which [New Mexico] has the capacity to exercise criminal jurisdiction." *Pataki*, 969 F. Supp. at 169–70.

Moreover, the nature of the Internet forecloses the argument that a statute such as section 30-37-3.2(A) applies only to intrastate communications. Even if it is limited to one-on-one e-mail communications, as defendants assert section 30-37-3.2(A) properly is limited, there is no guarantee that a message from one New Mexican to another New Mexican will not travel through other states en route. *See Pataki*, 969 F. Supp. at 171; *see also Cyberspace, Communications, Inc. [v. Engler]* 55 F. Supp. 2d [737, 757 (E.D. Mich.

1999)] ("virtually all Internet speech is...available everywhere"). Thus, section 30-37-3.2(A) "cannot effectively be limited to purely intrastate communications over the Internet because no such communications exist." *Pataki,* 969 F. Supp. at 171. We therefore agree with the district court that section 30-37-3.2(A) represents an attempt to regulate interstate conduct occurring outside New Mexico's borders, and is accordingly a per se violation of the Commerce Clause.

### b. Burden on interstate commerce compared to local benefit

We further agree, for the reasons outlined in *Pataki,* that section 30-37-3.2(A) is an invalid indirect regulation of interstate commerce because, under the balancing test of *Pike v. Bruce Church, Inc.,* 397 U.S. 137, 142, 90 S.Ct. 844, 25 L.Ed.2d 174 (1970), the burdens on interstate commerce imposed by section 30-37-3.2(A) exceed any local benefits conferred by the statute. *See V-1 Oil Co. v. Utah State Dep't of Pub. Safety,* 131 F.3d 1415, 1423–24 (10th Cir. 1997). Defendants' primary response to this argument is to reiterate the importance of the state's interest in protecting minors from sexually oriented materials which are "harmful to minors." We agree that the protection of minors from such materials is an undeniably compelling governmental interest, but the question in the context of the validity of section 30-37-3.2(A) is whether the means chosen to further that interest (§ 30-37-3.2(A)) excessively burden interstate commerce compared to the local benefits the statute actually confers. The local benefits of section 30-37-3.2(A), particularly as narrowly construed by defendants, are not huge. As the *Pataki* court noted with respect to the New York statute challenged in that case, section 30-37-3.2(A) "can have no effect on communications originating outside the United States." *Pataki,* 969 F. Supp. at 178.

Further, New Mexico's "prosecution of parties from out of state who have allegedly violated [section 30-37-3.2(A)], but whose only contact with [New Mexico] occurs via the Internet, is beset with practical difficulties, even if [New Mexico] is able to exercise criminal jurisdiction over such parties." *Id.* Finally, defendants' own interpretation of the statute—that it applies only to one-on-one communications between a sender in New Mexico and a recipient in New Mexico whom the sender knows to be a minor—renders it so narrow in scope that the actual benefit conferred is extremely small. As another district court has observed with respect to the CDA, which defendants argue is broader in scope than section 30-37-3.2(A):

> [The statute] will almost certainly fail to accomplish the Government's interest in shielding children from pornography on the Internet. Nearly half of Internet communications originate outside the United States, and some percentage of that figure represents pornography. Pornography from, say, Amsterdam will be no less appealing to a child on the Internet than pornography from [Albuquerque], and residents of Amsterdam have little incentive to comply with [the statute].

*ACLU v. Reno,* 929 F. Supp. 824, 882 (E.D. Pa. 1996), *aff'd,* 521 U.S. 844, 117 S.Ct. 2329, 138 L.Ed.2d 874 (1997). Balanced against those limited local benefits "is an extreme burden on interstate commerce." *Pataki,* 969 F. Supp. at 179. Thus, section 30-37-3.2(A) constitutes an invalid indirect regulation of interstate commerce.

### c. Inconsistent regulation

The third ground upon which the district court held section 30-37-3.2(A) violates the Commerce Clause is that it subjects the use of the Internet to inconsistent regulations. As we observed, *supra,* certain types of commerce have been recognized as requiring national regulation. *See, e.g., Wabash, St. L. & P. Ry. Co.,* 118 U.S. at 574–75, 7 S.Ct. 4 (noting that "[c]ommerce with foreign countries and among the states" requires "only one system of rules, applicable alike to the whole country"). The Internet is surely such a medium....

Plaintiffs have accordingly met their burden of demonstrating a likelihood that they will prevail on their claims that section 30-37-3.2(A) violates both the First Amendment and the Commerce Clause....

## B. Irreparable Harm

The district court held that "[p]laintiffs have made a sufficient showing that they will suffer irreparable injury—at a minimum the curtailment of their constitutionally protected speech—if the preliminary injunction is not granted." *Johnson,* 4 F. Supp. 2d at 1034. We agree. *See Elrod v. Burns,* 427 U.S. 347, 373, 96 S.Ct. 2673, 49 L.Ed.2d 547 (1976); *see also Pataki,* 969 F. Supp. at 168 (noting that the "[d]eprivation of the rights guaranteed under the Commerce Clause constitutes irreparable injury").

## C. Injury Outweighs Harm

We further agree with the district court's conclusion that "the threatened injury to Plaintiffs' constitutionally protected speech outweighs whatever damage the preliminary injunction may cause Defendants' inability to enforce what appears to be an unconstitutional statute." *Johnson,* 4 F. Supp. 2d at 1034.

## D. Public Interest

Finally, we further agree that "the preliminary injunction will not be adverse to the public interest as it will protect the free expression of the millions of Internet users both within and outside of the State of New Mexico." *Id.* ...

### CONCLUSION

For the forgoing reasons, we AFFIRM the issuance of a preliminary injunction against enforcement of section 30-37-3.2(A).

---

# CYBERSPACE COMMUNICATIONS, INC., *et al.* v. John ENGLER, *et al.*

United States District Court for the Eastern District of Michigan,
Southern Division
No. 99-cv-73150, 55 F. Supp. 2d 737
July 29, 1999

Opinion by: ARTHUR J. TARNOW

In 1978, the Michigan Legislature enacted a statute to protect children by prohibiting the distribution of obscene materials to children of this state. 1978 Public Act 33, M.C.L. 722.671, *et seq.;* M.S.A. 25.254(1), *et. seq.* In an effort to modernize the statute in light of current technology (and in an effort to make other improvements in the operation of the statute), the Legislature amended the statute by means of 1999 Public Act 33 (hereinafter referred to as the "Act"). The Act primarily attempts to do two things: 1) it adds criminal prohibitions against using computers or the Internet to disseminate sexually explicit materials to minors, and, 2) it changed the language of the statute so that the statute prohibits the dissemination of "sexually explicit" materials to minors rather than "obscene" materials.

The Act, amendments to M.C.L. 722.671 *et seq.*, was signed by Defendant, John Engler, the Governor of Michigan on June 1, 1999. It is set to take effect August 1, 1999. Plaintiffs represent a broad spectrum of organizations and individuals who use the Internet to communicate, disseminate, display and access a broad range of speech and ideas. Plaintiffs include speakers, content providers, and/or Internet service providers (ISPs).

Plaintiffs claim that the Act will adversely impact them because it is unconstitutionally vague or overbroad. They maintain it will have a chilling effect on their freedom of speech under the First Amendment. Plaintiffs communicate online both within and outside of the state of Michigan. Their speech is accessible within and outside of the state of Michigan. For this reason, Plaintiffs further argue that the Act violates the Commerce Clause of the United States Constitution. They have requested this Court issue a preliminary injunction to enjoin the amendments to the to enjoin the amendments to the statute.

## I. The Amended Statute

The central prohibition contained in the amended act is found in M.C.L. 722.675(1); M.S.A. 25.254(5)(1):

A person is guilty of disseminating sexually explicit matter to a minor if that person does either of the following:

    (a)  Knowingly disseminates to a minor sexually explicit visual or verbal material that is harmful to minors; or

    (b)  Knowingly exhibits to a minor a sexually explicit performance that is harmful to minors.

The Act redefines obscenity as "sexually explicit matter" The Act makes it unlawful to communicate, transmit, display, or otherwise make available by means of the Internet or a computer, computer program, computer system, or computer network this sexually explicit matter. M.C.L. 722.673; M.S.A. 25.254(3). Violation of the statute is a felony punishable by up to two years in prison and a fine of $ 10,000. 722.675(5); M.S.A. 25.254(5)(5). Finally, the Act threatens criminal sanctions "if the violation originates, terminates, or both originates and terminates" in the State of Michigan. (M.C.L. 722.675(8), M.S.A. 25.254(5)(8)).

The 1999 P.A. 33 amendments were specifically intended to apply the pre-existing statute's prohibition on the dissemination of sexually explicit matter to communication over the Internet. Because of the anonymous and borderless nature of the Internet, Plaintiffs fear the amendments will subject them to criminal prosecution for the expression of protected speech. They filed suit challenging the Act. Plaintiffs then asked to enjoin the Act's enforcement scheduled to begin August 1, 1999....

## The Interstate Nature of Online Communication

The Internet is wholly insensitive to geographic distinctions, and Internet protocols were designed to ignore rather than document geographic location. [*American Libraries Ass'n*] v. *Pataki*, 969 F. Supp. [160,] 167, 170 [(S.D.N.Y. 1997); *American Civil Liberties Union* v.] *Johnson*, 4 F. Supp. 2d [1029,] 1032 [(D.N.M. 1998), *appeal docketed*, No. 98-2199 (10th Cir. Aug. 7, 1998)].

While computers on the network do have "addresses," they are digital addresses on the network rather than geographic addresses in real space. The majority of Internet addresses contain no geographic indicators. *Pataki,* 969 F. Supp. at 170.

Like the nation's railways and highways, the Internet is by nature an instrument of interstate commerce. *Pataki,* 969 F. Supp. at 173; *Johnson,* 4 F. Supp. 2d at 1032. Just as goods and services travel over state borders by truck and train, information flows freely across state borders on the Internet. *Pataki,* 969 F. Supp. at 173.

It is this characteristic which has earned the Internet the nickname, "the information superhighway." *Pataki,* 969 F. Supp. at 161.

In fact, no aspect of the Internet can feasiblely be closed to users from another state. *Pataki,* 969 F. Supp. at 171; *Johnson,* 4 F. Supp. 2d at 1032. There is no way to stop or bar speech at Michigan's border.

An Internet user who posts a Web page cannot prevent Michiganians or Oklahomans or Iowans from accessing that page. They will not even know the state residency of any visitors to that site, unless the information is voluntarily (and accurately) given by the visitor. *Pataki,* 969 F. Supp. at 171; *Reno II,* 31 F. Supp. 2d at 495; *Johnson,* 4 F. Supp. 2d at 1032.

Participants in chat rooms and online discussion groups also have no way of knowing when participants from a particular state have joined the conversation. *Id; Johnson,* 4 F. Supp. 2d at 1032.

Because most e-mail accounts allow users to download their mail from anywhere, it is impossible for someone who sends an e-mail to know with certainty where the recipient is located geographically. *Pataki,* 969 F. Supp. at 171.

In addition, the Internet is a redundant series of linked computers over which information often travels randomly. *Pataki,* 969 F. Supp. at 164, 171. Thus, a message from an Internet user sitting at a computer in New York may travel via one or more other states—including Michigan—before reaching a recipient who is also sitting at a computer in New York. *Id; Johnson,* 4 F. Supp. 2d at 1032.

There is no way for an Internet user to prevent his or her message from reaching residents of any particular state. *Pataki,* 969 F. Supp. at 171; *Johnson,* 4 F. Supp. 2d at 1032. Similarly, "once a provider posts its content on the Internet, it cannot prevent that content from entering any community." *Reno I,* 117 S. Ct. at 2336 (quoting *ACLU v. Reno,* 929 F. Supp. at 844)....

## V. Violation of the Commerce Clause

The Commerce Clause, U.S. Const. Art. I, §8, cl. 3, contains an express authorization for Congress to "regulate Commerce with foreign Nations, and among the several States..." A "dormant" or "negative" aspect of this grant of power is that a state's power to impinge on interstate commerce may be limited in some situations. *Quill Corp. v. North Dakota,* 504 U.S. 298, 112 S.Ct. 1904, 119 L.Ed. 2d 91 (1992).

Defendants do not dispute that the Act reaches interstate commerce. Rather, they contend that the Act does not discriminate against out-of-state businesses in favor of Michigan businesses. Further, the government argues, any balancing of burdens on interstate commerce with local interests must tip in favor of the local interests asserted in the Act. These contentions fail for the reasons explained in *American Libraries Ass'n v. Pataki,* 969 F. Supp. 160 (S.D.N.Y. 1997).

First, Defendants focus solely on the line of cases which prohibit a state's discrimination against out-of-state businesses. The Commerce Clause reaches further than such discrimination alone. The Commerce Clause also operates to preclude "the application of a state statute to commerce that takes place wholly outside the State's borders, whether or not the commerce has effects within the state." *Pataki,* 969 F. Supp. at 175 (quoting *Healy v. The Beer Institute,* 491 U.S. 324, 336, 105 L. Ed. 2d 275, 109 S. Ct. 2491 (1989)). Although the Act by its terms regulates speech that "originates" or "terminates" in Michigan, virtually all Internet speech is, as stipulated by Defendants available everywhere including Michigan. A New York speaker must comply with the Act in order to avoid the risk of prosecution in Michigan even though (s)he does not intend his message to be read in Michigan. A publisher of a web page cannot limit the viewing of his site to everyone in the country except for those in Michigan. The Internet has no geographic boundaries. The Act is, as a direct regulation of interstate commerce, a *per se* violation of the Commerce Clause.

Moreover, even if this Court reaches the balancing of burdens on interstate commerce with local interests asserted in the Act, the Commerce Clause still requires the injunction of this Act. Assuming *arguendo* the validity of Michigan's interest in the Act, the Act will be wholly ineffective in achieving the asserted goal because nearly half of all Internet communications originate overseas. *Pataki,* 969 F. Supp. at 177. Just as in *Martin-Marietta Corp. v. Bendix Corp.,* 690 F.2d 558, 566 (6th Cir. 1982), where the Sixth Circuit said: "While protecting local investors is plainly a legitimate state objective, the state has no legitimate interest in protecting non-resident shareholders;" so too Michigan has no interest in regulating out-of-state communications.

As further explained in *Pataki,* the chilling effect on Internet communications outside of Michigan greatly outweighs any putative benefit inside Michigan. The Act, and other state statutes like it, would subject the Internet to inconsistent regulations across the nation. Information is a commodity and must flow freely. On this basis alone, the Act may be preliminarily enjoined as a violation of the Commerce Clause....

Having reached these findings of fact and conclusions of law, the Court concludes that the Plaintiffs have met their burden for a motion for a preliminary injunction. The threatened injury to Plaintiffs' constitutionally protected speech outweighs any claimed damage to the Defendants. Consequently, the Court grants the Plaintiffs' Motion for a Preliminary Injunction.

NOW, THEREFORE, IT IS HEREBY ORDERED THAT, pursuant to Fed. R. Civ. P. 65(d), the Defendants—as well as their officers, agents, servants, employees, and attorneys, and those persons in active concert or participation with Defendants—are hereby preliminarily enjoined from enforcing or threatening to enforce 1999 Public Act 33, which amends Sections 3, 5, 6 and 7 (Mich. Comp. Laws §§ 722.673, 722.675, 722.676, and 722.677) of 1978 Public Act 33, M.C. L. §§ 722.671–722.684.

---

# Filtering Devices

"Filters" are software tools utilized to block access to unwanted material. E-mail filters automatically delete "spam" (i.e., unwanted and unsolicited e-mail messages), and may be customized to delete incoming messages from particular sources. Site-blocking filters may screen out specified web-sites and web-sites containing specified keywords that the system presumes to relate to objectionable content. Site-blocking filters also may use a protocol developed by the W3 Consortium, called the Platform for Internet Content Selection ("PICS"). This protocol consists of an open-platform system that allows utilization of a ratings system, which often may be supplied by a web-site operator or other third-party vendor. PICS-based systems are imprecise because they do not target graphic material. As well, keyword searches cannot construe the context of the purportedly objectionable term, and thus are susceptible to screening out acceptable content along with information the user wishes to block.

Also controversial is the fact that, unlike certain "blocking" technologies, which cannot be implemented without the user's awareness, filtering technology can prevent access without the user's knowledge that a site has been blocked. These devices implicate First Amendment interests because they diminish the public's exposure to ideas; access to information may be thwarted even though it may not be unwelcome. Filtering devices also engender debate because they may be implemented by private entities, and thus evade the constitutional scrutiny that otherwise would be extended to governmental efforts to censor.

To what extent may the government supplant individual decision-making about content choice by compelling filtering? May the government implement screening mechanisms? Professor Lawrence Lessig draws an analogy to jurisprudence relating to the sending and receipt of mail. In *Bolger v. Youngs Drug Products Corp.*, 463 U.S. 60 (1983), for example, the Supreme Court struck a statute prohibiting the mailing of unsolicited advertisements for contraceptives. The Court explicitly "recognized the important interest in allowing addressees to give notice to a mailer that they wish no further mailings.... But we have never held that the government itself can shut off the flow of mailings to protect those recipients who might potentially be offended." *Id.* at 72. Lessig infers that the government is constrained in its power to aid individuals in the filtering of permissible speech. Individual discretion as to which material is the subject of filtering must be preserved. "The evil here is governmental facilitation of *ex ante* filtering, even where the filtering is what a majority would want." Lawrence Lessig, *Symposium— The State of the First Amendment at the Approach of the Millennium: The Constitution of Code: Limitations on Choice-Based Critiques of Cyberspace Regulation*, 5 Commlaw Conspectus 181, 190 (1997).

---

# MAINSTREAM LOUDOUN, *et al.* v. BOARD of TRUSTEES of the LOUDOUN COUNTY LIBRARY

United States District Court, Eastern District, Virginia, Alexandria Division.
No. Civ.A. 97-2049-A, 24 F. Supp. 2d 552
November 23, 1998

BRINKEMA, District Judge.

## BACKGROUND

[The plaintiffs, a non-profit organization suing on its own behalf and on behalf of its members, challenged a library's restrictions on access to sexually explicit Internet sites, and various web-site operators intervened.] At issue in this civil action is whether a public library may enact a policy prohibiting the access of library patrons to certain content-based categories of Internet publications.... [The] defendant passed a "Policy on Internet Sexual Harassment" (the "Policy") stating that the Loudoun County public libraries would provide Internet access to its patrons subject to the following restrictions: (1) the library would not provide e-mail, chat rooms, or pornography; (2) all library computers would be equipped with site-blocking software to block all sites displaying: (a) child pornography and obscene material; and (b) material deemed harmful to juveniles; (3) all library computers would be installed near and in full view of library staff; and (4) patrons would not be permitted to access pornography and, if they do so and refuse to stop, the police may be called to intervene. It is the second restriction in the Policy that lies at the heart of this action.

To effectuate the second restriction, the library has purchased X-Stop, commercial site-blocking software manufactured by Log-On Data Corporation. While the method by which X-Stop chooses sites to block has been kept secret by its developers, it is undisputed that it has blocked at least some sites that do not contain any material that is prohibited by the Policy.

If a patron is blocked from accessing a site that she feels should not be blocked under the Policy, she may request that defendant unblock the site by filing an official, written request with the librarian stating her name, the site she wants unblocked, and the reason why she wants to access the site. The librarian will then review the site and manually unblock it if he determines that the site should not be blocked under the Policy. There is no time limit in which a request must be handled and no procedure for notifying the patron of the outcome of a request. All unblocking requests to date have been approved. . . .

Defendant has . . . requested that we reconsider our earlier findings (1) that the Policy implicates the First Amendment and (2) that the appropriate standard of review is strict scrutiny.

## A. Implicating the First Amendment

Defendant first contends that the Policy should really be construed as a library acquisition decision, to which the First Amendment does not apply, rather than a decision to remove library materials. Plaintiffs and intervenors contend that this issue has already been decided by this Court and is the law of the case. *See Mainstream Loudoun v. Board of Trustees of the Loudoun County Library, et al.,* 2 F. Supp. 2d 783, 794–95 (E.D. Va. 1998) ("[T]he Library Board's action is more appropriately characterized as a removal decision;" "[W]e conclude that [*Pico*] stands for the proposition the First Amendment applies to, and limits, the discretion of a public library to place content-based restrictions on access to constitutionally protected materials within its collection.").

We addressed the acquisition/removal argument at length in our previous decision and defendant has not presented a single new argument or authority to support its position. Indeed, defendant's own expert, David Burt, undercuts its argument by acknowledging that "[f]iltering cannot be rightly compared to 'selection,' since it involves an active, rather than passive exclusion of certain types of content." Therefore, we decline to reconsider our earlier ruling on this issue.

## B. Forum Analysis

Next, defendant contends that even if the First Amendment does apply, we should apply a less stringent standard than strict scrutiny. Specifically, defendant argues that because the library is a non-public forum, the Policy should be reviewed by an intermediate scrutiny standard, examining whether it is reasonably related to an important governmental interest. Citing *Kreimer v. Bureau of Police*, 958 F.2d 1242 (3d Cir. 1992), defendant argues that public libraries are non-public fora and, therefore, content-based speech regulations are not subject to the strict scrutiny standard. Rather, it asserts, such regulations need only be "reasonable and viewpoint neutral" to be upheld. Plaintiffs and intervenors respond that defendant has misread *Kreimer* and moreover that the library is a limited public forum in which content-based regulations are subject to strict scrutiny.

Defendant concedes that the Policy is a content-based regulation of speech and that content-based regulations of speech in a limited public forum are subject to strict scrutiny. The only issue before us, then, is whether the library is a limited public forum or a non-public forum. In *Perry Education Ass'n v. Perry Local Educators' Ass'n*, 460 U.S. 37, 45–46, 103 S.Ct. 948, 74 L.Ed.2d 794 (1983), the Supreme Court identified three categories of fora for the purpose of analyzing the degree of protection afforded to speech. The first category is the traditional forum, such as a sidewalk or public park. These are "places which by long tradition or by government fiat have been devoted to assembly and debate." *Id.* at 45, 103 S.Ct. 948. Second is the limited or designated forum, such as a school board meeting or municipal theater. This category consists of "public property which the State has opened for use by the public as a place for expressive activity." *Id.* The last category is the non-public forum, such as a government office building or a teacher's mailbox, which is not "by tradition or designation a forum for public communication." *Id.* at 46, 103 S.Ct. 948. It is undisputed that the Loudoun County libraries have not traditionally been open to the public for all forms of expressive activity and, therefore, are not traditional public fora.

A limited public forum is created when the government voluntarily opens a particular forum to the public for expressive activity. *See id.* at 45, 103 S.Ct. 948. The government can create a limited public forum for all, some, or only a single kind of expressive activity. *See, e.g., Kreimer*, 958 F.2d at 1259 (finding that the government had made the public library a limited public forum for the expressive activity of "communication of the written word"). Even though it is not required to operate such a forum, once the government does so it "is bound by the same standards as apply in a traditional public forum." *Perry*, 460 U.S. at 46, 103 S.Ct. 948. Therefore, content-neutral time, place, and manner regulations on the expressive activity or activities allowed are permissible if narrowly tailored to serve a significant government interest while leaving open ample alternative channels of communication, *see Kreimer*, 958 F.2d at 1262. Any content-based restriction, however, must be "narrowly drawn to effectuate a compelling state interest." *Perry*, 460 U.S. at 46, 103 S.Ct. 948.

The only court to have examined whether a public library constitutes a limited public forum is the Third Circuit in *Kreimer*. In determining that the public library constituted a limited public forum, the court considered three factors: government intent; extent of use; and nature of the forum. *See id.* at 1259. We agree that these are the crucial factors in determining whether a forum is a limited or a non-public forum.

1. Government Intent

The record establishes that the Loudoun County government, through defendant library board, intended to create a public forum when it authorized its public library system. In a resolution it adopted in 1995 and reaffirmed last year, defendant declared that its "primary objective...[is] that the people have access to all avenues of ideas." *See* Loudoun County Library Board of Trustees Resolution, Freedom For Ideas—Freedom From Censorship, May 15, 1995 ("May 15 Resolution"). Furthermore, the same resolution states that the public interest requires "offering the widest possible diversity of views and expressions" in many different media, not diminishing the library collection simply because "minors might have access to materials with controversial content," not excluding any materials because of the nature of the information or views within, and not censoring ideas. *Id.* We find that defendant intended to designate the Loudoun County libraries as public fora for the limited purposes of the expressive activities they provide, including the receipt and communication of information through the Internet.

### 2. Extent of Use

As to the extent of use the government has allowed, defendant has designated the library for the use of "the people" and has declared that "[l]ibrary access and use will not be restricted nor denied to anyone because of age, race, religion, origin, background or views." *Id.* Defendant has opened the library to the use of the Loudoun County public at large and has significantly limited its own discretion to restrict access, thus indicating that it has created a limited public forum. *See Kreimer,* 958 F.2d at 1260 (finding that the extent of use inquiry favored concluding that the library was a limited public forum because the library "does not retain unfettered discretion governing admission").

### 3. Nature of the Forum

The final consideration is whether the nature of the forum is compatible with the expressive activity at issue. While the nature of the public library would clearly not be compatible with many forms of expressive activity, such as giving speeches or holding rallies, we find that it is compatible with the expressive activity at issue here, the receipt and communication of information through the Internet. Indeed, this expressive activity is explicitly offered by the library.

All three of these factors indicate that the Loudoun County libraries are limited public fora and, therefore, that defendant must "permit the public to exercise rights that are consistent with the nature of the Library and consistent with the government's intent in designating the Library as a public forum." *Id.* at 1262. The receipt and communication of information through the Internet is consistent with both.

Because the Policy at issue limits the receipt and communication of information through the Internet based on the content of that information, it is subject to a strict scrutiny analysis and will only survive if it is "necessary to serve a compelling state interest and...is narrowly drawn to achieve that end." *Perry,* 460 U.S. at 45, 103 S.Ct. 948 (citing *Carey v. Brown,* 447 U.S. 455, 461, 100 S.Ct. 2286, 65 L.Ed.2d 263 (1980)).

### C. *Renton*/Time, Place, and Manner

Defendant also argues in the alternative that the strict scrutiny standard should not apply because the Policy is more appropriately viewed as a time, place, and manner restriction pursuant to *City of Renton v. Playtime Theatres, Inc.,* 475 U.S. 41, 106 S.Ct. 925, 89 L.Ed.2d 29 (1986), than as a traditional content-based restriction on speech. Plaintiffs respond that this analysis is inapplicable to the Policy, which is designed to address the primary effects of Internet speech and which defendant admits restricts speech based on content.

In *Renton,* the Supreme Court found that a zoning ordinance prohibiting adult movie theaters from locating within 1000 feet of residential neighborhoods, churches, and specific other structures was a content-neutral time, place, and manner restriction because it could be justified without reference to the content of the speech in the theaters. The city justified the ordinance as necessary to address the sec-ondary effects of adult theaters in certain neighborhoods, namely preventing crime, protecting retail trade, maintaining property values, and preserving the quality of the neighborhoods, districts, and life. *See id.* at 48, 106 S.Ct. 925. The Court found that none of these secondary effects were related to the content of the movies shown at the theaters. Therefore, the Court found the ordinance to be constitutional. *See id.* at 54, 106 S.Ct. 925.

In a subsequent decision clarifying what it meant by "secondary effects," the Supreme Court held that "[r]egulations that focus on ... [l]isteners' reactions to speech are not the type of 'secondary effects' we referred to in *Renton*." *Boos v. Barry*, 485 U.S. 312, 321, 108 S.Ct. 1157, 99 L.Ed.2d 333 (1988). More recently, in construing the Communications Decency Act, the Court stated that "content-based blanket restric-tions on speech ... cannot be 'properly analyzed as a form of time, place, and manner regulation.'" *Reno v. ACLU*, 521 U.S. 844, 117 S.Ct. 2329, 2342, 138 L.Ed.2d 874 (1997).

Defendant contends that the Policy is designed to combat two secondary effects: cre-ating a sexually hostile environment and violating obscenity, child pornography, and harm to juveniles laws. Neither of these are secondary effects and neither can be justi-fied without reference to the content of the speech at issue. The defendant's concern that without installing filtering software, Internet viewing might lead to a sexually hos-tile environment is solely focused on the reaction of the audience to a certain category of speech. As the Supreme Court noted in *Boos,* this is not a secondary effect. The de-fendant's second concern is the possible violation of various criminal statutes that ad-dress materials deemed to be obscene, involve child pornography, or are harmful to ju-veniles. These criminal statutes define prohibited speech only by and because of its content. Far from addressing secondary effects of speech, these statutes focus on the very speech itself.

Indeed, the Fourth Circuit has recently observed that content-neutrality is a prereq-uisite to the constitutionality of time, place, and manner restrictions on expressive con-duct on public grounds. *See United States v. Johnson*, No. 97-5023, 159 F.3d 892, 1998 WL 781215, *3 (4th Cir. Oct. 28, 1998). Therefore, defendant's admission that the Pol-icy discriminates against speech based on content indicates that it would not be consti-tutional even if it were a time, place, and manner restriction.

## Constitutionality of the Policy

Defendant contends that even if we conclude that strict scrutiny is the appropriate standard of review, the Policy is constitutional because it is the least restrictive means to achieve two compelling government interests: "1) minimizing access to illegal pornog-raphy; and 2) avoidance of creation of a sexually hostile environment...." Plaintiffs and intervenors respond that there is no evidence that the Policy is necessary to further these interests nor that it is the least restrictive means available. Moreover, they argue that the Policy imposes an unconstitutional prior restraint on speech.

A content-based limitation on speech will be upheld only where the state demon-strates that the limitation "is necessary to serve a compelling state interest and that it is narrowly drawn to achieve that end." *Perry Educ. Ass'n. v. Perry Local Educators' Ass'n*, 460 U.S. 37, 45, 103 S.Ct. 948, 74 L.Ed.2d 794 (1983) (citing *Carey v. Brown*, 447 U.S. 455, 461, 100 S.Ct. 2286, 65 L.Ed.2d 263 (1980)). This test involves three distinct in-quiries: (1) whether the interests asserted by the state are compelling; (2) whether the limitation is necessary to further those interests; and (3) whether the limitation is narrowly drawn to achieve those interests.

### A. Whether the Defendant's Interests Are Compelling

Defendant argues that both of its asserted interests are compelling. Although plaintiffs and intervenors argue that these interests were not really the motivating factors behind the Policy and that they are not furthered by the Policy, they do not argue that the interests themselves are not compelling. For the purposes of this analysis, therefore, we assume that minimizing access to illegal pornography and avoidance of creation of a sexually hostile environment are compelling government interests.

### B. Whether the Policy is Necessary to Further Those Interests

To satisfy strict scrutiny, defendant must do more than demonstrate that it has a compelling interest; it must also demonstrate that the Policy is necessary to further that interest. In other words, defendant must demonstrate that in the absence of the Policy, a sexually hostile environment might exist and/or there would be a problem with individuals accessing child pornography or obscenity or minors accessing materials that are illegal as to them. Defendant "must demonstrate that the recited harms are real, not merely conjectural, and that the regulation will in fact alleviate these harms in a direct and material way." *Turner Broadcasting Sys., Inc. v. FCC*, 512 U.S. 622, 664, 114 S.Ct. 2445, 129 L.Ed.2d 497; *see also Johnson*, 865 F. Supp. at 1439 ("[S]imply alleging the need to avoid sexual harassment is not enough[;]...the defendant[ ] must show that the threat of disruption is actual, material, and substantial."). The defendant bears this burden because "[t]he interest in encouraging freedom of expression in a democratic society outweighs any theoretical but unproven benefit of censorship." *Reno v. ACLU*, 521 U.S. 844, 117 S.Ct. 2329, 2351, 138 L.Ed.2d 874 (1997).

The only evidence to which defendant can point in support of its argument that the Policy is necessary consists of a record of a single complaint arising from Internet use in another Virginia library and reports of isolated incidents in three other libraries across the country. In the Bedford County Central Public Library in Bedford County, Virginia, a patron complained that she had observed a boy viewing what she believed were pornographic pictures on the Internet. This incident was the only one defendant discovered within Virginia and the only one in the 16 months in which the Bedford County public library system had offered unfiltered public access to the Internet. After the incident, the library merely installed privacy screens on its Internet terminals which, according to the librarian, "work great." *Id*. at 4.

The only other evidence of problems arising from unfiltered Internet access is described by David Burt, defendant's expert, who was only able to find three libraries that allegedly had experienced such problems, one in Los Angeles County, another in Orange County, Florida, and one in Austin, Texas. There is no evidence in the record establishing that any other libraries have encountered problems....Significantly, defendant has not pointed to a single incident in which a library employee or patron has complained that material being accessed on the Internet was harassing or created a hostile environment. As a matter of law, we find this evidence insufficient to sustain defendant's burden of showing that the Policy is reasonably necessary. No reasonable trier of fact could conclude that three isolated incidents nationally, one very minor isolated incident in Virginia, no evidence whatsoever of problems in Loudoun County, and not a single employee complaint from anywhere in the country establish that the Policy is necessary to prevent sexual harassment or access to obscenity or child pornography.

C. Whether the Policy Is Narrowly Tailored to Achieve the Compelling Government Interests

Even if defendant could demonstrate that the Policy was reasonably necessary to further compelling state interests, it would still have to show that the Policy is narrowly tailored to achieve those interests. The parties disagree about several issues relating to whether the Policy is narrowly tailored: (1) whether less restrictive means are available; (2) whether the Policy is overinclusive; and (3) whether X-Stop, the filtering software used by defendant, is the least restrictive filtering software available.

### 1. Whether Less Restrictive Means Are Available

Defendant alleges that the Policy is constitutional because it is the least restrictive means available to achieve its interests. The only alternative to filtering, defendant contends, is to have librarians directly monitor what patrons view. Defendant asserts this system would be far more intrusive than using filtering software. Plaintiffs and intervenors respond that there are many less restrictive means available, including designing an acceptable use policy, using privacy screens, using filters that can be turned off for adult use, changing the location of Internet terminals, educating patrons on Internet use, placing time limits on use, and enforcing criminal laws when violations occur.

In *Sable Communications of Calif., Inc. v. FCC*, 492 U.S. 115, 126, 109 S.Ct. 2829, 106 L.Ed.2d 93 (1989), the Supreme Court noted that "[t]he Government may...regulate the content of constitutionally protected speech in order to promote a compelling interest if it chooses the least restrictive means to further the articulated interest." In *Sable* the Court declared unconstitutional a statute banning all "indecent" commercial telephone communications. The Court found that the government could not justify a total ban on communication that is harmful to minors, but not obscene, by arguing that only a total ban could completely prevent children from accessing indecent messages. *Id.* at 128, 109 S.Ct. 2829. The Court held that without evidence that less restrictive means had "been tested over time," the government had not carried its burden of proving that they would not be sufficiently effective. *Id.* at 128–29, 109 S.Ct. 2829.

We find that the Policy is not narrowly tailored because less restrictive means are available to further defendant's interests and, as in *Sable*, there is no evidence that defendant has tested any of these means over time. First, the installation of privacy screens is a much less restrictive alternative that would further defendant's interest in preventing the development of a sexually hostile environment. Second, there is undisputed evidence in the record that charging library staff with casual monitoring of Internet use is neither extremely intrusive nor a change from other library policies. Third, filtering software could be installed on only some Internet terminals and minors could be limited to using those terminals. Alternately, the library could install filtering software that could be turned off when an adult is using the terminal. While we find that all of these alternatives are less restrictive than the Policy, we do not find that any of them would necessarily be constitutional if implemented. That question is not before us.

### 2. Whether the Policy Is Overinclusive

Defendant contends that the Policy is neither overinclusive nor underinclusive because it is the least restrictive means available. Defendant also asserts that we should not focus on the specifics of what the Policy does and does not cover because that would detract from the broader issue of "whether a public library can or cannot filter obscene materials on its public Internet terminals and, if so, under what criteria and procedures.

In other words, the defendant asks this Court to consider a hypothetical situation that is not before us. The federal courts, however, may not provide advisory opinions; we may rule only on the Policy before us. Defendant cannot save its Policy by asking the Court to decide hypothetical questions for which there is no case or controversy.

In examining the specific Policy before us, we find it overinclusive because, on its face, it limits the access of all patrons, adult and juvenile, to material deemed fit for juveniles. It is undisputed that the Policy requires that "[i]f the Library Director considers a particular website to violate... [the Virginia Harmful to Juveniles Statute], the website should be blocked under the policy for adult as well as juvenile patrons." It has long been a matter of settled law that restricting what adults may read to a level appropriate for minors is a violation of the free speech guaranteed by the First Amendment and the Due Process Clause of the Fourteenth Amendment. *See Reno v. ACLU*, 521 U.S. 844, 117 S.Ct. 2329, 2346, 138 L.Ed.2d 874 (1997) ("It is true that we have repeatedly recognized the governmental interest in protecting children from harmful materials but that interest does not justify an unnecessarily broad suppression of speech addressed to adults.") (citations omitted); *Butler v. Michigan*, 352 U.S. 380, 383, 77 S.Ct. 524, 1 L.Ed.2d 412 (1957) (restricting adults to what is appropriate for juveniles is "not reasonably restricted to the evil with which it is said to deal").

... Because we have found that less restrictive alternatives are available to defendant and that defendant has not sufficiently tried to employ any of them, the Policy's limitation of adult access to constitutionally protected materials cannot survive strict scrutiny.

### 3. Whether X-Stop Is the Least Restrictive Filtering Software

Defendant claims that X-Stop is the least restrictive filtering software currently available and, therefore, the Policy is narrowly tailored as applied. Our finding that the Policy is unconstitutional on its face makes this argument moot. A facially overbroad government policy may nevertheless be saved if a court is able to construe government actions under that policy narrowly along the lines of their implementation, if the policy's text or other sources of government intent demonstrate "a clear line" to draw. *See Reno*, 117 S.Ct. at 2350–51. We find no such clear line here. Defendant has asserted an unconditional right to filter the Internet access it provides to its patrons and there is no evidence in the record that it has applied the Policy in a less restrictive way than it is written. Therefore, our finding that the Policy is unconstitutional on its face makes any consideration of the operation of X-Stop moot.

### Prior Restraint

Plaintiffs and intervenors allege that even if the Policy were to survive strict scrutiny analysis, the Court would have to find it unconstitutional under the doctrine of prior restraint because it provides neither sufficient standards to limit the discretion of the decisionmaker nor adequate procedural safeguards. Defendant responds that the Policy is not a prior restraint because it only prohibits viewing certain sites in Loudoun County public libraries, and not in the whole of Loudoun County.

Preventing prior restraints of speech is an essential component of the First Amendment's free speech guarantee. *See Freedman v. Maryland*, 380 U.S. 51, 58, 85 S.Ct. 734, 13 L.Ed.2d 649 (1965). "Permitting government officials unbridled discretion in determining whether to allow protected speech presents an unacceptable risk of both indefinitely suppressing and chilling protected speech." *11126 Baltimore Boulevard, Inc. v. Prince George's County*, 58 F.3d 988, 994 (4th Cir. 1995). In *11126*, the Fourth Circuit found that

[t]he guarantee of freedom of speech afforded by the First Amendment is abridged whenever the government makes the enjoyment of protected speech contingent upon obtaining permission from government officials to engage in its exercise under circumstances that permit government officials unfettered discretion to grant or deny the permission.... Such discretion exists when a regulation creating a prior restraint on speech fails to impose adequate standards for officials to apply in rendering a decision to grant or deny permission or when a regulation fails to impose procedural safeguards to ensure a sufficiently prompt decision.

[The following procedural safeguards have been required by the Supreme Court:] "(1) any restraint prior to judicial review can be imposed only for a specific brief period during which the status quo must be maintained; (2) expeditious judicial review of that decision must be available; and (3) the censor must bear the burden of going to court to suppress the speech and must bear the burden of proof once in court."

*Id.* at 996 (quoting *Freedman,* 380 U.S. at 58–60, 85 S.Ct. 734). In other words, even unprotected speech cannot be censored by administrative determination absent sufficient standards and adequate procedural safeguards. *See Southeastern Promotions, Ltd. v. Conrad,* 420 U.S. 546, 562, 95 S.Ct. 1239, 43 L.Ed.2d 448 (1975) ("Whatever the reasons may have been for the board's exclusion of the musical, it could not escape the obligation to afford appropriate procedural safeguards. We need not decide whether the... production is in fact obscene.").

Defendant argues that prior restraint cases are limited to situations in which a government tries to restrict all speech within its jurisdiction. Because Loudoun County residents are still permitted to obtain unfiltered Internet access in their homes or offices, defendant asserts, this situation is distinguishable from those cases. We find no legal support for this argument. *See Reno,* 117 S.Ct. at 2349 ("'[O]ne is not to have the exercise of his liberty of expression in appropriate places abridged on the plea that it may be exercised in some other place.'") (quoting *Schneider v. New Jersey,* 308 U.S. 147, 163, 60 S.Ct. 146, 84 L.Ed. 155 (1939)); *Southeastern Promotions,* 420 U.S. 546, 95 S.Ct. 1239, 43 L.Ed.2d 448. In *Southeastern Promotions,* a municipality had denied the use of a public facility for the production of the musical "Hair," which it deemed obscene. The Court found that "it does not matter... that the board's decision might not have had the effect of total suppression of the musical in the community. Denying use of the municipal facility under the circumstances present here constituted the prior restraint." 420 U.S. at 556, 95 S.Ct. 1239.

It is undisputed that the Policy lacks any provision for prior judicial determinations before material is censored. We find that the Policy includes neither sufficient standards nor adequate procedural safeguards. As to the first issue, the defendant's discretion to censor is essentially unbounded. The Policy itself speaks only in the broadest terms about child pornography, obscenity, and material deemed harmful to juveniles and fails to include any guidelines whatsoever to help librarians determine what falls within these broad categories. There are no standards by which a reviewing authority can determine if the decisions made were appropriate.

The degree to which the Policy is completely lacking in standards is demonstrated by the defendant's willingness to entrust all preliminary blocking decisions—and, by default, the overwhelming majority of final decision—to a private vendor, Log-On Data Corp. Although the defendant argues that X-Stop is the best available filter, a defendant cannot avoid its constitutional obligation by contracting out its decisionmaking to a private entity. Such abdication of its obligation is made even worse by the undisputed facts here. Specifically, defendant concedes that it does not know the criteria by which Log-On Data makes its blocking decisions. It is also undisputed that Log-On Data does not base its blocking decisions on any legal definition of obscenity or even on the parameters of defendant's Policy. Thus, on this record, we find that the defendant has not satisfied the first prong of prior restraint analysis, establishing adequate standards.

In addition, the Policy also fails to include adequate procedural safeguards. The three minimum procedural safeguards required are (1) a specific brief time period of imposition before judicial review; (2) expeditious judicial review; and (3) the censor bearing the burden of proof. The Policy, even including the alleged protections of the unofficial "unblocking policy," is inadequate in each of these respects. First, the Policy itself contains no provision for administrative review, no time period in which any review must be completed, and no provision for judicial review. Under the unofficial "unblocking policy," a library patron who finds herself blocked from an Internet site she believes contains protected speech is required to request in writing that the librarians unblock the specified site. If the librarian determines that the site does not fall within the Policy's prohibitions, he will unblock it, although there is no systematic way in which this is done. There is no time period during which this review must occur and there is no provision for notifying the requesting patron if and when a site has been unblocked.

The second required procedural safeguard is expeditious judicial review after the administrative decision is made. There is no provision whatsoever in the Policy for judicial review of any blocks. This makes the question of who carries the burden of proof in any judicial review proceeding, the third required procedural safeguard, moot. Because the Policy has neither adequate standards nor adequate procedural safeguards, we find it to be an unconstitutional prior restraint....

Because we have concluded that section 2 under the heading "Internet Services Provided" constitutes an unconstitutional prior restraint on speech, and that section 2 permeates the rest of the Policy, we hold that defendant's Policy on Internet Sexual Harassment is unconstitutional.

## Conclusion

Although defendant is under no obligation to provide Internet access to its patrons, it has chosen to do so and is therefore restricted by the First Amendment in the limitations it is allowed to place on patron access. Defendant has asserted a broad right to censor the expressive activity of the receipt and communication of information through the Internet with a Policy that (1) is not necessary to further any compelling government interest; (2) is not narrowly tailored; (3) restricts the access of adult patrons to protected material just because the material is unfit for minors; (4) provides inadequate standards for restricting access; and (5) provides inadequate procedural safeguards to ensure prompt judicial review. Such a policy offends the guarantee of free speech in the First Amendment and is, therefore, unconstitutional.

For these reasons, the intervenors' Motion to Substitute Parties will be GRANTED; the plaintiffs' and intervenors' motions for summary judgment will be GRANTED; and the defendant's Motion for Summary Judgment will be GRANTED as to the standing of John Ockerbloom d/b/a Banned Books On-Line and DENIED in all other respects. Defendant will be permanently enjoined from enforcing its Policy on Internet Sexual Harassment. An appropriate order will issue.

## *Notes and Questions*

1.  To what degree are government-sponsored filtering programs susceptible to political and social biases?

2.  Even though the Internet appears to be a single, integrated system from the user's perspective, no single organization or entity controls the Internet. Thus, there is no centralized point from which individual web-sites or services can be blocked from the World Wide Web.

3.  Does section 230 of the Communications Decency Act, 47 U.S.C. §230, *see* discussion *infra* at 203, shield governmental efforts to regulate Internet speech? *Compare Mainstream Loudoun v. Board of Trustees of the Loudoun County Library*, 2 F. Supp. 2d 783 (E.D. Va. 1998) *with Kathleen R. v. City of Livermore*, No. V-015266-4 (Cal. Super. Ct. filed May 28, 1998), *appeal* No. A086349 (Cal. Ct. App., 1st Div.) (reciting allegations by plaintiffs, a woman and her minor son, that the use of public funds to pay for children's access to pornography at a library constitutes a waste of public funds, and that the library's policy of not installing filtering software to block out material harmful to children on computers used by children constitutes a "nuisance"); *see also Judge Rules §230 Blocks the Livermore Library Suit*, Tech. L.J. (Oct. 21, 1998) <http://www.techlawjournal.com/censor/81021.htm>.

4.  Arizona was the first state to mandate filtering in its public schools and public libraries, restricting access by minors to sexually explicit material on the Internet. *See* Ariz. Rev. Stat. Ann. §§34-501, 34-502 (West 1999).

---

Ultimately, then,

> many find some of the speech on the Internet to be offensive, and amid the din of cyberspace many hear discordant voices that they regard as indecent. The absence of governmental regulation of Internet content has unquestionably produced a kind of chaos, but as one...put it with such resonance..., "[w]hat achieved success was the very chaos that the Internet is. The strength of the Internet is that chaos." Just as the strength of the Internet is chaos, so the strength of our liberty depends upon the chaos and cacophony of the unfettered speech the First Amendment protects.

*American Civil Liberties Union v. Reno,* 929 F. Supp. 824, 883 (E.D. Pa. 1996) (footnote omitted), *aff'd,* 521 U.S. 844 (1997).

# Chapter III

# Defamation

## Definition and Elements

Good name in man and woman, dear my lord,
Is the immediate jewel of their souls:
Who steals my purse steals trash; 'tis something, nothing;
'Twas mine, 'tis his, and has been slave to thousands;
But he that filches from me my good name
Robs me of that which not enriches him
And makes me poor indeed.

William Shakespeare, *Othello*, Iago to Othello, Act III, Scene 3.

Traditional libel law recognizes that the interest of the individual in preserving his public good name is worthy of protection. There is no general social value worthy of constitutional protection in the deliberate publication of defamatory falsehoods. "[T]hough a newspaper may publish without government censorship, it has never been entirely free from liability for what it chooses to print. Among other things, the press has not been wholly at liberty to publish falsehoods damaging to individual reputation.... [W]e have cherished the average citizen's reputation interest enough to afford him a fair chance to vindicate himself in an action for libel characteristically provided by state law." *Miami Herald Publ'g Co. v. Tornillo*, 418 U.S. 241, 261–62 (1974) (White, J., concurring). Nevertheless, the law of libel and slander subordinates the reputational interests of the individual in certain circumstances. So fundamentally significant is free speech to our notions of democratic ideals that some abuse is tolerated nonetheless.

Defamation is a tort that addresses damage to reputational interests. The defamatory material may be written, in which case the claim is denoted a "libel," or oral, in which case the claim is denoted a "slander." In general, a defamation is a communication to a third party that tends to hold the plaintiff up to hatred, contempt, or aversion, or to cause him to be shunned or avoided. A communication is defamatory if it tends to so harm the reputation of another as to induce an evil or unsavory opinion of him in the community. *See generally* Restatement (Second) of Torts, § 559, cmt. e (1997). The New York Court of Appeals has defined a defamatory statement as that which "'tends to expose a person to hatred, contempt or aversion, or to induce an evil or unsavory opinion of him in the minds of a substantial number in the community, even though it may impute no moral turpitude to him.'" *Nichols v. Item Publishers, Inc.*, 309 N.Y. 596, 600, 132 N.E.2d 860, 862 (1956) (quoting *Mencher v. Chelsey*, 297 N.Y. 94, 100 (1947)).

The Restatement (Second) of Torts, § 558, lists the elements of an action for defamation as (1) a false and defamatory statement concerning another; (2) an unprivileged publication to a third party; (3) fault amounting at least to negligence on the part of the publisher; and (4) either actionability of the statement irrespective of special harm or the existence of special harm caused by the publication. First Amendment expert Judge Robert Sack characterizes this list of enumerated elements as "deceptively simple." Robert D. Sack, *Sack on Defamation: Libel, Slander, and Related Problems* § 2.1.1 (3d ed. 1999). Application of these elements to each case's salient facts requires the integration of an extensive body of caselaw with an impressive constitutional gloss. One court envisaged the process by resorting to a "visual model" of "three interlocking circles":

> The first circle represents state defamation law and embodies the significant interest states have in providing tort remedies for injuries to reputation. The second circle, impinging on the first to varying degrees depending on language and interpretation, represents state constitutional guarantees of freedom of expression and freedom of the press. The third circle overlaps both the first and the second and embodies federal free expression and free press guarantees.

*West v. Thomson Newspapers,* 872 P.2d 999, 1004 (Utah 1994).

At the outset, courts generally look to whether there has been publication of the insult to another; otherwise, while the subject of the derogatory statement may have suffered hurt feelings, his reputation cannot have been harmed. In addition, the statement must be "of and concerning" the plaintiff; in other words, the plaintiff must show that others reasonably understood the insult to have been directed to him. Further, the statement must have been opprobrious; mere slights will not provide the requisite defamatory import. Additionally, the statement must be false. The defendant also must be shown to have acted with the requisite degree of fault, the standard for which generally is determined by the nature of the speech and the status of the plaintiff.

The Supreme Court has been mindful that damages awards may have detrimental effects on free speech values:

> The largely uncontrolled discretion of juries to award damages where there is no loss unnecessarily compounds the potential of any system of liability for defamatory falsehood to inhibit the vigorous exercise of First Amendment freedoms. Additionally, the doctrine of presumed damages invites juries to punish unpopular opinion rather than to compensate individuals for injury sustained by the pubication of a false fact. More to the point, the States have no substantial interest in securing for plaintiffs...gratuitious awards of money damages far in excess of any actual injury.

*Gertz v. Robert Welch, Inc.,* 418 U.S. 323, 349 (1974).

Punitive damages in particular "have an uneasy relationship with the law of defamation. They are punishment of expression...They are therefore a device peculiarly suited to use by judges and juries to avenge offending communications or to silence unpopular speakers." Robert D. Sack, *Sack on Defamation: Libel, Slander, and Related Problems* at § 10.3.5 (citations omitted). The Supreme Court has been troubled that juries often assess punitive awards "in wholly unpredictable amounts bearing no necessary relation to the actual harm caused." *Gertz v. Robert Welch, Inc.,* 418 U.S. at 350. The primary obstacle to a recovery of punitive damages is the constitutionally-rooted prerequisite that, at least as to claims against the media by public plaintiffs or by private plaintiffs where the communication at issue is a matter of public concern, actual malice must be proved. *See id.*

## Notes and Questions

1. Much of this country's First Amendment jurisprudence is premised upon the notion that censorship of political speech, even seditious libel, is antithetical to democratic freedoms. Moreover, protection for expression other than core political speech has been explicitly recognized by the Supreme Court. "Freedom of discussion, if it would fulfill its historic function in this nation, must embrace all issues about which information is needed or appropriate to enable the members of society to cope with the exigencies of their period." *Thornhill v. Alabama*, 310 U.S. 88, 102 (1940). "The guarantees for speech and press are not the preserve of political expression or comment upon public affairs." *Time, Inc. v. Hill*, 385 U.S. 374, 388 (1967). The citizenry has a legitimate and substantial interest in the conduct of its public figures, "and freedom of the press to engage in uninhibited debate about their involvement in public issues and events is as crucial as it is in the case of 'public officials.'" *Curtis Publ'g Co. v. Butts*, 388 U.S. 130, 164 (1967) (Warren, C.J., concurring).

2. Even when a plaintiff is able to make the requisite showing on all of the elements of the defamation tort, the media defendant nonetheless may have available to it a number of defenses. For example, the communication may be regarded as privileged on the theory that it was an accurate report of a judicial or governmental act or an accurate summary of official records. *See* discussion *infra* at 288.

# Publication

## 1. Publication to Another

Personal attacks on one's character, made directly to that person but not to others, cannot give rise to a defamation claim because there has been no reputational damage; the person attacked may have suffered hurt feelings, but he has not suffered a loss of esteem in the community.

In the traditional mass media context, the question of whether a statement has been "published" seldom serves as a battleground for dispute. In order to be actionable, the alleged defamation must have been communicated to a third person. Even a single viewer of a television program or a single reader of a book or article may be sufficient to sustain a *prima facie* case. While the number of persons to whom the falsehood has been published may bear on the level of damages awarded, a cognizable cause of action nonetheless exists if there is a single third-party recipient.

Has the defamatory statement been "published" if it is uttered in the course of dictating a letter to the subject of the defamation? In *Ostrowe v. Lee*, 256 N.Y. 36, 38, 175 N.E. 505, 506 (1931) ("*Ostrowe*"), the defendant dictated a letter, ostensibly unprotected by applicable privilege,[1] to the plaintiff, accusing him having committed the

---

1. Intra-corporate correspondence composed in the course of conducting business has been challenged as insufficient to constitute the requisite publication. Under an agency argument, for ex-

crime of larceny; the stenographer read the notes and transcribed them. The court stated:

> A defamatory writing is not published if it is read by no one but the one defamed. Published, it is, however, as soon as it is read by any one else. The reader may be a telegraph operator, or the compositor in a printing house, or the copyist who reproduces a longhand draft. The legal consequence is not altered where the symbols reproduced or interpreted are the notes of a stenographer. Publication there still is as a result of the dictation, at least where the notes have been examined or transcribed.

*Id.* at 38, 175 N.E. at 505 (citations omitted); *see also Hirschfeld v. Institutional Investor, Inc.,* 617 N.Y.S.2d 11, 208 A.D.2d 380 (App. Div. 1994); *Dixon v. Economy Co.,* 477 So.2d 353, 354 (Ala. 1985); *Berry v. City of New York Ins. Co.,* 210 Ala. 369, 98 So. 290, 292 (Ala. 1923) ("It is manifest that one who receives a dictation, takes notes, [and] reduces the same to typewriting, may be influenced in his or her estimate of the character of a person by libelous matter therein").

Transcription of the offending material, as opposed to having heard it uttered during the course of its dictation, seemed to be the focus of the court's inquiry. The *Ostrowe* court commented that "[v]ery often a stenographer does not grasp the meaning of dictated words till the dictation is over and the symbols have been read. This is particularly likely to be the case where a defamatory charge is made equivocally or with evasive innuendoes. The author who directs his copyist to read[ ] has displayed the writing to the reader as truly and effectively as if he had copied it himself." *Id.* 256 N.Y. at 39, 175 N.E. at 506.

How important is it that the dictated matter has been reduced to a tangible writing? In the Internet context, keying defamatory content in preparation for transmission of an e-mail message or posting on a discussion group that has not been viewed by others should not be characterized as a publication until the message has in fact been transmitted or posted and read by another.

The *Ostrowe* case was decided seven decades ago, long before the launch of Internet communications. The significance of the decision for the study of Internet speech lies in the court's emphasis on the dichotomy between slander and defamation. The court regarded less impunity attendant to speech that "is caught upon the wing and transmuted into print. What gives the sting to the writing is its permanence of form. The spoken word dissolves, but the written one abides and 'perpetuates the scandal.'" *Id.* (citation omitted).

In many jurisdictions, a person who has been slandered, unlike one who has been libeled, may recover only if he can prove that the statement caused actual pecuniary injury, unless the statement is defamatory *per se. See* discussion *infra* at 241. Rationales for permitting easier recovery for libel than for slander have been advanced—and debated.

---

ample, the corporation is depicted as simply engaged in communication with itself. Certain intracompany communications by a manager may constitute publication, however, on the theory that there has been damage to one's reputation within the corporate community. But even if such statements are deemed to have been published, they may be subject to the common interest privilege, which arises when a person makes a good faith, *bona fide* communication on a subject in which he has an interest or a legal, moral, or societal interest to speak to a person with a corresponding interest. *See, e.g., Sanderson v. Bellevue Maternity Hospital,* 259 A.D.2d 888, 889 (App. Div. 1999). "The rationale for applying the privilege in these circumstances is that so long as the privilege is not abused, the flow of information between persons sharing a common interest should not be impeded." *Liberman v Gelstein,* 80 N.Y.2d 429, 437 (1992).

Written statements arguably "leave[ ] a more permanent blot on one's reputation," and may evince "greater deliberation and intention." *See Spence v. Funk*, 396 A.2d 967, 970 (Del. 1978) (citing *Rice v. Simmons*, 2 Del. 417 (1836)); *see also Ward v. Zelkovsky*, 136 N.J. 516, 528, 643 A.2d 972, 978 (1994). Historically, "the written word" has been deemed "capable of wider circulation than that which is communicated orally." *Spence v. Funk*, 396 A. 2d at 970 (citation omitted).

How does this reasoning apply to digital dialogue? As to the relative permanency or transitory nature of communications, at first blush, a cyberspace communication appears to be ephemeral in nature, and thus closer to the slander analogue. Chat room participants, for instance, often regard electronic exchanges as casual conversation. But the words transmitted are in fact written out in some form; indeed, they may, at the recipient's discretion and possibly subject to the technical restrictions imposed by the author or host, even be downloaded or printed in tangible form.

Like written communications, electronic exchanges are deliberate, composed at a keyboard rather than through oral utterance, and are textual in nature. Further, computer storage systems have extensive archival capabilities, even when retention is not deliberately undertaken by the user. Whether a cyberspace communication is "premeditated" likely varies dramatically depending upon a wide variety of factors, such as the context in which the missive was dispatched, the person or entity to whom it was sent, the fervor with which it was written, and whether it was sent in response to a vituperative message.

Perhaps most suspect in its indiscriminate application to electronic speech is the presumption that "written" words are susceptible to greater dissemination. Internet communication may be sent simultaneously to any number of persons via a mail exploder or potentially to all those with access to the Internet via postings. Alternatively, a message may be sent to a single person, and even transmitted subject to encryption, password, or other restrictions specifically designed to contain its circulation.

----

# 2. *Publication by Conduits*

Defamation claims have been premised on publication of allegedly defamatory statements made by third parties. Under the "republication rule," one who repeats a defamatory statement may be held as liable as the original defamer. The rule is based on the legal fiction that the republisher "adopts" the defamatory statement as his own. Certainly a defense to an ensuing defamation claim is that the statement in issue was true. But if the press could avail itself of such a defense only when truth could be established, reporting of certain newsworthy events would be chilled.

At common law, one who repeats a defamatory statement made by another generally does so at his peril. *See, e.g., Cianci v. New Times Publ'g Co.*, 639 F.2d 54, 60–61 (2d Cir. 1980). The law regards one who republishes a defamatory statement made by another as having "adopted" the statement as his own, based on a theory that " 'tale bearers are as bad as tale makers.' " *Barry v. Time, Inc.*, 584 F. Supp. 1110, 1122 (N.D. Cal. 1984) (quoting *McDonald v. Glitsch, Inc.*, 589 S.W.2d 554, 556 (Tex. Civ. App. 1979). One cannot be held liable, however, unless he has " 'tak[en] a [r]esponsible part in the publication.' " *Lewis v. Time, Inc.*, 83 F.R.D. 455, 463 (E.D. Cal. 1979), *aff'd*, 710 F.2d 549 (9th Cir. 1983) (quoting *McGuire v. Brightman*, 79 Cal. App. 3d 776, 789 (1978)). The common law rule is subject to constitutionally-rooted limitations regarding the imposition of liability without fault. *See, e.g., Gertz v. Robert Welch, Inc.*, 418 U.S. 323, 347 (1974). The principle of protecting from liability those who merely deliver or transmit defamatory material previously published by another without knowledge or reason to know that the material was false and defamatory "is universally acknowledged." Robert D. Sack, *Sack on Defamation: Libel, Slander, and Related Problems* § 7.3.1 at 7-6 (3d ed. 1999).

Courts have distinguished among entities that publish or republish a defamatory statement. Traditional examples of "publishers" include newspapers, magazines, and broadcasters. When they create the content of their publications, they may be held accountable for them, subject to applicable defenses and privileges.

Those who deliver or transmit such material are characterized as "distributors." Such entities include bookstores, libraries, and newsstands, and generally are not deemed responsible for defamatory statements contained in the materials they distribute unless they knew or had reason to know that the material was defamatory. *See, e.g., Auvil v. CBS "60 Minutes,"* 800 F. Supp. 928, 931–32 (E.D. Wa. 1992). Distributors have no legal duty to examine publications prior to offering them for sale to ascertain whether they include defamatory content. *See, e.g., Lewis v. Time, Inc.*, 83 F.R.D. at 463.

"Common carriers," which provide facilities to enable the exchange of communications, historically have been exemplified by telephone companies. These entities are not held liable for the dissemination of defamatory material unless they are shown to have participated in the preparation of its content. *See, e.g., Anderson v. New York Telephone Co.*, 35 N.Y.2d 746, 748, 361 N.Y.S.2d 913, 915 (1974) (Gabrielli, J., concurring); *Lerman v. Chuckleberry Publ'g, Inc.*, 521 F. Supp. 228, 235 (S.D.N.Y. 1981), *rev'd on other grounds sub nom. Lerman v. Flynt Distrib. Co.*, 745 F.2d 123 (2d Cir. 1984), *cert. denied*, 471 U.S. 1054 (1985).

In some jurisdictions, conduits may be able to assert a "wire service defense," which precludes liability for republication of a news release from a reputable news agency without substantial change and without knowledge that the article was false. This defense parallels the constitutional prerequisite for liability based on a showing of fault. *See, e.g., Gertz v. Robert Welch, Inc.*, 418 U.S. 323. For example, CNN did not act grossly irresponsible under applicable New York fault standards by relying on information transmitted to it by the Canadian Broadcasting Company. *Bryks v. Canadian Broadcasting Corp.*, 928 F. Supp. 381 (S.D.N.Y. 1996).

This categorization reflects First Amendment values prohibiting the imposition of strict liability on such entities as booksellers. The consequent allocation of responsibilities ultimately advances the public's access to material, as it alleviates the otherwise inevitable timidity of distributors and common carriers to disperse material that might subject them to liability.

As technology advances, the means by which statements may be published proliferate. Perpetuation of information to larger sectors of the public frequently is accomplished by technical methodology that inevitably utilizes intermediary publishers. Emerging technologies increase, virtually instantaneously, the ability to publish and disseminate content. On-line communications conveyed through Internet service providers can render a statement available to millions of people, on a worldwide basis, simply because they have Internet access. Should the Internet service provider, whose facilities conveyed the communication, be held liable for defamatory content? Suppose that the Internet service provider is put on notice that the statement in issue in fact constitutes an actionable defamation? If a service provider enters into an agreement with an originator of content to license the content on the provider's service, is the provider accountable for the content? How can a service provider realistically monitor, investigate, and assess the potentially libelous content of communications which are so extensive, voluminous, and immediate in their availability?

Until the enactment of the Communications Decency Act, 47 U.S.C. § 230 (West Supp. 2000), courts had been grappling with these issues, with disparate results.

---

# CUBBY, INC. v. COMPUSERVE INC.

United States District Court, Southern District of New York
No. 90 Civ. 6571 (PKL), 776 F. Supp. 135
October 29, 1991

LEISURE, District Judge:

This is a diversity action for libel, business disparagement, and unfair competition, based on allegedly defamatory statements made in a publication carried on a computerized database. Defendant CompuServe Inc. ("CompuServe") has moved for summary judgment pursuant to Rule 56 of the Federal Rules of Civil Procedure. For the reasons stated below, CompuServe's motion is granted in its entirety.

## Background

CompuServe develops and provides computer-related products and services, including CompuServe Information Service ("CIS"), an on-line general information service or "electronic library" that subscribers may access from a personal computer or terminal. Subscribers to CIS pay a membership fee and online time usage fees, in return for which they have access to the thousands of information sources available on CIS. Subscribers may also obtain access to over 150 special interest "forums," which are comprised of electronic bulletin boards, interactive online conferences, and topical databases.

One forum available is the Journalism Forum, which focuses on the journalism industry. Cameron Communications, Inc. ("CCI"), which is independent of CompuServe, has contracted to "manage, review, create, delete, edit and otherwise control the contents" of the Journalism Forum "in accordance with editorial and technical standards and conventions of style as established by CompuServe."

One publication available as part of the Journalism Forum is Rumorville USA ("Rumorville"), a daily newsletter that provides reports about broadcast journalism and journalists. Rumorville is published by Don Fitzpatrick Associates of San Francisco ("DFA"), which is headed by defendant Don Fitzpatrick. CompuServe has no employment, contractual, or other direct relationship with either DFA or Fitzpatrick; DFA provides Rumorville to the Journalism Forum under a contract with CCI. The contract between CCI and DFA provides that DFA "accepts total responsibility for the contents" of Rumorville. The contract also requires CCI to limit access to Rumorville to those CIS subscribers who have previously made membership arrangements directly with DFA.

CompuServe has no opportunity to review Rumorville's contents before DFA uploads it into CompuServe's computer banks, from which it is immediately available to approved CIS subscribers. CompuServe receives no part of any fees that DFA charges for access to Rumorville, nor does CompuServe compensate DFA for providing Rumorville to the Journalism Forum; the compensation CompuServe receives for making Rumorville available to its subscribers is the standard online time usage and membership fees charged to all CIS subscribers, regardless of the information services they use. CompuServe maintains that, before this action was filed, it had no notice of any complaints about the contents of the Rumorville publication or about DFA.

In 1990, plaintiffs Cubby, Inc. ("Cubby") and Robert Blanchard ("Blanchard") (collectively, "plaintiffs") developed Skuttlebut, a computer database designed to publish and distribute electronically news and gossip in the television news and radio industries. Plaintiffs intended to compete with Rumorville; subscribers gained access to Skuttlebut through their personal computers after completing subscription agreements with plaintiffs.

Plaintiffs claim that, on separate occasions in April 1990, Rumorville published false and defamatory statements relating to Skuttlebut and Blanchard, and that CompuServe carried these statements as part of the Journalism Forum. The allegedly defamatory remarks included a suggestion that individuals at Skuttlebut gained access to information first published by Rumorville "through some back door;" a statement that Blanchard was "bounced" from his previous employer, WABC; and a description of Skuttlebut as a "new start-up scam."...

## Discussion

### ...A. The Applicable Standard of Liability

Plaintiffs base their libel claim on the allegedly defamatory statements contained in the Rumorville publication that CompuServe carried as part of the Journalism Forum. CompuServe argues that, based on the undisputed facts, it was a distributor of Rumorville, as opposed to a publisher of the Rumorville statements. CompuServe further contends that, as a distributor of Rumorville, it cannot be held liable on the libel claim because it neither knew nor had reason to know of the allegedly defamatory statements. Plaintiffs, on the other hand, argue that the Court should conclude that CompuServe is a publisher of the statements and hold it to a higher standard of liability.

Ordinarily, "'one who repeats or otherwise republishes defamatory matter is subject to liability as if he had originally published it.'" *Cianci v. New Times Publishing Co.*, 639 F.2d 54, 61 (2d Cir. 1980) (Friendly, J.) (quoting Restatement (Second) of Torts § 578 (1977)). With respect to entities such as news vendors, book stores, and libraries, however, "New York courts have long held that vendors and distributors of defamatory publications are not liable if they neither know nor have reason to know of the defamation." *Lerman v. Chuckleberry Publishing, Inc.*, 521 F. Supp. 228, 235 (S.D.N.Y. 1981); *accord Macaluso v. Mondadori Publishing Co.*, 527 F. Supp. 1017, 1019 (E.D.N.Y. 1981).

The requirement that a distributor must have knowledge of the contents of a publication before liability can be imposed for distributing that publication is deeply rooted in the First Amendment, made applicable to the states through the Fourteenth Amendment. "[T]he constitutional guarantees of the freedom of speech and of the press stand in the way of imposing" strict liability on distributors for the contents of the reading materials they carry. *Smith v. California*, 361 U.S. 147, 152–53, 80 S.Ct. 215, 218–19, 4 L.Ed.2d 205 (1959). In *Smith*, the Court struck down an ordinance that imposed liability on a bookseller for possession of an obscene book, regardless of whether the book-seller had knowledge of the book's contents. The Court reasoned that

> "Every bookseller would be placed under an obligation to make himself aware of the contents of every book in his shop. It would be altogether unreasonable to demand so near an approach to omniscience." And the bookseller's burden would become the public's burden, for by restricting him the public's access to reading matter would be restricted. If the contents of bookshops and periodi-cal stands were restricted to material of which their proprietors had made an inspection, they might be depleted indeed.

*Id.* at 153, 80 S.Ct. at 219 (citation and footnote omitted). Although *Smith* involved criminal liability, the First Amendment's guarantees are no less relevant to the instant action: "What a State may not constitutionally bring about by means of a criminal statute is likewise beyond the reach of its civil law of libel. The fear of damage awards... may be markedly more inhibiting than the fear of prosecution under a criminal statute." *New York Times Co. v. Sullivan,* 376 U.S. 254, 277, 84 S.Ct. 710, 724, 11 L.Ed.2d 686 (1964) (citation omitted).

CompuServe's CIS product is in essence an electronic, for-profit library that carries a vast number of publications and collects usage and membership fees from its sub-scribers in return for access to the publications. CompuServe and companies like it are at the forefront of the information industry revolution. High technology has markedly increased the speed with which information is gathered and processed; it is now possi-ble for an individual with a personal computer, modem, and telephone line to have in-stantaneous access to thousands of news publications from across the United States and around the world. While CompuServe may decline to carry a given publication alto-gether, in reality, once it does decide to carry a publication, it will have little or no edi-torial control over that publication's contents. This is especially so when CompuServe carries the publication as part of a forum that is managed by a company unrelated to CompuServe.

With respect to the Rumorville publication, the undisputed facts are that DFA up-loads the text of Rumorville into CompuServe's data banks and makes it available to ap-proved CIS subscribers instantaneously. CompuServe has no more editorial control over such a publication than does a public library, book store, or newsstand, and it would be no more feasible for CompuServe to examine every publication it carries for potentially defamatory statements than it would be for any other distributor to do so. "First Amendment guarantees have long been recognized as protecting distributors of publications.... Obviously, the national distributor of hundreds of periodicals has no duty to monitor each issue of every periodical it distributes. Such a rule would be an impermissible burden on the First Amendment." *Lerman v. Flynt Distributing Co.,* 745 F.2d 123, 139 (2d Cir. 1984), *cert. denied,* 471 U.S. 1054, 105 S.Ct. 2114, 85 L.Ed.2d 479 (1985); *see also Daniel v. Dow Jones & Co.,* 137 Misc.2d 94, 102, 520 N.Y.S.2d 334, 340 (N.Y.Civ.Ct. 1987) (computerized database service "is one of the modern, technologi-cally interesting, alternative ways the public may obtain up-to-the-minute news" and "is entitled to the same protection as more established means of news distribution").

Technology is rapidly transforming the information industry. A computerized data-base is the functional equivalent of a more traditional news vendor, and the inconsistent application of a lower standard of liability to an electronic news distributor such as CompuServe than that which is applied to a public library, book store, or newsstand would impose an undue burden on the free flow of information. Given the relevant

First Amendment considerations, the appropriate standard of liability to be applied to CompuServe is whether it knew or had reason to know of the allegedly defamatory Rumorville statements.

## B. CompuServe's Liability as a Distributor

CompuServe contends that it is undisputed that it had neither knowledge nor reason to know of the allegedly defamatory Rumorville statements, especially given the large number of publications it carries and the speed with which DFA uploads Rumorville into its computer banks and makes the publication available to CIS subscribers. The burden is thus shifted to plaintiffs, who "'must set forth specific facts showing that there is a genuine issue for trial.'" *Anderson v. Liberty Lobby, Inc.,* 477 U.S. 242, 250, 106 S.Ct. 2505, 2511, 91 L.Ed.2d 202 (1986) (quoting Fed.R.Civ.P. 56(e)). Plaintiffs have not set forth anything other than conclusory allegations as to whether CompuServe knew or had reason to know of the Rumorville statements, and have failed to meet their burden on this issue. Plaintiffs do contend that CompuServe was informed that persons affiliated with Skuttlebut might be "hacking" in order to obtain unauthorized access to Rumorville, but that claim is wholly irrelevant to the issue of whether CompuServe was put on notice that the Rumorville publication contained statements accusing the Skuttlebut principals of engaging in "hacking."

Plaintiffs have not set forth any specific facts showing that there is a genuine issue as to whether CompuServe knew or had reason to know of Rumorville's contents. Because CompuServe, as a news distributor, may not be held liable if it neither knew nor had reason to know of the allegedly defamatory Rumorville statements, summary judgment in favor of CompuServe on the libel claim is granted.…

## Conclusion

For the reasons stated above, CompuServe's motion for summary judgment pursuant to Fed. R. Civ. P. 56 is granted on all claims asserted against it.

---

Just four years after *Cubby, Inc. v. CompuServe, Inc.* was decided, a New York state court held that an Internet service provider's posture as "an on-line service that exercised editorial control over the content of messages posted on its computer bulletin boards" rendered it a "publisher." *Stratton Oakmont, Inc. v. Prodigy Services, Co.,* 63 U.S.L.W. 2765, 1995 WL 343710, 23 Media L. Rptr. (BNA) 1794 (N.Y. Sup. May 24, 1995) ("*Stratton Oakmont I*").

In *Strattton Oakmont I,* the plaintiffs, a securities investment banking firm and its president, claimed that they were defamed by statements that they had committed criminal and fraudulent acts in connection with an initial public offering. *Id.* at *1. The plaintiffs sued Prodigy Services Company ("Prodigy"), the owner and operator of the computer network service on which the statements had appeared. *Id.* The statements had been posted on "Money Talk," a bulletin board service devoted to discussion about stocks, investments, and other financial matters.

A threshold question for the New York Supreme Court was whether Prodigy could reasonably be considered a "publisher" of the statements in issue. In support of their argument that Prodigy had published the material in issue, the plaintiffs pointed to Prodigy's stated policy, which indicated that the company promoted itself as a family-oriented computer network. Proffer also was made of newspaper articles written by Prodigy personnel that likened Prodigy to a newspaper and described Prodigy as exercising editorial control over the content of messages posted on its bulletin board. *Id.* at *2. Additionally, Prodigy had promulgated "content guidelines," requesting users to refrain from posting insulting notes, and advising users that postings that harass, were in bad taste, repugnant to community standards, or harmful to the maintenance of a harmonious on-line community, would be removed when brought to Prodigy's attention. *Id.*

Prodigy, in its defense, relied on *Cubby, Inc. v. CompuServe, Inc.* The *Stratton Oakmont I* court deemed the case inapposite, however; CompuServe's role was distinguished as essentially an electronic for-profit library that assumed little or no editorial control over the contents of the publications it carried, and thus was regarded as the functional equivalent of a more traditional news vendor. *See id.* at *4. The *Stratton Oakmont I* court emphasized that Prodigy had held itself out to the public and its members as controlling the content of its computer bulletin boards and had implemented this control through a mandatory and automatic software screening program. *Id.* By making a "conscious choice" to "actively utilize technology and manpower" to delete offensive postings, "Prodigy [was] clearly making decisions as to content, and such decisions constitute editorial control." *Id.* at *4 (citation omitted).

As far as the court was concerned, the fact that the "control" exercised by Prodigy was inchoate and enforced erratically did "not minimize or eviscerate the simple fact that Prodigy has uniquely arrogated to itself the role of determining what is proper for its members to post and read on its bulletin boards." *Id.* Nor were policy arguments availing; the court eschewed contentions that its decision would compel other computer networks to abdicate control of their bulletin boards. The court surmised that market conditions likely would compensate a network for its increased control and resultant increased exposure. *Id.* at *5.

In a subsequent proceeding in which Prodigy moved for reargument and/or renewal of its motion for partial summary judgment, the court acknowledged that its initial decision in *Stratton Oakmont I* had received wide attention. *Stratton Oakmont, Inc. v. Prodigy Services Co.*, No. 31063/94, 1995 WL 805178 at *1 (N.Y. Sup. Dec. 11, 1995) ("*Stratton Oakmont II*"). Stratton Oakmont did not oppose the latter motion, amid media reports that the parties tentatively had decided to settle the case. The court noted that Prodigy apparently had insisted that any settlement be conditioned upon vacatur of the Court's earlier ruling. *Id.*

But the court denied the motion for rehearing and declined to vacate the order, stating that it would be inadvisable to allow private parties to demand that the court eradicate precedent they found unacceptable and threaten that burdensome litigation would ensue if the court refused. *Id.; see U.S. Bancorp Mortgage Co. v. Bonner Mall Partnership*, 513 U.S. 18, 27–28 (1994). The court was particularly disinclined to vacate its prior ruling in the face of a dearth of jurisprudence in this context, and thereby "remove the only existing New York precedent in this area[,] leaving the law even further behind the technology." *Stratton Oakmont II*, No. 31063/94, 1995 WL 801517 at *1.

The *Stratton Oakmont* decisions became the subject of Congressional attention. Debate on the bill that ultimately emerged as section 230 of the Communications Decency Act, 47 U.S.C.A. § 230 (West Supp. 2000) ("CDA"), included discussion of the enormous burden Internet service providers would suffer were they held accountable for problematic third-party content. *See, e.g.*, 141 Cong. Rec. H8460-01, H84-1 (daily ed. Aug. 4, 1995) (statement of Mr. Goodlatte) ("There is no way that any of those entities, like Prodigy, can take the responsibility to edit out information that is going to be coming in to them from all manner of sources onto their bulletin board. We are talking about something that is far larger than our daily newspaper. We are talking about some-thing that is going to be thousands of pages of information every day, and to have that imposition imposed on them is wrong.") Interestingly, in rejecting Prodigy's defense, the *Stratton Oakmont I* court presciently "note[d] that the issues addressed herein may ultimately be preempted by federal law if the Communications Decency Act of 1995, several versions of which are pending in Congress, is enacted." 63 U.S.L.W. 2765, 1995 WL 343710 at *5, 23 Media L. Rptr. (BNA) 1794 (citation omitted). Indeed, one of the purposes of section 230 was to explicitly overrule the *Stratton Oakmont I* decision. 142 Cong. Rec. H1078-03 (daily ed. Jan. 31, 1996).

Section 230 of the CDA is designed to contain the specter of tort liability in the In-ternet environment. Providers who exercise editorial judgments may not be effectively transmuted into publishers of the content. Section 230(c) expressly codifies protection for "good samaritan" blocking and screening of offensive material:

(1) No provider or user of an interactive computer service shall be treated as the publisher or speaker of any information provided by another information con-tent provider....

(2) No provider or user of an interactive computer service shall be held liable on account of —

(A) any action voluntarily taken in good faith to restrict access to or availabil-ity of material that the provider or user considers to be obscene, lewd, las-civious, filthy, excessively violent, harassing, or otherwise objectionable, whether or not such material is constitutionally protected; or

(B) any action taken to enable or make available to information content providers or others the technical means to restrict access to material de-scribed in paragraph (1).

47 U.S.C.A. § 230(c). This statutory construct furthers the legislative objective of pro-moting self-regulation by Internet service providers by addressing their fear that if they remove problematic content, they will incur liability. By encompassing "objectionable" speech within the statute, Congress evinced an intent to broadly cover within the scope of service providers' immunities defamatory material and other content that may of-fend sensibilities.

The policy underlying the CDA reflects a demonstrable disinclination to encumber electronic communications with governmental intervention: it is national policy "to promote the continued development of the Internet," and "to preserve the vibrant and competitive free market that presently exists for the Internet...unfettered by Federal or State regulation." 47 U.S.C. § 230(b)(1), (2).

The policy rationale underlying section 230 also reflects an empirical and pragmatic conceptualization of the unparalleled expanse of cyberspace as a medium for expres-sion. The sheer magnitude of speech conducted via the Internet clearly did not go un-noticed by Congress when it enacted section 230. As the Fourth Circuit explained, "the amount of information communicated via interactive computer services is...stagger-ing....It would be impossible for service providers to screen each of their millions of postings for possible problems." *Zeran v. America Online Inc.,* 129 F.3d 327, 333 (4th Cir. 1999), *cert. denied,* 524 U.S. 937 (1998). The pragmatic ramifications of holding such providers accountable for allegedly libelous statements they did not originate likely would have a profound effect on Internet access and usage; in such circumstances, providers would have little alternative other than to curtail the quantity and scope of matter transmitted over its facilities. Accordingly, on-line service providers who do not create the content in issue are accommodated by the statutory immunity, which helps promote extensive and robust electronic communication.

In this context, then, the nature of the Internet environment provides a legal rationale for obligations distinct from those imposed on other media. In traditional media environments, newspapers, magazines, books, and broadcasters have derived free speech protections in order to ensure that publications would be nurtured and speech would flourish. Conversely, the free speech protections afforded to service providers by virtue of CDA's section 230 are premised on a policy designed to ensure that the Internet's unprecedented, exponential growth and the prolific speech it facilitates would not be thwarted.

The rationales underlying section 230 also have been conceptualized as reflective of the fact that the Internet "has no 'gatekeepers'—no publishers or editors controlling the distribution of information." Bruce W. Sanford and Michael J. Lorenger, *Teaching an Old Dog New Tricks: The First Amendment in an Online World*, 28 Conn. L. Rev. 1137, 1141 (1996). Under this theory, the allocation of accountability crafted by the statute recognizes that interactive computer services are not engaged in normative publishing or editorial acitivity. To the contrary, "the users of Internet information are...its producers." *Id.* at 1142. It is appropriate, therefore, that the responsibility for the content they produce rests with them.

How does this approach compare to policies advocated in connection with the on-line dissemination of obscene material? In that context, Congress has been far more pro-active, enacting restrictive legislation (although more than one legislative initiative has been invalidated, *see* discussion *supra* at 159). Thus far, with respect to digital data mining practices, self-regulatory initiatives have been relied upon, except insofar as the information is culled from children. (As to minors under 13 years old, Congress has formulated a regulatory approach to address a number of privacy issues. *See* discussion *infra* at 335.) Why are there divergent approaches?

Perhaps the disparity reflects a belief that harm to reputation, unlike certain privacy transgressions, is more susceptible to effective redress through the judicial process. Regulatory proposals relating to obscene on-line content likely reflect a special sensitivity to the particular type of content, which leads to a more pronounced effort to curtail it. Generalized promotion of the mechanisms for the exchange of speech, by contrast, effectively endorses free speech values. Because abstract restraints on free expression are repugnant to societal interests in open and robust dialogue among an informed citizenry, and because the Internet offers "a forum for true diversity of political discourse, unique opportunities for cultural development, and myriad avenues for intellectual activity," 47 U.S.C.A. § 230(a)(3), those who provide the infrastrucutes for such speech to be transmitted and exchanged are worthy of protection so that speech on the Internet can flourish.

The policies that underlie section 230 also comport with principles relating to speech as a vehicle for attaining individual self-determination. Ultimately, decisions as to the scope of generally accessible content rest with the public. Section 230 was designed "to encourage the development of technologies which maximize *user control* over what information is received by individuals, families, and schools who use the Internet...." 47 U.S.C.A. § 230(b)(3) (emphasis supplied), and interactive computer services offer users a great deal of control over information they receive, and the potential for even greater control, *see* 47 U.S.C.A. § 230(a)(2). Consistent with this policy of autonomous decision-making in the selection of content is the statutory requirement that providers of interactive computer services must notify their customers that parental control protections (such as computer hardware, software, or filtering services) are commercially available. Such devices may assist the customer in limiting access to material that is harmful to minors. *See* 47 U.S.C.A. § 230(d). The providers' notice, which is to be underaken "in a manner deemed appropriate by the provider," is intended to provide the customer with access to information identifying current providers of parental control protections. *Id.* The notice effectively helps to inform the user that filtering mechanisms are available in the event the user wishes to self-screen available content. Thus, overall Congressional emphasis is placed on the individual's discretion in the use of the Internet because in this arena, Congress expressly found that "[t]he Internet and other interactive computer services have flourished, to the benefit of all Americans, with a minimum of government regulation." 47 U.S.C.A. § 230(a)(4).

---

# Kenneth M. ZERAN v. AMERICA ONLINE, INCORPORATED
United States Court of Appeals, Fourth Circuit
No. 97-1523, 129 F.3d 327
November 12, 1997

WILKINSON, Chief Judge:

Kenneth Zeran brought this action against America Online, Inc. ("AOL"), arguing that AOL unreasonably delayed in removing defamatory messages posted by an unidentified third party, refused to post retractions of those messages, and failed to screen for similar postings thereafter. The district court granted judgment for AOL on the grounds that the Communications Decency Act of 1996 ("CDA")—47 U.S.C. § 230—bars Zeran's claims. Zeran appeals, arguing that § 230 leaves intact liability for interactive computer service providers who possess notice of defamatory material posted through their services.... [W]e affirm the judgment of the district court.

"The Internet is an international network of interconnected computers," currently used by approximately 40 million people worldwide. *Reno v. ACLU*, —U.S. —, —, 117 S.Ct. 2329, 2334, 138 L.Ed.2d 874 (1997). One of the many means by which individuals access the Internet is through an interactive computer service. These services offer not only a connection to the Internet as a whole, but also allow their subscribers to access information communicated and stored only on each computer service's individual proprietary network. *Id.* AOL is just such an interactive computer service. Much of the information transmitted over its network originates with the company's millions of subscribers. They may transmit information privately via electronic mail, or they may communicate publicly by posting messages on AOL bulletin boards, where the messages may be read by any AOL subscriber.

The instant case comes before us on a motion for judgment on the pleadings, *see* Fed. R. Civ. P. 12(c), so we accept the facts alleged in the complaint as true. *Bruce v. Riddle*, 631 F.2d 272, 273 (4th Cir. 1980). On April 25, 1995, an unidentified person posted a message on an AOL bulletin board advertising "Naughty Oklahoma T-Shirts." The posting described the sale of shirts featuring offensive and tasteless slogans related to the April 19, 1995, bombing of the Alfred P. Murrah Federal Building in Oklahoma City. Those interested in purchasing the shirts were instructed to call "Ken" at Zeran's home phone number in Seattle, Washington. As a result of this anonymously perpetrated prank, Zeran received a high volume of calls, comprised primarily of angry and derogatory messages, but also including death threats. Zeran could not change his phone number because he relied on its availability to the public in running his business out of his home. Later that day, Zeran called AOL and informed a company representative of his predicament. The employee assured Zeran that the posting would be removed from AOL's bulletin board but explained that as a matter of policy AOL would not post a retraction. The parties dispute the date that AOL removed this original posting from its bulletin board.

On April 26, the next day, an unknown person posted another message advertising additional shirts with new tasteless slogans related to the Oklahoma City bombing. Again, interested buyers were told to call Zeran's phone number, to ask for "Ken," and to "please call back if busy" due to high demand. The angry, threatening phone calls intensified. Over the next four days, an unidentified party continued to post messages on AOL's bulletin board, advertising additional items including bumper stickers and key chains with still more offensive slogans. During this time period, Zeran called AOL repeatedly and was told by company representatives that the individual account from which the messages were posted would soon be closed. Zeran also reported his case to Seattle FBI agents. By April 30, Zeran was receiving an abusive phone call approximately every two minutes.

Meanwhile, an announcer for Oklahoma City radio station KRXO received a copy of the first AOL posting. On May 1, the announcer related the message's contents on the air, attributed them to "Ken" at Zeran's phone number, and urged the listening audience to call the number. After this radio broadcast, Zeran was inundated with death threats and other violent calls from Oklahoma City residents. Over the next few days, Zeran talked to both KRXO and AOL representatives. He also spoke to his local police, who subsequently surveilled his home to protect his safety. By May 14, after an Oklahoma City newspaper published a story exposing the shirt advertisements as a hoax and after KRXO made an on-air apology, the number of calls to Zeran's residence finally subsided to fifteen per day.

Zeran first filed suit on January 4, 1996, against radio station KRXO in the United States District Court for the Western District of Oklahoma. On April 23, 1996, he filed this separate suit against AOL in the same court. Zeran did not bring any action against the party who posted the offensive messages.[1]...

Because §230 was successfully advanced by AOL in the district court as a defense to Zeran's claims, we shall briefly examine its operation here. Zeran seeks to hold AOL liable for defamatory speech initiated by a third party. He argued to the district court that once he notified AOL of the unidentified third party's hoax, AOL had a duty to remove the defamatory posting promptly, to notify its subscribers of the message's false nature, and to effectively screen future defamatory material. Section 230 entered this litigation as an affirmative defense pled by AOL. The company claimed that Congress immunized interactive computer service providers from claims based on information posted by a third party.

The relevant portion of §230 states: "No provider or user of an interactive computer service shall be treated as the publisher or speaker of any information provided by an-

---

1. Zeran maintains that AOL made it impossible to identify the original party by failing to maintain adequate records of its users. The issue of AOL's record keeping practices, however, is not presented by this appeal.

other information content provider." 47 U.S.C. §230(c)(1).[2] By its plain language, §230 creates a federal immunity to any cause of action that would make service providers liable for information originating with a third-party user of the service. Specifically, §230 precludes courts from entertaining claims that would place a computer service provider in a publisher's role. Thus, lawsuits seeking to hold a service provider liable for its exercise of a publisher's traditional editorial functions—such as deciding whether to publish, withdraw, postpone or alter content—are barred.

The purpose of this statutory immunity is not difficult to discern. Congress recognized the threat that tort-based lawsuits pose to freedom of speech in the new and burgeoning Internet medium. The imposition of tort liability on service providers for the communications of others represented, for Congress, simply another form of intrusive government regulation of speech. Section 230 was enacted, in part, to maintain the robust nature of Internet communication and, accordingly, to keep government interference in the medium to a minimum. In specific statutory findings, Congress recognized the Internet and interactive computer services as offering "a forum for a true diversity of political discourse, unique opportunities for cultural development, and myriad avenues for intellectual activity." *Id.* §230(a)(3). It also found that the Internet and interactive computer services "have flourished, to the benefit of all Americans, with a minimum of government regulation." *Id.* §230(a)(4). Congress further stated that it is "the policy of the United States...to preserve the vibrant and competitive free market that presently exists for the Internet and other interactive computer services, unfettered by Federal or State regulation." *Id.* §230(b)(2).

None of this means, of course, that the original culpable party who posts defamatory messages would escape accountability. While Congress acted to keep government regulation of the Internet to a minimum, it also found it to be the policy of the United States "to ensure vigorous enforcement of Federal criminal laws to deter and punish trafficking in obscenity, stalking, and harassment by means of computer." *Id.* §230(b)(5). Congress made a policy choice, however, not to deter harmful online speech through the separate route of imposing tort liability on companies that serve as intermediaries for other parties' potentially injurious messages.

Congress' purpose in providing the §230 immunity was thus evident. Interactive computer services have millions of users. *See Reno v. ACLU,* — U.S. at —, 117 S.Ct. at 2334 (noting that at time of district court trial, "commercial online services had almost 12 million individual subscribers"). The amount of information communicated via interactive computer services is therefore staggering. The specter of tort liability in an area of such prolific speech would have an obvious chilling effect. It would be impossible for service providers to screen each of their millions of postings for possible problems. Faced with potential liability for each message republished by their services, interactive computer service providers might choose to severely restrict the number and type of messages posted. Congress considered the weight of the speech interests implicated and chose to immunize service providers to avoid any such restrictive effect.

---

2. Section 230 defines "interactive computer service" as "any information service, system, or access software provider that provides or enables computer access by multiple users to a computer server, including specifically a service or system that provides access to the Internet and such systems operated or services offered by libraries or educational institutions." 47 U.S.C. §230(e)(2). The term "information content provider" is defined as "any person or entity that is responsible, in whole or in part, for the creation or development of information provided through the Internet or any other interactive computer service." *Id.* §230(e)(3). The parties do not dispute that AOL falls within the CDA's "interactive computer service" definition and that the unidentified third party who posted the offensive messages here fits the definition of an "information content provider."

Another important purpose of § 230 was to encourage service providers to self-regulate the dissemination of offensive material over their services. In this respect, § 230 responded to a New York state court decision, *Stratton Oakmont, Inc. v. Prodigy Servs. Co.*, 1995 WL 323710 (N.Y. Sup. Ct. May 24, 1995). There, the plaintiffs sued Prodigy—an interactive computer service like AOL—for defamatory comments made by an unidentified party on one of Prodigy's bulletin boards. The court held Prodigy to the strict liability standard normally applied to original publishers of defamatory statements, rejecting Prodigy's claims that it should be held only to the lower "knowledge" standard usually reserved for distributors. The court reasoned that Prodigy acted more like an original publisher than a distributor both because it advertised its practice of controlling content on its service and because it actively screened and edited messages posted on its bulletin boards.

Congress enacted § 230 to remove the disincentives to self-regulation created by the *Stratton Oakmont* decision. Under that court's holding, computer service providers who regulated the dissemination of offensive material on their services risked subjecting themselves to liability, because such regulation cast the service provider in the role of a publisher. Fearing that the specter of liability would therefore deter service providers from blocking and screening offensive material, Congress enacted § 230's broad immunity "to remove disincentives for the development and utilization of blocking and filtering technologies that empower parents to restrict their children's access to objectionable or inappropriate online material." 47 U.S.C. § 230(b)(4). In line with this purpose, § 230 forbids the imposition of publisher liability on a service provider for the exercise of its editorial and self-regulatory functions.

Zeran argues, however, that the § 230 immunity eliminates only publisher liability, leaving distributor liability intact. Publishers can be held liable for defamatory statements contained in their works even absent proof that they had specific knowledge of the statement's inclusion. W. Page Keeton, *et al., Prosser and Keeton on the Law of Torts* § 113, at 810 (5th ed. 1984). According to Zeran, interactive computer service providers like AOL are normally considered instead to be distributors, like traditional news vendors or book sellers. Distributors cannot be held liable for defamatory statements contained in the materials they distribute unless it is proven at a minimum that they have actual knowledge of the defamatory statements upon which liability is predicated. *Id.* at 811 (explaining that distributors are not liable "in the absence of proof that they knew or had reason to know of the existence of defamatory matter contained in matter published").

Zeran contends that he provided AOL with sufficient notice of the defamatory statements appearing on the company's bulletin board. This notice is significant, says Zeran, because AOL could be held liable as a distributor only if it acquired knowledge of the defamatory statements' existence.

Because of the difference between these two forms of liability, Zeran contends that the term "distributor" carries a legally distinct meaning from the term "publisher." Accordingly, he asserts that Congress' use of only the term "publisher" in § 230 indicates a purpose to immunize service providers only from publisher liability. He argues that distributors are left unprotected by § 230 and, therefore, his suit should be permitted to proceed against AOL. We disagree. Assuming *arguendo* that Zeran has satisfied the requirements for imposition of distributor liability, this theory of liability is merely a subset, or a species, of publisher liability, and is therefore also foreclosed by § 230.

The terms "publisher" and "distributor" derive their legal significance from the context of defamation law. Although Zeran attempts to artfully plead his claims as ones of negligence, they are indistinguishable from a garden variety defamation action. Because the publication of a statement is a necessary element in a defamation action, only one who publishes can be subject to this form of tort liability. Restatement (Second) of Torts § 558(b) (1977); Keeton *et al., supra,* § 113, at 802. Publication does not only describe the choice by an author to include certain information. In addition, both the negligent communication of a defamatory statement and the failure to remove such a statement when first communicated by another party—each alleged by Zeran here under a negligence label—constitute publication. Restatement (Second) of Torts § 577; *see also Tacket v. General Motors Corp.,* 836 F.2d 1042, 1046–47 (7th Cir. 1987). In fact, every repetition of a defamatory statement is considered a publication. Keeton *et al., supra,* § 113, at 799.

In this case, AOL is legally considered to be a publisher. "[E]very one who takes part in the publication...is charged with publication." *Id.* Even distributors are considered to be publishers for purposes of defamation law:

> Those who are in the business of making their facilities available to disseminate the writings composed, the speeches made, and the information gathered by others may also be regarded as participating to such an extent in making the books, newspapers, magazines, and information available to others as to be regarded as publishers. They are intentionally making the contents available to others, sometimes without knowing all of the contents—including the defamatory content—and sometimes without any opportunity to ascertain, in advance, that any defamatory matter was to be included in the matter published.

*Id.* at 803. AOL falls squarely within this traditional definition of a publisher and, therefore, is clearly protected by § 230's immunity.

Zeran contends that decisions like *Stratton Oakmont* and *Cubby, Inc. v. CompuServe Inc.,* 776 F. Supp. 135 (S.D.N.Y. 1991), recognize a legal distinction between publishers and distributors. He misapprehends, however, the significance of that distinction for the legal issue we consider here. It is undoubtedly true that mere conduits, or distributors, are subject to a different standard of liability. As explained above, distributors must at a minimum have knowledge of the existence of a defamatory statement as a prerequisite to liability. But this distinction signifies only that different standards of liability may be applied within the larger publisher category, depending on the specific type of publisher concerned. *See* Keeton *et al., supra,* § 113, at 799–800 (explaining that every party involved is charged with publication, although degrees of legal responsibility differ). To the extent that decisions like *Stratton* and *Cubby* utilize the terms "publisher" and "distributor" separately, the decisions correctly describe two different standards of liability. *Stratton* and *Cubby* do not, however, suggest that distributors are not also a type of publisher for purposes of defamation law.

Zeran simply attaches too much importance to the presence of the distinct notice element in distributor liability. The simple fact of notice surely cannot transform one from an original publisher to a distributor in the eyes of the law. To the contrary, once a computer service provider receives notice of a potentially defamatory posting, it is thrust into the role of a traditional publisher. The computer service provider must decide whether to publish, edit, or withdraw the posting. In this respect, Zeran seeks to impose liability on AOL for assuming the role for which § 230 specifically proscribes liability—the publisher role.

Our view that Zeran's complaint treats AOL as a publisher is reinforced because AOL is cast in the same position as the party who originally posted the offensive messages. According to Zeran's logic, AOL is legally at fault because it communicated to third parties an allegedly defamatory statement. This is precisely the theory under which the original poster of the offensive messages would be found liable. If the original party is considered a publisher of the offensive messages, Zeran certainly cannot attach liability to AOL under the same theory without conceding that AOL too must be treated as a publisher of the statements.

Zeran next contends that interpreting § 230 to impose liability on service providers with knowledge of defamatory content on their services is consistent with the statutory purposes outlined in Part IIA. Zeran fails, however, to understand the practical implications of notice liability in the interactive computer service context. Liability upon notice would defeat the dual purposes advanced by § 230 of the CDA. Like the strict liability imposed by the *Stratton Oakmont* court, liability upon notice reinforces service providers' incentives to restrict speech and abstain from self-regulation.

If computer service providers were subject to distributor liability, they would face potential liability each time they receive notice of a potentially defamatory statement— from any party, concerning any message. Each notification would require a careful yet rapid investigation of the circumstances surrounding the posted information, a legal judgment concerning the information's defamatory character, and an on-the-spot editorial decision whether to risk liability by allowing the continued publication of that information. Although this might be feasible for the traditional print publisher, the sheer number of postings on interactive computer services would create an impossible burden in the Internet context. *Cf. Auvil v. CBS 60 Minutes*, 800 F. Supp. 928, 931 (E.D. Wash. 1992) (recognizing that it is unrealistic for network affiliates to "monitor incoming transmissions and exercise on-the-spot discretionary calls"). Because service providers would be subject to liability only for the publication of information, and not for its removal, they would have a natural incentive simply to remove messages upon notification, whether the contents were defamatory or not. See *Philadelphia Newspapers, Inc. v. Hepps*, 475 U.S. 767, 777, 106 S.Ct. 1558, 1564, 89 L.Ed.2d 783 (1986) (recognizing that fears of unjustified liability produce a chilling effect antithetical to First Amendment's protection of speech). Thus, like strict liability, liability upon notice has a chilling effect on the freedom of Internet speech.

Similarly, notice-based liability would deter service providers from regulating the dissemination of offensive material over their own services. Any efforts by a service provider to investigate and screen material posted on its service would only lead to notice of potentially defamatory material more frequently and thereby create a stronger basis for liability. Instead of subjecting themselves to further possible lawsuits, service providers would likely eschew any attempts at self-regulation.

More generally, notice-based liability for interactive computer service providers would provide third parties with a no-cost means to create the basis for future lawsuits. Whenever one was displeased with the speech of another party conducted over an interactive computer service, the offended party could simply "notify" the relevant service provider, claiming the information to be legally defamatory. In light of the vast amount of speech communicated through interactive computer services, these notices could produce an impossible burden for service providers, who would be faced with ceaseless choices of suppressing controversial speech or sustaining prohibitive liability. Because the probable effects of distributor liability on the vigor of Internet speech and on service provider self-regulation are directly contrary to § 230's statutory purposes, we will not assume that Congress intended to leave liability upon notice intact.

Zeran finally contends that the interpretive canon favoring retention of common law principles unless Congress speaks directly to the issue counsels a restrictive reading of the § 230 immunity here. *See United States v. Texas*, 507 U.S. 529, 534, 113 S.Ct. 1631, 1634–35, 123 L.Ed.2d 245 (1993). This interpretive canon does not persuade us to reach a different result. Here, Congress has indeed spoken directly to the issue by employing the legally significant term "publisher," which has traditionally encompassed distributors and original publishers alike.

The decision cited by Zeran, *United States v. Texas*, also recognized that abrogation of common law principles is appropriate when a contrary statutory purpose is evident. *Id.* This is consistent with the Court's earlier cautions against courts' application of the canon with excessive zeal: "'The rule that statutes in derogation of the common law are to be strictly construed does not require such an adherence to the letter as would defeat an obvious legislative purpose or lessen the scope plainly intended to be given to the measure.'" *Isbrandtsen Co. v. Johnson*, 343 U.S. 779, 783, 72 S.Ct. 1011, 1014, 96 L.Ed. 1294 (1952) (quoting *Jamison v. Encarnacion*, 281 U.S. 635, 640, 50 S.Ct. 440, 442, 74 L.Ed. 1082 (1930)); *cf. Astoria Fed. Sav. & Loan Ass'n v. Solimino*, 501 U.S. 104, 110–11, 111 S.Ct. 2166, 2170–71, 115 L.Ed.2d 96 (1991) (statute need not expressly delimit manner in which common law principle is abrogated). Zeran's argument flies in the face of this warning. As explained above, interpreting § 230 to leave distributor liability in effect would defeat the two primary purposes of the statute and would certainly "lessen the scope plainly intended" by Congress' use of the term "publisher."

Section 230 represents the approach of Congress to a problem of national and international dimension. The Supreme Court underscored this point in *Reno v. ACLU*, finding that the Internet allows "tens of millions of people to communicate with one another and to access vast amounts of information from around the world. [It] is 'a unique and wholly new medium of worldwide human communication.'" — U.S. at —, 117 S.Ct. at 2334 (citation omitted). Application of the canon invoked by Zeran here would significantly lessen Congress' power, derived from the Commerce Clause, to act in a field whose international character is apparent. While Congress allowed for the enforcement of "any State law that is consistent with [§ 230]," 47 U.S.C. § 230(d)(3), it is equally plain that Congress' desire to promote unfettered speech on the Internet must supersede conflicting common law causes of action. Section 230(d)(3) continues: "No cause of action may be brought and no liability may be imposed under any State or local law that is inconsistent with this section." With respect to federal-state preemption, the Court has advised: "[W]hen Congress has 'unmistakably…ordained,' that its enactments alone are to regulate a part of commerce, state laws regulating that aspect of commerce must fall. The result is compelled whether Congress' command is explicitly stated in the statute's language or implicitly contained in its structure and purpose." *Jones v. Rath Packing Co.*, 430 U.S. 519, 525, 97 S.Ct. 1305, 1309, 51 L.Ed.2d 604 (1977) (citations omitted). Here, Congress' command is explicitly stated. Its exercise of its commerce power is clear and counteracts the caution counseled by the interpretive canon favoring retention of common law principles.…

For the foregoing reasons, we affirm the judgment of the district court.

––––––––––

In March 1999, an English court considered a similar situation—and reached a different conclusion. In *Godfrey v. Demon Internet Limited*, [1999] E.M.L.R. 542 (Q.B. 1999), the High Court adjudicated the first defamation action in England involving the Internet. The plaintiff, Laurence Godfrey, a lecturer in physics, mathematics, and computer science, contended that false and defamatory e-mails were distributed by the defendant, Demon Internet, Limited ("Demon Internet"). A newsgroup known as "soc.culture.thai" was carried by Demon Internet, a service provider. Demon Internet stored postings for a couple of weeks in order to facilitate review by a newsgroup to whom it offered access. The court characterized the posting as "squalid, obscene and defamatory of the plaintiff." *Id.* The plaintiff notified Demon Internet that the posting was a forgery, but Demon Internet did not remove it. The High Court was confronted with the question of whether Demon Internet could reasonably be deemed a "publisher" of the defamatory posting.

The High Court relied on discussion during debate of the Defamation Bill, which provides a defense to a person who was not the author, editor, or publisher of the statement complained of, took reasonable care in relation to its publication, and did not know or have reason to believe that what he did caused or contributed to the publication of a defamatory statement. *See* Defamation Act, 1996 ch. 31, 1(1)(a–c) [Eng.]. But the court determined that this defense of innocent dissemination

> never provided an absolute immunity for distributors, however mechanical their contribution. It does not protect those who knew that the material they were handling was defamatory, or who ought to have known of its nature. Those safeguards are preserved, so that the defence is not available to a defendant who knew that his act involved or contributed to publication defamatory of the plaintiff. It is available only if, having taken all reasonable care, the defendant had no reason to suspect that his act had that effect.

Lord MacKay, L.C., Hansard, HL Apr. 2, 1996, col. 214, Defamation Bill. The defense was designed to exculpate "those who have unwittingly provided a conduit which has enabled another person to publish defamatory material. It is intended to provide a modern equivalent of the common law defence of innocent dissemination, recognising that there may be circumstances in which the unwitting contributor to the process of publication may have had no idea of the defamatory nature of the material he has handled or processed." *Id.*

The High Court analogized to another case, *Day v. Bream* (1837) 2 M. & r. 54, in which the jury was to decide whether a porter had knowledge that the contents of parcels he was to deliver were libelous. The court also considered *Byrne v. Deane* (1937) 1 K.B. 818, 837, where the appropriate inquiry was crafted as: "having regard to all the facts of the case is the proper inference that by not removing the defamatory matter the defendant really made himself responsible for its continued presence in the place where it had been put?"

The defendant referred the High Court to the holding in *Zeran v. America Online, Inc.,* 129 F.3d at 332, where the Fourth Circuit had concluded unequivocally that "[t]he simple fact of notice surely cannot transform one from an original publisher to a distributor in the eyes of the law." The defendant also cited other American decisional law that either preceded or did not rely upon the CDA, but the High Court ultimately concluded that such precedents were only of "marginal assistance because of the different approach to defamation across the Atlantic." *Godfrey v. Demon Internet Limited,* [1999] E.M.L.R. 542.

Interestingly, while the *Godfrey* court ultimately dismissed Demon Internet's defense on the ground that it was not a "publisher" as "hopeless," the court also offered that "[i]t may also be helpful to suggest that on the basis of the proposed amended defence any award of damages to the plaintiff is likely to be very small." *Id.*

A spokesperson for Demon Internet expressed disappointment about the court's ruling, stating, " 'If someone insulted you in a pub, would you sue the pub owner for housing the defamatory remark?' " *See* Jane Martinson, *U.S. Courts Free Internet Firms from*

*Libel Laws*, The Guardian (May 3, 2000) <http://www.globalarchive.ft.com/search-components/index.jsp>. Demon Internet decided not to appeal the ruling of Mr. Justice Morland and settled with Laurence Godfrey. In March, 2000, Demon reportedly agreed to pay Godfrey £15,000 plus legal costs, which were estimated to exceed £200,000. *See, e.g., id.*

According to FT.com, at least three web-sites closed following Demon's settlement agreement with Godfrey. *See Web Site Takes Fight for Free Speech to Europe[;] Internet Service Providers Close Sites, Prompting Fears of Growing Online Censorship*, Financial Times (Apr. 14, 2000) <http://www.globalarchive.ft.com/search-components/index.jsp>. The European Court of Human Rights may be asked to consider whether English libel laws violate the right to freedom of expression on the Internet. Arguments put to the European court likely will be based on the Defamation Act of 1996, and the scope of the defense of "innocent dissemination."

British libel law is significantly less hospitable to media defendants than is American libel law. *See* discussion *infra* at 252. Is the divergence in American and British caselaw on the question of Internet service provider liability the product of disparate reasoning founded upon conceptualization of providers as conduits? To what extent have American courts been influenced recently by the enactment of the CDA? Or are the different rulings reflective of more fundamental jurisprudential distinctions in libel law?

---

## Sidney BLUMENTHAL v. Matt DRUDGE and AMERICA ONLINE, INC.

United States District Court, District of Columbia
No. CIV.A. 97-1968 PLF, 992 F. Supp. 44
April 22, 1998

PAUL L. FRIEDMAN, District Judge.

This is a defamation case revolving around a statement published on the Internet by defendant Matt Drudge. On August 10, 1997, the following was available to all having access to the Internet:

> The DRUDGE REPORT has learned that top GOP operatives who feel there is a double-standard of only reporting republican shame believe they are holding an ace card: New White House recruit Sidney Blumenthal has a spousal abuse past that has been effectively covered up.
>
> The accusations are explosive.
>
> There are court records of Blumenthal's violence against his wife, one influential republican, who demanded anonymity, tells the DRUDGE REPORT.
>
> If they begin to use [Don] Sipple and his problems against us, against the Republican Party... to show hypocrisy, Blumenthal would become fair game. Wasn't it Clinton who signed the Violence Against Women Act?
>
> (There goes the budget deal honeymoon.)
>
> One White House source, also requesting anonymity, says the Blumenthal wife-beating allegation is a pure fiction that has been created by Clinton enemies. [The First Lady] would not have brought him in if he had this in his

background, assures the well placed staffer. This story about Blumenthal has been in circulation for years.

Last month President Clinton named Sidney Blumenthal an Assistant to the President as part of the Communications Team. He's brought in to work on communications strategy, special projects themeing—a newly created position.

Every attempt to reach Blumenthal proved unsuccessful.

...Sidney Blumenthal works in the White House as an Assistant to the President of the United States. His first day of work as Assistant to the President was Monday, August 11, 1997, the day after the publication of the alleged defamatory statement. Jacqueline Jordan Blumenthal, Sidney Blumenthal's wife, also works in the White House as Director of the President's Commission On White House Fellowships.

...[D]efendant Drudge created an electronic publication called the Drudge Report, a gossip column focusing on gossip from Hollywood and Washington, D.C.

Access to defendant Drudge's World Wide Web site is available at no cost to anyone who has access to the Internet at the Internet address of "www.drudge report.com."... Defendant Drudge has...placed a hyperlink on his web site, that, when activated, causes the most recently published edition of the Drudge Report to be displayed. The web site also contains numerous hyperlinks to other on-line news publications and news articles that may be of interest to readers of the Drudge Report. In addition, during the time period relevant to this case, Drudge developed a list of regular readers or subscribers to whom he e-mailed each new edition of the Drudge Report....

In late May or early June of 1997,...Drudge entered into a written license agreement with [America Online, Inc. ("AOL").] The agreement made the Drudge Report available to all members of AOL's service for a period of one year. In exchange, defendant Drudge received a flat monthly "royalty payment" of $3,000 from AOL....Under the licensing agreement, Drudge is to create, edit, update and "otherwise manage" the content of the Drudge Report, and AOL may "remove content that AOL reasonably determine[s] to violate AOL's then standard terms of service."...

Late at night on the evening of Sunday, August 10, 1997 (Pacific Daylight Time), defendant Drudge wrote and transmitted the edition of the Drudge Report that contained the alleged defamatory statement about the Blumenthals. Drudge transmitted the report from Los Angeles, California by e-mail to his direct subscribers and by posting both a headline and the full text of the Blumenthal story on his world wide web site. He then transmitted the text but not the headline to AOL, which in turn made it available to AOL subscribers....

After receiving a letter from plaintiffs' counsel on Monday, August 11, 1997, defendant Drudge retracted the story through a special edition of the Drudge Report posted on his web site and e-mailed to his subscribers[, and the following day, he]...e-mailed the retraction to AOL which posted it on the AOL service. Defendant Drudge later publicly apologized to the Blumenthals.[5]

---

5. AOL later removed the August 10 edition of the Drudge Report from the electronic archive of previous editions of the Drudge Report available to AOL subscribers.

## II. AOL's MOTION FOR SUMMARY JUDGMENT...

### Communications Decency Act of 1996, Section 230

In February of 1996, Congress made an effort to deal with some of these challenges in enacting the Communications Decency Act of 1996. While various policy options were open to the Congress, it chose to "promote the continued development of the Internet and other interactive computer services and other interactive media" and "to preserve the vibrant and competitive free market" for such services, largely "unfettered by Federal or State regulation...." 47 U.S.C. §230(b)(1) and (2). Whether wisely or not, it made the legislative judgment to effectively immunize providers of interactive computer services from civil liability in tort with respect to material disseminated by them but created by others. In recognition of the speed with which information may be disseminated and the near impossibility of regulating information content, Congress decided not to treat providers of interactive computer services like other information providers such as newspapers, magazines or television and radio stations, all of which may be held liable for publishing or distributing obscene or defamatory material written or prepared by others. While Congress could have made a different policy choice, it opted not to hold interactive computer services liable for their failure to edit, withhold or restrict access to offensive material disseminated through their medium.

Section 230(c) of the Communications Decency Act of 1996 provides:

> No provider or user of an interactive computer service shall be treated as the publisher or speaker of any information provided by another information content provider.

47 U.S.C. §230(c)(1). The statute goes on to define the term "information content provider" as "any person or entity that is responsible, in whole or in part, for the creation or development of information provided through the Internet or any other interactive computer service." 47 U.S.C. §230(e)(3). In view of this statutory language, plaintiffs' argument that the *Washington Post* would be liable if it had done what AOL did here—"publish Drudge's story without doing anything whatsoever to edit, verify, or even read it (despite knowing what Drudge did for a living and how he did it)" has been rendered irrelevant by Congress.

Plaintiffs concede that AOL is a "provider...of an interactive computer service" for purposes of Section 230, and that if AOL acted exclusively as a provider of an interactive computer service it may not be held liable for making the Drudge Report available to AOL subscribers. *See* 47 U.S.C. §230(c)(1). They also concede that Drudge is an "information content provider" because he wrote the alleged defamatory material about the Blumenthals contained in the Drudge Report. While plaintiffs suggest that AOL is responsible along with Drudge because it had some role in writing or editing the material in the Drudge Report, they have provided no factual support for that assertion. Indeed, plaintiffs affirmatively state that "no person, other than Drudge himself, edited, checked, verified, or supervised the information that Drudge published in the Drudge Report." It also is apparent to the Court that there is no evidence to support the view originally taken by plaintiffs that Drudge is or was an employee or agent of AOL, and plaintiffs seem to have all but abandoned that argument.

AOL acknowledges both that Section 230(c)(1) would not immunize AOL with respect to any information AOL developed or created entirely by itself and that there are situations in which there may be two or more information content providers responsible for material disseminated on the Internet—joint authors, a lyricist and a composer, for example. While Section 230 does not preclude joint liability for the joint development of content, AOL maintains that there simply is no evidence here that AOL had any role in creating or developing any of the information in the Drudge Report. The Court agrees. It is undisputed that the Blumenthal story was written by Drudge without any substantive or editorial involvement by AOL. AOL was nothing more than a provider of an interactive computer service on which the Drudge Report was carried, and Congress has said quite clearly that such a provider shall not be treated as a "publisher or speaker" and therefore may not be held liable in tort. 47 U.S.C. § 230(c)(1)....

The court in *Zeran* [*v. America Online, Inc.,* 129 F.3d 327 (4th Cir. 1997),] has provided a complete answer to plaintiffs' primary argument, an answer grounded in the statutory language and intent of Section 230.

Plaintiffs make the additional argument, however, that Section 230 of the Communications Decency Act does not provide immunity to AOL in this case because Drudge was not just an anonymous person who sent a message over the Internet through AOL. He is a person with whom AOL contracted, whom AOL paid $3,000 a month—$36,000 a year, Drudge's sole, consistent source of income—and whom AOL promoted to its subscribers and potential subscribers as a reason to subscribe to AOL. Furthermore, the license agreement between AOL and Drudge by its terms contemplates more than a passive role for AOL; in it, AOL reserves the "right to remove, or direct [Drudge] to remove, any content which, as reasonably determined by AOL...violates AOL's then-standard Terms of Service...." By the terms of the agreement, AOL also is "entitled to require reasonable changes to...content, to the extent such content will, in AOL's good faith judgment, adversely affect operations of the AOL network."

In addition, shortly after it entered into the licensing agreement with Drudge, AOL issued a press release making clear the kind of material Drudge would provide to AOL subscribers—gossip and rumor—and urged potential subscribers to sign onto AOL in order to get the benefit of the Drudge Report. The press release was captioned: "AOL Hires Runaway Gossip Success Matt Drudge." It noted that "[m]averick gossip columnist Matt Drudge has teamed up with America Online," and stated: "Giving the Drudge Report a home on America Online (keyword: Drudge) opens up the floodgates to an audience ripe for Drudge's brand of reporting....AOL has made Matt Drudge instantly accessible to members who crave instant gossip and news breaks." Why is this different, the Blumenthals suggest, from AOL advertising and promoting a new purveyor of child pornography or other offensive material? Why should AOL be permitted to tout someone as a gossip columnist or rumor monger who will make such rumors and gossip "instantly accessible" to AOL subscribers, and then claim immunity when that person, as might be anticipated, defames another?

If it were writing on a clean slate, this Court would agree with plaintiffs. AOL has certain editorial rights with respect to the content provided by Drudge and disseminated by AOL, including the right to require changes in content and to remove it; and it has affirmatively promoted Drudge as a new source of unverified instant gossip on AOL. Yet it takes no responsibility for any damage he may cause. AOL is not a passive conduit like the telephone company, a common carrier with no control and therefore no responsibility for what is said over the telephone wires. Because it has the right to exercise editorial control over those with whom it contracts and whose words it disseminates, it would seem only fair to hold AOL to the liability standards applied to a publisher or, at least, like a book store owner or library, to the liability standards applied to a distributor. But Congress has made a different policy choice by providing immunity even where the interactive service provider has an active, even aggressive role in making available content prepared by others. In some sort of tacit quid pro quo arrangement with the service provider community, Congress has conferred immunity from tort liability as an incentive to Internet service providers to self-police the Internet for obscenity and other offensive material, even where the self-policing is unsuccessful or not even attempted.

In Section 230(c)(2) of the Communications Decency Act, Congress provided:

> No provider or user of an interactive computer service shall be held liable on account of—
>
> (A) Any action voluntarily taken in good faith to restrict access to or availability of material that the provider or user considers to be obscene, lewd, lascivious, filthy, excessively violent, harassing, or otherwise objectionable, whether or not such material is constitutionally protected; or
>
> (B) any action taken to enable or make available to information content providers or others the technical means to restrict access to material described in paragraph (1).

47 U.S.C. § 230(c)(2).[13] As the Fourth Circuit stated in *Zeran*: "Congress enacted § 230 to remove…disincentives to self-regulation.…Fearing that the specter of liability would…deter service providers from blocking and screening offensive material.… § 230 forbids the imposition of publisher liability on a service provider for the exercise of its editorial and self regulatory functions." *Zeran v. America Online, Inc.*, 129 F.3d at 331.

Any attempt to distinguish between "publisher" liability and notice-based "distributor" liability and to argue that Section 230 was only intended to immunize the former would be unavailing. Congress made no distinction between publishers and distributors in providing immunity from liability. As the Fourth Circuit has noted: "If computer service providers were subject to distributor liability, they would face potential liability each time they receive notice of a potentially defamatory statement—from any party, concerning any message," and such notice-based liability "would deter service providers from regulating the dissemination of offensive material over their own services" by confronting them with "ceaseless choices of suppressing controversial speech or sustaining prohibitive liability"—exactly what Congress intended to insulate them from in Section 230. *Zeran v. America Online, Inc.*, 129 F.3d at 333. Cf. *Cubby, Inc. v. CompuServe, Inc.*, 776 F. Supp. 135, 139–40 (S.D.N.Y. 1991) (decided before enactment of Communications Decency Act). While it appears to this Court that AOL in this case has taken ad-

---

13. While this provision of the statute primarily addresses obscenity and violent material, it also references material that is "otherwise objectionable," a broad enough category to cover defamatory statements as well. Indeed, the legislative history makes clear that one of the primary purposes of Section 230 was to overrule the *Stratton Oakmont* decision of a New York State court that was itself a defamation case in which Prodigy Services, an Internet computer service like AOL, was held liable as a publisher of defamatory material. *See Stratton Oakmont, Inc. v. Prodigy Services Co.*, 1995 WL 323710 (N.Y. Sup. Ct. May 24, 1995). As the Conference Report stated:

> One of the specific purposes of this section is to overrule *Stratton Oakmont v. Prodigy* and any other similar decisions which have treated such providers and users as publishers or speakers of content that is not their own because they have restricted access to objectionable material. The conferees believe that such decisions create serious obstacles to the important federal policy of empowering parents to determine the content of communications their children receive through interactive computer services.

H.R. Conf. Rep. No. 104–458, at 194 (1996).

vantage of all the benefits conferred by Congress in the Communications Decency Act, and then some, without accepting any of the burdens that Congress intended, the statutory language is clear: AOL is immune from suit, and the Court therefore must grant its motion for summary judgment....

---

In *Lunney v. Prodigy Services Co.*, 94 N.Y.2d 242 (N.Y. 1999), *cert. denied*, 120 S.Ct. 1832 (2000), an imposter of the plaintiff, a boy scout, transmitted an e-mail message to a local scoutmaster. The New York Court of Appeals characterized the e-mail as "vulgar in the extreme." After receiving the e-mail, the scoutmaster alerted the local police, who investigated the matter and accepted that the plaintiff had not authored the message. While the investigation was underway, Prodigy notified the plaintiff that, based on the transmission of inappropriate material, it was terminating one of the accounts in his name. The plaintiff advised Prodigy that he did not send the message, and Prodigy apologized. The plaintiff sued nonetheless, claiming that Prodigy had been derelict in allowing the accounts to be opened in his name and had effectively defamed him. *Id.*

The Court assumed for purposes of its opinion that although he had not been directly attacked, the plaintiff was defamed by virtue of having been portrayed as the author of the "foul material." *Id.* at 248. But Prodigy could not be compelled to "examine and screen millions of e-mail communications, on pain of liability for defamation." *Id.* at 249. The Court of Appeals refused to deny Prodigy the common-law qualified privilege accorded to telephone and telegraph companies.

This principle was discussed in *Anderson v. New York Telephone Co.*, 35 N.Y.2d 746, 320 N.E.2d 647 (1974). There, a radio broadcast had urged listeners to call telephone numbers; listeners heard accusations against the plaintiff. The plaintiff sued the telephone company, from whom the equipment was leased. The New York Court of Appeals readily concluded that the telephone company did not publish the scandalous material, stating:

> The telephone company is not part of the "media" which puts forth informaton after processing it in one way or another. The telephone company is a public utility which is bound to make its equipment available to the public for any legal use to which it can be put and is privileged under its tariff restrictions to terminate service for cause only in certain prescribed circumstances none of which encompass the subscriber's dissemination of defamatory messages....It could not be said, for example, that International Business Machines, Inc., even if it had notice, would be liable were one of its leased typewriters used to publish a libel. Neither would it be said that the Xerox Corporation, even if it had notice, could be held responsible were one of its leased photocopy machines used to multiply a libel many times...The telephone company, if anything, would have even less control over the use of its leased equipment than would those companies...The latter are not public utilities and are ungoverned by the restrictions which devolve upon defendant; yet, as we have noted, it would not be seriously argued that they would be responsible for publication of a libel simply because their machines were used.

*Id.* at 750–51, 320 N.E.2d 649 (foonotes and citations omitted).

In *Lunney v. Prodigy Services Co.*, New York's highest court applied this rationale to communications conducted on electronic bulletin boards, observing that in some instances, they could be made to resemble a newspaper's editorial page. In other instances, they may function more like a chat room; i.e., a service designed to allow multiple users "talk" through simultaneous text postings. 94 N.Y.2d at 250 & n. 4.

In many respects, an [Internet service provider] bulletin board may serve much the same purpose as its ancestral version, but uses electronics in place of plywood and thumbtacks. Some electronic bulletin boards post messages instantly and automatically, others briefly delay posting so as not to become "chat rooms," while still others significantly delay posting to allow their operators an opportunity to edit the message or refuse posting altogether.

*Id.* at 250 (citations omitted). The Court of Appeals ruled that even if Prodigy had exercised the right it reserved under its membership agreements to edit certain bulletin board messages, Prodigy's "passive character" would not be altered in the millions of other messages in which it did not participate. In sum, Prodigy could not be compelled to guarantee the content of subscribers' messages.

Significantly, the Court of Appeals reached this conclusion without resorting to application of section 230 of the CDA. The issue had been briefed, and the Court acknowledged that "parties to a lawsuit, and surely others interested in the field, will look to decisions for points of guidance. For every new rule that a court sets down doubts are minimized, and practitioners are able to give counsel based on settled doctrine, rather than on open questions." *Id.* at 251–52. Nevertheless, the Court felt that it could not

go beyond the issues necessary to decide the case at hand. An ambition of that sort would entail something very much like drafting advisory opinions. Misdirected or misapplied, they can create the very kind of uncertainty, or confusion, that purposeful decisional law seeks to eliminate. These general observations apply even more compellingly when dealing with Internet law. Given the extraordinarily rapid growth of this technology and its developments, it is plainly unwise to lurch prematurely into emerging issues, given a record that does not at all lend itself to this determination.

*Id.* at 252.

This was to be the final word on the parties' dispute. On May 1, 2000, the Supreme Court denied the petition for certiorari in this case. 120 S.Ct. 1832 (2000).

---

## Jane DOE, mother, and legal guardian of John Doe, a minor v. AMERICA ONLINE, INC.

District Court of Appeal of Florida, Fourth District
No. 97-2587, 718 So.2d 385, 1998 Fla. App. LEXIS 12841
October 14, 1998

Dell, Judge.

Jane Doe appeals the trial court's order dismissing with prejudice her complaint against America Online, Inc. ("AOL"). She argues that the trial court erred when it considered matters outside the four corners of the complaint, when it denied her leave to amend, when it retroactively applied section 230 of the Communications Decency Act, 47 U.S.C. § 230, *et seq.* ("CDA"), to her complaint, and when it concluded that under the CDA, AOL is statutorily immune from her claims. We affirm.

On January 23, 1997, Doe filed a six count complaint against Richard Lee Russell and AOL to recover for emotional injuries suffered by her son, John Doe. She claimed that in early 1994, Russell lured John Doe (then eleven years old) and two other minor males to engage in sexual activity with each other and with Russell. She asserted that Russell photographed and videotaped these acts and utilized AOL's "chat rooms" to market the photographs and videotapes, and to later sell a videotape to a man in Arizona[, giving rise to a claim of negligence and violations of specified Florida statutes.]...

Doe...alleged that AOL, a "computer on-line, interactive information, communication and transaction service" promulgated "Terms of Service" ("TOS") and "Rules of the Road" ("ROR") and required its members to adhere to their terms. She claimed that the TOS and ROR prohibited members from posting or transmitting "unlawful, harmful...obscene...or otherwise objectionable" material on AOL, including material encouraging criminal conduct. She also claimed that AOL reserved the right to monitor the public areas and chat rooms to ensure that members adhered to the TOS and ROR and reserved the right to "prohibit conduct, communication, or content which it deems in its discretion to be harmful to individual members, the communities which make up the AOL Service, AOL, Inc.'s or other third party rights or to violate any applicable law." Further, she claimed that complaints had been communicated to AOL regarding Russell's transmitting obscene and unlawful photographs and/or images, and that although AOL reserved the right to terminate, without notice, the service of any member who did not abide by the TOS, AOL did not warn or advise Russell to stop, nor did it suspend or terminate his service. Doe did not allege that Russell transmitted photographs or images of her son....

Doe maintains that section 230 is inapplicable because she seeks to hold AOL liable as a distributor of child pornography, not as a publisher or a speaker. This is the same argument considered by the court in *Zeran* [*v. America Online, Inc.,* 129 F.3d 327 (4th Cir. 1997), *cert. denied,* 118 S.Ct. 2341 (1998)], Zeran argued that section 230 immunity eliminated publisher liability, but left distributor liability intact because the notice element for distributors permitted liability if AOL had sufficient notice. *Id.* at 331....

It is clear from the trial court's order that it concluded that section 230 preempted the statutory and common laws of the State of Florida. The trial court's conclusion is consistent with *Zeran....*

We hold that the trial court did not err when it denied Doe leave to amend because the complaint cannot be amended to overcome section 230 immunity. For the reasons expressed in *Zeran* as set forth in this opinion, we affirm the trial court's dismissal of Doe's complaint with prejudice.

We deem the questions raised as to the application of section 230 of the Communications Decency Act to be of great public importance and certify the following questions to the Florida Supreme Court:....

> [W]hether a computer service provider with notice of a defamatory third party posting is entitled to immunity under section 230 of the Communications Decency Act?

AFFIRMED.

---

## Notes and Questions

1. While the New York Court of Appeals in *Lunney v. Prodigy Services Co.,* 94 N.Y.2d 242, refused to impose liability on the service provider without even having to re-

sort to application of the CDA, the Florida appellate court in *Doe v. America On-line, Inc.*, 718 So.2d 385, 1998 Fla. App. LEXIS 12841, certified, among others, questions relating to the culpability of an Internet service provider who had received notice of the alleged defamation. The Florida Supreme Court granted review. 729 So.2d 390 (Fla. Apr. 12, 1999).

2.  Medphone Corp. sued for libel, claiming that its stock price dropped dramatically after the defendant posted allegedly disparaging comments on the "Money Talk" bulletin board. *Medphone Corp. v. DeNigris*, Civ. No. 92-3785, 1993 U.S. Dist. LEXIS 21266 (D.N.J. 1996). The plaintiff issued a press release, referring to its complaint and stating that the defendant had engaged in a "systematic program of defamation and trade disparagement" against the company. *Id.* at *2. The press release, made in the course of a judicial proceeding and bearing a relationship to the proceeding, was deemed privileged. *Id.* at *6–7; *see generally* discussion *infra* at 288.

3.  A California state court, in *Aquino v. ElectriCiti*, No. 984751, 26 Med. L. Rptr. (BNA) 1032 (Cal. Super. Ct. Sept. 23, 1997), dismissed an action brought against a service provider. The plaintiff alleged that the defendant Internet service provider had failed to take appropriate actions to restrict the dissemination of messages to a user group alleging that the plaintiff had been associated with a child-abuse investigation. The CDA preempted the plaintiff's state law claims and barred the imposition of liability on the Internet service provider.

4.  In *Ben Ezra, Weinstein and Co. v. America Online, Inc.*, No. 97-485 LH/LFG, 1999 WL 727402, 27 Med. L. Rptr. (BNA) 1794 (D.N.M. Mar. 1, 1999), the court dismissed a defamation and negligence suit against an Internet service provider that was alleged to have posted inaccurate stock quotes concerning the plaintiff. The stock quotes had been furnished by a third party to the Internet service provider, which had endeavored to correct erroneous quotes. The service provider had not assisted in creating or developing the information.

5.  Can the mere act of hyperlinking to a web-site containing libelous content constitute publication by the linking site? If the linking site endorses the defamatory material, knowing it to be such, may it be held accountable for the statements merely on the basis of the hyperlink?

————————

To what extent does section 230 of the CDA apply to entities other than Internet service providers? Are web hosts immune from liability under the legislation? As well, what happens if the aggrieved subject of an on-line posting cannot plead with specificity the role, if any, of a Web host in the creation of the offensive content?

————————

# John DOES 1 through 30 inclusive, and Unknown Illinois State University Football Players v. FRANCO PRODUCTIONS, Dan Franco, individually and d/b/a Franco Productions, *et al.*

United States District Court, Northern District of Illinois, Eastern Division
No. 99 C 7885, 2000 WL 816779
June 22, 2000

KOCORAS, J....

## BACKGROUND

The Plaintiffs in this matter were intercollegiate athletes who, without their knowledge or consent, were videotaped in various states of undress by hidden cameras in restrooms, locker rooms, or showers. The resulting videotapes were sold by various means, including web sites hosted by Genuity.net and TIAC.Net that included still images of the Plaintiffs taken from the videotapes. At no time did any of the Plaintiffs authorize the use of their images; in fact, they did not learn of the existence of the videotapes or that they were available for purchase until a newspaper article detailed the operation. They instituted this action to obtain monetary damages and injunctive relief for intrusion into the Plaintiffs' seclusion against the defendants, the allegd producers and distributors of the videotapes, andagainst defendants GTE Corporation and GTE Internetworking (together "GTE") and PSINet Inc. ("PSINet")....The Court dismissed Plaintiffs' previous complaint against GTE, finding that GTE was a service provider and therefore immune from suit under the Communications Decency Act of 1996, 47 U.S.C. §230 (the "CDA"). The Court also granted PSINet's oral motion to dismiss on April 20, 2000 for the same reason....

## DISCUSSION

...Plaintiffs push the boundaries of [Federal] Rule [of Civil Procedure] 11 by making such general and nonspecific allegations with respect to GTE and PSINet, which suggest that Plaintiffs did not conduct a reasonable preliminary inquiry before filing its third amended complaint.

For example, Plaintiffs allege:

> As web site hosts, GTE and PSI engage in varying degrees of designing or creating or maintaining the web site, ranging anywhere from completely creating, writing, organizing and originally editing content before it is posted and changing, updating, adding or deleting content thereafter, to providing the template or architecture of the web site. The exact degree of involvement by GTE and PSI in creating and designing the web sites at issue is known only to the defendants and cannot be ascertained by the Plaintiffs without the right of discovery, but after a reasonable opportunity for further investigation or discovery, there is likely to be evidentiary support that GTE and PSI were responsible at least in part for the creation or development or design of the web site or web pages, including the web pages which advertised the videos for sale.

Essentially, Plaintiffs are alleging that they have no idea what GTE and PSINet do in their capacity as web hosts and it could be just about anything, but if given the opportunity, Plaintiffs can figure out what GTE and PSINet do, and it will probably include at least partial responsibility for the creation or development or design of the web site or web pages, based upon which Plaintiffs seek to hold GTE and PSINet liable. Plaintiffs further allege in their third amended complaint, "depending on the exact range of involvement in the creation or design of the web site, GTE and PSI may have created or designed actual content of the web site." This allegation suggests that Plaintiffs do not even possess a current belief based on any information that GTE or PSI did create or design the actual content of the web site, but rather, they hope and speculate that they may be able to demonstrate it if they end up uncovering certain information. Moreover, Plaintiffs arguments in its response to GTE's and PSINet's motion to dismiss, seem to confirm that Plaintiffs do not have a reasonable belief that GTE and PSINet created the web site or contributed to its contents, but rather that it is probable that GTE and PSINet helped provide the framework necessary for others to create a web site. Thus, Plaintiffs argue that "the Host Server Defendants in their capacity as such more likely than not helped to create the web site, including by developing the graphics, the photo utilization, and the information and materials related to credit card transactions necessary to the sale for the illegal videotapes."

These allegations press the limits of the liberal pleading standards and come up against the provisions of Rule 11. They indicate little preliminary inquiry by Plaintiffs into their allegations before filing their third amended complaint and little known information upon which to base belief in certain factual allegations. However, the Court will not dismiss Plaintiffs' third amended complaint for its stretching of Rule 11's provisions. Sanctions are the appropriate remedy for violation of Rule 11, not dismissal. *See Chisolm[ v. Foothill Capital Corp.*], 940 F. Supp. [1273,] 1280–81 [(N.D. Ill. 1996)]. Because, however, the Court does not find that Plaintiffs' allegations are insufficient to place Defendants GTE and PSINet on notice as to the nature of Plaintiffs' claims, the Court will not dismiss Plaintiffs' third amended complaint based on pleading deficiencies under Rule 8. *See* Fed.R.Civ.P. 8; *Veazey v. Communications & Cable of Chicago, Inc.*, 194 F.3d 850, 854 (7th Cir. 1999).

Plaintiffs assert that they are not seeking to hold GTE and PSINet liable as publishers or speakers of information provided by another under §230(c)(1)[;] thus whatever immunity that section may supply is irrelevant. Rather, Plaintiffs assert that [they are] seeking to hold GTE and PSINet liable for their "own conduct" in "knowingly failing to restrict content" under §230(c)(2). Section 230(c)(2) provides immunity to those who restrict or enable restriction to objectionable material. *See* 47 U.S.C. §230(c). Thus, Plaintiffs reason because GTE and PSINet did not restrict or enable restriction of objectionable material, they are not entitled to immunity under this section. However, what Plaintiffs ignore is that by seeking to hold GTE and PSINet liable for their decision not to restrict certain content it is seeking to hold them liable in a publisher's capacity. Section 230(c)(1) provides, "No provider or user of an interactive computer service shall be treated as the publisher or speaker of any information provided by another information content provider." This "creates a federal immunity to any cause of action that would make service providers liable for information originating with a third-party user of the service…lawsuits seeking to hold a service provider liable for its exercise of a publisher's traditional editorial functions—such as deciding whether to publish, withdraw, postpone or alter content—are barred." *See Zeran v. America Online, Inc.*, 129 F.3d 327, 330 (4th Cir. 1997); *see also Ben Ezra, Weinstein, and Co. v. America Online, Inc.*, 206 F.3d 980, 985–86 (10th Cir. 2000) (§230 forbids imposition of liability for exercise of editorial functions). Thus, because Plaintiffs seek to hold GTE and PSINet liable for their "own conduct" as publishers, GTE and PSINet may avail themselves of the CDA's immunity in this action under §230(c)(1).

Moreover, Plaintiffs have recast the dismissed claims raised in their previous complaint by alleging that they are bringing the instant suit against GTE and PSINet in their capacity as "web site host[s]" rather than service providers. In this capacity as web hosts, Plaintiffs claim that GTE and PSINet acted as "information content provider[s]" and would, thus, not be immune from suit under the CDA. GTE and PSINet argue that Plaintiffs' amended claims still fail to state a claim because web site hosting activities are immunized under the CDA.

The Court agrees with Defendants GTE and PSINet. The CDA creates federal immunity against any state law cause of action that would hold computer service providers liable for information originating from a third party. *See Franco Productions*, No. 99 C 7885, at *4–5 (unpublished Apr. 20, 2000); *Ben Ezra*, 206 F.3d at 984–85. After the Court ruled that GTE as a service provider is immune from suit under the CDA, Plaintiffs severed out and focused on the allegedly separate role of web host played by GTE and PSINet, claiming that a suit against an entity based on its capacity as a web host is not barred by the CDA. This is because as web hosts GTE and PSINet are "information content provider[s]" according to Plaintiffs. Thus, Plaintiffs essentially argue that although GTE and PSINet are acting as service providers, they are also content providers in their role as web hosts and that in its third amended complaint Plaintiffs only seek to hold GTE and PSINet liable in their separate capacity as content providers as manifested in their role as web hosts. However, not only did the Court previously find that GTE was acting as a service provider for purposes of this action, but the Court specifically rejected the notion that GTE was acting as a content provider in this action as well. *See Franco Productions*, No. 99 C 7885, at *7. The Court reiterates its previous holding finding GTE, and now similarly PSINet, service providers whose immunity or status as service providers under the CDA is not vitiated because of their web hosting activities, whether viewed in combination with their roles as service providers or in isolation. Immunity under the CDA is not limited to service providers who contain their activity to editorial exercises or those who do not engage in web hosting, but rather, "Congress... provid[ed] immunity even where the interactive service provider has an active, even aggressive role in making available content prepared by others." *Blumenthal v. Drudge*, 992 F. Supp. 44, 52 (D.D.C. 1998).

Thus, Plaintiffs' new characterization of GTE's and PSINet's activities as web hosts do not alter this finding. The deficiency in Plaintiffs' allegations is the notion that involvement in web hosting activities transforms an entity into an information content provider. Plaintiffs believe that by focusing on Defendants GTE's and PSINet's web hosting activities, GTE and PSINet can essentially be characterized as information content providers. However, Plaintiff has pointed to no authority which provides that involvement in these web hosting activities makes an entity an information content provider.

Perhaps the Court is obtuse in its consistent "misunderstanding of Plaintiffs' cause of action," but it is still "at a loss to understand how GTE's [and PSINet's] role[s] in the descriptions or presentation of the images on the Web site impact the creation or development of the images and videotapes themselves." *Franco Productions*, No. 99 C 7885,*8–9. Plaintiffs' explain that "the culpable conduct is not only the taking of the videotapes but also disseminating them on the Internet and offering them for sale and selling them. The Plaintiffs were harmed, not just by the posting of their illegally taken images on the web page, but also by the sale and dissemination of the videotapes because of the web page." This makes no clearer Plaintiffs' theory that GTE and PSINet were somehow content providers. Plaintiffs do not allege that GTE or PSINet themselves sold or offered for sale the videotapes at issue. Plaintiffs simply allege that GTE and PSINet, as web hosts, provided a medium through which others could sell or offer for sale the videotapes at issue. However, by offering web hosting services which enable someone to create a web page, GTE and

PSINet are not magically rendered the creators of those web pages. *See* 47 U.S.C. [230] (c)(1).

As such, Plaintiffs' new characterization of GTE and PSINet as web hosts neither prevents these defendants from being deemed service providers protected by immunity under the CDA nor makes them content providers unprotected by the CDA's immunity. Moreover, this immunity extends to Plaintiffs' newly alleged public nuisance claim.

In addition, Plaintiffs' claims for injunctive relief, although not precluded by the CDA, fail to state a claim. *See Mainstream Loudoun v. Board of Trustees*, 24 F. Supp. 2d 552, 561 (E.D. Va. 1998). Plaintiffs fail to elucidate what activities of GTE and PSINet they seek to enjoin. It appears that the offending images at issue are no longer available on any web site hosted by GTE or PSINet. Moreover, Plaintiffs do not suggest that there is a likelihood that GTE or PSINet will engage in any offending activity against Plaintiffs. As such, Plaintiffs have failed to make allegations that would demonstrate their entitlement to injunctive relief....

## CONCLUSION

For the reasons set forth above, the Court grants Defendants GTE's and PSINet's motion to dismiss.

———————

# Tammy S. BLAKEY v. CONTINENTAL AIRLINES, INC.
### Supreme Court of New Jersey
### 164 N.J. 38, 751 A.2d 538
### June 1, 2000

The opinion of the Court was delivered by O'HERN, J.

...Should an employer, having actual or constructive knowledge that co-employees are posting harassing, retaliatory, and sometimes defamatory, messages about a co-employee on a bulletin board used by the company's employees, have a duty to prevent the continuation of such harassing conduct?...

It seems to us that if the facts are stated thus the answer[ ] to the question[ ] should be "yes." Because the facts may be somewhere in between, we cannot provide [a] categorical answer[ ] to the question[ ].

The case appears to have proceeded on the thesis that there could be no liability if the harassment by co-employees did not take place within the workplace setting at a place under the physical control of the employer. Although the electronic bulletin board may not have a physical location within a terminal, hangar or aircraft, it may nonetheless have been so closely related to the workplace environment and beneficial to Continental [Airlines, Inc. ("Continental")] that a continuation of harassment on the forum should be regarded as part of the workplace. As applied to this hostile environment workplace claim, we find that if the employer had notice that co-employees were engaged on such a work-related forum in a pattern of retaliatory harassment directed at a co-employee, the employer would have a duty to remedy that harassment. We find that the record is inadequate to determine whether the relationship between the bulletin board and the employer establishes a connection with the workplace sufficient to impose such liability on the employer. We remand that aspect of the matter to the Law Division for further proceedings in accordance with this opinion....

Tammy S. Blakey, a pilot for Continental Airlines since 1984, appears from the record to be a highly qualified commercial airline pilot. In December 1989, Blakey became that airline's first female captain to fly an Airbus or A300 aircraft (A300). The A300 is a widebody twin-engine jet aircraft seating 250 passengers. Airbus Industrie (visited March 13, 2000) <http:// www.airbus.com>. Plaintiff was one of five qualified A300 pilots in the service of Continental Airlines. Shortly after qualifying to be a captain on the A300, Blakey complained of sexual harassment and a hostile working environment based on conduct and comments directed at her by male co-employees.... According to Blakey, in February 1991, she began to file systematic complaints with various representatives of Continental about the conduct of her male co-employees. Specifically, Blakey complained to Continental's management concerning pornographic photographs and vulgar gender-based comments directed at her that appeared in the workplace, specifically in her plane's cockpit and other work areas.

In February 1993, Blakey filed a charge of sexual discrimination and retaliation in violation of Title VII of the Civil Rights Act of 1964 and the Civil Rights Act of 1991 against Continental with the Equal Employment Opportunity Commission in Seattle, Washington, her home state. She simultaneously filed a complaint in the United States District Court in Seattle, Washington, against Continental for its failure to remedy the hostile work environment....

In the midst of that federal litigation, her fellow pilots continued to publish a series of what plaintiff views as harassing gender-based messages, some of which she alleges are false and defamatory. From February to July 1995, a number of Continental's male pilots posted derogatory and insulting remarks about Blakey on the pilots on-line computer bulletin board called the Crew Members Forum ("Forum"). The Forum is accessible to all Continental pilots and crew member personnel through the Internet provider, CompuServe. When Continental employees access CompuServe, one of the menu selections listed in the "Continental Airlines Home Access" program includes an option called "Continental Forum." Like many other large corporations today, Continental's computer technology operations are "outsourced" or contracted-out, in this case to a company called Electronic Data Systems ("EDS"). EDS manages Continental's information systems including the CMS, which contains information on flights, crew member schedules, pay and pilot pairings. Continental requires that pilots and crew "access" the CMS in order to learn their flight schedules and assignments. To access such a system is, in essence, to call in through a computer or telephone.

Continental personnel access the CMS in three ways. Continental personnel may access the CMS through "dumb terminals"[3] located in crew locations throughout the Continental network through a direct line to Continental's main computer system that is managed by EDS and maintained on a mainframe computer in North Carolina. Flight crew members also may access CMS through a voice response system by dialing into the system on a regular telephone. The third means of access to the CMS is to con-

---

3. A "dumb terminal" is defined as "a display monitor that has no processing capabilities. A dumb terminal is simply an output device that accepts data from the [central processing unit or "brain" of the computer]. In contrast, a smart terminal is a monitor that has its own processor for special features, such as bold and blinking characters. Dumb terminals are not as fast as smart terminals, and they do not support as many display features, but they are adequate for most applications." Webopedia (visited March 30, 2000) <http://webopedia.com>.

nect to the system through an Internet service provider (ISP), in this case, CompuServe, a wholly owned subsidiary of America Online, Inc. (AOL). CompuServe is the ISP approved by Continental to provide pilot and crew access to the CMS. To access the CMS through CompuServe, Continental personnel simply need a personal computer, a modem (a device that connects the computer to a phone line), and a phone line. CompuServe provides "membership kits," containing customized computer software to all Continental personnel who may wish to connect to the CMS in this manner. The CompuServe software provides access to the CMS to any individual with a Continental employee identification number that identifies that individual as a pilot or crew member. As part of the package provided to pilots and crew personnel, CompuServe made the Crew Members Forum available for crew members to exchange ideas and information. According to Continental's witnesses, CompuServe charged $5.80 per hour to provide a direct connection between Continental's main computer system and CompuServe. Three percent of that charge is paid back to Continental to defray any costs incurred by Continental.

CompuServe charges pilots and crew members a monthly fee for Internet access. Perhaps to enhance the appeal of its product, CompuServe provides the Crew Members Forum for pilots and crew members to exchange messages. In the parlance of the Internet, this is described as a virtual community. Community is about communication and interaction among people of shared interests, objectives or purposes. When community members such as employees communicate with each other, they build relationships. *See* Steven L. Telleen, *What It Means To Have Virtual Communities on an Intranet*, Internet World, Nov. 16, 1998 (describing virtual communities and virtual workgroups). "Intranet communities are typically created to improve collaboration and knowledge sharing among employees." Joseph Cothrel, *Virtual Communities Today, The Journal of the Association for Global Strategic Information* (July 1999). The Crew Members Forum essentially serves as an Intranet system.

Access to the Crew Members Forum is available only through CompuServe. The Forum is not accessible through the dumb terminals. The Forum is like a bulletin board where employees can post messages or "threads" for each other. At the time of trial, the Law Division stated that "only 250 employees nationwide had access to the Forum at the time that [ ] defendants published their statements." System operators, or SYSOPS as they are called, provide technical assistance for the Forum. SYSOPS were Continental crew members who volunteered with CompuServe for the position and received no compensation from Continental for that work. Although it was said that Continental management was not permitted to post messages or reply to any messages on the Forum, its chief pilots and assistant chief pilots had access to the Forum if they signed up with CompuServe to utilize the CMS. Relying on deposition testimony of the Director of Crew Systems and Planning, plaintiff asserts that chief pilots are considered management within Continental.[5] Although Continental may have no duty to monitor the

---

5. We are not so certain that a chief pilot's knowledge of the harassing conduct can be imputed to Continental. *See Cavuoti v. New Jersey Transit*, 161 N.J. 107, 128–29, 735 A.2d 548 (1999) (generally reviewing tiers of management and holding "upper management would consist of those responsible to formulate the organization's anti-discrimination policies, provide compliance programs and insist on performance (its governing body, its executive officers), and those to whom the organization has delegated the responsibility to execute its policies in the workplace, who set the atmosphere or control the day-to-day operations of the unit (such as heads of departments, regional managers, or compliance officers)").

Forum, it is possible that a jury could find that Continental had knowledge, either direct or vicarious through managerial employees, of the content of certain messages posted on the Forum.

The...messages or "threads"[6] posted about Blakey by various male co-employees [include, as an example, the following:]

> Lawsuit, lawsuits lawsuits. That is all we hear about Tammy Blakey. You need to prey on a legal system that does not stand up to people who are vexatious and try to get even for their own lack of interpersonal skills....In my opinion, you are a wart (really bad choice of words with your ALLEGED problem) on the judicial system. I have zero respect for you and your kind....

...We do not purport to be experts on the complexities of the Internet or other forms of electronic communication, whether wired or wireless. We have made every effort, however, to describe the relationship between the Crew Members Forum and Continental Airlines in the language of those who do not possess a sophisticated knowledge of current computer technology.

To put the issue in perspective, we need to shrink the context a bit. There was a television series a few years ago called "Wings." Wings (NBC television broadcast, April 1990 through May 1997). The program concerned a small, regional airline, its pilots, ground crew and maintenance people. If there were at that small airport a lounge used exclusively by the pilots and crew of that airline and a bulletin board in that lounge contained the same or similar comments and asides by the pilots and crew, there would be little doubt that if management had notice of messages that met the required substantive criteria of being "sufficiently severe or pervasive to alter the conditions of employment and to create an intimidating, hostile, or offensive working environment," *Lehmann v. Toys 'R' Us, Inc.,* 132 N.J. 587, 592, 626 A.2d 445 (1993), a cause of action for hostile work environment sexual harassment could be asserted. And if there had been a nearby place frequented by senior management, pilots and crew where one of the crew was regularly subjected to sexually offensive insults and if that harassing conduct was a continuation of a pattern of harassment in the workplace, an employer that had notice of the pattern of severe and pervasive harassment in and out of the workplace, would not be entirely free to disregard the conduct.

The question in this more complex case is whether the Crew Members Forum is the equivalent of a bulletin board in the pilots' lounge or a work-related place in which pilots and crew members continue a pattern of harassment....

This Court has recognized that harassment by a supervisor that takes place outside of the workplace can be actionable. *American Motorists Ins. Co. v. L-C-A Sales Co.,* 155 N.J. 29, 42, 713 A.2d 1007 (1998)....

---

6. On the Internet..., a thread is a sequence of responses to an initial message posting. This enables you to follow or join an individual discussion in a [forum or] newsgroup from among the many that may be there. A thread is usually shown graphically as an initial message and successive messages "hung off" the original message. As a [forum or] newsgroup user, you contribute to a thread by specifying a "Reference" topic as part of your message.
[whatis?com (visited March 30, 2000) <http://whatis.com/index.htm >.]

Thus, standing alone, the fact that the electronic bulletin board may be located outside of the workplace (although not as closely affiliated with the workplace as was the cockpit in which similar harassing conduct occurred), does not mean that an employer may have no duty to correct off-site harassment by co-employees. Conduct that takes place outside of the workplace has a tendency to permeate the workplace. *See Schwapp v. Avon*, 118 F.3d 106, 111 (2d Cir. 1997) (finding that "[t]he mere fact that [the plaintiff] was not present when a racially derogatory comment was made will not render that comment irrelevant to his hostile work environment claim."). A worker need not actually hear the harassing words outside the workplace so long as the harassment contributes to the hostile work environment. *Ibid. See also* Young, Conaway, Stargatt & Taylor, *Six Sexual Harassment Myths Shattered*, 2 No. 4 Del. Employment L. Letter 1 (April 1997) (observing that "[i]t is clear today that the fact that the harassment occurred away from the workplace will carry little weight with the courts.")....

Our common experience tells us how important are the extensions of the workplace where the relations among employees are cemented or sometimes sundered. If an "old boys' network" continued, in an after-hours setting, the belittling conduct that edges over into harassment, what exactly is the outsider (whether black, Latino, or woman) to do? Keep swallowing the abuse or give up the chance to make the team? We believe that severe or pervasive harassment in a work-related setting that continues a pattern of harassment on the job is sufficiently related to the workplace that an informed employer who takes no effective measures to stop it, "sends the harassed employee the message that the harassment is acceptable and that the management supports the harasser." *Lehmann v. Toys 'R' Us, supra*, 132 N.J. at 623, 626 A.2d 445....

On remand, the trial court should first determine whether Continental derived a substantial workplace benefit from the overall relationship among CompuServe, the Forum and Continental.

The record does not disclose that Continental sought the Forum's inclusion on CompuServe's menu. Still, it appears to us that a business enterprise would derive the same benefits from having its employees connected as would a law firm, *see* Eric G. Kraft, *The Increasing Use of the Internet in the Practice of Law*, 69 J. Kan. B.A. 15, 17 (Feb. 2000), or the judiciary itself. We have become familiar with the process through which the judiciary's employees and its several jurisdictions may be connected by the Internet. That process is well known by now. *See* Dennis L. Greenwald, *The 21st Century Office...It's Not Your Father's Office Any More*, 14 Prob. & Prop. 9 (Feb. 2000) (observing that "high speed telecommunications, telecommuting and other 'live-work' models, the 'paperless workplace' and the personal computer as the 'virtual office' seem permanent fixtures of tomorrow's workplace"). The problems that developed in our fathers' offices are likely to develop in the offices of the future. Business counselors caution employers that they should have policies that deal with sexual harassment on the message centers of this changing world. Diana J.P. McKenzie, *Information Technology Policies: Practical Protection in Cyberspace*, 3 Stan. J.L. Bus. & Fin. 84 (Winter 1997). That does not mean that employers have a duty to monitor employees' mail. Grave privacy concerns are implicated. Todd M. Keebaugh, *The Virtual Office: Practical Considerations in Establishing and Implementing a Telecommuting Program*, 16 No. 5 ACCA Docket 16, 22 (Sept./Oct. 1998). It may mean that employers may not disregard the posting of offensive messages on company or state agency e-mail systems when the employer is made aware of those messages. Anne Sexton, *Parkway Suspends Three, and Others Squirm as E-Mail Is Reviewed*, Newark Star Ledger, March 15, 2000, at 1.

The Law Division should initially determine whether a triable issue of fact is presented concerning whether the Crew Members Forum should be considered sufficiently integrated with the workplace to require such a response by an employer. For example, the record does not contain the contract between CompuServe and Continental. In addition, at the time of these proceedings, use of the Internet was in the beginning stages. The number of current users would be relevant to the benefit that Continental might derive from the service. It appears to us likely that Continental crew members who subscribed to CompuServe did so because of access the CMS. In essence, Continental "outsourced" what another organization might call its own network. When a crew member accesses the CMS through CompuServe, the menu of options listed under the "Continental Airlines Home Access" includes both the "Crew Services/Forum" and "Continental Forum." The ability of Continental employees to access the information provided on the CMS benefits Continental by improving its efficiency and operations. *See* Paul M. Schwartz, *Privacy and Democracy in Cyberspace*, 52 Vand. L. Rev. 1609, 1620 n. 61 (November 1999) (citing Carl Shapiro & Hal R. Varian, *Information Rules: A Strategic Guide to the Network Economy* 13–14 1999) at 183–84, identifying the benefits of a network, which "include an increased access to information, an increased ease of communication, and a decrease in a variety of transaction and overhead costs"). The ability of the Continental employees to communicate with each other on the Forum would likewise appear to be a benefit.

CompuServe's role may thus be analogized to that of a company that builds an old-fashioned bulletin board. If the maker of an old-fashioned bulletin board provided a better bulletin board by setting aside space on it for employees to post messages, we would have little doubt that messages on the company bulletin board would be part of the workplace setting. Here, the Crew Members Forum is an added feature to the company bulletin board.[11]

To repeat, employers do not have a duty to monitor private communications of their employees; employers do have a duty to take effective measures to stop co-employee harassment when the employer knows or has reason to know that such harassment is part of a pattern of harassment that is taking place in the workplace and in settings that are related to the workplace. Besides, it may well be in an employer's economic best interests to adopt a proactive stance when it comes to dealing with co-employee harassment. The best defense may be a good offense against sexual harassment. "[W]e have afforded a form of a safe haven for employers who promulgate and support an active, anti-harassment policy." *Cavuoti, supra*, 161 N.J. at 121, 735 A.2d 548. Effective remedial steps reflecting a lack of tolerance for harassment will be "relevant to an employer's affirmative defense that its actions absolve it from all liability." *Payton v. New Jersey Turnpike Auth.*, 148 N.J. 524, 536–37, 691 A.2d 321 (1997). Surely an anti-harassment policy directed at any form of co-employee harassment would bolster that defense....

Having put the threshold issues in a more modest perspective, it is our hope that the parties, with assistance of active case management at the trial level, will approach the substantive issues with a similar outlook. Many of the messages complained of appear to us to be not capable of a defamatory meaning. Some of the messages appear to be

---

11. The corollary to this is that we should not hold the maker of the bulletin board liable for the statements that are placed on it. We therefore would hesitate to hold as did an English court that an Internet service provider should be liable for defamatory messages posted thereon by others. Sarah Lyall, *British Internet Provider to Pay Physicist Who Says E-Bulletin Board Libeled Him*, The New York Times, April 1, 2000, at A5.

expressions of opinion concerning the pending litigation, the truth of which simply cannot be assessed. *See Ward v. Zelikovsky*, 136 N.J. 516, 531, 643 A.2d 972 (1994) (holding that "[u]nless a statement explicitly or impliedly rests on false facts that damage the reputation of another, the alleged defamatory statement will not be actionable"). Some may be capable of a defamatory meaning in that they adversely reflect on plaintiff's fitness to conduct her profession, for example, that she destroyed company property....

[W]e would hope that an employer who cherishes its reputation for caring for its customers would use its good offices to resolve this long simmering disagreement among its key employees, whose harmony would appear crucial not only to efficient flight operations but to general public safety as well.

The judgment of the Appellate Division is reversed. The matter is remanded to the Law Division for further proceedings in accordance with this opinion. In view of our disposition, we do not consider the various motions filed by parties, the resolution of which should be left to the Law Division.

---

## 3.   Archived Materials

The Internet affords extensive archival capabilities. To what extent does access to archived materials give rise to a claim that the content has been "republished"? Under the "single publication rule," only one action may be brought to redress any particular publication, regardless of the number of copies of it that were distributed. *See* Restatement (Second) of Torts § 577A (1977). Barring the formation of a new edition, there is no republication. *See, e.g., Rinaldi v. Viking Penguin, Inc.*, 52 N.Y.2d 422, 420 N.E.2d 496 438 N.Y.S.2d 496 (1981); *Cox Enterprises, Inc. v. Gilreath*, 142 Ga.App. 297, 298, 235 S.E.2d 633, 634 (Ga. Ct. App. 1977) (publication of different editions of a daily newspaper were not deemed to be a single publication). Likewise, replenishing existing inventory with additional stock generally is not a "republication" or a new "edition."

Thus, an archived hard copy of a newspaper is considered part of the initial publication. Production of microfilm or microfiche copies of the newspaper, and access to such copies, similarly should be deemed part of the initial publication. *See* Restatement (Second) of Torts, § 577A, cmt. d (1977) ("The printing and distribution of extra copies... of a book may properly be treated as mere continued circulation of the first edition and hence as still part of the single publication, if it's done not long after the original publication as soon as the supply is exhausted").

In *Bartel v. Capital Newspapers*, 664 N.Y.S.2d 398, 25 Media L. Rptr. (BNA) 1959 (N.Y. City Ct. 1997), the plaintiff had, pursuant to an agreement with the *Times Union* newspaper, written articles that were published in its print edition. Several years later, complete copies of each issue of newspaper, without advertisements, were made available on-line. The court observed that:

> [i]n one sense the parties contemplated that [the plaintiff's] articles would appear only once in the *Times Union* on a particular publication date. However, it is also true that (1) a purchaser might mail the newspaper to a friend on the west coast; (2) a vendor might ship a supply of that day's papers for resale in another city; (3) the Albany Public Library might retain in paper form back copies

of the paper for viewing years later; and (4) the library, or the *Times Union* it-self, might retain on microfilm back copies of the paper for viewing years later. In each of the above examples, [the plaintiff's expert] conceded that no viola-tion of [the plaintiff's] rights would have occurred. The placement of each day's *Times Union* "on-line" in electronic format is in the court's view merely the modern-day equivalent of the former practice of microfilming, or before that, of simply saving extra copies of each day's paper in archives. While the on-line version of the *Times Union* did not exist back…[when the plaintiff agreed to write the articles], neither did microfilming back in 1925; in each case technol-ogy advanced and *the Times Union* was able to take advantage of that.

*Id., aff'd,* 26 Media L. Rptr. (BNA) 2500 (N.Y. County Ct. July 22, 1998).

Archival practices also bear on statute of limitations issues. In *Firth v. State,* No. 97999, 2000 WL 306865 (N.Y. Ct. Cl. March 23, 2000), for example, the New York Court of Claims readily confirmed that there is no rational basis upon which to distin-guish between the publication of a book or report through traditional printed media and the publication through electronic means simply because a copy was made available via the Internet. As there was no substantive alteration, there was no republication for statute of limitations purposes. *Id.* at 6. Likewise, in *Simon v. Arizona Bd. of Regents,* 28 Media L. Rptr. (BNA) 1240 (Ariz. Super. Ct. Oct. 25, 1999), the Arizona Superior Court held that the on-line publication of an allegedly defamatory article and the subsequent print edition of the article were a single publication for purposes of determining when the statute of limitations had begun to run.

In sum, archival materials that do not vary substantively from the original publica-tion should not be deemed to give rise to new actions or resuscitate an otherwise time-barred claim.

---

# Of and Concerning the Plaintiff

## 1. Identification

Another element critical to a *prima facie* case of defamation is a showing that the publication was "of and concerning" the plaintiff. Generally, the person who claims he was defamed is readily identifiable by the allegedly offending publication because he is specifically named. But what happens when the subject of the opprobrium is not named but arguably is described with such particularity that he has been, or is claimed to have been, recognized? Certainly it is no defense to a libel claim asserted by Bill Clinton that his name was omitted from a newspaper article published in 1999, where contempora-neous reference was made to "the incumbent President of the United States."

A claimant, while not named, may argue that enough information was set forth about him so as to render him recognizable. To support his claim, the plaintiff will scrutinize the offending passage to search for details that tend to point to him as the subject: physical characteristics, professional position held, relationship to others named, and the like. In *Bindrim v. Mitchell,* 92 Cal.App.3d 61, 155 Cal. Rptr. 29 (Ct. App.), *cert. denied,* 444 U.S. 984 (1979), for example, a novel depicted a fictitious therapist who bore no physical resemblance to the plaintiff-therapist and did not share the same name. Certain readers, however, were aware that the plaintiff had used relatively unique approaches in therapy sessions, which were described in the novel. The plaintiff proffered evidence of these extrinsic facts, which courts have characterized as "colloquium."

Governmental agencies generally have no cognizable claim for defamation, lest the suit be an action in seditious libel merely advanced in alternative nomenclature. "For good reason, 'no court of last resort in this country has ever held, or even suggested, that prosecutions for libel on government have any place in the American system of jurisprudence.'" *New York Times Co. v. Sullivan*, 376 U.S. 254, 291–92 (1964)) (quoting *City of Chicago v. Tribune Co.*, 307 Ill. 595, 601, 139 N.E. 86, 88, 28 A.L.R. 1368 (1923)).

If the criticism pertains to a governmental office, does a particular official have a viable claim that the statement reasonably was understood to refer to him? The Supreme Court has recognized that mere criticism of the performance of a governmental body cannot be transmuted into defamation of an unnamed governmental official who oversees that function. *See New York Times Co. v. Sullivan*, 376 U.S. 254.

Publications on a web-site arguably encompass a larger community. While the sphere of persons to whom the defamation potentially was published may be greater, the potential that an unnamed subject may reasonably be presumed to be within a contained community is diluted. Reasonable visitors to the site who viewed the defamatory statement would not presume that they recognized the subject of a posting who had been sketchily or imprecisely portrayed. Absent clear indicia that the statement referred to a particular person within the relevant context, mere commonality of a name or other shared attributes should not constitute identification.

---

## 2. Group Libel

A claimant may assert that he was included among a group of persons referred to in the article or posting in issue. In determining whether such claims are actionable, courts generally evaluate whether the group or class is so small that the statement may be reasonably understood to refer to the claimant. Under these circumstances, the plaintiff must show that he in fact is a member of the class defamed, and establish some reasonable personal application of the words to himself. No bright-line test exists for determining what constitutes a sufficiently "small" class such that the plaintiff may be understood, as a matter of law, to be included within it.

If the group is very large, the words may be deemed devoid of application to anyone in particular, lest "one might as well defame mankind." Restatement (Second) of Torts, § 112. Thus, the statement "all lawyers are liars" will not be subject to redress by any particular lawyer, because the putative class of lawyers is too large for the alleged defamer to be deemed to have pointed to any particular person. "If a class is sufficiently broad, no one member really suffers personal injury." *Auvil v. CBS "60 Minutes,"* 800 F. Supp. 928, 935 (E.D. Wash. 1992); *see also Khalid Abullah Tariq Al Mansour Faissal Fahd Al Talal v. Fanning*, 506 F. Supp. 186 (N.D. Cal. 1980) (class of 600 Muslims cannot claim each member was defamed).

Nor may all lawyers, joined together, challenge the statement "all lawyers are liars," because the alleged defamer could not reasonably have referred to every one of thousands of lawyers. "When an entire class is defamed, it is usually difficult to show that class-wide allegations could be said to be directed to each individual." *Auvil v. CBS "60 Minutes,"* 800 F. Supp. at 936. The general rule is that either the class must be small enough so that the derogatory communication may be reasonably understood to apply to each class member, or the circumstances of the publication must reasonably suggest that some particular member was targeted.[2]

---

# 3.  The Plaintiff with the Same Name

Lawsuits are sometimes premised upon claims that the defamatory report referenced an individual with the same name as the plaintiff, and thus was understood to have referred to the plaintiff. Litigation may also arise in the context of publication of works of fiction, when the author selects a name for a character that coincidentally belongs to a living person. An early English case dealt with a completely fictional character with an unusual name, "Artemus Jones," as the subject of a humorous article about a seemingly respectable lay officer of the Anglican Church who had engaged in a number of colorful activities in France. A lawyer with the same name claimed that he was subject to ridicule about what others believed to be his exploits. Even after the newspaper publicly confirmed that the subject of the article was entirely fictitious, the jury awarded the plaintiff £1,750 in damages. *E. Hulton & Co. v. Jones*, [1909] 2 K.B.D. 444.

Authors of fictional works often base their literary works — consciously or not — on real persons whom they have encountered. Noted author Carol Shields has commented that "[n]ovelists inevitably arrive at a recipe for their work: so many parts observation and experience combined with so many degrees of commitment to imagination. Stir well in a projected or real universe. Hope for a reader who understands what fiction really is and a critic who resist tying fictional gestures to autobiography." Carol Shields, *Opting for Invention Over the Injury of Invasion*, N.Y. Times (Apr. 10, 2000) at E1. If the author reasonably obscures the identity of the character and expressly disclaims resemblance to actual persons, the claim is rendered considerably less viable.

The Internet increases exponentially the risks of publication of fictitious names. For example, a college student was accused of posting three sexual fantasies on the Internet depicting the kidnapping, sodomy, and mutilation of a fictional victim, whom he had assigned the name of an actual female student. The student faced possible expulsion and federal criminal prosecution on charges of transmitting threats across state lines. *See* Philip Elmer-DeWitt, *Snuff Porn on the Net*, Time (Feb. 30, 1995) at 69.

---

2. Even though a CBS *60 Minutes* broadcast did not identify any particular apple grower in a report on chemicals sprayed on apples that may break down into carcinogenic agents, the federal court rejected CBS' effort to summarily dismiss the claim on the ground that the report was not of and concerning the apple growers. The court stated that "[t]he message 'apples give kids cancer' sounds an explicit, particularized and unmistakably concrete alarm to the consuming public to run, not walk, away from that apple stand." *Id.*

---

## 4.  The "Other Side" of Of and Concerning: Identifying the Originator of On-Line Content

A veritable hallmark of much of the communication that takes place in cyberspace is anonymity. Constitutional protection has been extended to anonymous communications. In *Talley v. California*, 362 U.S. 60 (1960), for example, the Supreme Court invalidated a Los Angeles ordinance that prohibited the distribution of any handbill in the city unless it included the name and address of the person who had prepared, distributed, or sponsored the handbill. The ordinance came under scrutiny when handbills were distributed, without the requisite attribution, to urge a boycott of certain Los Angeles merchants who allegedly had engaged in racially discriminatory employment practices. The Court rejected the argument that the law was a justifiable way to identify those responsible for fraud, false advertising, and libel, and deemed the ordinance void on its face, expressing concern that requiring the authors of handbills to identify themselves would tend to restrict freedom of expression. *See id.* at 64–65; *see also N.A.A.C.P. v. Alabama ex rel. Patterson*, 357 U.S. 449 (1958) (upholding the right of NAACP members to refuse to disclose their membership lists).

More recently, the Supreme Court invalidated a state campaign law that prohibited the distribution of anonymous campaign literature. *McIntyre v. Ohio Elections Comm'n*, 514 U.S. 334 (1995). Neither the state's interest in furnishing voters with information nor its objective of deterring libelous statements justified a writer being compelled to make "disclosures she would otherwise omit." *Id.* at 348.

Although protections for such speech have been questioned as "facilitat[ing] wrong by eliminating accountability," *id.* at 385 (Rehnquist, C.J., dissenting), a majority of the Supreme Court has concluded that:

> [u]nder our constitution, anonymous pamphleteering is not a pernicious, fraudulent practice, but an honorable tradition of advocacy and of dissent. Anonymity is a shield from the tyranny of the majority.... The right to remain anonymous may be abused when it shields fraudulent conduct. But political speech by its nature will sometimes have unpalatable consequences, and, in general, our society accords greater weight to the value of free speech than to the dangers of its misuse.

*Id.* at 357 (citations omitted).

What social values are served by anonymous speech? Motivations for withholding one's identity include fear of economic or other retaliation, of social ostracism, of reaction directed to one's family. Without protection for anonymous speech, its utterance may be quelled. "Persecuted groups and sects from time to time throughout history have been able to criticize oppressive practices and laws either anonymously or not at all." *Talley v. California*, 362 U.S. at 64. Indeed, while we now know that The Federalist Papers were the work of James Madison, John Jay, and Alexander Hamilton, the documents originally were published under the pseudonym "Publius."

Others may simply wish to preserve as much privacy as possible, and eschew the potential publicity attendant to the expression. In the Internet era in particular, anonymity quells some of the discomfort that may be experienced by extensive digital surveillance techniques to monitor on-line activity. Withholding one's name and other salient personal data may enhance the individual's sense of privacy and insulate the speaker from unauthorized efforts to probe his persona. Even casual inquiries may lead to unwanted e-mail communications that may distract the user from other computer activities.

Anonymity may also be important to those who seek access to information on sensitive or controversial topics, as in the case of a person requesting information from an organization that assists victims of sexual assault. *See, e.g., American Civil Liberties Union v. Reno*, 929 F. Supp. 824, 849 (E.D. Pa. 1996), *aff'd,* 521 U.S. 844 (1997). Absent some assurances that the identity of the speaker will remain confidential, the speaker may be deterred from seeking help or pursuing an inquiry for information. In the digital age, when data may be easily exchanged, a user may be reluctant to access web-sites relating to such topics as disease, based on perceptions that access of, subscription to, or exchanges with such sites may be disclosed to the user's insurer or employer.

As well, critics arguably may more objectively assess a work when they are not aware of the authors' identity. Furthermore, those who study an anonymous critique may be more likely to focus on its merits, as opposed to according the review either more or less credence based on the identity of the critic.

In addition to the myriad legitimate motives for engaging in anonymous speech, communications that cannot readily be traced raise serious concerns. Obfuscating identity may be exploited to evade detection when the speaker is engaged in hate speech, libelous speech, or violations of intellectual property rights. Anonymous on-line speech also has been a vexing problem for companies that have been the target of disparaging comments by unnamed authors.

So prevalent has anonymous posting of businesses become that the practice has acquired its own lexicon: "cybersmearing." In one case, an anonymous poster alleged that his employer, the subject of the poster's negative comments, terminated him in retaliation for the postings. He has asserted that Yahoo! improperly divulged his identity, thereby invading his privacy, breaching contractual obligations, and making negligent misrepresentations. *See* Michael Goldhaber, *Cybersmear Pioneer*, National L.J. (July 17, 2000) at A20.

In *Quad/Graphics, Inc. v. Southern Adirondack Library System*, 174 Misc. 2d 291, 664 N.Y.S.2d 225 (Sup. Ct. 1997), a corporation, Quad/Graphics, Inc., sought to compel pre-litigation disclosure of the names of certain of its employees whom it suspected had misappropriated corporate computer resources. The respondent, Southern Adirondack Library System, a cooperative system composed of member libraries operating an electronic information service known as "Library Without Walls," provided free 30-minute Internet access periods.

Quad/Graphics' employees were prohibited from using company computers for personal purposes. The company contended that certain employees nevertheless had used a computer feature during work hours to log onto the company's mainframe computer, access a long distance carrier, and telephone the library, allegedly resulting in considerable long distance telephone charges and the diversion of personnel resources. In denying Quad/Graphics' motion to compel disclosure regarding these employees, the court expressed concern that were Quad/Graphics' application granted, "the door would be open to other similar requests made, for example, by a parent who wishes to learn what a child is reading or viewing on the Internet...." *Id.* at 294, 664 N.Y.S.2d at 228.

Use of such devices as remailers, *see* discussion *infra* at 372, may effectively preclude identification of the posting's author. May the government permissibly require the speaker to accurately identify himself?

In *American Civil Liberties Union v. Miller*, 977 F. Supp. 1228 (N.D. Ga. 1997), a federal district court considered a statute that criminalized Internet transmissions that falsely identified the sender or that utilized trade names or logos without permission. The court granted a preliminary injunction, holding that the statute likely was a content-based regulation on speech that was not narrowly tailored. The statute was constitutionally infirm because it prohibited protected speech, such as the use of false identification to "avoid social ostracism, to prevent discrimination and harassment, and to protect privacy, as well as the use of trade names or logos in non-commercial educational speech, news, and commentary." *Id.* at 1233.

Speech generally may not be conditioned on having to identify oneself. But a somewhat different issue is presented when an aggrieved subject of defamation seeks to ascertain the identity of the speaker in order to redress the offending statement. With respect to defamation actions, the converse of the of and concerning element, the question of identifying the proponent of the speech in issue occurs far more frequently in the digital environment than in other media contexts. When a book is published, the publisher and the author (albeit occasionally under a pseudonym) are prominently displayed. But when an electronic bulletin board posting message appears on the Internet, the true identity of its author may not be readily apparent. Because the originator of content communicated on-line is not always readily discernable, the Internet context arguably presents yet an additional obstacle the defamation plaintiff must overcome to prevail on his claim; that is, identification of the putative defamer.

Plainly, the plaintiff's inability to proceed against a culpable party cannot render another liable for his misdeeds. Nor does a feasible solution lie in ad hoc resolutions of the competing interests at stake. As is the case with other libel claims, deserving plaintiffs, including some intentionally subjected to injury, will be unable to obtain redress. *Cf. Gertz. v. Robert Welch, Inc.*, 418 U.S. 323, 343–44 (1974) (recognizing that many plaintiffs with valid libel claims will be unable to surmount the barrier of the *New York Times* test).

In *Zeran v. America Online, Inc.*, 958 F. Supp. 1124 (E.D. Va. 1997), *aff'd*, 129 F.3d 327 (4th Cir. 1997), *cert. denied*, 524 U.S. 937 (1998), for instance, the plaintiff was besieged with harassing telephone calls after messages appeared on AOL, generated by an unidentified user, purporting to offer for sale by the plaintiff T-shirts, bumper stickers, and other merchandise that trivialized the horrific bombing in Oklahoma City. The FBI was even called in to investigate the identity of the message's author. As the court observed, the fact that liability could not be imposed on the Internet service provider over whose facilities the message was conveyed did not leave the plaintiff without redress; the pivotal inquiry required determining against whom the plaintiff could proceed.

If the posting was placed anonymously or pseudonymously, should the aggrieved subject of content be able to compel disclosure of the identity of the poster? *Columbia Insurance Co. v. Seescandy.com*, 185 F.R.D. 573 (N.D. Cal. 1999), albeit decided in the context of a different cause of action, offers one approach. There, the plaintiff sought to assert claims against anonymous defendants in order to object to the defendants' registration of the plaintiff's trademark as defendants' domain name. The court rejected the plaintiff's request for the issuance of a temporary restraining order until the complaint had been properly served on the defendants. The court balanced the public interest in providing redress with the valuable right to anonymously participate in on-line communications. To reconcile these competing interests, the court formulated a four-pronged test to determine when pre-complaint discovery legitimately could proceed: the plaintiff must (1) identify the missing party with sufficient specificity so that the court could determine that the defendant is the real person or entity who could be sued in federal court; (2) identify all previous steps taken to locate the elusive defendants; (3) establish that the plaintiff's suit would withstand a motion to dismiss; and (4) file a request for discovery with the court, as well as a statement of reasons justifying the specific discovery requested. *Id.* at 578–80.

Will this approach likely be applied to compel disclosure of information content providers in the context of libel claims? A Miami state court judge recently ordered America Online and Yahoo! to divulge the identity of the author of an anonymous and allegedly libelous message. The unnamed person had posted messages under such names as "justthefactsjack," indicating that the plaintiff had engaged in criminal conduct. *See* Chris Gaither, *Judge Orders AOL, Yahoo! To Identify Online Writer*, Miami Herald (May 26, 2000) at A(1)(1). The judge's views about shielding the identity of anonymous speakers were quite clear: "Give them anonymity and nothing holds them back. That's why the Ku Klux Klan wears hoods." *Id.* Some privacy advocates criticized the ruling; others countered that anonymity promotes the placing of irresponsible content on the Web. *See id.*

How should these interests be reconciled in the sphere of digital communications? One court commented:

> With the rise of the Internet has come the ability to commit certain tortious acts, such as defamation, copyright infringement, and trademark infringement, entirely on-line. The tortfeasor can act pseudonymously or anonymously and may give fictitious or incomplete identifying information. Parties who have been injured by these acts are likely to find themselves chasing the tortfeasor from Internet Service Provider (ISP) to ISP, with little or no hope of actually discovering the identity of the tortfeasor.
>
> In such cases the traditional reluctance for permitting filings against John Doe defendants or fictitious names and the traditional enforcement of strict compliance with service requirements should be tempered by the need to provide injured parties with a forum in which they may seek redress for grievances. However, this need must be balanced against the legitimate and valuable right to participate in online forums anonymously or pseudonymously. People are permitted to interact pseudonymously and anonymously with each other so long as those acts are not in violation of the law. This ability to speak one's mind without the burden of the other party knowing all the facts about one's identity can foster open communication and robust debate. Furthermore, it permits persons to obtain information relevant to a sensitive or intimate condition without fear of embarrassment. People who have committed no wrong should be able to participate online without fear that someone who wishes to harass or embarrass them can file a frivolous lawsuit and thereby gain the power of the court's order to discover their identity.

*Columbia Ins. Co. v. Seescandy.com*, 185 F.R.D. at 578 (footnote omitted).

# Kenneth L. COHEN v. John DOES 1 through 100

Circuit Court of Loudoun County, Virginia
No. 99-5116, 50 Va. Cir. 202, 1999 WL 1419239
August 17, 1999

HORNE, J.

This case came before the Court on the motion of defendants, collectively designated as John Does 1 through 100, by way of a special appearance, to quash a subpoena duces tecum addressed to America Online. The subpoena seeks subscriber information, documents, and communications in connection with a lawsuit presently pending in the State of Louisiana. Plaintiff has obtained Letters Rogatory from the Civil District Court for the Parish of Orleans, State of Louisiana, Division "L" for persons identified, inter alia, by ten e-mail addresses.

In the Louisiana litigation, Kenneth L. Cohen has claimed damages against "John Does 1 through 100" for alleged defamation through the use of an Internet message board. Plaintiff first sought to obtain information concerning the persons posting such alleged defamatory statements from Yahoo!, Inc., an Internet search engine. He contends that "Yahoo" reported to him that persons having an account with America Online did the postings. America Online is an Internet service provider located in Loudoun County, Virginia....

Production and inspection of the documents sought pursuant to the Louisiana commission is governed by the same procedures applicable to an action at law pending in the Commonwealth. §8.01-411, Code of Virginia. Upon the instant motion to quash, the Court has not considered matters raised by the defendants relating to privacy and to a claim of a First Amendment right to anonymity. *See McIntyre v. Ohio Elections Commission*, 514 U.S. 334 (1994). It is unclear whether such issues were raised at the time of the hearing before the Court in Louisiana. Although that is not the exclusive forum for resolving privilege claims in the instant case, it is the most appropriate. Otherwise, this Court would be required to address matters going to the very heart of the claims in ancillary proceedings: that is, are these defendants shielded from claims of defamation by reason of a privilege arising out of the publication of documents over the Internet?...

In accordance with the Rule 4.9(c) [of the Rules of the Supreme Court of Virginia,]... in addition to relevancy, there are three requirements antecedent to the issuance of the subpoena. They are a written request directed to the clerk, the existence of a pending action, and notice to counsel of record or to a party not represented by counsel.

Counsel for the plaintiff asserts that without the information requested, the parties cannot be identified. Such information is singularly relevant to the pursuit of the action and is reasonably calculated to lead to the discovery of admissible evidence. Rule 4:1(b)(1), Rules of Supreme Court of Virginia. The talisman for judging the instant request is the badge of relevancy. This is what the Rules mandate. By analogy, the test to be utilized by the Court in evaluating production of subscriber information in criminal cases is that of relevancy. §19.2-70.3, Code of Virginia....

[T]he Court must address the issue of notice. It is imperative that proper notice be given to each John Doe defendant who is identified by user name, "other identity," or by e-mail address in the instant subpoena. From the presence of such John Doe defendants by special appearance, such notice may be inferred. However, the Court will require

America Online, on or before September 1, 1999, to furnish to the Court a certificate that notice meeting the minimum requirements of Rule 4:9(c) has been given to those subscribers who can be identified from the subpoena request. It should include with such certificate a statement concerning the details as to the method by which such notice was given. Simultaneously with the filing of such statement, America Online shall file the requested documents with the clerk of this Court under seal. It shall furnish to counsel notice of such filing.

Plaintiff should furnish sufficient copies of the pleadings and papers is this cause (Law 22357, Circuit Court of Loudoun County), as well as the costs of any postage necessary, in order that they may be mailed to each of the subscribers to be notified.

Upon the filing of such documents, any one or more of the defendants may file an objection to the form of the notice given. Such objections shall be ruled on promptly by the Court at the request of any of the parties. . . .

## Notes and Questions

1.  Under what circumstances, if any, is it appropriate to compel a service provider or site host to disclose the identity of an anonymous or pseudonymous poster? Does the ostensible motivation for the posting or the nature of its content affect the analysis? For example, what if the posting divulges a trade secret or contains a threat to commit a violent act? Is the determination affected by whether the party seeking the disclosure is a governmental official?

2.  As global distribution of content increases, media defendants are becoming more conversant with distinctions not only in substantive libel law, but in foreign procedural law as well. In the Republic of Ireland, for instance, litigation practice does not contemplate the exchange of witness lists prior to the commencement of trial, as is the routine practice in the United States. Therefore, a media defendant may face, without advance preparation, a progression of witnesses who purportedly recognized an unnamed plaintiff from having read or viewed the allegedly defamatory statement. Noted Dublin solicitor Michael Kealey has commented that "[t]his approach facilitates 'trial by ambush.' Defendants, in particular, can often only anticipate the broad outlines of a plaintiff's case. With the burden of proof resting on a publisher, an unscrupulous plaintiff can often provide an innocent explanation of apparently damning evidence for the first time at trial, thereby affording his opposition little time or opportunity to check its accuracy." Michael Kealey, *Pre-Publication Review in the Republic of Ireland*, McCann FitzGerald. Under certain "exceptional circumstances," however, a court may order the unnamed plaintiff to specify in his pleading the identity of such witnesses.

# Defamatory Import

## 1.  The Per Se/Per Quod Distinction

The term "slander *per se*" relates to the nature of the charges made. Certain categories of statements have been characterized as slander *per se*: the imputation of crime; allegations that the plaintiff contracted a loathsome disease; and allegations that tend to injure the plaintiff in his business, trade, profession, office, or calling. *See* W. Page Keeton, *et al.*, *Prosser and Keeton on the Law of Torts*, § 112 at 788 (5th ed. 1984). An additional category, the imputation of unchastity, also has been recognized by state statutes and common law. *See* Restatement (Second) of Torts § 572, cmt. c (1977).

Imputation of a crime implicates the subject of the defamation in a potential criminal prosecution. The crime with which the subject of the defamation has been charged generally must be an offense that involves moral turpitude, possibly with an indictment or subjecting one to infamous or disgraceful punishment. Thus, a statement that a person has been imprisoned, committed a murder, or perjured himself generally is slanderous *per se.*

Characterizing statements that a person carried a loathsome disease as slander *per se* has its apparent origin in the presumption that such persons would have been shunned within the community. "Loathsome" diseases, therefore, do not consist of merely annoying or discomfiting illnesses or injury; tuberculosis, for example, generally is not deemed to be a loathsome disease, even though it is communicable. Similarly, a New York court has held that a statement about a professional person who was erroneously described as suffering from cancer did not import defamation. *Golub v. Enquirer/Star Group, Inc.*, 89 N.Y.2d 1074, 681 N.E.2d 1282 (1997). Typical examples of loathsome diseases instead include venereal diseases and leprosy.

Perhaps mindful that tradesmen and merchants depend upon their reputations for their livelihood, defaming one in his profession or business may constitute a slander *per se*. To come within the slander *per se* category, the challenged statement must go to the plaintiff's professional character, as opposed to more general traits. Thus, impugning a professional's honesty, skill, fitness, or financial acumen may give rise to a viable claim.

Unchastity also has been regarded by certain American legislatures and courts as actionable as slander *per se*. As to whether the gender of the plaintiff bears on the issue, a New York appellate court has stated that "the notion that while the imputation of sexual immorality to a woman is defamatory *per se*, but is not so with respect to a man has no place in modern jurisprudence. Such a distinction, having its basis in a gender-based classification, would violate constitutional precepts." *See Rejent v. Liberation Publications, Inc.*, 197 A.D.2d 240, 611 N.Y.S.2d 866 (App. Div. 1994).

Inclusion of unchastity as a category of slander *per se*, regardless of the plaintiff's gender, appears anachronistic. "There is no apparent reason why it should be slanderous *per se* to say that a woman has had sexual intercourse with her fiancé, but not slanderous *per se* to say that she has the intellect of a two-year-old or is habitually filthy and unkempt." Robert D. Sack, *Sack on Defamation: Libel, Slander, and Related Problems* § 2.8.2 at 2-91 (3d ed. 2000). Because community mores about what constitutes appropriate sexual conduct vary dramatically, statements relating to such conduct may be tested if they are published extensively, particularly over the World Wide Web, which effectively disseminates such statements internationally.

Courts sometimes classify a "libel *per se*" statement as one where the defamatory import is apparent from the face of the words themselves. "Libel *per quod*" statements are those that evince a defamatory meaning from the extrinsic knowledge of those to whom such words are published. "Libel *per quod*" also may refer to libel that arises from the context of the words. The significance of the libel *per se* category is that under the law of the relevant jurisdiction, the plaintiff may dispense with the requisite showing of proof of any actual harm to reputation. The law effectively recognizes that in these cases proof of the defamation itself establishes the existence of damage. All other defamatory words are actionable as libel or slander *per quod*, which constitute viable claims only upon a showing of proof of "special" damages. "Special" in this context means that the claim is supported by specific evidentiary proof that the plaintiff has suffered harm to his reputation.

The long-term viability of the distinction is unclear. Missouri, for example, has abandoned the *per se/per quod* distinction. The Missouri Supreme Court relegated the dichotomy to a "rule of the past [that] creates unjustifiable inequities for plaintiffs and defendants alike.... [P]laintiffs need not concern themselves with whether the defamation was *per se* or *per quod*, nor with whether special damages exist, but must prove actual damages in all cases. *Nazeri v. Missouri Valley College*, 860 S.W.2d 303, 313 (Mo. 1993) (footnote omitted).

While reported decisional law on Internet defamation has not addressed the *per se/ per quod* distinction, one can envision disputes arising over the availability of extrinsic facts that rendered the statement defamatory, and over the extent to which such information was accessed.

---

## 2. Defamatory Import in the Internet Context

To be actionable, the challenged statement must be opprobrious; mere slights will not suffice to sustain a claim.

> It would be highly impolitic to hold all language, wounding the feelings and affecting unfavorably the health and ability to labor, of another, a ground of action; for that would be to make the right of action depend often upon whether the sensibilities of a person spoken of are easily excited or otherwise; his strength of mind to disregard abusive, insulting remarks concerning him; and his physical strength and ability to bear them.

*Terwilliger v. Wands*, 17 N.Y. 54, 60 (1858). As a general matter, defamatory matter is "that which tends to injure 'reputation' in the popular sense; to diminish the esteem, respect, good will or confidence in which the plaintiff is held, or to excite adverse, derogatory or unpleasant feelings or opinions against him." W. Page Keeton, *et al., Prosser and Keeton on the Law of Torts,* § 111 at 773.

The context of the utterance bears upon the analysis of defamatory import. The Restatement (Second) of Torts at § 577 cmt. 15, suggests that a tavern owner would be liable if defamatory graffiti remained in a bathroom stall a single hour after its discovery. Half a century ago, in *Hellar v. Bianco*, 111 Cal. App. 2d 424, 244 P.2d 757 (Cal. App. 1952), Isabelle Hellar alleged that the defendants, who were the proprietors of a public tavern, did not promptly remove libelous matter from the men's restroom in the tavern. The graffiti indicated that Ms. Hellar "was an unchaste woman who indulged in illicit amatory ventures." *Id.* at 425. Ms. Hellar's husband called the tavern and demanded that the bartender, then in charge of the tavern, remove the defamatory writing. 111 Cal. App.2d at 426, 244 P.2d at 758. The court sustained the plaintiff's claim for a jury to determine whether, after knowledge that the graffiti existed, the tavern proprietors[3] negli-

---

3. The conduct was imputed to the tavern proprietors. *Id.*

gently permitted the graffiti "for so long a time as to be chargeable with its republication...." *Id.* at 427, 244 P.2d at 759.[4] To what extent might the *Hellar* court have been
influenced by the fact that the graffiti in issue presumably was placed there by invitees
of the defendants? *See Scott v. Hull,* 22 Ohio App.2d 141, 142, 259 N.E.2d 160, 161 (Ct.
App. 3d Dist. 1970).

In *Fogg v. Boston & L.R. Corp.,* 148 Mass. 513, 20 N.E. 109 (Mass. 1889), the defamatory matter was placed on a bulletin board maintained for public view by the defendant
railroad in its station. The court looked to whether there was evidence that the publication was made by the defendant's authority, ratified by it, or made by one of its agents
in the course of the business in which he was employed.

> [W]here liability is found to exist it is predicated upon actual publication by
> the defendant or on the defendant's ratification of a publication by another....
> Liability to respond in damages for the publication of a libel must be predi-
> cated on a positive act, on something done by the person sought to be charged,
> malfeasance in the case of an intentional defamatory publication and misfea-
> sance in the case of a negligent defamatory publication. Nonfeasance, on the
> other hand, is not a predicate to liability.

*Scott v. Hull,* 22 Ohio App.2d at 141–44, 259 N.E.2d at 161–62.

The "common law of washrooms" does not unwaveringly follow the Restatement's
suggestion. Courts have recognized "the steep discount that readers apply to such
statements and the high cost of hourly repaintings of bathroom stalls." *Tacket v. General Motors Corp.,* 836 F.2d 1042, 1046 (7th Cir. 1987) (citation omitted). While these
cases ostensibly analyze the publication element of the cause of action, their significance lies in their focus on the context of the challenged statement to assess its defamatory import.

Chat rooms and bulletin boards similarly are often the repository of a wide range of
casual, emotive, and imprecise speech. Rigid application of libel laws to comments
made in such an environment might well impose a "burden of constant vigilance
[that] greatly exceeds the benefits to be had." *See id.* Some commentators have opined
that the standard for determining what constitutes defamatory import should be different for on-line communications. *See, e.g.,* Mike Godwin, *Libel Law: Let It Die,* Wired
(Mar. 1996) <http://www.wired.com/wire/archives/4.03/letitdie.htm> (arguing that
defamation liability in the Internet arena is unnecessary because the Internet affords
such readily accessible and meaningful opportunities to rebut offensive speech). In addition to defensive theories under the Communications Decency Act, 47 U.S.C.A.
§ 230 (West Supp. 2000), and as articulated by the New York Court of Appeals in *Lunney v. Prodigy Services Co.,* 94 N.Y.2d 242, 723 N.E.2d 539 (1999), *cert. denied,* 120
S.Ct. 1832 (2000), a host's failure to monitor the chat and failure to remove the offensive statement upon notice and demand to do so may be characterized as constituting
no more than non-actionable nonfeasance. *See, e.g., Scott v. Hull,* 22 Ohio App.2d at
144, 259 N.E.2d at 162.

Further, the recipients of such statements do not necessarily attribute the same level
of credence to the statements than they would accord to statements made in other contexts. Note the discussion by the U.S. District Court for the Northern District of California of the libel plaintiff's contention in *Nicosia v. De Rooy,* 72 F. Supp. 2d 1093 (N.D.

---

4. Curiously, the putative "republication" was premised upon its display to Ms. Heller's husband
and the constable and others who went to the tavern at Ms. Heller's behest to investigate the matter.

Cal. 1999), that statements published on a web-site are a "condensed Internet version of a full-length book," and thus "are not quickly produced unconsidered cybertrash...." *Id.* at 1101–02 (citation omitted). The district court rejected the argument, however, on the ground that it did "not fundamentally alter the tenor of [the defendant's] articles." *Id.*

---

# Gerald NICOSIA v. Diane DE ROOY

United States District Court, Northern District of California
No. C98-3029 MMC, 72 F. Supp. 2d 1093
July 7, 1999

CHESNEY, District Judge.

### ...BACKGROUND

Plaintiff Gerald Nicosia ("Nicosia"), a California resident, brings the instant action for slander and libel in connection with statements De Rooy published about Nicosia on her web-site. According to the Complaint, De Rooy has called Nicosia a killer, an embezzler, a criminal, a fraud, a perjurer, and a liar, and, in particular, De Rooy has stated[, *inter alia*]:

> Gerald Nicosia is to the Beats (and Jan) what Charles Manson was to the hippies. Virtually everyone I've interviewed over the 17 months, including disinterested third parties, has said the same thing: Gerald Nicosia killed Jan Kerouac.

> [Nicosia used a Kerouac seminar] as a publicity stunt, in an effort to keep the public from noticing his embezzlement of at least $33,000 from Jan Kerouac's heirs.

> When I began my research 18 months ago, I had no idea I would discover that Gerry Nicosia's [sic] is a self-serving fraud and criminal....

> I thought [Nicosia] was maybe mentally unstable, from the stress of his crusade, perhaps. But I had to cross a line at some point into believing he was simply, deliberately, lying, including perjuring himself in court documents I'd gotten copies of.

> I have personal knowledge of the underhanded and deceitful practices of these two men. Although there is no controversy around the Jack Kerouac Estate, and his papers are in no danger whatsoever, Joe Grant and Gerald Nicosia persist in telling these lies because they are embittered believers in their own publicity.

> ...Jan is dead, but she is far from being laid to rest. Many people have unpublished points of view relating to Jan Kerouac's unfortunate association with Gerald Nicosia. These viewpoints clearly reveal a man with Napoleonic aspirations to conquer the literary kingdom; a man who believes he is more ethical than most people; a man who refuses to admit his own desires for money and fame; a man who has alienated, betrayed, or lied to everyone in the Beat community.

> [Nicosia] is far less well known for his biography of Jack Kerouac than he is for his role, many believe, as the Svengali who manipulated Kerouac's daughter,

Jan Two years after the death of Jan Kerouac, hardly a week goes by when Nicosia doesn't invoke the dead woman's name to shore up a sagging writing career.

Many people have unpublished points of view relating to Jan Kerouac's unfortunate association with Gerald Nicosia. These viewpoints clearly reveal a man with Napoleonic aspirations to conquer the literary kingdom....

Nicosia also alleges that De Rooy implied that he had forged a letter from Jan Kerouac and accused Nicosia of delivering a "heartless" speech about Jan at her memorial service.

## DISCUSSION

...Whether a statement is an assertion of fact or opinion is a question of law for the court. *Dworkin v. Hustler Magazine, Inc.*, 867 F.2d 1188, 1193 (9th Cir. 1989); *Baker v. Los Angeles Herald Examiner*, 42 Cal.3d 254, 260, 228 Cal.Rptr. 206, 209 (1986); *Gaeta v. Delta Airlines, Inc.*, 1997 WL 655953, at *4 (N.D. Cal. 1997). Pure opinions—"those that do not imply facts capable of being proved true or false"—are protected by the First Amendment. *Partington v. Bugliosi*, 56 F.3d 1147, 1153 fn. 10 (9th Cir. 1995). Assertions of fact and statements that "may imply a false assertion of fact," however, are not protected. *Id.* (quotes, citations, ellipses omitted). To determine whether a statement implies an assertion of fact, the Ninth Circuit applies the following three-part test:

We examine the totality of the circumstances in which it was made. First, we look at the statement in its broad context, which includes the general tenor of the entire work, the subject of the statement, the setting, and the format of the work. Next we turn to the specific context and content of the statement, analyzing the extent of figurative or hyperbolic language used and the reasonable expectations of the audience in that particular situation. Finally, we inquire whether the statement itself is sufficiently factual to be susceptible of being proved true or false.

*Underwager v. Channel 9 Australia*, 69 F.3d 361, 366 (9th Cir. 1995).

### a. Broad Context

Following the test articulated in *Underwager*, the Court first considers the general context of the allegedly defamatory statements. Nicosia does not dispute that De Rooy's statements were published on her personal web-site, and through Internet discussion groups, as part of a heated debate concerning a bitter legal dispute. Nicosia has fully engaged De Rooy in this debate.

In this context, readers are less likely to view statements as assertions of fact. *See Underwager*, at 366–67 (audience would likely view comments made in context of heated debate as "spirited critique" and "would expect emphatic language on both sides"); *Information Control v. Genesis One Computer Corp.*, 611 F.2d 781, 784 (9th Cir. 1980) (in context of legal dispute, "the audience may anticipate efforts by the parties to persuade others to their position by use of epithets, fiery rhetoric or hyperbole, [and thus] language which generally might be considered as statements of fact may well assume the character of statements of opinion.").

Nicosia argues that, despite the controversial subject matter of the debate, the general tenor of De Rooy's articles suggests that her statements are assertions of fact. Nicosia posits that words like "19 months of research," "first-hand experience," "findings," "definitive overview," "discover," and "truth" indicate assertions of fact, not opinion. These words, however, were not included in the articles containing the alleged defamation, but instead were contained in articles published after Nicosia filed the instant lawsuit. This post-litigation language cannot be considered part of the general context of the pre-litigation articles.

De Rooy does state in a pre-litigation article that the piece is just a "condensed Internet version of a full-length book." While this language suggests that, as Nicosia states, the articles "are not quickly produced unconsidered cybertrash," it does not fundamentally alter the tenor of De Rooy's articles.

### b. Specific Statements

The second prong of the totality of circumstances test considers the specific context and content of the allegedly defamatory statements, which includes the extent of figurative and hyperbolic language and the reasonable expectations of the readers. Of particular importance is the principal that "when an author outlines the facts available to him, thus making it clear that the challenged statements represent his own interpretation of those facts and leaving the reader free to draw his own conclusions, those statements are generally protected by the First Amendment." *Partington,* at 1156–57. The third prong of the test considers whether the statements are susceptible of being proved true or false. *Underwager,* at 366. In light of the general context discussed, the Court applies the second and third prongs of the test to each allegedly defamatory statement contained in Nicosia's complaint to determine whether such statement implies an assertion of fact.

#### 1) Allegations of Crimes

De Rooy's articles contain accusations that Nicosia committed murder, embezzlement, fraud, and perjury. The Court addresses each in turn.

##### a) Murder

...Nicosia argues that De Rooy's charge that he killed Jan Kerouac is an actionable assertion of fact. The disclosed, underlying facts, however, reveal that Shank understood De Rooy was using hyperbolic and figurative language, that De Rooy was merely expressing her opinion that Nicosia contributed to Jan's declining health by involving her in protracted litigation, and that De Rooy was not literally accusing Nicosia of murder. De Rooy's articles repeatedly criticized Nicosia for involving Jan in litigation while her health was failing. For example, De Rooy quoted Jan's biographer as writing that "Some, like her father's long-time friend, Beat poet Allen Ginsberg, suggested that she was killing herself by fighting an unnecessary battle...Part of Ginsberg's complaint about the lawsuit was that Gerry Nicosia and Tom Brill, Jan's lawyer in California, were taking advantage of a sick and vulnerable individual." In this context, Shank would understand that De Rooy was not literally accusing Nicosia of murder, but only alleging that the litigation contributed to Jan's decline in health.[6]...

##### b) Embezzlement

De Rooy wrote that Nicosia used a Kerouac seminar "as a publicity stunt, in an effort to keep the public from noticing his embezzlement of at least $33,000 from Jan Kerouac's heirs. De Rooy argues that the allegation is based on disclosed facts surrounding

---

6. Nicosia does not dispute that whether a course of action contributes to a decline in a person's health is a matter of opinion.

Nicosia's sale of Jan Kerouac's archives to the Bancroft library, and his licensing of Jack Kerouac's name to Levi Straus company. Nicosia responds that De Rooy failed to disclose any underlying facts, and to the extent any facts were disclosed, De Rooy omitted reference to the accounting Nicosia provided in relation to allegedly embezzled proceeds.

Nicosia argues that the embezzlement accusation must be read in isolation from De Rooy's other articles because the news group posting which contained the allegation did not include any underlying facts. However, the news group posting directed readers to specific articles on De Rooy's web-site and provided a hyperlink for immediate access to such articles.

These articles were at least as connected to the news group posting as the back page of a newspaper is connected to the front. Thus, the Court considers the articles part of the context of the embezzlement accusation.

In the articles, De Rooy provides the underlying basis for the embezzlement accusation. For example, she published a letter written by Jan's brother which stated in part:

> After sending the Bancroft Library in Berkeley notification that in the event of a sale of Jan's archives, 10 percent would go to Gerry (as per the codicil) and the remaining should be sent to the General Personal Representative to allot as needed, this notification was ignored. The sale happened. I called Gerry and asked him "Did you intend to call John or I?" No, he did not. "Where is the remaining 90?" He had it all. As this was not his money to keep, I call this embezzlement.
>
> [Nicosia] received $20,000 for the sale of Jan Kerouac's archive to the Bancroft Library at Berkeley, and $11,000 for licensing Jack Kerouac's name to Levi Straus. His first financial accounting to the heirs for these deals reveals that he has spent every dime of these proceeds, these "benefits Jan intended" for her heirs.

Similar references to the alleged misdeeds are contained throughout the article. Nicosia does not dispute that he sold Jan's archives to the Bancroft Library, licensed Jack Kerouac's name to Levi Strauss, and kept the proceeds from both transactions. Nor does Nicosia dispute that Jan's heirs filed suit against Nicosia for disgorgement alleging that Nicosia is only entitled to 10% of the proceeds. Nicosia merely argues that "De Rooy never discusses anywhere the fact that Nicosia did provide a full accounting of the money is [sic] supposedly took." This argument is not well-taken. First, in light of the language quoted above, it appears that De Rooy actually did mention an accounting relating to the subject transaction. Second, the record indicates that Nicosia provided this accounting only after a court ordered him to do so. As such, any omission with regard to the accounting would not be material to the accusation of embezzlement.

The Court finds that De Rooy adequately disclosed the facts underlying her conclusion that Nicosia embezzled money from Jan Kerouac's heirs. Accusations of criminal activity, like other statements, are not actionable if the underlying facts are disclosed. . . .

### c) Fraud, Criminal, Acting Illegally

. . . De Rooy argues that the statements accusing Nicosia of being a "fraud," a "criminal" and acting illegally are rhetorical hyperbole, and even if taken seriously, are still not actionable because she disclosed the underlying facts. Nicosia argues that De Rooy failed to disclose any underlying facts.

As discussed, De Rooy's articles are considered part of the context in which the news group's posting must be read. Like the embezzlement accusation discussed above, the "fraud" and "criminal" accusations would be understood by the average reader as referring to the sale of Jan Kerouac's archive, and the licensing of Jack Kerouac's name.... In light of the many criticisms, the average reader would understand "acted illegally" to be a hyperbolic expression intended to convey that De Rooy believed Nicosia had improperly challenged Jack Kerouac's estate. Such an assertion is too loose and hyperbolic to be susceptible of being proved true or false. In addition, De Rooy through her examples has revealed the underlying basis for her opinion, allowing readers to reach their own conclusions....

### d) Perjury

...De Rooy argues that she disclosed the facts underlying the perjury accusation. De Rooy, however, has not directed the Court to any statements in the relevant articles identifying the documents containing the alleged perjury or otherwise disclosing her basis for believing Nicosia lied in such documents.

Nicosia argues that De Rooy's failure to disclose renders the perjury accusation actionable. To support this contention, Nicosia relies on *Milkovich v. Lorain Journal Co.* 497 U.S. 1, 110 S.Ct. 2695, 111 L.Ed.2d 1 (1990). In *Milkovich*, the Supreme Court found that the defendants' statements accusing the plaintiff of lying under oath at a hearing were not "loose, figurative or hyperbolic," and were sufficiently factual to be susceptible to being proved true or false. *Id.*, 497 U.S. at 21–22, 110 S.Ct. at 2707. De Rooy posits that *Milkovich* is distinguishable from the instant case because, unlike *Milkovich*, De Rooy disclosed the facts underlying her accusation of perjury. For support, De Rooy cites *Phantom Touring, Inc. v. Affiliated Publications,* 953 F.2d 724, 730 (1st Cir. 1992), where the First Circuit distinguished *Milkovich* on these grounds. De Rooy's argument must fail as the basic premise is flawed—De Rooy did not identify the documents or otherwise disclose the basis for her conclusion that Nicosia had committed perjury.

De Rooy also argues that she sufficiently couched the perjury allegation in equivocal language—"I thought," "perhaps," "had to cross the line into believing"—so as to signal to the reader that what follows is opinion. While De Rooy's cautious phrasing is considered among the totality of circumstances, it is not sufficient to dispel the otherwise plain assertion of fact. *See Milkovich*, 497 U.S. at 18–19, 110 S.Ct. at 2705–06 (phrases like "in my opinion" and "I think" do not dispel defamatory implications). In addition, any mitigating effect this language might have is offset by De Rooy's inclusion of the phrase "in court documents I'd gotten copies of." This wording suggests that De Rooy based her conclusion on fact....

### 2) Allegations of Dishonesty

...Nicosia argues that De Rooy's accusations of dishonesty imply assertions of fact which were never disclosed. The record, however, is replete with examples where De Rooy identifies specific representations by Nicosia and then reveals her basis for believing that such representations are inaccurate or false. Indeed, an important, if not the primary focus of De Rooy's articles, is her disagreement with Nicosia's claims that he is carrying out the wishes of Jan Kerouac and that the Sampas family is threatening Jack Kerouac's estate. In discussing these matters, De Rooy provides facts, which Nicosia does not challenge, underlying her allegations that Nicosia is not telling the truth. De Rooy's readers could draw their own conclusions from the material presented, especially considering that De Rooy included Nicosia's contrary views in her articles.

Moreover, in the context of the heated debate on the Internet, readers are more likely to understand accusations of lying as figurative, hyperbolic expressions. *See Faltas v. State Newspaper*, 928 F. Supp. 637, 646–648 (D.S.C. 1996) (words "lie" and "liar" considered "hyperbole," in part because written in context of "highly controversial topic"), *aff'd*, 155 F.3d 557, 1998 WL 414238 (4th Cir. 1998). Indeed, the Ninth Circuit has found in a similar context that "the term 'lying' applies to a spectrum of untruths including white lies, partial truths, misinterpretation, and deception[,]and [a]s a result, the statement is no more than nonactionable rhetorical hyperbole, a vigorous epithet used by those who considered [the appellant's] position extremely unreasonable." *Underwager*, 69 F.3d at 367 (citations, internal quotations omitted)....

### 3) Other Allegations

De Rooy accused Nicosia of being a "manipulative" "Svengali," with "Napoleonic aspirations," who carried on an "exploitative business relationship" with Jan Kerouac and gave a "heartless speech" at Jan's funeral. De Rooy also makes statements, to which Nicosia objects, regarding one of Jan's letters and an application to trademark Jack Kerouac's name.

#### a) Manipulative Svengali

...Nicosia argues that De Rooy's accusation that he manipulated Jan Kerouac is or implies an assertion of fact. Manipulation, however, refers to subjective motivations and personality traits, which are not provable as true or false. *See Underwager*, [69 F.3d] at 367 (finding statements reflecting motivations and personality not provable). Further demonstrating the nonfactual character of De Rooy's accusation is the colorful, figurative language it contains and the controversial debate in which it appears....

#### c) Exploitative Business Relationship; Improper Author/Agent Agreement

...Nicosia argues that De Rooy's accusation that Nicosia had an "exploitative business relationship" with Jan is or implies an assertion of fact. Such a statement, however, is merely an evaluative judgment which is not provable true or false. *See PETA v. Bobby Berosini, Ltd.*, 111 Nev. 615, 895 P.2d 1269, 1275 (1995) (citing W. Page Keeton, *Prosser and Keeton on Torts*, 814 (5th Ed. 1984)) ("evaluative" judgments about the quality of a person's behavior, such as statements that plaintiff's actions were cruel or abusive are protected as a matter of law).

The Court finds that the language "exploitative business relationship"...is not and does not imply an assertion of fact, [and] is not actionable....

Nicosia also argues that De Rooy's accusation that Jan never signed the author/agent agreement is an assertion of fact. In contrast to the term "exploitative," whether or not Jan signed the agreement is provable as true or false—a copy of the alleged agreement would suffice to establish this assertion. In addition, De Rooy's statement regarding the author/agent agreement is not hyperbolic, or figurative, nor is it based on undisputed, disclosed facts.

The Court finds the allegation...indicating that Jan did not sign the author/agent agreement constitutes an assertion of fact....

#### d) Heartless Eulogy

De Rooy wrote that Nicosia spoke "heartlessly" against Jan Kerouac at her funeral. Nicosia argues that accusing him of presenting a "heartless" eulogy is or implies an assertion of fact. Whether a person speaks heartlessly is an evaluative judgment not provable true or false. Additionally, this statement appears in the context of a controversial debate on the Internet....

[T]he Court finds that Nicosia has failed to plead actual malice with the required specificity, and hereby GRANTS De Rooy's motion to dismiss for failure to state a claim. For the reasons expressed in the following section, leave to amend would be futile....

---

# Falsity

## 1. Substantial Truth

It is axiomatic that truth is a defense to a claim of defamation. Under American law, at least when matters of public interest are involved, the burden of proving that the press published a false statement rests with the plaintiff; the media defendant may defend against the claim on the ground that the utterance was "substantially true." A bedrock principle of American libel jurisprudence is the notion that "[a] rule compelling the critic of official conduct to guarantee the truth of all his factual assertions—and to do so on pain of libel judgments virtually unlimited in amount— leads to a comparable 'self-censorship.' Allowance of the defense of truth, with the burden of proving it on the defendant, does not mean that only false speech will be deterred." *New York Times Co. v. Sullivan*, 376 U.S. 254, 279 (1964) (footnote omitted).

In 1986, the Supreme Court, in a 5–4 decision, proclaimed that the "common-law presumption that defamatory speech is false cannot stand when a plaintiff seeks damages against a media defendant for speech of public concern." *Philadelphia Newspapers, Inc. v. Hepps*, 475 U.S. 767, 777 (1986). The *Hepps* decision evinces judicial regard for the notion that in order to achieve adequate protection, even some false speech must be protected to some degree.

The American judiciary has repeatedly acknowledged the difficulties of adducing legal proofs that the alleged libel was true in all its factual particulars. *See, e.g., Post Publ'g Co. v. Hallam*, 59 F. 530, 540 (6th Cir. 1893). Even when the substance of the speech is true, imposing the burden of proving it as such on the defendant may perniciously deter speech, "because of doubt whether it can be proved in court or fear of the expense of having to do so. [Publishers will] tend to make only statements which 'steer far wider of the unlawful zone.' The rule thus dampens the vigor and limits the variety of public debate." *New York Times Co. v. Sullivan*, 376 U.S. at 279 (citation omitted).

Thus, the common law of libel overlooks minor inaccuracies to determine whether the gist or the sting of the libelous charge is justified. *See, e.g., Masson v. New Yorker Magazine, Inc.*, 501 U.S. 496, 516–17 (1991). Media defendants are protected from liability for publishing false "details that, while not trivial, would not if corrected have altered the picture that the true facts paint." *Haynes v. Alfred A. Knopf, Inc.*, 8 F.3d 1222, 1228 (7th Cir. 1993).

Note that the majority view in *Hepps* confined its holding to media defendants, reserving judgment as to whether the rule it enumerated would apply to non-media defendants. Where is the appropriate line between media and non-media entities? As today's television programming runs the gamut from news broadcasts to weekly news magazines to documentaries to docudramas and informercials, which entities may reasonably be said to be engaged in media enterprises? Is one who launches a web-site and imparts newsworthy information a journalist? *See* discussion *supra* at 19.

International distribution of content via the Internet has profound implications on these issues. Disparities in applicable standards of fault and falsity, among other issues, create vexing concerns for media entities that routinely publish content on-line for global dissemination. "The Internet is eroding the barriers of communications. As a consequence, U.S. and foreign defamation laws are bound to clash." George B. Delta and Jeffrey H. Matsurra, *Law of the Internet,* § 7.04[D] at 7-47 (2000-2 Supp.). *Compare, e.g., Zeran v. America Online, Inc.,* 129 F.3d 327 (4th Cir. 1997), *cert. denied,* 524 U.S. 937 (1998) (applying American law to hold Internet service provider immune from liability relating to allegedly defamatory content), *with Godfrey v. Demon Internet,* [1999] E.M.L.R. 542 (Q.B. 1999) (applying English law to hold Internet service provider was not immune from liability relating to allegedly defamatory content).

American libel law differs significantly from English libel law, for example. Under English law, the plaintiff merely bears the burden of establishing that the words refer to him, were published by the defendant, and bear a defamatory meaning. *See* 28 Lord Hailsham of St. Marylebone, ed., *Halsbury's Laws of England* 9 (4th ed. 1979) (cited by *Ellis v. Time, Inc.,* 1997 WL 863267 at *13 (D.D.C. 1997)). Unlike the law in the United States, English libel law presumes that defamatory words are false and places the burden of proof on the defendant to prove that the statements in issue are true. *See id.* at *12–13; *McFarlane v. Sheridan Square Press,* 91 F.3d 1501, 1512 (D.D.C. 1996). Another distinction is that under English law, the libel defendant may be held liable even for statements he honestly believed to be true and published without negligence. *See Matusevitch v. Telnikoff,* 877 F. Supp. 1, 4 (D.D.C. 1995) (quoting Sir Brian Neill, ed., *Duncan and Neill on Defamation* 51 (1983)), *aff'd,* 159 F.3d 636 (D.D.C. 1998). Winston Churchill once remarked, "The United States is a land of free speech. Nowhere is speech freer—not even here [in Britain] where we sedulously cultivate it even in its most repulsive form." *See* John Bartlett, *Bartlett's Familiar Quotations* at 621(17) (16th ed. 1992).

---

# 2.  Opinion

The Supreme Court has eloquently stated that "[u]nder the First Amendment there is no such thing as a false idea. However pernicious an opinion may seem, we depend for its correction not on the conscience of judges and juries but on the competition of other ideas." *Gertz v. Robert Welch, Inc.,* 418 U.S. 323, 339–40 (1974). For several years thereafter, numerous federal and state courts had regarded these words as equivalent to a constitutional mandate that opinions are insulated from liability.

In 1990, the Supreme Court had occasion to consider the question of constitutional protection for opinions. The Court eschewed the contention that the *Gertz* language was "intended to create a wholesale exemption for anything that might be labeled 'opinion.'" *Milkovich v. Lorain Journal Co,* 497 U.S. 1, 18 (1990) ("*Milkovich*"). The Court clarified that the reference to "opinion" in *Gertz* is equivalent to the concept of "idea[s]" as used in the "marketplace of ideas" lexicon. *Id.* Constitutionally-rooted protection for the expression of opinions derives from the protection afforded to speech that "cannot 'reasonably [be] interpreted as stating actual facts.'" *Milkovich*, 497 U.S. at 17 (citation omitted). Thus, statements are imbued with protection when they cannot be proved false, provided that the factual statements upon which such opinions rest are accurately stated.

Rhetorical hyperbole and "loose, figurative" language also are protected because they similarly are employed to express the speaker's viewpoints. Courts look not only to whether invective was utilized, but also whether the language used—or the general tenor of the publication—negated the impression that the statement was advanced as fact. Again, the critical inquiry is whether the assertion is capable of being proved true or false. *See, e.g, Unelko Corp. v. Rooney*, 912 F.2d 1049 (9th Cir.), *cert. denied*, 499 U.S. 961 (1991). In sum, "if it is plain that the speaker is expressing a subjective view, an interpretation, a theory, conjecture, or surmise, rather than claiming to be in possession of objectively verifiable facts, the statement is not actionable." *Haynes v. Alfred A. Knopf, Inc.*, 8 F.3d 1222, 1227 (7th Cir. 1993).

One issue left open by *Milkovich* "is the scope of protection for opinion when the statement is not about a matter of public concern....It is not yet clear under what rubric and to what extent protection may be forthcoming....Also open...is whether the fact that the plaintiff is a public figure or public official enters into the opinion calculus." Robert D. Sack, *Sack on Defamation: Libel, Slander, and Related Problems* § 4.2.4.3 at 4-18 (3d ed. 1999).

Speech conducted in cyberspace takes many forms, of course. Where is the demarcation between speech that relates to matters of public—and speech that relates to private—concern? To a large degree, the analysis relating to the fact-opinion dichotomy focuses on the words themselves and their ordinary meanings, as well as the context in which they are used. While cloaking a statement with prefaces of "in my opinion" will not shield it automatically, determinations as to actionability are assisted by review of the statement's context.

To illustrate, critical comment, especially as to governmental or political affairs, has received special solicitude, which may well be reflective of the core values underlying general protections for free speech. Further, placement of the statement, such as in an editorial column, *see, e.g., Ollman v. Evans*, 750 F.2d 970 (D.C. Cir. 1984) (en banc), *cert. denied*, 471 U.S. 1127 (1985); or in a book review, *see, e.g., Moldea v. New York Times Co.*, 22 F.3d 310 (D.C. Cir.), *cert. denied*, 513 U.S. 875 (1994), helps alert the recipient that the statement is an opinion. This is particularly so when the statement bears a reasonable nexus to the event that is the subject of the comment or review. Signals indicating that the statement is the product of conjecture and rumor also help render challenged statements non-actionable. *See, e.g., Levin v. McPhee*, 119 F.3d 189 (2d Cir. 1997).

The decision in *Agora, Inc. v. Axxess, Inc.*, 90 F. Supp. 2d 697 (D. Md. 2000), illustrates a federal court's analysis of opinion in connection with statements posted on the Internet. The case involved a claim by an on-line securities newsletter against a Web-based financial publication. The defendant had set forth the facts underlying its characterization of the plaintiff as an "unpaid promoter": the newsletter's publishers "claim they are not paid by the companies for publishing reports, but acknowledge that they do or might trade in the shares of the companies they're writing about." *Id.* at 700. Other references challenged by the plaintiff, such as an invitation to visitors to "Please Read Stock Detective Guide to Pseudo-Research and Phony Financial Reports first," could not reasonably be interpreted as stating factual matter about the newsletter's publisher. Rather, when scrutinized in context, the statements "consist[ed] entirely of sub-jective, generalized statements about the importance of objectivity in financial report-ing through the use of 'irreverent and indefinite language.'" *Id.* at 703 (quoting *Bios-pherics, Inc. v. Forbes, Inc.*, 151 F.3d 180, 184–85 (4th Cir. 1998)). Thus, the U.S. District Court for the District of Maryland held that the statements in issue were protected as opinion because they were based on fully disclosed facts.

The district court also noted that facts upon which the defendant had based its opin-ion were contained within the plaintiff's own web-site, to which the defendant had hy-perlinked. Such linking practices may present a useful tool for the disclosure of relevant facts, as they enable web-sites to present a more comprehensive picture. Links to web-sites of the subject of the statements, as was done in the *Agora, Inc. v. Axxess, Inc.* case, promote presentation of the subject's countervailing viewpoints as well.

---

# 3. Matters of Public Concern

On-line speech proliferates, entrenches itself in our society, and increasingly dis-places other means of communication. Much of this speech relates to personal matters or mundane details of daily life; other communications are of profound interest to the general public. In connection with an adjudication of a defamation claim against a newspaper, Justice Goldberg acknowledged that "[i]n most cases,...there will be little difficulty in distinguishing defamatory speech relating to private conduct from that re-lating to official conduct. I recognize, of course, that there will be a gray area." *New York Times Co. v. Sullivan*, 376 U.S. 254, 302 n. 4 (1964) (Goldberg, J.). Under what circum-stances is the subject matter of cyberspace speech purely private? Put alternatively, what constitutes a matter of public concern?

---

### Defining Newsworthiness: Separating Matters of Legitimate Public Interest from Matters Which Simply Interest the Public

Kevin W. Goering

As courts struggle to adapt ancient common law and more recent constitutional libel law doctrine to the rapidly evolving "new media," judicial definitions of "newsworthi-ness" and "matters of public concern" pose a special threat to freedom of speech. Despite the Supreme Court's "doubts" expressed in *Gertz v. Robert Welch Inc.*, 418 U.S. 323, 346 (1974), regarding "the wisdom of committing this task to the conscience of the judges," courts are increasingly making case by case determinations as to whether a given state-ment is one "of legitimate public concern." With very little guidance from appellate courts on how to distinguish "public concerns" from "purely private matters," courts have reached logically inconsistent conclusions, undoubtedly motivated in part by the particular judges' views as to the appropriateness of the speaker and his or her speech.

The conclusion that a given statement discusses merely a matter of private concern may well determinate the outcome in a private figure defamation case. Depending upon the applicable state law, such a holding may mean a return to strict liability, where falsity and damages are presumed and lack of negligence is no defense. In most states it will permit an award of punitive damages without a showing of actual malice.

This essay discusses the history of the "public concern" doctrine and concludes that the doctrine should be applied with great caution in defamation cases. Specifically, courts should rule that speech is not of legitimate public concern only in very rare instances. Moreover, the trend (at least until very recently) toward rejecting a distinction between so called "media" and "non-media" speech should continue. *See* Annotation, *Application of* New York Times *to Non-Media Defendants*, 38 A.L.R. 4th 1114 (1995).

Determinations of the relative newsworthiness or "public interest" of given speech have long been features of the common law. For example, the common law defense of fair comment required that the defendant establish that its "comment" concerned a "matter of public interest." *E.g.*, A. Hanson, *Libel and Related Torts* ¶ 137 (1969). Similarly, a finding of "newsworthiness" has long been a defense to statutory and common law invasion of privacy actions. *E.g., Sidis v. F-R Publishing Corp.*, 113 F.2d 806 (2d Cir.), *cert. denied*, 311 U.S. 711 (1940*)*. *See Shulman v. Group W. Productions, Inc.*, 18 Cal. 4th 200, 955 P.2d 469 (Cal. 1998). Some states, such as New York and New Jersey, have construed their states' common law to require special fault standards in private figure libel actions which involve matters of public interest or concern. *Chapadeau v. Utica Observer-Dispatch*, 38 N.Y.2d 196 (1975) (gross irresponsibility); *Sisler v. Gannett*, 104 N.J. 256, 516 A.2d 1083 (1986) (actual malice).

In *Rosenbloom v. Metromedia*, 403 U.S. 29 (1971), a plurality of the Supreme Court voted to extend the actual malice rule of *New York Times v. Sullivan* to all matters of public concern, even where the plaintiff was not ruled to be a public figure. The Court retreated from this rule in *Gertz v. Robert Welch*, 418 U.S. 323 (1974), and held that only public figures are required to prove actual malice by convincing clarity to obtain compensatory damages. In *Gertz*, the Court further held that even private figures must prove *New York Times'* actual malice to obtain presumed or punitive damages, at least where a matter of public concern is involved.

From 1974 until 1985, the Court did not mention any independent "public concern" requirement in a libel case, although it did address repeatedly the "public controversy" element of the *Gertz* public figure text. *See, e.g., Wolston v. Reader's Digest Ass'n*, 443 U.S. 157 (1979); *Time, Inc. v. Firestone*, 424 U.S. 448 (1976). In *Dun & Bradstreet v. Greenmoss Builders*, 472 U.S. 748 (1985), however, a plurality of the Court upheld an upward of punitive damages which was not supported by a finding of actual malice based on the holding that a credit report disseminated to just five subscribers and which falsely referred to the plaintiff construction company's alleged bankruptcy filing was a matter of "purely private concern."

In cases decided since *Dun & Bradstreet*, the Court has consistently repeated its reference to "matters of public concern" as a necessary requirement to trigger certain constitutional protections. *See, e.g., Philadelphia Newspapers v. Hepps*, 475 U.S. 767 (1986) (requirement that private plaintiffs bear the burden of proving falsity). *See also Milkovich v. Lorain Journal*, 497 U.S. 1, 20 (1990) (rejecting an independent constitutional opinion privilege).

Prior to *Dun & Bradstreet*, a number of courts had distinguished between so-called "media" and "non-media" entities for purposes of applying First Amendment protections. *E.g., Denny v. Mertz*, 318 N.W. 2d 141 (Wisc.), *cert. denied*, 459 U.S. 883 (1983); *Harley-Davidson Motorsports v. Markley*, 568 P.2d 1359 (Ore. 1977). Although many courts rejected this distinction, those which recognized it refused to extend the *New*

*York Times* rule to "non-media" speech. Five members of the Court in *Dun & Bradstreet* rejected such a distinction. 472 U.S. at 773 (White, J. concurring); 472 U.S. at 784 (Brennan, J. dissenting). Courts in some states continued to adhere to the media/non-media distinction after *Dun & Bradstreet*. *E.g., Harris v. Quadracci*, 856 F. Supp. 413 (E.D. Wisc. 1994). Moreover, the Supreme Court in *Milkovich* has said the question as to such a distinction is still open. 497 U.S. at 206.

From 1985, when *Dun & Bradstreet* was decided, until recently, the "public concern" concept in the law of defamation received surprisingly little attention. One court "doubt[ed] that it is possible to have speech about a public figure but not of public concern." *Dworkin v. Hustler Magazine*, 867 F.2d 1188, 1197 (9th Cir. 1989). Some commentators opined (supported by language in *Hepps*) that a ruling that speech concerns a private person and a matter of private concern has the draconian consequence of permitting courts to return to strict liability under state common law. *E.g.,* R. Smolla, *Law of Defamation* § 3:5 (2d ed. 1997); R. Heinke, *Media Law* § 2.11(F), at 117 (1994). *See* Raysman, Brown & Neuburger, *Multimedia Law* § 9.05[3] (1995). A number of courts have ruled that the *Gertz* requirement that plaintiffs prove fault applies only in public concern cases. *See* Robert D. Sack, *Sack on Defamation: Libel, Slander, and Related Problems* § 6.6, at pp. 6-22 to 6-23 (3d ed. 1999).

Some courts have supported the view that even non-public figure plaintiffs in "private concern" cases are required to prove at least falsity and negligence to recover for defamation. *E.g., Newberry v. Allied Stores, Inc.*, 773 P.2d 1231, 1237 (N.D. 1989); *New England Tractor v. Globe Newspaper Co.*, 480 N.E. 2d 1005, 1009 (Mass. 1985); *Dunlap v. Wayne*, 716 P.2d 842, 859 (Wash. 1986); *Great Coastal Express Inc. v. Ellington*, 224 S.E. 2d 846, 853 (Va. 1985). *See also Fitzpatrick v. Milky Way Productions, Inc.*, 537 F. Supp. 165, 169 (E.D. Pa 1982) (Pollak, J.) (negligence standard applies to private figure of "private subject matter.") Unfortunately, a number of courts have returned to the common law and have held in such cases that falsity is presumed, that fault need not be shown, and even that presumed and punitive damages are recoverable without proof of actual malice. *E.g., Mutafis v. Erie Ins. Exchange*, 775 F.2d 593 (4th Cir. 1985); *Eckhaus v. Alfa-Laval, Inc.*, 764 F. Supp. 34, 37 n. 4 (S.D.N.Y. 1991); *Nelson v. Lapeyrouse Grain Corp.*, 534 So. 2d 1085 (Ala. 1988); *Phyfer v. Fiona Press*, 12 Media L. Rep. 2211 (N.D. Miss. 1986).

Over the years, the Supreme Court has done little to define matters of public concern other than to say that the issue is for the Court and turns on "the content, form, and turns on "the content, form, and context…as revealed by the whole record." *Dun & Bradstreet*, 472 U.S. at 761 (quoting *Connick v. Myers*, 461 U.S. 138 (1983)). How then do courts decide whether a given statement involves a matter of public concern?

One recent California Supreme Court decision reveals the difficulty courts face in defining matters of public concern. In *Shulman v. Group W Productions, Inc.*, 18 Cal. 4th 200, 955 P.2d 469 (Cal. 1998), the Court set forth a lengthy analysis of the concept of newsworthiness and concluded that a claim for public disclosure of private facts could not stand where the plaintiff was videotaped at the scene of an automobile accident and while en route to the hospital. The dissent disagreed and would have remanded for a trial on the newsworthiness issue and the "private facts" claim.

The question of whether speech is of public concern is frequently decided in the context of civil rights, retaliatory discharge or "whistle blower" cases. *E.g., West v. Brazos River Harbor Nav. Dist.*, 836 F. Supp. 1331, 1335 (S.D. Tex. 1993), *aff'd*, 32 F.3d 566 (5th Cir. 1994). Indeed, *Connick v. Myers* (quoted in *Dun & Bradstreet*) was a public employment case which turned on whether an employee was fired for commenting on a matter of public concern. In the employment context, the identity of the recipient of the statement often enters into the court's analysis, though the media's receipt of the speech is not determinative. *Kurtz v. Vickrey*, 855 F.2d 723, 727 (11th Cir. 1988)("employee's efforts to communicate his or her concerns to the public are relevant to a determination of whether or not the employee's speech relates to a matter of public concern."). *See* Note, *Employee Disclosures to the Media*, 15 Hastings Communications and Entertainment L.J. 357, 372–73 (1993) (collecting cases). In the employment context, to confuse matters further, some courts have held that a *portion* of a communication may qualify for special constitutional protection "even though other aspects of the communication may qualify for special constitutional protection "even though other aspects of the communication do not qualify as a public concern." *Hyland v. Wonder*, 972 F.2d 1129 (9th Cir. 1992), *cert. denied*, 113 S.Ct. 2337 (1993).

Since *Dun & Bradstreet*, the Supreme Court has not ruled that a "private concern" was involved in a defamation case, but a number of lower courts have. One court has said that, "whether a publication is a matter of public concern or purely private concern has proved to be a critical distinction in the Supreme Court's First Amendment jurisprudence." *Metcalf v. KFOR-TV*, 828 F. Supp. 1515 (W.D. Okla. 1992). *See Grossman v. Smart*, 807 F. Supp. 1404 (C.D. Ill. 1992)("defining what constitutes a matter of public concern proves problematic for courts").

Some commentators have criticized the lack of analysis in *Dun & Bradstreet* as to the "private concern" status of the credit report at issue in that case. *See* A. Langvardt, *Public Concern Revisited: A New Role for an Old Doctrine in the Constitutional Law of Defamation*, 21 Valparaiso U.S. Rev. 241 (1987). In a seemingly inconsistent result, the court in *Blue Ridge Bank v. Veribanc, Inc.*, 866 F.2d 681, 686 (4th Cir. 1989), held that a statement as to the financial condition of a federally insured bank raised a matter of public concern. *But see Sunward Corp. v. Dun & Bradstreet, Inc.*, 811 F.2d 511, 534 & n. 25 (10th Cir. 1987)(credit reports do not raise matters of public concern). One highly respected constitutional scholar has sharply criticized the Court's general definitions in this area. R. Post, *Constitutional Domains* 164–78 (1995).

In *Roffman v. Trump*, 754 F. Supp. 411, 418 (E.D. Pa. 1990), the court held that Donald Trump's statements about an investment analyst which were published in six media publications, including the *Wall Street Journal, Business Week, Fortune* and the *New York Post* were not subject to First Amendment protections because they were "matters pertinent to [plaintiff] himself that are of no concern to the general public." This unappealed District Court decision may demonstrate the public concern doctrine's potential for mischief. Six editors believed that Trump's statements were of concern to their readers but a United States District Judge disagreed and stripped the statements of First Amendment protection.

Unfortunately, the result in *Roffman* is consistent with a number of other lower court decisions. For example, a United States District Court in Connecticut implicitly found that statements which appeared in book reviews "in a number of periodicals in the United States" lacked "public concern" in *Katz v. Gladstone*, 673 F. Supp. 76, 83 (D. Conn. 1987) (holding that defendant had the burden of proving truth). At least two courts in New York have held that the defendants in slander actions where matters of "purely private concern" are involved have the burden of proving truth as defense. *Technology Consortium v. Digital Communications*. 757 F. Supp. 197 (E.D.N.Y. 1991); *King v. Tanner*, 142 Misc. 2d 1004, 539 N.Y.S. 2d 617 (Sup. Ct. West. Cty. 1989). Two other courts have found that presumed damages are available in such cases without a showing of actual malice. *Yasner v. Spinner*, 765 F. Supp. 48 (E.D.N.Y. 1991) (letter to court reporter association accusing plaintiff court reporter of incompetence); *60 Minute Man Ltd. v. Kossman*, 161 A.D.2d 574, 555 N.Y.S.2d 152 (2d Dep't 1990) (oral statement that plaintiff used and sold drugs). *See also Ross v. Bricker*, 770 F. Supp. 1038 (D.V.I. 1991) (oral allegation that dentist "steals" patients); *Sleem v. Yale University*, 843 F. Supp. 57 (W.D.N.C. 1993) (false imputation of H.I.V. infection in class reunion mailing not a matter of public concern). In *Ramirez v. Rogers*, 540 A.2d 475 (Me. 1988), the court found no public concern in a statement by a school owner to a television personality that a competing school was being investigated ty the state attorney general's office.

Some courts have taken a much broader view of what is of legitimate public concern. *Stolz v. KSFM 102 FM*, 23 Media L. Rep. 1233, 1238 (Cal. App. 1994) ("irresponsibility in radio broadcasting "is matter of public concern). *See also Gaeta v. New Yorker News, Inc.*, 62 N.Y.2d 340 (1984). In *Metcalf v. KFOR-TV*, 828 F. Supp. 1515, 1533 (W.D. Okla. 1992), the Court found that statements in a television broadcast about a doctor's qualifications to do breast enhancement surgery addressed of matters of public concern. *See also Unelko v. Rooney*, 912 F.2d 1049, 1057 (9th Cir. 1990) (statement that windshield product did not work was of public concern); *Cunningham v. United Bank of Washington*, 710 F. Supp. 861 (D.D.C. 1989) (oral and written accusations that bank officer had been fired involve matter of public concern); *Pearce v. E.F. Hutton Group, Inc.*, 664 F. Supp. 1490, 1504 (D.D.C. 1987). Similarly, in invasion of privacy actions, the concept of newsworthiness has consistently been very broadly construed. *E.g., Time, Inc. v. Sand Creek Partners*, 825 F. Supp. 210 (S.D. Ind. 1993); *Arrington v. New York Times Co.*, 55 N.Y.2d 433 (1982), *cert. denied*, 459 U.S. 1146 (1983).

Many of the defamation cases in which courts have found matters of purely private concern have arisen in the employment context, where courts have focused on the limited scope of the publication but have given virtually no other reasons for their holdings. *E.g., Staheli v. Smith*, 548 So. 2d 1299 (Miss. 1989). For example, an oral accusation in a small group that an assault was the cause for the discharge of a station agent for an airline company was viewed by a panel of the Second Circuit Court of Appeals as not raising an issue of public concern. *Weldy v. Piedmont Airlines, Inc.*, 985 F.2d 57 (2d Cir. 1993). Similarly, the limited publication of a statement that a worker at a nuclear power plant was a security risk led to a finding of a lack of public concern in *Cooper v. PGE*, 824 P.2d 1152, 1155 (Ore. App. 1992). *See also Weissman v. Sri Lanka Curry House*, 469 N.W.2d 471 (Minn. App. 1991); *Miles v. Perry*, 11 Conn. App. 584, 14 Media L. Rep. 1985 (1987) (accusations of misappropriation against church finance committee member at a church board meeting was not "of public concern"); *Davis v. Ross*, 107 F.R.D. 326 (S.D.N.Y. 1985) (no public concern in statement made by employer about former employee's performance); *Hagel v. Vera Sims Food*, 713 P.2d 736 (Wash. App. 1986) (flyer mailed to 100 potential customers accusing car dealer and principals of being "thieves"); *Great Coastal Express v. Ellington*, 334 S.E. 2d 846 (Va. 1985) (employer's statement accusing employee of offering bribe not a matter of public concern). *Cf. Burroughs v. FFP Operating Partners, L.P.*, 28 F.3d 543, 549 (5th Cir. 1994) (*Hepps* rule on burden of proof as to falsity applies in slander case where plaintiff was accused of theft by employer)....

Two very recent judicial developments in New York should give the media cause for hope and, perhaps, for concern. The New York Court of Appeals ruled unanimously on December 20, 1999 that three articles in the "Hot Copy" column of the New York *Daily News* involved content which was "arguably a matter of legitimate public concern" and thus was entitled to the protection of the "gross irresponsibility" standard. *Huggins v.*

*Moore,* N.Y. Ct. App., No. 1 No. 198 (Slip Op. 12/20/99). The articles in *Huggins* concerned a popular actress's allegations of plaintiff's betrayal of trust during a failed marriage. The Appellate Division, First Department, had ruled that the parties' divorce and related matters were "essentially private affairs" and that, as a result, a negligence standard would apply.

In reversing, the Court of Appeals in *Huggins* distinguished between "the realm of mere gossip and private interest," where the publication is "directed only to a limited, private audience" from matters "reasonably related to information warranting public exposition." *Id.* Slip Op. at 4–5. The court specifically noted that "absent clear abuse, the courts defer to the news editor's determination of whether the portions of the article to which plaintiff objects" involve matters of public concern. *Id.* at 5. The result in *Huggins* is particularly interesting in the light of the Appellate Division, First Department's June 1998 ruling that a similar discussion by the tabloid, *The Globe,* of the divorce of television celebrity Joan Lunden did not involve matters of legitimate public concern. *Krauss v. Globe International,* 251 A.D.2d 191 (1st Dep't 1998). That case was settled before trial, but the Appellate Division's ruling on the public concern issue appears to be overruled by *Huggins.* . . . It is impossible to predict how the courts will distinguish "media" from "non-media" entities, much less how they will apply the "public concern" and "public audience" tests. In view of the expansive definition set forth in *Huggins, supra,* the media can only hope that the lower courts will continue to apply the weighty presumption that matters published to more than a very private audience are entitled to constitutional and common law protections.

## Conclusion

Until the Supreme Court revisits the issue, lower courts will continue to struggle with definitions of newsworthiness in private figure libel cases. Until then, courts should be urged to err on the side of protecting First Amendment freedoms by refusing to subject any speaker, whether or not a member of the traditional media, to the strict liability standards of the common law.

---

# The Requisite Degree of Fault

The First Amendment has been construed to ameliorate the harsh effects that historically ensued from holding the press strictly liable for defamatory statements by, among other ways, taking into account the status of the claimant pursuing the suit. Propelling this jurisprudence is a recognition that there is a constitutionally-rooted and significant public interest in robust and vigorous dialogue about matters of public concern.

The fault requirement seeks to accommodate the need for self-censorship by an otherwise timorous press faced with the prospect of civil liability for injurious falsehood. Thus, incorporation of fault as an element of a defamation claim accommodates, at least to some degree, the tension that necessarily exists between the societal interest in a vigorous and uninhibited press and the legitimate public interest in redressing defamatory falsehoods.

---

# The NEW YORK TIMES COMPANY v. L. B. SULLIVAN

Supreme Court of the United States
Nos. 39, 40, 376 U.S. 254
March 9, 1964

Mr. Justice BRENNAN delivered the opinion of the Court.

We are required in this case to determine for the first time the extent to which the constitutional protections for speech and press limit a State's power to award damages in a libel action brought by a public official against critics of his official conduct.

Respondent L. B. Sullivan is one of the three elected Commissioners of the City of Montgomery, Alabama. He testified that he was "Commissioner of Public Affairs and the duties are supervision of the Police Department, Fire Department, Department of Cemetery and Department of Scales." He brought this civil libel action against the four individual petitioners, who are Negroes and Alabama clergymen, and against petitioner the New York Times Company, a New York corporation which publishes the *New York Times*, a daily newspaper. A jury in the Circuit Court of Montgomery County awarded him damages of $500,000, the full amount claimed, against all the petitioners, and the Supreme Court of Alabama affirmed....

Respondent's complaint alleged that he had been libeled by statements in a full-page advertisement that was carried in the *New York Times* on March 29, 1960. Entitled "Heed Their Rising Voices," the advertisement began by stating that "As the whole world knows by now, thousands of Southern Negro students are engaged in widespread non-violent demonstrations in positive affirmation of the right to live in human dignity as guaranteed by the U.S. Constitution and the Bill of Rights." It went on to charge that "in their efforts to uphold these guarantees, they are being met by an unprecedented wave of terror by those who would deny and negate that document which the whole world looks upon as setting the pattern for modern freedom...."

[The respondent challenged the following paragraphs:]

> In Montgomery, Alabama, after students sang "My Country, 'Tis of Thee" on the State Capitol steps, their leaders were expelled from school, and truck-loads of police armed with shotguns and tear-gas ringed the Alabama State College Campus. When the entire student body protested to state authorities by refusing to re-register, their dining hall was padlocked in an attempt to starve them into submission.

> Again and again the Southern violators have answered Dr. King's peaceful protests with intimidation and violence. They have bombed his home almost killing his wife and child. They have assaulted his person. They have arrested him seven times—for "speeding," "loitering" and similar "offenses." And now they have charged him with "perjury"—a felony under which they could imprison him for *ten years....*"

Although neither of these statements mentions respondent by name, he contended that the word "police" in the third paragraph referred to him as the Montgomery Commissioner who supervised the Police Department, so that he was being accused of "ringing" the campus with police. He further claimed that the paragraph would be read as imputing to the police, and hence to him, the padlocking of the dining hall in order to starve the students into submission.... [He also] contended that since arrests are ordinarily made by the police, the statement "They have arrested [Dr. King] seven times" would be read as referring to him; he further contended that the "They" who did the arresting would be equated with the "They" who committed the other described acts and with the "Southern violators." Thus, he argued, the paragraph would be read as accusing the Montgomery police, and hence him, of answering Dr. King's protests with "intimidation and violence," bombing his home, assaulting his person, and charging him with perjury. Respondent and six other Montgomery residents testified that they read some or all of the statements as referring to him in his capacity as Commissioner.

It is uncontroverted that some of the statements contained in the two paragraphs were not accurate descriptions of events which occurred in Montgomery. Although Negro students staged a demonstration on the State Capital steps, they sang the National Anthem and not "My Country, 'Tis of Thee." Although nine students were expelled by the State Board of Education, this was not for leading the demonstration at the Capitol, but for demanding service at a lunch counter in the Montgomery County Courthouse on another day. Not the entire student body, but most of it, had protested the expulsion, not by refusing to register, but by boycotting classes on a single day; virtually all the students did register for the ensuing semester. The campus dining hall was not padlocked on any occasion, and the only students who may have been barred from eating there were the few who had neither signed a preregistration application nor requested temporary meal tickets. Although the police were deployed near the campus in large numbers on three occasions, they did not at any time "ring" the campus, and they were not called to the campus in connection with the demonstration on the State Capitol steps, as the third paragraph implied. Dr. King had not been arrested seven times, but only four; and one of the officers who made the arrest denied that there was such an assault....

## II.

Under Alabama law as applied in this case, a publication is "libelous *per se*" if the words "tend to injure a person...in his reputation" or to "bring (him) into public contempt," the trial court stated that the standard was met if the words are such as to "injure him in his public office, or impute misconduct to him in his office, or want of official integrity, or want of fidelity to a public trust...." The jury must find that the words were published "of and concerning" the plaintiff, but where the plaintiff is a public official his place in the governmental hierarchy is sufficient evidence to support a finding that his reputation has been affected by statements that reflect upon the agency of which he is in charge. Once "libel *per se*" has been established, the defendant has no defense as to stated facts unless he can persuade the jury that they were true in all their particulars. *Alabama Ride Co. v. Vance*, 235 Ala. 263, 178 So. 438 (1938); *Johnson Publishing Co. v. Davis*, 271 Ala. 474, 494–495, 124 So.2d 441, 457–458 (1960). His privilege of "fair comment" for expressions of opinion depends on the truth of the facts upon which the comment is based. *Parsons v. Age-Herald Publishing Co.*, 181 Ala. 439, 450, 61 So. 345, 350 (1913). Unless he can discharge the burden of proving truth, general damages are presumed, and may be awarded without proof of pecuniary injury. A showing of actual malice is apparently a prerequisite to recovery of punitive damages, and the defendant may in any event forestall a punitive award by a retraction meeting the statutory requirements. Good motives and belief in truth do not negate an inference of malice, but are relevant only in mitigation of punitive damages if the jury chooses to accord them weight. *Johnson Publishing Co. v. Davis, supra,* 271 Ala. at 495, 124 So.2d at 458.

The question before us is whether this rule of liability, as applied to an action brought by a public official against critics of his official conduct, abridges the freedom of speech and of the press that is guaranteed by the First and Fourteenth Amendments.

... Like insurrection, contempt, advocacy of unlawful acts, breach of the peace, obscenity, solicitation of legal business, and the various other formulae for the repression of expression that have been challenged in this Court, libel can claim no talismanic immunity from constitutional limitations. It must be measured by standards that satisfy the First Amendment.

The general proposition that freedom of expression upon public questions is secured by the First Amendment has long been settled by our decisions.... Thus we consider this case against the background of a profound national commitment to the principle that debate on public issues should be uninhibited, robust, and wide-open, and that it may well include vehement, caustic, and sometimes unpleasantly sharp attacks on government and public officials. See *Terminiello v. Chicago,* 337 U.S. 1, 4, 69 S.Ct. 894, 93 L.Ed. 1131; *De Jonge v. Oregon,* 299 U.S. 353, 365, 57 S.Ct. 255, 81 L.Ed. 278. The present advertisement, as an expression of grievance and protest on one of the major public issues of our time, would seem clearly to qualify for the constitutional protection. The question is whether it forfeits that protection by the falsity of some of its factual statements and by its alleged defamation of respondent.

Authoritative interpretations of the First Amendment guarantees have consistently refused to recognize an exception for any test of truth—whether administered by judges, juries, or administrative officials—and especially one that puts the burden of proving truth on the speaker. *Cf. Speiser v. Randall,* 357 U.S. 513, 525–526, 78 S.Ct. 1332, 2 L.Ed.2d 1460. The constitutional protection does not turn upon "the truth, popularity, or social utility of the ideas and beliefs which are offered." *N.A.A.C.P. v. Button,* 371 U.S. 415, 445, 83 S.Ct. 328, 344, 9 L.Ed.2d 405. As Madison said, "Some degree of abuse is inseparable from the proper use of every thing; and in no instance is this more true than in that of the press." 4 Elliot's Debates on the Federal Constitution (1876), p. 571. In *Cantwell v. Connecticut,* 310 U.S. 296, 310, 60 S.Ct. 900, 906, 84 L.Ed. 1213, the Court declared:

> In the realm of religious faith, and in that of political belief, sharp differences arise. In both fields the tenets of one man may seem the rankest error to his neighbor. To persuade others to his own point of view, the pleader, as we know, at times, resorts to exaggeration, to vilification of men who have been, or are, prominent in church or state, and even to false statement. But the people of this nation have ordained in the light of history, that, in spite of the probability of excesses and abuses, these liberties are, in the long view, essential to enlightened opinion and right conduct on the part of the citizens of a democracy.

... Injury to official reputation error affords no more warrant for repressing speech that would otherwise be free than does factual error. Where judicial officers are involved, this Court has held that concern for the dignity and reputation of the courts does not justify the punishment as criminal contempt of criticism of the judge or his decision. *Bridges v. California,* 314 U.S. 252, 62 S.Ct. 190, 86 L.Ed. 192. This is true even though the utterance contains "half-truths" and "misinformation." *Pennekamp v. Florida,* 328 U.S. 331, 342, 343, n. 5, 345, 66 S.Ct. 1029, 90 L.Ed. 1295. Such repression can be justified, if at all, only by a clear and present danger of the obstruction of justice. *See also Craig v. Harney*, 331 U.S. 367, 67 S.Ct. 1249, 91 L.Ed. 1546; *Wood v. Georgia*, 370 U.S. 375, 82 S.Ct. 1364, 8 L.Ed.2d 569. If judges are to be treated as "men of fortitude, able to thrive in a hardy climate," *Craig v. Harney, supra*, 331 U.S. at 376, 67 S.Ct. at 1255, 91 L.Ed. 1546, surely the same must be true of other government officials, such as elected city commissioners. Criticism of their official conduct does not lose its constitutional protection merely because it is effective criticism and hence diminishes their official reputations....

The state rule of law is not saved by its allowance of the defense of truth. A defense for erroneous statements honestly made is no less essential here than was the requirement of proof of guilty knowledge which, in *Smith v. California*, 361 U.S. 147, 80 S.Ct. 215, 4 L.Ed.2d 205, we held indispensable to a valid conviction of a bookseller for possessing obscene writings for sale. We said:

> For if the bookseller is criminally liable without knowledge of the contents,... he will tend to restrict the books he sells to those he has inspected; and thus the State will have imposed a restriction upon the distribution of constitutionally protected as well as obscene literature....And the bookseller's burden would become the public's burden, for by restricting him the public's access to reading matter would be restricted....[H]is timidity in the face of his absolute criminal liability, thus would tend to restrict the public's access to forms of the printed word which the State could not constitutionally suppress directly. The bookseller's self-censorship, compelled by the State, would be a censorship affecting the whole public, hardly less virulent for being privately administered. Through it, the distribution of all books, both obscene and not obscene, would be impeded.

(361 U.S. 147, 153–154, 80 S.Ct. 215, 218, 4 L.Ed.2d 205.)

A rule compelling the critic of official conduct to guarantee the truth of all his factual assertions—and to do so on pain of libel judgments virtually unlimited in amount—leads to a comparable "self-censorship." Allowance of the defense of truth, with the burden of proving it on the defendant, does not mean that only false speech will be deterred. Even courts accepting this defense as an adequate safeguard have recognized the difficulties of adducing legal proofs that the alleged libel was true in all its factual particulars. *See, e.g., Post Publishing Co. v. Hallam*, 59 F. 530, 540 (C.A.6th Cir. 1893); *see also* Noel, *Defamation of Public Officers and Candidates*, 49 Col. L. Rev. 875, 892 (1949). Under such a rule, would-be critics of official conduct may be deterred from voicing their criticism, even though it is believed to be true and even though it is in fact true, because of doubt whether it can be proved in court or fear of the expense of having to do so. They tend to make only statements which "steer far wider of the unlawful zone." *Speiser v. Randall, supra*, 357 U.S. at 526, 78 S.Ct. at 1342, 2 L.Ed.2d 1460. The rule thus dampens the vigor and limits the variety of public debate. It is inconsistent with the First and Fourteenth Amendments.

The constitutional guarantees require, we think, a federal rule that prohibits a public official from recovering damages for a defamatory falsehood relating to his official conduct unless he proves that the statement was made with "actual malice"—that is, with knowledge that it was false or with reckless disregard of whether it was false or not....

Such a privilege for criticism of official conduct is appropriately analogous to the protection accorded a public official when he is sued for libel by a private citizen. In *Barr v. Matteo*, 360 U.S. 564, 575, 79 S.Ct. 1335, 1341, 3 L.Ed.2d 1434, this Court held the utterance of a federal official to be absolutely privileged if made "within the outer perimeter" of his duties. The States accord the same immunity to statements of their highest officers, although some differentiate their lesser officials and qualify the privilege they enjoy. But all hold that all officials are protected unless actual malice can be proved. The reason for the official privilege is said to be that the threat of damage suits would otherwise "inhibit the fearless, vigorous, and effective administration of policies of government" and "dampen the ardor of all but the most resolute, or the most irresponsible, in the unflinching discharge of their duties." *Barr v. Matteo, supra*, 360 U.S. at 571, 79 S.Ct. at 1339, 3 L.Ed.2d 1434. Analogous considerations support the privilege for the citizen-critic of government. It is as much his duty to criticize as it is the official's duty to administer. *See Whitney v. California*, 274 U.S. 357, 375, 47 S.Ct. 641, 648, 71 L.Ed. 1095 (concurring opinion of Mr. Justice Brandeis), quoted *supra*, pp. 720, 721. As Madison said, *see supra*, p. 723, "the censorial power is in the people over the Government, and not in the Government over the people." It would give public servants an unjustified preference over the public they serve, if critics of official conduct did not have a fair equivalent of the immunity granted to the officials themselves.

We conclude that such a privilege is required by the First and Fourteenth Amendments.

### III.

We hold today that the Constitution delimits a State's power to award damages for libel in actions brought by public officials against critics of their official conduct. Since this is such an action, the rule requiring proof of actual malice is applicable. While Alabama law apparently requires proof of actual malice for an award of punitive damages, where general damages are concerned malice is "presumed." Such a presumption is inconsistent with the federal rule. "The power to create presumptions is not a means of escape from constitutional restrictions," *Bailey v. Alabama*, 219 U.S. 219, 239, 31 S.Ct. 145, 151, 55 L.Ed. 191; "[t]he showing of malice required for the forfeiture of the privilege is not presumed but is a matter for proof by the plaintiff...." *Lawrence v. Fox*, 357 Mich. 134, 146, 97 N.W.2d 719, 725 (1959)....

As to the *Times*, we similarly conclude that the facts do not support a finding of actual malice. The statement by the *Times'* Secretary that, apart from the padlocking allegation, he thought the advertisement was "substantially correct," affords no constitutional warrant for the Alabama Supreme Court's conclusion that it was a "cavalier ignoring of the falsity of the advertisement (from which) the jury could not have but been impressed with the bad faith of the *Times*, and its maliciousness inferable therefrom." The statement does not indicate malice at the time of the publication; even if the advertisement was not "substantially correct"—although respondent's own proofs tend to show that it was—that opinion was at least a reasonable one, and there was no evidence to impeach the witness' good faith in holding it. The *Times'* failure to retract upon respondent's demand, although it later retracted upon the demand of Governor Patterson, is likewise not adequate evidence of malice for constitutional purposes. Whether or not a failure to retract may ever constitute such evidence, there are two reasons why it does not here. First, the letter written by the *Times* reflected a reasonable doubt on its part as to whether the advertisement could reasonably be taken to refer to respondent at all. Second, it was not a final refusal, since it asked for an explanation on this point—a request that respondent chose to ignore. Nor does the retraction upon the demand of the Governor supply the necessary proof. It may be doubted that a failure to retract which is not itself evidence of malice can retroactively become such by virtue of a retraction subsequently made to another party. But in any event that did not happen here, since the explanation given by the *Times'* Secretary for the distinction drawn between respondent and the Governor was a reasonable one, the good faith of which was not impeached.

Finally, there is evidence that the *Times* published the advertisement without checking its accuracy against the news stories in the *Times'* own files. The mere presence of the stories in the files does not, of course, establish that the *Times* "knew" the advertisement was false, since the state of mind required for actual malice would have to be brought home to the persons in the *Times'* organization having responsibility for the publication of the advertisement. With respect to the failure of those persons to make the check, the record shows that they relied upon their knowledge of the good reputation of many of those whose names were listed as sponsors of the advertisement, and upon the letter from A. Philip Randolph, known to them as a responsible individual, certifying that the use of the names was authorized. There was testimony that the persons handling the advertisement saw nothing in it that would render it unacceptable under the *Times'* policy of rejecting advertisements containing "attacks of a personal character;" their failure to reject it on this ground was not unreasonable. We think the evidence against the *Times* supports at most a finding of negligence in failing to discover the misstatements, and is constitutionally insufficient to show the recklessness that is required for a finding of actual malice. *Cf. Charles Parker Co. v. Silver City Crystal Co.,* 142 Conn. 605, 618, 116 A.2d 440, 446 (1955); *Phoenix Newspapers, Inc. v. Choisser,* 82 Ariz. 271, 277—278, 312 P.2d 150, 154–155 (1957)....

The judgment of the Supreme Court of Alabama is reversed and the case is remanded to that court for further proceedings not inconsistent with this opinion.

Mr. Justice BLACK, with whom Mr. Justice DOUGLAS joins (concurring).

I concur in reversing this half-million-dollar judgment against the New York Times Company and the four individual defendants. In reversing the Court holds that "the Constitution delimits a State's power to award damages for libel in actions brought by public officials against critics of their official conduct." *Ante,* p. 727. I base my vote to reverse on the belief that the First and Fourteenth Amendments not merely "delimit" a State's power to award damages to "public officials against critics of their official conduct" but completely prohibit a State from exercising such a power. The Court goes on to hold that a State can subject such critics to damages if "actual malice" can be proved against them. "Malice," even as defined by the Court, is an elusive, abstract concept, hard to prove and hard to disprove. The requirement that malice be proved provides at best an evanescent protection for the right critically to discuss public affairs and certainly does not measure up to the sturdy safeguard embodied in the First Amendment. Unlike the Court, therefore, I vote to reverse exclusively on the ground that the *Times* and the individual defendants had an absolute, unconditional constitutional right to publish in the *Times* advertisement their criticisms of the Montgomery agencies and officials....

The half-million-dollar verdict does give dramatic proof, however, that state libel laws threaten the very existence of an American press virile enough to publish unpopular views on public affairs and bold enough to criticize the conduct of public officials. The factual background of this case emphasizes the imminence and enormity of that threat. One of the acute and highly emotional issues in this country arises out of efforts of many people, even including some public officials, to continue state-commanded segregation of races in the public schools and other public places, despite our several holdings that such a state practice is forbidden by the Fourteenth Amendment. Montgomery is one of the localities in which widespread hostility to desegregation has been

manifested. This hostility has sometimes extended itself to persons who favor desegregation, particularly to so-called "outside agitators," a term which can be made to fit papers like the *Times*, which is published in New York. The scarcity of testimony to show
that Commissioner Sullivan suffered any actual damages at all suggests that these feelings of hostility had at least as much to do with rendition of this half-million-dollar verdict as did an appraisal of damages. Viewed realistically, this record lends support to an
inference that instead of being damaged Commissioner Sullivan's political, social, and
financial prestige has likely been enhanced by the *Times*' publication. Moreover, a second half-million-dollar libel verdict against the *Times* based on the same advertisement
has already been awarded to another Commissioner. There a jury again gave the full
amount claimed. There is no reason to believe that there are not more such huge ver-
dicts lurking just around the corner for the *Times* or any other newspaper or broadcaster which might dare to criticize public officials. In fact, briefs before us show that in
Alabama there are now pending eleven libel suits by local and state officials against the
*Times* seeking $5,600,000, and five such suits against the Columbia Broadcasting System
seeking $1,700,000. Moreover, this technique for harassing and punishing a free press—
now that it has been shown to be possible—is by no means limited to cases with racial
overtones; it can be used in other fields where public feelings may make local as well as
out-of-state newspapers easy prey for libel verdict seekers.

In my opinion the Federal Constitution has dealt with this deadly danger to the press
in the only way possible without leaving the free press open to destruction—by granting the press an absolute immunity for criticism of the way public officials do their public duty. *Compare Barr v. Matteo*, 360 U.S. 564, 79 S.Ct. 1335, 3 L.Ed.2d 1434. Stopgap
measures like those the Court adopts are in my judgment not enough. This record certainly does not indicate that any different verdict would have been rendered here whatever the Court had charged the jury about "malice," "truth," "good motives," "justifiable
ends," or any other legal formulas which in theory would protect the press. Nor does the
record indicate that any of these legalistic words would have caused the courts below to
set aside or to reduce the half-million-dollar verdict in any amount....

An unconditional right to say what one pleases about public affairs is what I consider
to be the minimum guarantee of the First Amendment.

I regret that the Court has stopped short of this holding indispensable to preserve
our free press from destruction.

Mr. Justice GOLDBERG, with whom Mr. Justice DOUGLAS joins (concurring in the
result).

...In my view, the First and Fourteenth Amendments to the Constitution afford to
the citizen and to the press an absolute, unconditional privilege to criticize official conduct despite the harm which may flow from excesses and abuses.... It may be urged that
deliberately and maliciously false statements have no conceivable value as free speech.
That argument, however, is not responsive to the real issue presented by this case,
which is whether that freedom of speech which all agree is constitutionally protected
can be effectively safeguarded by a rule allowing the imposition of liability upon a jury's
evaluation of the speaker's state of mind. If individual citizens may be held liable in
damages for strong words, which a jury finds false and maliciously motivated, there can
be little doubt that public debate and advocacy will be constrained. And if newspapers,
publishing advertisements dealing with public issues, thereby risk liability, there can
also be little doubt that the ability of minority groups to secure publication of their
views on public affairs and to seek support for their causes will be greatly diminished....

This is not to say that the Constitution protects defamatory statements directed against the private conduct of a public official or private citizen. Freedom of press and of speech insures that government will respond to the will of the people and that changes may be obtained by peaceful means. Purely private defendant has little to do with the political ends of a self-governing society. The imposition of liability for private defamation does not abridge the freedom of public speech or any other freedom protected by the First Amendment....

---

In *Garrison v. Louisiana*, the Supreme Court addressed the absolute privilege endorsed by concurring opinions *in New York Times Co. v. Sullivan*, 376 U.S. 254, stating:

> Although honest utterance, even if inaccurate, may further the fruitful exercise of the right of free speech, it does not follow that the lie, knowingly and deliberately published about a public official, should enjoy a like immunity. At the time the First Amendment was adopted, as today, there were those unscrupulous enough and skillful enough to use the deliberate or reckless falsehood as an effective political tool to unseat the public servant or even topple an administration. That speech is used as a tool for political ends does not automatically bring it under the protective mantle of the Constitution. For the use of the known lie a tool is at once at odds with the premises of democratic government and with the orderly manner in which economic, social, or political change is to be effected. Calculated falsehood falls into that class of utterances which "are no essential part of any exposition of ideas, and are of such slight social value as a step to truth that any benefit that may be derived from them is clearly outweighed by the social interest in order and morality."

*Garrison v. Louisiana*, 379 U.S. 64, 75 (1964) (citations omitted).

---

## Elmer GERTZ v. ROBERT WELCH, INC.
### Supreme Court of the United States
### No. 72-617, 418 U.S. 323
### June 25, 1974

Mr. Justice POWELL delivered the opinion of the Court.

This Court has struggled for nearly a decade to define the proper accommodation between the law of defamation and the freedoms of speech and press protected by the First Amendment. With this decision we return to that effort. We granted certiorari to reconsider the extent of a publisher's constitutional privilege against liability for defamation of a private citizen.

I

In 1968 a Chicago policeman named Nuccio shot and killed a youth named Nelson. The state authorities prosecuted Nuccio for the homicide and ultimately obtained a conviction for murder in the second degree. The Nelson family retained petitioner Elmer Gertz, a reputable attorney, to represent them in civil litigation against Nuccio.

Respondent publishes *American Opinion*, a monthly outlet for the views of the John Birch Society. Early in the 1960's the magazine began to warn of a nationwide conspiracy to discredit local law enforcement agencies and create in their stead a national police force capable of supporting a Communist dictatorship. As part of the continuing effort to alert the public to this assumed danger, the managing editor of *American Opinion* commissioned an article on the murder trial of Officer Nuccio. For this purpose he engaged a regular contributor to the magazine. In March 1969 respondent published the resulting article under the title "FRAME-UP: Richard Nuccio And The War On Police." The article purports to demonstrate that the testimony against Nuccio at his criminal trial was false and that his prosecution was part of the Communist campaign against the police.

In his capacity as counsel for the Nelson family in the civil litigation, petitioner attended the coroner's inquest into the boy's death and initiated actions for damages, but he neither discussed Officer Nuccio with the press nor played any part in the criminal proceeding. Notwithstanding petitioner's remote connection with the prosecution of Nuccio, respondent's magazine portrayed him as an architect of the "frame-up." According to the article, the police file on petitioner took "a big, Irish cop to lift." The article stated that petitioner had been an official of the "Marxist League for Industrial Democracy, originally known as the Intercollegiate Socialist Society, which has advocated the violent seizure of our government." It labeled Gertz a "Leninist" and a "Communist-fronter."...

These statements contained serious inaccuracies. The implication that petitioner had a criminal record was false. Petitioner had been a member and officer of the National Lawyers Guild some 15 years earlier, but there was no evidence that he or that organization had taken any part in planning the 1968 demonstrations in Chicago. There was also no basis for the charge that petitioner was a "Leninist" or a "Communist-frontier." And he had never been a member of the "Marxist League for Industrial Democracy" or the "Intercollegiate Socialist Society."

The managing editor of *American Opinion* made no effort to verify or substantiate the charges against petitioner. Instead, he appended an editorial introduction stating that the author had "conducted extensive research into the Richard Nuccio Case."...

## II

The principal issue in this case is whether a newspaper or broadcaster that publishes defamatory falsehoods about an individual who is neither a public official nor a public figure may claim a constitutional privilege against liability for the injury inflicted by those statements....

## III

We begin with the common ground. Under the First Amendment there is no such thing as a false idea. However pernicious an opinion may seem, we depend for its correction not on the conscience of judges and juries but on the competition of other ideas.[8] But there is no constitutional value in false statements of fact. Neither the intentional lie nor the careless error materially advances society's interest in "uninhibited, robust, and wide-open" debate on public issues. *New York Times Co. v. Sullivan*, 376 U.S.

---

8. As Thomas Jefferson made the point in his first Inaugural Address: "If there be any among us who would wish to dissolve this Union or change its republican form, let them stand undisturbed as monuments of the safety with which error of opinion may be tolerated where reason is left free to combat it."

at 270, 84 S.Ct., at 721. They belong to that category of utterances which "are no essential part of any exposition of ideas, and are of such slight social value as a step to truth that any benefit that may be derived from them is clearly outweighed by the social interest in order and morality." *Chaplinsky v. New Hampshire*, 315 U.S. 568, 572, 62 S.Ct. 766, 769, 86 L.Ed. 1031 (1942).

Although the erroneous statement of fact is not worthy of constitutional protection, it is nevertheless inevitable in free debate. As James Madison pointed out in the Report on the Virginia Resolutions of 1798: "Some degree of abuse is inseparable from the proper use of every thing; and in no instance is this more true than in that of the press." 4 J. Elliot, *Debates on the Federal Constitution* of 1787, p. 571 (1876). And punishment of error runs the risk of inducing a cautious and restrictive exercise of the constitutionally guaranteed freedoms of speech and press. Our decisions recognize that a rule of strict liability that compels a publisher or broadcaster to guarantee the accuracy of his factual assertions may lead to intolerable self-censorship. Allowing the media to avoid liability only by proving the truth of all injurious statements does not accord adequate protection to First Amendment liberties. As the Court stated in *New York Times Co. v. Sullivan, supra*, 376 U.S. at 279, 84 S.Ct., at 725: "Allowance of the defense of truth, with the burden of proving it on the defendant, does not mean that only false speech will be deterred." The First Amendment requires that we protect some falsehood in order to protect speech that matters.

The need to avoid self-censorship by the news media is, however, not the only societal value at issue. If it were, this Court would have embraced long ago the view that publishers and broadcasters enjoy an unconditional and indefeasible immunity from liability for defamation. *See New York Times Co. v. Sullivan, supra*, at 293, 84 S.Ct. at 733 (Black, J., concurring); *Garrison v. Louisiana*, 379 U.S. at 80, 85 S.Ct. at 218 (1964) (Douglas, J., concurring); *Curtis Publishing Co. v. Butts*, 388 U.S. at 170, 87 S.Ct. at 1999 (opinion of Black, J.). Such a rule would, indeed, obviate the fear that the prospect of civil liability for injurious falsehood might dissuade a timorous press from the effective exercise of First Amendment freedoms. Yet absolute protection for the communications media requires a total sacrifice of the competing value served by the law of defamation.

The legitimate state interest underlying the law of libel is the compensation of individuals for the harm inflicted on them by defamatory falsehood. We would not lightly require the State to abandon this purpose, for, as Mr. Justice Stewart has reminded us, the individual's right to the protection of his own good name

> reflects no more than our basic concept of the essential dignity and worth of every human being—a concept at the root of any decent system of ordered liberty. The protection of private personality, like the protection of life itself, is left primarily to the individual States under the Ninth and Tenth Amendments. But this does not mean that the right is entitled to any less recognition by this Court as a basic of our constitutional system.

*Rosenblatt v. Baer*, 383 U.S. 75, 92, 86 S.Ct. 669, 679, 15 L.Ed.2d 597 (1966) (concurring opinion).

Some tension necessarily exists between the need for a vigorous and uninhibited press and the legitimate interest in redressing wrongful injury. As Mr. Justice Harlan stated, "some antithesis between freedom of speech and press and libel actions persists, for libel remains premised on the content of speech and limits the freedom of the publisher to express certain sentiments, at least without guaranteeing legal proof of their substantial accuracy." *Curtis Publishing Co. v. Butts, supra*, 388 U.S. at 152, 87

S.Ct. at 1990. In our continuing effort to define the proper accommodation between these competing concerns, we have been especially anxious to assure to the freedoms of speech and press that "breathing space" essential to their fruitful exercise. *N.A.A.C.P. v. Button,* 371 U.S. 415, 433, 83 S.Ct. 328, 338, 9 L.Ed.2d 405 (1963). To that end this Court has extended a measure of strategic protection to defamatory falsehood.

The *New York Times* standard defines the level of constitutional protection appropriate to the context of defamation of a public person. Those who, by reason of the notoriety of their achievements or the vigor and success with which they seek the public's attention, are properly classed as public figures and those who hold governmental office may recover for injury to reputation only on clear and convincing proof that the defamatory falsehood was made with knowledge of its falsity or with reckless disregard for the truth. This standard administers an extremely powerful antidote to the inducement to media self-censorship of the common-law rule of strict liability for libel and slander. And it exacts a correspondingly high price from the victims of defamatory falsehood. Plainly many deserving plaintiffs, including some intentionally subjected to injury, will be unable to surmount the barrier of the *New York Times* test. Despite this substantial abridgment of the state law right to compensation for wrongful hurt to one's reputation, the Court has concluded that the protection of the *New York Times* privilege should be available to publishers and broadcasters of defamatory falsehood concerning public officials and public figures. *New York Times Co. v. Sullivan, supra; Curtis Publishing Co. v. Butts, supra.* We think that these decisions are correct, but we do not find their holdings justified solely by reference to the interest of the press and broadcast media in immunity from liability. Rather, we believe that the *New York Times* rule states an accommodation between this concern and the limited state interest present in the context of libel actions brought by public persons. For the reasons stated below, we conclude that the state interest in compensating injury to the reputation of private individuals requires that a different rule should obtain with respect to them.

Theoretically, of course, the balance between the needs of the press and the individual's claim to compensation for wrongful injury might be struck on a case-by-case basis. As Mr. Justice Harlan hypothesized, "it might seem, purely as an abstract matter, that the most utilitarian approach would be to scrutinize carefully every jury verdict in every libel case, in order to ascertain whether the final judgment leaves fully protected whatever First Amendment values transcend the legitimate state interest in protecting the particular plaintiff who prevailed." *Rosenbloom v. Metromedia, Inc.,* 403 U.S. at 63, 91 S.Ct. at 1829 (footnote omitted). But this approach would lead to unpredictable results and uncertain expectations, and it could render our duty to supervise the lower courts unmanageable. Because an ad hoc resolution of the competing interests at stake in each particular case is not feasible, we must lay down broad rules of general application. Such rules necessarily treat alike various cases involving differences as well as similarities. Thus it is often true that not all of the considerations which justify adoption of a given rule will obtain in each particular case decided under its authority.

With that caveat we have no difficulty in distinguishing among defamation plaintiffs. The first remedy of any victim of defamation is self-help — using available opportunities to contradict the lie or correct the error and thereby to minimize its adverse impact on reputation. Public officials and public figures usually enjoy significantly greater access to the channels of effective communication and hence have a more realistic opportunity to counteract false statements then private individuals normally enjoy.[9] Private individuals are therefore more vulnerable to injury, and the state interest in protecting them is correspondingly greater.

More important than the likelihood that private individuals will lack effective opportunities for rebuttal, there is a compelling normative consideration underlying the distinction between public and private defamation plaintiffs. An individual who decides to seek governmental office must accept certain necessary consequences of that involvement in public affairs. He runs the risk of closer public scrutiny than might otherwise be the case. And society's interest in the officers of government is not strictly limited to the formal discharge of official duties. As the Court pointed out in *Garrison v. Louisiana*, 379 U.S. at 77, 85 S.Ct. at 217, the public's interest extends to "anything which might touch on an official's fitness for office.... Few personal attributes are more germane to fitness for office than dishonesty, malfeasance, or improper motivation, even though these characteristics may also affect the official's private character."

Those classed as public figures stand in a similar position. Hypothetically, it may be possible for someone to become a public figure through no purposeful action of his own, but the instances of truly involuntary public figures must be exceedingly rare. For the most part those who attain this status have assumed roles of especial prominence in the affairs of society. Some occupy positions of such persuasive power and influence that they are deemed public figures for all purposes. More commonly, those classed as public figures have thrust themselves to the forefront of particular public controversies in order to influence the resolution of the issues involved. In either event, they invite attention and comment.

Even if the foregoing generalities do not obtain in every instance, the communications media are entitled to act on the assumption that public officials and public figures have voluntarily exposed themselves to increased risk of injury from defamatory falsehood concerning them. No such assumption is justified with respect to a private individual. He has not accepted public office or assumed an "influential role in ordering society." *Curtis Publishing Co. v. Butts*, 388 U.S. at 164, 87 S.Ct. at 1996 (Warren, C.J., concurring in result). He has relinquished no part of his interest in the protection of his own good name, and consequently he has a more compelling call on the courts for redress of injury inflicted by defamatory falsehood. Thus, private individuals are not only more vulnerable to injury than public officials and public figures; they are also more deserving of recovery.

For these reasons we conclude that the States should retain substantial latitude in their efforts to enforce a legal remedy for defamatory falsehood injurious to the reputation of a private individual. The extension of the *New York Times* test proposed by the *Rosenbloom* plurality would abridge this legitimate state interest to a degree that we find unacceptable. And it would occasion the additional difficulty of forcing state and federal judges to decide on an ad hoc basis which publications address issues of "general or public interest" and which do not—to determine, in the words of Mr. Justice Marshall, 'what information is relevant to self-government." *Rosenbloom v. Metromedia, Inc.*, 403 U.S. at 79, 91 S.Ct. at 1837. We doubt the wisdom of committing this task to the conscience of judges. Nor does the Constitution require us to draw so thin a line between

---

9. Of course, an opportunity for rebuttal seldom suffices to undo harm of defamatory falsehood. Indeed, the law of defamation is rooted in our experience that the truth rarely catches up with a lie. But the fact that the self-help remedy of rebuttal, standing alone, is inadequate to its task does not mean that it is irrelevant to our inquiry.

the drastic alternatives of the *New York Times* privilege and the common law of strict liability for defamatory error. The "public or general interest" test for determining the applicability of the *New York Times* standard to private defamation actions inadequately serves both of the competing values at stake. On the one hand, a private individual whose reputation is injured by defamatory falsehood that does concern an issue of public or general interest has no recourse unless he can meet the rigorous requirements of *New York Times*. This is true despite the factors that distinguish the state interest in compensating private individuals from the analogous interest involved in the context of public persons. On the other hand, a publisher or broadcaster of a defamatory error which a court deems unrelated to an issue of public or general interest may be held liable in damages even if it took every reasonable precaution to ensure the accuracy of its assertions. And liability may far exceed compensation for any actual injury to the plaintiff, for the jury may be permitted to presume damages without proof of loss and even to award punitive damages.

We hold that, so long as they do not impose liability without fault, the States may define for themselves the appropriate standard of liability for a publisher or broadcaster of defamatory falsehood injurious to a private individual.[10] This approach provides a more equitable boundary between the competing concerns involved here. It recognizes the strength of the legitimate state interest in compensating private individuals for wrongful injury to reputation, yet shields the press and broadcast media from the rigors of strict liability for defamation. At least this conclusion obtains where, as here, the substance of the defamatory statement "makes substantial danger to reputation apparent." This phrase places in perspective the conclusion we announce today. Our inquiry would involve considerations somewhat different from those discussed above if a State purported to condition civil liability on a factual misstatement whose content did not warn a reasonably prudent editor or broadcaster of its defamatory potential. *Cf. Time, Inc. v. Hill*, 385 U.S. 374, 87 S.Ct. 534, 17 L.Ed.2d 456 (1967). Such a case is not now before us, and we intimate no view as to its proper resolution.

## IV

Our accommodation of the competing values at stake in defamation suits by private individuals allows the States to impose liability on the publisher or broadcaster of defamatory falsehood on a less demanding showing than that required by *New York Times*. This conclusion is not based on a belief that the considerations which prompted

---

10. Our caveat against strict liability is the prime target of Mr. Justice White's dissent. He would hold that a publisher or broadcaster may be required to prove the truth of a defamatory statement concerning a private individual and, failing such proof, that the publisher or broadcaster may be held liable for defamation even though he took every conceivable precaution to ensure the accuracy of the offending statement prior to its dissemination. *Post*, at 3031–3033. In Mr. Justice White's view, one who publishes a statement that later turns out to be inaccurate can never be "without fault" in any meaningful sense, for "[i]t is he who circulated a falsehood that he was not required to publish." *Post*, at 3033.

...Mr. Justice White asserts that our decision today "trivializes and denigrates the interest in reputation," *Miami Herald Publishing Co. v. Tornillo*, 418 U.S. at 262, 94 S.Ct. at 2842 (concurring opinion), that it "scuttle[s] the libel laws of the States in...wholesale fashion" and renders ordinary citizens "powerless to protect themselves." *Post*, at 3022. In light of the progressive extension of the knowing-or-reckless-falsity requirement detailed in the preceding paragraph, one might have viewed today's decision allowing recovery under any standard save strict liability as a more generous accommodation of the state interest in comprehensive reputational injury to private individuals than the law presently affords.

the adoption of the *New York Times* privilege for defamation of public officials and its extension to public figures are wholly inapplicable to the context of private individuals. Rather, we endorse this approach in recognition of the strong and legitimate state interest in compensating private individuals for injury to reputation. But this countervailing state interest extends no further than compensation for actual injury. For the reasons stated below, we hold that the States may not permit recovery of presumed or punitive damages, at least when liability is not based on a showing of knowledge of falsity or reckless disregard for the truth.

The common law of defamation is an oddity of tort law, for it allows recovery of purportedly compensatory damages without evidence of actual loss. Under the traditional rules pertaining to actions for libel, the existence of injury is presumed from the fact of publication. Juries may award substantial sums as compensation for supposed damage to reputation without any proof that such harm actually occurred. The largely uncontrolled discretion of juries to award damages where there is no loss unnecessarily compounds the potential of any system of liability for defamatory falsehood to inhibit the vigorous exercise of First Amendment freedoms. Additionally, the doctrine of presumed damages invites juries to punish unpopular opinion rather than to compensate individuals for injury sustained by the publication of a false fact. More to the point, the States have no substantial interest in securing for plaintiffs such as this petitioner gratuitous awards of money damages far in excess of any actual injury.

We would not, of course, invalidate state law simply because we doubt its wisdom, but here we are attempting to reconcile state law with a competing interest grounded in the constitutional command of the First Amendment. It is therefore appropriate to require that state remedies for defamatory falsehood reach no farther than is necessary to protect the legitimate interest involved. It is necessary to restrict defamation plaintiffs who do not prove knowledge of falsity or reckless disregard for the truth to compensation for actual injury. We need not define "actual injury," as trial courts have wide experience in framing appropriate jury instructions in tort actions. Suffice it to say that actual injury is not limited to out-of-pocket loss. Indeed, the more customary types of actual harm inflicted by defamatory falsehood include impairment of reputation and standing in the community, personal humiliation, and mental anguish and suffering. Of course, juries must be limited by appropriate instructions, and all awards must be supported by competent evidence concerning the injury, although there need be no evidence which assigns an actual dollar value to the injury.

We also find no justification for allowing awards of punitive damages against publishers and broadcasters held liable under state-defined standards of liability for defamation. In most jurisdictions jury discretion over the amounts awarded is limited only by the gentle rule that they not be excessive. Consequently, juries assess punitive damages in wholly unpredictable amounts bearing no necessary relation to the actual harm caused. And they remain free to use their discretion selectively to punish expressions of unpopular views. Like the doctrine of presumed damages, jury discretion to award punitive damages unnecessarily exacerbates the danger of media self-censorship, but, unlike the former rule, punitive damages are wholly irrelevant to the state interest that justifies a negligence standard for private defamation actions. They are not compensation for injury. Instead, they are private fines levied by civil juries to punish reprehensible conduct and to deter its future occurrence. In short, the private defamation plaintiff who establishes liability under a less demanding standard than that stated by

*New York Times* may recover only such damages as are sufficient to compensate him for actual injury.

## V

Notwithstanding our refusal to extend the *New York Times* privilege to defamation of private individuals, respondent contends that we should affirm the judgment below on the ground that petitioner is either a public official or a public figure. There is little basis for the former assertion. Several years prior to the present incident, petitioner had served briefly on housing committees appointed by the mayor of Chicago, but at the time of publication he had never held any remunerative governmental position. Respondent admits this but argues that petitioner's appearance at the coroner's inquest rendered him a "*de facto* public official." Our cases recognized no such concept. Respondent's suggestion would sweep all lawyers under the *New York Times* rule as officers of the court and distort the plain meaning of the "public official" category beyond all recognition. We decline to follow it.

Respondent's characterization of petitioner as a public figure raises a different question. That designation may rest on either of two alternative bases. In some instances an individual may achieve such pervasive fame or notoriety that he becomes a public figure for all purposes and in all contexts. More commonly, an individual voluntarily injects himself or is drawn into a particular public controversy and thereby becomes a public figure for a limited range of issues. In either case such persons assume special prominence in the resolution of public questions.

Petitioner has long been active in community and professional affairs. He has served as an officer of local civic groups and of various professional organizations, and he has published several books and articles on legal subjects. Although petitioner was consequently well known in some circles, he had achieved no general fame or notoriety in the community. None of the prospective jurors called at the trial had ever heard of petitioner prior to this litigation, and respondent offered no proof that this response was atypical of the local population. We would not lightly assume that a citizen's participation in community and professional affairs rendered him a public figure for all purposes. Absent clear evidence of general fame or notoriety in the community, and pervasive involvement in the affairs of society, an individual should not be deemed a public personality for all aspects of his life. It is preferable to reduce the public-figure question to a more meaningful context by looking to the nature and extent of an individual's participation in the particular controversy giving rise to the defamation.

In this context it is plain that petitioner was not a public figure. He played a minimal role at the coroner's inquest, and his participation related solely to his representation of a private client. He took no part in the criminal prosecution of Officer Nuccio. Moreover, he never discussed either the criminal or civil litigation with the press and was never quoted as having done so. He plainly did not thrust himself into the vortex of this public issue, nor did he engage the public's attention in an attempt to influence its outcome. We are persuaded that the trial court did not err in refusing to characterize petitioner as a public figure for the purpose of this litigation.

We therefore conclude that the *New York Times* standard is inapplicable to this case and that the trial court erred in entering judgment for respondent. Because the jury was allowed to impose liability without fault and was permitted to presume damages without proof of injury, a new trial is necessary. We reverse and remand for further proceedings in accord with this opinion.

Mr. Justice BLACKMUN, concurring.

...The Court today refuses to apply *New York Times* to the private individual, as contrasted with the public official and the public figure. It thus withdraws to the factual limits of the pre-*Rosenbloom* cases. It thereby fixes the outer boundary of the *New York Times* doctrine and says that beyond that boundary, a State is free to define for itself the appropriate standard of media liability so long as it does not impose liability without fault. As my joinder in *Rosenbloom*'s plurality opinion would intimate, I sense some illogic in this.

The Court, however, seeks today to strike a balance between competing values where necessarily uncertain assumptions about human behavior color the result. Although the Court's opinion in the present case departs from the rationale of the *Rosenbloom* plurality, in that the Court now conditions a libel action by a private person upon a showing of negligence, as contrasted with a showing of willful or reckless disregard, I am willing to join, and do join, the Court's opinion and its judgment for two reasons:

1. By removing the specters of presumed and punitive damages in the absence of *New York Times* malice, the Court eliminates significant and powerful motives for self-censorship that otherwise are present in the traditional libel action. By so doing, the Court leaves what should prove to be sufficient and adequate breathing space for a vigorous press. What the Court has done, I believe, will have little, if any, practical effect on the functioning of responsible journalism.

2. The Court was sadly fractionated in *Rosenbloom*. A result of that kind inevitably leads to uncertainty. I feel that it is of profound importance for the Court to come to rest in the defamation area and to have a clearly defined majority position that eliminates the unsureness engendered by *Rosenbloom*'s diversity. If my vote were not needed to create a majority, I would adhere to my prior view. A definitive ruling, however, is paramount. *See Curtis Publishing Co. v. Butts*, 388 U.S. at 170, 87 S.Ct. at 1999 (Black, J., concurring); *Time, Inc. v. Hill*, 385 U.S. 374, 398, 87 S.Ct. 534, 547, 17 L.Ed.2d 456 (1967) (Black, J., concurring); *United States v. Vuitch*, 402 U.S. 62, 97, 91 S.Ct. 1294, 1311, 28 L.Ed.2d 601 (1971) (separate statement).

For these reasons, I join the opinion and the judgment of the Court.

Mr. Chief Justice BURGER, dissenting.

The doctrines of the law of defamation have had a gradual evolution primarily in the state courts. In *New York Times Co. v. Sullivan*, 376 U.S. 254, 84 S.Ct. 710, 11 L.Ed.2d 686 (1964), and its progeny this Court entered this field.

Agreement or disagreement with the law as it has evolved to this time does not alter the fact that it has been orderly development with a consistent basic rationale. In today's opinion the Court abandons the traditional thread so far as the ordinary private citizen is concerned and introduces the concept that the media will be liable for negligence in publishing defamatory statements with respect to such persons. Although I agree with much of what Mr. Justice White states, I do not read the Court's new doctrinal approach in quite the way he does. I am frank to say I do not know the parameters of a "negligence" doctrine as applied to the news media. Conceivably this new doctrine could inhibit some editors, as the dissents of Mr. Justice Douglas Mr. Justice Brennan suggest. But I would prefer to allow this area of law to continue to evolve as it has up to now with respect to private citizens rather than embark on a new doctrinal theory which has no jurisprudential ancestry.

The petitioner here was performing a professional representative role as an advocate in the highest tradition of the law, and under that tradition the advocate is not to be invidiously identified with his client. The important public policy which underlies this tradition—the right to counsel—would be gravely jeopardized if every lawyer who takes an "unpopular" case, civil or criminal, would automatically become fair game for irresponsible reporters and editors who might, for example, describe the lawyer as a "mob mouthpiece" for representing a client with a serious prior criminal record, or as an "ambulance chaser" for representing a claimant in a personal injury action.

I would reverse the judgment of the Court of Appeals and remand for reinstatement of the verdict of the jury and the entry of an appropriate judgment on that verdict.

Mr. Justice DOUGLAS, dissenting.

The Court describes this case as a return to the struggle of "defin[ing] the proper accommodation between the law of defamation and the freedoms of speech and press protected by the First Amendment." It is indeed a struggle, once described by Mr. Justice Black as "the same quagmire" in which the Court "is now helplessly struggling in the field of obscenity." *Curtis Publishing Co. v. Butts,* 388 U.S. 130, 171, 87 S.Ct. 1975, 2000, 18 L.Ed.2d 1094 (concurring opinion). I would suggest that the struggle is a quite hopeless one, for, in light of the command of the First Amendment, no "accommodation" of its freedoms can be "proper" except those made by the Framers themselves.

Unlike the right of privacy which, by the terms of the Fourth Amendment, must be accommodated with reasonable searches and seizures and warrants issued by magistrates, the rights of free speech and of a free press were protected by the Framers in verbiage whose prescription seems clear. I have stated before my view that the First Amendment would bar Congress from passing any libel law. This was the view held by Thomas Jefferson[2] and it is one Congress has never challenged through enactment of a civil libel statute. The sole congressional attempt at this variety of First Amendment muzzle was in the Sedition Act of 1798—a criminal libel act never tested in this Court and one which expired by its terms three years after enactment. As President, Thomas Jefferson pardoned those who were convicted under the Act, and fines levied in its prosecution were repaid by Act of Congress. The general consensus was that the Act constituted a regrettable legislative exercise plainly in violation of the First Amendment.

With the First Amendment made applicable to the States through the Fourteenth, I do not see how States have any more ability to "accommodate" freedoms of speech or of the press than does Congress. This is true whether the form of the accommodation is civil or criminal since "[w]hat a State may not constitutionally bring about by means of a criminal statute is likewise beyond the reach of its civil law of libel." *New York Times Co. v. Sullivan,* 376 U.S. 254, 277, 84 S.Ct. 710, 724, 11 L.Ed.2d 686. Like Congress, States are without power "to use a civil libel law or any other law to impose damages for merely discussing public affairs." *Id.* at 295, 84 S.Ct. at 734 (Black, J., concurring).[6]

---

2. In 1798 Jefferson stated:
"[The First Amendment] thereby guard[s] in the same sentence, and under the same words, the freedom of religion, of speech, and of the press: insomuch, that whatever violates either, throws down the sanctuary which covers the others, *and that libels, falsehood, and defamation, equally with heresy and false religion, are withheld from the cognizance of federal tribunals....*"
8 *The Works of Thomas Jefferson* 464–465 (Ford ed. 1904) (emphasis added).
6. Since this case involves a discussion of public affairs, I need not decide at this point whether the First Amendment prohibits all libel actions. "An unconditional right to say what one pleases about public affairs is what I consider to be the minimum guarantee of the First Amendment." *New*

Continued recognition of the possibility of state libel suits for public discussion of public issues leaves the freedom of speech honored by the Fourteenth Amendment a diluted version of First Amendment protection. This view is only possible if one accepts the position that the First Amendment is applicable to the States only through the Due Process Clause of the Fourteenth, due process freedom of speech being only that freedom which this Court might deem to be "implicit in the concept of ordered liberty."[7] But the Court frequently has rested state free speech and free press decisions on the Fourteenth Amendment generally rather than on the Due Process Clause alone. The Fourteenth Amendment speaks not only of due process but also of "privileges and immunities" of United States citizenship. I can conceive of no privilege or immunity with a higher claim to recognition against state abridgment than the freedoms of speech and of the press. In our federal system we are all subject to two governmental regimes, and freedoms of speech and of the press protected against the infringement of only one are quite illusory. The identity of the oppressor is, I would think, a matter of relative indifference to the oppressed.

There can be no doubt that a State impinges upon free and open discussion when it sanctions the imposition of damages for such discussion through its civil libel laws. Discussion of public affairs is often marked by highly charged emotions, and jurymen, not unlike us all, are subject to those emotions. It is indeed this very type of speech which is the reason for the First Amendment since speech which arouses little emotion is little in need of protection. The vehicle for publication in this case was the *American Opinion*, a most controversial periodical which disseminates the views of the John Birch Society, an organization which many deem to be quite offensive. The subject matter involved "Communist plots," "conspiracies against law enforcement agencies," and the killing of a private citizen by the police. With any such amalgam of controversial elements pressing upon the jury, a jury determination, unpredictable in the most neutral circumstances, becomes for those who venture to discuss heated issues, a virtual roll of the dice separating them from liability for often massive claims of damage.

It is only the hardy publisher who will engage in discussion in the face of such risk, and the Court's preoccupation with proliferating standards in the area of libel increases the risks. It matters little whether the standard be articulated as "malice" or "reckless disregard of the truth" or "negligence," for jury determinations by any of those criteria are virtually unreviewable. This Court, in its continuing delineation of variegated mantles of First Amendment protection, is, like the potential publisher, left with only speculation on how jury findings were influenced by the effect the subject matter of the publication had upon the minds and viscera of the jury. The standard announced today

---

*York Times Co. v. Sullivan*, 376 U.S. 254, 297, 84 S.Ct. 710, 735, 11 L.Ed.2d 686 (Black, J., concurring). But "public affairs" includes a great deal more than merely political affairs. Matters of science, economics, business, art, literature, etc., are all matters of interest to the general public. Indeed, any matter of sufficient general interest to prompt media coverage may be said to be a public affair. Certainly police killings, "Communist conspiracies," and the like qualify....

7. *See Palko v. Connecticut*, 302 U.S. 319, 325, 58 S.Ct. 149, 152, 82 L.Ed. 288. As Mr. Justice Black has noted, by this view the test becomes "whether the government has an interest in abridging the right involved and, if so, whether that interest is of sufficient importance, in the opinion of a majority of the Supreme Court, to justify the government's action in doing so. Such a doctrine can be used to justify almost any government suppression of First Amendment freedoms. As I have stated many times before, I cannot subscribe to this doctrine because I believe that the First Amendment's unequivocal command that there shall be no abridgment of the rights of free speech shows that the men who drafted our Bill of Rights did all the 'balancing' that was to be done in this field." H. Black, *A Constitutional Faith* 52 (1969).

leaves the States free to "define for themselves the appropriate standard of liability for a publisher or broadcaster" in the circumstances of this case. This of course leaves the simple negligence standard as an option, with the jury free to impose damages upon a finding that the publisher failed to act as "a reasonable man." With such continued erosion of First Amendment protection, I fear that it may well be the reasonable man who refrains from speaking.

Since in my view the First and Fourteenth Amendments prohibit the imposition of damages upon respondent for this discussion of public affairs, I would affirm the judgment below.

Mr. Justice BRENNAN, dissenting.

I agree with the conclusion, expressed in Part V of the Court's opinion, that, at the time of publication of respondent's article, petitioner could not properly have been viewed as either a "public official" or "public figure;" instead, respondent's article, dealing with an alleged conspiracy to discredit local police forces, concerned petitioner's purported involvement in "an event of public or general interest." *Rosenbloom v. Metromedia, Inc.,* 403 U.S. 29, 31–32, 91 S.Ct. 1811, 1814, 29 L.Ed.2d 296 (1971); *see ante,* at 3002 n. 4. I cannot agree, however, that free and robust debate—so essential to the proper functioning of our system of government—is permitted adequate "breathing space," *N.A.A.C.P. v. Button,* 371 U.S. 415, 433, 83 S.Ct. 328, 338, 9 L.Ed.2d 405 (1963), when, as the Court holds, the States may impose all but strict liability for defamation if the defamed party is a private person and "the substance of the defamatory statement 'makes substantial danger to reputation apparent.'" *Ante,* at 3011.[1] I adhere to my view expressed in *Rosenbloom v. Metromedia, Inc., supra,* that we strike the proper accommodation between avoidance of media self-censorship and protection of individual reputations only when we require States to apply *the New York Times Co. v. Sullivan,* 376 U.S. 254, 84 S.Ct. 710, 11 L.Ed.2d 686 (1964), knowing-or-reckless-falsity standard in civil libel actions concerning media reports of the involvement of private individuals in events of public or general interest.

The Court does not hold that First Amendment guarantees do not extend to speech concerning private persons' involvement in events of public or general interest. It recognizes that self-governance in this country perseveres because of our "profound national commitment to the principle that debate on public issues should be uninhibited, robust, and wide-open." *Id.* at 270, 84 S.Ct. at 721. Thus, guarantees of free speech and press necessarily reach "far more than knowledge and debate about the strictly official activities of various levels of government," *Rosenbloom v. Metromedia, Inc., supra,* 403 U.S. at 41, 91 S.Ct. at 1818 for "[f]reedom of discussion, if it would fulfill its historic function in this nation, must embrace all issues about which information is needed or appropriate to enable the members of society to cope with the exigencies of their period." *Thornhill v. Alabama,* 310 U.S. 88, 102, 60 S.Ct. 736, 744, 84 L.Ed. 1093 (1940).

The teaching to be distilled from our prior cases is that, while public interest in events may at times be influenced by the notoriety of the individuals involved, "[t]he public's primary interest is in the event[,]...the conduct of the participant and the content, effect, and significance of the conduct...." *Rosenbloom, supra,* 403 U.S. at 43, 91 S.Ct. at 1819. Matters of public or general interest do not "suddenly become less so

---

1. *A fortiori* I disagree with my Brother *White*'s view that the States should have free rein to impose strict liability for defamation in cases not involving public persons.

merely because a private individual is involved, or because in some sense the individual did not 'voluntarily' choose to become involved." *Ibid. See Time, Inc. v. Hill,* 385 U.S. 374, 388, 87 S.Ct. 534, 542, 17 L.Ed.2d 456 (1967).

Although acknowledging that First Amendment values are of no less significance when media reports concern private persons' involvement in matters of public concern, the Court refuses to provide, in such cases, the same level of constitutional protection that has been afforded the media in the context of defamation of public persons. The accommodation that this Court has established between free speech and libel laws in cases involving public officials and public figures—that defamatory falsehood be shown by clear and convincing evidence to have been published with knowledge of falsity or with reckless disregard of truth—is not apt, the Court holds, because the private individual does not have the same degree of access to the media to rebut defamatory comments as does the public person and he has not voluntarily exposed himself to public scrutiny.

While these arguments are forcefully and eloquently presented, I cannot accept them, for the reasons I stated in *Rosenbloom:*

> The *New York Times* standard was applied to libel of a public official or public figure to give effect to the [First] Amendment's function to encourage ventilation of public issues, not because the public official has any less interest in protecting his reputation than an individual in private life. While the argument that public figures need less protection because they can command media attention to counter criticism may be true for some very prominent people, even then it is the rare case where the denial overtakes the original charge. Denials, retractions, and corrections are not "hot" news, and rarely receive the prominence of the original story. When the public official or public figure is a minor functionary, or has left the position that put him in the public eye..., the argument loses all of its force. In the vast majority of libels involving public officials or public figures, the ability to respond through the media will depend on the same complex factor on which the ability of a private individual depends: the unpredictable event of the media's continuing interest in the story. Thus the unproved, and highly improbable, generalization that an as yet (not fully defined) class of "public figures" involved in matters of public concern will be better able to respond through the media than private individuals also involved in such matters seems too insubstantial a reed on which to rest a constitutional distinction.

403 U.S. at 46–47, 91 S.Ct. at 1821.

Moreover, the argument that private persons should not be required to prove *New York Times* knowing-or-reckless falsity because they do not assume the risk of defamation by freely entering the public arena "bears little relationship either to the values protected by the First Amendment or to the nature of our society." *Id.* at 47, 91 S.Ct. at 1822. Social interaction exposes all of us to some degree of public view. This Court has observed that "[t]he risk of this exposure is an essential incident of life in a society which places a primary value on freedom of speech and of press." *Time, Inc. v. Hill,* 385 U.S. at 388, 87 S.Ct. at 543. Therefore,

> [v]oluntarily or not, we are all "public" men to some degree. Conversely, some aspects of the lives of even the most public men fall outside the area of matters of public or general concern. *See Griswold v. Connecticut,* 381 U.S. 479, 85 S.Ct. 1678, 14 L.Ed.2d 510 (1965). Thus, the idea that certain "public" figures have voluntarily exposed their entire lives to public inspection, while private indi-

viduals have kept theirs carefully shrouded from public view is, at best, a legal fiction. In any event, such a distinction could easily produce the paradoxical result of dampening discussion of issues of public or general concern because they happen to involve private citizens while extending constitutional encouragement to discussion of aspects of the lives of "public figures" that are not in the area of public or general concern.

*Rosenbloom, supra,* 403 U.S. at 48, 91 S.Ct. at 1822 (footnote omitted).

To be sure, no one commends publications which defame the good name and reputation of any person: "In an ideal world, the responsibility of the press would match the freedom and public trust given it." *Id.* at 51, 91 S.Ct. at 1823.[2] Rather, as the Court agrees, some abuse of First Amendment freedoms is tolerated only to insure that would-be commentators on events of public or general interest are not "deterred from voicing their criticism, even though it is believed to be true and even though it is in fact true, because of doubt whether it can be proved in court or fear of the expense of having to do so." *New York Times Co. v. Sullivan,* 376 U.S. at 279, 84 S.Ct. at 725.... Today's decision will exacerbate the rule of self-censorship of legitimate utterance as publishers "steer far wider of the unlawful zone," *Speiser v. Randall,* 357 U.S. 513, 526, 78 S.Ct. 1332, 1342, 2 L.Ed.2d 1460 (1958).

We recognized in *New York Times Co. v. Sullivan, supra,* 376 U.S. at 279, 84 S.Ct. at 725, that a rule requiring a critic of official conduct to guarantee the truth of all of his factual contentions would inevitably lead to self-censorship when publishers, fearful of being unable to prove truth or unable to bear the expense of attempting to do so, simply eschewed printing controversial articles. Adoption, by many States, of a reasonable-care standard in cases where private individuals are involved in matters of public interest—the probable result of today's decision—will likewise lead to self-censorship since publishers will be required carefully to weigh a myriad of uncertain factors before publication. The reasonable-care standard is "elusive," *Time, Inc. v. Hill, supra,* 385 U.S. at 389, 87 S.Ct. at 543; it saddles the press with "the intolerable burden of guessing how a jury might assess the reasonableness of steps taken by it to verify the accuracy of every reference to a name, picture or portrait." *Ibid.* Under a reasonable-care regime, publishers and broadcasters will have to make prepublication judgments about juror assessment of such diverse considerations as the size, operating procedures, and financial condition of the newsgathering system, as well as the relative costs and benefits of insti-

---

2. A respected commentator has observed that factors other than purely legal constraints operate to control the press:

> Traditions, attitudes, and general rules of political conduct are far more important controls. The fear of opening a credibility gap, and thereby lessening one's influence, holds some participants in check. Institutional pressures in large organizations, including some of the press, have a similar effect; it is difficult for an organization to have an open policy of making intentionally false accusations.

T. Emerson, *The System of Freedom of Expression* 538 (1970).

Typical of the press' own ongoing self-evaluation is a proposal to establish a national news council, composed of members drawn from the public and the journalism profession, to examine and report on complaints concerning the accuracy and fairness of news reporting by the largest newsgathering sources. Twentieth Century Fund Task Force Report on a National News Council, *A Free and Responsive Press* (1973). *See also* Comment, *The Expanding Constitutional Protection for the News Media from Liability for Defamation: Predictability and the New Synthesis,* 70 Mich. L. Rev. 1547, 1569–1570 (1972).

tuting less frequent and more costly reporting at a higher level of accuracy. *See The Supreme Court, 1970 Term*, 85 Harv. L. Rev. 3, 228 (1971)....

The Court does not discount altogether the danger that jurors will punish for the expression of unpopular opinions. This probability accounts for the Court's limitation that "the States may not permit recovery of presumed or punitive damages, at least when liability is not based on a showing of knowledge of falsity or reckless disregard for the truth. But plainly a jury's latitude to impose liability for want of due care poses a far greater threat of suppressing unpopular views than does a possible recovery of presumed or punitive damages....

Since petitioner failed, after having been given a full and fair opportunity, to prove that respondent published the disputed article with knowledge of its falsity or with reckless disregard of the truth, *see ante*, n. 2, I would affirm the judgment of the Court of Appeals.

---

Note that *Gertz* sets forth the minimum fault standard for adjudication of defamation claims consistent with constitutional norms. Some states have adopted the actual malice rule even as to private plaintiffs when the subject matter is within the sphere of public concern. New York has fashioned another standard, requiring private plaintiffs to prove that the publisher acted in a grossly irresponsible manner without due consideration for the standards of information gathering and dissemination ordinarily followed by responsible parties. *See Chapadeau v. Utica Observer-Dispatch, Inc.*, 38 N.Y.2d 196, 341 N.E.2d 569 (1975).

What fault standards should be applicable to libel claims asserted against non-media defendants? Consider Justice White's statement that it "makes no sense to give the most protection to those publishers who reach the most readers and therefore pollute the channels of communication with the most misinformation and do the most damage to private reputation." *Dun & Bradstreet, Inc. v. Greenmoss Builders, Inc.*, 472 U.S. 749, 784 (1985) (White, J., concurring). Justice Brennan has cautioned that "protection for the speech of nonmedia defendants is essential to ensure a diversity of perspectives." *Id.* at 773 n. 9 (Brennan, J, dissenting).

A critical threshold question in adjudications of Internet defamation claims is the determination of who is a public figure. Justice Powell justified the distinction for traditional mass communications purposes on the ground that public figures have significantly greater access to the channels of effective communication and hence have a more realistic means of counteracting false statements without resort to judicial intervention. *See Gertz v. Robert Welch, Inc.*, 418 U.S. at 344.

The Internet affords significant fora—as well as considerable opportunity to create fora—for rebuttal speech. Access to Internet resources is relatively inexpensive, and once access is achieved, the capacity for speech is virtually unbounded. One who objects to the substance of an electronic message posted on a bulletin board or in a chat room often can post a rebuttal message. Charges and responses in the cyberspace environment are so commonplace that the process has its own lexicon: when the dialog becomes acrimonious, it is referred to as "flame wars."

The degree to which the rebuttal message reaches the same or a similar audience may depend in large part on how quickly the message is posted; a reply posted virtually contemporaneously with the original posting likely will reach more of the same chat room participants or bulletin board visitors. Subjects of opprobrious speech may benefit, however, from having some time to marshal substantive support for arguments that the challenged statement is false, to allow time for emotional reactions to the posting to dissipate, and to craft the tone and content of the rebuttal.*

Aggrieved subjects of such messages have other options, as well. In addition to posting rebuttal messages in chat rooms and bulletin boards, responses can be placed on existing sites. Additionally, new web-sites can be fashioned to set forth alternative viewpoints in a more developed or less defensive mode.

One commentator has opined that this avenue offers scant relief for an aggrieved subject of opprobrium. "The ability to reply in cyberspace, just like in the real world, depends not just on one's access to the Internet, but also on the ability and willingness of others to access one's reply.... Finding a particular Web page from a local computer requires an affirmative step, either typing in the Internet address, searching for a relevant term using a search engine, or linking from a page that has already discovered the Web page." Michael Hadley, Note, *The Gertz Doctrine and Internet Defamation*, 84 Va. L. Rev. 477, 492 (1998).

Structural features of the World Wide Web appreciably enhance a parity of reply, however, when such exchanges occur among a known universe of recipients. The response arguably will reach the initial audience at least to the same degree as a retraction or clarification included in a newspaper, magazine, or television or radio broadcast. Further, a cyberspace communicant invariably has more control over whether his viewpoint will be published than an aggrieved subject who requests a newspaper, magazine, or broadcaster to air his response. *See, e.g., Miami Herald Publ'g Co. v. Tornillo*, 418 U.S. 241 (1974).

Justice Powell also justified the public/private figure dichotomy on the ground that public figures may have entered into a debate over public issues, resulting in a "compelling normative consideration underlying the distinction between public and private defamation plaintiffs." *Gertz v. Robert Welch, Inc.*, 418 U.S. at 344. Is one who engages in on-line postings automatically a public figure?

In *Kassel v. Gannet Co., Inc.*, 875 F.2d 935, 939–40 (1st Cir. 1989), the First Circuit envisaged a test for determining whether the plaintiff is a public official that rested on a "tripodal base." First, discussion of issues of public importance must be "uninhibited, robust, and wide-open;" because the inherent attributes of policymakers, upper-level administrators, and supervisors occupy niches of "apparent importance," they are public officials. Second, government workers who, by virtue of their employment, may easily defuse erroneous or misleading reports without the intervention of the judiciary, are more susceptible to ranking as public officials. Third, persons who actively sought positions of influence in public life have effectively assumed the risk that a diminution in privacy will ensue. How do these rationales apply in the digital communications era?

With respect to public figures when claims have been asserted in traditional media contexts, some courts look to whether: (1) the controversy at issue is public in the sense that it is the subject of discussion and people other than the immediate participants are likely to feel the impact of its resolution; (2) the plaintiff had more than a trivial or tan-

---

* The Supreme Court has observed that "an opportunity for rebuttal seldom suffices to undo harm of defamatory falsehood. Indeed, the law of defamation is rooted in our experience that the truth rarely catches up with a lie. But the fact that the self-help remedy of rebuttal, standing alone, is inadequate to its task does not mean that it is irrelevant to our inquiry." *Id.* at 344 n. 9.

gential role in the controversy; and (3) the alleged defamation was germane to the plaintiff's participation in the controversy. *See Trotter v. Jack Anderson Enterprises, Inc.*, 818 F.2d 431, 433–34 (5th Cir. 1987) (footnote omitted); *see also Waldbaum v. Fairchild Pub., Inc.*, 627 F.2d 1287, 1296–98 (D.C. Cir. 1980). Do multiple, independent chat room discussions about the same subject matter tend to support a finding on the test's first prong? Do extensive or multiple postings on the Web by the plaintiff tend to support findings on the second and third prongs of the test?

In *Ellis v. Time, Inc.*, No. Civ. A. 94-1755, 1997 WL 863267 at *1 (D.D.C. 1997), the plaintiff, a Reuters photographer, posted a series of messages on CompuServe in the National Press Photographers Association discussion group. The plaintiff's postings stated that certain photographs featured in a *Time* magazine article had been staged. *Id.* at *2. *Time* published a letter from its managing editor, questioning the plaintiff's efforts to "attempt to induce [one of the subjects of the photographs] to change his story for money....," and then subsequently published a letter to its readers referencing the denial of one of the photographs' subjects and expressing regret about *Time*'s "error" in having "run these pictures." *Id.* The plaintiff argued, among other things, that he was defamed by *Time*'s editorial comments.

The court summarily dismissed the libel claim, concluding that the plaintiff was a limited purpose public figure because he had thrust himself into the controversy surrounding the veracity of the photographs in order to influence the resolution of the issue. *Id.* at *3–6. He had, for example, posted messages for discussion by the press and met with the head of the prostitution ring. *Id.* at *5. The court evidently was persuaded by the extent of the plaintiff's overall participation in the debate and by the nexus between the plaintiff's posted comments and the underlying controversy. The court observed that "[w]hile on-line postings, even on controversial topics, will, under ordinary circumstances, likely be seen by few people, [the plaintiff] posted his message in a forum for journalists who, predictably, publicized the story." *Id.* at *5. The court indicated, however, that one who posts messages on an electronic bulletin board is not "by definition a limited purpose public figure. In this unusual case, the message was disseminated far beyond the Internet." *Id.* at *6.

---

## Notes and Questions

1. How does reliance on on-line sources affect determinations as to whether the defendant acted with the requisite degree of fault? To what extent is it appropriate for journalists and others to assess whether a source is funded by a particular interest group, for example? Does extensive use of hyperlinking capability — providing seamless transition among independently operated web-sites — tend to dilute the degree to which users are focusing on the source of the information reviewed? How do posted disclaimers, such as statements indicating that a web-site consists of "rumor" or "gossip," affect reliance on the substance of the site by others?

2. American jurisprudence has evinced a profound antipathy to the imposition of liability without fault in defamation claims. What standards should apply to content distributed on a global basis by an American information provider? Conversely, what standards should apply to content distributed into the United States by a foreign information provider?

---

# Gerald NICOSIA v. Diane DE ROOY

United States District Court, Northern District of California

No. C98-3029 MMC, 72 F. Supp. 2d 1093

July 7, 1999

CHESNEY, District Judge.

[For the background of this case, *see supra* at 245.]

[In addition to contending that the statements are matters of opinion,] De Rooy... moves to dismiss pursuant to Rule 12(b)(6) on the independent ground that Nicosia has failed to adequately plead actual malice. Public figures must prove actual malice in order to recover on defamation claims. *New York Times v. Sullivan*, 376 U.S. 254, 279–80, 84 S.Ct. 710, 11 L.Ed.2d 686 (1964). Actual malice means that the defamatory statement was made with "knowledge that it was false or with reckless disregard of whether it was false or not." *Id.* Reckless disregard means that the publisher "in fact entertained serious doubts as to the truth of his publication." *St. Amant v. Thompson*, 390 U.S. 727, 731, 88 S.Ct. 1323, 20 L.Ed.2d 262 (1968). To prove actual malice, a plaintiff must "demonstrate with clear and convincing evidence that the defendant realized that his statement was false or that he subjectively entertained serious doubts as to the truth of his statement." *Bose Corp. v. Consumers Union of U.S., Inc.,* 466 U.S. 485, 511 n. 30, 104 S.Ct. 1949, 80 L.Ed.2d 502 (1984).

Nicosia does not dispute that he is a limited-purpose public figure subject to the actual malice standard. Nor does Nicosia dispute that actual malice must be pled with specificity. *See Barger v. Playboy Enterprises, Inc.,* 564 F. Supp. 1151, 1156 (N.D. Cal. 1983) (requiring heightened pleading standard for malice; dismissing case with prejudice for failure to satisfy requirement). Instead, Nicosia presents two arguments to demonstrate that his complaint satisfies the heightened pleading standard.

First, Nicosia contends that his allegations that De Rooy was "motivated by a desire to advance her career, her book/calendar project, and by an animus toward him" sufficiently plead malice. The Court disagrees. Economic interests of the defendant and animus toward the plaintiff cannot serve as a basis for actual malice. *Harte-Hanks Comm. Inc. v. Connaughton*, 491 U.S. 657, 665, 109 S.Ct. 2678, 105 L.Ed.2d 562 (1989) ("Motive in publishing a story... cannot provide a sufficient basis for finding actual malice.") "[T]he actual malice standard is not satisfied merely through a showing of ill will or 'malice' in the ordinary sense of the term." *Id.* at 666, 109 S.Ct. 2678. "Nor can the fact that the defendant published the defamatory material in order to increase its profits suffice to prove actual malice." *Id.* at 667, 109 S.Ct. 2678.

Second, Nicosia argues malice is sufficiently pled because De Rooy is a self-proclaimed expert on the subject events and therefore De Rooy must have knowingly stated the falsehoods or at least been reckless with regard to the truth. There are two problems with this contention. One, Nicosia does not direct the Court to language in the complaint reflecting the above allegations. Two, even if the complaint did allege as much, conclusory statements that De Rooy should have known the truth does not satisfy the heightened pleading standard. In *Bose Corp. v. Consumers Union,* 466 U.S. 485, 512–13, 104 S.Ct. 1949, 80 L.Ed.2d 502 (1984), the Supreme Court rejected a similar argument proffered by the plaintiff in that case. The Supreme Court found that the trial court erred in finding actual malice based on the argument that the writer "must have realized the statement was inaccurate at the time he wrote it" because the writer was an expert in the field and the information upon which he relied did not support his conclusion. *Id.* Likewise, the Ninth Circuit has stated that a "must" or "should have" known argument "is an objective negligence test while the actual malice test…is deliberately subjective." *Newton v. NBC, Inc.,* 930 F.2d 662, 680 (9th Cir. 1990).

Accordingly, the Court finds that Nicosia has failed to plead actual malice with the required specificity, and hereby GRANTS De Rooy's motion to dismiss for failure to state a claim. For the reasons expressed in the following section, leave to amend would be futile.…

# Retractions and Clarifications

The extent to which a claimant has meaningful access to avenues of rebuttal is a significant factor in both the analytical rationale for the public/private figure dichotomy and the determination as to the claimant's status within this framework. *See* discussion *supra* at 281. In *Norris v. Bangor Publ'g Co.,* 53 F. Supp. 2d 495, 499, 504 (D. Me. 1999), for instance, the court deemed the plaintiff, a political opposition researcher, a limited purpose public figure in part because of his access to both traditional and electronic media. A plaintiff who frequents a particular chat room or posts messages to the electronic bulletin board where the allegedly defamatory statements appear may be a public figure with respect to that cyberspace community, even if he is not well known outside that community.

Many states have retraction statutes, which may affect the amount of damages a plaintiff can recover. Statutes that were enacted prior to the advent of extensive electronic communication do not expressly address application to on-line content. Certain retraction statutes, on their face, apply only to newspapers and other traditional print media; certain statutes refer only to newspapers and radio and television stations; and other statutes apply to all media.

Are newspaper web-sites covered by retraction statutes that apply to "newspapers"? Is the analysis affected if the web-site's content is different from its print counterpart? Courts confronting such issues may find guidance in the legislative intent underlying the retraction statutes. *Compare, e.g.,* Fla. Stat. Ann. § 770.02 (West 2000) (indicating application to publication or broadcast in a newspaper or periodical) *and Davies v. Bossert,* 449 So.2d 418, 420 (Fla. Dist. Ct. App. 1984) *with* Mont. Code Ann. § 27-1-818 (1999) *and Fitfield v. American Auto Ass'n,* 262 F. Supp. 253, 257–58 (D. Mont. 1967) (indicating application to "defamatory publication in or broadcast on any newspaper, magazine, periodical, radio or television station, or cable television system" to members of the media that are capable of publishing a quick and effective retraction). A retraction statute designed to cover media that can expeditiously correct an error has been held not to apply to a book publisher. *See id.* at 257–58. As book publishers enter the on-line arena, however, might such a statute have disparate application as to the print publication and its electronic counterpart of the same content?

In *It's In the Cards, Inc. v. Fuschetto, d/b/a Triple Play Collectibles,* 193 Wis. 2d 429 (Ct. App. 1995) ("*Fuschetto*"), the court considered a Wisconsin statute that provided that a libel plaintiff could not commence a civil action against a "newspaper, magazine, or periodical" unless he first demanded a correction and the challenged publication failed to publish a correction. When messages are posted to an electronic bulletin board, does the bulletin board come within the definition of a "newspaper, magazine, or periodi-cal?" The state appellate court held that random communications posted sporadically by bulletin board users were not "periodicals" under the ordinary meaning of the term because they were not published at regular intervals. In addition, the court stated that "the nature of bulletin board postings on computer network services cannot be classi-fied as print." *Id.* at 437, 535 N.W.2d at 14.

In *Fuschetto,* the court was required to assess only the Sports Net bulletin board. In-ternet publishers increasingly are offering multiple or hybrid products, however. A newspaper or magazine web-site may include a chat room, or provide a forum for post-ing notes and comments. Will the judicial analysis regarding application of particular statutes focus on the specific role the publisher assumed with respect to the challenged material? Such an approach may mean that identical content in one aspect of the elec-tronic publication would be subject to statutory corrective measures and in another as-pect might not. It is likely, then, that legislatures that have enacted retraction statutes eventually will resolve the issue by clarifying the statutory language, thereby providing clear guidance to the courts.

How do retraction statutes apply to Internet service providers? Under the Communi-cations Decency Act, 47 U.S.C.A. §230(c) (West Supp. 2000), providers and users of in-teractive computer services are not "publishers" or "speakers" of information furnished by another content provider. *See* discussion *supra* at 203. The liability of service providers who fail to correct or retract defamatory statements should be deemed to par-allel the contours of service providers' liability for the original content; therefore, Inter-net service providers should not be disadvantaged if they fail to implement corrective measures, unless the challenged content originated with that service provider.

---

# Robert ZELINKA v. AMERICARE
# HEALTHSCAN, INC., *et al.*

District Court of Appeal of Florida, Fourth District.
No. 99-3030, 2000 Fla. App. LEXIS 500
January 26, 2000

STEVENSON, J.

The issue in this case is whether a plaintiff in a libel action which is based on the posting of allegedly false and defamatory statements on an internet "message board" is required to comply with the presuit notice requirements of Florida Statutes chapter 770 (1999). The trial court determined that the statutory presuit notice requirements did not apply and denied petitioner's motion to dismiss respondents' defamation action where no presuit notice was alleged in the complaint. We deny the ensuing petition for writ of certiorari and conclude that the trial court did not depart from the essential re-quirements of the law in denying the motion to dismiss since petitioner, a mere inter-net-using, private individual, is not a "media defendant" to which the presuit notice re-quirements apply.

Respondents, Americare Healthscan, Inc., Americare Diagnostics, Inc., and Dr. Joseph P. D'Angelo, filed a four-count complaint against petitioner, Robert Zelinka, and other defendants, alleging in counts I and II libel *per se* and libel *per quod* based on the publication of allegedly false and defamatory statements on an internet "message board." The complaint alleges that the board where the messages were posted is maintained for the purpose of transmitting information about Technical Chemicals and Products, Inc., a corporation which was involved in litigation with the respondents. Zelinka was not alleged to be the owner or operator of the web site where the bulletin board was located.

The message board is described in the complaint as follows:

Yahoo! is accessed through the World Wide Web and is a bulletin board system which provides a means of communication between people all over the world wishing to communicate with other people regarding certain subjects or message boards that are maintained by Yahoo!. The messages posted on the Yahoo! board are disseminated among millions of people every day who use the Yahoo! bulletin board system to either communicate or to publish information regarding a subject of their choosing.

Florida Statutes section 770.01 requires that, in certain circumstances, notice must be given to a potential defendant before a libel action can be filed:

Notice condition precedent to action or prosecution for libel or slander. — Before any civil action is brought for publication or broadcast, in a newspaper, periodical, *or other medium*, of a libel or slander, the plaintiff shall, at least 5 days before instituting such action, serve notice in writing on the defendant, specifying the article or broadcast and the statements therein which he or she alleges to be false and defamatory. (emphasis supplied)

Section 770.02 allows the defendants to whom section 770.01 is applicable the right to avoid punitive damages by the timely publication of a correction, apology, or retraction.

In its original form, section 770.01 applied only to newspapers and periodicals. The Florida Supreme Court found that the notice requirement was designed to allow for the timely retraction of erroneous information in an attempt to balance the individual's right to be free from defamation against the public's "interest in the free dissemination of news." *Ross v. Gore*, 48 So.2d 412, 415 (Fla. 1950) (rejecting an equal protection claim). After looking at the underlying purpose for the legislation, the Court concluded that "[t]he provision for retraction is peculiarly appropriate to newspapers and periodicals, as distinguished from private persons." *Id.* at 414. The Court went on to note that "the Legislature might well have included radio broadcasting stations within the terms of the statute," but chose not to do so in that earlier version of the statute. *Id.*

In 1976, the statute was amended to include reference to "broadcasts" in addition to "publications" and to "other mediums" in addition to newspapers and periodicals. That was the last substantive amendment to section 770.01. The Third District interpreted the term "other medium" to refer to television and radio broadcasting stations, concluding that the section did not apply to broadcasts over the citizen's band radio. *See Davies v. Bossert*, 449 So.2d 418, 420 (Fla. 3d DCA 1984). *Compare Gifford v. Bruckner*, 565 So.2d 887 (Fla. 2d DCA 1990) (holding that section does not apply to defendant who flew airplane towing banner with alleged defamatory statements).

Petitioner asserts that this court should find that the internet is an "other medium" within the meaning of the statute, akin to broadcasts, periodicals, newspapers and the like. Petitioner argues that it is the responsibility of the courts to "'modernize traditional principals of tort law...as society and technology change,'" quoting *King v. Cutter Laboratories, Division of Miles, Inc.*, 714 So.2d 351, 355 (Fla.) (quoting *Conley v. Boyle Drug Co.*, 570 So.2d 275, 284 (Fla. 1990)), *review dismissed*, 725 So.2d 1108 (Fla. 1998).

Here, we need not reach the issue of whether the internet is a "medium" within the meaning of section 770.01. Even if an internet bulletin board was a "medium" within the scope of the statute, no precedent would allow this court to extend the statutory notice requirement to a private individual who merely posts a message on the board.

Every Florida court that has considered the question has concluded that the presuit notice requirement applies only to "media defendants," not private individuals. *See Tobkin v. Jarboe*, 695 So.2d 1257, 1258–59 (Fla. 4th DCA 1997) (holding that notice requirement does not apply to client who made Bar complaint), *approved on other grounds*, 710 So.2d 975 (Fla. 1998); *Gifford*, 565 So.2d at 887 (*see* discussion above); *Della-Donna v. Gore Newspapers Co.*, 463 So.2d 414 (Fla. 4th DCA 1985) (holding that section does not apply to non-media defendants); *Davies*, 449 So.2d at 418 (*see* discussion above); *Bridges v. Williamson*, 449 So.2d 400 (Fla. 2d DCA 1984) (holding that section does not apply even where individuals' statements were republished in a newspaper); *Ross*, 48 So.2d at 412 (*see* discussion above). *But see Laney v. Knight-Ridder Newspapers, Inc.*, 532 F. Supp. 910, 913 (S.D. Fla. 1982) (stating that "it would be grossly unfair...to deny non-media defendants [notice and] the opportunity to mitigate actual damages" by retraction), *expressly disapproved in Bridges and Davies.*

The terms media and non-media defendants are meant to distinguish between "third parties who are not engaged in the dissemination of news and information through the news and broadcast media from those who are so engaged." *Mancini*, 702 So.2d at 1380. In *Mancini*, this court concluded that the notice requirement applied to a newspaper columnist who allegedly made defamatory statements in her column, as well as to the newspaper itself, but not to private individuals. Based on the overwhelming authority going against petitioner on this point, we conclude that the notice requirement does not apply to a private individual who posts a message on a computer service that is owned and operated by someone else. The petitioner in this case is in the same position as that of the private individuals in the *Davies, Bridges* and *Gifford* cases, whose statements were "broadcast" to the public, but who themselves were not members of "the media."

It may well be that someone who maintains a web site and regularly publishes internet "magazines" on that site might be considered a "media defendant" who would be entitled to notice. Zelinka does not fall into that category; he is a private individual who merely made statements on a web site owned and maintained by someone else. Accordingly, we hold that the trial court did not depart from the essential requirements of the law in denying the motion to dismiss. The petition for writ of certiorari is, therefore, denied.

---

## Notes and Questions

1.  In addition to the constitutional limitations on defamation claims, certain additional defenses are available to media entities through the common law. Such defenses include the judicial and fair report privileges. The United States Supreme Court has observed that "perhaps the largest share of news concerning the doings of government appears in the form of accounts of reports, speeches, press conferences, and the like." *Time, Inc. v. Pape*, 401 U.S. 279, 286 (1971).

2.  Courts have long recognized a privilege to report on judicial and other official proceedings, even when the reputations of individuals may be adversely affected by the publication. The rule ameliorates the chilling effect of reporting on newsworthy

governmental actions, by relieving the press of the burden of having to establish the truth of the statements reported.

Analytically, the privilege is analogous to the defense of truth in that both defenses rest on the veracity of the report in issue. Unlike defending against a libel action on the basis that the challenged statement is substantially true, the fair report privilege may be defeated by a showing that the publisher acted solely for the purpose of harming the person defamed. Various rationales have been advanced for the privilege.

The agency theory is premised upon the notion that one who reports on a public official proceeding acts as a surrogate, or agent, for persons who had a right to attend, and informs them of what they might have seen for themselves. "The privilege rests upon the idea that any member of the public, if he were present, might see and hear for himself so that the reporter is merely a substitute for the public eye—this, together with the obvious public interest in having public affairs made known to all." W. Page Keeton, *et al., Prosser and Keeton on the Law of Torts,* § 115 at 836 (5th ed. 1984). In an early English case, *Curry v. Walker,* 126 Eng. Rep. 1046 (C.P. 1796), for example, Chief Justice Eyre instructed the jury that it is not unlawful to publish "a true account of what took place in a court of justice which is open to the world." The analytical impediment to this theory, however, is that it does not account for application of the privilege to proceedings or reports which are not open to the public.

The informational rationale for the privilege rests on the public interest in learning of important matters. The actions of governmental officials are of legitimate public concern and thus appropriately scrutinized.

Alternatively, a theory of public supervision has been advanced as a rationale. As Justice Holmes explained, the privilege is justified by

the security which publicity gives for the proper administration of justice.... It is desirable that the trial of causes should take place under the public eye, not because the controversies of one citizen with another are of public concern, but because it is of the highest moment that those who administer justice should always act under the sense of public responsibility and that every citizen should be able to satisfy himself with his own eyes as to the mode in which a public duty is performed.

*Cowley v. Pulsifer,* 137 Mass. 392, 394 (1884).

3. Once the privilege has been invoked successfully with respect to the publication of a defamatory statement, the burden is shifted back to the libel plaintiff to demonstrate that the defendant abused the privilege. The privilege may be defeated if the account of official reports was inaccurate.

4. How will the advent of sophisticated research capabilities on the Internet, and thus more facile access to a wide range of judicial records, likely affect the ability of the press to invoke this privilege as a defense?

5. What if the statement alleged to be defamatory is included in an official report but the report was not the reporter's source for his information? May the reporter still rely on the privilege if his account of the events, fortuitously, is a fair and reliable summary of the contents of an official report? In *Medico v. Time, Inc.,* 643 F.2d 134 (3d Cir. 1980), *cert. denied,* 454 U.S. 836 (1981), the plaintiff contended that there was a genuine issue of fact as to whether *Time* employees utilized the FBI materials

when they prepared the magazine article. The Third Circuit, applying Pennsylvania law, rejected this argument. *Id.* at 146–47. A Pennsylvania court had held that "[h]ow a reporter gathers his information concerning a judicial proceeding is immaterial provided his story is a fair and substantially accurate portrayal of the events in question." *Binder v. Triangle Publications, Inc.,* 442 Pa. 319, 327, 275 A.2d 53, 58 (1971) (*"Binder"*). The Second Circuit disagreed with this approach, holding that the fact that the Associated Press did not rely on official records in preparing its reports (but rather discovered them in the course of litigation) is dispositive of the issue. *Bufalino v. Associated Press,* 692 F.2d 266 (2d Cir. 1982), *cert. denied,* 462 U.S. 111 (1983). The Second Circuit acknowledged the Third Circuit's reliance on *Binder,* but pointed out that there the reporter ultimately had relied on information obtained at an official proceeding, albeit through an intermediary. "[W]here the media does not directly or indirectly rely upon official records, the policy underlying the privilege is inapplicable and the privilege itself should not be applied." *Bufalino v. Associated Press,* 692 F.2d at 271; *see also Phillips v. Evening Newspaper Co.,* 424 A.2d 78, 89 (D.C. App. 1980), *cert. denied,* 451 U.S. 989 (1981).

6.  Does the privilege apply to reports of foreign governments? The need for clear guidance on this issue likely will become more pronounced as the Internet is accessed to retrieve information about foreign countries.

In *Lee v. Dong-A Ilbo,* 849 F.2d 876 (4th Cir. 1988), *cert. denied,* 489 U.S. 1067 (1989), a South Korean citizen sued newspapers and a public television station, alleging that he had been libeled by their reports of a South Korean government press release identifying him as a North Korean agent. The Fourth Circuit reversed the Virginia district court's summary dismissal of the case and held that domestic reports of the press release were not privileged. The appellate court analyzed the rationales underlying the privilege, stating that the agency rationale is weakened because the information was available only in Korea, and the public supervision rationale applies only indirectly. By contrast, the informational rationale applies to all matters of importance, no matter what their source. *Id.* at 879. The privilege typically is extended because of the nature of the relationship the public shares with its government, which in turn is accountable to the citizenry for its actions. "Foreign governments, like nongovernmental sources of information, are not necessarily familiar, open, reliable, or accountable. Therefore, we think it unwise to provide a blanket privilege to those who report the activities of foreign governments." *Id.* at 879.

In *Corporate Training Unlimited, Inc. v. National Broadcasting Co., Inc.,* 868 F. Supp. 501 (E.D.N.Y. 1994), *summary judgment granted by* 981 F. Supp. 112 (E.D. N.Y. 1997), NBC sought to rely on criminal proceedings conducted in Iceland that its reporter attended. The district court noted that "[t]he fact that this was an Icelandic, as opposed to American, trial raises an intriguing question: whether the... privilege applies with equal force to reports of foreign judicial, legislative, or official proceedings." *Id.* at 509 n. 5. The court rejected NBC's defense, however, viewing the connection between the challenged broadcast and the proceedings as too attenuated. Despite specific mention in the challenged broadcast of the legal proceedings conducted in Iceland, the court felt that "[t]he ordinary viewer of the Broadcast would not have been under the impression that he was being presented with a report of the Icelandic judicial proceedings let alone a fair and true report of those proceedings." *Id.* at 509.

Compare these decisions with *Sharon v. Time, Inc.*, 599 F. Supp. 538 (S.D.N.Y. 1984), in which the plaintiff challenged *Time*'s republication of an Israeli commission's conclusion regarding the plaintiff's involvement in a Beirut massacre. The court stated in dicta that the plaintiff "did not base his suit on the overall thrust of *Time*'s critical article, most of which is absolutely protected either as opinion or as the fair report of a judicial proceeding." *Id.* at 543–44.

In *Friedman v. Israel Labour Party*, 957 F. Supp. 701 (E.D. Pa. 1997), the plaintiff challenged a statement that he was defamed by a press release announcing that the Israeli government had barred him and six other Americans from entering Israel, and by press coverage of the press release. In discussing the application of the fair report privilege to the official acts by foreign governments, the court stated:

> [T]ransnational supervision is arguably similar to the effect of the supervision that citizens in one state exert over citizens of a different state, and the publication of a different state's official reports in a second state is protected by the fair report privilege. In addition, as the success of many international human rights groups and the United Nations demonstrates, indirect supervision, i.e., public pressure, can play a large role in the affairs of foreign governments....

> Information concerning a United States citizen who is allegedly planning "illegal activities in Israel" is of legitimate and significant interest to the American public. Such information is neither "idle gossip," nor scandalous information, but important public security information conveyed to an audience eager to absorb it. With regard to the agency rationale, it too supports the existence and application of a qualified fair report privilege here. Although the statements [in issue] and the Israeli government's press release were available for public inspection to anyone in the world, most people chose to rely on the international press to disseminate the information worldwide....

> [Further,] the absence of the fair report privilege would effectively stand international news reporting on its head. Without the privilege, the news media who report international news would find it incredibly difficult, if not impossible, to publish reports of official acts of foreign governments without subjecting themselves to intolerable defamation liability....

> Recognizing the fair report privilege therefore allows the news media to continue to cover international stories without the fear of overwhelming defamation liability and also ensures that media markets, large and small, will continue to be provided with access to important international news and information.

*Id.* at 713 (citations and footnote omitted). In an effort to ameliorate concerns that the qualified privilege would be transmuted into a blanket privilege because a foreign official report would have the imprimatur of public interest, the court endorsed an ad hoc factual approach to assess the public's interest in particular defendants' news reports. *See id.* at 713–14.

# Chapter IV

# Privacy Interests

## Fundamental Principles of Privacy

The term "privacy" is not susceptible to facile definition in the field of communications. As one court observed, invasion of privacy torts are imbued with a "legally amorphous character." *Hill v. National Collegiate Athletic Ass'n,* 7 Cal. 4th 1, 25, 865 P.2d 633, 647 (1994). Privacy issues in the communications context often require a balancing between the right to engage in free speech and the right of individuals to "be let alone." While a wide range of issues relating to privacy has been the subject of judicial analysis and legislative initiative, an express right to privacy is not defined in either the original United States Constitution or the Bill of Rights.

Nonetheless, the concept of privacy is deeply embedded in the nation's political heritage, and is abstractly affirmed by the Bill of Rights' constraints on the government's power to interfere with individual liberty. Personal autonomy has been conceptualized as subsisting in penumbras that emanate from specific guarantees in the Bill of Rights. *See, e.g., Griswold v. Connecticut,* 381 U.S. 479, 484 (1965) (striking down a Connecticut statute that prohibited married couples from using contraceptives on the ground that the law impermissibly intruded on marital relationships). Encompassed in the notion of information privacy is the claim by "individuals, groups, or institutions to determine for themselves when, how, and to what extent information about them is communicated to others." Alan F. Westin, *Privacy and Freedom* 7 (1967). Autonomous control over disclosures of personal information has been a thematic element of privacy long before the advent of digital media: "for the individual, there is a need to keep some facts about himself wholly private, and to feel free to decide for himself who shall know other facts, at what time, and under what conditions." *Id.* at 368.

The judiciary has long recognized that "the right to keep information private was bound to clash with the right to disseminate information to the public." *Briscoe v. Reader's Digest Association, Inc.,* 4 Cal. 3d 529, 534, 93 Cal. Rptr. 866, 483 P.2d 34 (1971). "[I]t has long been apparent that the desire for privacy must at many points give way before our right to know, and the news media's right to investigate and relate, facts about the events and individuals of our time." *Shulman v. Group W Productions, Inc.,* 18 Cal. 4th 200, 208, 955 P.2d 469, 474, *reh'g denied,* 18 Cal. 4th 1034 (1998). The Supreme Court has acknowledged that "[e]xposure of the self to others in varying degrees is a concomitant of life in a civilized community. The risk of this exposure is an essential incident of life in a society which places a primary value on freedom of speech and of press." *Time, Inc. v. Hill,* 385 U.S. 374, 388 (1967). Intervening and technological changes notwithstanding, the fundamental analytical problems inherent in delimiting the parameters of a right of privacy remain; one court has opined that "if anything, [they have] intensified." *Shulman v. Group W Productions, Inc.*, 18 Cal. App. 4th at 208, 955 P.2d at 474. In the context of traditional media law, the term "privacy" has been used to connote a general right "to be left alone."

Precise definition of the right of the news media to gather and report on "private" matters remains elusive in the digital environment as well. Common law claims also have been advanced to redress perceived invasions of privacy arising from digital communications, and likely will continue to be fertile ground for dispute. *See* discussion *infra* at 294. Thus far, concerns about privacy relating to the Internet have focused primarily on the acquisition and use of information and on the security of private communications exchanged with others. Much of the attention on privacy issues relating to on-line communications and attendant legislative action have dealt with the commercial collection and exploitation of personal information. *See* discussion *infra* at 320. Some have predicted that:

> [p]rivacy of personal data will become an increasingly volatile legal issue as the commercial demand for that information grows. Individuals seeking to protect their personal data and organizations attempting to obtain access to that material for commercial purposes will both place pressure on the legal system to control the scope and terms of access to personal data.

George B. Delta and Jeffrey H. Matsuura, *Law of the Internet*, § 6.03 at 6-34 (2000).

---

# Common Law Privacy Claims

The genesis of the formulation of invasion of privacy causes of action is widely attributed to a law review article written in 1890 by Samuel D. Warren and Louis D. Brandeis, entitled *The Right to Privacy*, published by The Harvard Law Review. According to legend, in 1890, Mrs. Samuel D. Warren, "a young matron of Boston,...held at her home a series of social entertainments on an elaborate scale." The *Saturday Evening Gazette* covered her parties "in highly personal and embarrassing detail....The matter came to a head when the newspapers had a field day on the occasion of the wedding of a daughter and Mr. Warren became annoyed." Prosser, *Privacy*, 48 Cal. L. Rev. 383 (1960) (footnotes omitted). *But see* J. McCarthy, *The Rights of Publicity and Privacy*, § 1.3[C] (4th ed. 1999) (questioning the account).

The Warren and Brandeis article argued that the common law implicitly recognized a right of privacy. The authors asserted that:

> The press is overstepping in every direction the obvious bounds of propriety and of decency. Gossip is no longer the resource of the idle and of the vicious, but has become a trade, which is pursued with industry as well as effrontery. To satisfy a prurient taste the details of sexual relations are spread broadcast in the columns of the daily papers. To occupy the indolent, column upon column is filled with idle gossip, which can only be procured by intrusion upon the domestic circle. The intensity and complexity of life, attendant upon advancing civilization, have rendered necessary some retreat from the world, and man,

under the refining influence of culture, has become more sensitive to publicity, so that solitude and privacy have become more essential to the individual, but modern enterprise and invention have, through invasions upon his privacy, subjected him to mental pain and distress, far greater than could be inflicted by mere bodily injury.

Samuel D. Warren and Louise D. Brandeis, *The Right to Privacy*, 4 Harv. L. Rev. 193, 196 (1890). Warren and Brandeis conceded limitations on the parameters of the "right to be let alone," *id.* at 205, such as a privilege to publish matters of general or public interest, *id.* at 214.

While invasion of privacy claims met with some resistance initially, *see, e.g., Roberson v. Rochester Folding Box Co.*, 171 N.Y. 538, 64 N.E. 442 (1902), courts and legislatures began to recognize the tort in one or more forms. Four basic causes of action have been recognized by various states: false light, misappropriation, public disclosure of private facts, and intrusion on seclusion.

While all four torts use the lexicon of "invasion of privacy," they are founded upon disparate analyses. One commentator has characterized privacy as "a chameleon that shifts meaning depending on context." Jerry Kang, *Information Privacy in Cyberspace Transactions*, 50 Stan. L. Rev. 1193, 1202 (1998). Invasion of privacy allegations may arise from the alleged usurping of personal choice about the way the individual is portrayed to the public, transgressing of space, or interfering with control over the flow of personal information. All of these concerns play a role in privacy aspects of digital media as well.

---

# 1.  False Light

The gravamen of the false light cause of action is that the claimant has been placed in a "false light;" that is, in a manner that would be highly offensive to a reasonable person or a person of ordinary sensibilities. The tort is closely analogous to defamation, but is designed to redress false speech that injures feelings rather than reputation. Thus, the statement in issue need not necessarily be defamatory in order to be actionable, but nonetheless must be "offensive." While "trivial indignities" will not suffice to establish a claim, *see Godbehere v. Phoenix Newspapers Inc.*, 162 Ariz. 335, 340, 783 P.2d 781, 786 (1989), there must be "such a major misrepresentation of [the plaintiff's] character, history, activities or beliefs that serious offense may reasonably be expected to be taken by a reasonable man in [the plaintiff's] position," *Lane v. Random House*, 985 F. Supp. 141 (D.D.C. 1995) (quoting Restatement (Second) of Torts, §652E, cmt. c (1977)). Elements of false light claims include publication of the statement in issue; a statement that is "of and concerning" the plaintiff, *see* discussion *supra* at 233; a statement that is substantially false; and a showing that the defendant acted with the requisite degree of fault.

In *Time, Inc. v. Hill*, 385 U.S. 374, 387–88 (1967), the Supreme Court held that the constitutional protections for speech and press preclude recovery for invasion of privacy to redress false reports of matters of public interest in the absence of proof of actual malice; i.e., that the defendant published the report with knowledge of its falsity or in reckless disregard of the truth. Thus, whether the plaintiff was a public official or public figure was immaterial; the Court looked instead to whether the challenged publication concerned a matter of public interest. In a subsequent privacy case decided by the Supreme Court, *Cantrell v. Forest City Pub'g Co.*, 419 U.S. 245 (1974), the Court declined to decide whether all privacy cases about matters of public concern required a showing of actual malice, because such a showing had been made by the plaintiff in any event.

---

# Kenneth M. ZERAN v. DIAMOND BROADCASTING INC.

United States District Court, Western Division Oklahoma.
No. Civ-96-0008-T, 19 F. Supp. 2d 1249
December 29, 1997

RALPH G. THOMPSON, District Judge.

Plaintiff Kenneth M. Zeran instituted this action against defendant Diamond Broadcasting Inc. d/b/a KRXO Radio ("KRXO"), asserting [among other claims,] false light invasion of privacy....

The defendant owns and operates radio station KRXO in Oklahoma; its signal covers the Oklahoma City metropolitan area and can be heard a maximum radius of approximately seventy-five miles. In 1995, KRXO aired "Shannon and Spinozi," a weekday morning "drive time" talk show from 5:30 a.m. until 9:00 a.m. The show's hosts, Mark Shannon and Ron Benton, did not report the news during their morning program, but occasionally commented about news items. During this time period, the plaintiff resided in Seattle, Washington, where he was engaged in several business projects or ventures, including publishing *The Apartment Special*, a free guide which listed apartments available for rent in the Seattle area. He officed and had a business telephone in a room in his parent's home, where he lived.

Beginning on April 25, 1995, advertisements bearing the plaintiff's business phone number and the name "Ken ZZ03," or some variation of it, appeared as postings on American Online ("AOL").[3] The ads were for t-shirts and other items that made offensive references to the bombing of the A.P. Murrah Building in Oklahoma City. Interested buyers were told to call and "Ask for Ken." The plaintiff neither subscribed to AOL nor posted the message but, because of the advertisements, began to receive nasty, threatening phone calls.

On April 29, 1995, an AOL subscriber using the screen name "EckieA" and identifying himself as "Eck" (Hollywood) Prater, e-mailed a copy of the April 25 AOL posting to Mark Shannon, who first saw it either late on April 30 or early in the morning on May 1. Shannon, who did not know Prater, tried unsuccessfully to e-mail Ken ZZ03 through AOL. The response he received indicated that Ken ZZ03 was not an AOL member or was no longer using that screen name. Shannon did not try and call the phone number listed on the advertisement because it was before normal business hours.

On May 1, 1995, during the morning broadcast, Shannon commented on the ad being on AOL and read portions of the posting on the air, including the slogans purportedly displayed on the t-shirts. He urged listeners to call the plaintiff's telephone number, which he read repeatedly on the air, and let the seller know what Oklahomans

---

3. The person posting the first advertisement, which appeared on April 25, used the screen name "Ken ZZ03;" in the second advertisement, which followed on April 26, "KEN ZZ033" was used. In the final three ads, which were all posted on April 28, the screen name was "KEN Z033."

thought of him. He also engaged in a dialogue with his co-host, Spanoza, about the posting. Shannon attested that he believed that the ad was real, that someone actually was selling the t-shirts.[7]

Although the plaintiff had already received numerous calls prior to May 1, 1997, as a result of the broadcast the calls increased. Following the broadcast, the plaintiff also received death threats. The plaintiff called KRXO on May 1, 1995 and advised the station's general manager, Vance Harrison, Jr., that he had nothing to do with the AOL posting and requested that the station broadcast a retraction. Harrison told the plaintiff that KRXO would state on the air that the person at the phone number given out during the morning show had claimed he was not connected to the t-shirt sales. This was announced twice during the May 1, 1995 afternoon drive time show and once the next morning during the Shannon and Spinozi show.

The plaintiff does not know of anyone who knows him or knows of him by the name Ken Zeran, who saw the AOL postings, heard the May 1 broadcast on KRXO, or associated him with "Ken Z" or the phone number on the AOL advertisements. He "admits that he cannot identify by name anyone who thinks less of him today than they did before the postings."

On April 28, 1995, the plaintiff contacted the FBI about the advertisements and phone calls and subsequently notified the local police department. As a result of the postings and KRXO broadcast, the plaintiff suffered sleep deprivation and anxiety. He saw his family physician once and was prescribed an anxiety drug/sleeping pills. The plaintiff was unable to identify any specific interferences with his businesses or projects that were caused by the AOL postings and the KRXO broadcast....

In *Colbert* [*v. World Pub. Co.,*] 747 P.2d [286,] 290 [(Okla. 1987)], the Oklahoma Supreme Court specified the elements of a false light invasion of privacy claim:

> One who gives publicity to a matter concerning another that places the other before the public in a false light is subject to liability to the other for invasion of his privacy, if
>
> (a) the false light in which the other was placed would be highly offensive to a reasonable person, and
>
> (b) the actor had knowledge or acted in reckless disregard as to the falsity of the publicized matter and the false light in which the other would be placed.

*Id.* (quoting *McCormack v. Oklahoma Pub. Co.,* 613 P.2d 737, 740 (Okla. 1980)). Mere negligence is not sufficient to establish the requisite fault necessary to hold a defendant liable for false light invasion of privacy—the defendant must have "had a high degree of awareness of probable falsity or in fact entertained serious doubts as to the truth of the publication." *Colbert,* 747 P.2d at 291. While the defendant's employees acted negligently, there is no proof that they knew that the ads were fictitious or acted "recklessly," as that term is defined by the controlling authorities. *Cf. Harte-Hanks Communications v. Connaughton,* 491 U.S. 657, 688, 109 S.Ct. 2678, 105 L.Ed.2d 562 (1989) (in a libel action involving a public figure, "failure to investigate before publishing, even when a reasonably prudent person would have done so, is not sufficient to establish reckless

---

7. Shannon admitted during his deposition that had he been able to talk to the plaintiff before the broadcast and had he learned the facts, including that AOL had confirmed that the plaintiff was not Ken ZZ03 and that the FBI was investigating the matter, that, while he still would have read the posting, he would not have announced the phone number.

disregard"). The plaintiffs own expert attested, in essence, that the defendant's conduct did not satisfy the level of culpability necessary to impose liability: "Mark Shannon and Ron Benton were extremely negligent and violated standards of professional conduct when hosting the Shannon and Spinozi Show on May 1, 1995" and "failed to perform at a minimally acceptable level of professionalism." [The expert] notably avoided using the term "reckless." KRXO is, therefore, entitled to summary judgment on the plaintiff's false light invasion of privacy claim....

Accordingly, the defendant's motion for summary judgment is granted.[16]

----

### Notes and Questions

1. In affirming the district court's decision in *Zeran v. Diamond Broadcasting, Inc.,* the Tenth Circuit rejected the plaintiff's argument that by accepting the posting "at face value and failing to verify its authenticity," the defendants had acted with actual malice. Plaintiff's expert affidavit was deemed irrelevant, because he could not possibly have had personal knowledge as to whether the defendants' radio personnel had an actual, subjective awareness that what they were repeating on the air "was probably false." 203 F.3d 714, 720 (10th Cir. 2000).

2. Are causes of action sounding in defamation and false light redundant?

3. The Fourth Circuit stated in *Zeran v. America Online, Inc.,* 129 F.3d 327, 330 (4th Cir.) (footnotes omitted), *cert. denied,* 524 U.S. 937 (1998), that "lawsuits seeking to hold a service provider liable for its exercise of a publisher's traditional editorial functions—such as deciding whether to publish, withdraw, postpone or alter content—are barred." Would the originator of the content have any viable claim against the Internet service provider for having mis-edited the work so as to make it appear that the content provider had, for example, endorsed prejudiced viewpoints?

4. New York is among those states that do not recognize a false light invasion of privacy claim. How does this affect forum shopping in light of the geographically indiscriminate publication by digital media?

----

## 2. Misappropriation

The tort of misappropriation is premised upon a showing that one has appropriated to his own use or benefit the name or likeness of another. *See generally* Restatement (Second) of Torts, §652C (1977). The tort most frequently is asserted to protect from appropriation the valuable property right in names and likenesses. This right has been blurred with references to a "right of publicity," which signifies a property right in the value of an individual's personality.

Undoubtedly, the most notable right of publicity case is *Zacchini v. Scripps-Howard Broadcasting Co.,* 433 U.S. 562 (1977). There, the plaintiff, who had a fifteen-second act

----

16. The court is not, by its rulings, condoning, in the slightest, the behavior of the radio station's employees, but is constrained by the applicable law to reach these decisions on the plaintiff's claims.

in which he was shot from a canon, challenged the defendant's broadcast of his act. The Supreme Court held that the First Amendment did not prevent a state from protecting the performer's interest in the economic value of his performance when the defendant had broadcast the performance in its entirety. "[T]he State's interest in permitting a 'right of publicity' is in protecting the proprietary interest of the individual in his act in part to encourage such entertainment." *Id.* at 573. Note that the "[p]etitioner [did] not seek to enjoin the broadcast of his performance; he simply want[ed] to be paid for it." *Id.* at 578.

Like copyright laws, *see* discussion *infra* at 389, the appropriation tort safeguards incentives to create expression by protecting the economic value derived from the work.[1] Analogous to the fair use defense to claims of copyright infringement, *see* discussion *infra* at 425, uses that are merely "incidental" to protected content are not actionable. *See, e.g., Lane v. Random House, Inc.,* 985 F. Supp. 141 (D.D.C. 1995) (using Kennedy assassination conspiracy theorist's picture to advertise book about conspiracy theories protected from common law appropriation claim).

The incidental use exception was first adopted in New York in *Humiston v. Universal Film Mfg. Co.,* 189 A.D. 467, 178 N.Y.S. 752 (App. Div. 1919). There, a news disseminator was held to be entitled to display the name and likeness of a woman who was the subject of the disseminator's newsreel for purposes of promoting and selling the film. The use of the plaintiff's name and picture in the advertisement was "incidental to the exhibition of the film itself." *Id.* at 467, 178 N.Y.S. at 759. This provides an important safeguard for free speech, so that misappropriation sanctions will "not...apply to publications concerning newsworthy events or matters of public interest." *Creel v. Crown Publishers, Inc.,* 115 A.D.2d 414, 415, 496 N.Y.S.2d 219, 220 (App. Div. 1985).

Underlying this protection is a recognition that the use of the name or likeness helps "to inform potential readers about the contents [of the news product] and induce them to purchase it...." *Groden v. Random House, Inc.,* No. 94 Civ. 1074, 1994 WL 455555 at *4 (S.D.N.Y. 1994), *aff'd,* 61 F.3d 1045 (2d Cir. 1995). Application of this rationale demands that matters of public interest be broadly defined. *See Arrington v. New York Times Co.,* 55 N.Y.2d 433, 440, 434 N.E.2d 1319, 1322 (1982), *cert. denied,* 459 U.S. 1146 (1983). Thus, the words "advertising purposes" and for the "purposes of trade" are to be "construed narrowly and not used to curtail the right of free speech, or free press, or to shut off the publication of matters of newsworthy or of public interest, or to prevent comment on matters in which the public has an interest or the right to be informed." *Rand v. Hearst Corp.,* 31 A.D.2d 406, 408, 298 N.Y.S.2d 405 (App. Div. 1969), *aff'd,* 26 N.Y.2d 806, 257 N.E.2d 895 (1970).

Further, claims based on "collateral" uses, such as in the form of advertisements with prominent use of a name, have been unavailing. Thus, the use by *Sports Illustrated* of photographs of Joe Namath, former quarterback of the Jets, in promotional material that was printed adjacent to a subscription application for the magazine, did not constitute a violation of Namath's right of privacy in contravention of New York law. *Namath v. Sports Illustrated,* 80 Misc. 2d 531, 533, 363 N.Y.S.2d 276, 279 (Sup. Ct.), *aff'd,* 48

---

1. Indeed, because of the doctrinal relationship, issues sometimes arise as to whether copyright laws preempt misappropriation and right of publicity claims. *See, e.g., Wendt v. Host Intern., Inc.,* 125 F.3d 806 (9th Cir. 1997), *petition for reh'g en banc denied,* 197 F.3d 1284 (9th Cir. 1999) (determining claim by actors who had appeared in the television series "Cheers" that animatronic robots, allegedly based on actors' likenesses, violated actors' right of publicity; the defendant had secured a license from Paramount, the copyright holder).

A.D.2d 487, 371 N.Y.S.2d 10 (App. Div. 1975), *aff'd*, 39 N.Y.2d 897, 352 N.E.2d 584 (1976). The court acknowledged that it was

> understandable that Namath desires payment for the use of his name and likeness in advertisements for the sale of publications in which he has appeared as newsworthy just as he is paid for collateral endorsement of commercial products. This he cannot accomplish under the existing law of our State and Nation. Athletic prowess is much admired and well paid in this country. It is commendable that freedom of speech and the press under the First Amendment transcends the right to privacy. This is so particularly when a petitioner seeks remuneration for what is basically a property right—not a right to privacy.

*Id.* at 535, 363 N.Y.S.2d at 280.

---

# KNB ENTERPRISES v. Greg W. MATTHEWS
Court of Appeal of California, Second Appellate District, Division One
78 Cal. App. 4th 362, 92 Cal. Rptr. 2d 713
February 17, 2000

OPINION BY: ORTEGA

In *Fleet v. CBS, Inc.* (1996) 50 Cal. App. 4th 1911, the appellate court held that unpaid film actors' claims for misappropriation of name, photograph, or likeness under section 3344 of the Civil Code were preempted by federal copyright law, where the only misappropriation alleged was the film's authorized distribution by the exclusive distributor, CBS. Here, we must decide whether photography models' misappropriation claims under [Cal. Civ. Code] section 3344 are preempted by federal copyright law, where the alleged exploitation was the unauthorized display, for profit, of the models' erotic photographs on defendant's internet website featuring sexually explicit photographs.

Plaintiff KNB Enterprises...seeks section 3344 damages for the commercial appropriation of the models' photographs caused by their unauthorized commercial display on defendant Greg W. Matthew's website, Justpics. The models' section 3344 rights that plaintiff asserts in this action were obtained by contractual assignment.

We conclude that because a human likeness is not copyrightable, even if captured in a copyrighted photograph, the models' section 3344 claims against the unauthorized publisher of their photographs are not the equivalent of a copyright infringement claim and are not preempted by federal copyright law. Accordingly, we reverse the summary judgment for defendant and remand for further proceedings.

## BACKGROUND

For purposes of their cross-motions for summary judgment only, the parties stipulated to the following facts.

There are 417 erotic photographs at issue. The photographs depict 452 models, all of whom have assigned their section 3344 rights to plaintiff. Plaintiff owns the copyright to all the photographs.

Plaintiff displays erotic photographs on its own website. To promote its website, plaintiff intermittently posts its copyrighted photographs to certain Usenet newsgroups.

By posting its photographs on the Usenet, plaintiff is not placing them in the public domain or permitting their unauthorized commercial use, display, or publication.

Defendant uses a software program to identify and copy sexually explicit photographs posted on the Usenet. Using this software, defendant, over a period of time, copied and displayed the models' photographs, without plaintiff's permission, on defendant's commercial website, Justpics. Justpics is not a newsgroup or bulletin board system. Justpics charges its customers a monthly membership fee to view the erotic photographs retrieved by Justpics from the Usenet. The models' photographs were displayed on Justpics in their original state, but without plaintiff's accompanying text, captions, and headers.

Defendant concedes that Justpics' unauthorized display of the models' photographs is not protected by any privilege afforded to news reporting or commentary on matters of public interest. None of the models depicted in the photographs is a known celebrity. Similarly, none of the photographers is recognized "as a master of the genre."

Plaintiff concedes that defendant did not use the models' photographs in a manner that implied the existence of a commercial endorsement of defendant's actions: "Neither the models, photographers, nor (Plaintiff) KNB Enterprises has been used by defendants as a "spokesman" or presented as endorsing the actions of defendants in any way."

## DISCUSSION

The right to prevent others from appropriating one's photograph for commercial gain has evolved from the common law right of privacy.... This action concerns the fourth category, appropriation for the defendant's advantage of the models' photographs, which is also referred to as the right of publicity. (*Wendt v. Host Intern., Inc.* (9th Cir. 1997) 125 F.3d 806, 811.)

The right of publicity has come to be recognized as distinct from the right of privacy. In the commercial arena, celebrity endorsements are often considered a valuable marketing tool. What may have originated as a concern for the right to be left alone has become a tool to control the commercial use and, thus, protect the economic value of one's name, voice, signature, photograph, or likeness. In 1971, California enacted section 3344, a commercial appropriation statute which complements the common law tort of appropriation.

Section 3344, subdivision (a) provides in relevant part:

> Any person who knowingly uses another's name, voice, signature, photograph, or likeness, in any manner, on or in products, merchandise, or goods, or for purposes of advertising or selling, or soliciting purchases of, products, merchandise, goods or services, without such person's prior consent... shall be liable for any damages sustained by the person or persons injured as a result thereof. In addition, in any action brought under this section, the person who violated the section shall be liable to the injured party or parties in an amount equal to the greater of seven hundred fifty dollars ($750) or the actual damages suffered by him or her as a result of the unauthorized use, and any profits from the unauthorized use that are attributable to the use and are not taken into account in computing the actual damages....

Although the unauthorized appropriation of an obscure plaintiff's name, voice, signature, photograph, or likeness would not inflict as great an economic injury as would be suffered by a celebrity plaintiff, California's appropriation statute is not limited to celebrity plaintiffs. Section 3344 provides for minimum damages of $750, even if no actual damages are proven. In discussing a similar Nevada statute, the Nevada Supreme Court noted that the legislative purpose for providing a minimum recovery for non-celebrities is "to discourage such appropriation." (*Hetter v. District Court* (1994) 110 Nev. 513, 519, 874 P.2d 762, 765).

In this case, none of the models is a celebrity. Their anonymity, however, is allegedly a valuable asset in the marketing of erotic photographs. Plaintiff alleged in the complaint: "...Although it is hard to measure how much the defendants profited by their acts, they profited in three ways. First, they got sales. The additional photos encouraged consumers to buy access to their sites—i.e., memberships—and also helped the defendants retain existing members. The photos were especially valuable because many of the models were new to modeling, and 'new faces' are prized in the adult field and difficult to find. Second, the defendants saved money. Their copying—rather than creation or purchase—of photos, saved the costs of scouting for and casting models, photographer fees, model fees, film and processing, studios, photo scanning and digitizing, and other direct and incidental expenses. Third, the defendants saved time—by substituting a few moments of copying for what could have been days or weeks of work in hiring photographers, casting models, processing and scanning photos, and other activities."

The issue we face is whether the non-celebrity models' section 3344 claims, which plaintiff asserts by right of assignment, are preempted by federal copyright law. "California law concerning right to publicity, as any state statute or law, is subject to preemption under the supremacy clause of the United States Constitution if it "actually conflicts with a valid federal statute" or "'stands as an obstacle to the accomplishment and execution of the full purposes and objectives of Congress.'" (*Edgar v. MITE Corp.* (1982) 457 U.S. 624, 631, 73 L. Ed. 2d 269, 102 S. Ct. 2629....) In addition, "when acting within constitutional limits, Congress is empowered to pre-empt state law by so stating in express terms. [Citation.]" (*California Federal S. & L. Assn. v. Guerra* (1987) 479 U.S. 272, 280, 93 L. Ed. 2d 613, 107 S. Ct. 683....).

17 United States Code section 301, part of the 1976 Copyright Act...expressly prohibits states from legislating in the area of copyright law....Thus, for preemption to occur under the Act, two conditions must be met: first, the subject of the claim must be a work fixed in a tangible medium of expression and come within the subject matter or scope of copyright protection as described in sections 102 and 103 of 17 United States Code, and second, the right asserted under state law must be equivalent to the exclusive rights contained in section 106. [Citations.]" (*Fleet v. CBS, Inc., supra,* 50 Cal. App. 4th at pp. 1918–1919, 58 Cal. Rptr. 2d 645.)

There can be no dispute that photographs are copyrightable. According to the Nimmer treatise on copyright law: "Photographs clearly fall within the Section 102(a)(5) classification of "pictorial, graphic and sculptural works." The Copyright Act does not contain a definition of a photograph, but subject to the fixation requirement, it would appear to include any product of the photographic process, whether in print or negative form, including filmstrips, slide films and individual slides.....It is, of course, fundamental that copyright in a work protects against unauthorized copying, not only in the original medium in which the work was produced, but also in any other medium as well. Thus, copyright in a photograph will preclude unauthorized copying by drawing or in any other form, as well as by photographic reproduction." (1 *Nimmer on Copyright* (1999) § 2.08[E], pp. 2-128–2-129, fns. omitted.)

It is also undisputed that the unauthorized commercial display of the copyrighted photographs on defendant's website constituted an infringement of plaintiff's exclusive

17 United States Code section 106 rights. The question that remains, however, is whether plaintiff's statutory appropriation claim based on the violation of the models' section 3344 rights is the equivalent of a copyright infringement claim.

The facts of this case do not quite fit those of other similar cases....

[I]n a New York decision, *Russell v. Marboro Books* (1959) 18 Misc. 2d 166 [183 N.Y.S.2d 8], Mary Jane Russell, a famous professional model, signed an unrestricted release allowing a well-known photographer, Richard Avedon, to use a photograph of the model taken for a bookstore's advertising campaign. The photograph was published for its intended purpose without incident. Thereafter, however, the bookstore asked Avedon for the negative, falsely claiming that more bookstore posters were needed. The bookstore sold the negative to a bedsheet manufacturer, which altered the photograph to give the false appearance that Russell "had posed for a bedsheet advertisement portraying a willing call girl waiting to be used by a stranger whetting his sexual appetite." (18 Misc. 2d at p. 171.) The New York court held that Russell was entitled to sue for violation of her statutory right of publicity. The court found that although plaintiff had given an unrestricted release permitting the use of her photograph without her inspection and approval, she did not, as a matter of law, agree to "the dissemination of all types of altered pictures or of libelous material." (*Id.* at p. 182.)

In this case, the models released their rights in the photographs to plaintiff. Plaintiff did not, however, consent to defendant's unauthorized use of the photographs.... [T]his case from Fleet because this is not a situation where the models are asserting a right of publicity claim against the exclusive copyright holder in an effort to halt the authorized distribution of their photographs. This case is closer, although not entirely similar, to... *Russell*, in that plaintiff is asserting the models' statutory right of publicity claim to halt the unauthorized display of the photographs. In this case, although the models consented to have plaintiff display, copy, publish, or assign the photographs as he pleased, plaintiff did not assign those rights to defendant.

Defendant contends that in this case, the models' statutory right of publicity claims are indistinguishable from plaintiff's copyright infringement claim because the only wrong alleged was the unauthorized publication of the copyrighted photographs, or an infringing use.... Professor Nimmer's treatise and others [have been cited] as authority... [for the point that] "...a right is equivalent to rights within the exclusive province of copyright when it is infringed by the mere act of reproducing, performing, distributing, or displaying the work at issue. A claim asserted to prevent nothing more than the reproduction, performance, distribution, or display of a dramatic performance captured on film is subsumed by copyright law and preempted." (*Fleet v. CBS, Inc., supra,* 50 Cal. App. 4th at p. 1924.)

The actual language of Nimmer's treatise, however, leads us to a different conclusion. The passage from *Nimmer* relied upon by the court in Fleet states: "Abstracting to the realm of principle, if under state law the act of reproduction, performance, distribution, or display, no matter whether the law includes all such acts or only some, will in itself infringe the state-created right, then such right is pre-empted. But if qualitatively other elements are required, instead of, or in addition to, the acts of reproduction, performance, distribution, or display, in order to constitute a state-created cause of action, then the right does not lie "within the general scope of copyright," and there is no preemption." (1 *Nimmer on Copyright, supra,* § 1.01[B][1], p. 1-13, fns. omitted.)

*Fleet* failed to mention, however, Nimmer's caveat that right of publicity claims generally are not preempted by the Copyright Act. According to Nimmer: "Invasion of privacy may sometimes occur by acts of reproduction, distribution, performance, or display, but inasmuch as the essence of the tort does not lie in such acts, pre-emption should not apply. The same may be said of the right of publicity.... A persona can hardly be said to constitute a 'writing' of an 'author' within the meaning of the Copyright Clause of the Constitution. *A fortiori*, it is not a 'work of authorship' under the Act. Such name and likeness do not become a work of authorship simply because they are embodied in a copyrightable work such as a photograph." (1 *Nimmer on Copyright*, *supra*, § 1.01[B][1][c], pp. 1-22–1-23, fns. omitted.)

Accordingly, we would limit *Fleet's* broad language regarding preemption of the actors' section 3344 claims to the unique facts of that case. In our view, a section 3344 claim is preempted under *Fleet* where an actor or model with no copyright interest in the work seeks to prevent the exclusive copyright holder from displaying the copyrighted work. We do not believe a section 3344 claim is preempted under *Fleet* where, as here, the defendant has no legal right to publish the copyrighted work.

Returning to the two-part test for determining preemption (the subject of the claim must be a work fixed in a tangible medium of expression and come within the subject matter or scope of copyright protection, and the right asserted under the state law must be equivalent to the exclusive rights contained in 17 United States Code section 106), we conclude neither condition has been met in this case. First, the subjects of the claims are the models' likenesses, which are not copyrightable even though "embodied in a copyrightable work such as a photograph." (1 *Nimmer on Copyright*, *supra*, § 1.01[B][1][c], p. 1-23, fn. omitted.) Second, the right asserted under the state statute, the right of publicity, does not fall within the subject matter of copyright. (*Id.* at pp. 1-22–1-23.) Accordingly, we conclude the models' section 3344 claims are not preempted by federal copyright law.

## DISPOSITION

We reverse the summary judgment for defendant and remand for further proceedings. Plaintiff is awarded costs on appeal.

---

The Internet provides vast opportunities for the display of names, images, and likenesses. Are these displays subject to the same guidelines as so-called traditional media uses? In *Stern v. Delphi Internet Services*, 165 Misc. 2d 21, 626 N.Y.S.2d 694 (Sup. Ct. 1995), radio talk show host Howard Stern objected to the display of an advertisement that included a "flamboyant" photograph of him "in leather pants which largely exposed his buttocks." *Id.* at 22, 626 N.Y.S.2d at 695. The ad, along with a caption that read "Should this man be the next governor of New York?" was placed on an on-line bulletin board service the defendant had established for comment about Stern's candidacy for governor of New York. *Id.* The ad promoted the defendant's bulletin board service, encouraging visitors to the site to "tell the world exactly what you think. The Internet's the one frontier even the King of (Almost) All Media hasn't conquered. And Delphi's where you get aboard. The on-line service that 'leads the way in Internet access.'" *Id.* at 22, 626 N.Y.S.2d at 696.

Stern complained that the use of the photograph commercially misappropriated his name and likeness, citing New York's statute, N.Y. Civ. Rights Law §§ 50–51 (McKinney 1992). It was undisputed that the defendant used Stern's name and image without his permission for advertising purposes. But inclusion of the photograph within the advertisement was deemed lawful under the incidental use exception. *See Stern v. Delphi Internet Services*, 165 Misc. 2d at 29, 626 N.Y.S.2d at 700.

A preliminary issue for the *Stern* court was whether the electronic bulletin board service operated by the defendant constituted a news dissemination service analogous to those provided by news vendors and bookstores; the latter are not burdened with a duty to monitor the content of all of its distributions. The *Stern* court reasoned that such protection similarly should be afforded to on-line computer services when they are engaged in traditional news dissemination. *Id.* at 26, 696 N.Y.S.2d at 697–98; *see also Daniel v. Dow Jones & Co.,* 137 Misc. 2d 94, 102, 520 N.Y.S.2d 334, 340 (Civ. Ct. 1987). Such dissemination—whether of books, periodicals, or other publications—requires purchase of materials for the public to gain access to the information contained within them. *See Stern v. Delphi Internet Services Corp.,* 165 Misc. 2d at 24, 626 N.Y.S.2d at 697. "[I]t is clear that what drives the 'incidental use' exception is the First Amendment interest in protecting the ability of news disseminators to publicize, to make public, their own communications." *Id.* at 29, 626 N.Y.S.2d at 700 (citations omitted). The court even noted that "it is ironic that Stern, a radio talk show host (as well as author and would-be politician) seeks to silence the electronic equivalent of a talk show, an on-line computer bulletin board service." *Id.* at 30, 626 N.Y.S.2d at 700. Accordingly, the court readily concluded that the incidental advertising exception to New York's commercial misappropriation statute applies to all news disseminators, including those made available electronically. *Id.* Stern's candidacy, a matter of electoral politics, was unquestionably within the range of subjects of public interest. Because Stern's name and likeness were placed on the defendant's bulletin board service in a fashion related to the content of the news within the service, the use was within the ambit of the incidental use exception. *Id.*

---

## Kimberly LEARY v. Debra PUNZI, *et al.*

Supreme Court, Suffolk County, New York
1999 N.Y. Slip Op. 99124, 179 Misc.2d 1025, 687 N.Y.S.2d 551
February 16, 1999

ELIZABETH H. EMERSON, J.

[The plaintiff, a former employee of defendant Long Island Ballet Center Inc., alleged that the defendants misappropriated the use of her name. She asserted that after her employment was terminated, an article appeared in *Suffolk Life* newspaper and on defendant's web-site identifying her as the manager for the defendant. The web-site was based upon information provided by the parties in 1995 to Millennium Productions, Inc., an organization that apparently created the site on behalf of the defendants.] ...

[New York] Civil Rights Law § 51 authorizes a civil action for injunctive relief and damages where the name or likeness of any living person is used for advertising or trade purposes without the written consent of that person in violation of Civil Rights Law § 50 (*see Kane v. Orange County Publications,* 232 A.D.2d 526, 649 N.Y.S.2d 23 [2d Dept. 1996]). Civil Rights Law §§ 50 and 51 "were drafted narrowly to encompass only the commercial use of an individual's name or likeness and no more" (*Kane v. Orange County Publications, supra* at 527, 649 N.Y.S.2d 23, quoting *Arrington v. New York Times Co.,* 55 N.Y.2d 433, 439, 449 N.Y.S.2d 941, 434 N.E.2d 1319, *cert. denied,* 459 U.S. 1146, 103 S.Ct. 787, 74 L.Ed.2d 994). A name is used "for advertising purposes" if it appears in a publication which, taken in its entirety, was distributed for use in, or as part of, an advertisement or solicitation for patronage of a particular product or service (*see Bever-*

*ley v. Choices Women's Medical Center, Inc.,* 78 N.Y.2d 745, 579 N.Y.S.2d 637, 587 N.E.2d 275). "Trade purposes" is more difficult to define *(see Davis v. High Society Magazine,* 90 A.D.2d 374, 457 N.Y.S.2d 308 [2d Dept. 1982]), and involves use which would draw trade to the defendant *(see Kane v. County Publications, supra; Flores v. Mosler Safe Co.,* 7 N.Y.2d 276, 196 N.Y.S.2d 975, 164 N.E.2d 853). However, courts have carved out exceptions so that the statute does not apply to publications concerning newsworthy events or matters of public interest *(see Stephano v. News Group Publications, Inc.,* 64 N.Y.2d 174, 184, 485 N.Y.S.2d 220, 474 N.E.2d 580; *Creel v. Crown Publishers, Inc.,* 115 A.D.2d 414, 496 N.Y.S.2d 219 [1st Dept. 1985]).

Here, the web site in question was not a home page created by the defendants for the purpose of advertising or promotion. Rather, the record indicates that the defendants provided information at no cost to a third party which created web sites for arts organizations under the listing "www.arts-online.com." Thus, there is nothing in the record to indicate that the defendants were responsible for creating or maintaining the web site. Moreover, a web site on the Internet providing information about arts organizations is certainly a matter of some public interest. Even assuming, however, that the web site constitutes advertising or trade purposes within the meaning of the statute, it is well settled that where a reference to an individual is "fleeting and incidental," it will not be actionable under Civil Rights Law § 51 *(see Marks v. Elephant Walk, Inc.,* 156 A.D.2d 432, 548 N.Y.S.2d 549 [2d Dept. 1989]; *Delan v. CBS, Inc.,* 91 A.D.2d 255, 458 N.Y.S.2d 608 [2d Dept. 1983]). Whether a particular use is incidental is determined through an assessment of the "relationship of the references to a particular individual to the main purpose and subject of the [work in issue] *(Delan v. CBS, Inc., supra* at 260, 458 N.Y.S.2d 608, quoting *Ladany v. Morrow & Co.,* 465 F. Supp. 870, 882 (S.D.N.Y. 1978)). In this case, the plaintiff's name was not used in a manner directly related to the product or service. The plaintiff was not identified as a dancer or performer promoting the organization, but only as a contact person to call for additional information. Therefore, under these circumstances, any potential rewards for using the plaintiff's name were too remote and speculative to sustain her claim *(see Marks v. Elephant Walk, Inc., supra; Griffin v. Harris, Beach, Wilcox, Rubin & Levey,* 112 A.D.2d 514, 490 N.Y.S.2d 919 [3d Dept. 1985]).

Accordingly, the defendants' motion for summary judgment is granted, the plaintiff's cross-motion is denied and the complaint is dismissed.

---

# 3. Public Disclosure of Private Facts

Perhaps the formulation of the tort with which Warren and Brandeis were most concerned was the claim that evolved as invasion of privacy by public disclosure of private facts. *See* Samuel D. Warren and Louis D. Brandeis, *The Right to Privacy,* 4 Harv. L. Rev. 193, 196 (1890), *see supra* at 294. Elements of the public disclosure of private facts tort include publication, about an identifiable plaintiff, of facts that are private, the disclosure of which would be highly offensive to reasonable persons and which are not legitimate matters of public interest or concern. Unlike defamation and false light invasion of privacy claims, then, the public disclosure of private facts tort presupposes that the disclosure is true.

Truthful speech generally has been protected in a variety of contexts. Truth is a defense to a claim of defamation, for example. In order to temper the potentially vague and troublesome aspects of a tort premised upon accurate publication of an event, the cause of action generally cannot proceed absent a showing that the matter publicized is such that would be highly offensive to a reasonable person and is not of legitimate public concern. *See generally* Restatement (Second) of Torts, § 652D (1977).

Because the gravamen of the tort is the divulgence of facts that are private, to state an actionable claim, the plaintiff must show that the facts were not already known or available from public records. With respect to Internet communications, information that may be freely accessed would negate an inference of privacy.

Publication of newsworthy statements generally do not give rise to liability. This principle has sometimes been characterized as a "newsworthiness privilege," or conceptualized as a defense to the tort. First Amendment expert Judge Robert Sack believes that the better approach recognizes newsworthiness to be an element of the tort itself, because information of legitimate public interest is not legally private. Robert D. Sack, *Sack on Defamation: Libel, Slander, and Related Problems* § 12.4.5 at 12-40-41 (3d ed. 1999).

He also regards the term "newsworthy" to be a misnomer. "Protection is not limited to publication of 'news;' it is afforded for dissemination of anything within the boundaries of legitimate public interest or concern. The term 'general interest' is more accurate." *Id.*

In alleging that a particular matter was not newsworthy, plaintiffs sometimes argue that the facts disclosed were too "stale" to be of legitimate public interest. In *Briscoe v. Reader's Digest Association*, 4 Cal. 3d 529, 93 Cal. Rptr. 866, 483 P.2d 34 (1971), for instance, the plaintiff challenged an article describing his conviction for a truck hijacking, which had occurred more than a decade before the article's publication. Since the crime, the plaintiff had not been involved in criminal conduct, and his prior conviction had not been known to his family and friends. Although the incident was the subject of public records, the California Supreme Court expressed doubt that "identification of the actor in reports of long past crimes usually serves... [an] independent public purpose." *Id.* 4 Cal. 3d at 537, 93 Cal. Rptr. at 872. Significantly, the lower court subsequently summarily dismissed the claim on grounds of newsworthiness. *Briscoe v. Reader's Digest Association, Inc.,* 1 Media L. Rptr. (BNA) 1852 (C.D. Cal. 1972).

In another case, the plaintiff had been convicted of murder twice, and pardoned twice. *Bernstein v. National Broadcasting Co.,* 129 F. Supp. 817, 828 (D.D.C. 1955), *aff'd*, 232 F.2d 369 (D.C. Cir.), *cert. denied*, 352 U.S. 945 (1956). Twenty years later, the defendant broadcast an account of a named reporter's efforts to secure the plaintiff's release. The plaintiff's name was not disclosed in the broadcast. The court acknowledged that once an individual was involved in a public event, he could not be protected from subsequent disclosures. However, the public identification of a person's current position might give rise to a new disclosure, which if unwarranted, could lead to an invasion of privacy claim.

To some degree, the courts appear less troubled by subsequent discussion of events themselves than by the identification of the actor with the event. How does a publisher determine when identification of the individuals who played relevant roles in the incident described is gratuitous? Might the identification help lend credence to the accuracy of the report? In the digital age of communications, information that is stored on websites or in databases may be readily retrieved. Does intervening attention to such matters, as where users access archived information in the time period between the event and the challenged disclosure, undermine the viability of a claim?

The occasional judicial reticence to dismiss privacy claims arising from disclosures of dated events may be the product of sympathy toward plaintiffs who have undergone rehabilitation since the event in question. But aspects of the plaintiff's status other than rehabilitation may be relevant to the inquiry. As to private figures, the closer the nexus of the facts disclosed to the newsworthy component of the publication in issue, the more likely its disclosure will be protected. If the claimant is a public figure or a public official, his life inevitably gives rise to significant public interest. The depth of the intrusion into the plaintiff's private affairs and the manner in which the information is divulged on-line may, as the following case illustrates, be a factor in the court's consideration.

## Bret MICHAELS v. INTERNET ENTERTAINMENT GROUP, INC., *et al.*

United States District Court, Central District of California

No. CV 98-0583 DDP (CWX), 5 F. Supp. 2d 823

April 27, 1998

PREGERSON, District Judge.

This matter comes before the Court on the motions of the plaintiff, Bret Michaels ("Michaels"), and the intervenor, Pamela Anderson Lee ("Lee") (collectively, the "plaintiffs"), for a preliminary injunction to prevent dissemination of a videotape ("the Tape") in which Michaels and Lee claim a copyright. Dissemination of the Tape by defendant Internet Entertainment Group, Inc. ("IEG") is currently prohibited by this Court's Temporary Restraining Order ("TRO"), issued February 27, 1998. IEG has consented to several extensions of the TRO....

Michaels is a musician, best known as the lead singer of the rock band "Poison." Michaels asserts that he is now engaged in a second career as a feature film director. Lee is a well-known television and film actor.

Defendant IEG is a corporation involved in the distribution of adult entertainment material through a subscription service on the Internet.

On or about October 31, 1994, Michaels and Lee recorded the Tape, which depicts them having sex.

On December 31, 1997, Michaels received a letter from IEG claiming that IEG had acquired the Tape and all rights necessary to publish the Tape...[and Michaels, through his attorney, wrote to IEG to object to any display of the Tape on the Internet.]...

The elements of the tort of public disclosure of private facts are (1) public disclosure (2) of a private fact (3) which would be offensive and objectionable to the reasonable person and (4) which is not of legitimate public concern. [citation omitted]

[T]he public disclosure...tort[ is] subject to a newsworthy privilege, which protects the First Amendment freedom to report on matters of public concern. See *Diaz* [*v. Oakland Tribune, Inc.*, 139 Cal.App.3d 118, 188 Cal.Rptr. 762, 767 (1983)]. Newsworthiness is defined broadly to include not only matters of public policy, but any matter of public concern, including the accomplishments, everyday lives, and romantic involvements of famous people. See *Eastwood* [*v. Superior Court (National Enquirer)*, 149 Cal.App.3d 409, 198 Cal.Rptr. 342, 350 (1983)].

The privilege to report newsworthy information is not without limit. "Where the publicity is so offensive as to constitute a morbid and sensational prying into private lives for its own sake, it serves no legitimate public interest and is not deserving of protection." *Diaz,* 188 Cal. Rptr. at 767 (internal quotation marks omitted); *Virgil v. Time, Inc.,* 527 F.2d 1122, 1129 (9th Cir. 1975); Restatement 2d Torts § 652D cmt. h.

## 1. Likelihood of Success on the Merits

Here, distribution of the Tape on the Internet would constitute public disclosure. The content of the Tape—Michaels and Lee engaged in sexual relations—constitutes a set of private facts whose disclosure would be objectionable to a reasonable person.

IEG makes three related contentions based on Lee's status as a "sex symbol." First, IEG contends that matters regarding sex should not be considered private with regard to Lee because her acting career is in part based on sex. Second, IEG contends that because a foreign Internet source has already released part of the Tape, the facts it contains are no longer private. Third, IEG contends that Lee's status as a sex symbol, and Michaels's status as a rock star make the sex acts depicted on the Tape newsworthy.

### a. Do Sex Symbols Have Privacy?

IEG contends that because Lee has appeared nude in magazines, movies and publicly distributed videotapes, the facts contained on the Tape depicting her having sex are no longer private. IEG's contention unreasonably blurs the line between fiction and reality. Lee is a professional actor. She has played roles involving sex and sexual appeal. The fact that she has performed a role involving sex does not, however, make her real sex life open to the public. *See Virgil,* 527 F.2d at 1131; *Briscoe v. Reader's Digest Ass'n,* 4 Cal.3d 529, 93 Cal. Rptr. 866, 869, 483 P.2d 34 (1971) (noting that even for non-actors, public life requires the assumption of various roles, and that "[l]oss of control over which 'face' one puts on may result in literal loss of self-identity [citations], and is humiliating beneath the gaze of those whose curiosity treats a human being as an object.").

IEG contends that the wide distribution of a different videotape, one depicting sexual relations between Lee and her husband Tommy Lee, negates any privacy interest that Lee might have in the Tape depicting sexual relations with Michaels. The facts depicted on the Tommy Lee tape, however, are different from the facts depicted on the Michaels Tape. Sexual relations are among the most personal and intimate of acts. The Court is not prepared to conclude that public exposure of one sexual encounter forever removes a person's privacy interest in all subsequent and previous sexual encounters.

It is also clear that Michaels has a privacy interest in his sex life. While Michaels's voluntary assumption of fame as a rock star throws open his private life to some extent, even people who voluntarily enter the public sphere retain a privacy interest in the most intimate details of their lives. *See Virgil,* 527 F.2d at 1131 ("[A]ccepting that it is, as matter of law, in the public interest to know about some area of activity, it does not necessarily follow that it is in the public interest to know private facts about the persons who engage in that activity."); Restatement 2d Torts § 652D cmt. h.

The Court notes that the private matter at issue here is not the fact that Lee and Michaels were romantically involved. Because they sought fame, Lee and Michaels must tolerate some public exposure of the fact of their involvement. *See Eastwood,* 198 Cal. Rptr. at 351. The fact recorded on the Tape, however, is not that Lee and Michaels were romantically involved, but rather the visual and aural details of their sexual relations, facts which are ordinarily considered private even for celebrities. For this reason,

IEG's reliance on *Carlisle v. Fawcett Publications, Inc.*, 201 Cal.App.2d 733, 20 Cal. Rptr. 405 (1962), is misplaced. *Carlisle*, like *Eastwood*, involved publicity about the fact of a famous person's romantic involvement, as well as some of the details of that involvement. Neither case, however, involved graphic depictions of the most intimate aspects of the relationships.

In short, the Court concludes that the private facts depicted on the Michaels Tape have not become public either by virtue of Lee's professional appearances as an actor, or by dissemination of the Tommy Lee videotape.

### b. Publication of a 148-Second Section of the Tape on the Dutch Internet Site

IEG presents evidence that a 148-second clip from the Tape was posted on the Internet on or about April 16, 1998. IEG contends that the publication of this clip converts the intimate activities depicted on the Tape to matters of public knowledge, and that, therefore, the plaintiffs no longer have a privacy interest to assert in the Tape. *See Lee v. Penthouse Int'l Ltd.*, 25 Med. L. Rptr. 1651, 1656 (C.D. Cal. 1997) (granting defendant's motion for summary judgment on claim for disclosure of private facts because photographs at issue had already been published); *Sipple v. Chronicle Publ'g Co.*, 154 Cal. App. 3d 1040, 201 Cal. Rptr. 665 (1984) (holding that plaintiff's sexual orientation was no longer a private fact because it had previously been published).

In *Sipple* and Lee, however, all of the matters in which the plaintiffs asserted privacy were already well-known before the defendants re-published the information. Here, however, exposure of a small portion of the Tape began to occur ten days ago. The Court cannot conclude from this recent publication that the contents of the 148-second clip are now matters of public knowledge. Additionally, in *Sipple* and *Lee* the previously published information corresponded exactly to the information in which the plaintiffs asserted a privacy interest. *Sipple*, 201 Cal. Rptr. at 669; *Lee*, 25 Med. L. Rptr. at 1652. Here, the plaintiffs assert a privacy interest in all of the intimate activity depicted on the Tape. The plaintiffs' privacy interest in the unreleased portions of the Tape is undiminished.

The Court also notes that the ability of the plaintiffs to assert a privacy interest in the 148-second segment of the Tape does not affect the preliminary injunctive relief to which the plaintiffs are entitled. While the plaintiffs' privacy interest in the 148-second clip might be diminished, the plaintiffs' copyright in this portion of the Tape is unaffected. Any loss of privacy interest therefore provides no basis for relaxing this preliminary injunction's prohibition on copying, reproducing, publishing, disseminating, distributing or circulating the 148-second portion of the Tape. Additionally, prior publication of the 148-second segment does not negate the plaintiffs' right to exploit their names, likenesses, and identities for their own benefit. The publication of the 148-second segment therefore provides no basis for modifying the prohibition on marketing, advertising or promoting the Tape.

### c. Newsworthiness Privilege

In order to determine whether the contents of the Tape are covered by the privilege for reporting private but newsworthy information, the Court must balance (1) the social value of the facts published; (2) the depth of the intrusion into ostensibly private affairs; and (3) the extent to which the party voluntarily acceded to a position of public notoriety. *Diaz*, 188 Cal. Rptr. at 772; *Capra v. Thoroughbred Racing Ass'n of North America, Inc.*, 787 F.2d 463, 464 (9th Cir. 1986). At trial or at summary judgment, the burden is on the plaintiffs to prove that the information they seek to protect is not newsworthy. *Diaz*, 188 Cal. Rptr. at 769.

The first factor, the social value of the facts published, weighs against a finding of newsworthiness. It is difficult if not impossible to articulate a social value that will be advanced by dissemination of the Tape.

The second factor, depth of intrusion, also weighs against a finding of newsworthiness. This factor is to be applied with an eye toward community mores as to the depth of intrusion. *See Virgil*, 527 F.2d at 1131. At trial, it will be for the finder of fact to determine the state of community mores regarding the depth of intrusion. *Id.* For purposes of this motion, the Court determines that the plaintiffs are likely to convince the finder of fact that sexual relations are among the most private of private affairs, and that a video recording of two individuals engaged in such relations represents the deepest possible intrusion into such affairs.

The third factor, voluntary accession to fame, weighs in favor of a finding of newsworthiness. Michaels and Lee declare that they have cultivated fame throughout their careers. In Lee's case, her fame arises in part from television and movie roles based on sex and sexual appeal.

The first two factors weigh heavily against a finding of newsworthiness for the contents of the Tape. The third factor weighs somewhat in favor of a finding of newsworthiness for the contents of the Tape. Weighing the factors together, the Court concludes that the plaintiffs have demonstrated a likelihood of success in meeting their burden to show that the contents of the Tape are not covered by the newsworthiness privilege.

The Court notes, however, a critical distinction which IEG has attempted to blur in its papers. The fact that the Tape exists and that it is the focus of this dispute is newsworthy. While the fact of the Tape's existence is somewhat intrusive into the plaintiffs' privacy, this intrusion is outweighed by the strong public interest in litigation concerning individuals' right to privacy. Although this preliminary injunction prohibits IEG from violating the plaintiffs' right to privacy by disseminating the contents of the Tape, the injunction does not restrict IEG's ability to participate in public discussion about the Tape or this litigation.

2. Irreparable Injury

By definition, an actionable disclosure of private facts must be highly offensive to a reasonable person. The injury inflicted is therefore to the plaintiffs' "human dignity and peace of mind." 2 McCarthy § 11.7[A]. Although monetary damages are available for such injuries, they are difficult to quantify, and such injuries are to some extent irreparable. Furthermore, the privacy of the acts depicted on the Tape cannot be restored by monetary damages after the Tape becomes public. The nature of the Internet aggravates the irreparable nature of the injury. Once the Tape is posted on IEG's web site, it will be available for instant copying and further dissemination by IEG's subscribers.

In light of the foregoing, the Court concludes that the plaintiffs are entitled to a preliminary injunction prohibiting the dissemination of the Tape in order to prevent a violation of the plaintiffs' state law right of privacy in the contents of the Tape....

IT IS HEREBY ORDERED that, pending final judgment or dismissal of this action, defendant IEG and its agents, officers, employees, attorneys, and those acting in concert with them are temporarily restrained from:

1. Selling, attempting to sell, causing to be sold, permitting any other individual or entity to sell, copying, reproducing, preparing derivative works, publishing, disseminat-

ing, distributing, circulating, promoting, marketing, and advertising of the Michaels/Lee videotape (the "Tape");

2. Selling, attempting to sell, causing to be sold, permitting any other individual or entity to sell, copying, reproducing, preparing derivative works, publishing, disseminating, distributing, circulating, promoting, marketing, and advertising of still photographs from the Tape, captured images from the Tape displayed on the Internet, and/or any downloaded hard copies of images from the Tape;

3. Selling, attempting to sell, causing to be sold, permitting any other individual or entity to sell, copying, reproducing, preparing derivative works, publishing, disseminating, distributing, circulating, promoting, marketing, and advertising of all advertising, promotional material, or packaging referring to the Tape;

4. Taking orders for copies of the Tape through the Internet or any other means;

5. Shipping copies of the Tape to those purchasers who already have placed orders for copies of the Tape, or to anyone else; and

6. Using Michaels's or Lee's name, likeness or identity in any manner, on or in products, merchandise, or goods, or for purposes of advertising or selling, or soliciting purchases of, products, merchandise, goods or services....

---

## 4.  Intrusion on Seclusion

Intrusion on the plaintiff's physical solitude is the only invasion of privacy tort that arises in the context of gathering—rather than disseminating—information. Intrusion claims are predicated on an allegation that the plaintiff's right to seclusion has been transgressed. The California Supreme Court has opined that "it is in the intrusion cases that invasion of privacy is most clearly seen as an affront to individual dignity." *Shulman v. Group W Productions, Inc.,* 18 Cal. 4th 200, 230, 955 P.2d 469, 489 (1998).

Such claims often are broadly conceptualized to include trespass. The unauthorized entry onto physical property by journalists in pursuit of newsworthy information has been challenged as a trespass. *Compare Florida Publ'g Co. v. Fletcher,* 340 So. 2d 914, 917–18 (Fla. 1976), *cert. denied,* 431 U.S. 930 (1977) (upholding newspaper photographer's entry into house, which was the scene of a fire, as implied from common usage, custom, and practice) *with Wilson v. Layne,* 526 U.S. 603 (1999) (holding that police violate the Fourth Amendment by bringing the media into a home during the execution of a warrant when the latter's presence is not in aid of the execution of the warrant) *and Green Valley School, Inc. v. Cowles Florida Broadcasting, Inc.,* 327 So. 2d 810, 819 (Fla. Dist. Ct. App. 1976) (reversing summary dismissal of the plaintiff's trespass claim against a television station, rejecting the defendant's assertion that entry had been sanctioned by "the request of and with the consent of the State Attorney" and with the "common usage and custom in Florida," which "could well bring to the citizenry of this state the hobnail boots of a Nazi stormtrooper equipped with glaring lights invading a couple's bedroom at midnight with the wife hovering in her nightgown in an attempt to shield herself from the scanning TV camera.").

The gravamen of traditional trespass claims lies in an unauthorized entry onto physical property. Claims of invasion of privacy by intrusion, by contrast, can arise in situations where there is no transgression of property rights. In *Galella v. Onassis,* 487 F.2d

986, 995 (2d Cir. 1973), for instance, the Second Circuit reasoned that a photographer's pursuit of Jacqueline Kennedy Onassis and her children was so "obtrusive and intruding" that it reasonably placed them in fear that their personal safety would be jeopardized. When the former First Lady was engaged in private activities, such as visiting a friend, walking in the park, or shopping, she still was a public figure and thus subject to news coverage. *Id.* But the First Amendment provided no "wall of immunity protecting newsmen" from liability for torts committed while gathering news, and the court felt that the photographer's conduct went "far beyond the reasonable bounds of news gathering."*Id.*[2]

When the intrusion challenges the surreptitious procuring of a conversation, the defendant generally must be shown to have penetrated some zone of physical or sensory privacy surrounding, or obtained unwanted access to data about, the plaintiff. The tort is sustained only if the plaintiff had an objectively reasonable expectation of seclusion or solitude in the place, conversation, or data source. *See* Restatement (Second) Torts § 652B, cmt. c. The Michigan Supreme Court has emphasized that the appropriate inquiry is whether the plaintiff intended and reasonably expected that the *conversation* would be private, as opposed to whether *the subject matter* of the conversation was intended to be private. *See Dickerson v. Rafael,* 601 N.W.2d 108 (Mich. 1999). The Supreme Court of California similarly distinguished between an accident victim's lack of reasonable expectation of privacy at the accident scene, which was within the sight and hearing of members of the public where conversations may have been overheard "with unaided ears," and "amplifying and recording what [the victim] said and heard," which may have been conversations the parties could reasonably expected to be private. *Shulman v. Group W Productions, Inc.,* 18 Cal. 4th at 233, 955 P.2d at 491 (deferring to the jury questions as to whether the plaintiff expected her conversations with rescuers to remain private and whether any such expectation was reasonable). The decisions' rationale may be predicated, at least in part, on preserving the speaker's ability to control the nature and extent of the firsthand dissemination of his statement.

---

## Notes and Questions

1.  In *Ribas v. Clark,* 38 Cal. 3d 355, 696 P.2d 637 (1985), a wife asked the defendant to listen in on an extension telephone when the wife spoke with her husband, from whom she was estranged. The defendant then testified about the conversation she had overheard. The court, in considering the statutory and common law claims asserted by the plaintiff, stated that "[w]hile one who imparts private information risks the betrayal of his confidence by the other party, a substantial distinction has been recognized between the secondhand repetition of the contents of a conversation and its simultaneous dissemination to an unannounced second auditor, whether that auditor be a person or mechanical device." *Id.* at 360–361, 696 P.2d at 640. Is this situation distinguishable from one where a married individual accesses his spouse's private e-mail account to review his messages?

2.  Will a cause of action for intrusion lie if identification of the plaintiff, by name or image, can be shown to have added no significance to the news report? Who is the appropriate party to make that determination? If on-line data is collected and dis-

---

2. Claims challenging newsgathering techniques as intrusive increasingly have been premised on a variety of theories. *See, e.g., Veilleux v. National Broadcasting Co.,* 206 F.3d 92 (1st Cir. 2000) (misrepresentation); *Ayeni v. CBS,* 848 F. Supp. 362 (E.D.N.Y. 1994) (*Bivens* claim).

persed independently of personal identifiers, are meaningful privacy interests implicated?

3.  What "reasonable expectations" of privacy do employees have in their e-mail communications made through corporate computers? In *Smyth v. Pillsbury Co.*, 914 F. Supp. 97, 101 (E.D. Pa. 1996), the U.S. District Court for the Eastern District of Pennsylvania declined to find that the employee had a reasonable expectation in such messages made voluntarily to his supervisor over the company e-mail system, notwithstanding assurances that such communications would not be intercepted by management. The court further noted that even if the employee had a reasonable expectation of privacy in the contents of his e-mail communications, the employer's interception of the messages would not constitute a substantial and highly offensive invasion of privacy.

---

How have claims of intrusion been asserted in the Internet context? In some instances, nascent theories advancing intrusion claims have been premised on a theory that the "matter" that has been intruded upon is a "chattel."

Trespass to chattel is a tort action that, relative to claims of trespass to land, is esoteric and has been largely dormant until recently. Trespass to chattel claims presuppose substantial interference with property, such as removal, damage, or other impairment. *See* Restatement (Second) of Torts §217-18 (1965). The essence of the offense is the intentional use or "intermeddling" with a chattel in the possession of another. *Id.* at §217(b). The claim is closely akin to one of conversion, which generally requires wrongful appropriation of some tangible item.[3] The gravamen of a trespass to chattel claim bears a closer analytical relationship to a misappropriation claim than it does to other types of privacy claims, because the inherent interest to be protected is not so much a "privacy" right as it is a right to enjoy an unencumbered interest in one's chattel.

In *Thrifty-Tel, Inc. v. Bezenek*, 46 Cal. App. 4th 1559, 54 Cal. Rptr. 2d 468 (1996), a long-distance telephone provider asserted a claim of conversion against the parents of minor children[4] who had engaged in "phreaking;" i.e., the unauthorized use of telephone services. The teenage children had utilized computer technology in their efforts to crack the plaintiff's access and authorization codes and make long distance phone calls without paying for them. *Id.* at 1563, 54 Cal. Rptr. 2d at 471. Initially the teenagers gained entry into Thrifty-Tel's system with a confidential access code and then conducted manual random searches for the authorization code; eventually they acquired and utilized computer software to expedite the process. *Id.* at 1563–64, 54 Cal. Rptr. 2d at 472. The court eschewed the provider's claim of conversion, indicating that it was not necessary to reach this issue of first impression of California, and instead analyzed the children's conduct under a theory of trespass to chattels. *Id.* at 1565–66. The court

---

3. Conversion consists of an unauthorized or wrongful act of dominion exercised over another's personal property that deprives the owner of his property permanently or for an indefinite period of time. In *Mundy v. Decker*, No. A-97-882, 1999 WL 14479 (Neb. Ct. App. Jan. 5, 1999), an employer claimed that his former secretary's irrevocable destruction of a WordPerfect directory amounted to a conversion.

4. The parents' efforts to evade vicarious liability for the willful torts of their minor children were unavailing. *See id.* at 1571–72, 54 Cal. Rptr. 2d at 476.

noted that the electronic signals in issue were "sufficiently tangible to support a trespass cause of action." *Id.* at 1567 & n. 6, 54 Cal. Rptr. 2d at 473 & n. 6.

This was the first time a California court had applied a trespass theory to computer hacking. *Id.* at 1567 n. 7, 54 Cal. Rptr. 2d at 473 n. 7. The Indiana Supreme Court had earlier stated in dicta that a hacker's unauthorized access to a computer was more in the nature of trespass than criminal conversion. *State v. McGraw,* 480 N.E.2d 552, 554 (Ind. 1985). The State of Washington made unauthorized computer access a criminal offense under the rubric of "computer trespass." *See, e.g., State v. Riley,* 121 Wash.2d 22, 35–36, 846 P.2d 1365, 1373 (1993).

After the court ruled in *Thrifty-Tel, Inc. v. Bezenek,* a trespass to chattels cause of action was advanced by a proprietary network system against a commercial service that transmitted "spam;" i.e., unsolicited bulk e-mail messages, to thousands of users on the system's network. *CompuServe Inc. v. Cyber Promotions, Inc.,* 962 F. Supp. 1015 (S.D. Ohio 1997). The court enjoined the spam on the ground that the system had demonstrated an interference by the defendant that impaired the value of the chattel. The spam burdened the system's equipment by exploiting available memory space and consuming computer processing resources. Also, the system's resources, including the attention of its personnel, were diverted in efforts to thwart the defendant's e-mail messages. *Id.* at 1022.

In *America Online, Inc. v. IMS,* 24 F. Supp. 2d 548 (E.D. Va. 1998), the plaintiff successfully advanced such a cause of action, claiming the defendant had sent more than 60 million e-mail messages in less than a one-year period. The messages were alleged to have diverted the plaintiff's technical and personnel resources and damaged its good will among its members. *See id.*

As a general matter, consent is a defense to intrusion claims, including claims of trespass. In *CompuServe Inc. v. Cyber Promotions, Inc.,* the defendant argued that it permissibly transmitted its e-mail messages because the system provider had connected its service to the Internet, thereby tacitly acquiescing to the transmission of e-mail via its system. 962 F. Supp. at 1023–24. The court refused to apply the consent defense to bulk e-mail messages, pointing to the exclusion of unsolicited e-mails in the system's posted policy statement. *Id.* at 1024.

In *Intel Corp. v. Hamidi,* No. 98AS05067, 1999 WL 450944 (Cal. App. Dep't Super. Ct. Cal. Sacramento Cty. Apr. 28, 1999), the plaintiff, Intel Corporation, complained that the defendant, an Intel employee, sent e-mail messages concerning Intel's employment practices to over 30,000 Intel employees at their corporate e-mail addresses. *Id.* at *1. The employee refused Intel's requests to cease sending such messages, and employed surreptitious means to circumvent the company's efforts to block entry of his messages into Intel's system. *Id.*

The defendant-employee argued that his e-mail messages and use of the employee e-mail list did not amount to a trespass to chattels because he had sent his messages through an Internet server. The court rejected this argument, stating that a trespass may be committed through an agency. *Id.*

Nor was the court persuaded that Intel's trespass to chattels claim could be defeated on the ground that the e-mail messages allegedly did not cause damage to Intel's e-mail system. The court focused not on whether the system had been physically harmed, but on whether Intel's system had been impaired in value. *Id.* at *2. Intel had been injured by the diminished productivity of its personnel and by the diversion of its corporate resources to block the defendant's efforts and to address employees about the defendant's e-mails. *Id.* These injuries were deemed adequate to support Intel's cause of action.[5] *Id.; see also Hotmail v. Van$ Money Pie Inc.,* No. C 98-20064, 1998 WL 388389 at *2 (N.D. Cal. 1998) (by causing misdirected e-mail messages to be transmitted to the plaintiff without its authorization, thereby depleting its computer storage space and threatening to damage its ability to service its legitimate customers, the defendant has damaged the plaintiff in terms of added costs for personnel to sort through and respond to the misdirected e-mails, and in terms of harm to its business reputation and goodwill).

At least one commentator, Professor Dan Burk, has opined that the conventional trespass claim is "mutating from an innovative claim to deter commercial spam into a more general claim to deter unwanted messages." Dan L. Burk, *The Trouble With Trespass,* 4 J. Small and Emerging Bus. L. 27, 32 (2000). First, he states, the element of physical interference with a chattel required by trespass to chattels claim is contrived in the physical contact in the passage of electrons over the service provider's system. Second, the alleged impairment is too trivial a contact to evoke the requisite interference of traditional physical seizures of chattel. Third, the alleged "intermeddling" arguably is privileged, as the service providers have invited public usage of their equipment. *Id.*

Professor Trotter Hardy views trespass actions as grounded in protecting an owner's control over real property, which is merely "a particular species of 'property.' There is no inherent reason that a Web site could not be considered a species of 'property.'" *See* I. Trotter Hardy, *The Ancient Doctrine of Trespass to Web Sites,* 1996 J. Online L. art. 7, par. 57 <http://www.wm.edu/law/publications/jol/hardy.html>. The application of traditional trespass concepts to cyberspace is illustrative of efforts by litigants and courts alike to utilize existing frameworks to analyze allegedly wrongful conduct.

---

# Patrick E. DWYER v. AMERICAN EXPRESS COMPANY, *et al.*

Appellate Court of Illinois, First District, First Division.
No. 1-92-3944, 273 Ill. App. 3d 742, 652 N.E.2d 1351, 210 Ill. Dec. 375
June 30, 1995

Justice BUCKLEY delivered the opinion of the court:

Plaintiffs, American Express cardholders, appeal the circuit court's dismissal of their claims for invasion of privacy and consumer fraud against defendants, American Express Company, American Express Credit Corporation, and American Express Travel Related Services Company, for their practice of renting information regarding cardholder spending habits.

On May 13, 1992, the New York Attorney General released a press statement describing an agreement it had entered into with defendants. The following day, newspapers reported defendants' actions which gave rise to this agreement. According to the news articles, defendants categorize and rank their cardholders into six tiers based on spending habits and then rent this information to participating merchants as part of a tar-

---

5. The court also rejected the employee's First Amendment defense on the ground that Intel is not a governmental entity or a public forum. The court held that limited access to the e-mail system for specific purposes did not convert Intel into a public forum. Nor was there evidence that the Internet server utilized by the employee functioned as a public postal service. *Id.* at *3.

geted joint-marketing and sales program. For example, a cardholder may be characterized as "Rodeo Drive Chic" or "Value Oriented." In order to characterize its cardholders, defendants analyze where they shop and how much they spend, and also consider behavioral characteristics and spending histories. Defendants then offer to create a list of cardholders who would most likely shop in a particular store and rent that list to the merchant.

Defendants also offer to create lists which target cardholders who purchase specific types of items, such as fine jewelry. The merchants using the defendants' service can also target shoppers in categories such as mail-order apparel buyers, home-improvement shoppers, electronics shoppers, luxury lodgers, card members with children, skiers, frequent business travelers, resort users, Asian/European travelers, luxury European car owners, or recent movers. Finally, defendants offer joint-marketing ventures to merchants who generate substantial sales through the American Express card. Defendants mail special promotions devised by the merchants to its cardholders and share the profits generated by these advertisements.

On May 14, 1992, Patrick E. Dwyer filed a class action against defendants. His complaint alleges[, among other things,] that defendants intruded into their cardholders' seclusion....

As a preliminary matter, we note that a cause of action for intrusion into seclusion has never been recognized explicitly by the Illinois Supreme Court. In *Lovgren v. Citizens First National Bank* (1989), 126 Ill. 2d 411, 128 Ill. Dec. 542, 534 N.E.2d 987, the supreme court discussed this tort as enunciated by the Restatement and *Prosser*, but stated that its discussion did not imply a recognition of the action by the court. (*Lovgren*, 126 Ill. 2d at 416–17, 128 Ill. Dec. at 543–44, 534 N.E.2d at 988–89.) The court concluded that the defendants' alleged actions in that case did not constitute an unreasonable intrusion into the seclusion of another and declined to address the conflict among the appellate court districts as to whether the cause of action should be recognized in this State. *Lovgren*, 126 Ill. 2d at 417, 128 Ill. Dec. at 544, 534 N.E.2d at 989.

In 1979, this district declined to entertain a cause of action for intrusion into the seclusion of another in *Kelly v. Franco* (1979), 72 Ill. App.3d 642, 28 Ill. Dec. 855, 391 N.E.2d 54. In *Kelly,* the plaintiffs contended that the defendant repeatedly made phone calls to their home, only to hang up when one of the plaintiffs answered. The plaintiffs also alleged that the defendant verbally threatened and abused them and harassed their son. (*Kelly*, 72 Ill. App.3d at 644, 28 Ill. Dec. at 857, 391 N.E.2d at 56.) This court noted that the law in Illinois was inconsistent on this matter and held that even if it were to recognize such a cause of action the plaintiff's allegations were insufficient to support a cause of action for unreasonable intrusion into another's seclusion. *Kelly*, 72 Ill. App. 3d at 646–47, 28 Ill. Dec. at 859, 391 N.E.2d at 58.

The third district recognized the intrusion tort in *Melvin v. Burling* (1986), 141 Ill. App. 3d 786, 95 Ill. Dec. 919, 490 N.E.2d 1011, seven years after *Kelly*. In *Melvin*, the court set out four elements which must be alleged in order to state a cause of action: (1) an unauthorized intrusion or prying into the plaintiff's seclusion; (2) an intrusion which is offensive or objectionable to a reasonable man; (3) the matter upon which the intrusion occurs is private; and (4) the intrusion causes anguish and suffering. (*Melvin*, 141 Ill. App. 3d at 789, 95 Ill. Dec. at 921–22, 490 N.E.2d at 1013–14.)...

Plaintiffs' allegations fail to satisfy the first element, an unauthorized intrusion or prying into the plaintiffs' seclusion. The alleged wrongful actions involve the defendants' practice of renting lists that they have compiled from information contained in their own records. By using the American Express card, a cardholder is voluntarily, and necessarily, giving information to defendants that, if analyzed, will reveal a cardholder's spending habits and shopping preferences. We cannot hold that a defendant has committed an unauthorized intrusion by compiling the information voluntarily given to it and then renting its compilation.

Plaintiffs claim that because defendants rented lists based on this compiled information, this case involves the disclosure of private financial information and most closely resembles cases involving intrusion into private financial dealings, such as bank account transactions. Plaintiffs cite several cases in which courts have recognized the right to privacy surrounding financial transactions. See *Zimmermann v. Wilson* (3d Cir. 1936), 81 F.2d 847 (holding examination of information in taxpayers' bank books would violate the taxpayers' privacy rights); *Brex v. Smith* (1929), 104 N.J.Eq. 386, 146 A. 34 (upholding claim for unauthorized intrusion into the plaintiff's bank account); *Hickson v. Home Federal* (N.D. Ga. 1992), 805 F. Supp. 1567 (finding bank disclosure to credit bureau of borrower's loan payment delinquency could violate borrower's right to privacy); *Suburban Trust Co. v. Waller* (1979), 44 Md.App. 335, 408 A.2d 758 (holding bank cannot reveal information about customers' account or transaction unless compelled by legal process); *Mason v. Williams Discount Center, Inc.* (Mo. 1982), 639 S.W.2d 836 (finding store's posting of names of bad check risks invades plaintiff's privacy).

However, we find that this case more closely resembles the sale of magazine subscription lists, which was at issue in *Shibley v. Time, Inc.* (1975), 45 Ohio App.2d 69, 341 N.E.2d 337. In *Shibley*, the plaintiffs claimed that the defendant's practice of selling and renting magazine subscription lists without the subscribers' prior consent "constitut[ed] an invasion of privacy because it amount[ed] to a sale of individual 'personality profiles,' which subjects the subscribers to solicitations from direct mail advertisers." (*Shibley*, 45 Ohio App. 2d at 71, 341 N.E.2d at 339.) The plaintiffs also claimed that the lists amounted to a tortious appropriation of their names and "personality profiles." The trial court dismissed the plaintiffs' complaint and the Court of Appeals of Ohio affirmed. *Shibley*, 45 Ohio App.2d at 71, 341 N.E.2d at 339.

The *Shibley* court found that an Ohio statute, which permitted the sale of names and addresses of registrants of motor vehicles, indicated that the defendant's activity was not an invasion of privacy. The court considered a Federal district court case from New York, *Lamont v. Commissioner of Motor Vehicles* (S.D.N.Y. 1967), 269 F. Supp. 880, *aff'd*, (2d Cir. 1967), 386 F.2d 449, *cert. denied*, (1968), 391 U.S. 915, 88 S.Ct. 1811, 20 L.Ed.2d 654, to be insightful. In *Lamont*, the plaintiff claimed an invasion of privacy arising from the State's sale of its list of names and addresses of registered motor-vehicle owners to mail-order advertisers. The *Lamont* court held that however "noxious" advertising by mail might be, the burden was acceptable as far as the Constitution is concerned. (*Lamont*, 269 F. Supp. at 883.) The *Shibley* court followed the reasoning in *Lamont* and held:

> The right to privacy does not extend to the mailbox and therefore it is constitutionally permissible to sell subscription lists to direct mail advertisers. It necessarily follows that the practice complained of here does not constitute an invasion of privacy even if appellants' unsupported assertion that this amounts to the sale of "personality profiles" is taken as true because these profiles are only used to determine what type of advertisement is to be sent.

*Shibley*, 45 Ohio App.2d at 73, 341 N.E.2d at 339–40.

Defendants rent names and addresses after they create a list of cardholders who have certain shopping tendencies; they are not disclosing financial information about particular cardholders. These lists are being used solely for the purpose of determining what type of advertising should be sent to whom. We also note that the Illinois Vehicle Code authorizes the Secretary of State to sell lists of names and addresses of licensed drivers and registered motor-vehicle owners. (625 ILCS 5/2—123 (West 1992).) Thus, we hold that the alleged actions here do not constitute an unreasonable intrusion into the seclusion of another. We so hold without expressing a view as to the appellate court conflict regarding the recognition of this cause of action....

Affirmed.

---

# Data Mining and Data Protection Directives, Policies, and Legislation

## 1.  Data Collection Techniques

Various technological devices can be used to monitor and record Internet activities. Clickstream data, for instance, is comprised of information collected when a user surfs the World Wide Web. The data culled may be used to create records of a user's on-line communications and transactions, as well as of particular web-sites visited, pages or advertising accessed, and purchases made. An Internet Protocol Address, known as an "IP Address," which references a number assigned to the user's computer, may be traced to the user's service provider or, in certain circumstances, to the computer's owner. Globally Unique Identifiers, known as "GUIDs," are alphanumeric identifiers for the unique installation of software. Such devices similarly yield information about the user, in terms of the software or other files created or downloaded on the user's hard drive.

By utilizing "cookies," commercial web-sites can collect personal information about visitors to particular web-sites. Cookies essentially consist of small data files sent to the user's browser when he visits a site, and typically include the IP address of the user's on-line provider, the type of the user's browser, and the user's operating system. This facilitates rapid retrieval of files from web-sites a user frequently visits. Cookies may also include data that the user furnished, such as the user's name and e-mail address. The device is also used to enable a server to resume a partially completed transaction interrupted by a computer or communications failure.

Cookies may be considered to be helpful by consumers who want the web-site's server to recall certain information. Retention of such items as billing address, size, and preferred method of payment may expedite the transaction. The devices are often used by marketers to target advertising to users who have previously visited related sites, and thus are presumed to have an interest in related merchandise. In addition to facilitating the user's selection of available merchandise by, for example, retaining a customer's prior selections on a customized page and indicating them on the page when the user next visits the site, cookies may also be used for marketing purposes by tracking users' buying habits and preferences. Among other practices, utilization of cookies technology enables commercial web-sites and advertisers to deliver individually tailored banner advertisements to their browsers.

Another common method of data collection is the retention of information that the user has deliberately furnished to the web-site by completing an on-line subscription or registration form. Certain web-sites make access to the interior of their site contingent on providing such information. The specific information sought typically consists of the user's name and postal and e-mail addresses, but may also include significantly more data, such as the user's occupation, age, income level, and product preferences.

The cookies device, when used without the aid of other data sources, generally enables the web-site server to gather data about the user without ascertaining the user's identity. When a user also registers with the site, such as by furnishing his name and other information, the registration information may be associated with the cookie to personally identify the user to the host server.

In addition, personal information may be divulged in chat rooms, on bulletin boards, or through other posted comments. These bits of information may be viewed in conjunction with cookies and registration information, providing an amalgamated image of the Internet user.

These are illustrative of the practices by which web-sites collect and obtain user information, share such information with others, and track individual users' interest in particular subjects. The resultant portrait of the individual has considerable economic value. Such "on-line profiling" practices are particularly prevalent among companies and agencies that place advertisements on the Internet and then record and monitor the individual's on-line interest and purchasing habits. The data is deemed so valuable that it has effectively become a commodity, producing a flourishing trade in data for profit. In consequence, the Internet has dramatically increased the quantity and range of the commercial availability and use of personal information relating to individual behavior, and has concomitantly reduced the zones of privacy and anonymity attendant to such data. A critical factor in data collection practices is that, when technological countervailing measures have not been implemented, users may lack control over the collection and subsequent dissemination of data relating to the users.

As discussed previously, *see* discussion *supra* at 312–13, common law intrusion torts incorporate consideration of the reasonableness of the individual's expectation of privacy into the analysis. Have expectations of privacy in the digital environment yet been well formed? Are individuals adequately savvy about technical devices to understand the functionalities and capabilities of data mining practices, and the ways in which the collection of data can be aggregated to create a more complete portrait? To what extent has decisional and statutory law delimited the reasonableness of any such expectations? Ultimately, cyberspace's nascent evolution has heightened uncertainty, and therefore concern, about how such data may be used, manipulated, and conveyed to others, as well as the extent to which users must be made aware of such practices.

---

## 2.  Data Mining Controversies

Although privacy issues arise regularly in the context of more conventional communications, the most controversial and highly publicized privacy issues in the Internet arena concern the practices of data mining and on-line profiling. Privacy advocates, industry groups, and government regulators have focused considerable attention on these issues, which have often been referred to as "information privacy."

Such concerns relate to an individual's control over the flow and processing of personal information. President Clinton's Information Infrastructure Task Force utilizes the term information privacy to refer to "an individual's claim to control the terms under which personal information — information identifiable to the individual — is acquired, disclosed, and used." Information Infrastructure Task Force, *Privacy and the National Information Infrastructure: Principles for Providing and Using Personal Information* (1995) <http://www.iitf.doc.gov>.

Concerns about the use of personal data have heightened in the face of security breaches. For instance, a hacker threatened an on-line music retailer with the public disclosure of thousands of customers' names and credit card account numbers that he had accessed from the retailer's database. When the company refused to pay the sum demanded by the hacker, he reportedly followed through on his threat to post the customer information on a site. *See* Troy Wolverton, *FBI Probes Extortion Case at CD Store*, CNET-News.com (Jan. 10, 2000) <http://news.cnet.com/news/0-1007-200-1519088.html>.

Another recent event troublesome to privacy advocates was an effort to sell customer information to a third party, in violation of the company's posted privacy policy, as an asset in a bankruptcy proceeding. *See* Elinor Abreu, *TRUSTe to File Antiprivacy Brief Against Toysmart*, Standard (June 30, 2000) <http://www.thestandard.com/article/display/0,1151,6577,00.html>. Toysmart.com's creditors filed an involuntary bankruptcy petition in the U.S. Bankruptcy Court for the District of Massachusetts in June 2000, and Toysmart.com filed its assent a couple of weeks thereafter. Federal Trade Commission, Press Release, *FTC Sues Failed Website, Toysmart.com, for Deceptively Offering for Sale Personal information of Website Visitors*, (July 10, 2000) <http//www.ftc.gov/opa/2000/07/toysmart.htm>. In the wake of the public outcry, the Commission sued Toysmart.com, alleging that it violated section 5 of the Federal Trade Commission Act by having misrepresented to consumers that personal information would never be shared with third parties. *Id.* A coalition of 39 states filed objections to Toysmart.com's proposed sale of its customer list. *See* Melanie Austria Farmer, *39 States Object to Sale of Toysmart's Customer List*, CNET News.com (July 21, 2000) <http://news.cnet.com/news/0-1007-200-2307727.htm>.

In July 2000, the Commission announced that it had reached a settlement with the defunct retailer. The proposed compromise permits a sale of the confidential customer list, provided it is sold in conjunction with the remainder of the web-site, and is sold only to a purchaser in a related market who agrees to comply with Toysmart.com's stated privacy policy. *See Today's News Update*, N.Y.L.J. (July 24, 2000) at 1, col. 1.

Illustrative of the controversy surrounding data collection practices are the complaints filed by a coalition of consumer groups and civil liberties advocates with the Federal Trade Commission, asking it to investigate the data collection practices of DoubleClick, Inc., an Internet advertising firm. DoubleClick reportedly utilized cookies to track the on-line activities of Internet users in order to develop personal profiles for a national marketing database. In 1999, DoubleClick merged with Abacus Direct Corporation, which had culled personal information about consumers through more traditional means, such as direct mail marketing and catalog subscription lists. DoubleClick announced a plan to reference user data mined on-line with actual names and addresses that were collected off-line. The program was designed to target customized advertising to consumers. The program sparked public reaction by privacy advocates, and the following month, DoubleClick announced that it would suspend its plans to link consumer data with the user profiles it had compiled and maintained in a database. *See, e.g.,* Jeffrey L. Seglin, *The Right Thing; Who is Minding Your Own Business?* N.Y. Times (Mar. 19, 2000) at 4 col. 2.

In addition to self-imposed restraints on data mining practices, privacy guidelines are being developed by various trade associations. The Internet Advertising Bureau, for example, is working to establish privacy policies for businesses that engage in on-line advertising. Such policies include notice and disclosure as to how personal information will be collected, choice and consent for the collection, and the implementation of security measures designed to preclude improper use of personally identifiable information. *See* David McGuire, *Web Publishing Group Unveils Privacy Guidelines,* Newsbytes <http://www.newsbyte.com/pubNews/00/151676.html>. Third-party monitoring organizations have been formed, such as BBBOnLine, a wholly-owned subsidiary of the Council of Better Business Bureaus. BBBOnLine features a privacy "seal" program that incorporates the guidelines outlined by the Federal Trade Commission. *See* BBBOnline, *available at* <http://www.bbbonline.com>. TRUSTe utilizes a "trustmark" seal program to signify the subscribing web-site's commitment to disclose its privacy policies. *See* TRUSTe, Press Release, *TRUSTe Testifies Before House Judiciary Committee* (May 27, 1999) <http://www.truste.org/about_committee.html>. The American Institute of Certified Public Accountants and the Canadian Institute of Chartered Accountants created the CPA Web-Trust. *See* program description, *available at* <http://www.cpawebtrust.org>. The British government recently supported a TrustUK scheme, designed to monitor on-line commerce in the United Kingdom. *See* Mark Ward, *Putting Trust Online,* BBC News (July 18, 2000) <http://news6.thdo.bbc.co.uk/hi/english/business/newsid_905F839000/839112.sti>.

---

# 3. Theories of Concern about Privacy in On-Line Communications

Privacy frequently is cited as the most important issue facing the Internet. *See, e.g.,* Heather Green, *et. al., A Little Net Privacy, Please,* Business Week Online, ¶ 3 (March 16, 1998) <http://www.businessweek.com/common_frames/bws.htm?http://>. Why is there such ardent concern about the privacy implications of data mining and on-line profiling?

Professor Jerry Kang explores several values relevant to privacy interests. For example, "[a]n individual's capacity to disclose personal information selectively...supports her ability to modulate intimacy....Without information privacy, we would be less able to disclose on a case-by-case basis the nonpublic facets of our personality. Thus, we would lack the 'moral capital' needed to construct intimacy." Jerry Kang, *Information Privacy in Cyberspace Transactions,* 50 Stan. L. Rev. 1193, 1212–13 (1998) (footnotes omitted).

To some degree, "[o]ne of the more insidious aspects of modern surveillance technology is its passivity. Those who do not know that they are being spied on cannot complain of it." Adam J. Tutaj, Comment, *Intrusion Upon Seclusion: Bringing An "Otherwise" Valid Cause of Action Into the 21st Century,* 82 Marq. L. Rev. 665, 666 (1999). Professor Lawrence Lessig posits that:

> [i]f you walked into a store, and the guard at the store recorded your name; if cameras tracked your every step, noting what items you looked at and what

items you ignored; if an employee followed you around, calculating the time you spent in any given aisle; if before you could purchase an item you selected, the cashier demanded that you reveal who you were—if any or all of these thing happened in real space, you would notice....In cyberspace, you would not.

Lawrence Lessig, *The Law of the Horse: What Cyberlaw Might Teach*, 113 Harv. L. Rev. 501, 504–05 (1999).

Perhaps it seems presumptuous to try to profile an image of an individual merely on the basis of such on-line activities as a few recent purchases. And even these items may have been chosen at the behest of or as gifts for another—thereby distorting depiction founded upon these selections. The individual risks the loss of multi-dimensional facets, and becomes trivialized, reduced to a shoe size, a price range, a color preference. Further, the motives of a person who has satisfied a fleeting curiosity about a controversial subject—sexual practices, terrorist activities, effects of controlled substances—may be misperceived by others who later retrieve the information.

Conversely, on-line communication may facilitate a more complete picture of an individual, because electronic data may be more comprehensive and more readily aggregated with information acquired off-line. Digital records may be more revealing than other conventional types of business records. For example, hard copies of transactional records might disclose an actual purchase; on-line transactions, by contrast, may generate, in addition to such purchase information, data about items browsed, product information requested, and advertising information accessed.

There is also the concern that because personal information is stored and archived, it is made available for retrieval for purposes not originally contemplated by the person who has divulged it. Disclosing one's measurements in the course of purchasing a garment may not have been intended as a wholesale divulgence, without regard to the nature of the entity subsequently obtaining such information or the purposes for which such information was obtained.

In *Dietemann v. Time, Inc.*, 449 F.2d 245 (9th Cir. 1971), decided long before the emergence of routine on-line communication, the Ninth Circuit observed:

"Men fear exposure not only to those closest to them; much of the outrage underlying the asserted right to privacy is a reaction to exposure to persons known only through business or other secondary relationships. The claim is not so much one of total secrecy as it is of the right to define one's circle of intimacy— to choose who shall see beneath the quotidian mask. Loss of control over which 'face' one puts on may result in literal loss of self-identity, and is humiliating beneath the gaze of those whose curiosity treats a human being as an object."

*Id.* at 248 (quoting *Briscoe v. Reader's Digest Ass'n, Inc.*, 4 Cal. 3d 529 n. 4, 483 P.2d 34, 37 n. 4 (1971)). Residual trails of data left by Web surfers provide information about the surfer, and the surfer may lack control over the timing and circumstances of the disclosures of such information. The compilation of bits of data about an individual for the purpose of contriving an amalgamated image similarly reduces the individual's control over the circumstances of these disclosures. "The danger in a limitless surveillance of expression in cyberspace is that it can corrupt individual decisionmaking about the elements of one's identity." Paul M. Schwartz, *Privacy and Democracy in Cyberspace*, 52 Vand. L. Rev. 1609, 1657 (1999). Control over the receipt and dissemination of information is a theme that pervades judicial decisions considering the parameters of privacy interests in the electronic arena. The Ninth Circuit observed in a non-Internet case that:

[o]ne who invites another to his home or office takes a risk that the visitor may not be what he seems, and that the visitor may repeat all he hears and observes when he leaves. But he does not and should not be required to take the risk that what is heard and seen will be transmitted...to the public at large or to any segment of it that the visitor may select.

*Dietemann v. Time, Inc.*, 449 F.2d at 249.

In *United States v. Maxwell*, 45 M.J. 406 (C.A.A.F. 1996), the Court of Appeals for the Armed Forces considered these rationales with respect to e-mail messages:

[O]nce [a first-class mail] letter is received and opened, the destiny of the letter then lies in the control of the recipient of the letter, not the sender, absent some legal privilege. Similarly, the maker of a telephone call has a reasonable expectation that police officials will not intercept and listen to the conversation; however, the conversation itself is held with the risk that one of the participants may reveal what is said to others. Drawing from these parallels, we can say that the transmitter of an e-mail message enjoys a reasonable expectation that police officials will not intercept the transmission without probable cause and a search warrant. However, once the transmissions are received by another person, the transmitter no longer controls its destiny. In a sense, e-mail is like a letter. It is sent and lies sealed in the computer until the recipient opens his or her computer and retrieves the transmission. The sender enjoys a reasonable expectation that the initial transmission will not be intercepted by the police. The fact that an unauthorized "hacker" might intercept an e-mail message does not diminish the legitimate expectation of privacy in any way.

*Id.* at 417–18 (citations omitted).

In addition to concerns that residual data may lead to a lessening of abstract privacy and of personal autonomy over the circumstances of disclosure, users fear that data will be corrupted by others. Manipulative practices may render users vulnerable to such problematic consequences as harassing spam messages or misuse of credit information. Such problems existed before the onset of widespread Internet use, of course. Junk mail preceded spam, and abuse of credit account information was accomplished by retrieval of carbon copy receipts. While the concerns may be more conspicuous in the digital environment, are they more serious?

Countervailing social values relating to data collection and information privacy exist as well. Individuals may reap benefits from the release of personal data in certain circumstances. With respect to commerce, those who have divulged certain interests and preferences may become the target of more specific and desired marketing endeavors. This leads some to conclude that "[i]nformation privacy does not mandate informational quarantine; it merely requires that the individual exercise control within reasonable constraints over whether, and what type of, quarantine should exist." *See* Jerry Kang, *Information Privacy in Cyberspace Transactions*, 50 Stan. L. Rev. at 1218.

The press often is concerned with instances of differentiated public and private visages, particularly insofar as such personae are deliberately manipulated by politicians for purposes of self-interest. While such differences are not necessarily the product of nefarious deception, ascertaining the motivations for shielding information may give rise to legitimate journalistic inquiry.

What are the implications of legislatively mandated privacy protections for the press? Would one engaged in newsgathering endeavors be compelled first to seek express permission from those about whom data was collected before the information could be disclosed within a publication? Would compliance with access provisions require a reporter to afford interview subjects an opportunity to review and correct data maintained about them in the reporter's files?

The European Union Directive on Data Protection, *see* discussion *infra* at 329, attempts to accommodate the issue by obliging member states to provide exemptions or derogations "for the processing of personal data carried out solely for journalistic purposes... only if they are necessary to reconcile the right to privacy with the rules governing freedom of expression." Council Directive 95/46 of 24 October 1995, The Protection of Individuals with Regard to the Processing of Personal Data and on the Free Movement of Such Data, art. 9, 1996 O.J. (L 281). As one First Amendment expert pointed out, the imposition of such a regulatory scheme in the United States would encounter "at least two significant First Amendment obstacles." Jane E. Kirtley, *The EU Data Protection Directive and the First Amendment: Why a "Press Exemption" Won't Work*, 80 Iowa L. Rev. 639, 648 (March 1995). First, inquiries by the government into how the news media contemplated utilizing such data "would be of doubtful constitutionality." *See id.* at 648 & n. 75. Second, such a regulatory scheme would necessitate delineation of standards for determining the eligibility to come within the exemption; "courts might find the system of exemptions to be tantamount to a system of licensing, and thus facially unconstitutional." *See id.* at 648 & n. 76.

---

# Privacy and Democracy in Cyberspace
# Paul M. Schwartz[*]
### 52 Vand. L. Rev. 1609 (1999)[†]

A right to privacy is not generally recognized on the Internet.[1]

Cyberspace is our new arena for public and private activities. It reveals information technology's great promise: to form new links between people and to marshal these connections to increase collaboration in political and other activities that promote democratic community. In particular, cyberspace has a tremendous potential to revitalize democratic self-governance at a time when a declining level of participation in communal life endangers civil society in the United States.

Yet, information technology in cyberspace also affects privacy in ways that are dramatically different from anything previously possible. By generating comprehensive records of online behavior, information technology can broadcast an individual's secrets in ways that she can neither anticipate nor control. Once linked to the Internet, the computer on our desk becomes a potential recorder and betrayer of our confidences. In the absence of strong privacy rules, cyberspace's civic potential will never be attained.

At present, however, no successful standards, legal or otherwise, exist for limiting the collection and utilization of personal data in cyberspace. The lack of appropriate and

---

* Professor of Law, Brooklyn Law School....
1. *Microsoft Press Computer Dictionary* 382 (3d ed. 1997).

enforceable privacy norms poses a significant threat to democracy in the emerging Information Age. Indeed, information privacy concerns are the leading reason why individuals not on the Internet are choosing to stay off.[7]

The stakes are enormous; the norms that we develop for personal data use on the Internet will play an essential role in shaping democracy in the Information Age. Nevertheless, the Clinton Administration and legal commentators increasingly view the role of the Internet law of privacy as facilitating wealth-creating transmissions of information, including those of personal data. This Article takes a different tack. It does not oppose a commercial function for cyberspace, but calls for something other than shopping on the Internet. Moreover, it argues that unfettered participation in democratic and other fora in cyberspace will not take place without the right kinds of legal limits on access to personal information....

## The Law's Domain

Both the market and self-regulation have important roles to play in privacy protection on the Internet. Yet, reliance on these forces alone will not create effective privacy standards for cyberspace. The four fair information practices that this Article has developed[, i.e., (1) defined obligations that limit the use of personal data; (2) transparent processing systems; (3) limited procedural and substantive rights; and (4) external oversight] should be expressed in federal legislation. Enactment of this law would be an ideal follow-up to congressional enactment in 1998 of the Children's Online Privacy Act. This legislative imposition of fair information practices for cyberspace will lead to three significant benefits: (1) the prevention of a lock-in of poor privacy standards, (2) the creation of the preconditions for effective market and self-regulatory contributions to privacy protection, and (3) the ending of United States intransigence on the wrong side of ongoing negotiations with the European Union about trans-Atlantic transfers of personal data.

The timing of strategic moves in the Information Age is critical, and the likely result of delay in the expression of privacy standards will be to lock in the current privacy horror show in cyberspace. If we wait, American society may follow the path indicated by

---

7. *See A Little Privacy, Please*, Bus. Wk., Mar. 16, 1998, at 98 [hereinafter Business Week Poll]. This Business Week/Harris poll also found that of people who already use the Internet, "78% say they use the Web more if privacy were guaranteed." *Id.*

The Graphic, Visualization, and Usability Center's ("GVU") Tenth World Wide Web User Survey also revealed a high level of public concern for information privacy. Graphic, Visualization & Usability Center, *Tenth World Wide Survey Results* (visited Oct. 1998) <http:www.gvu.gatech.edu/user)_surveys/>. This survey, which relied on the self-reporting of visitors to the GVU Web site, found that over seventy-five percent of Internet users rated privacy as more important than convenience, and seventy percent agreed that a need existed for Internet privacy laws. *Id.* In addition, eighty percent of Internet users disagreed that content providers had a right to resell user information. *Id.*

Americans are also highly concerned with privacy issues when they are off-line. For example, a 1996 poll found that eigthy percent of Americans were either very or somewhat concerned about threats to their personal privacy. *See* Alan F. Westin, *"Whatever Works": The American Public's Attituds Toward Regulation on Consumer Privacy Issues*, in National Telecomm & Info. Admin., U.S. Dep't of Commerce, Privacy and Self-Regulation in the Information Age 55 (1997) [hereinafter NTIA Report]. This poll also found that "[a] rising large percentage of the public feels that consumers have 'lost all control over how personal information about them is circulated and used by companies.'" *Id.*

Scott McNealy and "get over" its loss of privacy on the Internet.[515] This path would be more than unfortunate because privacy rules are a critical means of constituting both individuals and community. The promotion of cyberspace as a new arena for civic life and the maintenance of a populace capable of self-determination requires the right kind of restrictions on different kinds of access to personal information. The four fair information practices that this Article advocates, if expressed in law, will be the best first step in establishing the necessary data topography of Internet privacy. This legal expression of privacy norms will also promote democratic deliberation and individual self-determination in cyberspace.

A further benefit of a legislative expression of privacy norms, paradoxically, will be to heighten the effectiveness of the market and self-regulatory mechanisms. The Clinton Administration's policies in this area have largely encouraged a consensus in the industry around norms that do not benefit society as a whole. As the industry is currently configured, it benefits from standards that accomplish the following: promote maximum disclosure of personal data; establish a poor level of transparency; offer no effective procedural or substantive rights; and establish hollow oversight. In a similar fashion in the past, the legal system's deference to the direct marketing industry's weak code of conduct has permitted it to stave off effective regulation.

A legal expression of fair information practices would create an environmental shock to industry's privacy self-regulatory groups and its current consensus. The legislative enactment of fair information practices would prevent firms from viewing personal data as a public good; instead, companies would be forced to engage in privacy price discrimination. Already, software and other Information Age companies have become highly sophisticated at capturing revenues by customizing their products and services to charge each customer the price that she is willing to pay, and no more. Such price discrimination sometimes takes place by selling to different users at different prices, by letting users choose the version of a product they wish, and by making discounts available to certain groups. Compared to this effort, companies do not generally seek privacy price discrimination because the law, technology, and social practices create an information subsidy in their favor. From this perspective, a legislative enactment of fair information practices would end a socially unproductive subsidy to online industry. In addition, greater industry interest in such Trusted Third Parties as infomediaries and privacy seal organizations would be likely to develop.

Finally, enactment of an online privacy protection law in the United States would help resolve a conflict with the European Union ("EU"). The stakes in this clash are high; at present, the Commission of the EU is threatening to block the flow of personal data to the United States. European nations have spent decades in creating high levels of protection for personal data through legal regulations at the domestic and trans-European level. In an age of international data flows, however, these measures would be doomed to failure if their reach ended at the borders of Europe.

In response to this increase in extra-territorial activities involving the personal data of their citizens, many European nations have extended their domestic laws to regulate international transmissions of personal data. At the trans-European level, moreover, the Member States of the EU enacted a Data Protection Directive that seeks both to harmo-

---

515. Polly Sprenger, *Sun on Privacy: Get Over It*, at 1 (visited Jan. 26, 1999) <www.wired-com/news/print_version/politics/story/17538.html?wnpg=all>.

nize their national data protection laws at a high level and to restrict transfers of personal data to third-party nations that lack "an adequate level of protection." In cases where such adequate protection is not present, the Directive provides exceptions that permit transfers if, among other circumstances, the individual affected has "unambiguously" consented, or if the party receiving the data has agreed by contract to provide adequate protection.

These national and European-wide measures for information privacy pose significant challenges to the free flow of personal data to the United States.[527] Whether or not the United States generally has "adequate" information privacy is a complex question. An answer to it requires examination of the protections available for a specific data transfer, including the safeguards offered by law and relevant business practices. Nevertheless, the European view regarding United States privacy standards has been appropriately skeptical.

In response to EU pressure, Clinton Administration officials followed an initial period of inaction with the U.S. Commerce Department's drafting of weak "safe harbor" standards for privacy The Commerce Department's plan is to obtain EU agreement to waive sanctions against any American companies that follow these standards. Yet, the "safe harbor" principles largely track the worst aspects of the industry codes of conduct that this Article has already criticized. In addition, to the extent that the Commerce Department is attempting to move the American online industry in the direction of stronger fair information practices for European citizens, it faces opposition from business. The American online industry is fearful of domestic precedential value if it agrees to provide European citizens who visit its Web sites with fair information practices superior to those given to Americans at these same sites. One particular contentious area concerns improving the access to one's personal data that is collected in cyberspace.

The EU's Data Protection Directive is only part of a larger international effort at privacy protection.[536] The United government is not helping in this effort. Rather, it is increasing the problem by its intransigence in favor of industry self-regulation, which is an approach that will not work under current conditions.

## Conclusion

This Article has depicted the widespread, silent collection of personal information in cyberspace. At present, it is impossible to know the fate of the personal data that one generates online. This state of affairs is bad for the health of a deliberative democracy. It cloaks in dark uncertainty the transmutation of Internet activity into personal data that

---

527. As Peter Swire and Robert Litan write,

> The Directive could have far-reaching effects on business practices within the United States and other "third countries" (countries that are not part of the European Union). Mainframes and Web sites in the United States might be cut off from data from Europe. Marketing and management practices that are routine in the United States might be disrupted.

Peter P. Swire & Robert E. Litan, *None of Your Business: World Data Flows, Electronic Commerce, and the European Directive* at 3 (1998).

536. For example, countries in Latin America that are developing information privacy laws include Argentina, Brazil, and Chile. Alastair Tempest, *The Globalization of Data Privacy*, DMNews Int'l, Mar. 15, 1999, at 5. As part of the international effort at improving privacy in cyberspace, Germany has enacted the Teleservices Data Protection Act of 1997. *See Privacy Law Sourcebook*, 299–300 [Marc Rotenberg ed. 1998].

will follow one into other areas and discourage civic participation. This situation also has a negative impact on individual self-determination; it makes it difficult to engage in the necessary thinking out loud and deliberation with others upon which choice-making depends. In place of the existing privacy horror show, we need multidimensional rules that set out fair information practices for personal data in cyberspace.

This Article has argued that the necessary practices must embody four requirements: (1) defined obligations that limit the use of personal data; (2) transparent processing systems; (3) limited procedural and substantive rights; and (4) external oversight. Neither the market nor industry self-regulation is likely, however, to put these four practices in place. In particular, despite the Clinton Administration's favoring of industry self-regulation, this method is an unlikely candidate for success. Industry self-regulation about privacy is a negotiation about "the rules of play" for the use of personal data. In deciding on these rules, industry is likely to be most interested in protecting its stream of revenues. It will therefore benefit if it develops norms that preserve the current status quo of maximum information disclosure.

This Article advocates a legislative enactment of its four fair information practices. This legal expression of privacy norms is the best first step in promoting democratic deliberation and individual self-determination in cyberspace. It will further the attainment of cyberspace's potential as a new realm for collaboration in political and personal activities. Enactment of such a federal law would be a decisive move to shape technology so it will further—and not harm—democratic self-governance.

---

## Notes and Questions

1. How does the commercial marketplace affect normative conduct about information privacy?

2. When Sun Microsystems announced that it was introducing a technological system to connect digital appliances and allow them to communicate with one another, some privacy advocates voiced concern that the collection of personal information and the online tracking of users would similarly be facilitated. Sun Microsystem's chairman and chief executive Scott McNealey reportedly responded, "You already have zero privacy—get over it." *See* Richard Raysman and Peter Brown, *Update on On-Line Privacy*, N.Y.L.J. (Nov. 9, 1999) at 3, col. 1.

3. With respect to values underlying the protection of anonymous and pseudonymous speech on the Internet, *see* discussion *supra* at 236.

---

# 4.  Data Protection Paradigms

## a. The European Union Model

Concerns about data collection and on-line profiling have been particularly evident in Europe, where conventions about privacy often are more strident than in the United States. In 1995, the European Union adopted a directive on "The Protection of Individuals with Regard to the Processing of Personal Data and on the Free Movement of Such Data," Council Directive 95/46, 1996 O.J. (L 281) 31–50 ("Directive"). This Directive, which became effective in October 1998, was designed to harmonize among member states protections relating to the mining of personal data. The Directive requires member states to adopt laws embodying principles espoused by the Organization for Economic Cooperation and Development.

In general, the Directive's safe harbor principles include requirements relating to:

- notice as to why information is collected, how to complain about such collection, and identification of third parties who receive the information;

- opt-out provisions to avoid making disclosures other than that for which the information originally was collected;

- disclosure to third parties that is consistent with the notice and opt-out provisions;

- reasonable measures to ensure security so as to avoid loss, misuse, unauthorized access, and the like;

- the processing of only data relevant to the purpose of collection, with efforts to ensure that such data is accurate, complete, and current;

- access by individuals to data about themselves with a means to correct inaccurate information; and

- compliance mechanisms regarding these requirements.

## b. American Approaches

At first blush, it would appear that the Directive applies only to those countries that are members of the European Union. However, American and other companies have been concerned that, in the event their respective protection devices did not satisfy the Directive's requirements, their ability to conduct business on-line and avoid liability in Europe would be impaired. The Directive prohibits European organizations from transacting with countries that do not provide "adequate" safeguards for personal data. Directive 95/46, art. 25(1), 1996 O.J. (L 281). Determination as to whether a particular country's protections are "adequate" rests with individual member states, upon review of the circumstances relating to the transfer of the data. *Id.* at arts. 25(1), (2). Such circumstances include "the nature of the data, the purpose and duration of the proposed processing operation or operations, the country of origin and country of final destination, the rules of law, both general and sectoral, in force in the third country in question and the professional rules and security measures which are complied with in those countries." *Id.* at art. 25(2).

An exception to these requirements occurs when the user "unambiguously" consents. *See id.* at art. 7(a). Thus, personal data may be transferred to a country that lacks "adequate" protection under the Directive if the individual furnishing the information has clearly consented to the proposed transfer. *See generally* http://www.ita.doc.gov/ecom/menu.htm>. Among other exemptions, personal data also may be transferred to a country that lacks the requisite protections if the transfer is necessary for the performance of a contract between the individual and the entity collecting the information. Directive 95/46, art. 7(b), 1996 O.J. (L 281).[6]

---

6. Recently, the European Commission also considered implementing regulations on the use of spam and cookies. The measures would require opt-in procedures for spam and restrictions on the use of cookies.

Some American businesses have been responding by establishing practices that conform to the Directive's exceptions, such as by conditioning data collection on consent from the user. In addition, the International Trade Administration of the U.S. Department of Commerce has negotiated a "safe harbor" privacy arrangement with European Union officials to ensure "adequate privacy protection" and compliance with the Directive's criteria. *See* <http://www.ita.doc.gov./td/ecom/menu.html> (setting forth final safe harbor principles approved by the European Commission on July 27, 2000). This coordination may portend efforts to globally harmonize laws and practices relating to on-line communications and transactions in order to avoid the vagaries of disparate application of regulatory schemes.

The viability of this joint United States-European Union data privacy protocol remains unclear as of the writing of this book, however. Despite approval by the European Commission and fifteen member nations of the European Union, opponents of the protocol have challenged the safe harbor provisions of the protocol. Specifically, the Parliament's Committee on Citizens' Freedoms and Rights expressed concern that compliance essentially is on a voluntary basis because enforcement by the Federal Trade Commission against safe-harbor violators is discretionary. *See generally* Keith Perine, *U.S.-EU Net Privacy Proposal in Jeopardy,* Standard (June 26, 2000) <http://www.thestandard.com/article/display/0,1151,16387,00.html>; *see also* Letter from John Mogg, Director-General of DGXV, to Robert LaRussa, Under Secretary for International Trade of the United States Dep't of Commerce (July 28, 2000) (on file with International Trade Administration <http://www.ita.doc.gov/ecom/ menu.htm>) (discussing European Commission decision C(2000) 2441, which provides that data controllers in the European Union can transfer personal data processed in accordance with Member States' law, without providing additional safeguards to ensure their protection, to U.S.-based organizations that adhere to safe harbor principles, provided the organizations are subject to the statutory powers of a public body empowered to investigate complaints and to obtain relief against unfair or deceptive practices or otherwise effectively ensure compliance with the principles).

In June 1998, the Federal Trade Commission issued a report entitled "Privacy Online: A Report to Congress," which examined information practices of commercial sites on the World Wide Web and the industry's efforts to implement self-regulatory programs to protect consumers' on-line privacy. The Commission had conducted a survey of more than 1400 commercial web sites; of these, more than 85 percent collected information from consumers, but only 14 percent of the Commission's random sample furnished any privacy notice as to their information practices. *See* Federal Trade Commission, *Privacy Online: A Report to Congress* (June 1998) <http://www.ftc.gov/reports/privacy3/toc.htm>. Shortly after the Commission issued its report, Congress enacted the Children's Online Privacy Protection Act of 1998 ("COPPA"). *See* discussion *infra* at 335.

The following year, in July 1999, the Commission issued another report, entitled "Self-Regulation and Privacy Online." Federal Trade Commission, *Self-Regulation and Privacy Online*, Prepared Statement Before the Subcom. on Telecommunications, Trade, and Consumer Protection of the Committee on Commerce, U.S. House of Representatives (July 13, 1999) <http://www.ftc.gov.ox/1999/9907/pt071399.htm>. This latter report assessed the putative progress made to protect consumers' on-line privacy. Essentially, the Commission opined that self-regulation is the "least intrusive and most efficient means to ensure fair information practices online, given the rapidly evolving nature of the Internet and computer technology." *Id.* The Commission pointed to a number of laudable self-regulatory initiatives, but lamented that "[o]nly a small minority of commercial Web sites...have joined these programs to date." *Id.* Nevertheless, the Commission recommended that legislation to address on-line privacy "is not appropriate at this time....[T]he present challenge is to educate those companies which still do not understand the importance of consumer privacy and to create incentives for further progress toward effective, widespread implementation." *Id.*

Thereafter, in May 2000, the Federal Trade Commission shifted its position and recommended that Congress enact legislation to require operators of web-sites to display privacy policies; allow visitors to choose how their personal information would be used by the web-sites; afford access to data collected about the user by the web-site; and implement adequate measures to safeguard the security of data collected by the sites. Federal Trade Commission, *Final Report of the FTC Advisory Committee on Online Access and Security* (May 15, 2000) <http://www.ftc.gov/acoas/papers/finalreport.htm>.

Later, in the summer of 2000, the Federal Trade Commission once again endorsed a self-regulatory approach by endorsing a plan submitted by the Network Advertising Initiative, a consortium of major Internet advertising companies. The proposal contemplates that consumers be given "reasonable access" to personally identifiable information collected about them, receive notice of Internet profiling activities, and have a choice as to whether certain data can be stored and used by advertisers. *See* Associated Press, *FTC Backs Internet Privacy Deal* <http://legalnews.findlaw.com/news/s/20000727/privacy.htm>.

The Federal Trade Commission has a broad mandate to enforce the Federal Trade Commission Act. Section 5 of the Act, 15 U.S.C.A. § 45(a) (West 1997), prohibits "deceptive acts or practices in or affecting commerce." In August 1998, for example, the Commission entered into a settlement with GeoCities, against whom the Commission had asserted its first Internet privacy case. The Commission charged that GeoCities had misrepresented the way that it would use personal registration information collected on its site. *See* Complaint for Federal Trade Commission (No. C-3849) <http://www.ftc.gov/os/1998/9808/geo-cmpl.htm>. Specifically, the Commission complained that, rather than using the information exclusively to provide the site's members with specific advertising and/or product information the members had requested, GeoCities had disclosed the information to third parties who used it to target promotional messages to the site's members. The Commission was also troubled by GeoCities' representations regarding the maintenance of data collected from children who participated in the site's "GeoKidz Club," because third parties had access to and maintained this data.

Pursuant to the settlement, GeoCities agreed to post a clear and prominent privacy notice on its site. The notice is designed to inform members about the information that GeoCities intends to collect, the purpose for which such information is collected, those to whom the information may be disclosed, and the methods by which consumers can access and remove the information. Additionally, with respect to visitors to the site who are under 13 years of age, GeoCities agreed to secure parental consent before collecting personal data from the children. *See GeoCities,* Agreement Containing Proposed Consent Order (No. 9823015) <http://www.ftc.gov/os/1998/9808.geo-ord.htm>.

To a large degree, the terms of GeoCities's settlement with the Federal Trade Commission effectively implement the basic precepts of privacy protection that the Commission has opined should govern privacy protection. The Commission noted that government agencies in the United States, Canada, and Europe studied data collection practices, and issued a series of reports, guidelines, and model codes.

Common to all of these initiatives are five "core principles" of privacy protection:

(1) Notice/Awareness: The Commission believes that there should be notice to consumers as to when, how, and for what purposes personal data will be collected. The Commission characterizes this as "[t]he most fundamental principle." Federal Trade Commission, *Fair Information Practice Principles* (June 4, 1998) <http://www.ftc.gov/reports/privacy3/fairinfo.htm>. The scope and content of the notice would depend on the entity's substantive information practices, but likely would include: identification of the entity collecting the data, the uses to be made of the data, any potential recipients of the data, the nature of the data collected, and the means by which it is collected; specification of the consequences of a refusal to provide the requested information; and delineation of the steps taken by the collector of the data to ensure the confidentiality and quality of the data collected.

(2) Choice/Consent: The Commission believes that consumers should be given an option as to how any personal information collected from them may be used. Consumers should also have control as to any secondary uses of information; that is, the uses that exceed those necessary to complete the contemplated transaction. Choice paradigms typically take the form of either "opt-in" or "opt-out" schemes. The former require affirmative steps by the consumer to *allow* the collection and use of information; the latter require affirmative steps to *prevent* such collection or use.

(3) Access/Participation: The Commission believes that an individual should have the ability both to access data about himself by viewing the data maintained by the collecting entity, and to contest the data's accuracy and completeness. "To be meaningful, access must encompass timely and inexpensive access to data, a simple means for contesting inaccurate or incomplete data, a mechanism by which the data collector can verify the information, and the means by which corrections and/or consumer objections can be added to the data file and sent to all data recipients." *Id.*

(4) Integrity/Security: This precept is designed to promote the accuracy and security of the data collected. The Commission believes that reasonable steps should be taken by collectors to ensure data integrity. For example, reputable sources of data and cross-referencing data against multiple sources should be used, and untimely data should be destroyed. Managerial measures (such as internal restrictions on access to data) and technical measures (such as encryption in the transmission and storage of data and the storage of data on secure servers or computers that are inaccessible by modem) should be undertaken to protect the data against loss, unauthorized access, destruction, and disclosure.

(5) Enforcement/Redress: The Commission has opined that the core principles of privacy protection can only be effective if there is a mechanism in place to enforce them. Among available enforcement approaches are industry self-regulation, legislation, and/or regulatory schemes. *See id.*

The ostensible consensus on these principles notwithstanding, as of mid-2000, American privacy policies of general application may be found largely in legislation relating to data collection practices for information concerning children, *see* discussion *infra* at 335, and in the safe harbor guidelines governing the receipt and use of information originating in the European Union. The FTC's enforcement function has been manifested by the prosecution, as unfair and deceptive practices, of the failure of web-site operators to adhere to those privacy practices and policies they profess to maintain.

## Notes and Questions

1.  In addition to the proceeding brought against GeoCities, the Federal Trade Commission charged Liberty Financial Companies, Inc. with having misrepresented how information furnished by children in connection with a game would be used, and with having enticed children to provide such information by offering non-existent contests. The proposed consent order contemplates injunctive relief, without admission of guilt. *See* Liberty Financial, Agreement Containing Proposed Consent Order (No. 9823522) <http://www.ftc.gov/opa/1999/9905/younginvestor.htm>.

2.  On January 6, 2000, ReverseAuction.com settled charges brought against it by the Commission. The site had been accused of violating consumers' privacy by harvesting their personal information from a competitor auction site, eBay.com, and then sending unsolicited e-mail messages to eBay.com's members. The messages purported to warn of imminent expiration of their eBay.com accounts, and encouraged that site's members to visit ReverseAuction.com's site. The consent order entered into by ReverseAuction.com prohibits that company from engaging in similar practices in the future. *See* Federal Trade Commission, Press Release, *Online Auction Site Settles FTC Privacy Charges* (Jan. 6, 2000) <http://www.ftc.gov/opa/2000/01/reverse4.htm>. In addition, ReverseAuction.com is required to delete data relating to the consumers who had received the e-mail messages. *Id.* ReverseAuction.com also must inform consumers that their eBay.com accounts were not about to expire and that eBay.com neither knew nor authorized ReverseAuction.com's dissemination of the e-mail messages.

3.  The Federal Trade Commission has also charged operators of a group of on-line pharmacies as violating federal laws with, among other things, issuing privacy and confidentiality assurances with which they did not comply. Federal Trade Commission, Press Release, *Online Pharmacies Settle FTC Charges: Viagra, Propecia Prescriptions Promoted with False Medical Claims Consumers' Medical and Financial Data Collected with False Privacy Assurances* (July 12, 2000) <http://www.ftc.gov/opa/2000/07/iog.htm>. The parties resolved the dispute; the settlement prohibits deceptive claims, proscribes disclosure of the information collected from consumers with their authorization, and requires the promoters to notify consumers of their practices regarding the collection and use of consumers' personal identifying information. *See id.* Specifically, the settlement prohibits the defendants from "selling, renting, leasing, transferring or disclosing the personal information that was collected from their customers without express authorization from the customer." *See id.* The directed privacy practices mirror the Commission's core principles on this issue. The FTC also is entitled pursuant to the settlement to monitor compliance with its order. *See* Federal Trade Commission, Press Release, *Online Pharmacies Settle FTC Charges: Viagra, Propecia Prescriptions Promoted with False Medical Claims Consumers' Medical and Financial Data Collected with False Privacy Assurances* (July 12, 2000) <http://www.ftc.gov/opa/2000/07/iog.htm>.

4.  *Brill's Content* recently reported on a Web bug (i.e., a computer code that cannot be viewed by the naked eye but allows on-line monitoring) that indicated that DoubleClick, Inc. was collecting information about a visit to a porn-related site. Mark Boal, *Click Click Trick,* Brill's Content (July/Aug. 2000) at 40. "Company officials say emphatically that [DoubleClick] won't link information about an individual's website visits with his or her name. Yet the sort of Web bug coding...DoubleClick

[was found to be] using on various porn and health sites is ideally suited to linking a person's name to his or her computer." *Id.* at 41.

5.   What are the implications of out-sourcing data collection tasks to a third party? Should the relationship be disclosed to visitors to the site? Is the analysis affected if the site is targeted to minors?

--------

## c. Data Collection Protections Relating to Children

Data collection practices relating to information supplied by and maintained about children have been viewed with a heightened level of concern by many privacy advocates and government regulators. Information may be collected from children as they register for contests, play on-line games, complete surveys, and participate in chat rooms. The Federal Trade Commission has stated that:

> The most potentially serious safety concern is presented by the posting of personal identifying information by and about children — i.e., information that can be used to identify children, such as name, postal or e-mail address — in interactive public areas, like chat rooms and bulletin boards, that are accessible to all online users. These activities enable children to communicate freely with strangers, including adults. The FBI and Justice Department's "Innocent Images" investigation has revealed that online services and bulletin boards are quickly becoming the most powerful resources used by predators to identify and contact children. Further, anecdotal evidence indicates that many children surfing the Web claim to have experienced problems such as attempted password theft and inappropriate advances by adults in children's chat rooms.

> Traditionally, parents have instructed children to avoid speaking with strangers. The collecting or posting of personal information in chat rooms and on bulletin boards online runs contrary to that traditional safety message. Children are told by parents not to talk to strangers whom they meet on the street, but they are given a contrary message by Web sites that encourage them to interact with strangers in their homes via the Web. The dangers in the Web environment are heightened by the fact that children cannot determine whether they are dealing with another child or an adult posing as a child.

> In addition to these safety issues are privacy concerns raised by commercial Web sites' collection of personal information from children for marketing purposes.... [T]he practice is widespread and includes the collection of personal information from even very young children without any parental involvement or awareness.

Federal Trade Commission, *Privacy Online: A Report to Congress* (June 1998) <http://www.ftc.gov/reports/privacy3/history.htm#Children's Privacy Online>.

In 1998, the Federal Trade Commission expressed concern that 89 percent of the children's web-sites surveyed by the Commission in its sample of 1400 sites collect personal information from children. *See id.* "Few" of the sites reportedly took any steps to provide "meaningful" parental involvement in the process. *See id.* For example, only ten percent of the sites surveyed provided for parental control over the collection and/or use of information from children. *See id.*

These concerns led to enactment of the Children's Online Privacy Protection Act of 1998, 15 U.S.C. §§ 6501–6506 (West 2000) ("COPPA"), which became effective in April 2000. The Act is designed to prohibit unfair and deceptive acts and practices in connection with the collection and use of personally identifiable information retrieved from and about children via the Internet. For purposes of COPPA, "children" refers to persons under the age of 13.

The Federal Trade Commission has indicated that COPPA is designed to enhance parental involvement in the child's on-line activities in order to promote the privacy and safety of children in the electronic environment. The Act also is intended to maintain the security of data collected about children over the Internet.

Compliance with COPPA's provisions requires web-site operators to furnish notice to parents of the site's information practices; obtain prior parental consent for the collection, use, and/or disclosure of personal information from children; provide an opportunity for parental review of the information collected from the child and an opportunity to refuse permission for the operator's further use or maintenance of data from the child; and establish and maintain reasonable procedures to protect the confidentiality, security, and integrity of the data collected. *See* 15 U.S.C.A. § 6502 (West Supp. 2000). In addition, the Act limits the web-site operator's collection of personal information for a child's on-line participation in a game, prize offer, and other activities to information that is reasonably necessary for the activity in question. *See id.; see generally How to Comply with the Children's Online Privacy Protection Rule* (Nov. 1999) <http://www.ftc.gov/bcp/conline/pubs/buspubs/coppa.htm>.

COPPA is directed not only to web-sites and on-line services targeted to children, but also to such operators and service providers connected with a general audience web-site that have actual knowledge that the site is collecting personal information from children. *See id.* Implementation of COPPA's provisions is under the auspices of the Federal Trade Commission, which adopted a rule effective April 21, 2000. The rule requires relevant operators of web-sites and on-line services to (1) prominently indicate how they collect, use, and disclose personal information from children; (2) with certain exceptions, notify parents that they wish to collect information and obtain parental consent before collecting, using, and disclosing such information; (3) refrain from conditioning a child's participation in on-line activities on the provision of more personal information than is reasonably necessary to participate in the activity; (4) allow parents the opportunity to review and to have their children's information deleted and prohibit further collection from the child; and (5) establish procedures to protect the confidentiality, security, and integrity of personal information they collect from children. The rule also provides a safe harbor for operators following Commission-approved self-regulatory guidelines. *See* 16 C.F.R. § 312 (2000).

The Federal Trade Commission has been sending e-mails to "scores" of web-sites directed to children to alert them that they are obligated to comply with COPPA's requirements. Federal Trade Commission, Press Release, *Web Sites Warned to Comply with Children's Online Privacy Law* (July 17, 2000) <http://www.ftc.gov/opa/2000/07/coppacompli.htm>. "Protecting children's privacy is a priority for the FTC. We intend to ensure that Web sites collecting personal information from kids are complying with COPPA and that kids' information is protected, not exploited," said the Director of the Commission's Bureau of Consumer Protection. *Id.*

## Notes and Questions

1. From the perspective of consumers, is there a difference between a privacy seal site that approves a company that operates a web-site, as opposed to a seal that approves a web-site?

2. Children have been treated specially by the legal system in a number of contexts. Recall the discussion as to the statutory provisions designed to protect minors from indecent and offensive communications on the Internet. *See* discussion *supra* at 158.

3. Web-site operators are increasingly engaging in the practice of posting their privacy protection and security measures. "Perhaps the most effective approaches to safeguarding on-line privacy will be those based on education of individual users of the Internet and of commercial enterprises that deal with consumers in the on-line environment." George B. Delta and Jeffry H. Matsuura, *Law of the Internet*, § 6.03 at 6-38 (2000).

---

### d. Legislative Privacy Protections

By mid-2000, hundreds of legislative initiatives were proposed at the state and federal level to address cyberspace communications and transactions. Included within the patchwork of federal legislation existing at that time was the Privacy Protection Act of 1980, 42 U.S.C.A. § 2000aa (West 1994), which deals with, among other things, efforts to obtain information gathered by the press. The Act gives journalists and publishers notice and an opportunity to be heard before materials they are preparing for publication may be seized by law enforcement personnel. The Act refers to "a person reasonably believed to have a purpose to disseminate to the public a newspaper, book, broadcast or other similar form of public communication." *Id.* As on-line content providers proliferate, who is engaged in such publishing activities for purposes of the Act's protection? *See* discussion *supra* at 19.

---

## Anthony A. DAVIS, *et al.* v. Anthony GRACEY, *et al.*

United States Court of Appeals, Tenth Circuit
No. 95-6245, 111 F.3d 1472
April 21, 1997

Before SEYMOUR, Chief Judge, BARRETT and LIVELY, Senior Circuit Judges.

SEYMOUR, Chief Judge.

Anthony Davis operated a large computer bulletin board system [whereby subscribers could dial in using a modem, then use the syustem to send and receive messages via e-mail, access the Internet, utilize on-line database, and download or upload software.] After Mr. Davis sold obscene CD-ROMs to an undercover officer, a warrant was obtained to search his business premises. During the execution of the warrant, police officers determined pornographic CD-ROM files could be accessed through the bulletin board and seized the computer equipment used to operate it. Following his criminal conviction and civil forfeiture of the computer equipment in state court proceedings, Mr. Davis, his related businesses, and several users of electronic mail (e-mail) on his bulletin board brought this action in federal court against the officers who executed the search, alleging that the seizure of the computer equipment, and e-mail and software stored on the system, violated several constitutional and statutory provisions. The district court granted summary judgment for the officers. We affirm.

### Background

Mr. Davis operated the Oklahoma Information Exchange, a computer bulletin board system.... The officer never actually saw the computer equipment used to operate the bulletin board. In his affidavit for a search warrant, the officer did not mention the possibility that a bulletin board was being operated on the premises, or the possibility that this bulletin board could be used to distribute or display pornographic images.... During the search, the officers discovered the bulletin board. Attached to it were CD-ROM drives housing sixteen CD-ROM discs, including four discs identified by Mr. Davis to the officers as containing pornographic material. The officers believed from the configuration of the bulletin board computers that the files accessible via the bulletin board included files from the four pornographic CD-ROMs. The officers called for assistance from officer Gregory Taylor, who was reputed to be more knowledgeable about computers than they were. He confirmed that the pornographic CD-ROMs could be accessed via the bulletin board. The officers seized the computer equipment used to operate the bulletin board, including two computers, as well as monitors, keyboards, modems, and CD-ROM drives and changers. The seizure of this computer equipment is the subject of the federal proceedings in this case.

At the time of the seizure, the computer system contained approximately 150,000 e-mail messages in electronic storage, some of which had not yet been retrieved by the intended recipients. The hard drive of the computer system also contained approximately 500 megabytes of software which had been uploaded onto the bulletin board by individual subscribers. Mr. Davis intended to republish this "shareware" on a CD-ROM for sale to the public. Mr. Davis had previously published three such compilations of shareware on CD-ROM.

Mr. Davis was convicted of several counts of possessing and distributing obscenity, and of using a computer to violate Oklahoma statutes. His conviction was upheld on appeal. *Davis v. State*, 916 P.2d 251, 254 (Okla.Crim.App. 1996). The State also obtained civil forfeiture of the computer equipment used to operate the bulletin board. *State ex rel. Macy v. One (1) Pioneer CD-ROM Changer*, 891 P.2d 600, 607 (Okla.Ct.App. 1994). Law enforcement officials have apparently disclaimed any interest in the materials in electronic storage, either for purposes of evidence or forfeiture.

Mr. Davis, Gayla Davis, John Burton, and TSI Telecommunications Specialists, Inc., filed the instant suit in federal court alleging claims under 42 U.S.C. § 1983 for violation of First and Fourth Amendment rights, and under the Privacy Protection Act (PPA), 42 U.S.C. §§ 2000aa–2000aa-12, and the Electronic Communications Privacy Act (ECPA), 18 U.S.C. §§ 2510–2711. The crux of the complaint is that the seizure of the equipment was illegal because the warrant was not sufficiently particular and because the seized computer system contained e-mail intended for private subscribers to the bulletin board, and software intended for future publication by Mr. Davis. Plaintiffs contend these stored electronic materials were outside the scope of the warrant, and are protected by several congressional enactments....

## Privacy Protection Act

Plaintiffs assert that the seizure of the stored electronic materials constituted a violation of the Privacy Protection Act (PPA), 42 U.S.C. §§ 2000aa–2000aa-12. The PPA provides that

> it shall be unlawful for a government officer or employee, in connection with the investigation or prosecution of a criminal offense, to search for or seize any work product materials possessed by a person reasonably believed to have a purpose to disseminate to the public a newspaper, book, broadcast, or other similar form of publication.

42 U.S.C. § 2000aa(a).[7] The PPA requires law enforcement officers, absent exigent circumstances, *id.* § 2000aa(a)(2), to rely on subpoenas to acquire materials intended for publication unless "there is probable cause to believe that the person possessing [work product] materials has committed or is committing the criminal offense to which the materials relate," *id.* § 2000aa(a)(1).

The statute creates a civil cause of action for damages resulting from a search or seizure of materials in violation of the Act. *Id.* § 2000aa-6. This cause of action is available against the United States, against a State (if the State has waived sovereign immunity), or against "any other governmental unit." *Id.* § 2000aa-6(a)(1). A cause of action is available against the officers or employees of a State only if the State has not waived its sovereign immunity. *Id.* 2000aa6(a)(2). The Act provides that "[i]t shall be a complete defense to a civil action [against a government officer or employee] that the officer had a reasonable good faith belief in the lawfulness of his conduct." 42 U.S.C. § 2000aa-6(b). The district court here granted summary judgment for the officers, holding them entitled to the good faith defense due to their reliance on a warrant.

We hold instead that we lack subject matter jurisdiction over defendant officers under the PPA. The statute provides:

> The remedy provided by [section 2000aa-6(a)(1)] against the United States, a State, or any other governmental unit is exclusive of any other civil action or proceeding for conduct constituting a violation of this chapter, against the officer or employee whose violation gave rise to the claim, or against the estate of such officer or employee.

*Id.* § 2000aa-6(d). Thus, an action under the PPA may only be brought against the governmental entity, unless the state has not waived sovereign immunity in which event state employees may be sued. *Id.* § 2000aa-6(a)(2). The PPA by its terms does not authorize a suit against municipal officers or employees in their individual capacities. The statute therefore provides no cause of action against these defendants. Although the parties stipulated below to subject-matter jurisdiction, "no action of the parties can confer subject-matter jurisdiction upon a federal court," *Insurance Corp. of Ireland v. Compagnie des Bauxites de Guinee*, 456 U.S. 694, 702, 102 S.Ct. 2099, 2104, 72 L.Ed.2d 492 (1982). We dismiss the PPA claim for lack of subject-matter jurisdiction. . . .

---

7. The PPA also provides protection to "documentary materials, other than work product materials," which are not themselves intended for publication but which are "possessed . . . in connection with a purpose to disseminate" a public communication. 42 U.S.C. § 2000aa(b).

### Conclusion

We hold that...we lack subject matter jurisdiction over plaintiffs' asserted claim against the officers under the PPA. We AFFIRM the district court's entry of summary judgment for the officers.

---

## Notes and Questions

1.  Legislation relating to the privacy of financial and credit records includes the Right to Financial Privacy Act of 1978, 12 U.S.C.A. §§ 3401–02 (West 1989), which protects the privacy of certain individual customer records maintained by financial institutions. Such institutions are permitted under the Act to respond to requests for information submitted pursuant to valid warrants or if there is reason to believe that the records sought are relevant to a legitimate law enforcement inquiry and the customer has been properly served with notice.

2.  The Fair Credit Reporting Act of 1996, 15 U.S.C.A. §§ 1681a–u (West 1997 & Supp.), which applies to databases and communications involving consumer credit card information, also deals with privacy interests in financial and credit records. The Act authorizes access by individuals, upon request, to information from credit companies and affords a mechanism for the correction of errors. When a consumer reporting agency prepares reports, it must follow "reasonable procedures to assure maximum possible accuracy of information concerning the individual about whom the report relates." 15 U.S.C.A. § 1681e(b). The agency may be held liable if it negligently fails to comply with the Act's requirements. *See* 15 U.S.C. § 1681o, *see also Thompson v. San Antonio Retail Merchants Ass'n,* 682 F.2d 509 (5th Cir. 1982).

3.  The Gramm-Leach-Bliley Act (Financial Services Modernization Act of 1999), Pub. L. No. 106-102, 113 Stat. 1338 (1999) (codified as amended §§ 12 U.S.C.A. 24a, 248b, 1828b, 1831v, 1848a, 2908, 4809 (West Supp. 2000) and 15 U.S.C.A. §§ 80b–10a, 6701, 6711–17, 6735–37, 6751–66, 6781, 6801–09, 6821–27, 6901–10 (West Supp. 2000), was signed into law in November 1999. The Act is designed to enhance competition in the financial services industry. The preamble to the Act states that "it is the policy of Congress that each financial institution has an affirmative and continuing obligation to respect the privacy of its customers and to protect the security and confidentiality of 'nonpublic personal information' of those customers." 15 U.S.C.A. § 6801. Specific privacy provisions included in the Act require financial institutions to provide notice to consumers of their privacy policies regarding personal information. 15 U.S.C.A. § 6802. The Act includes an "opt-out" mechanism, whereby consumers can choose not to have disclosures made of personal data. *Id.*

4.  Several bills have been proposed to address privacy issues relating to health care information. The U.S. Department of Health and Human Services recently issued proposed regulations to create national standards to protect health information that is transmitted and maintained electronically. The regulations envision limitations on the release of medical information for purposes unrelated to treatment and payment absent written consent. The proposed regulations represent an effort to balance individual privacy interests and the public interest in protecting health, conducting medical research, improving health care, and combating health care fraud and abuse.

To what extent may these objectives be served without engaging in the use of personal identifiers tied to the data? Does the disclosure of data devoid of names or other identifying details still implicate cognizable privacy interests? How is this analysis affected by technological developments in instrumental mapping, which keys information (such as social security numbers) to particular individuals?

5. The Cable Communications Policy Act of 1984, 47 U.S.C.A. § 551 (West 1991), addresses various privacy issues that relate to subscribers of cable services and other services provided by cable operators. Such issues include notice to subscribers regarding the cable operator's practices that concern personally identifiable information, the scope of permissible information that may be collected by the cable operator, disclosure by the cable operator absent the subscriber's consent, and access to personally identifiable information collected by the cable operator. *See* 47 U.S.C.A. § 551(a-e). How do these provisions affect cable operators that offer access to the Internet?

6. The Video Privacy Protection Act, 18 U.S.C.A. § 2710 (West 2000), governs the use of personal data generated by the purchase and rental of videocassettes.

---

An extensive web of statutory authority also exists with respect to eavesdropping, wiretapping, and the interception of telephonic and other communications. In addition to legislation enacted by states, the federal government has promulgated regulations of such conduct as the recording of telephone conversations. The Omnibus Crime Control and Safe Streets Act of 1968, 18 U.S.C.A. §§ 2510–2520 (West 2000), for example, prohibits "any person" who, without a warrant, "willfully intercepts" any "wire or oral communication."

With respect to on-line communications, the Electronic Communications Privacy Act of 1986, 18 U.S.C. §§ 2701–2711 (West 2000) ("ECPA"), is among the statutes that regulates electronic communications from unauthorized interception. The legislation amended Title II of the 1968 Omnibus Crime Control and Safe Streets Act in an effort to accommodate new technologies.

One aspect of the ECPA is known as the "Wiretap Act," which prohibits the interception of oral, wire, and electronic communications while such communications are in transit. Intentional interception of such communications may be punished by the imposition of fines, imprisonment, or both. The statute also provides for a private civil action in favor of persons whose oral, wire, or electronic communications have been intercepted. 18 U.S.C.A. § 2511(a).

Another aspect of legislation protects communications both during transmission and while the content of the communications is in electronic storage. The law proscribes unauthorized access of e-mail messages, bulletin board transmissions, and communications between remote computing services and their customers. Essentially, the ECPA prohibits accessing an electronic communication computer facility to acquire information which has not been authorized to be disclosed to the recipient, and divulging the contents of such information. Remedies similarly include civil actions and penal sanctions of fines, imprisonment, or both. *See* 18 U.S.C.A. § 2701(a), (b).

There are mulitple exceptions to the statute's prohibitions. Not surprisingly, interception of communications in transit or access to stored communictions is permitted with consent. *See* 18 U.S.C.A. § 2511(a)(2)(d), 2701(c)(1), (2) (West 2000). Of course, the contents of a communication may also be divulged to an addressee or intended recipient of the communication. *See* 18 U.S.C. § 2702(b)(1),(3),(4).

Additionally, providers of a communications system are permitted to intercept communications in the normal course of employment while an employee is engaged in any activity that is a necessary incident to the rendition of his service, or to protect the rights or property of the provider. *See* 18 U.S.C.A. § 2511(a)(i). This exception has been referred to as the "business use exception." Another aspect of the statute, the "provider exception," allows those who provide a wire or electronic communications service to authorize access to stored communications on that system. *See* 18 U.S.C.A. § 2701(c)(1). A system operator may also divulge to a law enforcement agency when the system operator inadvertently obtained the contents of the communication and those contents appear to pertain to the commission of a crime. *See* 18 U.S.C.A. § 2702(b)(6).

Controversies arising in the cyberspace context relate to the disparity in permissible disclosures to the government and to others. Under the ECPA, the government generally can obtain the content of stored on-line communications, provided such disclosure is sought pursuant to a valid criminal warrant, subpoena, or court order. *See* 18 U.S.C.A. § 2703(c)(1)(c). Such court process generally is authorized when the material sought appears to relate to the commission of a crime. Electronic communications service providers may, but are not required to, disclose subscriber record information to non-governmental persons or entities.

Privacy interests have traditionally been placed in a delicate balance with the pursuit of criminal investigations. With respect to digital information, such interests have collided with efforts to execute search warrants for computer-related materials. In *Steve Jackson Games, Inc. v. United States Secret Service*, 36 F.3d 457 (5th Cir. 1994), for example, officers seized computers, disks, and other items from a bulletin board operator pursuant to a search warrant. Did the seizure of the computer, on which undelivered private e-mails were stored, constitute an unlawful interception? The court construed Title I of the ECPA as excluding stored electronic communications. *See id.* at 462.

Under what circumstances are private individuals and the government entitled to obtain information from an on-line service provider about one of its customers or the content of the customer's electronic communication?

---

# Terry JESSUP-MORGAN v. AMERICA ONLINE, INC.

United States District Court, Eastern District of Michigan, Southern Division
No. 98-70676, 20 F. Supp. 2d 1105
July 23, 1998

FEIKENS, District Judge.

## BACKGROUND

In June, 1995 Phillip Morgan filed a suit for divorce from Barbara Smith-Morgan (now Barbara Smith) in the Oakland County Circuit Court in Michigan. That court granted the divorce in May 1996. Within weeks of the divorce judgment, Terry Jessup (Jessup) (now Terry Jessup-Morgan, plaintiff in this case), married Phillip Morgan.

Jessup and Phillip Morgan began a relationship some time prior to January 1996, while Phillip Morgan and Barbara Smith were still married. On January 11, 1996 Jessup (then an America Online (AOL) member) used her AOL account to post publicly on the Internet a message meant to harass and injure Barbara Smith. Jessup posted the message under the "screen name" (*i.e.,* alias) of "Barbeeedol." The message read as follows:

Subject: * * * * * CALL ME * * * * *

From: barbeeedol@aol.com (Barbeeedol)

Date: 11 Jan 1996 15:01:36 -0500

Message-ID: d3qb0$bb7@newsbf02.news.aol.com

Call me.....I'm single, lonely, horny and would love to have either phone sex or a[sic] in person sexual relationship....

My name is Barbara and I'm a single white female looking for just about any kind of sex I can have with someone other than myself... If you can help, call me....

The [telephone number set forth]...was the phone number of Barbara Smith's parents' home, with whom Barbara Smith and her two young children were residing pending resolution of the divorce suit. Jessup posted the message in an Internet usenet newsgroup entitled "alt.amazon-women.admirers," a public electronic bulletin board containing messages accessible to, and read by, a potential 40 million persons worldwide.

As intended by Jessup, posting this message resulted in persons Barbara Smith did not know calling her parents' home to request sexual liaisons with "Barbara." This gravely disturbed and distressed Barbara Smith and her parents. From the nature of the calls, and from the information callers supplied about how they obtained her parents' home phone number, Barbara Smith concluded that she was the intended target of the person(s) who posted a message on the Internet. Barbara Smith enlisted the aid of her brother, Kenton Smith, an experienced interactive computer services and Internet user. Kenton Smith was himself an AOL member at that time. He used a computer "search engine" to locate the posting of the offensive message on the Internet. He deduced from the posting's screen name and the "Message-ID" line that it was posted by another AOL member.

On January 12, 1996 Kenton Smith sent an e-mail message to AOL describing the posting and the calls to his parents' home. He asked AOL for information as to the identity of the person who posted the message. AOL reviewed Kenton Smith's complaint and the "Barbeeedol" message, and determined that the posting originated from Jessup's AOL account, which constituted an egregious breach of the AOL Member Agreement signed by Jessup. AOL, therefore, terminated its contract with Jessup on February 2, 1996, and closed her AOL account. AOL's records list the grounds for this termination as "excessive USENET abuse." The same day, AOL sent Kenton Smith two messages. The first message explained that, for confidentiality reasons, AOL could not disclose information about actions it took against other AOL members. The second message explained that as a matter of AOL policy, information identifying the AOL member who posted the offensive message could only be released in response to a subpoena.

On February 16, 1996 Barbara Smith's divorce attorney, Kathleen M. Dilger, served AOL with a civil subpoena for information which would identify the AOL member who authored the injurious message. On February 23, 1996, in compliance with the subpoena, AOL sent to Dilger a two-page summary containing basic identity information on the AOL account from which the "Barbeeedol" message originated. The summary revealed that Jessup was the holder of the account.

Terry Jessup-Morgan now brings suit against AOL, claiming that AOL's compliance with the subpoena was unlawful, tortious, and a breach of contract. Specifically, Jessup alleges (1) that AOL's release of stored electronic information violated the Electronic Communication Privacy Act, 18 U.S.C. § 2707; (2) that AOL breached its contract with her, and its implied and express warranties; (3) that AOL's release of the information was negligent; (4) that AOL engaged in fraud and misrepresentation in its contract with her; (5) that AOL invaded her privacy and disclosed private facts about her; (6) that AOL violated the Michigan Consumer Protection Act; and (7) that AOL violated the Michigan Pricing and Advertising of Consumer Items Act. Jessup does not deny that she perpetrated the offense against Barbara Smith (by posting the fraudulent Internet message). However, she complains that AOL's disclosure that she committed the offense affected her child custody hearings, "her future husband's [Phillip Morgan's] divorce hearing, and other personal matters." Jessup also complains that AOL's disclosure affected her "reputation in the community...and her reputation among her friends."

She requests various damages in excess of $47 million.

Defendant AOL moves that I (1) grant AOL judgment on the pleadings pursuant to Fed. R. Civ. P. 12(c) on Jessup's claim that AOL violated the Electronic Communication Privacy Act; (2) grant AOL summary judgment on Jessup's breach of contract and implied and express warranties claim; (3) grant AOL judgment on the pleadings on Jessup's negligence claim; (4) dismiss Jessup's fraud and misrepresentation claim pursuant to Fed. R. Civ. P. 9(b); (5) grant AOL judgment on the pleadings or summary judgment on Jessup's invasion of privacy/disclosure of private facts claim; (6) dismiss Jessup's Michigan Consumer Protection Act claim; and (7) dismiss Jessup's Michigan Pricing and Advertising of Consumer Items Act claim....

## AOL MEMBER AGREEMENT

To obtain her AOL service, Jessup executed a Member Agreement (Agreement) with AOL. The Agreement is governed by the AOL Terms of Service (TOS) and the AOL Rules of the Road (ROR). The TOS provides for AOL or Member termination of their contract at any time. Terms of Service, § 9. The TOS provides that it is governed by the laws of the Commonwealth of Virginia, and by executing the Agreement Jessup and AOL agreed to submit to these laws. Terms of Service, § 10.[1]

The ROR provides that:

> AOL Inc. does not disclose to private persons or companies information that identifies a Member's AOL screen name(s) with Member's actual name or other identity information, *unless required to do so by law or legal process served on AOL Inc. AOL Inc. reserves the right to make exceptions to this policy* of non-disclosure in exceptional circumstances (such as a suicide threat, or instances of suspected fraud) on a case by case basis and *at AOL's sole discretion.*

Rules of the Road, § 2.B(iv) (emphasis added).

By executing the Agreement, Jessup agreed to use her AOL account only for lawful purposes. The ROR specifically prohibits using AOL services to:

> (1) harass, threaten, embarrass, or cause distress, unwanted attention or discomfort upon another Member or user of AOL or other person or entity,

---

1. Because of federal question and supplemental jurisdiction, I apply either federal law or Virginia law as appropriate. Under the terms of the Agreement, Jessup's Michigan state law claims are moot.

(2) post or transmit sexually explicit images or other content which is deemed by AOL Inc. to be offensive,

(3) *transmit any* unlawful, harmful, threatening, abusive, harassing, defamatory, vulgar, obscene, hateful, ethnically or otherwise objectionable Content,...

(5) impersonate any person... or communicate under a false name or a name that you are not entitled or authorized to use,...

(10) intentionally or unintentionally violate any applicable local, state, national or international law, including but not limited to any regulations having the force of law.

Rules of the Road, § 2.C(a).

## DISCUSSION

1. Violation of Electronic Communication Privacy Act claim.

The prohibitions of the Electronic Communication Privacy Act (ECPA), 18 U.S.C. §§ 2701 *et seq.*, are inapplicable. The ECPA prohibits disclosure of the contents of an electronic communication to any person or entity (18 U.S.C. § 2702) or to the government (18 U.S.C. § 2703) without first meeting certain restrictions. 18 U.S.C. § 2711 states that the definitions in 18 U.S.C. § 2510 apply to the ECPA's provisions. 18 U.S.C. § 2510 states that "'contents,' when used with respect to any wire, oral, or electronic communication, includes any information concerning the substance, purport, or meaning of that communication," [not information concerning the identity of the author of the communication]. 18 U.S.C. § 2510(8). The "content" of a communication is not at issue in this case. Disclosure of information identifying an AOL electronic communication account customer is at issue. In 18 U.S.C. § 2703(c)(1)(C) this identifying information is specifically acknowledged as separate from the "content" of electronic communications. The ECPA actually authorizes AOL's disclosure:

> Except as provided in subparagraph (B), a provider of electronic communication service or remote computing service *may* disclose a record or other information pertaining to a subscriber to or customer of such service (not including the contents of communications covered by subsection (a) or (b) of this section) to any person *other than a governmental entity.*

8 U.S.C. § 2703(c)(1)(A) (emphasis added) (subsections (a) and (b) do not apply to the AOL disclosure). AOL made the disclosure, not to the public, but to a private individual, Barbara Smith's attorney, pursuant to a properly executed subpoena. Because the prohibitions of the ECPA do not apply to the AOL disclosure in this case, Jessup's claim that AOL violated the Electronic Communication Privacy Act fails, and AOL is entitled to dismissal of this claim because of her failure to state a claim upon which relief can be granted. Fed. R. Civ. P. 12.

2. Breach of contract and implied and express warranties claim.

Jessup breached her contract with AOL, particularly section 2.C(a), by posting the message which invited third persons to seek sexual liaisons with Barbara Smith. Jessup's breach of the Agreement prior to any alleged breach of the same contract by AOL bars her claim against AOL for breach of contract and implied and express warranties. Under Virginia law, when the initial breach is substantial, the party who breaches a contract first is barred from maintaining an action against another contracting party for its subsequent breach of, or failure to perform under, the contract. *Horton v. Horton*, 487 S.E.2d 200, 203–04 (Va. 1997); *Federal Ins. Co. v. Starr Elec. Co.*, 242 Va. 459, 467–68, 410 S.E.2d 684, 688–89 (Va. 1991). Here, Jessup's impersonation of Barbara Smith, and her posting of the message to harass and cause distress to Barbara, is certainly a substantial and material breach of the Agreement.

AOL did not breach the Agreement. According to the terms of the Agreement, AOL, at its discretion, could terminate a Member's account because the Member committed the acts Jessup did. AOL did so in this instance. In providing identifying information to Barbara Smith's lawyer pursuant to a civil subpoena, AOL complied with applicable law. The Agreement clearly provides for this compliance with proper legal process.

Jessup committed an egregious and intentionally harmful (to a third party) breach of the contract, and AOL acted responsibly in terminating her account and in providing information identifying her as the account holder that posted the harassing message on the Internet. Jessup provides no evidence that AOL breached any implied or express warranties. AOL is thus entitled to summary judgment on Jessup's breach of contract and implied and express warranties claim.

### 3. Negligence claim.

Under Virginia law, in a contract case a tort claim must rest on a breach of duty distinct from the breach of contract. *Foreign Mission Bd. of the S. Baptist Convention v. Wade*, 242 Va. 234, 240–41, 409 S.E.2d 144, 148 (1991). The duty Jessup claims AOL breached—not to release information identifying her as the author of the injurious message—is a contractual one. Therefore, Jessup's negligence claim must fail, and AOL is entitled to dismissal of this claim because she failed to state a claim upon which relief can be granted. Fed. R. Civ. P. 12(b)(6).

### 4. Fraud, misrepresentation claim.

AOL is entitled to dismissal of this claim because Jessup failed to plead fraud and misrepresentation with particularity, as required by Fed. R. Civ. P. 9(b). "[A] plaintiff must at a minimum allege the time, place and contents of the misrepresentation(s) upon which he relied." *Bender v. Southland Corp.*, 749 F.2d 1205, 1216 (6th Cir. 1984). Jessup did not meet these minimum requirements in stating her fraud/misrepresentation claim against AOL.

### 5. Invasion of privacy and disclosure of private facts claim.

Virginia law does not recognize the tort of invasion of privacy as alleged by Jessup (whether intrusion upon seclusion or disclosure of private facts). *Brown v. American Broad. Co., Inc.*, 704 F.2d 1296, 1302–03 (4th Cir. 1983). Jessup's claim of invasion of privacy and disclosure of private facts fails, and AOL is entitled to dismissal of this claim because she failed to state a claim upon which relief can be granted. Fed. R. Civ. P. 12(b)(6).

### 6. Violation of Michigan Consumer Protection Act claim, and
### 7. Violation of Michigan Pricing and Advertising of Consumer Items Act claim.

Because Michigan law is inapplicable, Jessup's claims under the Michigan Consumer Protection Act and the Michigan Pricing and Advertising of Consumer Items Act are moot. AOL is entitled to dismissal of these claims because of Jessup's failure to state a claim upon which relief can be granted. Fed. R. Civ. P. 12(b)(6).

## CONCLUSION

For the reasons stated herein all of the above cited AOL motions are hereby GRANTED.

---

# Timothy R. McVEIGH v. William S. COHEN, *et al.*

United States District Court, District of Columbia
No. CIV. A. 98-116, 983 F. Supp. 215
January 1998

SPORKIN, District Judge.

This matter comes before the Court on Plaintiff's Motion for a Preliminary Injunction. Plaintiff Timothy R. McVeigh, who bears no relation to the Oklahoma City bombing defendant, seeks to enjoin the United States Navy from discharging him under the statutory policy colloquially known as "Don't Ask, Don't Tell, Don't Pursue." *See* 10 U.S.C. § 654 ("new policy"). In the course of investigating his sexual orientation, the Plaintiff contends that the Defendants violated his rights under the Electronic Communications Privacy Act ("ECPA"), 18 U.S.C. § 2701 *et seq.*, the Administrative Procedure Act ("APA") 5 U.S.C. § 706, the Department's own policy, and the Fourth and Fifth Amendments of the U.S. Constitution. Absent an injunction, the Plaintiff avers that he will suffer irreparable injury from the discharge, even if he were ultimately to prevail on the merits of his claims.

## STATEMENT OF FACTS

The Plaintiff, Senior Chief Timothy R. McVeigh, is a highly decorated seventeen-year veteran of the United States Navy who has served honorably and continuously since he was nineteen years old. At the time of the Navy's decision to discharge him, he was the senior-most enlisted man aboard the United States nuclear submarine U.S.S. Chicago.

On September 2, 1997, Ms. Helen Hajne, a civilian Navy volunteer, received an electronic mail ("email") message through the America Online Service ("AOL") regarding the toy-drive that she was coordinating for the Chicago crew members' children. The message box stated that it came from the alias "boysrch," but the text of the email was signed by a "Tim." Administrative Record ("AR") at 110. Through an option available to AOL subscribers, the volunteer searched through the "member profile directory" to find the member profile for this sender. The directory specified that "boysrch" was an AOL subscriber named Tim who lived in Honolulu, Hawaii, worked in the military, and identified his marital status as "gay." Although the profile included some telling interests such as "collecting pics of other young studs" and "boy watching," it did not include any further identifying information such as full name, address, or phone number. However, on other occasions, Hajne had communicated with the Plaintiff about his participation in the drive.

Ms. Hajne proceeded to forward the email and directory profile to her husband, who, like Plaintiff, was also a noncommissioned officer aboard the U.S.S. Chicago. The material eventually found its way to Commander John Mickey, the captain of the ship and Plaintiff's commanding officer. In turn, Lieutenant Karin S. Morean, the ship's principal legal adviser and a member of the Judge Advocate General's ("JAG")

Corps was called in to investigate the matter. By this point, the Navy suspected the "Tim" who authored the email might be Senior Chief Timothy McVeigh. Before she spoke to the Plaintiff and without a warrant or court order, Lieutenant Morean requested a Navy paralegal on her staff, Legalman First Class Joseph M. Kaiser, to contact AOL and obtain information from the service that could "connect" the screen name "boysrch" and accompanying user profile to McVeigh. Legalman Kaiser called AOL's toll-free customer service number and talked to a representative at technical services. Legalman Kaiser did not identify himself as a Naval serviceman. According to his testimony at the administrative hearing, he stated that he was "a third party in receipt of a fax sheet and wanted to confirm the profile sheet, [and] who it belonged to." The AOL representative affirmatively identified Timothy R. McVeigh as the customer in question.

Upon verification from AOL, Lieutenant Morean notified Senior Chief McVeigh that the Navy had obtained "some indication[ ] that he made a statement of homosexuality" in violation of §654(b)(2) of "Don't Ask, Don't Tell." In light of the Uniform Code of Military Justice prohibition of sodomy and indecent acts, she then advised him of his right to remain silent. Shortly thereafter, in a memorandum dated September 22, 1997, the Navy advised Plaintiff that it was commencing an administrative discharge proceeding (termed by the Navy as an "administrative separation") against him. The reason stated was for "homosexual conduct, as evidenced by your statement that you are a homosexual."

On November 7, 1997, the Navy conducted an administrative discharge hearing before a three-member board. At the hearing, the Plaintiff made an unsworn oral statement that explained the substance of his email to Ms. Hajne, and thus by inference confirmed his authorship of the correspondence. The Plaintiff presented evidence of a prior engagement to a woman and several other heterosexual relationships to rebut the presumption of homosexuality, pursuant to §654(b)(2). This evidence was rejected by the Board. At the conclusion of the administrative hearing, the board held that the government had sufficiently shown by a preponderance of the evidence that Senior Chief McVeigh had engaged in "homosexual conduct," a dischargeable offense.

The Navy accelerated Plaintiff's separation to take effect at 5:00 a.m. EST on Friday, January 16, 1998. On January 15, Plaintiff commenced this lawsuit and the government postponed his separation until Wednesday, January 20. This Court held a hearing on that Wednesday morning. There, the Navy initially declined to honor this Court's request for an additional amount of time to consider this matter. The Plaintiff was scheduled to be discharged on Friday, January 23. However, on January 22, the Navy extended the time for this Court to render a decision until Tuesday, January 27, when Plaintiff is now scheduled to be discharged barring relief from this Court.

## ANALYSIS
### Standard for Preliminary Injunction

To prevail on a request for preliminary injunction, the plaintiff must demonstrate 1) a substantial likelihood of success on the merits; 2) irreparable harm or injury absent an injunction; 3) less harm or injury to the other parties involved; and 4) the service of the public interest. *See Dendy v. Washington Hosp. Center*, 581 F.2d 990, 992 (D.C. Cir. 1978) (footnote omitted); *Washington Metro. Area Transit Comm'n v. Holiday Tours, Inc.*, 559 F.2d 841, 843 (D.C. Cir. 1977). For the reasons set forth below, this Court concludes that the Plaintiff is entitled to the relief that he seeks at this time, a preliminary injunction barring his discharge.

I. Substantial Likelihood of Success on the Merits

Plaintiff in this case demonstrates a likely success to prevail on the merits. At its core, the Plaintiff's complaint is with the Navy's compliance, or lack thereof, with its new regulations under the "Don't Ask, Don't Tell, Don't Pursue" policy. Plaintiff contends that he did not "tell," as prescribed by the statute, but that nonetheless, the Navy impermissibly "asked" and zealously "pursued."

In short, this case raises the central issue of whether there is really a place for gay officers in the military under the new policy, "Don't Ask, Don't Tell, Don't Pursue." Although there have been a series of challenges to the constitutionality of the statute that codifies the policy, see e.g., Philips v. Perry, 106 F.3d 1420 (9th Cir. 1997); Thomasson v. Perry, 80 F.3d 915 (4th Cir. 1996), cert. denied, — U.S. —, 117 S.Ct. 358, 136 L.Ed.2d 250 (1996); Richenberg v. Perry, 97 F.3d 256 (8th Cir. 1996), cert. denied, — U.S. —, 118 S.Ct. 45, 139 L.Ed.2d 12 (1997); Able v. United States, 88 F.3d 1280 (2d Cir. 1996), civil courts thus far have not interpreted the requirements of the statute assuming its constitutionality. The limits on the Navy's right to investigate sexual orientation and the restrictions on an officer's right to be a gay man or woman in the military—i.e., what it practically means not to ask, not to tell, and not to pursue—have yet to be litigated in the courts.

In 1993, leaders of Congress and the President reached a compromise designed to recognize the important role that officers who happen to be gay play in the defense of our nation. See Policy Concerning Homosexuality in the Armed Forces: Hearings Before the Senate Committee on Armed Services, 103d Cong. 595 et seq. (1993) (statements of General Colin Powell, Chair of the Joint Chiefs of Staff, Admiral David Jeremiah, Navy, and General Merrill McPeak, Air Force). While the heads of the Armed Forces expressed fear that unit cohesion and military preparedness would be compromised by openly gay conduct, they acknowledged that homosexuality itself was not necessarily incompatible with military service. The statute that came to embody this position, "Don't Ask, Don't Tell, Don't Pursue," was specifically drafted to allow members of the military to live private lives as gay men and women, so long as their sexual orientation remained unspoken.

The facts as stated above clearly demonstrate that the Plaintiff did not openly express his homosexuality in a way that compromised this "Don't Ask, Don't Tell" policy. Suggestions of sexual orientation in a private, anonymous email account did not give the Navy a sufficient reason to investigate to determine whether to commence discharge proceedings. In its actions, the Navy violated its own regulations. See Guidelines for Fact-Finding Inquiries Into Homosexual Conduct, Department of Defense Directive No. 1332.14 ("Guidelines"). An investigation into sexual orientation may be initiated "only when [a commander] has received credible information that there is a basis for discharge," such as when an officer "has said that he or she is a homosexual or bisexual, or made some other statement that indicates a propensity or intent to engage in homosexual acts." Id. Yet in this case, there was no such credible information that Senior Chief McVeigh had made such a statement. Under the Guidelines, "credible information" requires more than "just a belief or suspicion" that a Service member has engaged in homosexual conduct. Id. In the examples provided, the Guidelines state that "credible information" would exist in this case only if "a reliable person" stated that he or she directly observed or heard a Service member make an oral or written statement that "a reasonable person would believe was intended to convey the fact that he or she engages in or has a propensity or intent to engage in homosexual acts." Id.

Clearly, the facts as stated above in this case demonstrate that there was no such "credible information." All that the Navy had was an email message and user profile that it suspected was authored by Plaintiff. Under the military regulation, that information alone should not have triggered any sort of investigation. When the Navy affirmatively took steps to confirm the identity of the email respondent, it violated the very essence of "Don't Ask, Don't Pursue" by launching a search and destroy mission. Even if the Navy had a factual basis to believe that the email message and profile were written by Plaintiff, it was unreasonable to infer that they were necessarily intended to convey a propensity or intent to engage in homosexual conduct. Particularly in the context of cyberspace, a medium of "virtual reality" that invites fantasy and affords anonymity, the comments attributed to McVeigh do not by definition amount to a declaration of homosexuality. At most, they express "an abstract preference or desire to engage in homosexual acts." *See* Guidelines. Yet the regulations specify that a statement professing homosexuality so as to warrant investigation must declare "more than an abstract preference or desire;" they must indicate a likelihood actually to carry out homosexual acts. *Id.*

The subsequent steps taken by the Navy in its "pursuit" of the Plaintiff were not only unauthorized under its policy, but likely illegal under the Electronic Communications Privacy Act of 1986 ("ECPA"). The ECPA, enacted by Congress to address privacy concerns on the Internet, allows the government to obtain information from an online service provider — as the Navy did in this instance from AOL — but only if a) it obtains a warrant issued under the Federal Rules of Criminal Procedure or state equivalent; or b) it gives prior notice to the online subscriber and then issues a subpoena or receives a court order authorizing disclosure of the information in question. *See* 18 U.S.C. § 2703(b)(1)(A)–(B), (c)(1)(B).

In soliciting and obtaining over the phone personal information about the Plaintiff from AOL, his private on-line service provider, the government in this case invoked neither of these provisions and thus failed to comply with the ECPA. From the record, it is undisputed that the Navy directly solicited by phone information from AOL. Lieutenant Karin S. Morean, the ship's principal legal counsel and a member of the JAG Corp, personally requested Legalman Kaiser to contact AOL and obtain the identity of the subscriber. Without this information, Plaintiff credibly contends that the Navy could not have made the necessary connection between him and the user profile which was the sole basis on which to commence discharge proceedings.

The government, in its defense, contends that the Plaintiff cannot succeed on his ECPA claim. It argues that the substantive provision of the statute that Plaintiff cites, 18 U.S.C. § 2703(c)(1)(B), puts the obligation on the online service provider to withhold information from the government, and not vice versa. In support of its position, Defendants cite to the Fourth Circuit opinion in *Tucker v. Waddell*, 83 F.3d 688 (4th Cir. 1996), which held that § 2703(c)(1)(B) only prohibits the actions of online providers, not the government. Accordingly, Defendants allege that Plaintiff has no cause of action against the government on the basis of the ECPA.

Under the circumstances of this case, it is unlikely that the government will prevail on this argument. Section 2703(c)(1)(B) must be read in the context of the statute as a whole. In comparison, § 2703(a) and (b) imposes on the government a reciprocal obligation to obtain a warrant or the like before requiring disclosure. It appears from the face of the statute that all of the subsections of § 2703 were intended to work in tandem to protect consumer privacy. Even if, however, the government ultimately proves to be right in its assessment of §2703(c)(1)(B), the Plaintiff has plead §2703(a) and (b) as alternative grounds for relief. In his claim that the government, at the least, solicited a violation of the ECPA by AOL, the Court finds that there is likely success on the merits with regard to this issue. The government knew, or should have known, that by turning over the information without a warrant, AOL was breaking the law. Yet the Navy, in this case, directly solicited the information anyway. What is most telling is that the Naval investigator did not identify himself when he made his request. While the government makes much of the fact that §2703(c)(1)(B) does not provide a cause of action against the government, it is elementary that information obtained improperly can be suppressed where an individual's rights have been violated. In these days of "big brother," where through technology and otherwise the privacy interests of individuals from all walks of life are being ignored or marginalized, it is imperative that statutes explicitly protecting these rights be strictly observed.

The government has produced no evidence that would indicate that it would have proceeded without this information from AOL affirmatively linking the email to Senior Chief McVeigh. That the Plaintiff may have made incriminating statements at the subsequent administrative hearing does not bootstrap the Navy out of its legal dilemma of not only violating its own policy, but also a federal statute in its attempt to charge the Plaintiff with homosexuality.

In Plaintiff's case, this Court finds that the Navy has gone too far. The "Don't Ask, Don't Tell, Don't Pursue" policy was clearly aimed at accommodating gay men and women in the military. In effect, it was intended to bring our nation's armed forces in line with the rest of society, which finds discrimination of virtually every form intolerable. It is self-evident that a person's sexual orientation does not affect that individual's performance in the workplace. At this point in history, our society should not be deprived of the many accomplishments provided by people who happen to be gay. The "Don't Ask, Don't Tell, Don't Pursue" policy was a bow to society's growing recognition of this fact. For the policy to be effective, it has to be implemented in a sensitive, balanced manner. Under the policy as it stands today, gay service members must be permitted to serve their country honorably, so long as they are discrete in pursuing their personal lives.

In this case, the Plaintiff has had an exemplary service record for some seventeen years. Indeed, he has risen in the ranks to become the most senior non-commissioned officer on his ship. His evaluations have been of the highest order. Nothing has been produced before this Court which would in any way suggest that his sexual orientation has adversely affected his job performance. Senior Chief McVeigh's place in the Navy might even be characterized by some to be the very essence of what was hoped to be achieved by those who conceived the policy. The Plaintiff is no less an officer today than he was on January 5, 1998, the day before he was told of his imminent discharge from the Navy because of his sexual orientation.

As this Court stated in *Elzie v. Aspin*, 897 F. Supp. 1, 3 (1995), it cannot understand why the Navy would seek to discharge an officer who has served his country in a distinguished manner just because he might be gay. Plaintiff's case "vividly underscores the folly...of a policy that systematically excludes a whole class of persons who have served this country proudly and in the highest tradition of excellence." *Id.* at 4. Although this case specifically does not reach any of the constitutional issues underscoring the "Don't Ask, Don't Tell, Don't Pursue" policy, *see Able v. United States*, 968 F. Supp. 850 (E.D.N.Y. 1997), the Court must note that the defenses mounted against gays in the military have been tried before in our nation's history—against blacks and women. *See*

*Elzie v. Aspin,* 841 F. Supp. 439, 443 (D.D.C. 1993). Surely, it is time to move beyond this vestige of discrimination and misconception of gay men and women.

## II. Irreparable Harm

Without this Court's immediate intervention, the Plaintiff will lose his job, income, pension, health and life insurance, and all the other benefits attendant with being a Naval officer. Having served honorably for the last seventeen years, Plaintiff will be separated from a position which is central to his life on the sole ground that he has been labeled a "homosexual," and thus by definition unfit for service. The stigma that attaches to such an accusation without substantiation is significant enough that this Court believes it must grant the injunctive relief sought. In cases nearly identical to this, courts have accordingly granted a preliminary injunction, *see Elzie v. Aspin,* 841 F. Supp. 439, 443 (D.D.C. 1993) (loss of benefits and "rights as a Marine" constitute irreparable harm); *May v. Gray,* 708 F. Supp. 716, 719 (E.D.N.C. 1988) (same); *see also Saunders v. George Washington University,* 768 F. Supp. 843, 845 (D.D.C. 1991); *Huynh v. Carlucci,* 679 F. Supp. 61, 67 (D.D.C. 1988).

## III. Harm to Other Parties

In contrast to the serious injury that Plaintiff immediately faces if discharged, there is no appreciable harm to the Navy if Senior Chief McVeigh is permitted to remain in active service. Indeed, the Navy will only be enhanced by being able to retain the Plaintiff's seventeen years of service experience.

## IV. Public Interest

Certainly, the public has an inherent interest in the preservation of privacy rights as advanced by Plaintiff in this case. With literally the entire world on the world-wide web, enforcement of the ECPA is of great concern to those who bare the most personal information about their lives in private accounts through the Internet. In this case in particular, where the government may well have violated a federal statute in its zeal to brand the Plaintiff a homosexual, the actions of the Navy must be more closely scrutinized by this Court. It is disputed in the record exactly as to how the Navy represented itself to AOL when it requested information about the Plaintiff. The Defendants contend that Legalman Kaiser merely asked for confirmation of a fax sheet bearing Plaintiff's account. Plaintiff contends, and AOL confirms, however, that the Naval officer "mislead" AOL's representative by "both failing to disclose the identity and purpose [of his request] and by portraying himself as a friend or acquaintance of Senior Chief McViegh's." At the final injunction hearing, this issue should be fully explored.

The Court believes that when this case is finally determined, it will become clear that the case will be able to be disposed on the basis of the "Don't Ask, Don't Tell, Don't Pursue" policy. This provision draws a fine balance between the interests of gay service members and the Armed Forces. It is a way of permitting gay women and men to serve in the Armed Forces, a right that the military did not provide them prior to the adoption of "Don't Ask, Don't Tell, Don't Pursue."

To make the policy work requires each of the parties to refrain from taking certain actions. Under the provisions of the policy, if the gay member agrees to remain silent about his or her sexual orientation, he or she is permitted to serve. For its part under the policy, the military is required to refrain from asking any of its members about their sexual orientation or pursuing an inquiry into a member's sexual orientation without a reasonable basis in fact. So far, pursuant to the record developed in this case, while

Plaintiff complied with the requirements imposed upon him under "Don't Ask, Don't Tell, Don't Pursue," the Defendant went further than the policy permits. Although Officer McVeigh did not publicly announce his sexual orientation, the Navy nonetheless impermissibly embarked on a search and "outing" mission. Therefore, when this case is finally heard, if the record remains as it is now, the Plaintiff will likely prevail. It is accordingly for this reason that a preliminary injunction will issue. An appropriate order follows....

## Notes and Questions

1. Are the policies underlying the court's concerns about the Navy's conduct in *McVeigh v. Cohen*, 983 F. Supp. 215, heightened because the government—as opposed to a private litigant—sought disclosure of the information? *Cf. Boggs v. Rubin*, 161 F.3d 37, 40 (D.C. Cir. 1998), *cert. denied*, 120 S.Ct. 45 (1999) (stating that "[t]he Supreme Court has indeed held law enforcement officers to a higher standard when presumptively expressive materials are involved because of the risk of prior restraint and censorship.").

2. How do expectations about privacy factor into judicial rulings on these issues? In *United States v. Charbonneau*, 979 F. Supp. 1177, 1185 (S.D. Ohio 1997), the defendant moved to suppress on-line statements regarding his possession of child pornography. The district court observed that the expectation of privacy in electronic mail was largely dependent upon the type of e-mail and the recipient. The court denied the defendant's motion, holding that messages sent to others in a chat room were not reasonably susceptible to an expectation of privacy. In *United States v. Maxwell*, 45 M.J. 406, 417 (C.A.A.F. 1996), the court held that the defendant had a reasonable, albeit limited, expectation of privacy in e-mail messages he sent and received through a computer subscription service. Passwords and other restrictive measures may help support an argument that a subject of compelled disclosure sought to preserve the communication as private.

## ANDERSEN CONSULTING LLP v. UOP, *et al.*

United States District Court, Northern District of Illinois, Eastern Division
No. 97 C 5501, 991 F. Supp. 1041
January 23, 1998

BUCKLO, District Judge.

Plaintiff, Andersen Consulting LLP ("Andersen"), brought an eight count complaint against the defendants, UOP and its counsel, the law firm of Bickel & Brewer. In Count I, Andersen alleges that the defendants knowingly divulged, or caused to be divulged, the contents of Andersen's e-mail messages in violation of the Electronic Communications Privacy Act ("ECPA"), 18 U.S.C. §2701, *et seq....*

### Background

UOP hired Andersen to perform a systems integration project in 1992. During the project, Andersen employees had access to and used UOP's internal e-mail system to communicate with each other, with UOP, and with third parties.

Dissatisfied with Andersen's performance, UOP terminated the project in December 1993. Subsequently UOP hired Bickel and Brewer and brought suit in Connecticut state court charging Andersen with breach of contract, negligence, and fraud....

While these three cases were pending, UOP and Bickel and Brewer divulged the contents of Andersen's e-mail messages on UOP's e-mail system to the *Wall Street Journal*. *The Journal* published an article on June 19, 1997 titled "E-Mail Trail Could Haunt Consultant in Court." The article excerpted some of Andersen's e-mail messages made during the course of its assignment at UOP. This disclosure of the e-mail messages and their subsequent publication is the basis of this suit.

### ECPA Claim

18 U.S.C. §2702(a)(1) states that "a person or entity providing an electronic communication service to the public shall not knowingly divulge to any person or entity the contents of a communication while in electronic storage by that service." Andersen claims that the defendants violated this section by knowingly divulging the contents of its e-mail message to the *Wall Street Journal*.

To be liable for the disclosure of Andersen's e-mail messages, UOP must fall under the purview of the Act: UOP must provide "electronic communication service to the public." 18 U.S.C. §2702(a)(1). The statute defines "electronic communication service" as "any service which provides to users thereof the ability to send or receive wire or electronic communications." 18 U.S.C. §2510(15). The statute does not define "public."[1] The word "public," however, is unambiguous. Public means the "aggregate of the citizens" or "everybody" or "the people at large" or "the community at large." *Black's Law Dictionary* 1227 (6th ed. 1990). Thus, the statute covers any entity that provides electronic communication service (e.g., e-mail) to the community at large.

Andersen attempts to render the phrase "to the public" superfluous by arguing that the statutory language indicates that the term "public" means something other than the community at large. It claims that if Congress wanted public to mean the community at large, it would have used the term "general public." However, the fact that Congress used both "public" and "general public" in the same statute does not lead to the conclusion that Congress intended public to have any other meaning than its commonly understood meaning. *Compare* 18 U.S.C. §2511(2)(g) (using the term "general public") *with id.* §§2511(2)(a)(i), (3)(a), (3)(b), (4)(c)(ii) (using the term "public").

Andersen argues that the legislative history indicates that a provider of electronic communication services is subject to Section 2702 even if that provider maintains the system primarily for its own use and does not provide services to the general public. This legislative history argument is misguided. "A court's starting point to determine the intent of Congress is the language of the statute itself." *United States v. Hayward*, 6 F.3d 1241, 1245 (7th Cir. 1993). If the language is "clear and unambiguous," the court must give effect to the plain meaning of the statute. *Id.* Since the meaning of "public" is clear, there is no need to resort to legislative history.

Even if the language was somehow ambiguous, the legislative history does not support Andersen's interpretation. The legislative history indicates that there is a distinction between public and proprietary. In describing "electronic mail," the legislative history stated that "[e]lectronic mail systems may be available for public use or may be proprietary, such as systems operated by private companies for internal cor-

---

1. Further, there is no case law interpreting the word "public" as used in the ECPA.

respondence." S. Rep. No. 99-541, at 8 (1986), reprinted in 1986 U.S.C.C.A.N. 3555, 3562. Thus, Andersen must show that UOP's electronic mail system was available for public use.

In its complaint, Andersen alleges that UOP "is a general partnership which licenses process technologies and supplies catalysts, specialty chemicals, and other products to the petroleum refining, petrochemical, and gas processing industries." UOP is not in the business of providing electronic communication services. It does, however, have an e-mail system for internal communication as e-mail is a necessary tool for almost any business today. *See State Wide Photocopy v. Tokai Fin. Servs., Inc.,* 909 F. Supp. 137, 145 (S.D.N.Y. 1995) (finding that defendant was in the business of financing and that the mere use of fax machines and computers, as necessary tools of business, did not make it an electronic communication service provider).

UOP hired Andersen to provide services in connection with the integration of certain computer systems. As part of the project, "UOP provided an electronic communication service for Andersen to use. That electronic communication service could be used, and was used by Andersen and UOP personnel, to electronically communicate with (i.e., send e-mail messages to, and receive e-mail messages from) other Andersen personnel, UOP personnel, third-party vendors and other third-parties both in and outside of Illinois."

Based on these allegations, Andersen claims that UOP provides an electronic communication service to the public. However, giving Andersen access to its e-mail system is not equivalent to providing e-mail to the public. Andersen was hired by UOP to do a project and as such, was given access to UOP's e-mail system similar to UOP employees. Andersen was not any member of the community at large, but a hired contractor. Further, the fact that Andersen could communicate to third-parties over the Internet and that third-parties could communicate with it did not mean that UOP provided an electronic communication service to the public. UOP's internal e-mail system is separate from the internet. UOP must purchase internet access from an electronic communication service provider like any other consumer; it does not independently provide internet services....

### Conclusion

Defendants' motion to dismiss all counts of Andersen's complaint is granted.

----------

## 5. Access to Information

Privacy interests often conflict with other significant interests, such as the access to or use of governmental records to gather information regarding individuals about whom the government maintains records, and for purposes of assessing the agencies' performance. Enactment of the Privacy Act of 1974, as amended, 5 U.S.C.A. §552(a) (West 1996 & Supp. 2000), for example, was prompted by the rapid expansion of computerized databases. The statute constrains the federal government's use of information it maintains on individuals by prohibiting agencies of the federal government from divulging to any person—or even to another government agency—data about an individual without the individual's written consent to such disclosure. 5 U.S.C.A. §552a(b). Maintenance of data is confined to records that are "relevant" and "necessary" to the agency's mandate. 5 U.S.C. §552a(e)(1). Significantly, this limitation restricts the maintenance of "records," which in turn is defined to mean documents that identify the individual, such as by name, photograph, or fingerprints. 5 U.S.C. § 552a(a)(4). Therefore, compilation of information, either in composite form or without identifying material, is not constrained.

Another statute also deals with interaction among governmental agencies. The Computer Matching and Privacy Protection Act of 1988, 5 U.S.C.A. § 552a (West 1996 & Supp. 2000), limits governmental "cross-matching;" i.e., the comparison of data maintained by governmental agencies about the same individual. In order to cross-match, agencies must satisfy a number of prerequisites, such as execute a written agreement specifying the purpose of the matching program, the legal authority for the program, the records to be matched, the verification procedures established, and the notification procedures to be implemented. See 5 U.S.C.A. § 552a(o)(1). The Act covers only matching programs that are intended to verify eligibility for federal benefit programs or to recoup monies owed under such programs; the Act does not cover matching programs relating to law enforcement or foreign intelligence investigations. See 5 U.S.C.A. § 552a(8)(A). Like the Privacy Act of 1974, the Computer Matching and Privacy Protection Act of 1988 does not constrain the maintenance of databases of information devoid of personal identifiers. See 5 U.S.C.A. § 552a(a)(8)(B).

The Freedom of Information Act, 5 U.S.C.A. § 552 (West 1996) ("FOIA"), establishes a public right of access to records of federal agencies. FOIA is founded upon the notion that open government provides a vital check against corruption, rendering "governors accountable to the governed." *National Labor Relations Board v. Robbins Tire & Rubber Co.*, 437 U.S. 214, 242 (1978). FOIA's legislative history makes it "crystal clear" that FOIA is designed to "pierce the veil of administrative secrecy and to open agency action to the light of public scrutiny." *Department of the Air Force v. Rose*, 425 U.S. 352, 361 (1976) (citation omitted).

In furtherance of these policies, FOIA requires applicable agencies to publish in the Federal Register a description of their organization, a list of personnel from whom the public may request information, and the procedures by which such requests will be processed. FOIA does not, however, obligate governmental agencies to create records to respond to an information request.

The federal government is believed to be the largest single producer, collector, consumer, and disseminator of information in the United States. *See* Office of Management and the Budget, Management of Federal Information Resources Notice, 7a, 59 Fed. Reg. 37,906, 37,901 (July 25, 1994) (OMB Circular A-130). Access to governmental records pursuant to FOIA has led to significant disclosures. Records released by the government revealed such information as action taken by the Federal Aviation Administration in connection with a fatal airplane crash; the lead content of tap water in Washington, D.C.; and the U.S. government's treatment of South Vietnamese commandos who fought in a CIA-sponsored army in the early 1960s. *See, e.g.*, 142 Cong. Rec. S10713-03 (daily ed. Sept. 17, 1996) (statement of Sen. Leahy).

Exemptions to FOIA include:

(1) information to be kept secret by Executive order in the interest of national defense or foreign policy;

(2) information related solely to the internal personnel rules and practices of an agency;

(3) information that is specifically exempted from disclosure by statute;

(4) trade secrets and commercial or financial information that are privileged or confidential;

(5) inter-agency or intra-agency memoranda or letters that would otherwise be available only through litigation with the agency;

(6) "personnel and medical files and similar files the disclosure of which would constitute a clearly unwarranted invasion of personal privacy;"

(7) records or information compiled for law enforcement purposes if, among other circumstances, their disclosure could interfere with enforcement proceedings, deprive a person of a right to a fair trial, "could reasonably be expected to constitute an unwarranted invasion of personal privacy," could reasonably be expected to disclose a confidential source or law enforcement techniques, or could reasonably be expected to endanger the life or physical safety of an individual;

(8) documents related to examination reports for an agency that regulates or supervises financial institutions; and

(9) certain geological and geophysical information.

5 U.S.C.A. § 552, as amended. Several of these provisions are designed to promote privacy in the documents maintained by agencies, so that public access to such records is not unlimited.

---

# UNITED STATES DEPARTMENT of JUSTICE, *et al.* v. REPORTERS COMMITTEE for FREEDOM of the PRESS, *et al.*

Supreme Court of the United States
No. 87-1379, 489 U.S. 749
March 22, 1989

Justice STEVENS delivered the opinion of the Court.

The Federal Bureau of Investigation (FBI) has accumulated and maintains criminal identification records, sometimes referred to as "rap sheets," on over 24 million persons. The question presented by this case is whether the disclosure of the contents of such a file to a third party "could reasonably be expected to constitute an unwarranted invasion of personal privacy" within the meaning of the Freedom of Information Act (FOIA), 5 U.S.C. § 552(b)(7)(C) (1982 ed., Supp. V).

I

In 1924, Congress appropriated funds to enable the Department of Justice ("Department") to establish a program to collect and preserve fingerprints and other criminal identification records. 43 Stat. 217. That statute authorized the Department ot exchange such information with "officials of States, cities and other institutions." *Ibid.* Six years later Congress created the FBI's identification division, and gave it responsibility for "acquiring, collecting, classifying, and preserving criminal identification and other crime records and the exchanging of said criminal identification records with the duly authorized officials of governmental agencies, of States, cities, and penal institutions." Ch. 455, 46 Stat. 554 (codified at 5 U.S.C. § 340 (1934 ed.); *see* 28 U.S.C. § 534(a)(4) (providing for exchange of rap-sheet information among "authorized officials of the Federal Government, the States, cities, and penal and other institutions"). Rap sheets compiled pursuant to such authority contain certain descriptive information, such as date of birth and physical characteristics, as well as a history of arrests, charges, convictions, and incarcerations of the subject. Normally a rap sheet is preserved until its subject attains age 80. Because of the volume of rap sheets, they are sometimes incorrect or incomplete and sometimes contain information about other persons with similar names.

The local, state, and federal law enforcement agencies throughout the Nation that exchange rap-sheet data with the FBI do so on a voluntary basis. The principal use of the information is to assist in the detection and prosecution of offenders; it is also used by courts and corrections officials in connection with sentencing and parole decisions. As a matter of executive policy, the Department has generally treated rap sheets as confidential and, with certain exceptions, has restricted their use to government purposes. Consistent with the Department's basic policy of treating these records as confidential, Congress in 1957 amended the basic statute to provide that the FBI's exchange of rap-sheet information with any other agency is subject to cancellation "if dissemination is made outside the receiving departments or related agencies." 71 Stat. 61; *see* 28 U.S.C. § 534(b)....

## II

The statute known as the FOIA is actually a part of the Administrative Procedure Act (APA). Section 3 of the APA as enacted in 1946 gave agencies broad discretion concerning the publication of governmental records. In 1966 Congress amended that section to implement " 'a general philosophy of full agency disclosure.' " The amendment required agencies to publish their rules of procedure in the Federal Register, 5 U.S.C. § 552(a)(1)(C), and to make available for public inspection and copying their opinions, statements of policy, interpretations, and staff manuals and instructions that are not published in the Federal Register, § 552(a)(2). In addition, § 552(a)(3) requires every agency "upon any request for records which...reasonably describes such records" to make such records "promptly available to any person." If an agency improperly withholds any documents, the district court has jurisdiction to order their production. Unlike the review of other agency action that must be upheld if supported by substantial evidence and not arbitrary or capricious, the FOIA expressly places the burden "on the agency to sustain its action" and directs the district courts to "determine the matter de novo."

Congress exempted nine categories of documents from the FOIA's broad disclosure requirements. Three of those exemptions are arguably relevant to this case. Exemption 3 applies to documents that are specifically exempted from disclosure by another statute. § 552(b)(3). Exemption 6 protects "personnel and medical files and similar files the disclosure of which would constitute a clearly unwarranted invasion of personal privacy." § 552(b)(6). Exemption 7(C) excludes records or information compiled for law enforcement purposes, "but only to the extent that the production of such [materials]...could reasonably be expected to constitute an unwarranted invasion of personal privacy." § 552(b)(7)(C).

Exemption 7(C)'s privacy language is broader than the comparable language in Exemption 6 in two respects [because, unlike Exemption 6, Exemption 7(C) does not contain the word "clearly," and, unlike Exemption 6, Exemption 7(C) encompasses any disclosure that "could reasonably be expected to constitute" an invasion....Thus, the standard for evaluating a threatened invasion of privacy interests resulting from the disclosure of records compiled for law enforcement purposes is somewhat broader than the standard applicable to personnel, medical, and similar files.

## III

This case arises out of requests made by a CBS news correspondent and the Reporters Committee for Freedom of the Press (respondents) for information concerning the criminal records of four members of the Medico family. The Pennsylvania Crime Commission had identified the family's company, Medico Industries, as a legitimate business dominated by organized crime figures. Moreover, the company allegedly had obtained a number of defense contracts as a result of an improper arrangement with a corrupt Congressman.

The FOIA requests sought disclosure of any arrests, indictments, acquittals, convictions, and sentences of any of the four Medicos. Although the FBI originally denied the requests, it provided the requested data concerning three of the Medicos after their deaths. In their complaint in the District Court, respondents sought the rap sheet for the fourth, Charles Medico (Medico), insofar as it contained "matters of public record."...

## IV

Exemption 7(C) requires us to balance the privacy interest in maintaining, as the Government puts it, the "practical obscurity" of the rap sheets against the public interest in their release.

The preliminary question is whether Medico's interest in the nondisclosure of any rap sheet the FBI might have on him is the sort of "personal privacy" interest that Congress intended Exemption 7(C) to protect. As we have pointed out before, "[t]he cases sometimes characterized as protecting 'privacy' have in fact involved at least two different kinds of interests. One is the individual interest in avoiding disclosure of personal matters, and another is the interest in independence in making certain kinds of important decisions." *Whalen v. Roe*, 429 U.S. 589, 598–600, 97 S.Ct. 869, 875–877, 51 L.Ed.2d 64 (1977) (footnotes omitted). Here, the former interest, "in avoiding disclosure of personal matters," is implicated. Because events summarized in a rap sheet have been previously disclosed to the public, respondents contend that Medico's privacy interest in avoiding disclosure of a federal compilation of these events approaches zero. We reject respondents' cramped notion of personal privacy.

To begin with, both the common law and the literal understandings of privacy encompass the individual's control of information concerning his or her person. In an organized society, there are few facts that are not at one time or another divulged to another. Thus the extent of the protection accorded a privacy right at common law rested in part on the degree of dissemination of the allegedly private fact and the extent to which the passage of time rendered it private.[15] According to Webster's initial definition,

---

15. *See* Warren & Brandeis, *The Right to Privacy*, 4 Harv. L. Rev. 193, 198 (1890–1891) ("The common law secures to each individual the right of determining, ordinarily, to what extent his thoughts, sentiments, and emotions shall be communicated to others.... [E]ven if he has chosen to give them expression, he generally retains the power to fix the limits of the publicity which shall be given them"). The common law recognized that one did not necessarily forfeit a privacy interest in matters made part of the public record, albeit the privacy interest was diminished and another who obtained the facts from the public record might be privileged to publish it. *See Cox Broadcasting Corp. v. Cohn*, 420 U.S. at 494–495, 95 S.Ct. at 1046 ("[T]he interests in privacy fade when the information involved already appears on the public record"). *See also* Restatement (Second) of Torts § 652D, pp. 385–386 (1977) ("[T]here is no liability for giving publicity to facts about the plaintiff's life that are matters of public record, such as the date of his birth...On the other hand, if the record is one not open to public inspection, as in the case of income tax returns, it is not public and there is an invasion of privacy when it is made so"); W. Keeton, D. Dobbs, R. Keeton, & D. Owens, *Prosser & Keeton on Law of Torts* § 117, p. 859 (5th ed. 1984) ("[M]erely because [a fact] can be found in a

information may be classified as "private" if it is "intended for or restricted to the use of a particular person or group or class of persons; not freely available to the public."[16] Recognition of this attribute of a privacy interest supports the distinction, in terms of personal privacy, between scattered disclosure of the bits of information contained in a rap sheet and revelation of the rap sheet as a whole. The very fact that federal funds have been spent to prepare, index, and maintain these criminal-history files demonstrates that the individual items of information in the summaries would not otherwise be "freely available" either to the officials who have access to the underlying files or to the general public. Indeed, if the summaries were "freely available," there would be no reason to invoke the FOIA to obtain access to the information they contain. Granted, in many contexts the fact that information is not freely available is no reason to exempt that information from a statute generally requiring its dissemination. But the issue here is whether the compilation of otherwise hard-to-obtain information alters the privacy interest implicated by disclosure of that information. Plainly there is a vast difference between the public records that might be found after a diligent search of courthouse files, county archives, and local police stations throughout the country and a computerized summary located in a single clearinghouse of information.

This conclusion is supported by the web of federal statutory and regulatory provisions that limits the disclosure of rap-sheet information. That is, Congress has authorized rap-sheet dissemination to banks, local licensing officials, the securities industry, the nuclear-power industry, and other law enforcement agencies. Further, the FBI has permitted such disclosure to the subject of the rap sheet and, more generally, to assist in the apprehension of wanted persons or fugitives. Finally, the FBI's exchange of rap-sheet information "is subject to cancellation if dissemination is made outside the receiving departments or related agencies." 28 U.S.C. § 534(b). This careful and limited pattern of authorized rap-sheet disclosure fits the dictionary definition of privacy as involving a restriction of information "to the use of a particular person or group or class of persons." Moreover, although perhaps not specific enough to constitute a statutory exemption under FOIA Exemption 3, 5 U.S.C. § 552(b)(3), these statutes and regulations, taken as a whole, evidence a congressional intent to protect the privacy of rap-sheet subjects, and a concomitant recognition of the power of compilations to affect personal privacy that outstrips the combined power of the bits of information contained within.

Other portions of the FOIA itself bolster the conclusion that disclosure of records regarding private citizens, identifiable by name, is not what the framers of the FOIA had in mind. Specifically, the FOIA provides that "[t]o the extent required to prevent a clearly unwarranted invasion of personal privacy, an agency may delete identifying details when it makes available or publishes an opinion, statement of policy, interpretation, or staff manual or instruction." 5 U.S.C. § 552(a)(2). Additionally, the FOIA assures that "[a]ny reasonably segregable portion of a record shall be provided to any

---

public recor[d] does not mean that it should receive widespread publicity if it does not involve a matter of public concern").

16. *See Webster's Third New International Dictionary* 1804 (1976). *See also* A. Breckenridge, *The Right to Privacy* 1 (1970) ("Privacy, in my view, is the rightful claim of the individual to determine the extent to which he wishes to share of himself with others....It is also the individual's right to control dissemination of information about himself"); A. Westin, *Privacy and Freedom* 7 (1967) ("Privacy is the claim of individuals...to determine for themselves when, how, and to what extent information about them is communicated to others"); Project, Government Information and the Rights of Citizens, 73 Mich. L. Rev. 971, 1225 (1974–1975) ("[T]he right of privacy is the right to control the flow of information concerning the details of one's individuality").

person requesting such record after deletion of the portions which are exempt under [§(b)]." 5 U.S.C. §552(b) (1982 ed., Supp. V). These provisions, for deletion of identifying references and disclosure of segregable portions of records with exempt information deleted, reflect a congressional understanding that disclosure of records containing personal details about private citizens can infringe significant privacy interests.

Also supporting our conclusion that a strong privacy interest inheres in the nondisclosure of compiled computerized information is the Privacy Act of 1974, codified at 5 U.S.C. §552a (1982 ed. and Supp. V). The Privacy Act was passed largely out of concern over "the impact of computer data banks on individual privacy." H.R. Rep. No. 93-1416, p. 7 (1974). The Privacy Act provides generally that "[n]o agency shall disclose any record which is contained in a system of records...except pursuant to a written request by, or with the prior written consent of, the individual to whom the record pertains." 5 U.S.C. §552a(b) (1982 ed., Supp. V). Although the Privacy Act contains a variety of exceptions to this rule, including an exemption for information required to be disclosed under the FOIA, see 5 U.S.C. §552a(b)(2), Congress' basic policy concern regarding the implications of computerized data banks for personal privacy is certainly relevant in our consideration of the privacy interest affected by dissemination of rap sheets from the FBI computer.

Given this level of federal concern over centralized data bases, the fact that most States deny the general public access to their criminal-history summaries should not be surprising. As we have pointed out, in 47 States nonconviction data from criminal-history summaries are not available at all, and even conviction data are "generally unavailable to the public." State policies, of course, do not determine the meaning of a federal statute, but they provide evidence that the law enforcement profession generally assumes—as has the Department of Justice—that individual subjects have a significant privacy interest in their criminal histories. It is reasonable to presume that Congress legislated with an understanding of this professional point of view.

In addition to the common-law and dictionary understandings, the basic difference between scattered bits of criminal history and a federal compilation, federal statutory provisions, and state policies, our cases have also recognized the privacy interest inherent in the nondisclosure of certain information even where the information may have been at one time public. Most apposite for present purposes is our decision in *Department of Air Force v. Rose,* 425 U.S. 352, 96 S.Ct. 1592, 48 L.Ed.2d 11 (1976). New York University law students sought Air Force Academy Honor and Ethics Code case summaries for a law review project on military discipline. The Academy had already publicly posted these summaries on 40 squadron bulletin boards, usually with identifying names redacted (names were posted for cadets who were found guilty and who left the Academy), and with instructions that cadets should read the summaries only if necessary. Although the opinion dealt with Exemption 6's exception for "personnel and medical files and similar files the disclosure of which would constitute a clearly unwarranted invasion of personal privacy," and our opinion today deals with Exemption 7(C), much of our discussion in *Rose* is applicable here. We explained that the FOIA permits release of a segregable portion of a record with other portions deleted, and that in camera inspection was proper to determine whether parts of a record could be released while keeping other parts secret. *See id.* at 373–377, 96 S.Ct. at 1604–1607; 5 U.S.C. §§552(b) and (a)(4)(B) (1982 ed. and Supp. V). We emphasized the FOIA's segregability and *in camera* provisions in order to explain that the case summaries, with identifying names redacted, were generally disclosable. We then offered guidance to lower courts in determining whether disclosure of all or part of such case summaries would constitute a "clearly unwarranted invasion of personal privacy" under Exemption 6:

Respondents sought only such disclosure as was consistent with [the Academy tradition of keeping identities confidential within the Academy]. Their request for access to summaries "with personal references or other identifying information deleted," respected the confidentiality interests embodied in Exemption 6. As the Court of Appeals recognized, however, what constitutes identifying information regarding a subject cadet must be weighed not only from the viewpoint of the public, but also from the vantage of those who would have been familiar, as fellow cadets or Academy staff, with other aspects of his career at the Academy. Despite the summaries' distribution within the Academy, many of this group with earlier access to summaries may never have identified a particular cadet, or may have wholly forgotten his encounter with Academy discipline. And the risk to the privacy interests of a former cadet, particularly one who has remained in the military, posed by his identification by otherwise unknowing former colleagues or instructors cannot be rejected as trivial. We nevertheless conclude that consideration of the policies underlying the Freedom of Information Act, to open public business to public view when no "clearly unwarranted" invasion of privacy will result, requires affirmance of the holding of the Court of Appeals...that although "no one can guarantee that all those who are 'in the know' will hold their tongues, particularly years later when time may have eroded the fabric of cadet loyalty," it sufficed to protect privacy at this stage in these proceedings by enjoining the District Court...that if in its opinion deletion of personal references and other identifying information 'is not sufficient to safeguard privacy, then the summaries should not be disclosed to [respondents].'

425 U.S. at 380–381, 96 S.Ct. at 1608. *See also id.* at 387–388, 96 S.Ct. at 1611–1612 (Blackmun, J., dissenting); *id.* at 389–390, 96 S.Ct. at 1612 (Rehnquist, J., dissenting). In this passage we doubly stressed the importance of the privacy interest implicated by disclosure of the case summaries. First: We praised the Academy's tradition of protecting personal privacy through redaction of names from the case summaries. But even with names redacted, subjects of such summaries can often be identified through other, disclosed information. So, second: Even though the summaries, with only names redacted, had once been public, we recognized the potential invasion of privacy through later recognition of identifying details, and approved the Court of Appeals' rule permitting the District Court to delete "other identifying information" in order to safeguard this privacy interest. If a cadet has a privacy interest in past discipline that was once public but may have been "wholly forgotten," the ordinary citizen surely has a similar interest in the aspects of his or her criminal history that may have been wholly forgotten.

We have also recognized the privacy interest in keeping personal facts away from the public eye. In *Whalen v. Roe*, 429 U.S. 589, 97 S.Ct. 869, 51 L.Ed.2d 64 (1977), we held that "the State of New York may record, in a centralized computer file, the names and addresses of all persons who have obtained, pursuant to a doctor's prescription, certain drugs for which there is both a lawful and an unlawful market." *Id.* at 591, 97 S.Ct. at 872. In holding only that the Federal Constitution does not prohibit such a compilation, we recognized that such a centralized computer file posed a "threat to privacy":

We are not unaware of the threat to privacy implicit in the accumulation of vast amounts of personal information in computerized data banks or other massive government files. The collection of taxes, the distribution of welfare and social security benefits, the supervision of public health, the direction of our Armed Forces, and the enforcement of the criminal laws all require the orderly preservation of great quantities of information, much of which is personal in character and potentially embarrassing or harmful if disclosed.

The right to collect and use such data for public purposes is typically accompanied by a concomitant statutory or regulatory duty to avoid unwarranted disclosures. Recognizing that in some circumstances that duty arguably has its roots in the Constitution, nevertheless New York's statutory scheme, and its implementing administrative procedures, evidence a proper concern with, and protection of, the individual's interest in privacy.

*Id.* at 605, 97 S.Ct. at 879 (footnote omitted); *see also id.* at 607, 97 S.Ct. at 880 (Brennan, J., concurring) ("The central storage and easy accessibility of computerized data vastly increase the potential for abuse of that information...").

In sum, the fact that "an event is not wholly 'private' does not mean that an individual has no interest in limiting disclosure or dissemination of the information." Rehnquist, *Is an Expanded Right of Privacy Consistent with Fair and Effective Law Enforcement?*, Nelson Timothy Stephens Lectures, University of Kansas Law School, pt. 1, p. 13 (Sept. 26–27, 1974). The privacy interest in a rap sheet is substantial. The substantial character of that interest is affected by the fact that in today's society the computer can accumulate and store information that would otherwise have surely been forgotten long before a person attains age 80, when the FBI's rap sheets are discarded.

### V

Exemption 7(C), by its terms, permits an agency to withhold a document only when revelation "could reasonably be expected to constitute an unwarranted invasion of personal privacy." ...

[W]hether disclosure of a private document under Exemption 7(C) is warranted must turn on the nature of the requested document and its relationship to "the basic purpose of the Freedom of Information Act 'to open agency action to the light of public scrutiny.'" *Department of Air Force v. Rose,* 425 U.S. at 372, 96 S.Ct. at 1604, rather than on the particular purpose for which the document is being requested. In our leading case on the FOIA, we declared that the Act was designed to create a broad right of access to "official information." *EPA v. Mink,* 410 U.S. 73, 80, 93 S.Ct. 827, 832, 35 L.Ed.2d 119 (1973). In his dissent in that case, Justice Douglas characterized the philosophy of the statute by quoting this comment by Henry Steele Commager:

"The generation that made the nation thought secrecy in government one of the instruments of Old World tyranny and committed itself to the principle that a democracy cannot function unless the people are permitted to know *what their government is up to.*"

*Id.* at 105, 93 S.Ct. at 845 (quoting from *The New York Review of Books,* Oct. 5, 1972, p. 7) (emphasis added).

This basic policy of "'full agency disclosure unless information is exempted under clearly delineated statutory language,'" *Department of Air Force v. Rose,* 425 U.S. at 360–361, 96 S.Ct. at 1599 (quoting S. Rep. No. 813, 89th Cong., 1st Sess., 3 (1965)), indeed focuses on the citizens' right to be informed about "what their government is up to." Official information that sheds light on an agency's performance of its statutory duties falls squarely within that statutory purpose. That purpose, however, is not fostered by disclosure of information about private citizens that is accumulated in various governmental files but that reveals little or nothing about an agency's own conduct. In this case—and presumably in the typical case in which one private citizen is seeking information about another—the requester does not intend to discover anything about the conduct of the agency that has possession of the requested records. Indeed, response to this request would not shed any light on the conduct of any Government agency or official.

The point is illustrated by our decision in *Rose, supra.* As discussed earlier, we held that the FOIA required the United States Air Force to honor a request for in camera submission of disciplinary-hearing summaries maintained in the Academy's Honors and Ethics Code reading files. The summaries obviously contained information that would explain how the disciplinary procedures actually functioned and therefore were an appropriate subject of a FOIA request. All parties, however, agreed that the files should be redacted by deleting information that would identify the particular cadets to whom the summaries related. The deletions were unquestionably appropriate because the names of the particular cadets were irrelevant to the inquiry into the way the Air Force Academy administered its Honor Code; leaving the identifying material in the summaries would therefore have been a "clearly unwarranted" invasion of individual privacy. If, instead of seeking information about the Academy's own conduct, the requests had asked for specific files to obtain information about the persons to whom those files related, the public interest that supported the decision in *Rose* would have been inapplicable. In fact, we explicitly recognized that "the basic purpose of the [FOIA is] to open agency action to the light of public scrutiny." *Id.* at 372, 96 S.Ct. at 1604.

Respondents argue that there is a two-fold public interest in learning about Medico's past arrests or convictions: He allegedly had improper dealings with a corrupt Congressman, and he is an officer of a corporation with defense contracts. But if Medico has, in fact, been arrested or convicted of certain crimes, that information would neither aggravate nor mitigate his allegedly improper relationship with the Congressman; more specifically, it would tell us nothing directly about the character of the Congressman's behavior. Nor would it tell us anything about the conduct of the Department of Defense (DOD) in awarding one or more contracts to the Medico Company. Arguably a FOIA request to the DOD for records relating to those contracts, or for documents describing the agency's procedures, if any, for determining whether officers of a prospective contractor have criminal records, would constitute an appropriate request for "official information."

Conceivably Medico's rap sheet would provide details to include in a news story, but, in itself, this is not the kind of public interest for which Congress enacted the FOIA. In other words, although there is undoubtedly some public interest in anyone's criminal history, especially if the history is in some way related to the subject's dealing with a public official or agency, the FOIA's central purpose is to ensure that the Government's activities be opened to the sharp eye of public scrutiny, not that information about private citizens that happens to be in the warehouse of the Government be so disclosed. Thus, it should come as no surprise that in none of our cases construing the FOIA have we found it appropriate to order a Government agency to honor a FOIA request for information about a particular private citizen.

What we have said should make clear that the public interest in the release of any rap sheet on Medico that may exist is not the type of interest protected by the FOIA. Medico may or may not be one of the 24 million persons for whom the FBI has a rap sheet. If respondents are entitled to have the FBI tell them what it knows about Medico's criminal history, any other member of the public is entitled to the same disclosure—whether for writing a news story, for deciding whether to employ Medico, to rent a house to him, to extend credit to him, or simply to confirm or deny a suspicion. There is, unquestionably, some public interest in providing interested citizens with answers to their questions about Medico. But that interest falls outside the ambit of the public interest that the FOIA was enacted to serve.

Finally, we note that Congress has provided that the standard fees for production of documents under the FOIA shall be waived or reduced "if disclosure of the information is in the public interest because it is likely to contribute significantly to public understanding of the operations or activities of the government and is not primarily in the commercial interest of the requester." 5 U.S.C. § 552(a)(4)(A)(iii) (1982 ed., Supp. V). Although such a provision obviously implies that there will be requests that do not meet such a "public interest" standard, we think it relevant to today's inquiry regarding the public interest in release of rap sheets on private citizens that Congress once again expressed the core purpose of the FOIA as "contribut[ing] significantly to public understanding of *the operations or activities of the government*." ...

---

FOIA was enacted in 1974, at a time when computerized databases were far less prevalent than they are today. In 1986, a Congressional report on the collection and dissemination of electronic information stated that:

> A principal goal of government information policy is the maintenance of general public availability of information in the possession of the government except where confidentiality is appropriate in order to protect a legitimate governmental or privacy interest. The report finds that there is a risk that agencies may be able to exert greater control over information in electronic information systems than is possible with data maintained in traditional, hard copy formats.

> Legal ambiguities, practical limitations, and economic constraints may allow Federal agencies to restrict unduly the public availability of government data maintained electronically. The result could be diminished public access to federally operated public data bases; increased agency power over data users and information system contractors; and unnecessary government interference in the marketplace for information products and services.

House Committee on Government Operations, *Electronic Collection and Dissemination of Information by Federal Agencies: A Policy Overview*, 99th Cong., 2d Sess. at 1–2 (1986).

In 1996, the Electronic Freedom of Information Improvement Act ("EFOIIA") was enacted, requiring increased electronic access to federal agency records and application of FOIA to electronic material. 5 U.S.C.A. § 552 (West 1996 & Supp 2000). Congressional policy underlying EFOIIA encourages governmental agencies to use new technology to enhance public access to agency records and information, and to maximize the usefulness of agency records and information collected, maintained, used, retained, and disseminated by the federal government. EFOIIA specifies that electronic records are accessible under FOIA, requires agencies to provide electronic formats when technically feasible, and encourages agencies to implement on-line access when possible. *See* 5 U.S.C.A. § 552(a)(2–3), (f).

In discussing FOIA, the Supreme Court cautioned that the exceptions are "limited," and should "not obscure the basic policy that disclosure, not secrecy, is the dominant objective of the act." *Department of the Air Force v. Rose*, 495 U.S. at 263. Compare this pronouncement with that of Justice Stevens in *United States Dep't of Justice v. Reporters Committee for Freedom of the Press*, 489 U.S. at 774: FOIA's "central purpose is to ensure that the government's activities be opened to the sharp eye of public scrutiny, not that information about private citizens that happens to be in the warehouse of the government be so disclosed."

In the *Reporters Committee* case, the Supreme Court distinguished computerized compilations of records from rap sheets that "would otherwise have surely been forgotten long before a person attains the age of 80, when the FBI's rap sheets are discarded." *Id.* at 771. Was Justice Stevens apparently influenced more by the comprehensiveness of the compilation, or by its putative permanency? To what degree does a compilation, as opposed to the underlying component documents, reflect less on an agency's performance? In this era of rapid computerization, does the formation, maintenance, and retention of computerized database records reflect on the conduct of government officials? One reporter opined that "it is poor public policy for Congress to allow the conflict between the FOIA and the 1989 *Reporters Committee* ruling to remain unresolved for so long.... The problem is that the Supreme Court's narrow interpretation of the FOIA's purpose can potentially undermine the very policy that [EFOIIA]...was intended to advance." Martin E. Halstuk, *Bits, Bytes, and the Right to Know: How the Electronic Freedom of Information Act Holds the Key to Public Access to a Wealth of Useful Government Databases*, 15 Computer & High Tech. L.J. 73, 105 (1999). EFOIIA broadens public access rights, but the *Reporters Committee* decision suggests that disclosure is required only when the official information sought sheds light on an agency's performance, which is a conflict that "can be likened to driving a car with one foot on the gas pedal and one foot on the brake...." *Id.*

Has public reaction to data collection issues in the private sector affected the landscape of access to governmental records? The American Civil Liberties Union recently filed a FOIA request with the Federal Bureau of Investigation, asking for information about the agency's "Carnivore" surveillance system. The FBI's system is designed to monitor traffic on Internet service provider networks. The request is believed to be the first that seeks a source code for a program. *See* Elinor Abreu, *ACLU Investigating "Carnivore's" Diet*, Standard (July 17, 2000) <http://www.thestandard.com/article/display/0,1151,16877,00.htm>. As of mid-August 2000, the FBI stated that it would begin releasing documents after review by the FBI to determine whether any should be withheld as classified information, and after review by companies to determine whether they had objections on the ground that the documents contained trade secrets. *See* Associated Press, *FBI to Release Email Surveillance System Papers*, CNETNews.com (Aug. 16, 2000) <http://news.cnet.com/new/0-1005-200-2538368.htm>.

---

# QUAD/GRAPHICS, INC. v. SOUTHERN ADIRONDACK LIBRARY SYSTEM

1997 N.Y. Slip Op. 97573, 174 Misc. 2d 291, 664 N.Y.S.2d 225
Supreme Court, Saratoga County, New York
September 30, 1997

WILLIAM H. KENIRY, J.

In a case of first impression, petitioner corporation seeks to compel prelitigation disclosure of the names of certain of its employees whom it suspects have misappropriated corporate computer resources. Quad/Graphics, Inc. is a major national commercial printing company. Its headquarters is in Wisconsin. It maintains a large plant (1,000 employees) in Saratoga Springs, New York. Petitioner uses computers extensively in its business. Examination of relatively high longdistance telephone bills led the corporation to suspect that its computers were being misused.

The respondent in the case is Southern Adirondack Library System (SALS). SALS is a cooperative system composed of 30 member libraries located in four upstate New York counties. Respondent operates, from its headquarters in Saratoga Springs, New York, an electronic information service known as "Library Without Walls." Users of "Library Without Walls" (LWW) possessing a valid library card and a personal identification number issued by any one of SALS' participating libraries may access the "Internet." A library-based computer or a personally owned computer can be used to log on-line. Access is free for 30-minute periods.

Quad/Graphics employees are prohibited from using Quad/Graphics computers for personal purposes. Petitioner's Saratoga computer terminals do not have the capability of directly accessing outside telephone lines. However a computer operator in the Saratoga Springs plant may log into the company's mainframe computer located in Wisconsin. The terminal user can cause the mainframe by the use of a Quad/Graphics password to access long distance. Then by telephoning the library in Saratoga Springs and providing a correct library password the employee-caller accomplishes a hookup with the LWW (third party) computer network.

Petitioner contends that a cadre of its Saratoga Springs-based employees employed the library feature during working hours to effect the hookup and explore the "Internet" for personal purposes. Petitioner, after examining its long distance telephone billing records, asserts that unauthorized use between April 1995 and December 1996 has resulted in petitioner incurring over $23,000 in long distance telephone charges to the "LWW" telephone line and in petitioner losing 1,770 Saratoga Springs employee manhours in devotion to personal use of the "Internet." Petitioner, through internal investigative techniques, has been able to decipher nine distinct 13-digit identification numbers which were used to access "LWW" from its computer system.

Petitioner, in an effort to learn the identity of the individuals to whom those nine identification numbers were issued, made a request under the Freedom of Information Law (Public Officers Law, art. 6) to the Saratoga Springs Public Library for such information. Petitioner's request was rejected by the library on the basis that such information is confidential and may not be voluntarily disclosed.[1]

In this application petitioner contends that SALS as a quasi-municipal agency is subject to and bound by the Freedom of Information Law and is required to disclose the names it seeks.

SALS contends that under CPLR 4509 the identities are required to be kept confidential.

Section 4509 of the Civil Practice Law and Rules, first enacted in 1982 (L.1982, ch. 14) and broadened in 1988 (L.1988, ch. 112), provides as follows:

> Library records, which contain names or other personally identifying details regarding the users of public, free association, school, college and university libraries and library systems of this state, including but not limited to records

---

1. The Saratoga Springs Public Library was originally named as the respondent in this proceeding. An order, based upon a written stipulation, was made and entered substituting SALS as respondent since "LWW" was and is a program of SALS and not of the Saratoga Springs Public Library.

related to the circulation of library materials, computer database searches, interlibrary loan transactions, reference queries, requests for photocopies of library materials, title reserve requests, or the use of audio-visual materials, films or records, shall be confidential and shall not be disclosed except that such records may be disclosed to the extent necessary for the proper operation of such library and shall be disclosed upon request or consent of the user or pursuant to subpoena, court order or where otherwise required by statute.

The court has reviewed the legislative history of CPLR 4509 as contained in the bill jackets for the original enactment and the subsequent amendment. The supporting memorandum issued by the Assembly of the State of New York when the law was enacted, states:

> The New York State Legislature has a strong interest in protecting the right to read and think of the people of this State. The library, as the unique sanctuary of the widest possible spectrum of ideas, must protect the confidentiality of its records in order to insure its readers' right to read anything they wish, free from the fear that someone might see what they read and use this as a way to intimidate them. Records must be protected from the self-appointed guardians of public and private morality and from officials who might overreach their constitutional prerogatives. Without such protection, there would be a chilling effect on our library users as inquiring minds turn away from exploring varied avenues of thought because they fear the potentiality of others knowing their reading history.

(Mem. of Assemblyman Sanders, 1982 N.Y. Legis. Ann., at 25.)...

It is clear that CPLR 4509 does not grant an absolute privilege prohibiting the disclosure of library records. The law is intended to allow limited disclosure pursuant to court order. A court order is precisely what petitioner seeks. The salient issue is whether or not petitioner's expressed desire to learn the identity of individuals who are alleged to have misused its computer system and misappropriated its property, in order to initiate civil legal proceedings, is a proper basis for release of the library system's records.

It is the court's determination that disclosure of the information sought should not be permitted. Petitioner certainly has an internal security problem involving the unauthorized use of its computer equipment and resources. However a criminal complaint is not before this court and apparently has not been made. Were this application to be granted, the door would be open to other similar requests made, for example, by a parent who wishes to learn what a child is reading or viewing on the "Internet" via "LWW" or by a spouse to learn what type of information his or her mate is reviewing at the public library.

The court recognizes the significance of the problem that petitioner faces and the difficulty that petitioner has encountered in trying to identify the users. The Legislature has expressed, in rather direct and unequivocal fashion, a public policy that the confidentiality of a library's records should not be routinely breached and this court, in denying the petitioner's request, is following the clearly expressed legislative purpose of CPLR 4509.

One of the petitioner's other arguments deserves brief comment. Petitioner contends that disclosure of the records sought is required under CPLR 4509 since it, as the owner of the computer equipment and telephone lines utilized to access the Internet, should be considered the "user" of "LWW" and thus it is entitled to the information as a matter of right. The argument is specious. The operation of a computer is controlled by the person who gives it commands. The users in this case are the individuals who actually operated the computers guiding them through the Internet.

Petitioner's application is denied without costs.

---

# The PUTNAM PIT, INC., *et al.* v. CITY of COOKEVILLE, TENNESSEE, *et al.*

United States Court of Appeals for the Sixth Circuit
No. 98-6438, 2000 U.S. App. LEXIS 17305; 2000 FED App. 0235P
July 19, 2000,

Before: JONES, BOGGS, and COLE, Circuit Judges.

OPINION BY: R. GUY COLE, JR.

Plaintiff, Geoffrey Davidian, appeals the district court's grant of summary judgment on his claims that the City of Cookeville, Tennessee, and its city manager, Jim Shipley, violated his First Amendment rights by[, among other things,] failing to provide him copies of or access to electronic information held by the city.... For the following reasons, we AFFIRM the grant of summary judgment with regard to the records challenge, but REVERSE and REMAND for a trial on the hypertext link claim.

The Putnam Pit, a small, free tabloid and Web page published and edited by Davidian, is a self-appointed eye on government corruption for the City of Cookeville. Davidian, who does not live in Tennessee, originally became interested in Cookeville in 1995 because of an unsolved murder that occurred in the area. Over the past few years, Davidian, as editor of The Putnam Pit, has made extensive requests for public information from the city. For example, a city administrative employee who handled many of Davidian's requests, estimated that from May 1995 to August 1997, Davidian's requests occupied 75 to 80 hours of city employee time. Except for those which are the subject of this suit, most of these requests, even some which duplicated prior requests, were filled by the city.

Specifically, in July 1997, Davidian requested a copy of the computer files of the outstanding parking tickets issued by the city. The city did not provide these files in electronic form, but gave them to Davidian in hard copy....

In September 1997, the city passed an ordinance regarding public access to records, including a specification that the city is not obliged to provide electronic copies of information when it is not kept in that format in the normal course of business....

Davidian alleges that the City of Cookeville violated his First Amendment freedom of the press by denying him access to city parking ticket records in electronic form.

The collection of information is an important aspect of First Amendment freedoms. *See Branzburg v. Hayes,* 408 U.S. 665, 728, 33 L. Ed. 2d 626, 92 S. Ct. 2646 (1972) (stating that "without freedom to acquire information the right to publish would be impermissibly compromised"). This ability to collect information is not absolute, however. Although the First Amendment protects information gathering, it does not provide blanket access to information within the government's control. *See Houchins v. KQED, Inc.,* 438 U.S. 1, 8, 57 L. Ed. 2d 553, 98 S. Ct. 2588 (1978).

First, "the First Amendment does not guarantee the press a constitutional right of special access to information not available to the public generally." *Branzburg,* 408 U.S. at 684. Although some circumstances may dictate distinguishing journalists from the general public, the difficulty of this court's determining who may be considered "press" is obvious. *See Branzburg,* 408 U.S. at 704; *see also Smith v. Plati,* 56 F. Supp. 2d 1195, 1203 (D. Colo. 1999) (rejecting claim of a publisher of an Internet Web site on University of Colorado athletics who alleged, among other things, that he had been denied press privileges by a university media liaison). In this case, Davidian, by publishing The Putnam Pit, is akin to a twenty-first century "lonely pamphleteer," *Branzburg,* 408 U.S. at 704, whose access to information must be equal to that granted to members of the public. There is no indication in the record that access to parking ticket records in electronic form had ever been allowed by the city. Davidian has no greater right to this information than the general public; accordingly, the city does not have an affirmative duty to provide this information to him. *See Pell v. Procunier,* 417 U.S. 817, 834–35, 41 L. Ed. 2d 495, 94 S. Ct. 2800 (1974).

Davidian admits that he had access to the parking tickets in hard copy, although he complains of being denied the information in electronic form and being harassed by city officials, and on one occasion, arriving at city offices and being told that no one could help him that day. Davidian wrote a story for The Putnam Pit based on the parking tickets he reviewed. Davidian, however, asserts that, given the changing nature of the information he sought, electronic access was necessary.

Davidian has no First Amendment right to government information in a particular form, as long as the information sought is made available as required by the First Amendment. *See United States v. McDougal,* 103 F.3d 651, 659 (8th Cir. 1996) (denying the press and public access to videotapes of President Clinton's deposition, where access to the information contained on these tapes was readily available). This holds regardless of whether Davidian is considered a member of the press or not. *Cf. Nixon v. Warner Communications, Inc.,* 435 U.S. 589, 55 L. Ed. 2d 570, 98 S. Ct. 1306 (1978) (finding that the press had no First Amendment right to copies of White House tapes, when it unquestionably had access to the contents of the tapes and when the public at large was not given physical access to copies).

Davidian also alleges harm because of the expense and inconvenience of the one time he traveled to Tennessee from his home in California to view the ticket records but no one was available to help him. On this occasion, Davidian sent an e-mail to Shipley notifying him of Davidian's intent to visit Cookeville to obtain public records later that week. The next day, Shipley replied that the city employee who could provide those records would not be available on that date, so Davidian should come on a different day. When Davidian arrived, he was told that he could not be helped that day. The denial of access to records on one day does not rise to the level of a constitutional violation. See *Monell v. Department of Social Servs.,* 436 U.S. 658, 691, 56 L. Ed. 2d 611, 98 S. Ct. 2018 (1978) (requiring that a practice "be so permanent and well settled as to constitute a 'custom or usage' with the force of law" for purposes of § 1983 liability). Accordingly, we reject Davidian's argument.

In sum, we AFFIRM the district court's grant of summary judgment on Davidian's First Amendment freedom of the press claim....

———————

## Notes and Questions

1.  How does the act of disseminating information in electronic form differ, qualitatively, from the dissemination of its print counterpart? To what extent are privacy concerns alleviated by ensuring that disclosure of information about individuals is devoid of personal identifiers?

2. Does the posting of required personal information on the Internet transgress cognizable privacy interests? In *Lorig v. Medical Board*, 78 Cal. App. 4th 462, 92 Cal. Rptr. 2d 862 (Cal. Ct. App. 2000), state-employed physicians sought declaratory and injunctive relief, claiming that the Medical Board violated the Information Privacy Act and the California Public Records Act by posting the doctors' names and addresses of record on its web-site. *Id.* at 464, 92 Cal. Rptr. 2d at 864. The court denied the relief requested, observing that the posting serves significant—in some respects, even compelling—public interests: it facilitates the location of medical records maintained by patients' former physicians; it establishes a certain and reliable location for effecting service of process on the licensee; and it helps to more accurately identify a particular physician about whom a prospective or former patient may wish to inquire. *Id.* at 467, 92 Cal. Rptr. 2d at 866.

   The *Lorig* court also observed that the physicians did not explain how posting the physicians' addresses of record on the Internet should be regarded as any more dangerous than the previous system of disclosure upon telephonic inquiry by an anonymous requester. *Id.* at 465 n. 1, 92 Cal. Rptr. 2d at 864 n. 1. Nevertheless, the court was willing to accept "for the sake of argument" that the ability to access address information on the Internet "around the clock, with a higher level of anonymity and without leaving a trail of 'hard' evidence, will make it marginally easier for a hostile or dangerous patient to find and injure a physician who uses his or her home address as an address of record." *Id.*

3. In December 1999, APBnews.com, a national news service, filed suit against members of the Judicial Conference's Committee on Financial Disclosure, challenging its decision to bar the plaintiff from receiving public financial disclosure statements of federal judges that the plaintiff wanted to post on its web-site. Financial disclosure forms are filed on an annual basis by all federal judges, specifying assets and income for the judges and their immediate families. Judges may not preside over cases in which they or their immediate families have a meaningful financial interest. Disclosure forms are generally available to the public upon request. The Committee had argued that disclosure to anyone who had not made a written request to the federal bench was prohibited. APBnews.com challenged the security concerns delineated by the Committee, contending that any such concerns did not warrant blanket removal of public display of the documents. In May 2000, Chief Justice William Rehnquist issued a letter, challenging the premises for opposing the disclosure, and pointing out that an exemption for judicial disclosure lacks parity with the disclosure obligations of other governmental officials. In June 2000, the first batch of financial disclosure forms for federal judges appeared on APBnews.com's site. Among the first postings were redacted 1998 forms for all nine Supreme Court justices.

4. "No reasonable jury" could have found that the posting of several judges names and home addresses on a site bearing the headline "Alternate Revenge" could be anything other than a "true threat," however. *Mourad v. Bojekian*, 205 F.3d 1329 (3d Cir. 1999); *see* 28 Med. L. Rptr. (BNA) 1170 (1999). The Third Circuit dismissed a civil rights action filed by the plaintiff pursuant to 42 U.S.C.A. § 1983 (West 1994 & Supp. 2000) contesting his arrest for allegedly having created a nuisance as violative of his First Amendment rights. The court stated that the Internet, "unlike the county recorder of deeds where this information is publicly available, is accessed by millions of people everyday. And, also unlike the county recorder of deeds, [the posted information] links the idea of revenge with the judges' home ad-

dresses. This endangers the judges' safety as [the individual posting the information] knew it would." 28 Med. L. Rptr. (BNA) 1170.

---

# Technological Privacy Protections

"Unsigned" communications on the Internet assume hierarchical levels of anonymity. Messages may be sent without a comprehensibly identifiable address; while the message or posting may disclose certain digitally recognizable details, the sender's name is not readily discerned. A. Michael Froomkin characterizes a remailer that discloses no details about the sender's identity directly to the recipient but leaves such information intact with a single intermediary as "traceable anonymity." A. Michael Froomkin, *Anonymity and Its Enmities*, 1995 J. Online L. art. 4, ¶ 14 <http://www.WM.edu/law/publications/jol/froomkin.html.>

A higher level of security is rendered to communications as to which the author is not identifiable because his message is routed through a series of anonymous remailers. Encryption, utilized in conjunction with such "chained mailing," is another technique designed to safeguard not only the content of the message but its transmission. *See generally id.* at ¶¶ 19–25.

"Cryptography" is a means of securing communications; essentially, it is the science of secret writing, "a science that has roots stretching back hundreds, and perhaps thousands, of years." *See Bernstein v. United States Dep't of Justice*, 176 F.3d 1132, 1136 (9th Cir.), *reh'g en banc granted, opinion withdrawn*, 192 F.3d 1308 (9th Cir. 1999). Encryption has been used for decades although the methods of encryption have changed. Until the end of World War II, mechanical devices, such as Nazi Germany's Enigma machines, were used to encrypt messages. Today, computers and electronic devices have largely replaced mechanical encryption. Throughout history, cryptography has been the "jealously guarded" province of governments and militaries. *Id.* at 1137. In the past few decades, however, the science has become increasingly relevant to other organizations, especially as modern information technologies facilitate communication in a digital sphere.

Cryptographers seek secure methods to encrypt messages, rendering them unintelligible to all except the intended recipients. The science basically involves running a readable message, known as "plaintext," through a computer program that translates the message according to an equation or algorithm into unreadable "ciphertext." "Decryption" is the translation back to plaintext when the message is received by someone with an appropriate "key." *See Bernstein*, 974 F. Supp. 1288, 1292 (N.D. Cal. 1997), *aff'd*, 176 F.3d 1132, *reh'g en banc granted, opinion withdrawn*, 192 F.3d 1308 (9th Cir. 1999). In addition to promoting security, encryption has applications for ensuring data integrity, authenticating users, and facilitating non-repudiation (e.g., linking a specific message to a specific sender). Thus, through encryption, users seek to prevent the unauthorized interception, viewing, tampering, and forging of data. Without encryption, information sent by a computer may be unsecured, such that persons other than the intended recipient may view sensitive information. *Bernstein*, 176 F.3d at 1146.

The government has expressed trepidation about the use of encryption to code communications relating to national security. *Id.* at 1137 (citations omitted). The interception and deciphering of foreign communications has long played an important part in our nation's national security efforts.

In the words of a high-ranking State Department official: Policies concerning the export control of cryptographic products are based on the fact that the proliferation of such products will make it easier for foreign intelligence targets to deny the United States Government access to information vital to national security interests. Cryptographic products and software have military and intelligence applications. As demonstrated throughout history, encryption has been used to conceal foreign military communications, on the battlefield, aboard ships and submarines, or in other military settings. Encryption is also used to conceal other foreign communications that have foreign policy and national security significance for the United States. For example, encryption can be used to conceal communications of terrorists, drug smugglers, or others intent on taking hostile action against U.S. facilities, personnel, or security interests. As increasingly sophisticated and secure encryption methods are developed, the government's interest in halting or slowing the proliferation of such methods has grown keen.

*Id.* (citation omitted).

May the government permissibly regulate the use of cryptographic devices? Does encryption merit protection as expressive speech? The courts have been working to resolve this issue.

---

## Peter JUNGER v. William M. DALEY, *et al.*

United States District Court, Northern District of Ohio, Eastern Division
No. 1:96-CV-1723, 8 F. Supp. 2d 708
July 2, 1998

GWIN, District Judge.

In October and November 1997, Plaintiff Peter Junger ("Junger") and Defendants United States Secretary of Commerce, *et al.* ("the government") filed cross-motions for summary judgment in this First Amendment case. In his motion for judgment, Plaintiff Junger seeks injunctive and declaratory relief from the government's enforcement of export controls on encryption software. In support of his motion for injunctive relief, Junger claims the Export Administration Regulations ("Export Regulations"), 15 C.F.R. pt. 730 *et seq.,* violate rights protected by the First Amendment.

The government denies that the Export Regulations implicate First Amendment rights. The government says its licensing requirement seeks only to restrict the distribution of encryption software itself, not ideas on encryption. Stated otherwise, the government says it seeks to control only the engine for encrypting data. The government says it controls the distribution of sophisticated encryption software for valid national security purposes.

For the reasons that follow, the Court denies Plaintiff Junger's motion for summary judgment, and grants the government's motion for summary judgment....

Background

A. Description of claims made

Plaintiff Junger claims the Export Regulations violate rights protected by the First Amendment[, because licensing requirements for exporting encryption software work a prior restraint; the Export Regulations are unconstitutionally overbroad and vague; the regulations engage in unconstitutional content discrimination by subjecting certain types of encryption software to more stringent export regulations than other items; the regulations restrict his ability to exchange software by infringing his First Amendment rights to academic freedom and freedom of association; and executive regulation of encryption software under the International Emergency Economic Powers Act, 50 U.S.C. § 1701 *et seq.*, is a violation of the separation of powers doctrine.]...

The Court finds that the Export Regulations are constitutional because encryption source code is inherently functional, because the Export Regulations are not directed at source code's expressive elements, and because the Export Regulations do not reach academic discussions of software, or software in print form. For these reasons, the Court grants the government's motion for summary judgment and denies Junger's motion for summary judgment.

### B. Cryptography

Once almost the exclusive province of military and governmental bodies, cryptography is now increasingly available to businesses and private individuals wishing to keep their communications confidential. *See Bernstein v. United States Dep't of State*, 974 F. Supp. 1288, 1292 (N.D. Cal. 1997) (*"Bernstein III "*), *aff'd*, 176 F.3d 1139, *reh'g en banc granted, withdrawn*, 192 F.3d 1308 (9th Cir. 1999). To keep their communications confidential, users encrypt and decrypt communications, records and other data....

In using electronic devices, encryption can be done with dedicated hardware (such as a telephone scrambler's electronic circuitry) or with computer software. Encryption software carries out a cryptographic "algorithm," which is a set of instructions that directs computer hardware to encrypt plaintext into an encoded ciphertext. Mathematical functions or equations usually make up the instructions.

Like all software, encryption programs can take two general forms: object code and source code. Source code is a series of instructions to a computer in programming languages such as BASIC, PERL, or FORTRAN. Object code is the same set of instructions translated into binary digits (1's and 0's). Thus, source code and object code are essentially interchangeable. While source code is not directly executable by a computer, the computer can easily convert it into executable object code with "compiler" or "interpreter" software.[3]

### C. Regulatory background

On November 15, 1996, President Clinton issued Executive Order 13026. With that order, he transferred jurisdiction over export controls on nonmilitary encryption products and related technology from the State Department to the Commerce Department.[4] The order specified that encryption products formerly designated as defense articles on the United States Munitions List after that would be subjected to Commerce Department regulations (the "Export Regulations"). In his order, the President found that "the

---

3. Software in source code, a "high level language," is unintelligible to most, but it can be understood by computer scientists, mathematicians, programmers and others with knowledge of the particular language in which the program is written.

4. Encryption items that are "specifically designed, developed, configured, adapted or modified for military applications (including command, control and intelligence applications)" remain under State Department jurisdiction on the International Traffic in Arms Regulations ("ITAR"), 22 C.F.R. §§ 120 *et seq. See* 61 Fed.Reg. 68633 (1996).

export of encryption software, like the export of other encryption products described in this section, must be controlled because of such software's functional capacity, rather than because of any possible informational value of such software...." Exec. Order No. 13026, 1996 WL 666563. The Export Regulations remain in effect.[5]

The Export Regulations control the "export" of certain software. The Export Regulations define "export" of controlled encryption source code and object code software as "downloading, or causing the downloading of, such software to locations...outside the United States...unless the person making the software available takes precautions adequate to prevent unauthorized transfer of such code outside the United States." 15 C.F.R. § 734.2(b)(9).

The Export Regulations forbid the transfer of certain encryption software outside the United States. Unless very difficult precautions are taken, posting software on the Internet is an export. See 15 C.F.R. § 734.2(b)(9)(ii)(B). However, it is nearly impossible for most Internet users to carry out or verify the precautions. Because of the difficulty of the precautions, almost any posting of software on the Internet is an export.

The Export Regulations set up procedures to obtain approval for exporting items on the Control List. To export any item listed on the Commerce Control List, one must first submit a commodity classification request to the Bureau of Export Administration. See 15 C.F.R. Pts. 740–44. All items on the Commerce Control List are given an Export Control Classification Number, and Bureau of Export Administration regulations specify three categories of controlled Encryption Items.

Export Classification Number 5A002 covers encryption commodities (such as circuitry and hardware products), Export Classification Number 5D002 covers encryption software,[7] and Export Classification Number 5E002 covers encryption technology. See 15 C.F.R. § 774 Supp. I. Although the Export Administration Act defines "technology" to include software, 50 U.S.C.App. § 2415(4), Bureau of Export Administration regulations treat encryption software the same as encryption commodities. 15 C.F.R. Part 774, Note following 5D002.

For software falling under Export Classification Numbers 5A002, 5D002 and 5E002, the Export Regulations requires licenses for export to all destinations except Canada. See 15 C.F.R. § 742.15(a). As later described, Plaintiff Junger's application involves software classified under Classification Number 5D002. As to this classification number, licensing is required except for encryption source code in a book or other printed material, 15 C.F.R. § 734.3, Notes to Paragraphs (b)(2) and (b)(3). Encryption source code in printed form is not subject to the Export Regulations and, thus, is outside the scope of the licensing requirement.

### D. Junger's commodity classification requests

Plaintiff Junger is a law professor. He teaches a course titled "Computers and the Law" at Case Western Reserve University Law School in Cleveland, Ohio. Junger maintains

---

5. The Export Regulations implemented the Export Administration Act of 1979, 50 U.S.C. § 2401 et seq. When that Act lapsed in 1994, the President extended the Export Regulations pursuant to the International Emergency Economic Powers Act. The International Powers Act requires the President to renew the extension each year. He has done so.

7. Encryption software is defined as "[c]omputer programs that provide capability of encryption functions or confidentiality of information or information systems. Such software includes source code, object code, applications software, or system software." 15 C.F.R. pt. 772.

sites on the World Wide Web that include information about courses that he teaches, including a computers and law course. His web sites also set out documents involved with this litigation. Plaintiff Junger uses his web site to describe the process of this litigation through press releases and filed materials. Besides descriptions of this lawsuit, the web site has information from Junger's courses and other topics of interest to him.

Plaintiff Junger wishes to post to his web site various encryption programs that he has written to show how computers work. Such a posting is an export under the Export Regulations. *See* 15 C.F.R. §734.2(b)(9).

On June 12, 1997, Plaintiff Junger submitted three applications to the Commerce Department requesting determination of commodity classifications for encryption software programs and other items. With these applications, Plaintiff Junger sought a Commerce Department determination whether they restricted the materials from export. On July 4, 1997, the Bureau of Export Administration told Junger that Export Classification Number 5D002 covered four of the five software programs he had submitted, and therefore were subject to the Export Regulations. Although it found that four programs were subject to the Export Regulations, the Commerce Department found that the first chapter of Junger's textbook, Computers and the Law, was an allowed unlicenced export. While deciding that the printed book chapter containing encryption code could be exported, the Commerce Department said that export of a software program itself would need a license. After receiving the classification determination, Junger has not applied for a license to export his classified encryption software....

### First Amendment Scrutiny

The scrutiny the Court will apply to the Export Regulations depends upon whether the export of encryption source code is expressive, and whether the Export Regulations are directed at the content of ideas. Prior restraints on expressive materials bear a heavy presumption against their constitutional validity, and are subject to the strictest judicial scrutiny. *See New York Times Co. v. United States,* 403 U.S. 713, 714, 91 S.Ct. 2140, 29 L.Ed.2d 822 (1971) (*per curiam*).

If a law distinguishes among types of speech based on their content of ideas, the Court reviews it under strict scrutiny. *See Turner Broadcasting System, Inc. v. FCC,* 512 U.S. 622, 642, 114 S.Ct. 2445, 129 L.Ed.2d 497 (1994). To survive strict scrutiny, the government must employ narrowly tailored means that are necessary to advance a compelling government interest. *See id.*

If a law does not distinguish among types of speech based upon the content of the speech, the law will not be subject to strict scrutiny. *Turner,* 512 U.S. at 658, 114 S.Ct. 2445 (laws favoring broadcast programs over cable programs are not subject to strict scrutiny unless the laws reflect government preference for the content of one speaker). As described in Turner: "It would be error to conclude, however, that the First Amendment mandates strict scrutiny for any speech regulation that applies to one medium (or a subset thereof) but not others." *Id.* at 660, 114 S.Ct. 2445.

If the Export Regulations are not expressive and if the Export Regulations are not aimed at the content of the ideas, then the Court reviews the regulations under an intermediate scrutiny standard. *See id.* at 662, 114 S.Ct. 2445. Under intermediate scrutiny, a law is constitutional if it furthers a substantial governmental interest, if the interest is unrelated to the suppression of free expression, and if the restriction is no greater than is essential to the furtherance of that interest. *See id.* (citing *United States v. O'Brien,* 391 U.S. 367, 377, 88 S.Ct. 1673, 20 L.Ed.2d 672 (1968)).

*Does the First Amendment protect export of software?*

The most important issue in the instant case is whether the export of encryption software source code is sufficiently expressive to merit First Amendment protection. This is a matter of first impression in the Sixth Circuit. Indeed, the Court is aware of only two other courts in the United States that have addressed this question, and they reached opposite results.[12] This Court finds that although encryption source code may occasionally be expressive, its export is not protected conduct under the First Amendment.

As the Supreme Court observed in *Roth v. United States,* 354 U.S. 476, 77 S.Ct. 1304, 1 L.Ed.2d 1498 (1957), the First Amendment was adopted to foster the spread of ideas: "The protection given speech and press was fashioned to assure unfettered interchange of ideas for the bringing about of political and social changes desired by the people." *Id.* at 484, 77 S.Ct. 1304 (upholding a federal statute that prohibited mailing obscene materials). Conversely, speech that is "so far removed from any exposition of ideas, and from truth, science, morality, and arts in general, in its diffusion of liberal sentiments on the administration of Government" lacks First Amendment protection. *Virginia State Bd. of Pharmacy v. Virginia Citizens Consumer Council, Inc.,* 425 U.S. 748, 762, 96 S.Ct. 1817, 48 L.Ed.2d 346 (1976) (ruling that commercial speech is not wholly without First Amendment protection).

In reviewing governmental regulation of computer software, the Court need examine the software involved. Certain software is inherently expressive. Such expressive software contains an "exposition of ideas." *Chaplinsky v. State of New Hampshire,* 315 U.S. 568, 572, 62 S.Ct. 766, 86 L.Ed. 1031 (1942). In contrast, other software is inherently functional. With such software, users look to the performance of tasks with scant concern for the methods employed or the software language used to control such methods.

Among computer software programs, encryption software is especially functional rather than expressive. Like much computer software, encryption source code is inherently functional; it is designed to enable a computer to do a designated task. Encryption source code does not merely explain a cryptographic theory or describe how the software functions. More than describing encryption, the software carries out the function of encryption. The software is essential to carry out the function of encryption. In doing this function, the encryption software is indistinguishable from dedicated computer hardware that does encryption.

In the overwhelming majority of circumstances, encryption source code is exported to transfer functions, not to communicate ideas. In exporting functioning capability, encryption source code is like other encryption devices. For the broad majority of persons receiving such source code, the value comes from the function the source code does.

The Court now examines the relationship between source code's inherent functionality and First Amendment protection. In *Bernstein v. United States Dep't of State,* 922 F. Supp. 1426 (N.D. Cal. 1996) ("*Bernstein I*"), *aff'd,* 176 F.3d 1139, *reh'g en banc granted, withdrawn,* 192 F.3d 1308 (9th Cir. 1999), the district court held that the inherent func-

---

12. *Compare Karn v. United States Dep't of State,* 925 F. Supp. 1, 9 n. 19 (D.D.C. 1996) (assuming that computer source code is protected by the First Amendment when joined with commentary, but observing that source code alone is "merely a means of commanding a computer to perform a function") *with Bernstein v. United States Dep't of State,* 922 F. Supp. 1426, 1436 (N.D. Cal. 1996) ("*Bernstein I* ") (finding that source code is speech for the purposes of First Amendment analysis). Reargument has been ordered in *Karn* to consider the constitutional effect of transferring jurisdiction over export controls from the State Department to the Commerce Department. *Bernstein* has been appealed and is presently pending before the Ninth Circuit.

tionality of software does not vitiate its status as protected speech: instructions, do-it-yourself manuals, and recipes "are often purely functional," but they are also protected as speech because they are written in a language. *Bernstein I,* 922 F. Supp. at 1435.

That court's ruling rested on its conclusion that anything written in a language necessarily is protected speech: "[l]anguage is by definition speech, and the regulation of any language is the regulation of speech." *Id.* at 1435 (quoting *Yniguez v. Arizonans for Official English,* 69 F.3d 920, 935 (9th Cir. 1995), *vacated on other grounds,* 520 U.S. 43, 117 S.Ct. 1055, 137 L.Ed.2d 170 (1997)). Whether the alleged "speech" is actually expressive is immaterial if it is communicated through language. A court "need only assess the expressiveness of conduct in the absence of 'the spoken or written word.'" *Id.* at 1434 (construing *Texas v. Johnson,* 491 U.S. 397, 404, 109 S.Ct. 2533, 105 L.Ed.2d 342 (1989)).[13]

The *Bernstein* court's assertion that "language equals protected speech" is unsound. "Speech" is not protected simply because we write it in a language. Instead, what determines whether the First Amendment protects something is whether it expresses ideas. *See Roth v. United States,* 354 U.S. at 484; *Virginia Citizens Consumer Council,* 425 U.S. at 762, 96 S.Ct. 1817.

"Fighting words" are written or spoken in a language. While spoken or written in language, they are excluded from First Amendment protection. *See, e.g., Sandul v. Larion,* 119 F.3d 1250, 1255 (6th Cir.), *cert. dismissed,* — U.S. —, 118 S.Ct. 439, 139 L.Ed.2d 377 (1997) (observing that words "which by their very utterance inflict injury or tend to incite an immediate breach of the peace" are not protected because they "are no essential part of any exposition of ideas....") (quoting *Chaplinsky,* 315 U.S. at 572, 62 S.Ct. 766). Similarly, commercial advertisements are written in a language, but are afforded a lesser level of protection under the First Amendment. *See Central Hudson Gas & Elec. Corp. v. Public Serv. Comm'n of New York,* 447 U.S. 557, 566, 100 S.Ct. 2343, 65 L.Ed.2d 341 (1980) (acknowledging that the government may ban forms of communication more likely to deceive the public than to inform).

Furthermore, the court in *Bernstein I* misunderstood the significance of source code's functionality. Source code is "purely functional," 922 F. Supp. at 1435, in a way that the *Bernstein* Court's examples of instructions, manuals, and recipes are not. Unlike instructions, a manual, or a recipe, source code actually performs the function it describes. While a recipe provides instructions to a cook, source code is a device, like embedded circuitry in a telephone, that actually does the function of encryption.

While finding that encryption source code is rarely expressive, in limited circumstances it may communicate ideas. Although it is all but unintelligible to most people, trained computer programmers can read and write in source code. Moreover, people such as Plaintiff Junger can reveal source code to exchange information and ideas about cryptography.

Therefore, the Court finds that exporting source code is conduct that can occasionally have communicative elements. Nevertheless, merely because conduct is occasionally expressive, does not necessarily extend First Amendment protection to it. As the

---

13. The *Bernstein* court's interpretation of *Johnson* appears misguided. *Johnson* does not "strongly imply" that the First Amendment extends to anything written in language regardless of its expressiveness. *Bernstein I,* 922 F. Supp. at 1434. Rather, it simply observes that the First Amendment's "protection does not end at the spoken or written word." *Johnson,* 491 U.S. at 404, 109 S.Ct. 2533.

Supreme Court has observed, "[i]t is possible to find some kernel of expression in almost every activity—for example, walking down the street or meeting one's friends at the shopping mall—but such a kernel is not sufficient to bring the activity within the protection of the First Amendment." *City of Dallas v. Stanglin*, 490 U.S. 19, 25, 109 S.Ct. 1591, 104 L.Ed.2d 18 (1989).

In *Spence v. State of Washington*, 418 U.S. 405, 94 S.Ct. 2727, 41 L.Ed.2d 842 (1974) (*per curiam*), the Supreme Court established guidelines for determining whether occasionally expressive conduct is "sufficiently imbued with the elements of communication to fall within the scope of the First...Amendment." *Id.* at 409–10, 94 S.Ct. 2727. "An intent to convey a particularized message [must be] present, and in the surrounding circumstances the likelihood [must be] great that the message would be understood by those who viewed it." *Id.* at 411, 94 S.Ct. 2727. For example, in *Johnson*, an individual desecrated an American flag during the Republican National Convention, and the "overtly political nature of this conduct was both intentional and overwhelmingly apparent." *Johnson*, 491 U.S. at 406, 109 S.Ct. 2533. Similarly, in *Tinker v. Des Moines Independent Community School Dist.*, 393 U.S. 503, 89 S.Ct. 733, 21 L.Ed.2d 731 (1969), a student's black arm band "conveyed an unmistakable message" about his stance on the Vietnam war, a "contemporaneous issue of intense political concern." *Id.* at 505–06, 89 S.Ct. 733.

Applying this standard, it is evident that exporting encryption source code is not sufficiently communicative. In both *Johnson* and *Tinker*, the expressive nature of the conduct was clear. Unlike *Tinker*, encryption source code does not convey "an unmistakable message." Unlike *Johnson*, the communicative nature of encryption source code is not "overwhelmingly apparent." Instead, source code is by design functional: it is created and, if allowed, exported to do a specified task, not to communicate ideas. Because the expressive elements of encryption source code are neither "unmistakable" nor "overwhelmingly apparent," its export is not protected conduct under the First Amendment.

*Prior Restraint*

Plaintiff Junger urges that the Export Regulations are invalid on their face as an unconstitutional prior restraint on the export of encryption source code. Specifically, he alleges that the Export Regulations function as a prior restraint by requiring prepublication review and licensing of inherently expressive encryption software. Junger further argues that the Export Regulations lack adequate procedural safeguards to prevent the licensing officials' abuse of discretion. The Court finds that a facial challenge is inappropriate, and holds that the Export Regulations do not serve as a prior restraint on expressive conduct.

Prior restraints on publication of expressive materials are anathema to American constitutionalism. As the Supreme Court has recognized, "it has been generally, if not universally, considered that it is the chief purpose of the [First Amendment's free press] guaranty to prevent previous restraints upon publication." *Near v. State of Minnesota ex rel. Olson*, 283 U.S. 697, 713, 51 S.Ct. 625, 75 L.Ed. 1357 (1931). It is for this reason that "[a]ny prior restraint on expression comes to this Court with a 'heavy presumption' against its constitutional validity." *Organization for a Better Austin v. Keefe*, 402 U.S. 415, 419, 91 S.Ct. 1575, 29 L.Ed.2d 1 (1971) (citations omitted).

In order for a licensing law to be invalidated by a prior restraint facial challenge, it "must have a close enough nexus to expression, or to conduct commonly associated with expression, to pose a real and substantial threat" of censorship. *City of Lakewood v. Plain Dealer Publ'g Co.*, 486 U.S. 750, 759, 108 S.Ct. 2138, 100 L.Ed.2d 771 (1988). The mere fact that regulated conduct possibly can be expressive is not enough to invalidate a law on its face on prior restraint grounds. *See Roulette v. City of Seattle*, 97 F.3d 300, 303 (9th Cir. 1996) (although sitting on city sidewalks may occasionally be expressive, city ordinance prohibiting sitting is not subject to facial challenge). As described above, the Court has found that exporting encryption software has little expressive nature. A facial attack upon legislation on First Amendment grounds is appropriate only where the challenged statute "is directed narrowly and specifically at expression or conduct commonly associated with expression." *See Lakewood*, 486 U.S. at 760, 108 S.Ct. 2138.

Exporting encryption source code is not an activity that is "commonly associated with expression." Source code is a set of instructions to a computer that is commonly distributed for the wholly non-expressive purpose of controlling a computer's operation. It may, as the Court has noted, occasionally be exported for expressive reasons. Nevertheless, the prior restraint doctrine is not implicated simply because an activity may on occasion be expressive.

In *Roulette*, the Ninth Circuit recognized that Seattle's anti-sitting ordinance impaired the unquestionably expressive acts of a registrar of voters, a street musician, the Freedom Socialist Party, and the National Organization for Women. 97 F.3d at 302. Nevertheless, the law was not an unconstitutional prior restraint because neither sitting nor lying on the sidewalk are "integral to, or commonly associated with, expression." *Id.* at 304.

As in *Roulette*, exporting encryption software is not integral to expression. Because encryption software is not typically expression, a facial challenge does not succeed. Even if the Export Regulations have impaired the isolated expressive acts of academics like Plaintiff Junger, exporting software is typically non-expressive.

Neither are the Export Regulations "directed narrowly and specifically" at the expressive export of encryption source code. *Lakewood*, 486 U.S. at 760, 108 S.Ct. 2138. The Export Regulations do not single out encryption software. Instead, all types of devices that have the capacity to encrypt data, whether software or hardware, are subject to licensing. *See* 15 C.F.R. § 742.15. The Export Regulations are not "directed quite specifically" to "an entire field of scientific research and discourse." *Bernstein III*, 974 F. Supp. at 1305. Instead, the Export Regulations allow academic discussion and descriptions of software in print media while restricting the export of software that can actually encrypt data.

The Court, therefore, finds that Plaintiff Junger's facial challenge to the Export Regulations' licensing scheme fails. Because the Court finds that the Export Regulations are not narrowly directed at expressive conduct, and therefore not a prior restraint, considering Junger's claim that the Export Regulations lack adequate procedural safeguards is unnecessary. *See, e.g., Lakewood*, 486 U .S. at 772, 108 S.Ct. 2138.

*Overbreadth and vagueness*

Plaintiff Junger argues that he is entitled to bring a facial challenge to the export regulatory scheme as unconstitutionally overbroad and vague. The Court finds that a facial challenge on overbreadth grounds is inappropriate because Junger fails to show that the Export Regulations injure third parties in a manner different from the way they affect the plaintiff. Also, the Court finds that the Export Regulations are not vague.

Overbreadth challenges are an exception to the usual requirement that a plaintiff "must assert his own legal rights and interests." *Warth v. Seldin*, 422 U.S. 490, 499, 95 S.Ct.

2197, 45 L.Ed.2d 343 (1975). An overbreadth challenge allows a plaintiff to attack laws alleged to be unconstitutional under any circumstances, not merely as applied to the plaintiff's own circumstances. *See New York State Club Ass'n, Inc. v. City of New York*, 487 U.S. 1, 14, 108 S.Ct. 2225, 101 L.Ed.2d 1 (1988). Overbreadth challenges are "strong medicine" that should be used "sparingly and only as a last resort." *Id.* (quoting *Broadrick v. Oklahoma*, 413 U.S. 601, 613, 93 S.Ct. 2908, 37 L.Ed.2d 830 (1973)).

The overbreadth rule arises from the purpose of the doctrine. The overbreadth doctrine allows a challenge to laws having the potential to repeatedly chill the exercise of expressive activity by many individuals. To make the overbreadth challenge, there must be a realistic danger that the statute will significantly compromise recognized First Amendment protections of parties not before the Court. *Members of City Council of City of Los Angeles v. Taxpayers for Vincent*, 466 U.S. 789, 800, 104 S.Ct. 2118, 80 L.Ed.2d 772 (1984). Under *Vincent*, to prevail on a facial overbreadth challenge, the plaintiff must show that the challenged law is "substantially overbroad." *Id.* at 801, 104 S.Ct. 2118. To establish substantial overbreadth, a plaintiff must show that the law will have a significant and different impact on third parties' free speech interests than it has on his own. *See id.* A challenge on overbreadth grounds requires a showing that the governmental action impair third parties' free speech rights in a manner different from the law's effect on the plaintiff. The overbreadth doctrine does not apply where the law affects the plaintiff and third parties in the same manner. *See id.* at 802–803, 104 S.Ct. 2118 (observing that "appellees' attack on the ordinance is basically a challenge to the ordinance as applied to their activities").

Junger does not show any difference between his professed injuries and those of parties not before the Court. The heart of his overbreadth argument is that the Export Regulations control the distribution of encryption software among fellow academics, and that such distribution does not pose a threat to United States security interests. But the resulting injury to other academics is the very same injury that Junger allegedly suffers. Because the Export Regulations potentially injure other academics in the same manner as Junger, their injury cannot be the basis of an overbreadth challenge.

Plaintiff Junger's overbreadth challenge fails because he does not show that the Export Regulations injure parties not before the Court in a manner different from the way they affect Junger. Even if Junger could bring the overbreadth challenge, he does not show the Export Regulations significantly compromise recognized First Amendment protections through a challenged law that is "substantially overbroad."

Junger also alleges that the Export Regulations' controls are vague because they do not give fair notice of what items are subject to the licensing requirement. The Court finds that the Export Regulations are not vague. The Export Regulations provide adequate notice. The regulations are quite detailed in describing which encryption software programs are subject to export licensing, and those that are not. Indeed, the Export Regulations even contain a description of the key length in "bits" for regulated programs. *See* 15 C.F.R. § 742.15(b)(3)(i)–(ii).

*Content discrimination*

...Because the regulations are content neutral, they are subject to intermediate scrutiny....

Junger first alleges that the Export Regulations discriminate because of content because they treat other types of software more favorably than encryption software. Plaintiff Junger is correct that the government subjects encryption software to heightened licensing regulations that do not apply to other types of software. Under the Export Administration Act, all types of software are regulated as "technology." 50 U.S.C.App. §2415(4). However, encryption software is categorized under the stricter "commodity" standard. 15 C.F.R. Part 774, note following 5D002.

The Export Regulations are not content based, however, because the regulations burden encryption software without reference to any views it may express. As the President has made clear, encryption software is regulated because it has the technical capacity to encrypt data and by that jeopardize American security interests, not because of its expressive content. Exec. Order No. 13026, 1996 WL 666563. The regulatory distinction between encryption software and other types of software does not turn on the content of ideas. Instead, it turns on the ability of encryption software to actually do the function of encrypting data.

That the Export Regulations are not directed at the content of ideas is further suggested because the Export Regulations do not attempt to restrict the free flow of public information and ideas about cryptography. Publicly available information that can be used to design or operate encryption products is not subject to the Export Regulations and may be freely exported. 15 C.F.R. §734.3(b)(3). More important, the Export Regulations exclude books, magazines, and other printed materials, by that imposing no controls on the export of publications on cryptography. 15 C.F.R. §734.3(b)(2).

The plaintiff also argues that the Export Regulations are content based because they discriminate based upon media: export of encryption software in print form is not subject to the Export Regulations' licensing requirement, whereas software exported electronically is subject to licensing. The plaintiff argues that *Reno v. ACLU*, 521 U.S. 844, 117 S.Ct. 2329, 138 L.Ed.2d 874 (1997), forecloses any distinction between Internet and print publications. There, the Supreme Court held that "our cases provide no basis for qualifying the level of First Amendment scrutiny that should be applied to [the Internet]." *Id.* at 2344.

Plaintiff's argument is misguided for two reasons. First, as discussed above, the media distinction is not content-based discrimination because it is not directed at the content of ideas. Second, *Reno* is distinguishable....

In *Reno*, the court found the government could not restrict the transmission of indecent (but not obscene) communication. In so finding, the Court held the Decency Act was "a content-based blanket restriction on [indecent] speech." *Id.* at 2343. But obscenity does not have the functional ability that encryption software does. In other words, the function of a given lascivious photograph is the same whether on a computer screen or in a magazine. Software, by contrast, is functionally different in electronic form than when in print. When in print, encryption source code is simply a description of instructions. When in electronic form, encryption source code is a functional device that directs a computer to perform specified tasks. Unlike *Reno*, the regulated item is fundamentally and functionally different when in electronic form than when in print form.

Finally, Junger contends that the Export Regulations discriminate based on content by excepting certain mass market and key-recovery software from export regulations. *See* 15 C.F.R. §742.15(b)(1)–(2). This argument does not persuade. The government distinguishes among software based upon its functional ability. These distinctions are not directed at the content of ideas. 40-bit mass market and key-recovery software pose a lesser threat to American security interests than more complex types of encryption software. Plaintiff's argument only proves that the government tailors the licensing requirements to the risks presented, with less restrictive requirements for exports that pose lesser risks.

Because the Export Regulations are content neutral, the Court must evaluate the licensing scheme under intermediate scrutiny. *Turner,* 512 U.S. at 662, 114 S.Ct. 2445. A content neutral government regulation passes constitutional muster if " 'it furthers an important or substantial governmental interest; if the governmental interest is unrelated to the suppression of free expression; and if the incidental restriction of alleged First Amendment freedoms is no greater than is essential to the furtherance of that interest.' " *Id.* (quoting *United States v. O'Brien,* 391 U.S. 367, 377, 88 S.Ct. 1673, 20 L.Ed.2d 672 (1968)).

The "important interest" prong is satisfied because the government is properly concerned with controlling the export of encryption software to potentially hostile countries or individuals to protect national security. The use of encryption products by foreign intelligence targets can have "a debilitating effect" on the National Security Agency's "ability to collect and report...critical foreign intelligence." Without the Export Regulations' licensing requirements, domestic producers of encryption software could export their products, without restriction, to any person abroad for any reason, no matter a particular encryption product's strength and its usefulness to hostile interests abroad.

The government's important interest in controlling the spread of encryption software is not diminished even if certain forms of encryption software are already available abroad. Whatever the present foreign availability of encryption software, the government has a substantial interest to limit future distribution. The government also has an interest in ensuring that the most complex and effective encryption programs, such as 128-bit key length software, are not widely released abroad.

The Export Regulations, furthermore, are "unrelated to the suppression of free expression." *O'Brien,* 391 U.S. at 377. Plaintiff Junger argues that the Export Regulations are related to the suppression of expression because they limit the publication of software. This argument is off the mark. A regulation is not "related" to the suppression of free expression simply because it may have the effect of suppressing expression. Such an interpretation of the *O'Brien* test would render it a nullity, for any law that had the incidental effect of burdening expression would violate the First Amendment. Instead, a law violates the "unrelated" prong if it is "directed at the communicative nature of conduct." *Johnson,* 491 U.S. at 406, 109 S.Ct. 2533. In other words, the government cannot prohibit particular conduct to reach its expressive elements. *Id.*

The Export Regulations are "unrelated to the suppression of free expression," *O'Brien,* 391 U.S. at 377, 88 S.Ct. 1673, for the same reasons that they are content neutral. The Export Regulations are not designed to limit the free exchange of ideas about cryptography. Instead, the government regulates encryption software because it does the function of actually encrypting data.

Besides meeting the "important interest" and "unrelated" prongs, the Export Regulations also satisfy the "narrow tailoring" requirement. The narrow tailoring prong does not require that the government employ the least speech-restrictive means to achieve its purposes. Instead, narrow tailoring requires that the law not "burden substantially more speech than is necessary to further the government's legitimate interests." *Ward,* 491 U.S. at 799, 109 S.Ct. 2746. Accordingly, the requirement is satisfied if the government's interests "would be achieved less effectively absent the regulation." *Id.*

The government's interest in controlling the spread of encryption software and gathering foreign intelligence surely would be "achieved less effectively" absent the export controls. Encryption software posted on the Internet or on computer diskette can be converted from source code into workable object code with a single keystroke. Elimination of export controls would permit the unrestricted export of encryption software to any person, organization, or country, without regard to the strength of the software, the identity of the recipients, or the uses to which it might be put.

The export controls at issue do not "burden substantially more speech than is necessary to further the government's legitimate interests," *Ward*, 491 U.S. at 799, 109 S.Ct. 2746, for the same reason they are not overbroad. Export controls are targeted at precisely the activity that threatens the government's legitimate interests. First, the Export Regulations do not prohibit exporting encryption products altogether, but only those inconsistent with American national security and foreign policy interests. *See* 15 C.F.R. §742.15(b). The licensing requirements are tailored to the risks presented, with less restrictive requirements for exports that pose lesser risks, such as 40-bit mass market and key-recovery software. *See* 15 C.F.R. §742.15(b)(1)–(2). Finally, the Export Regulations do not reach print publications. Thus, they "leave open ample alternative channels of communication," *Ward*, 491 U.S. at 802, 109 S.Ct. 2746, for the exchange of information and ideas regarding cryptography.

Because the content neutral export regulations at issue enable the government to collect vital foreign intelligence, are not directed at a source code's ideas, and do not burden more speech than necessary, they satisfy intermediate scrutiny....

## Conclusion

For these reasons, plaintiff's motion for summary judgment is denied, and defendants' motion for summary judgment is granted.

----

## Peter D. JUNGER v. William DALEY, *et al.*,

United States Court of Appeals for the Sixth Circuit
No. 98-4045, 209 F.3d 481
April 4, 2000

Before: MARTIN, Chief Judge; CLAY, Circuit Judge; WEBER, District Judge.

OPINION BY: BOYCE F. MARTIN, JR., Chief Judge.

This is a constitutional challenge to the provisions of the Export Administration Regulations, 15 C.F.R. Parts 730–74, that regulate the export of encryption software. Peter D. Junger appeals the district court's grant of summary judgment in favor of Secretary Daley and the other defendants.

The district court found that encryption source code is not sufficiently expressive to be protected by the First Amendment, that the Export Administration Regulations are permissible content-neutral restrictions, and that the Regulations are not subject to a facial challenge as a prior restraint on speech. Subsequent to the district court's holding and the oral arguments before this Court, the Bureau of Export Administration issued an interim final rule amending the regulations at issue. *See* Revisions to Encryption Items, 65 Fed. Reg. 2492 (2000) (to be codified at 15 C.F.R. Parts 734, 740, 742, 770, 772, 774). Having concluded that the First Amendment protects computer source code, we reverse the district court and remand this case for further consideration of Junger's constitutional claims in light of the amended regulations....

The issue of whether or not the First Amendment protects encryption source code is a difficult one because source code has both an expressive feature and a functional feature. The United States does not dispute that it is possible to use encryption source code to represent and convey information and ideas about cryptography and that encryption source code can be used by programmers and scholars for such informational purposes. Much like a mathematical or scientific formula, one can describe the function and design of encryption software by a prose explanation; however, for individuals fluent in a computer programming language, source code is the most efficient and precise means by which to communicate ideas about cryptography.

The district court concluded that the functional characteristics of source code overshadow its simultaneously expressive nature. The fact that a medium of expression has a functional capacity should not preclude constitutional protection. Rather, the appropriate consideration of the medium's functional capacity is in the analysis of permitted government regulation.

The Supreme Court has explained that "all ideas having even the slightest redeeming social importance, "including those concerning "the advancement of truth, science, morality, and arts" have the full protection of the First Amendment. *Roth v. United States*, 354 U.S. 476, 484, 1 L. Ed. 2d 1498, 77 S. Ct. 1304 (1957) (quoting 1 *Journals of the Continental Congress* 108 (1774)). This protection is not reserved for purely expressive communication. The Supreme Court has recognized First Amendment protection for symbolic conduct, such as draft-card burning, that has both functional and expressive features. *See United States v. O'Brien*, 391 U.S. 367, 20 L. Ed. 2d 672, 88 S. Ct. 1673 (1968).

The Supreme Court has expressed the versatile scope of the First Amendment by labeling as "unquestionably shielded" the artwork of Jackson Pollack, the music of Arnold Schoenberg, or the Jabberwocky verse of Lewis Carroll. *Hurley v. Irish-American Gay, Lesbian and Bisexual Group*, 515 U.S. 557, 569, 132 L. Ed. 2d 487, 115 S. Ct. 2338 (1995). Though unquestionably expressive, these things identified by the Court are not traditional speech. Particularly, a musical score cannot be read by the majority of the public but can be used as a means of communication among musicians. Likewise, computer source code, though unintelligible to many, is the preferred method of communication among computer programers.

Because computer source code is an expressive means for the exchange of information and ideas about computer programming, we hold that it is protected by the First Amendment.

The functional capabilities of source code, and particularly those of encryption source code, should be considered when analyzing the governmental interest in regulating the exchange of this form of speech. Under intermediate scrutiny, the regulation of speech is valid, in part, if "it furthers an important or substantial governmental interest." *O'Brien*, 391 U.S. at 377. In *Turner Broadcasting System v. FCC*, 512 U.S. 622, 664, 129 L. Ed. 2d 497, 114 S. Ct. 2445 (1994), the Supreme Court noted that although an asserted governmental interest may be important, when the government defends restrictions on speech "it must do more than simply 'posit the existence of the disease sought to be cured.'" *Id.* (quoting *Quincy Cable TV, Inc. v. FCC*, 248 U.S. App. D.C. 1, 768 F.2d 1434, 1455 (D.C. Cir. 1985)). The government "must demonstrate that the recited harms are real, not merely conjectural, and that the regulation will in fact alleviate these harms in a direct and material way." *Id.* We recognize that national security interests can outweigh the interests of protected speech and require the regulation of speech. In the present case, the record does not resolve whether the exercise of presidential power in furtherance of national security interests should overrule the interests in allowing the free exchange of encryption source code.

Before any level of judicial scrutiny can be applied to the Regulations, Junger must be in a position to bring a facial challenge to these regulations. In light of the recent amendments to the Export Administration Regulations, the district court should examine the new regulations to determine if Junger can bring a facial challenge.

For the foregoing reasons, we REVERSE the district court and REMAND the case to the district court for consideration of Junger's constitutional challenge to the amended regulations.

---

In *Bernstein v. United States Dep't of Justice*, 176 F.3d 1132 (9th Cir. 1999), the government appealed the grant of summary judgment to the plaintiff, Professor Daniel Bernstein, that enjoined the enforcement of certain Export Administration Regulations limiting Bernstein's ability to distribute encryption software. The Ninth Circuit found that the regulations operated as a pre-publication licensing scheme that burdens scientific expression. The Supreme Court had treated licensing schemes that act as prior restraints on speech with suspicion, because such restraints incurred risks that self-censorship would be encouraged and illegitimate abuses of censorial power would be concealed. The appellate court concluded that Bernstein was entitled to facially attack the regulations, because the regulations accorded the government unbridled discretion to deny licenses whenever export might be inconsistent with "U.S. national security and foreign policy interests." *See* 15 C.F.R. § 742.15(b) (2000). The Ninth Circuit had no difficulty concluding that the regulatory constraint offered inadequate guidance.

More troublesome for the court was the question as to whether the challenged regulations exhibited a close enough nexus to expression. After reviewing the nature of source code, the court considered declarations submitted by Bernstein from cryptographers and computer programmers that explained that cryptographic ideas and algorithms are conveniently expressed in source code. Source codes effectively enable cryptographers to express algorithmic ideas with precise methodology that might otherwise be difficult to achieve. The Ninth Circuit was persuaded that cryptographers use source code to express their scientific ideas in much the same way that mathematicians use equations or economists use graphs. The government's argument, that source code is different from other forms of expression (such as blueprints, recipes, and "how-to" manuals) because it can be used to control the operation of a computer without conveying information to the user, was unavailing. This led the court to conclude that encryption software, in its source code form and as employed by those in the field of cryptography, must be viewed as expressive for First Amendment purposes, and thus is entitled to the protections of the prior restraint doctrine.

Having framed the inquiry for analysis, the Ninth Circuit then applied the doctrine of prior restraint to determine whether the regulations were permissible. The court reasoned that the regulations were flawed because they did not require that a licensing decision be made by the government within a reasonably short, specified time period. The regulatory regime also was deemed to offend First Amendment requirements because it denied a disappointed applicant appropriate opportunity for judicial review.

The court concluded its decision by cautioning that its decision was narrow, emphasizing that it was not ruling that all software was expressive. The court commented that insofar as the regulations on encryption software inhibited the spread of secure encryption methods to foreign nations, the regulatory scheme retarded the progress of cryptography as a science.

Pragmatic aspects of digital communications did not go unnoticed by the court. Reliance on electronic media has brought with it a dramatic diminution in the capacity for private communication, the court observed. Access to secure encryption mechanisms

> may offer an opportunity to reclaim some portion of the privacy we have lost. Government efforts to control encryption thus may well implicate not only the First Amendment rights of cryptographers intent on pushing the boundaries of their science, but also the constitutional rights of each of us as potential recipients of encryption's bounty. Viewed from this perspective, the government's efforts to retard progress in cryptography may implicate the Fourth Amendment, as well as the right to speak anonymously.

*Bernstein v. United States Dep't of Justice*, 176 F.3d at 1146.

Only a few months after the Ninth Circuit's decision was issued, the court withdrew its opinion and ordered the case to be reheard by the court en banc. 192 F.3d 1308 (9th Cir. 1999). Judge Bright, concurring in the appellate court's earlier decision observed, perhaps presciently, that "[t]he importance of this case suggests that it may be appropriate for review by the United States Supreme Court." *Bernstein v. United States Dep't of Justice*, 176 F.3d at 1147.

---

## Notes and Questions

1. In *Karn v. United States Dep't of State,* 925 F. Supp. 1 (D.D.C. 1996), *remanded per curiam,* 107 F.3d 923 (D.C. Cir. 1997), the plaintiff challenged the State Department's denial of permission to export a diskette containing the code of encryption algorithms. The encryption matter had been published in a book, the export of which was not prohibited. 925 F. Supp. at 3.

2. Professor Ronald Rivest of the Massachusetts Institute of Technology developed a new protocol for promoting the security of electronically transmitted data, known as "chaffing and winnowing." This method utilizes electronic authentication, as opposed to encryption. Messages are sent electronically in a combination of packets, which represent authenticating information (the "wheat") and extraneous, irrelevant information (the "chaff"). Rivest analogizes the concept underlying the methodology to the signals used in baseball: "a coach will signal to a runner by giving a sequence of signals, but the real signal is the one immediately following a previously agreed-upon authenticator signal." Ronald L. Rivest, *Chaffing and Winnowing: Confidentiality Without Encryption* at 7 <http://theory.lcs.mit.edu/~rivest/chaffing.txt>. Is this method subject to the current federal regulatory scheme?

3. Federal efforts to regulate encryption include establishing standards accessible to law enforcement authorities by court order to address terrorism, drug trafficking, foreign espionage, and the like. The initiative, known as the "Clipper Chip," has been abandoned. *See* A. Michael Froomkin, *The Metaphor is the Key: Cryptography, the Clipper Chip, and the Constitution,* 143 U. Pa. L. Rev. 709 (1995); Kurt M. Saunders, *The Regulation of Internet Encryption Technologies: Separating the Wheat from the Chaff,* 17 J. Marshall J. Computer & Info. L. 945, 950–51 (1999). In 1998, the Clinton Administration persuaded parties to the Wassenaar Arrangement on Ex-

port Controls for Conventional Arms and Dual Use Goods and Technologies, *see* <http://www.wassenaar.org/>, to apply to encryption software the same export controls applied to munitions. *See* Kurt M. Saunders, *The Regulation of Internet Encryption Technologies: Separating the Wheat from the Chaff*, 17 J. Marshall J. Computer & Info. L. at 959.

# Chapter V

# Proprietary Interests in Content

## Copyright

### 1. Fundamental Principles of Copyright

Copyright protection extends to "original works of authorship fixed in any tangible medium of expression." 17 U.S.C.A. § 102 (West 1995). Copyright subsists in such creative works of expression as books, movies, plays, paintings, and photographs. *Id.* The copyright owner enjoys exclusive rights to reproduce the work, to create derivative works, to distribute the work, to perform the work publicly, and to display the work publicly. Any or all of these rights may be licensed by the author to a third party.

A "derivative work" is one that is based upon one or more pre-existing works, such as editorial revisions, annotations, elaborations, or other modifications which, as a whole, represent an original work of authorship. Copyright law thus constrains unauthorized uses and transformations of authors' original works. *See* 17 U.S.C.A. § 101 (West 1995 & Supp. 2000). Under the copyright laws, to "display" a work means "to show a copy of it" directly or through "a film, slide, television image, or any other device or process...." *Id.* Copyright holders are protected from unauthorized displays of their works that are made publicly.

"Unlike a patent, a copyright gives no exclusive right to the art disclosed; protection is given only to the expression of the idea—not the idea itself." *Mazer v. Stein,* 347 U.S. 201, 217 (1954) (footnote omitted), *reh'g denied,* 347 U.S. 949 (1954). Recognition of the dichotomy between ideas and expression is entrenched in the Copyright Act itself, which explicitly precludes copyright protection for "any idea." 17 U.S.C.A. § 102(b). "This provision was not intended to enlarge or contract the scope of copyright protection but 'to restate...that the basic dichotomy between expression and idea remains unchanged.'" *Apple Computer, Inc. v. Franklin Computer Corp.,* 714 F.2d 1240, 1252 (3d Cir. 1983) (quoting H.R. Rep. No. 1476, 94th Cong., 2d Sess. 54, reprinted in 1976 U.S.C.C.A.N. 5659, 5670), *cert. dismissed,* 464 U.S. 1033 (1984). Similarly, copyright protection does not extend to facts. *See, e.g., Feist Publications, Inc. v. Rural Telephone Serv. Co.,* 499 U.S. 340 (1991). Rather, copyright protects only the creative manner in which the facts are expressed. *See, e.g., id.*

The monopoly privileges conferred by the copyright laws "are neither unlimited nor primarily designed to provide a special private benefit. Rather, the limited grant is a means by which an important public purpose may be achieved. It is intended to motivate the creative activity of authors and inventors by the provision of a special reward, and to allow the public access to the products of their genius after the limited period of exclusive control has expired." *Sony Corp. v. Universal City Studios, Inc.*, 464 U.S. 417, 429 (1984).

Copyright protection is statutorily defined, deriving its basis from concepts embedded in the U.S. Constitution, U.S. Const. art. I, § 8; free speech protection was codified thereafter, in the Bill of Rights, U.S. Const. amend. I. Copyright has been envisaged as an "engine of free expression," *Harper & Row, Publishers, Inc. v. Nation Enterprises*, 471 U.S. 539, 558 (1985), "infused with First Amendment values," William F. Patry, *The Fair Use Privilege in Copyright Law* 576 (2d ed. 1995). "By establishing a marketable right to the use of one's expression, copyright supplies the economic incentive to create and disseminate ideas." *Harper & Row, Publishers, Inc. v. Nation Enterprises*, 471 U.S. at 558. "The glory of copyright is that it sustains not only independent, idiosyncratic, and iconoclastic authors, but also fosters daring, innovative, and risk-taking publishers. Without such publishers, authors are as mute as if they did not speak at all. Without them, authors do not speak at all…." David Ladd, *The Harm of the Concept of Harm in Copyright*, 30 J. Copyright Soc'y 421, 428 (1983).

Analytically, then, copyright protection has been conceptualized fundamentally less as an exception to First Amendment protection than as a legal, albeit intangible, device by which the dissemination of information is achieved. "Where the First Amendment removes obstacles to the free flow of ideas, copyright law adds positive incentives to encourage the flow." *Pacific & Southern Co. v. Duncan*, 744 F.2d 1490, 1499 n. 14 (11th Cir. 1984), *cert. denied*, 471 U.S. 1004 (1985), *on remand*, 618 F. Supp. 469 (N.D. Ga. 1985), *aff'd*, 792 F.2d 1013 (11th Cir. 1986).

There is nonetheless an inherent tension between free speech and proprietary interests. One way this conflict is accommodated is by establishing an analytical demarcation between ideas and expression. The Copyright Act expressly precludes protection to "any idea,…concept, [or] principle,…regardless of the form in which it is described, explained, illustrated, or embodied in such work." 17 U.S.C.A. § 102(b) (West 1995). "[T]here is no attempt to make a monopoly of the ideas expressed. The law confines itself to a particular, cognate, and well-known form of reproduction." *Kalem Co. v. Harper Bros.*, 222 U.S. 55, 63 (1911). The dichotomy serves to limit the scope of an author's control over his work. Were an author able to prevent subsequent authors from using concepts, ideas, or facts contained in his work, the creative process would be jeopardized and scholars would be relegated to the unproductive replication of research by their predecessors.

More significantly, the limitation is consonant with First Amendment values. Broad dissemination of principles, ideas, and factual information is crucial to robust public debate and an informed citizenry, which are essential to self-government. Allowing authors to monopolize ideas and information would negate these objectives, and thwart efforts to marshal ideas and facts in the pursuit of advocacy of political and social choice.

Distinguishing between ideas and their expression is another matter, however. As Judge Learned Hand observed, "[n]obody has ever been able to fix [the] boundary [between ideas and expression], and nobody ever can." *Nichols v. Universal Pictures Corp.*, 45 F.2d 119, 121 (2d Cir. 1930), *cert. denied*, 282 U.S. 902 (1931). Determinations as to whether an infringing appropriation of literary form has occurred, as opposed to a taking of information or ideas, may prove elusive in practice. "Decisions must therefore inevitably be ad hoc." *Peter Pan Fabrics, Inc. v. Martin Weiner Corp.*, 274 F.2d 487, 489 (2d Cir. 1960).

# 2. Injunctive Relief and First Amendment Implications

The impetus for copyright protection may be found in the invention of the printing press, and had its early beginnings in British censorship laws. "'The fortunes of the law of copyright have always been closely connected with freedom of expression, on the one hand, and with technological improvements in means of dissemination, on the other. Successive ages have drawn different balances among the interest of the writer in the control and exploitation of his intellectual property, the related interest of the publisher, and the competing interest of society in the untrammeled dissemination of ideas.'" *Sony Corp. v. Universal City Studios, Inc.*, 464 U.S. at 431 n. 12 (quoting foreword to B. Kaplan, *An Unhurried View of Copyright* vii–viii (1967)).

As the Supreme Court has stated with respect to efforts to squelch the content of speech, "'[a]ny system of prior restraints of expression comes to this Court bearing a heavy presumption against its constitutional validity.'" *New York Times Co. v. United States*, 403 U.S. 713, 714 (1971) (quoting *Bantam Books, Inc. v. Sullivan*, 372 U.S. 58, 70 (1963)). In the copyright arena, however, injunctive relief to enjoin publication of pirated material is far more common. The Copyright Act of 1976 specifically authorizes courts to grant "temporary and final injunctions on such terms as [they] may deem reasonable to prevent or restrain infringement of a copyright." 17 U.S.C.A. §502 (West 1995).

"Not all injunctions that may incidentally affect expression, however, are 'prior restraints' in the sense that that term was used in *New York Times Co.* [*v. United States*, 403 U.S. 713 (1971),] or *Vance* [*v. Universal Amusement Co.*, 445 U.S. 308 (1980) (per curiam) (holding that Texas public nuisance statute which authorized state judges, on the basis of a showing that a theater had exhibited obscene films in the past, to enjoin its future exhibition of films not yet found to be obscene was unconstitutional as authorizing an invalid prior restraint)]." *Madsen v. Women's Health Center, Inc.*, 512 U.S. 753, 764 n. 2 (1994). Thus, an injunction entered against anti-abortion protesters was distinguished from a prior restraint on the ground that the petitioners were not prevented from expressing their message in any one of several different ways, and because the injunction was issued not because of the content of their expression, but because of prior unlawful conduct. *Id.* Constitutional infirmity may be avoided if the injunction has a content-neutral justification and does not represent an absolute bar on a particular expression. *See National Basketball Association v. Sports Team Analysis & Tracking Systems, Inc.*, 939 F. Supp. 1071, 1087 (S.D.N.Y. 1996).

In *Dallas Cowboys Cheerleaders, Inc. v. Pussycat Cinema, Ltd.*, 604 F.2d 200, 206 (2d Cir. 1979), for example, the Second Circuit rejected the contention that issuance of an injunction constituted an impermissible prior restraint. The court stated, "[t]his is not a case of government censorship, but a private plaintiff's attempt to protect its property rights;" because the court regarded the applicable statutory provision to be content neutral, the injunction "does not arouse the fears that trigger the application of constitutional 'prior restraint' principles." *Id.*

The extent to which divergent approaches to the issuance of prior restraints in speech and intellectual property situations are well-founded remains the subject of debate. In the Internet sphere, the disparate paradigms for speech and proprietary interests appear to be commensurate with their conventional counterparts. Section 230 of the Communications Decency Act, 17 U.S.C.A. §230 (West Supp. 2000), *see* discussion *supra* at 203, immunizes Internet service providers from liability even if the Internet service provider is on notice of the defamatory posting. By contrast, the Digital Millennium Copyright Infringement Act, 17 U.S.C.A. § 1201 (West Supp. 2000), *see* discussion *infra* at 402, shelters Internet service providers from liability for infringing material of which they were unaware, or which they timely removed once on notice of its existence. While both statutes provide meaningful protections for service providers, enhanced protections may be found in the Communications Decency Act. Such statutory provisions address conduct that impinges on the substance of the expressive speech, while the Digital Millennium Copyright Act's safe harbors relate to proprietary interests in content.

---

# Freedom of Speech and Injunctions in Intellectual Property Cases
## Mark A. Lemley and Eugene Volokh
### 48 Duke L.J. 147 (1998)*

Say we think a new book is going to libel us, and we ask a court for a preliminary injunction against the book's publication. We argue that we're likely to succeed on the merits of our libel claim, and that failure to enjoin the speech would cause us irreparable harm.

Too bad, the court will certainly say; a content-based preliminary injunction of speech would be a blatantly unconstitutional prior restraint. Maybe after a trial on the merits and a judicial finding that the speech is in fact constitutionally unprotected libel, we could get a permanent injunction, though even that's not clear. But we definitely could not get a preliminary injunction, based on mere likelihood of success. Likewise for preliminary injunctions against obscenity and other kinds of speech, despite the fact that such speech, if ultimately found to be unprotected at trial, could be criminally or civilly punished.

In copyright cases, though, preliminary injunctions are granted pretty much as a matter of course, even when the defendant has engaged in creative adaptation, not just literal copying. How can this be? True, the Supreme Court has held that copyright law is a constitutionally permissible speech restriction; though copyright law restricts what we can write or record or perform, the First Amendment doesn't protect copyright-infringing speech against such a restraint. But libel law and obscenity law are likewise constitutionally valid restrictions on speech, and yet courts refuse to allow preliminary injunctions there. The "First Amendment due process" rule against prior restraints applies even to speech that's alleged to be constitutionally unprotected. Why, then, not to allegedly infringing speech? ...

Several things are notable about the law of copyright preliminary injunctions. First, the modern U.S. practice is unquestionably more favorable to plaintiffs than to defendants, and it is more favorable in copyright cases than in most other contexts. Copyright plaintiffs can dispense with most of the normal requirements for obtaining a preliminary injunction, and disputed issues are regularly resolved in their favor.

Second, in many cases it is the defendant, not the plaintiff, who effectively bears the burden of proof with respect to such injunctions. Bond practice reinforces this shift — it

---

* © 1998 Mark A. Lemley and Eugene Volokh.

is the defendant who is presumed to be compensable by money damages if an injunction wrongly issues, while plaintiffs are conclusively presumed to suffer irreparable harm if an injunction does not issue.

Finally, while the pro-plaintiff trend in copyright injunctions has historic antecedents in early English practice, they are not lineal antecedents. Early U.S. copyright practice differed markedly from both the traditional English rule and the modern U.S. rule. Only in the 1900s have preliminary injunctions come to be an expected part of U.S. copyright cases.

Copyright law restricts speech: it restricts you from writing, painting, publicly performing, or otherwise communicating what you please. If your speech copies ours, and if the copying uses our "expression," not merely our ideas or facts that we have uncovered, the speech can be enjoined and punished, civilly and sometimes criminally.

And copyright law applies to creative adaptation as well as to literal copying, so it's no answer to say that the copiers aren't themselves originating the speech. Writers are barred from creating works, even works based on real events, whose plots are too similar to what others have done. Artists are forbidden from creating artworks that are too similar to others' art. Musicians are restricted from using "vocal percussion effects" that are too similar to those of other artists. Indeed, in some cases basing even a small bit of an otherwise original work on others' copyrighted expression can subject a defendant to liability, as when movie producers are held liable for including copyrighted posters, sculptures, or even furniture in brief scenes from the film. Copyright law seriously restricts speakers' ability to express themselves the way they want.

.... [C]ould it be that copyright law is somehow specially immune from the normal concerns surrounding other speech restrictions? We've often heard this view among copyright lawyers. While copyright law is clearly a speech restriction, to many it lacks that speech restriction flavor. It doesn't sound like censorship, just people enforcing their lawful property rights. Still, while many have this intuition, is there some specific reason underlying it, some reason that can justify setting aside the normal First Amendment procedural guarantees?

1. Property Rights. The argument that copyright law should be exempted from standard First Amendment procedural rules because it protects property rights strikes us as a non sequitur. Free speech guarantees can't be avoided simply by characterizing a speech restriction as an "intellectual property law.".…

[C]ontent-based laws, specifically targeted at speech, must be seen as speech restrictions regardless of whether one frames them as "property" rules. They may be substantively valid speech restrictions, but calling them property rules doesn't justify exempting them from the normal First Amendment procedural principles, especially when they ban people from saying a particular thing anywhere, at any time, and not just on others' land.

.... [C]onsumption of intellectual property, unlike consumption of tangible property, is "nonrivalrous"—one person's use of a work does not prevent others from using it as well. This makes intellectual property sufficiently unlike tangible property that some courts that have faced the issue directly have even concluded that copyrights and trademarks are not "property" within the meaning of the Takings Clause. Whether or not that's correct, the nonrivalrous aspect of intellectual property infringement weakens the property rights argument. Generally speaking, writing graffiti on someone else's building damages the building owner in a different way than making a copy of a book injures the author. One might perhaps think of both as using another's private property to facilitate one's speech, but graffiti, unlike unauthorized copying, interferes with the owner's use of his own property. This isn't to say that copyright law is unjustifiable or an unconstitutional speech restriction, only that the constitutional questions surrounding it can't be avoided merely by invoking the tangible property cases.

2. Private Enforcement. Because copyright law is largely enforced by private litigation rather than government prosecution, some argue that it's much less likely to turn into an engine of government censorship. But of course libel law is also enforced almost exclusively by private litigation. Despite this, courts correctly ban preliminary injunctions in libel cases, even those brought by people who aren't public officials. Libel law is a government-imposed restriction that uses government power to restrict speech that people want to see restricted; this is troublesome enough that the Court has insisted on strict procedural safeguards to make sure such a restriction is applied correctly. The same should be true for copyright cases.

3. Content-Neutrality. It's also incorrect to argue that intellectual property law is content-neutral and should therefore be subject to laxer rules. Copyright liability turns on the content of what is published. It's true that copyright law draws no ideological distinctions: just like libel law, obscenity law, and fighting words law, it applies equally to speech advocating democracy, speech advocating communism, and speech with no ideological message at all. But while this might make the law viewpoint-neutral, it doesn't make it content-neutral, and it doesn't avoid the prohibition on preliminary injunctions, which applies even to viewpoint-neutral restrictions such as libel law.

4. Subject Matter of the Jeopardized Speech. Some suggest that injunctions in copyright cases pose less of a threat to free speech because they typically involve nonpolitical matters; after all, would it be such a big deal if a court erroneously concluded that Battlestar Galactica infringes the plot of Star Wars? When the risk of error or chill falls only on such nonpolitical material, the argument goes, there's no need for special procedural protections.

This argument, though, runs counter to fifty years of First Amendment precedents that give art, entertainment, comedy, and the like the same level of protection that is given to political speech. The Court has never suggested that the risk of erroneous restriction is less important as to these materials than as to political advocacy....

And of course quite a few copyright cases do involve political or other socially significant speech... and quite a few libel cases involve material that seems to be as much "entertainment" as a typical movie or novel. A law that precludes news organizations from publishing the film of an assassination, or the audiotape of a White House intern, certainly affects "core" protected speech.

5. Copyright Law Furthers Free Speech Values. Nor can copyright law be exempted from the general prior restraint rules on the grounds that "copyright itself [can] be the engine of free expression." Copyright law's speech-enhancing effect, coupled with the specific constitutional authorization for copyright law, may justify holding copyright law to be a substantively valid speech restriction, though even this is in large part true because copyright law is limited in the powers it gives copyright owners.[193] But the point

---

193. As Jessica Litman notes, "the harmony between the First Amendment and copyright doesn't inhere in their essential nature; rather, it derives from accommodations and restrictions we have built into copyright to enhance its role as an engine of free expression." [Jessica Litman, *Reforming Information Law in Copyright's Image*, 22 U. Dayton L. Rev. 587, 619 (1997)]....

Justin Hughes has offered a first Amendment defense of copyright based on the listener's as well as the speaker's need for integrity, arguing that "freedom of expression is meaningless without assurances that the expression will remain unadulterated." Justin Hughes, *The Philosophy of Intellec-*

of procedural rules, such as the prior restraint doctrine, is precisely to make sure that even substantively valid speech restrictions don't end up restricting speech that should remain protected....

6. The Copyright and Patent Clause. Unlike libel and obscenity law, copyright laws have a specific textual hook in the Constitution: Article I, Section 8 of the Constitution authorizes Congress "[t]o promote the Progress of Science and useful Arts, by securing for limited Times to Authors and Inventors the exclusive Right to their respective Writings and Discoveries." In *Harper & Row*, the Court mentioned this as one reason why copyright law is a constitutionally permissible speech restriction. But the existence of the congressional power can't exempt copyright law from all First Amendment scrutiny. The Copyright and Patent Clause grants power to Congress, but the point of the Bill of Rights is to restrain the federal government in the exercise of its enumerated powers. In exercising its other powers, Congress is subject to First Amendment constraints: For instance, the government has the enumerated power to run the post office, but this doesn't mean it can refuse to carry communist propaganda; the government has power to regulate interstate commerce, but this doesn't mean it can impose content-based restrictions on the interstate distribution of newspapers. Likewise, in exercising its copyright power, Congress is bound by the Fourth, Fifth, and Sixth Amendments. Copyright law must be bound by the First Amendment too.

That is not to say that the presence of the Copyright and Patent Clause is irrelevant to the First amendment inquiry. We agree that it would be unsound to read the First Amendment as entirely eliminating the copyright power created by the Framers only two years earlier....[C]ourts ought not, in their zeal to protect speech, eviscerate the incentive that copyright law provides....

But this argument hardly shows that copyright law ought to be free of the traditional procedural protections available in all other First Amendment cases. A general ban on preliminary injunctions wouldn't eviscerate or even greatly diminish the incentive provided by copyright law, just as such a ban doesn't eviscerate libel law or obscenity law; it would merely require the law to be enforced in a slightly different way.

7. Importance of the Government Interest. The interest promoted by copyright law—the interest in providing an incentive for the dissemination of ideas—is, even without regard to its constitutional status, quite important. One might even go so far as to call it "compelling," a term of constitutional significance.

But many speech restrictions—for instance, those aimed at protecting individual reputation, preventing harms caused by the distribution of child pornography, protecting national security, and preventing violent acts incited by violent advocacy—are justified by important (perhaps even compelling) interests, too. The requirement that speech be finally adjudicated to be unprotected before it can be enjoined doesn't prevent these important interests from being served; it just requires that they be served through a certain set of procedures. True, the procedures might in some cases make the process of vindicating these interests a bit less effective. But the general First

---

*tual Property*, 77 Geo. L.J. 287, 359 (1988). Hughes takes as his paradigm cases instances which defendants have altered an author's work in ways the author finds objectionable, and then attributed the adulterated work to the original author. *See id.* at 36–65. The cases he discusses are troubling, but primarily because they involve misrepresentations as to the source of various parts of the work. Such deceptive speech may in some situations constitute a "false designation of origin" actionable under the trademark laws; whether or not it does, we would distinguish misrepresentations about the source of speech from additions, deletions, or changes to the speech itself.

Amendment judgment underlying the prior restraint doctrine is that this extra burden is justified by the interest in preventing the punishment of constitutionally protected speech.

8. Irreparable Harm. Courts often stress that copyright infringements presumptively cause "irreparable injury," harm that can't be remedied by an eventual damages award. And to a certain extent that's true: preventing illegal behavior is generally more effective than is trying to compensate for the harms after they have occurred.[207]

But this is true for virtually all kinds of harmful speech; for some kinds, such as libel, it's even more true than for copyright infringement. Copyright law is aimed primarily at ensuring that authors are economically rewarded so that they and others will continue to create new works of authorship—damages can generally reward authors relatively adequately and are often not terribly hard to estimate. Reputation, on the other hand, once sullied can never be perfectly repaired. Damages are only a highly imperfect palliative, may be impossible to get from an indigent defendant, and in any event are very hard to estimate, even roughly. Further, one might reasonably contend that enriching plaintiffs is not really the point of libel law, as it is with copyright: certainly one sees many cases of copyright owners licensing their rights in exchange for money, while it is harder to imagine people regularly selling others the right to defame them. Yet despite all this, libels may not be preliminarily enjoined.

And even if the harm caused by copyright infringement really were "irreparable," this shouldn't matter. The point of the prior restraint doctrine is that prevention of potentially harmful speech isn't allowed without a final judicial finding that the speech is unprotected. This necessarily causes some harm to the government interest (and to the private plaintiff's interest), whether it's the interest in protecting people's reputations, in preventing the moral harms caused by obscenity, or in preventing competitive injury to copyright owners. But under the prior restraint doctrine, it's a harm that must be borne. It certainly is borne by libel victims; why not copyright owners?

9. Ideas Can Be Expressed in Another Way. Copyright law, properly applied, generally restricts expression and not ideas or facts. Even a preliminarily enjoined speaker may be able to communicate the gist of his message, so long as he expresses it differently enough. Thus, some have suggested that copyright law is not a speech restriction because it leaves open adequate alternate channels of communication by allowing defendants to choose different words to express their ideas.

But obscenity law likewise restricts expression more than idea....Furthermore, while a damages award or a permanent injunction should by definition punish or restrict only copying of expression, preliminary injunctions may well enjoin even speech that will ultimately turn out to copy only facts or ideas. This is the nature of preliminary relief: because the test for entering a preliminary injunction turns on a reasonable likelihood of success on the merits, some fraction of preliminary injunctions will eventually prove to have enjoined speech that's not infringing—speech that copies only facts or ideas, or speech that's a fair use. So preliminary injunctions in copyright cases, like preliminary injunctions in libel cases, may often suppress facts and ideas, and not just particular modes of expression.

---

207. We are skeptical that this is necessarily true, however, and might therefore question the *Cadence* court's conclusion that the presumption of irreparable harm can never be rebutted in a copyright case by a showing that monetary damages would be adequate. *See* [*Cadence Design Sys., Inc. v. Avant! Corp.*, 125 F.3d 824, 829 (1997)].

10. "The Only Question Is Who Gets to Do the Publishing." Some might argue that copyright law is unlike other restrictions because it doesn't actually suppress speech: the expression involved will in due course be published, but by the copyright owner and to his financial benefit. An injunction won't deprive the public of the speech; it will just cause the speech to come from a different person. As with the right of publicity, the argument would go, "the only question is who gets to do the publishing."

In cases of nonliteral copying, though, this factual claim will often be wrong. Nonliteral copiers, even when they use another's expression, are by definition creating something different from (albeit in some ways similar to) the copyright owner's work. Sometimes the differences are quite dramatic; copying can be infringement even when the copier adds a great deal, and thus only part of the copy is substantially similar to the original.... And when the expression is enjoined, the public will only see what the copyright owner is saying, not what the would-be copier wanted to say.

What's more, even if the copying is literal or close to it, a copyright injunction may well prevent the expression from reaching the public altogether, at least for the many decades that the copyright lasts; some copyright owners use copyright law precisely for this purpose. The whole point of a copyright injunction, as opposed to a suit for damages, is not merely to redistribute the profits, but to prevent dissemination of defendant's work. There might be good reasons, in the copyright owner's mind or even the public's, to restrict distribution of the new work, but it seems hard to argue that such an injunction isn't really a speech restriction.

11. No Need for Timeliness. Some might argue that brief, temporary injunctions of movies or books pose little danger to free speech because such media, unlike newspapers or demonstrations, aren't particularly time-sensitive: it doesn't much matter whether you see a movie or read a book today or a week or two later.

This is a plausible argument, and is perhaps the best defense (though maybe still not an adequate defense) of the Court's toleration of prescreening systems for books and movies, so long as such systems really do create only a brief delay. It might justify some preliminary injunctions in copyright cases, and perhaps even libel cases, involving non-time-sensitive media.

But even for these injunctions,... preliminary injunctions in copyright cases can last for many months.... And the timeliness argument can't justify any preliminary injunctions of more time-sensitive publications, such as newspaper articles or television programs or even articles in weekly magazines.

12. Tradition: "A Copyright Question, Not a Free Speech Question." Finally, we've heard some people argue that it's a mistake—a form of "constitutional law imperialism"—to disrupt, on recently discovered First Amendment grounds, a balance carefully established over 200 years. Whether preliminary injunctions should be available in copyright cases should be seen, the argument goes, as a copyright law question, not as a free speech question.

Constitutional law imperialism, however, isn't our invention. The theory of *Marbury v. Madison* is that all U.S. laws are subject to the U.S. Constitution; and as the Court has clearly held, no "formulae for the repression of expression" can claim "talismanic immunity from constitutional limitations." Tradition alone cannot prevent constitutional scrutiny, as the Court made clear with respect to obscenity law and libel law, which had long been seen as not "rais[ing] any Constitutional problem" but which were ultimately held to be restrained by free speech principles. Sometimes, as in *Harper & Row*, the Court will conclude that a speech restriction passes constitutional muster; but all speech restrictions, regardless of their historical provenance, must be tested by First Amendment standards....

We thus see no compelling normative reason to treat copyright differently from other speech restrictions, restrictions that are likewise substantively valid but that nonetheless require certain procedural safeguards. And we see a good reason not to treat copyright more favorably than other speech restraints....

Any special preference for copyright law must...be justified by some substantial difference between copyright and other speech restrictions. Where, as here, no such difference exists, favoritism for a particular kind of speech restriction risks corroding public respect for First Amendment law more generally. And, ironically, publishers and producers—the very people who often benefit from the way copyright law now ignores First Amendment protections—have the most to lose from any corrosion of First Amendment protection outside copyright....

---

### Notes and Questions

1. The nature of the content at issue also may impinge on the analysis. In *Universal City Studios, Inc. v. Reimerdes*, No. 00 Civ. 0277, 2000 U.S. Dist. LEXIS 11696 at *112 & n. 231 (S.D.N.Y. Aug. 17, 2000), for example, Judge Lewis Kaplan cited the article authored by Professors Mark Lemley and Eugene Volokh, and stated that "even academic commentators who take the extreme position that most injunctions in intellectual property cases are unconstitutional prior restraints concede that there is no First Amendment obstacle to injunctions barring distribution of copyrighted code or restraining the construction of a new building based on copyrighted architectural drawings because the functional aspects of these types of information are 'sufficiently nonexpressive.'"

2. With respect to the impact of the fair use doctrine on prior restraint analysis in the copyright area, *see* discussion *infra* at 425.

---

## 3. Copyright Infringement Claims

Digitization permits instantaneous, facile copying of matter that appears nearly identical to the original. A publisher can develop original content for display on the Internet or can display content as to which it holds the applicable rights. Additionally, publishers may license content furnished by others for display. Content also may be made available through the use of linking and framing practices, which sometimes lead to contention. *See* discussion *infra* at 481. Disputes also may arise as to the scope of a publisher's rights in a collective work that is made available on an electronic database.

In *Ryan v. Carl Corp.*, 23 F. Supp. 2d 1146 (N.D. Cal. 1998), for instance, authors of articles published in collective works claimed that the defendant, who operated a document retrieval and delivery business, infringed on copyrights in the authors' individual articles. The defendant maintained an Internet database that contained the titles, but not the text, of millions of articles from periodicals. *Id.* at 1147. The defendant furnished articles to customers, and paid copyright fees to the publishers of the collective works, but did not make payments to the plaintiffs. *Id.* The court determined that the authors of the individual articles published in collective works — as opposed to the publisher of the work — held the privilege of reproducing the articles. *Id.* at 1150.

Claims of copyright infringement can be filed only in federal court. 28 U.S.C.A. § 1338(a) (West 1993 & Supp. 2000). Such actions may be brought by the owner of the copyright, or, in certain circumstances, by an exclusive licensee. 17 U.S.C.A. § 501 (West 1995 & Supp. 2000).

The remedies available to a copyright owner to redress infringement in civil lawsuits include: (1) seizure, impounding, and destruction of the infringing articles; (2) actual damages and profits of the infringer or, for copyrights that were registered in a timely manner, statutory damages; (3) court costs and, for copyrights that were registered in a timely manner, attorney's fees; and (4) injunctive relief in the form of a temporary restraining order, a preliminary injunction, or a permanent injunction. *See* 17 U.S.C.A. §§ 502–05 (West 1995).[1]

The Internet's capabilities offer unprecedented opportunity for illicit copying of others' material, and thus claims of infringement have already arisen. Use of others' copyrighted material can give rise to various types of infringement claims, which may be affected by the role the defendant has played and, more recently, by whether the defendant has complied with the Digital Millennium Copyright Act, Digital Millennium Copyright Act, Pub. L. No. 105-304, 112 Stat. 2860 (1998) (codified as amended at 17 U.S.C.A. §§ 512, 1201–05, 1301–22 (West Supp. 2000) and 24 U.S.C.A. § 4001 (West Supp. 2000), *see* discussion *infra* at 402.

In order to prevail on a claim of direct copyright infringement, the copyright owner must prove ownership of a valid copyright and the unauthorized exercise of any of the exclusive rights reserved to the copyright owner. *See, e.g., Feist Publications, Inc. v. Rural Telephone Serv. Co.,* 499 U.S. 340, 361 (1991). This has frequently been referred to by courts as "unlawful copying." Direct evidence of unlawful copying is not always available. The more typical copyright claim is premised upon evidence that (1) the defendant had access to the copyrighted work in question; and (2) there is a substantial similarity between the copyrighted work and the allegedly infringing work.

In addition to claims of direct copyright infringement, other types of infringement claims may be asserted. "Contributory infringement" claims are predicated upon allegations that the defendant knew of the infringing activity and materially contributed to it. Such claims may arise when one who controls the copyrighted works allows use without permission from the copyright owner. *See Sony Corp. v. Universal City Studios, Inc.,* 464 U.S. at 437. This type of infringement may be committed by "one who, with knowledge of the infringing activity, induces, causes or materially contributes to the infringing conduct of another." *See Gershwin Publ'g Corp. v. Columbia Artists Management, Inc.,* 443 F.2d 1159, 1162 (2d Cir. 1971) (citing *Fortnightly Corp. v. United Artists Television, Inc.,* 392 U.S. 390, 396–97 (1968)). "Vicarious infringement" occurs when the defen-

---

1. Criminal actions may be brought by the U.S. Attorney to redress copyright infringement. As well, the U.S. Customs Service is empowered to exclude "piratical" articles (i.e., copies made without authorization of the copyright owner) from entry into the United States. *See* 17 U.S.C.A. § 506 (West 1995).

dant has the right or ability to control the infringer's activities and derives financial benefit from them.

For example, courts have assessed the liability of various Internet participants when copyrighted works were alleged to have been displayed. In *Playboy Enterprises, Inc. v. Webbworld, Inc.*, 968 F. Supp. 1171 (N.D. Tex. 1997), *aff'd*, 168 F.3d 486 (5th Cir. 1999), for instance, the defendant, who operated a web-site, made available images originally created by or for the plaintiff that previously had appeared in one of the plaintiff's copyrighted magazines. The court determined that the defendant was liable for direct copyright infringement. The display right was implicated because the images had been shown on a Web server.

In *Playboy Enterprises v. Fena*, 839 F. Supp. 1552, 1554 (M.D. Fla. 1993) ("*Frena*"), the plaintiff sued the owner of a bulletin board system, claiming, among other things, that the defendant had committed direct copyright infringement by making photographs, to which the plaintiff held the rights, available to the defendants' subscribers. Display rights were broadly defined to include "the projection of an image on a screen or other surface by any method, the transmission of an image by electronic or other means, and the showing of an image on a cathode ray tube, or similar viewing apparatus connected with any sort of information storage and retrieval system." *Id.* (citing H.R. Rep. No. 1476, 94th Cong., 2d Sess. 64 (Sept. 3, 1976), reprinted in U.S. Code Cong. & Admin. News 5659, 5677)). The court concluded that the defendant had distributed the photographs by providing the space in which they were uploaded and downloaded, and rejected the defendant's argument that he was not culpable because he had not made the copies himself. *See Frena*, 839 F. Supp. at 1556. Professor Alfred Yen has stated that *Frena* "is the only case that supports this result. Subsequent case law and commentary have properly discredited it." Alfred C. Yen, *Internet Service Provider Liability for Subscriber Copyright Infringement, Enterprise Liability, and the First Amendment*, 88 Georgetown L.J. 1833, 1841 (2000).

In *Playboy Enterprises, Inc. v. Russ Hardenburgh, Inc.*, 982 F. Supp. 503, 513 (N.D. Ohio 1997), the court confronted the question of whether a computer bulletin board system operator was liable for, among other things, direct copyright infringement with respect to graphic image files that were alleged to unlawfully contain copies of photographs to which the plaintiff held the rights, and allegedly were made available to paying customers of the bulletin board service. The court ruled that a finding of direct copyright infringement requires some element of direct action or participation, and that "[s]etting up" a computer bulletin board system does not suffice to state a claim for direct infringement. "Merely *encouraging* or *facilitating* those activities is not proscribed by the [copyright] statute." *Id.* at 512 (emphasis in original). The court went on to hold, however, that

> Defendants "*themselves... distributed* and *displayed* copies of [the plaintiff's] photographs in derogation of [the plaintiff's] copyrights. This finding hinges on two crucial facts: (1) Defendants' policy of encouraging subscribers to upload files, including adult photographs, onto the system, and (2) Defendants' policy of using a screening procedure in which [the Defendants'] employees *viewed* all files in the upload file and *moved them* into the generally available files for subscribers.
>
> These two facts transform Defendants from passive providers of a space in which infringing activities happened to occur to active participants in the process of copyright infringement. Defendants admit that they were operating a service where the quantity of adult files available to customers increased the attractiveness of the service. Defendants actively encouraged their subscribers

to upload such files. Defendants had control over which files were discarded and which files were moved into the general system. Defendants knew that there was a possibility that [the Plaintiff's] photographs were being uploaded onto the system, but failed to adopt procedures which ensured that any and all [of the Plaintiff's] photographs would be discarded. It is inconsistent to argue that one may actively encourage and control the uploading and dissemination of adult files, but cannot [be] held liable for copyright violations because it is too difficult to determine which files infringe upon someone else's copyrights.

Distributing unlawful copies of a copyrighted work violates the copyright owner's distribution right and, as a result, constitutes copyright infringement. In order to establish "distribution" of a copyrighted work, a party must show that an unlawful copy was disseminated "to the public." The phrase "to the public," in this sense, includes paying subscribers to an otherwise publicly available service....

Similarly, Defendants violated [the Plaintiff's] right of public display....Defendants displayed copies of [the Plaintiff's] photographs to the public by adopting a policy which allowed their employees to place those photographs in files available to subscribers.

*Id.* at 513 (emphasis in original).

In *Religious Technology Center v. Netcom On-Line Communications Services, Inc.,* 907 F. Supp. 1361 (N.D. Cal. 1995), the plaintiff, the Church of Scientology, sued a former Church member, claiming that his distribution over the Internet of Church material violated the plaintiff's copyright. The plaintiff also sued the operator of the bulletin board on which the material had been posted, and Netcom, the Internet access provider for the bulletin board service.[2] The Church demanded that the defendants remove the material in issue; when they refused, suit ensued.

The federal court considered whether Netcom had committed direct, contributory, or vicarious infringement. The court held that Netcom's act of designing or implementing a system that automatically and uniformly creates temporary copies of all data sent through it is not unlike that of the owner of a copying machine who lets the public make copies with it. *Id.* at 1369. The court repudiated the approach taken by the *Frena* court and declined to sustain the plaintiff's claim that Netcom directly infringed on the plaintiff's rights, stating that "[w]here the infringing subscriber is clearly directly liable for the same act, it does not make sense to adopt a rule that could lead to the liability of countless parties whose role in the infringement is nothing more than setting up and operating a system that is necessary for the functioning of the Internet. Such a result is unnecessary as there is already a party directly liable for causing the copies to be made." *Id.* at 1372.

The plaintiffs' claim of contributory infringement against Netcom was then analyzed by the court. If the plaintiffs could prove that Netcom knew or should have known that plaintiffs' copyrights were being infringed, Netcom would be liable for contributory infringement "since its failure to simply cancel [the] infringing message and thereby stop an infringing copy from being distributed worldwide constitutes substantial participation in [the direct infringer's] public distribution of the message." *Id.* at 1374 (citation omitted). The court noted that the defendant had retained control over how its system

---

2. The former Church member posted messages on the BBS, with whom he had contracted; the BBS in turn arranged for access to the Internet through Netcom. *See id.* at 1375 n. 22, 1367–68.

was used, and "[t]hus, it is fair, assuming Netcom is able to take simple measures to prevent further damage to plaintiff's copyrighted works, to hold Netcom liable for contributory infringement where [it] has knowledge of [the] infringing postings yet continues to aid in the accomplishment of [the infringer's] purpose of publicly distributing the postings." *Id.* at 1375. Netcom was free to try to demonstrate at trial that its lack of knowledge of the infringement, even after receipt of notice, was reasonable in light of the nature of the purported infringement.

The court then considered the possibility that Netcom might be liable on a theory of vicarious infringement. Such a claim is premised on a showing that the defendant (1) has the right and ability to control the acts of the primary infringer; and (2) receives a direct financial benefit from the infringement. *See, e.g., Shapiro, Bernstein & Co. v. H.L. Green Co.,* 316 F.2d 304, 306 (2d Cir. 1963). Unlike contributory infringement, knowledge is not an element of the vicarious infringement claim. *See Religious Technology Center v. Netcom On-Line Communications Services, Inc.,* 907 F. Supp. at 1375. While there was a question as to whether Netcom had the right and ability to exercise contol over its subscribers, the plaintiff's vicarious infringement claim nonetheless was flawed because there was no evidence that the alleged infringement enhanced the value of Netcom's services to subscribers or attracted new subscribers. Therefore, there was no proof that Netcom received a direct financial benefit from the allegedly infringing activities of its users. *Id.* at 1376–77.

The court also held that the plaintiff had not adequately alleged direct infringement against the bulletin board service operator because there was no averment that he "took any affirmative steps to cause the copies to be made." *Id.* at 1381. Nor was the bulletin board service operator vicariously liable, as he was not alleged to have profited from allowing the end user to infringe the copyrights. *See id.* at 1382. The plaintiff's contributory claim against the bulletin board service operator was not dismissed, however, on the ground that he allegedly knew or should have known of the infringing actions. *See id.*

As these cases illustrate, courts have been grappling with the appropriate standards of liability for varied Internet participants. Bulletin board service operators and Internet access providers are among those who need frameworks to predictably assess their potential exposure for permitting content to be distributed and displayed, or for providing the facilities over which such content was conveyed. As well, predictability is needed to evaluate when such entities could, with impunity, remove allegedly infringing content. Congress recognized that, in light of technology's constant evolution, the law must adapt in order to make digital networks "safe places to disseminate and exploit copyrighted materials." S. Rep. No. 105-190, 105th Cong., 2d Sess. (1998). Legislation was enacted to provide "this protection and create[ ] the legal platform for launching the global digital on-line marketplace for copyrighted works." *Id.*

----

## 4.   The Digital Millennium Copyright Act

The Digital Millennium Copyright Act, Pub. L. No. 105-304, 112 Stat. 2860 (1998) (codified as amended at 17 U.S.C.A. §§ 512, 1201–05, 1301–22 (West. Supp. 2000) and 24 U.S.C.A. § 4001 (West Supp. 2000)) ("DMCA"), was signed into law by President Bill Clinton in October 1998. The legislation implements two 1996 World Intellectual Property Organization ("WIPO") treaties: the WIPO Copyright Treaty and the WIPO Performances and Phonograms Treaty.

The intricate statutory framework of the DMCA may, at first blush, seem inconsistent with the approach Congress took when it insulated service providers from liability for defamation. *See* 17 U.S.C.A. § 230 (West Supp. 2000); *see* discussion *supra* at 203. Enactment of section 230 of the Communications Decency Act was expressly premised on a policy of preserving the vibrant free market for interactive computer services, unfettered by Federal or State regulation. 17 U.S.C.A. § 230(b)(2). The DMCA's elaborate structure delineates the circumstances under which an Internet service provider may be held responsible for temporarily storing copies of third-party content on its system in order to facilitate display; for displaying infringing material posted on the provider's system by its subscribers; for using subscriber devices that circumvent technological mechanisms designed to prevent copying; and for removing copyright management information.

The DMCA actually is designed to comport with overall Congressional policy; by articulating the parameters by which service providers may operate without incurring liability for copyright infringement, the DMCA effectively preserves the market for the Internet, promotes its continued development, and encourages technological innovations. President Clinton expressly encouraged ratification of the Act to "provide clear international standards for intellectual property protection in the digital environment and protect U.S. copyrighted works, musical performances and sound recordings from international piracy.... Th[e Act was intended to] extend intellectual protection into the digital era while preserving fair use and limiting infringement liability for providers of basic communication services." Statement by President Bill Clinton at the Office of the Press Secretary (Oct. 12, 1998). The framework of the DMCA thus reflects the general legislative approach to copyright issues, which endeavors to stimulate the creation of works by protecting the author's rights in such work, balanced with promotion of the free flow of ideas.

The framework of the DMCA covers a panoply of protections for "on-line service providers" from charges of copyright liability. The DMCA defines a service provider as "an entity offering the transmission, routing, or providing of connections for digital online communications, between or among points specified by a user, of material of the user's choosing, without modification to the contents of the material as sent or received." 17 U.S.C.A. § 512(k)(1)(A) (West Supp. 2000).[3]

---

### a. On-Line Copyright Infringement Liability Limitation

The Act delineates methods by which service providers may limit their liability when allegedly infringing content is posted on the provider's system by a subscriber. Service providers generally are protected by the DMCA when they act as mere transitory conduits of the data. There are four specific types of on-line service provider activities covered by the DMCA safe harbors:

(1) transitory digital network communications (when the service provider acts as a conduit to transmit, route, or provide connections for material);

---

3. With respect to other limitations on liability, "service provider" more broadly refers to a provider of on-line services, of network access, or of the operator of such facilities. 17 U.S.C.A. § 512(k)(*l*)(B).

(2) caching (when the service provider temporarily stores material in order to more efficiently supply data);

(3) providing storage space on a system or network (when the service provider stores, at the direction of a user, material that resides on a provider's system); and

(4) providing information locator tools (when the service provider refers or links users to an Internet location that contains infringing material by using search engines, links, or other information location tools).

The DMCA also is designed to avoid having service providers choose between implementing procedures designed to reduce their liability on the one hand, and preserving the privacy of their subscribers on the other. Accordingly, the statute explicitly states that the on-line copyright infringement liability limitations do not require a service provider to monitor its service or access material in violation of any law in order to remain eligible for the safe harbor protections of the Act. *See* 17 U.S.C.A. § 512(m).

Although the DMCA does not require on-line service providers to affirmatively monitor infringements on their sites, 17 U.S.C.A. § 512(m)(1), the provider must adopt and reasonably implement a policy for terminating the accounts of repeat infringers, and it must communicate the policy to repeat infringers, 17 U.S.C.A. § 512(i)(1). In addition, the service provider must accommodate "standard technical measures," which are those used by copyright owners to identify or protect copyrighted works. Such measures have been developed pursuant to a broad consensus of copyright owners and service providers, and are openly available on reasonable, non-discriminatory terms at insubstantial cost. 17 U.S.C.A. § 512(i). To avail itself of the safe harbor provision, the service provider must designate an agent to receive notification of alleged infringements. 17 U.S.C.A. § 512(c)(2).

The DMCA provides other protections for on-line service providers who in good faith remove or disable access to allegedly infringing material, delineating procedures to re-post the material if requested by the copyright holder. 17 U.S.C.A. § 512(g). Service providers must take such action expeditiously once they have actual knowledge that the posted data or activity using the material is infringing, or become aware of "facts and circumstances from which the infringing character of the activity is apparent." 17 U.S.C.A. § 512(b)(2)(E); *see also* 17 U.S.C.A. §§ 512(c)(1)(c), (d)(3).

The safe harbors enunciated by the Act do not displace defenses available under other laws. 17 U.S.C.A. § 1201(c) (West Supp. 2000). Thus, the failure of a service provider to qualify for any of the limitations set forth in the statute does not necessarily render it liable for copyright infringement; the copyright owner must still demonstrate that the provider has infringed, and the provider may still avail itself of any applicable defenses. The Act also sets forth several exemptions relating to non-profit libraries and educational institutions; law enforcement, intelligence, and other governmental activities; reverse engineering; encryption research; security testing activities; and the protection of personal identifying information. 17 U.S.C.A. §§ 1201(d)–(i).[4]

---

4. In the event, however, that the service provider is not in compliance with the DMCA's safe harbor requirements, the copyright owner may pursue an infringement claim against the service provider. The copyright owner may request that the clerk of a federal district court issue a subpoena to a service provider for identification of an alleged infringer without having to first initiate suit. *See* 17 U.S.C.A. § 512(h).

Professor Alfred Yen cautions that the DMCA "ossifies and perpetuates ambiguities in existing law that encourage ISPs to indiscriminately remove material from the Internet." Alfred C. Yen, *Internet Service Provider Liability for Subscriber Copyright Infringement, Enterprise Liability, and the First Amendment*, 88 Georgetown L.J. at 1888.

Application of the on-line copyright liability limitations of the DMCA has occurred most conspicuously in the realm of music software:

# A & M RECORDS, INC., *et al.* v. NAPSTER, INC.
United States District Court, Northern District of California
No. C 99-05183 MHP, 2000 WL 573136, 54 U.S.P.Q.2d 1746
May 5, 2000

PATEL, Chief J.

On December 6, 1999, plaintiff record companies filed suit alleging contributory and vicarious federal copyright infringement and related state law violations by defendant Napster, Inc. ("Napster"). Now before this court is defendant's motion for summary adjudication of the applicability of a safe harbor provision of the Digital Millennium Copyright Act ("DMCA"), 17 U.S.C. section 512(a), to its business activities. Defendant argues that the entire Napster system falls within the safe harbor and, hence, that plaintiffs may not obtain monetary damages or injunctive relief, except as narrowly specified by subparagraph 512(j)(1)(B). In the alternative, Napster asks the court to find subsection 512(a) applicable to its role in downloading MP3 music files, as opposed to searching for or indexing such files. Having considered the parties' arguments and for the reasons set forth below, the court enters the following memorandum and order.

## BACKGROUND

Napster—a small Internet start-up based in San Mateo, California—makes its proprietary MusicShare software freely available for Internet users to download. Users who obtain Napster's software can then share MP3 music files with others logged-on to the Napster system. MP3 files, which reproduce nearly CD-quality sound in a compressed format, are available on a variety of websites either for a fee or free-of-charge. Napster allows users to exchange MP3 files stored on their own computer hard-drives directly, without payment, and boasts that it "takes the frustration out of locating servers with MP3 files."

Although the parties dispute the precise nature of the service Napster provides, they agree that using Napster typically involves the following basic steps: After downloading MusicShare software from the Napster website, a user can access the Napster system from her computer. The MusicShare software interacts with Napster's server-side software when the user logs on, automatically connecting her to one of some 150 servers that Napster operates. The MusicShare software reads a list of names of MP3 files that the user has elected to make available. This list is then added to a directory and index, on the Napster server, of MP3 files that users who are logged-on wish to share. If the user wants to locate a song, she enters its name or the name of the recording artist on the search page of the MusicShare program and clicks the "Find It" button. The Napster software then searches the current directory and generates a list of files responsive to the search request. To download a desired file, the user highlights it on the list and clicks the "Get Selected Song(s)" button. The user may also view a list of files that exist on another user's hard drive and select a file from that list. When the requesting user clicks on the name of a file, the Napster server communicates with the requesting user's and host user's MusicShare browser software to facilitate a connection between the two users and initiate the downloading of the file without any further action on either user's part.

According to Napster, when the requesting user clicks on the name of the desired MP3 file, the Napster server routes this request to the host user's browser. The host user's browser responds that it either can or cannot supply the file. If the host user can supply the file, the Napster server communicates the host's address and routing information to the requesting user's browser, allowing the requesting user to make a connection with the host and receive the desired MP3 file. The parties disagree about whether this process involves a hypertext link that the Napster server-side software provides. However, plaintiffs admit that the Napster server gets the necessary IP address information from the host user, enabling the requesting user to connect to the host. The MP3 file is actually transmitted over the Internet, but the steps necessary to make that connection could not take place without the Napster server.

The Napster system has other functions besides allowing users to search for, request, and download MP3 files. For example, a requesting user can play a downloaded song using the MusicShare software. Napster also hosts a chat room.

Napster has developed a policy that makes compliance with all copyright laws one of the "terms of use" of its service and warns users that:

> Napster will terminate the accounts of users who are repeat infringers of the copyrights, or other intellectual property rights, of others. In addition, Napster reserves the right to terminate the account of a user upon any single infringement of the rights of others in conjunction with use of the Napster service.

However, the parties disagree over when this policy was instituted and how effectively it bars infringers from using the Napster service. Napster claims that it had a copyright compliance policy as early as October 1999, but admits that it did not document or notify users of the existence of this policy until February 7, 2000....

## DISCUSSION

Section 512 of the DMCA addresses the liability of online service and Internet access providers for copyright infringements occurring online. Subsection 512(a) exempts qualifying service providers from monetary liability for direct, vicarious, and contributory infringement and limits injunctive relief to the degree specified in subparagraph 512(j)(1)(B). Interpretation of subsection 512(a), or indeed any of the section 512 safe harbors, appears to be an issue of first impression.[3]

Napster claims that its business activities fall within the safe harbor provided by subsection 512(a). This subsection limits liability "for infringement of copyright by

---

3. In *Universal City Studios, Inc. v. Reimerdes*, 82 F. Supp. 2d 211, 217 & n. 17 (S.D.N.Y. 2000), one defendant sought protection under subsection 512(c). Although the court noted in passing that the defendant offered no evidence that he was a service provider under subsection 512(c), it held that he could not invoke the safe harbor because plaintiffs claimed violations of 17 U.S.C. section 1201(a), which applies to circumvention products and technologies, rather than copyright infringement.

reason of the [service] provider's transmitting, routing, or providing connections for, material through a system or network controlled or operated by or for the service provider, or by reason of the intermediate and transient storage of that material in the course of such transmitting, routing, or providing connections," if five conditions are satisfied:

(1) the transmission of the material was initiated by or at the direction of a person other than the service provider;

(2) the transmission, routing, provision of connections, or storage is carried out through an automatic technical process without selection of the material by the service provider;

(3) the service provider does not select the recipients of the material except as an automatic response to the request of another person;

(4) no copy of the material made by the service provider in the course of such intermediate or transient storage is maintained on the system or network in a manner ordinarily accessible to anyone other than the anticipated recipients, and no such copy is maintained on the system or network in a manner ordinarily accessible to such anticipated recipients for a longer period than is reasonably necessary for the transmission, routing, or provision of connections; and

(5) the material is transmitted through the system or network without modification of its content.

17 U.S.C. § 512(a).

Citing the "definitions" subsection of the statute, Napster argues that it is a "service provider" for the purposes of the 512(a) safe harbor. See 17 U.S.C. § 512(k)(1)(A).[4] First, it claims to offer the "transmission, routing, or providing of connections for digital online communications" by enabling the connection of users' hard-drives and the transmission of MP3 files "directly from the Host hard drive and Napster browser through the Internet to the user's Napster browser and hard drive." Second, Napster states that users choose the online communication points and the MP3 files to be transmitted with no direction from Napster. Finally, the Napster system does not modify the content of the transferred files. Defendant contends that, because it meets the definition of "service provider," it need only satisfy the five remaining requirements of the safe harbor to prevail in its motion for summary adjudication.

Defendant then seeks to show compliance with these requirements by arguing: (1) a Napster user, and never Napster itself, initiates the transmission of MP3 files; (2) the transmission occurs through an automatic, technical process without any editorial input from Napster; (3) Napster does not choose the recipients of the MP3 files; (4) Napster does not make a copy of the material during transmission; and (5) the content of the material is not modified during transmission. Napster maintains that the 512(a)

---

4. Subparagraph 512(k)(1)(A) provides:

As used in subsection (a), the term "service provider" means an entity offering the transmission, routing, or providing of connections for digital online communications, between or among points specified by a user, of material of the user's choosing, without modification to the content of the material sent or received.

Subparagraph 512(k)(1)(B) states:

As used in this section, other than subsection (a), the term "service provider" means a provider of online services or network access, or the operator of facilities therefor, and includes an entity described in subparagraph (A).

safe harbor thus protects its core function—"transmitting, routing and providing connections for sharing of the files its users choose."

Plaintiffs disagree. They first argue that subsection 512(n) requires the court to analyze each of Napster's functions independently and that not all of these functions fall under the 512(a) safe harbor. In their view, Napster provides information location tools—such as a search engine, directory, index, and links—that are covered by the more stringent eligibility requirements of subsection 512(d), rather than subsection 512(a).

Plaintiffs also contend that Napster does not perform the function which the 512(a) safe harbor protects because the infringing material is not transmitted or routed through the Napster system, as required by subsection 512(a). They correctly note that the definition of "service provider" under subparagraph 512(k)(1)(A) is not identical to the prefatory language of subsection 512(a). The latter imposes the additional requirement that transmitting, routing, or providing connections must occur "through the system or network." Plaintiffs argue in the alternative that, if users' computers are part of the Napster system, copies of MP3 files are stored on the system longer than reasonably necessary for transmission, and thus subparagraph 512(a)(4) is not satisfied.

Finally, plaintiffs note that, under the general eligibility requirements established in subsection 512(i), a service provider must have adopted, reasonably implemented, and informed its users of a policy for terminating repeat infringers. Plaintiffs contend that Napster only adopted its copyright compliance policy after the onset of this litigation and even now does not discipline infringers in any meaningful way. Therefore, in plaintiffs' view, Napster fails to satisfy the DMCA's threshold eligibility requirements or show that the 512(a) safe harbor covers any of its functions.

## I. Independent Analysis of Functions

Subsection 512(n) of the DMCA states:

> Subsections (a), (b), (c), and (d) describe separate and distinct functions for purposes of applying this section. Whether a service provider qualifies for the limitation on liability in any one of those subsections shall be based solely on the criteria in that subsection and shall not affect a determination of whether that service provider qualifies for the limitations on liability under any other such subsections.

Citing subsection 512(n), plaintiffs argue that the 512(a) safe harbor does not offer blanket protection to Napster's entire system. Plaintiffs consider the focus of the litigation to be Napster's function as an information location tool—eligible for protection, if at all, under the more rigorous subsection 512(d). They contend that the system does not operate as a passive conduit within the meaning subsection 512(a). In this view, Napster's only possible safe harbor is subsection 512(d), which applies to service providers "referring or linking users to an online location containing infringing material or infringing activity, by using information location tools, including a directory, index, reference, pointer, or hypertext link...." Subsection 512(d) imposes more demanding eligibility requirements because it covers active assistance to users.

Defendant responds in two ways. First, it argues that subsection 512(a), rather than 512(d), applies because the information location tools it provides are incidental to its core function of automatically transmitting, routing, or providing connections for the MP3 files users select. In the alternative, defendant maintains that, even if the court decides to analyze the information location functions under 512(d), it should hold that the 512(a) safe harbor protects other aspects of the Napster service.

Napster undisputedly performs some information location functions. The Napster server stores a transient list of the files that each user currently logged-on to that server wants to share. This data is maintained until the user logs off, but the structure of the index itself continues to exist. If a user wants to find a particular song or recording artist, she enters a search, and Napster looks for the search terms in the index. Napster's Vice President of Engineering, admitted in his deposition that, at least in this context, Napster functions as a free information location tool. [He stated] that "Napster operates exactly like a search engine or information location tool to the user"[.] Napster software also has a "hot list" function that allows users to search for other users' log-in names and receive notification when users with whom they might want to communicate have connected to the service. In short, the parties agree on the existence of a searchable directory and index, and Napster representatives have used the phrase "information location tool," which appears in the heading for subsection 512(d), to characterize some Napster functions.

There the agreement ends. According to Napster, the information location tools upon which plaintiffs base their argument are incidental to the system's core function of transmitting MP3 music files, and for this reason, the court should apply subsection 512(a). Napster also disputes the contention that it organizes files or provides links to other Internet sites in the same manner as a search engine like Yahoo!. Consequently, it deems subsection 512(d) inapplicable to its activities. *Cf.* H.R. Rep. No. 105-551(II), 105th Cong., 2d Sess. (1998), 1998 WL 414916, at *147 (using Yahoo! as an example of an information location tool covered by 512(d)). Napster contrasts its operations, which proceed automatically after initial stimuli from users, with search engines like Yahoo! that depend upon the "human judgment and editorial discretion" of the service provider's staff. *Id.*

Napster's final and most compelling argument regarding subsection 512(d) is that the DMCA safe harbors are not mutually exclusive. According to subsection 512(n), a service provider could enjoy the 512(a) safe harbor even if its information location tools were also protected by (or failed to satisfy) subsection 512(d). *See* 17 U.S.C. § 512(n) ("Whether a service provider qualifies for the limitation on liability in any one of those subsections... shall not affect a determination of whether that service provider qualifies for the limitations on liability under any other such subsections.") Similarly, finding some aspects of the system outside the scope of subsection 512(a) would not preclude a ruling that other aspects do meet 512(a) criteria.

Because the parties dispute material issues regarding the operation of Napster's index, directory, and search engine, the court declines to hold that these functions are peripheral to the alleged infringement, or that they should not be analyzed separately under subsection 512(d). Indeed, despite its contention that its search engine and indexing functions are incidental to the provision of connections and transmission of MP3 files, Napster has advertised the ease with which its users can locate "millions of songs" online without "wading through page after page of unknown artists." Such statements by Napster to promote its service are tantamount to an admission that its search and indexing functions are essential to its marketability. Some of these essential functions—including but not limited to the search engine and index-should be analyzed under subsection 512(d).

However, the potential applicability of subsection 512(d) does not completely foreclose use of the 512(a) safe harbor as an affirmative defense. *See* 17 U.S.C. § 512(n). The court will now turn to Napster's eligibility for protection under subsection 512(a). It notes at the outset, though, that a ruling that subsection 512(a) applies to a given function would not mean that the DMCA affords the service provider blanket protection.

II. Subsection 512(a)

Plaintiffs' principal argument against application of the 512(a) safe harbor is that Napster does not perform the passive conduit function eligible for protection under this subsection. As defendant correctly notes, the words "conduit" or "passive conduit" appear nowhere in 512(a), but are found only in the legislative history and summaries of the DMCA. The court must look first to the plain language of the statute, "construing the provisions of the entire law, including its object and policy, to ascertain the intent of Congress." *United States v. Hockings*, 129 F.3d 1069, 1071 (9th Cir. 1997) (quoting *Northwest Forest Resource Council v. Glickman*, 82 F.3d 825, 830 (9th Cir. 1996)) (internal quotation marks omitted). If the statute is unclear, however, the court may rely on the legislative history. *See Hockings*, 129 F.3d at 1071. The language of subsection 512(a) makes the safe harbor applicable, as a threshold matter, to service providers "transmitting, routing or providing connections for, material through a system or network controlled or operated by or for the service provider...." 17 U.S.C. § 512(a). According to plaintiffs, the use of the word "conduit" in the legislative history explains the meaning of "through a system."

Napster has expressly denied that the transmission of MP3 files ever passes through its servers. Indeed, Kessler declared that "files reside on the computers of Napster users, and are transmitted directly between those computers." MP3 files are transmitted "from the Host user's hard drive and Napster browser, through the Internet to the recipient's Napster browser and hard drive." The Internet cannot be considered "a system or network controlled or operated by or for the service provider," however. 17 U.S.C. § 512(a). To get around this problem, Napster avers (and plaintiffs seem willing to concede) that "Napster's servers and Napster's MusicShare browsers on its users' computers are all part of Napster's overall system." Defendant narrowly defines its system to include the browsers on users' computers. In contrast, plaintiffs argue that either (1) the system does not include the browsers, or (2) it includes not only the browsers, but also the users' computers themselves.

Even assuming that the system includes the browser on each user's computer, the MP3 files are not transmitted "through" the system within the meaning of subsection 512(a). Napster emphasizes the passivity of its role—stating that "[a]ll files transfer directly from the computer of one Napster user through the Internet to the computer of the requesting user." It admits that the transmission bypasses the Napster server. This means that, even if each user's Napster browser is part of the system, the transmission goes from one part of the system to another, or between parts of the system, but not "through" the system. The court finds that subsection 512(a) does not protect the transmission of MP3 files.

The prefatory language of subsection 512(a) is disjunctive, however. The subsection applies to "infringement of copyright by reason of the provider's transmitting, routing, or providing connections through a system or network controlled or operated by or for the service provider." 17 U.S.C. § 512(a). The court's finding that transmission does not occur "through" the system or network does not foreclose the possibility that subsection 512(a) applies to "routing" or "providing connections." Rather, each of these functions must be analyzed independently.

Napster contends that providing connections between users' addresses "constitutes the value of the system to the users and the public." This connection cannot be established without the provision of the host's address to the Napster browser software installed on the requesting user's computer. The central Napster server delivers the host's address. While plaintiffs contend that the infringing material is not transmitted through the Napster system, they provide no evidence to rebut the assertion that Napster supplies the requesting user's computer with information necessary to facilitate a connection with the host.

Nevertheless, the court finds that Napster does not provide connections "through" its system. Although the Napster server conveys address information to establish a connection between the requesting and host users, the connection itself occurs through the Internet. The legislative history of section 512 demonstrates that Congress intended the 512(a) safe harbor to apply only to activities "in which a service provider plays the role of a 'conduit' for the communications of others." H.R. Rep. No. 105-551(II), 105th Cong., 2d Sess. (1998), 1998 WL 414916, at *130. Drawing inferences in the light most favorable to the non-moving party, this court cannot say that Napster serves as a conduit for the connection itself, as opposed to the address information that makes the connection possible. Napster enables or facilitates the initiation of connections, but these connections do not pass through the system within the meaning of subsection 512(a).

Neither party has adequately briefed the meaning of "routing" in subsection 512(a), nor does the legislative history shed light on this issue. Defendant tries to make "routing" and "providing connections" appear synonymous—stating, for example, that "the central Napster server routes the transmission by providing the Host's address to the Napster browser that is installed on and in use by Userl's computer." However, the court doubts that Congress would have used the terms "routing" and "providing connections" disjunctively if they had the same meaning. It is clear from both parties' submissions that the route of the allegedly infringing material goes through the Internet from the host to the requesting user, not through the Napster server. The court holds that routing does not occur through the Napster system.

Because Napster does not transmit, route, or provide connections through its system, it has failed to demonstrate that it qualifies for the 512(a) safe harbor. The court thus declines to grant summary adjudication in its favor.

III. Copyright Compliance Policy

Even if the court had determined that Napster meets the criteria outlined in subsection 512(a), subsection 512(i) imposes additional requirements on eligibility for any DMCA safe harbor. This provision states:

> The limitations established by this section shall apply to a service provider only if the service provider —
> (A) has adopted and reasonably implemented, and informs subscribers and account holders of the service provider's system or network of, a policy that provides for the termination in appropriate circumstances of subscribers and account holders of the service provider's system or network who are repeat infringers; and
> (B) accommodates and does not interfere with standard technical measures.

17 U.S.C. § 512(i).

Plaintiffs challenge Napster's compliance with these threshold eligibility requirements on two grounds. First, they point to evidence...that Napster did not adopt a written policy of which its users had notice until on or around February 7, 2000—two months after the filing of this lawsuit.... [The deponent testified] that, although Napster had a copyright compliance policy as early as October 1999, he is not aware that this policy was reflected in any document, or communicated to any user. Congress did not intend to require a service provider to "investigate possible infringements, monitor its service or make difficult judgments as to whether conduct is or is not infringing," but the notice requirement is designed to insure that flagrant or repeat infringers "know that there is a realistic threat of losing [their] access." H.R. Rep. 105-551(II), 1998 WL 414916, at *154.

Napster attempts to refute plaintiffs' argument by noting that subsection 512(i) does not specify when the copyright compliance policy must be in place. Although this characterization of subsection 512(i) is facially accurate, it defies the logic of making formal notification to users or subscribers a prerequisite to exemption from monetary liability. The fact that Napster developed and notified its users of a formal policy after the onset of this action should not moot plaintiffs' claim to monetary relief for past harms. Without further documentation, defendant's argument that it has satisfied subsection 512(i) is merely conclusory and does not support summary adjudication in its favor.

Summary adjudication is also inappropriate because Napster has not shown that it reasonably implemented a policy for terminating repeat infringers. *See* 17 U.S.C. § 512(i)(A) (requiring "reasonable" implementation of such a policy). If Napster is formally notified of infringing activity, it blocks the infringer's password so she cannot log on to the Napster service using that password. Napster does not block the IP addresses of infringing users, however, and the parties dispute whether it would be feasible or effective to do so.

Plaintiffs aver that Napster wilfully turns a blind eye to the identity of its users—that is, their real names and physical addresses—because their anonymity allows Napster to disclaim responsibility for copyright infringement. Hence, plaintiffs contend, "infringers may readily reapply to the Napster system to recommence their infringing downloading and uploading of MP3 music files." Plaintiffs' expert, computer security researcher Daniel Farmer, declared that he conducted tests in which he easily deleted all traces of his former Napster identity, convincing Napster that "it had never seen me or my computer before." Farmer also cast doubt on Napster's contention that blocking IP addresses is not a reasonable means of terminating infringers. He noted that Napster bans the IP addresses of users who runs "bots"[8] on the service.

Hence, plaintiffs raise genuine issues of material fact about whether Napster has reasonably implemented a policy of terminating repeat infringers. They have produced evidence that Napster's copyright compliance policy is neither timely nor reasonable within the meaning of subparagraph 512(i)(A).

## CONCLUSION

This court has determined above that Napster does not meet the requirements of subsection 512(a) because it does not transmit, route, or provide connections for allegedly infringing material through its system. The court also finds summary adjudication inappropriate due to the existence of genuine issues of material fact about Napster's compliance with subparagraph 512(i)(A), which a service provider must satisfy to enjoy the protection of any section 512 safe harbor. Defendant's motion for summary adjudication is DENIED.

---

8. Farmer informed that court that "A 'bot' is a robot, or program, that performs actions continuously, in a sort of manic or robotic fashion."

In late July 2000, Judge Patel granted a preliminary injunction to enjoin Napster's on-line music service from permitting the exchange of copyrighted music owned by major music labels. Judge Patel concluded that Napster users were engaged in "wholesale infringing." *See* Transcript of Judge Marilyn Hall Patel's ruling, CNET News (Aug. 1, 2000) <http://news.cnet.com/news/0-1005-201-2426706-0.htm>. Napster has announced that it plans to appeal the decision. *See, e.g.*, Matt Richtel, *In Victory for Recording Industry, Judge Bars Online Music Sharing*, N.Y. Times (July 27, 2000) at A1; *Napster Ruling Shifts Balance of Web Power Back to Music Industry*, Wall. St. J. (July 28, 2000) at A1. The Ninth Circuit granted emergency motions to stay the preliminary injunction and to expedite the appeal. *A&M Records, Inc. v. Napster, Inc.*, No. 00-16401, No. 00-16403, 2000 U.S. App. LEXIS 18688 (9th Cir. July 28, 2000).

## b. Circumvention of Technological Protection Measures

Other sections of the DMCA generally offer protection to copyright holders who use technological measures to prevent copying of their protected works. The DMCA prohibits the making or selling of devices or services that are used to circumvent the unauthorized access or copying of copyrighted works. The Act includes several exemptions, but generally proscribes circumvention devices or services that: (1) are primarily designed to circumvent a technological measure to protect a copyrighted work; (2) have only limited commercially significant use other than to circumvent those protections; or (3) are marketed for use in circumventing those protections. 17 U.S.C.A. § 1201 (West Supp. 2000).

The DMCA distinguishes between technological measures that prevent unauthorized *access* to a copyrighted work, and measures that prevent unauthorized *copying* of a copyrighted work. The Act specifies prohibitions for the making or selling of devices or services that can circumvent either technological measure, but prohibits circumvention only of measures that prevent unauthorized access. The rationale underlying the distinction relates to the fair use doctrine. *See* discussion *infra* at 425. "Th[e] distinction was employed to assure that the public will have the continued ability to make fair use of copyrighted works. Because copying of a work may be a fair use under appropriate circumstances, section 1201 does not prohibit the act of circumventing a technological measure that prevents copying. By contrast, since the fair use doctrine is not a defense to the act of gaining unauthorized access to a work, the act of circumventing a technological measure in order to gain access is prohibited." U.S. Copyright Office, Summary, *The Digital Millennium Copyright Act of 1998* at 4 (Dec. 1998) (on file with the Library of Congress <http://www.loc.gov/copyright/legislation/dmca.pdf>).

When motion picture companies release movies on digital versatile disks ("DVDs"), the digital format of the disks may increase the risk of unauthorized reproduction. If the companies use an encryption-based security and authentication system to reduce such risks, is a system designed to decrypt the protections and copy the DVDs' content a violation of the DMCA? What sort of evidence might persuade a court that the technology used to override the companies' security mechanisms was utilized to engage in reverse engineering studies, to conduct encryption research, or to perform security testing? The U.S. District Court for the Southern District of New York granted the motion by eight movie studios for a preliminary injunction barring the defendants from posting the circumvention devices. *Universal City Studios, Inc. v. Reimerdes*, 82 F. Supp. 2d

211 (S.D.N.Y. 2000). Subsequent motions to expand the preliminary injunction to linking and to vacate it were consolidated with a trial on the merits, *see Universal City Studios, Inc. v. Reimerdes*, No. 00 Civ. 0277, 2000 U.S. Dist. LEXIS 11696 at *2 n. 2
(S.D.N.Y. Aug. 17, 2000), and on August 17, 2000, the court issued its decision:

---

# UNIVERSAL CITY STUDIOS, INC, *et al.* v.
## Shawn C. REIMERDES, *et al.*

United States District Court, Southern District of New York
No. 00 Civ. 0277 (LAK), 55 U.S.P.Q.2d 1873, 2000 U.S. Dist. LEXIS 11696
February 2, 2000

OPINION BY: Lewis A. Kaplan

Plaintiffs, eight major United States motion picture studios, distribute many of their
copyrighted motion pictures for home use on digital versatile disks ("DVDs"), which
contain copies of the motion pictures in digital form. They protect those motion pictures
from copying by using an encryption system called CSS. CSS-protected motion pictures
on DVDs may be viewed only on players and computer drives equipped with licensed
technology that permits the devices to decrypt and play—but not to copy—the films.

Late last year, computer hackers devised a computer program called DeCSS that circumvents the CSS protection system and allows CSS-protected motion pictures to be
copied and played on devices that lack the licensed decryption technology. Defendants
quickly posted DeCSS on their Internet web site, thus making it readily available to
much of the world. Plaintiffs promptly brought this action under the Digital Millennium Copyright Act (the "DMCA") to enjoin defendants from posting DeCSS and to
prevent them from electronically "linking" their site to others that post DeCSS. Defendants responded with what they termed "electronic civil disobedience"—increasing
their efforts to link their web site to a large number of others that continue to make
DeCSS available.

Defendants contend that their actions do not violate the DMCA....This is the
Court's decision after trial, and the decision may be summarized in a nutshell.

Defendants argue first that the DMCA should not be construed to reach their conduct,
principally because the DMCA, so applied, could prevent those who wish to gain access to
technologically protected copyrighted works in order to make fair—that is, non-infringing—use of them from doing so. They argue that those who would make fair use of technologically protected copyrighted works need means, such as DeCSS, of circumventing
access control measures not for piracy, but to make lawful use of those works.

Technological access control measures have the capacity to prevent fair uses of copyrighted works as well as foul. Hence, there is a potential tension between the use of such
access control measures and fair use. Defendants are not the first to recognize that possibility. As the DMCA made its way through the legislative process, Congress was preoccu-
pied with precisely this issue. Proponents of strong restrictions on circumvention of access control measures argued that they were essential if copyright holders were to make
their works available in digital form because digital works otherwise could be pirated too
easily. Opponents contended that strong anticircumvention measures would extend the
copyright monopoly inappropriately and prevent many fair uses of copyrighted material.

Congress struck a balance. The compromise it reached, depending upon future technological and commercial developments, may or may not prove ideal. But the solution it enacted is clear. The potential tension to which defendants point does not absolve them of liability under the statute. There is no serious question that defendants' posting of DeCSS violates the DMCA....

Digital files may be stored on several different kinds of storage media, some of which are readily transportable. Perhaps the most familiar of these are so called floppy disks or "floppies," which now are 3 1/2 inch magnetic disks upon which digital files may be recorded. For present purposes, however, we are concerned principally with two more recent developments, CD-ROMs and digital versatile disks, or DVDs.

A CD-ROM is a five-inch wide optical disk capable of storing approximately 650 MB of data. To read the data on a CD-ROM, a computer must have a CD-ROM drive.

DVDs are five-inch wide disks capable of storing more than 4.7 GB of data. In the application relevant here, they are used to hold full-length motion pictures in digital form. They are the latest technology for private home viewing of recorded motion pictures and result in drastically improved audio and visual clarity and quality of motion pictures shown on televisions or computer screens.

CSS, or Content Scramble System, is an access control and copy prevention system for DVDs developed by the motion picture companies, including plaintiffs. It is an encryption-based system that requires the use of appropriately configured hardware such as a DVD player or a computer DVD drive to decrypt, unscramble and play back, but not copy, motion pictures on DVDs. The technology necessary to configure DVD players and drives to play CSS-protected DVDs has been licensed to hundreds of manufacturers in the United States and around the world.

DeCSS is a software utility, or computer program, that enables users to break the CSS copy protection system and hence to view DVDs on unlicenced players and make digital copies of DVD movies. The quality of motion pictures decrypted by DeCSS is virtually identical to that of encrypted movies on DVD.

DivX is a compression program available for download over the Internet. It compresses video files in order to minimize required storage space, often to facilitate transfer over the Internet or other networks.

Plaintiffs are eight major motion picture studios. Each is in the business of producing and distributing copyrighted material including motion pictures. Each distributes, either directly or through affiliates, copyrighted motion pictures on DVDs. Plaintiffs produce and distribute a large majority of the motion pictures on DVDs on the market today.

Defendant Eric Corley is viewed as a leader of the computer hacker community and goes by the name Emmanuel Goldstein, after the leader of the underground in George Orwell's classic, *1984*. He and his company, defendant 2600 Enterprises, Inc., together publish a magazine called *2600: The Hacker Quarterly*, which Corley founded in 1984, and which is something of a bible to the hacker community. The name "2600" was derived from the fact that hackers in the 1960's found that the transmission of a 2600 hertz tone over a long distance trunk connection gained access to "operator mode" and allowed the user to explore aspects of the telephone system that were not otherwise accessible. Mr. Corley chose the name because he regarded it as a "mystical thing," commemorating something that he evidently admired. Not surprisingly, *2600: The Hacker Quarterly* has included articles on such topics as how to steal an Internet domain name, access other people's e-mail, intercept cellular phone calls, and break into the computer systems at Costco stores and Federal Express. One issue contains a guide to the federal criminal justice system for readers charged with computer hacking. In addition, defendants operate a web site located at <http://www.2600.com> ("2600.com"), which is managed primarily by Mr. Corley and has been in existence since 1995.

Prior to January 2000, when this action was commenced, defendants posted the source and object code for DeCSS on the 2600.com web site, from which they could be downloaded easily. At that time, 2600.com contained also a list of links to other web sites purporting to post DeCSS....

In the early 1990's... the major movie studios began to explore distribution to the home market in digital format, which offered substantially higher audio and visual quality and greater longevity than video cassette tapes. This technology, which in 1995 became what is known today as DVD, brought with it a new problem—increased risk of piracy by virtue of the fact that digital files, unlike the material on video cassettes, can be copied without degradation from generation to generation. In consequence, the movie studios became concerned as the product neared market with the threat of DVD piracy.... In 1996, Matsushita Electric Industrial Co. ("MEI") and Toshiba Corp. presented—and the studios adopted—CSS.

CSS involves encrypting, according to an encryption algorithm, the digital sound and graphics files on a DVD that together constitute a motion picture. A CSS-protected DVD can be decrypted by an appropriate decryption algorithm that employs a series of keys stored on the DVD and the DVD player. In consequence, only players and drives containing the appropriate keys are able to decrypt DVD files and thereby play movies stored on DVDs.

As the motion picture companies did not themselves develop CSS and, in any case, are not in the business of making DVD players and drives, the technology for making compliant devices, i.e., devices with CSS keys, had to be licensed to consumer electronics manufacturers. In order to ensure that the decryption technology did not become generally available and that compliant devices could not be used to copy as well as merely to play CSS-protected movies, the technology is licensed subject to strict security requirements. Moreover, manufacturers may not, consistent with their licenses, make equipment that would supply digital output that could be used in copying protected DVDs. Licenses to manufacture compliant devices are granted on a royalty-free basis subject only to an administrative fee. At the time of trial, licenses had been issued to numerous hardware and software manufacturers, including two companies that plan to release DVD players for computers running the Linux operating system.

With CSS in place, the studios introduced DVDs on the consumer market in early 1997. All or most of the motion pictures released on DVD were, and continue to be, encrypted with CSS technology. Over 4,000 motion pictures now have been released in DVD format in the United States, and movies are being issued on DVD at the rate of over 40 new titles per month in addition to rereleases of classic films. Currently, more than five million households in the United States own DVD players, and players are projected to be in ten percent of United States homes by the end of 2000....

In late September 1999, Jon Johansen, a Norwegian subject then fifteen years of age, and two individuals he "met" under pseudonyms over the Internet, reverse engineered a licensed DVD player and discovered the CSS encryption algorithm and keys. They used this information to create DeCSS, a program capable of decrypting or "ripping" encrypted DVDs, thereby allowing playback on non-compliant computers as well as the copying of decrypted files to computer hard drives. Mr. Johansen then posted the executable code on his personal Internet web site and informed members of an Internet mailing list that he had done so. Neither Mr. Johansen nor his collaborators obtained a license from the DVD CCA....

In November 1999, defendants' web site began to offer DeCSS for download. It established also a list of links to several web sites that purportedly "mirrored" or offered DeCSS for download. The links on defendants' mirror list fall into one of three categories. By clicking the mouse on one of these links, the user may be brought to a page on the linked-to site on which there appears a further link to the DeCSS software. If the user then clicks on the DeCSS link, download of the software begins. This page may or may not contain content other than the DeCSS link. Alternatively, the user may be brought to a page on the linked-to site that does not itself purport to link to DeCSS, but that links, either directly or via a series of other pages on the site, to another page on the site on which there appears a link to the DeCSS software. Finally, the user may be brought directly to the DeCSS link on the linked-to site such that download of DeCSS begins immediately without further user intervention.... At least some of the links currently on defendants' mirror list lead the user to copies of DeCSS that, when downloaded and executed, successfully decrypt a motion picture on a CSS-encrypted DVD....

The net of all this is reasonably plain. DeCSS is a free, effective and fast means of decrypting plaintiffs' DVDs and copying them to computer hard drives. DivX, which is available over the Internet for nothing, with the investment of some time and effort, permits compression of the decrypted files to sizes that readily fit on a writeable CD-ROM. Copies of such CD-ROMs can be produced very cheaply and distributed as easily as other pirated intellectual property. While not everyone with Internet access now will find it convenient to send or receive DivX'd copies of pirated motion pictures over the Internet, the availability of high speed network connections in many businesses and institutions, and their growing availability in homes, make Internet and other network traffic in pirated copies a growing threat.

These circumstances have two major implications for plaintiffs. First, the availability of DeCSS on the Internet effectively has compromised plaintiffs' system of copyright protection for DVDs, requiring them either to tolerate increased piracy or to expend resources to develop and implement a replacement system unless the availability of DeCSS is terminated. It is analogous to the publication of a bank vault combination in a national newspaper. Even if no one uses the combination to open the vault, its mere publication has the effect of defeating the bank's security system, forcing the bank to reprogram the lock. Development and implementation of a new DVD copy protection system, however, is far more difficult and costly than reprogramming a combination lock and may carry with it the added problem of rendering the existing installed base of compliant DVD players obsolete.

Second, the application of DeCSS to copy and distribute motion pictures on DVD, both on CD-ROMs and via the Internet, threatens to reduce the studios' revenue from the sale and rental of DVDs. It threatens also to impede new, potentially lucrative initiatives for the distribution of motion pictures in digital form, such as video-on-demand via the Internet.

In consequence, plaintiffs already have been gravely injured. As the pressure for and competition to supply more and more users with faster and faster network connections grows, the injury will multiply.

*The Digital Millennium Copyright Act*

...The DMCA contains two principal anticircumvention provisions. The first, Section 1201(a)(1), governs "the act of circumventing a technological protection measure put in place by a copyright owner to control access to a copyrighted work," an act described by Congress as "the electronic equivalent of breaking into a locked room in order to obtain a copy of a book." The second, Section 1201(a)(2), which is the focus of this case, "supplements the prohibition against the act of circumvention in paragraph (a)(1) with prohibitions on creating and making available certain technologies...developed or advertised to defeat technological protections against unauthorized access to a work." As defendants are accused here only of posting and linking to other sites posting DeCSS, and not of using it themselves to bypass plaintiffs' access controls, it is principally the second of the anticircumvention provisions that is at issue in this case....

In this case, defendants concededly offered and provided and, absent a court order, would continue to offer and provide DeCSS to the public by making it available for download on the 2600.com web site. DeCSS, a computer program, unquestionably is "technology" within the meaning of the statute. "Circumvent a technological measure" is defined to mean descrambling a scrambled work, decrypting an encrypted work, or "otherwise to avoid, bypass, remove, deactivate, or impair a technological measure, without the authority of the copyright owner," so DeCSS clearly is a means of circumventing a technological access control measure. In consequence, if CSS otherwise falls within paragraphs (A), (B) or (C) of Section 1201(a)(2), and if none of the statutory exceptions applies to their actions, defendants have violated and, unless enjoined, will continue to violate the DMCA by posting DeCSS.

During pretrial proceedings and at trial, defendants attacked plaintiffs' Section 1201(a)(2)(A) claim, arguing that CSS, which is based on a 40-bit encryption key, is a weak cipher that does not "effectively control" access to plaintiffs' copyrighted works. They reasoned from this premise that CSS is not protected under this branch of the statute at all. Their post-trial memorandum appears to have abandoned this argument. In any case, however, the contention is indefensible as a matter of law.

First, the statute expressly provides that "a technological measure 'effectively controls access to a work' if the measure, in the ordinary course of its operation, requires the application of information or a process or a treatment, with the authority of the copyright owner, to gain access to a work." One cannot gain access to a CSS-protected work on a DVD without application of the three keys that are required by the software. One cannot lawfully gain access to the keys except by entering into a license with the DVD CCA under authority granted by the copyright owners or by purchasing a DVD player or drive containing the keys pursuant to such a license. In consequence, under the express terms of the statute, CSS "effectively controls access" to copyrighted DVD movies. It does so, within the meaning of the statute, whether or not it is a strong means of protection....

The House Judiciary Committee section-by-section analysis of the House bill, which in this respect was enacted into law, makes clear that a technological measure "effectively controls access" to a copyrighted work if its *function* is to control access....Further, the House Commerce Committee made clear that measures based on encryption or scrambling "effectively control" access to copyrighted works, although it is well known that what may be encrypted or scrambled often may be decrypted or unscrambled. As CSS, in the ordinary course of its operation—that is, when DeCSS or some other decryption program is not employed—"actually works" to prevent access to the protected work, it "effectively controls access" within the contemplation of the statute.

Finally, the interpretation of the phrase "effectively controls access" offered by defendants at trial—*viz.*, that the use of the word "effectively" means that the statute protects only successful or efficacious technological means of controlling access—would gut the statute if it were adopted. If a technological means of access control is circumvented, it is, in common parlance, ineffective. Yet defendants' construction, if adopted, would limit the application of the statute to access control measures that thwart circumvention, but withhold protection for those measures that can be circumvented. In other words, defendants would have the Court construe the statute to offer protection where none is needed but to withhold protection precisely where protection is essential. The Court declines to do so. Accordingly, the Court holds that CSS effectively controls access to plaintiffs' copyrighted works.

As CSS effectively controls access to plaintiffs' copyrighted works, the only remaining question under Section 1201(a)(2)(A) is whether DeCSS was designed primarily to circumvent CSS. The answer is perfectly obvious. By the admission of both Jon Johansen, the programmer who principally wrote DeCSS, and defendant Corley, DeCSS was created solely for the purpose of decrypting CSS—that is all it does. Hence, absent satisfaction of a statutory exception, defendants clearly violated Section 1201(a)(2)(A) by posting DeCSS to their web site.

As the only purpose or use of DeCSS is to circumvent CSS, the foregoing is sufficient to establish a *prima facie* violation of Section 1201(a)(2)(B) as well.

Perhaps the centerpiece of defendants' statutory position is the contention that DeCSS was not created for the purpose of pirating copyrighted motion pictures. Rather, they argue, it was written to further the development of a DVD player that would run under the Linux operating system, as there allegedly were no Linux compatible players on the market at the time. The argument plays itself out in various ways as different elements of the DMCA come into focus. But it perhaps is useful to address the point at its most general level in order to place the preceding discussion in its fullest context.

As noted, Section 1201(a) of the DMCA contains two distinct prohibitions. Section 1201(a)(1), the so-called basic provision, "aims against those who engage in unauthorized circumvention of technological measures... [It] focuses directly on wrongful conduct, rather than on those who facilitate wrongful conduct...." Section 1201(a)(2), the anti-trafficking provision at issue in this case, on the other hand, separately bans offering or providing technology that may be used to circumvent technological means of controlling access to copyrighted works. If the means in question meets any of the three prongs of the standard set out in Section 1201(a)(2)(A), (B), or (C), it may not be offered or disseminated.

As the earlier discussion demonstrates, the question whether the development of a Linux DVD player motivated those who wrote DeCSS is immaterial to the question whether the defendants now before the Court violated the anti-trafficking provision of the DMCA. The inescapable facts are that (1) CSS is a technological means that effectively controls access to plaintiffs' copyrighted works, (2) the one and only function of DeCSS is to circumvent CSS, and (3) defendants offered and provided DeCSS by posting it on their web site. Whether defendants did so in order to infringe, or to permit or encourage others to infringe, copyrighted works in violation of other provisions of the Copyright Act simply does not matter for purposes of Section 1201(a)(2). The offering or provision of the program is the prohibited conduct—and it is prohibited irrespective of why the program was written, except to whatever extent motive may be germane to determining whether their conduct falls within one of the statutory exceptions....

*Conclusion*

In the final analysis, the dispute between these parties is simply put if not necessarily simply resolved.

Plaintiffs have invested huge sums over the years in producing motion pictures in reliance upon a legal framework that, through the law of copyright, has ensured that they will have the exclusive right to copy and distribute those motion pictures for economic gain. They contend that the advent of new technology should not alter this long established structure.

Defendants, on the other hand, are adherents of a movement that believes that information should be available without charge to anyone clever enough to break into the computer systems or data storage media in which it is located. Less radically, they have raised a legitimate concern about the possible impact on traditional fair use of access control measures in the digital era.

Each side is entitled to its views. In our society, however, clashes of competing interests like this are resolved by Congress. For now, at least, Congress has resolved this clash in the DMCA and in plaintiffs' favor. Given the peculiar characteristics of computer programs for circumventing encryption and other access control measures, the DMCA as applied to posting and linking here does not contravene the First Amendment. Accordingly, plaintiffs are entitled to appropriate injunctive and declaratory relief.

----

# REALNETWORKS, INC. v. STREAMBOX, INC.

United States District Court, Western District of Washington
No. 2:99CV02070, 2000 U.S. Dist. LEXIS 1889
January 18, 2000

Pechman, J.

Plaintiff RealNetworks, Inc. ("RealNetworks")...claims that Defendant Streambox has violated provisions of the Digital Millennium Copyright Act ("DMCA"), 17 U.S.C. § 1201, *et seq.*, by distributing and marketing products known as the Streambox VCR and the Ripper. RealNetworks also contends that another Streambox product, known as the Ferret, is unlawfully designed to permit consumers to make unauthorized modifications to a software program on which RealNetworks holds the copyright.

On December 21, 1999, RealNetworks applied for a temporary restraining order to bar Streambox from manufacturing, distributing, selling, or marketing the VCR, the Ripper, and the Ferret. On December 23, 1999, Chief Judge Coughenour of this Court entered a Temporary Restraining Order, finding RealNetworks was likely to succeed on the merits of its claims and that it was suffering irreparable harm from Streambox's conduct. The Court also ordered Streambox to show cause as to why the restraints contained in the Temporary Restraining Order should not be continued as a preliminary injunction.

...RealNetworks offers products that enable consumers to access audio and video content over the Internet through a process known as "streaming." When an audio or video clip is "streamed" to a consumer, no trace of the clip is left on the consumer's computer, unless the content owner has permitted the consumer to download the file.

Streaming is to be contrasted with "downloading," a process by which a complete copy of an audio or video clip is delivered to and stored on a consumer's computer. Once a consumer has downloaded a file, he or she can access the file at will, and can generally redistribute copies of that file to others.

In the digital era, the difference between streaming and downloading is of critical importance. A downloaded copy of a digital audio or video file is essentially indistinguishable from the original, and such copies can often be created at the touch of a button. A user who obtains a digital copy may supplant the market for the original by distributing copies of his or her own. To guard against the unauthorized copying and redistribution of their content, many copyright owners do not make their content available for downloading, and instead distribute the content using streaming technology in a manner that does not permit downloading....

[The plaintiff's product technologically precluded, at the option of the content owner, the downloading of streamed material. This protection was known as the "Secret Handshake" program, which consisted of an authentication sequence that allowed the streaming of media files; and another security measure called a "Copy Switch," that contained the content owner's preference as to whether the stream could be copied by end-users. RealNetworks proffered declarations from copyright owners, indicating that they relied on RealNetworks' security measures to protect their copyrighted works on the Internet.

The] Streambox VCR circumvents both the access control and copy protection measures....

The Streambox VCR poses a threat to RealNetworks' relationships with existing and potential customers who wish to secure their content for transmission over the Internet and must decide whether to purchase and use RealNetworks' technology....

Streambox also manufactures and distributes a product called the Streambox Ripper....

The Ripper operates on files which are already resident on the hard disk of the user's computer. The Ripper permits users to convert files that they have already created or obtained (presumably through legitimate means) from one format to another....

In conjunction with the Secret Handshake, the Copy Switch is a "technological measure" that effectively protects the right of a copyright owner to control the unauthorized copying of its work. *See* 17 U.S.C. § 1201(b)(2)(B) (measure "effectively protects" right of copyright holder if it "prevents, restricts or otherwise limits the exercise of a right of a copyright owner"); 17 U.S.C. § 106(a) (granting copyright holder exclusive right to make copies of its work). To access a RealMedia file distributed by a RealServer, a user must use a RealPlayer. The RealPlayer reads the Copy Switch in the file. If the Copy Switch in the file is turned off, the RealPlayer will not permit the user to record a copy as the file is streamed. Thus, the Copy Switch may restrict others from exercising a copyright holder's exclusive right to copy its work.

Under the DMCA, a product or part thereof "circumvents" protections afforded a technological measure by "avoiding, bypassing, removing, deactivating or otherwise impairing" the operation of that technological measure. 17 U.S.C. §§ 1201(b)(2)(A), 1201(a)(2)(A). Under that definition, at least a part of the Streambox VCR circumvents the technological measures RealNetworks affords to copyright owners. Where a RealMedia file is stored on a RealServer, the VCR "bypasses" the Secret Handshake to gain access to the file. The VCR then circumvents the Copy Switch, enabling a user to make a copy of a file that the copyright owner has sought to protect.

Given the circumvention capabilities of the Streambox VCR, Streambox violates the DMCA if the product or a part thereof: (i) is primarily designed to serve this function; (ii) has only limited commercially significant purposes beyond the circumvention; or (iii) is marketed as a means of circumvention. 17 U.S.C. §§ 1201(a)(2)(A–C), 1201(b)(b)(A–C). These three tests are disjunctive. *Id.* A product that meets only one of the three independent bases for liability is still prohibited. Here, the VCR meets at least the first two.

The Streambox VCR meets the first test for liability under the DMCA because at least a part of the Streambox VCR is primarily, if not exclusively, designed to circumvent the access control and copy protection measures that RealNetworks affords to copyright owners. 17 U.S.C. §§ 1201(a)(2)(A), 1201(b)(c)(A).

The second basis for liability is met because portion of the VCR that circumvents the Secret Handshake so as to avoid the Copy Switch has no significant commercial purpose other than to enable users to access and record protected content. 17 U.S.C. § 1201(a)(2)(B), 1201(b)(d)(B). There does not appear to be any other commercial value that this capability affords.

Streambox's primary defense to Plaintiff's DMCA claims is that the VCR has legitimate uses. In particular, Streambox claims that the VCR allows consumers to make "fair use" copies of RealMedia files, notwithstanding the access control and copy protection measures that a copyright owner may have placed on that file.

The portions of the VCR that circumvent the secret handshake and copy switch permit consumers to obtain and redistribute perfect digital copies of audio and video files that copyright owners have made clear they do not want copied. For this reason, Streambox's VCR is not entitled to the same "fair use" protections the Supreme Court afforded to video cassette recorders used for "time-shifting" in *Sony Corp. v. Universal City Studios, Inc.,* 464 U.S. 417 (1984).... [In that case, there was a finding that substantial numbers of copyright holders who broadcast their works either had authorized or would not objected to having their works time-shifted by private viewers. In the instant case, copyright owners have specifically chosen to prevent the copying enabled by the Streambox VCR by putting their content on RealServers and leaving the Copy Switch off.]

Moreover, the Sony decision did not involve interpretation of the DMCA. Under the DMCA, product developers do not have the right to distribute products that circumvent technological measures that prevent consumers from gaining unauthorized access to or making unauthorized copies of works protected by the Copyright Act. Instead, Congress specifically prohibited the distribution of the tools by which such circumvention could be accomplished. The portion of the Streambox VCR that circumvents the technological measures that prevent unauthorized access to and duplication of audio and video content therefore runs afoul of the DMCA....

As set forth above, the Streambox VCR falls within the prohibitions of sections 1201(a)(2) and 1201(b)(1). Accordingly, Section 1201(c)(3) affords Streambox no defense.

...RealNetworks has demonstrated that it would likely suffer irreparable harm if the Streambox VCR is distributed. The VCR circumvents RealNetworks' security measures, and will necessarily undermine the confidence that RealNetworks' existing and potential customers have in those measures. It would not be possible to determine how many of RealNetworks' existing or potential customers declined to use the company's products because of the perceived security problems created by the VCR's ability to circumvent RealNetworks' security measures.

An injunction against the VCR also would serve the public interest because the VCR's ability to circumvent RealNetworks' security measures would likely reduce the willingness of copyright owners to make their audio and video works accessible to the public over the Internet....

## CONCLUSION

Consistent with the findings of fact and conclusions of law above, the Court hereby ORDERS that:

During the pendency of this action, Defendant Streambox, Inc. and its officers, agents, servants, employees and attorneys, and those persons in active concert and participation with Streambox, Inc. who receive actual notice of this Preliminary Injunction, are restrained and enjoined from manufacturing, importing, licensing, offering to the public, or offering for sale:

a) versions of the Streambox VCR or similar products that circumvent or attempt to circumvent RealNetworks' technological security measures, and from participating or assisting in any such activity;

b) versions of the Streambox Ferret or similar products that modify RealNetworks' RealPlayer program, including its interface, its source code, or its object code, and from participating or assisting in any such activity....

---

### c. Copyright Management Information Provisions

The DMCA also prohibits the removal of "copyright management information" and the dissemination of copies of works knowing that the copyright management information has been removed or altered. 17 U.S.C.A. § 1202 (West Supp. 2000). Copyright management information includes the work, writer, director, terms and conditions of use, and any other information that the Register of Copyrights may prescribe by regulation (although information concerning users of works is excluded from the definition). Statutory exemptions also are provided for, among others, law enforcement and intelligence. 17 U.S.C.A. § 1202(d). Under what circumstances might the operator of a site that displays reduced images of protected content, where the copyright management information is available through links, have reasonable grounds to know that infringements would ensue?

---

# Leslie A. KELLY, *et al.* v. ARRIBA SOFT CORP., *et al.*

United States District Court, Central District of California
No. SACV99560GLT [JW], 77 F. Supp. 2d 1116
December 15, 1999

Taylor, District Judge.

[For the background of this case, *see infra* at 432.]

...Enacted on October 28, 1998, the Digital Millennium Copyright Act (DMCA) implements two earlier World Intellectual Property Organization treaties. Section 1202 of the DMCA governs "integrity of copyright management information."[9] Section 1202(a) prohibits falsification of copyright management information with the intent to aid copyright infringement. Section 1202(b) prohibits, unless authorized, several forms of knowing removal or alteration of copyright management information. Section 1203 creates a federal civil action for violations of these provisions.

Plaintiff argues Defendant violated § 1202(b) by displaying thumbnails of Plaintiff's images without displaying the corresponding copyright management information consisting of standard copyright notices in the surrounding text. Because these notices do not appear in the images themselves, the Ditto crawler did not include them when it indexed the images. As a result, the images appeared in Defendant's index without the copyright management information, and any users retrieving Plaintiff's images while using Defendant's Web site would not see the copyright management information.

Section 1202(b)(1) does not apply to this case. Based on the language and structure of the statute, the Court holds this provision applies only to the removal of copyright management information on a plaintiff's product or original work. Moreover, even if § 1202(b)(1) applied, Plaintiff has not offered any evidence showing Defendant's actions were intentional, rather than merely an unintended side effect of the Ditto crawler's operation.

Here, where the issue is the absence of copyright management information from copies of Plaintiff's works, the applicable provision is § 1202(b)(3). To show a violation of that section, Plaintiff must show Defendant makes available to its users the thumbnails and full-size images, which were copies of Plaintiff's work separated from their copyright management information, even though it knows or should know this will lead to infringement of Plaintiff's copyrights. There is no dispute the Ditto crawler removed Plaintiff's images from the context of Plaintiff's Web sites where their copyright management information was located, and converted them to thumbnails in Defendant's index. There is also no dispute the Arriba Vista search engine allowed full-size images to be viewed without their copyright management information.

Defendant's users could obtain a full-sized version of a thumbnailed image by clicking on the thumbnail. A user who did this was given the name of the Web site from which Defendant obtained the image, where any associated copyright management information would be available, and an opportunity to link there. Users were also informed on Defendant's Web site that use restrictions and copyright limitations may apply to images retrieved by Defendant's search engine.[13]

---

9. "Copyright management information" is defined, in relevant part, as:
[A]ny of the following information conveyed in connection with copies... of a work... or displays of a work, including in digital form...:
  (1) The title and other information identifying the work, including the information set forth on a notice of copyright.
  (2) The name of, and other identifying information about, the author of a work.
  (3) The name of, and other identifying information about, the copyright owner of the work, including the information set forth in a notice of copyright.
17 U.S.C. § 1202(c).

13. Plaintiff argues Defendant's warnings are insufficient because they do not appear with the thumbnail images on the search result pages produced by the search engine. The Arriba Vista Web site only offered a warning if users clicked on a link to its "Copyright" page. This warning may arguably have been placed in the wrong place to deter some potential copyright infringers. But this does not necessarily mean Defendant "knew" or "should have known" for the purposes of a DMCA violation, especially since Plaintiff offers no evidence of any actual copyright infringement about which Defendant "should have known."

Based on all of this, the Court finds Defendant did not have "reasonable grounds to know" it would cause its users to infringe Plaintiff's copyrights. Defendant warns its users about the possibility of use restrictions on the images in its index, and instructs them to check with the originating Web sites before copying and using those images, even in reduced thumbnail form.

Plaintiff's images are vulnerable to copyright infringement because they are displayed on Web sites. Plaintiff has not shown users of Defendant's site were any more likely to infringe his copyrights, any of these users did infringe, or Defendant should reasonably have expected infringement.

There is no genuine issue of material fact requiring a trial on Plaintiff's DMCA claims, and summary adjudication is appropriate. The Court finds there was no violation of DMCA § 1202. Defendant's motion is GRANTED and Plaintiff's motion is DENIED on the DMCA claim.

---

# 4. The Fair Use Defense

Copyright law is designed "[t]o promote the Progress of Science and useful Arts." Const. art. I, § 8. Readily reconcilable with this policy is the notion that certain copying is permissible. De minimis use of protected material is not actionable, for example. The inquiry turns on how much material is used; as Judge Learned Hand declared, "no plagiarist can excuse the wrong by showing how much of his work he did not pirate." *Sheldon v. Metro-Goldwyn Pictures Corp.*, 81 F.2d 49, 56 (2d Cir. 1936).

In addition to de minimis uses, "fair uses" are sanctioned. The fair use defense is codified in the Copyright Act, 17 U.S.C.A. § 107 (West 1995), in order to balance the need to protect the author's interest in his work with the public's interest in the free flow of ideas. Thus, limited amounts of a protected work may be used without the copyright holder's permission for certain purposes, such as criticism, comment, news reporting, teaching, scholarship, and research.

There is no bright-line test for determining when a use qualifies as "fair." The task, "like the doctrine it recognizes, calls for case-by-case analysis." *Campbell v. Acuff-Rose Music, Inc.*, 510 U.S. 569, 577 (1994) (citations omitted). Courts are statutorily directed to consider four factors in evaluating the use:

(1) the purpose and character of the use, including whether such use is of a commercial nature or is for nonprofit educational purposes;
(2) the nature of the copyrighted work;
(3) the amount and substantiality of the portion used in relation to the copyrighted work as a whole; and
(4) the effect of the use upon the potential market for or value of the copyrighted work.

17 U.S.C.A. § 107.

All four factors "are to be explored, and the results weighed together, in light of the purposes of copyright." *Campbell v. Acuff-Rose Music, Inc.*, 510 U.S. at 578. Nor are the factors necessarily the exclusive determinants of the fair use inquiry; they are designed to provide guidance to courts as they undertake fact-specific inquiries in each case.

The statute expressly states that the fact that a work is unpublished does not alone bar a finding of fair use. *See* 17 U.S.C.A. § 107. Further, no particular type of use is itself dispositive; the statutory preamble cites such purposes as criticism, comment, news reporting, teaching, scholarship, and research as illustrations.

In addition to the rationales for upholding injunctive relief in copyright infringement claims discussed previously, *see* discussion *supra* at 391, courts have rejected First Amendment challenges to injunctions in such cases on the ground that free speech concerns "are protected by and coextensive with the fair use doctrine." *Nihon Keizai Shimbun, Inc. v. Comline Buiness Data, Inc.*, 166 F.3d 65, 74 (2d Cir. 1999) (citations omitted); *see also New Era Publications International v. Henry Holt and Co., Inc.*, 873 F.2d 576, 584 (2d Cir. 1989) ("[o]ur observation that the fair use doctrine encompasses all claims of first amendment in the copyright field, *Roy Export Co. Establishment v. Columbia Broadcasting System, Inc.*, 672 F.2d 1095–100 (2d Cir.), *cert. denied*, 459 U.S. 826, 103 S.Ct. 60, 74 L.Ed.2d 63 (1982), never has been repudiated.") "An author's expression of an idea, as distinguished from the idea itself, is not considered subject to the public's 'right to know.'" *Id.* (citation omitted).

One expert on the fair use defense has noted that "[c]opyright in the United States was not born from the 'interstices' of censorship but, to the contrary, out of fervently held beliefs that freedom of expression could flourish only when it was not subject to government control and that the system of private ownership of property represented the best possible mechanism for providing the citizenry with the security necessary to accomplish that lofty goal." William F. Patry, *The Fair Use Privilege in Copyright Law* (2d ed. 1995) at 574–75. James Madison, author of both the First Amendment and the Constitution's general grant of power from which copyright protections are derived, viewed free speech principles and proprietary interests as in coincident service of the public good. *See id.* at 575 & n. 15. As a former Register of Copyrights observed:

> The basic purpose of copyright is the public interest, to make sure that the wellsprings of creation do not dry up through lack of incentive, and to provide an alternative to the evils of an authorship dependent upon private or public patronage. As the founders of this country were wise enough to see, the most important elements of any civilization include its independent creators—its authors, composers and artists—who create as a matter of personal initiative and spontaneous expression rather than as a result of patronage or subsidy. A strong, practical copyright is the only assurance we have that this creative activity will continue.

Copyright Law Revisions: Hearings Before the Subcomm. On Patents, Trademarks, and Copyrights of the Comm. on the Judiciary on § 1006, 89th Cong., 1st Sess. 65 (1965) (statement of Abraham Kaminstein).

Thus the copyright holder has a property interest in preventing others from reaping the fruits of his labor, but not in preventing others from building upon his advances. The fair use defense presupposes that the process of creation is often an incremental one, where advances that build on past developments often are more common than the formation of radical new concepts. *See Lewis Galoob Toys, Inc. v. Nintendo of America, Inc.*, 964 F.2d 965 (9th Cir. 1992). When the infringement is small relative to the new work created, the fair user is profiting largely from his own creative efforts rather than free-riding on another's work. The defense is premised on the notion that an absolute prohibition on all copying would stifle the free flow of ideas without serving any legitimate interest of the copyright holder.

Fair use principles have been applied to digital communications. The U.S. District Court for the Northern District of California, for instance, observed that:

> The temporary copying involved in browsing is only necessary because humans cannot otherwise perceive digital information. It is the functional equivalent of reading, which does not implicate the copyright laws.... Absent a commercial or profit-depriving use, digital browsing is probably a fair use.... [U]sers should hardly worry about a finding of direct infringement; it seems highly unlikely from a practical matter that a copyright owner could prove such infringement or would want to sue such an individual.

*Religious Technology Center v. Netcom On-line Communication Services, Inc.*, 907 F. Supp. 1361, 1378 n. 25 (N.D. Cal. 1995). Note that the succinct passage encompasses multiple rationales for the court's conclusion: temporary copying in the course of browsing the Web is regarded as a functional necessity, potential claimants are deemed likely to have little incentive to proceed against numerous users, and the available evidence that could be marshaled to support such a claim is questionable. Which of these theories provides the most persuasive analytical support for the conclusion? Is this copying the functional equivalent of reading, as the court suggests? Does the ability to download the Web page document affect the analogy? Perhaps the court's conclusion also takes into account prevailing Internet practices, which may include implicit assent to such temporary copying during browsing by virtue of having permitted unrestricted access.

---

# LOS ANGELES TIMES, *et al.* v. FREE REPUBLIC, *et al.*

United States District Court, Central District of California
Case No. CV 98-7840 MMM (AJWx), 2000 U.S. Dist. LEXIS 5669
March 31, 2000

OPINION BY: MARGARET M. MORROW

Plaintiffs Los Angeles Times and The Washington Post Company publish newspapers in print and online versions. Defendant Free Republic is a "bulletin board" website whose members use the site to post news articles to which they add remarks or commentary. Other visitors to the site then read the articles and add their comments. For the most part, Free Republic members post the entire text of articles in which they are interested; among these are verbatim copies of articles from the Los Angeles Times and Washington Post websites. Plaintiffs' complaint alleges that the unauthorized copying and posting of the articles on the Free Republic site constitutes copyright infringement.

Defendants...assert that the copying of news articles onto their website is protected by the fair use doctrine....

Plaintiffs publish the *Los Angeles Times* and *The Washington Post* in print and online at "http://www.latimes.com" and "http://www.washingtonpost.com." Their respective websites contain the current edition of the newspaper, which can be viewed free of charge, and archived articles that users must pay to view. The *Times* charges $1.50 to view an archived article, while the *Post* charges from $1.50 to $2.95 depending on the time of day. In addition to income generated in this fashion, the websites also produce advertising and licensing revenue for the papers. Because advertising is sold "CPM" (cost per thousand), the revenue generated from this source depends on the volume of traffic the sites experience during a given period. The parties dispute the extent to which being able to access archived articles at a different site for free affects plaintiffs' ability to advertise, license, and sell the archived articles....

Plaintiffs contend that "perfect copies" of news articles appearing in their publications and on their websites are posted to the Free Republic site. Defendants maintain that the posted articles are merely "purported copies" of the original, and assert that one can verify that a posting is an exact copy only by visiting plaintiffs' websites. Defendants nonetheless apparently concede that *some* of the postings are verbatim copies of original articles....

The parties...dispute whether the posting of plaintiffs' news articles to the Free Republic site causes an increase or decrease in traffic at the Times and Post websites, whether it diminishes the available market for sale of plaintiffs' news articles, and whether it has a negative impact on plaintiffs' ability to license the works. Defendants assert that plaintiffs' websites actually gain viewers because people go to them after visiting the Free Republic site. Plaintiffs maintain they lose traffic when Internet users read an article posted on freerepublic.com rather than visiting the *Times* or *Post* websites. They further assert that their ability to sell copies of the archived articles and their ability to license the works is diminished by having copies made freely available on the Free Republic site.

...Because the parties address the availability of a *defense* to copyright infringement, their motions assume for present purposes that such a claim can be proved. The court expresses no opinion as to whether this is so, given that the "copying" of news articles at issue in this case is to a large extent copying by third-party users of the Free Republic site. The court also makes no determination as to whether plaintiffs have in any manner consented to the copying of their articles....

There is little transformative about copying the entirety or large portions of a work verbatim....Defendants' first argument—that the copies of plaintiffs' articles found on the Free Republic site do not substitute for those on plaintiffs' sites—focuses on readers' ability to access and review specific articles in which they are interested. Defendants contend that using the Free Republic site to read current articles would be impractical since there is a delay between the time information is posted to the site and the time it is indexed by third-party search engines. Additionally, they assert that the imprecision of search language makes it difficult to locate archived articles at the site. These arguments overlook the fact that the Free Republic site has its own search engine that apparently has immediate search capability.

Even were this not true, the articles posted on the Free Republic site ultimately serve the same purpose as "that [for which] one would normally seek to obtain the original—to have it available...for ready reference if and when [website visitors adding comments] need to look at it." *American Geophysical Union v. Texaco, Inc.*, 60 F.3d 913, 918 (2d Cir. 1995) (the court held that the first fair use factor weighed against a defendant that encouraged its employees to make unauthorized photocopies of articles in scientific and medical journals and keep them in their offices for ready reference).

Defendants' web page acknowledges this. It states, *inter alia*, that the Free Republic site is a place where visitors "can often find breaking news and up to the minute updates." Indeed, it is clear from the content of the representative pages submitted by defendants that visitors can read copies of plaintiffs' current and archived articles at the Free Republic site. For those who visit the site regularly, therefore, the articles posted there serve as substitutes for the originals found on plaintiffs' websites or in their newspapers.

Defendants next argue that their use of plaintiffs' works is transformative because registered Free Republic users add comments and criticism concerning the articles following a posting. Copying portions of a copyrighted work for the purpose of criticism or commentary is often considered fair use....

Since the first posting of an article to the Free Republic site often contains little or no commentary, it does not significantly transform plaintiffs' work....

Additionally, even where copying serves the "criticism, comment and news reporting" purposes highlighted in § 107, its extent cannot exceed what is necessary to the purpose....

Here, it seems clear that the primary purpose of the postings to the Free Republic site is to facilitate discussion, criticism and comment by registered visitors.... Defendants' assertion that links expire after a period of time is presumably a reference to the fact that articles are available on plaintiffs' websites free of charge only for a certain number of days. Thereafter, there is a charge for viewing and/or printing them. That this is so does not make linking plaintiffs' websites to the Free Republic site "impractical." It merely requires that Free Republic visitors pay a fee for viewing plaintiffs' articles just as other members of the public do. Similarly, defendants' suggestion that articles are posted to the Free Republic site long after they are published is not supported by the representative postings they have submitted. These reflect that the vast majority of comments are posted the same day the articles appear or within one to three days afterwards. Finally, defendants' assertion that unsophisticated Internet users would be confused by links is unpersuasive. Linking is familiar to most Internet users, even those who are new to the web....

The fact that linking the text of an article as it appears on plaintiffs' websites to the Free Republic site, or summarizing the article's text, is not as easy or convenient for Free Republic users as full text posting does not render the practice a fair use....

Defendants have not met their burden of demonstrating that verbatim copying of all or a substantial portion of plaintiffs' articles is necessary to achieve their critical purpose. They argue that the purpose of full text posting is to enable Free Republic users to criticize the manner in which the media covers current events. The statement or purpose found on the website, however, is somewhat different. There, defendants state that visitors to the Free Republic site "are encouraged to comment on the news of the day... and... to contribute whatever information they may have to help others better understand a particular story." In fact, a review of the representative articles submitted by defendants reveals that visitors' commentary focuses much more on the news of the day than it does on the manner in which the media reports that news. This is significant, since the extent of copying that might be necessary to comment on the nature of the media's coverage of a news event is arguably greater than the amount needed to facilitate comment on the event itself. Commentary on news events requires only recitation of the underlying facts, not verbatim repetition of another's creative expression of those facts in a news article. So too, the fact that a particular media outlet published a given story, or approached that story from a particular angle can be communicated to a large degree without posting a full text copy of the report. For this reason, the court concludes that verbatim posting of plaintiffs' articles is "more than is necessary" to further defendants' critical purpose. *See Castle Rock Entertainment* [*Inc. v. Carol Publishing Group, Inc.,* 150 F.3d 132, 144 (2d Cir. 1998)]. *See also Hustler Magazine, Inc. v. Moral Majority, Inc.,* 796 F.2d 1148, 1153 (9th Cir. 1986) (examining whether defendant copied "more than was necessary" in responding to a parody)....

[D]efendants' operation possesses many characteristics of a non-profit entity. It does not market or sell a product, and does not generate revenue in the traditional sense....

Here, while the Free Republic operation has commercial aspects, its overall character is more properly viewed as non-commercial.

Additionally, the Free Republic site provides a public service by fostering debate and discussion regarding the issues of the day. This too is a factor that should be taken into account in assessing the character of defendants' use of plaintiffs' copyrighted material....

Defendants do not generate revenue or profits from posting plaintiffs' articles on the Free Republic website. At most, they derive indirect economic benefit by enhancing the website's cachet, increasing registrations, and hence increasing donations and other forms of support. Coupled with the fact that Free Republic has many of the attributes of a non-profit organization, this indirect benefit argues against a finding that the use is strictly commercial. Rather, it is more appropriate to conclude that, while defendants do not necessarily "exploit" the articles for commercial gain, their posting to the Free Republic site allows defendants and other visitors to avoid paying the "customary price" charged for the works. *See Harper & Row* [*Publishers, Inc. v. Nation Enterprises,* 471 U.S. 539, 562 (1985)]....

Here, the court has found that defendants' copying of plaintiffs' articles is minimally, if at all, transformative. The comments of the individual who posts an article generally add little by way of comment or criticism to its substance. The extent of the copying is more than is necessary to foster the critical purpose it is designed to serve. Because the copying is verbatim, encompasses large numbers of articles, and occurs on an almost daily basis, the evidence supports a finding that defendants (and visitors to the Free Republic page) engage in extensive, systematic copying of plaintiffs' works.

Weighed against the essentially non-transformative nature of defendants' use is the fact that they do not directly derive revenue or profit from the posting of plaintiffs' articles, and the fact that their operation of the Free Republic website has many characteristics of a non-profit venture. So too, their use of plaintiffs' articles appears to be intended more for public benefit than for private commercial gain.

Since the "central purpose" of the inquiry on the first fair use factor is to determine "whether the new work merely 'supersede[s]' the objects' of the original creation,... or instead adds something new" (*Campbell* [*v. Acuff-Rose Music, Inc.,* 510 U.S. 569, 579 (1994)], the court finds that the non-transformative character of the copying in this case tips the scale in plaintiffs' favor, and outweighs the non-profit/public benefit nature of the purpose for which the copying is performed. This is particularly true since the posting of plaintiffs' articles to the Free Republic site amounts to "systematic...multiplying [of] the available number of copies" of the articles, "thereby serving the same purpose" for which licenses are sold or archive charges imposed. *See American Geophysical, supra,* 60 F.3d at 924. The first fair use factor thus favors plaintiffs....

[Second,] while plaintiffs' news articles certainly contain expressive elements, they are predominantly factual. Consequently, defendants' fair use claim is stronger than it would be had the works been purely fictional. *See Sony* [*Corporation of America v. Universal City Studios,* 464 U.S. 417, 455 n. 40 (1984)]("Copying a news broadcast may have a stronger claim to fair use than copying a motion picture"). The court concludes that the second factor weighs in favor of a finding a fair use of the news articles by defendants in this case....

[Third, the] fact that exact copies of plaintiffs' article are posted to the Free Republic site weighs strongly against a finding of fair use in this case. *See American Geophysical, supra,* 60 F.3d at 926 (defendant's copying of entire copyrighted articles militated against a finding of fair use and led the court to conclude that the third factor weighed in plaintiffs' favor); *Hustler, supra,* 796 F.2d at 1155 ("although wholesale copying does not preclude fair use *per se,*" reproducing an entire parody was the type of wholesale copying that "militated against a finding of fair use"); *Supermarket of Homes, Inc. v. San Fernando Valley Board of Realtors,* 786 F.2d 1400, 1409 (9th Cir. 1986) ("generally, no more of a work may be taken than is necessary to make the accompanying comment understandable"); *Television Digest, supra,* 841 F. Supp. at 10 (because an entire copyrighted work was used, the court concluded that the third factor weighed against a finding of fair use); *Nimmer, supra,* § 13.05[A][3] ("whatever the use, generally, it may not constitute a fair use if the entire work is reproduced")....

[D]efendants have not offered a persuasive argument that full-text copying is essential to the critical purpose of the Free Republic site. Contrasted with the purpose and character of the use, the wholesale copying of plaintiffs' articles weighs against a finding of fair use....

[With respect to the fourth factor,] the undisputed evidence shows that the Free Republic website has approximately 20,000 registered users, receives as many as 100,000 hits per day, and attracts between 25 and 50 million page views each month. The evidence also shows that visitors to the site are able to read full text copies of articles from plaintiffs' newspapers and archives without purchasing the papers, visiting plaintiffs' websites or paying the fee plaintiffs charge for retrieving an article from their archives. While defendants argue that the Free Republic site is a "poor substitute" for locating plaintiffs' articles on their websites, the court has found that for those individuals who visit the site, the articles posted to freerepublic.com do substitute for the original works. Given the number of registered visitors, hits and page views Free Republic attracts, the court cannot accept defendants' assertion that the site has only a de minimis effect on plaintiffs' ability to control the market for the copyrighted works....

[D]efendants' argument here—that the Free Republic site is small in comparison to the sites operated by plaintiffs, is not known to the general public, and thus could not divert a substantial amount of business from plaintiffs. As the copyright holders, however, plaintiffs have the "right to control" access to the articles, and defendants' activities affect a market plaintiffs currently seek to exploit....

Here, plaintiffs have shown that they are attempting to exploit the market for viewing their articles online, for selling copies of archived articles, and for licensing others to display or sell the articles. Defendants' use "substitutes" for the originals, and has the potential of lessening the frequency with which individuals visit plaintiffs' websites, of diminishing the market for the sale of archived articles, and decreasing the interest in licensing the articles. *See Hustler, supra,* 796 F.2d at 1155–56 (if the copying "fulfill[s] 'the demand for the original' works and 'diminish[es] or prejudice[s]' their potential sale," this justifies a finding that the fourth fair use factor favors the copyright holder); *Wainwright Securities, supra,* 558 F.2d at 96 (defendant's abstracts filled the demand for plaintiff's financial reports)....

Defendants also contend that plaintiffs actually benefit from having their articles posted verbatim on the Free Republic site. While they argue that plaintiffs' sites receive "literally tens of thousands, if not hundreds of thousands of hits per month" as a result of referrals from the Free Republic site, this overstates their expert's quantification of the number of referral hits. In his declaration, Richard Stout states that the *Los Angeles Times'* website receives approximately 20,000 hits per month from users who visit the Free Republic site before accessing the *Times'* site. Stout estimates that these referral hits generate approximately $1,000 in revenue for the paper each month. Defendants argue that this information regarding referral hits demonstrates that plaintiffs' advertising revenue is not diminished because of a reduction in the number of hits to their sites. Stout's declaration, however, does not address how many hits are *diverted* from plaintiffs' websites as a consequence of the posting of articles to the Free Republic site, and this is the pertinent inquiry in terms of potential market harm.

Defendants assert the evidence regarding referral hits demonstrates that Free Republic is creating a demand for plaintiffs' works. Even if this is the case, it does not mandate a conclusion that the fourth fair use factor favors defendants. Courts have routinely rejected the argument that a use is fair because it increases demand for the plaintiff's copyrighted work....

In short, plaintiffs have demonstrated that they are attempting to exploit the market for viewing their articles online, for selling copies of archived articles, and for licensing others to display or sell the articles. They have demonstrated that the availability of verbatim copies of the articles at the Free Republic site has the potential to interfere with these markets, particularly if it becomes a widespread practice....

In sum, three of the four fair use factors weigh in plaintiffs' favor. Moreover, the factor that favors defendants — the nature of the copyrighted work — does not provide strong support for a fair use finding, since defendants copied both the factual *and* the expressive elements of plaintiffs' news articles. Conversely, the amount and substantiality of the copying and the lack of any significant transformation of the articles weigh heavily in favor of plaintiffs on this issue. The court thus finds that defendants may not assert a fair use defense to plaintiffs' copyright infringement claim....

## CONCLUSION

For the foregoing reasons, plaintiffs' motion for summary adjudication with respect to fair use is granted, and defendants' motion is denied.

---

## Leslie A. KELLY, *et al.* v. ARRIBA SOFT CORP., *et al.*

United States District Court, Central District of California
No. SACV99560GLT [JW], 77 F. Supp. 2d 1116
December 15, 1999

Taylor, District Judge.

On apparent first impression, the Court holds the use by an Internet "visual search engine" of others' copyrighted images is a prima facie copyright violation, but it may be justified under the "fair use" doctrine. The Court finds that, under the particular circumstances of this case, the "fair use" doctrine applies....

### I. BACKGROUND

Defendant Ditto (formerly known as Arriba) operates a "visual search engine" on the Internet. Like other Internet search engines, it allows a user to obtain a list of related Web content in response to a search query entered by the user. Unlike other Internet search engines, Defendant's retrieves images instead of descriptive text. It produces a list of reduced, "thumbnail" pictures related to the user's query.

During the period when most of the relevant events in this case occurred, Defendant's visual search engine was known as the Arriba Vista Image Searcher. By "clicking" on the desired thumbnail, an Arriba Vista user could view the "image attributes" window displaying the full-size version of the image, a description of its dimensions, and an address for the Web site where it originated.[1] By clicking on the address, the user could link to the originating Web site for the image.

Ditto's search engine (in both of its versions) works by maintaining an indexed database of approximately two million thumbnail images. These thumbnails are obtained through the operation of Ditto's "crawler," a computer program that travels the Web in search of images to be converted into thumbnails and added to the index. Ditto's employees conduct a final screening to rank the most relevant thumbnails and eliminate inappropriate images.

Plaintiff Kelly is a photographer specializing in photographs of California gold rush country and related to the works of Laura Ingalls Wilder. He does not sell the photographs independently, but his photographs have appeared in several books. Plaintiff also maintains two Web sites, one of which (www.goldrush1849.com) provides a "virtual tour" of California's gold rush country and promotes Plaintiff's book on the subject, and the other (www.showmethegold.com) markets corporate retreats in California's gold rush country.

In January 1999, around thirty five of Plaintiff's images were indexed by the Ditto crawler and put in Defendant's image database. As a result, these images were made available in thumbnail form to users of Defendant's visual search engine.

After being notified of Plaintiff's objections, Ditto removed the images from its database, though due to various technical problems some of the images reappeared a few times. Meanwhile Plaintiff, having sent Defendant a notice of copyright infringement in January, filed this action in April....

## II. DISCUSSION...

In order to show copyright infringement, Plaintiff must show ownership of a valid copyright and invasion of one of the exclusive rights of copyright holders. 17 U.S.C. § 106. Defendant does not dispute the validity of Plaintiff's copyrights or his ownership of them. Defendant also does not dispute it reproduced and displayed Plaintiff's images in thumbnail form without authorization. Plaintiff thus has shown a *prima facie* case of copyright infringement unless the fair use doctrine applies.

"Fair use" is a limitation on copyright owners' exclusive right "to reproduce the copyrighted work in copies." 17 U.S.C. § 106(1). It is codified at 17 U.S.C. § 107....

Fair use is an affirmative defense, and defendants carry the burden of proof on the issue. *American Geophysical Union v. Texaco Inc.*, 60 F.3d 913, 918 (2d Cir. 1995); *Columbia Pictures Ind. v. Miramax Films Corp.*, 11 F. Supp. 2d 1179, 1187 (C.D. Cal. 1998) ("[b]ecause fair use is an affirmative defense, Defendants bear the burden of proof on all of its factors"). Based on an analysis of the factors, the Court finds there is fair use here.

---

1. This full-size image was not technically located on Defendant's Web site. It was displayed by opening a link to its originating Web page. But only the image itself, and not any other part of the originating Web page, was displayed on the image attributes page. From the user's perspective, the source of the image matters less than the context in which it is displayed.

### 1. Purpose and Character of the Use

The first factor considers the nature of the use, including whether the use is commercial or educational. This, however, does not end the inquiry. "Purpose and character" also involve an assessment of whether "the new work merely supersedes the objects of the original creation, or instead adds something new, with a further purpose or different character, altering the first with new expression, meaning, or message; it asks, in other words, whether and to what extent the new work is transformative." *Campbell v. Acuff-Rose Music*, 510 U.S. 569, 579, 114 S.Ct. 1164, 127 L.Ed.2d 500 (1994) (citation omitted). "[T]he more transformative the new work, the less will be the significance of other factors, like commercialism, that may weigh against a finding of fair use." *Id.* at 579, 114 S.Ct. 1164.

There is no dispute Defendant operates its Web site for commercial purposes. Plaintiff's images, however, did not represent a significant element of that commerce, nor were they exploited in any special way.[5] They were reproduced as a result of Defendant's generally indiscriminate method of gathering images. Defendant has a commercial interest in developing a comprehensive thumbnail index so it can provide more complete results to users of its search engine. The Ditto crawler is designed to obtain large numbers of images from numerous sources without seeking authorization. Plaintiff's images were indexed as a result of these methods. While the use here was commercial, it was also of a somewhat more incidental and less exploitative nature than more traditional types of "commercial use."

The most significant factor favoring Defendant is the transformative nature of its use of Plaintiff's images. Defendant's use is very different from the use for which the images were originally created. Plaintiff's photographs are artistic works used for illustrative purposes. Defendant's visual search engine is designed to catalog and improve access to images on the Internet. The character of the thumbnail index is not esthetic, but functional; its purpose is not to be artistic, but to be comprehensive.

To a lesser extent, the Arriba Vista image attributes page also served this purpose by allowing users to obtain more details about an image. The image attributes page, however, raises other concerns. It allowed users to view (and potentially download) full-size images without necessarily viewing the rest of the originating Web page. At the same time, it was less clearly connected to the search engine's purpose of finding and organizing Internet content for users. The presence of the image attributes page in the old version of the search engine somewhat detracts from the transformative effect of the search engine. But, when considering purpose and character of use in a new enterprise of this sort, it is more appropriate to consider the transformative purpose rather than the early imperfect means of achieving that purpose. The Court finds the purpose and character of Defendant's use was on the whole significantly transformative.

The Court finds the first factor weighs in favor of fair use.

### 2. Nature of the Copyrighted Work

The second factor in § 107 is an acknowledgment "that some works are closer to the core of intended copyright protection than others, with the consequence that fair use is more difficult to establish when the former works are copied." *Campbell, supra* 510 U.S.

---

5. The use in this case is commercial, but it is unusual and less serious than many other commercial uses. If, for example, Plaintiff's images were used without authorization in advertising for Defendant's Web site, a finding of fair use would be much less likely.

at 586, 114 S.Ct. 1164. Artistic works like Plaintiff's photographs are part of that core. The Court finds the second factor weighs against fair use.

### 3. Amount and Substantiality of the Portion Used

The third factor assesses whether the amount copied was "reasonable in relation to the purpose of the copying." *Id.* The analysis focuses on "the persuasiveness of a [copier's] justification for the particular copying done, and the inquiry will harken back to the first of the statutory factors, for…the extent of permissible copying varies with the purpose and character of the use." *Id.* at 586–587, 114 S.Ct. 1164.

In the thumbnail index, Defendant used Plaintiff's images in their entirety, but reduced them in size. Defendant argues it is necessary for a visual search engine to copy images in their entirety so users can be sure of recognizing them, and the reduction in size and resolution mitigates damage that might otherwise result from copying. As Defendant has illustrated in its brief, thumbnails cannot be enlarged into useful images. Use of partial images or images further reduced in size would make images difficult for users to identify, and would eliminate the usefulness of Defendant's search engine as a means of categorizing and improving access to Internet resources.

As with the first factor, the Arriba Vista image attributes page presents a greater problem because it displayed a full-size image separated from the surrounding content on its originating Web page. Image attributes (e.g., dimensions and the address of the originating site) could have been displayed without reproducing the full-size image, and the display of the full image was not necessary to the main purposes of the search engine.[8]

If only the thumbnail index were at issue, Defendant's copying would likely be reasonable in light of its purposes. The image attributes page, however, was more remotely related to the purposes of the search engine. The Court finds the third factor weighs slightly against fair use.

### 4. Effect of the Use on the Potential Market or Value

The fourth factor inquiry examines the direct impact of the defendant's use and also considers "whether unrestricted and widespread conduct of the sort engaged in by the defendant…would result in a substantially adverse impact on the potential market for the original." *Campbell, supra,* 510 U.S. at 590, 114 S.Ct. 1164 (citation omitted).

The relevant market is Plaintiff's Web sites as a whole. The photographs are used to promote the products sold by Plaintiff's Web sites (including Plaintiff's books and corporate tour packages) and draw users to view the additional advertisements posted on those Web sites. The fourth factor addresses not just the potential market for a particular photo, but also its "value." The value of Plaintiff's photographs to Plaintiff could potentially be adversely affected if their promotional purposes are undermined.

Defendant argues there is no likely negative impact because its search engine does not compete with Plaintiff's Web sites and actually increases the number of users finding their way to those sites.

Plaintiff argues the market for his various products has been harmed. Defendant's conduct created a possibility that some users might improperly copy and use Plaintiff's

---

8. The newer search engine, ditto.com, appears to lessen this problem by eliminating the image attributes page and simultaneously opening the originating Web page along with a full-size image.

images from Defendant's site. Defendant's search engine also enabled users to "deep link" directly to the pages containing retrieved images, and thereby bypass the "front page" of the originating Web site. As a result, these users would be less likely to view all of the advertisements on the Web sites or view the Web site's entire promotional message. However, Plaintiff has shown no evidence of any harm or adverse impact.

In the absence of any evidence about traffic to Plaintiff's Web sites or effects on Plaintiff's businesses, the Court cannot find any market harm to Plaintiff. The Defendant has met its burden of proof by offering evidence tending to show a lack of market harm, and Plaintiff has not refuted that evidence. The Court finds the fourth factor weighs in favor of fair use.

### 5. Conclusion—Fair Use

The Court finds two of the four factors weigh in favor of fair use, and two weigh against it. The first and fourth factors (character of use and lack of market harm) weigh in favor of a fair use finding because of the established importance of search engines and the "transformative" nature of using reduced versions of images to organize and provide access to them. The second and third factors (creative nature of the work and amount or substantiality of copying) weigh against fair use.

The first factor of the fair use test is the most important in this case. Defendant never held Plaintiff's work out as its own, or even engaged in conduct specifically directed at Plaintiff's work. Plaintiff's images were swept up along with two million others available on the Internet, as part of Defendant's efforts to provide its users with a better way to find images on the Internet. Defendant's purposes were and are inherently transformative, even if its realization of those purposes was at times imperfect. Where, as here, a new use and new technology are evolving, the broad transformative purpose of the use weighs more heavily than the inevitable flaws in its early stages of development.

The Court has weighed all of the § 107 factors together. The Court finds Defendant's conduct constituted fair use of Plaintiff's images. There is no triable issue of material fact remaining to be resolved on the question of fair use, and summary adjudication is appropriate. Defendant's motion is GRANTED and Plaintiff's motion is DENIED as to the copyright infringement claims....

---

# UMG RECORDINGS, INC., *et al.* v. MP3.COM, INC.

United States District Court, Southern District of New York
No. 00 Civ. 472 (JSR), 92 F. Supp. 2d 349
May 4, 2000

RAKOFF, District Judge.

The complex marvels of cyberspatial communication may create difficult legal issues; but not in this case. Defendant's infringement of plaintiffs' copyrights is clear. Accordingly, on April 28, 2000, the Court granted defendant's motion for partial summary judgment holding defendant liable for copyright infringement. This opinion will state the reasons why.

The pertinent facts, either undisputed or, where disputed, taken most favorably to defendant, are as follows:

The technology known as "MP3" permits rapid and efficient conversion of compact disc recordings ("CDs") to computer files easily accessed over the Internet. *See generally Recording Industry Ass'n of America v. Diamond Multimedia Systems Inc.,* 180 F.3d 1072, 1073–74 (9th Cir. 1999). Utilizing this technology, defendant MP3.com, on or around January 12, 2000, launched its "My.MP3.com" service, which is advertised as permitting subscribers to store, customize and listen to the recordings contained on their CDs from any place where they have an Internet connection. To make good on this offer, defendant purchased tens of thousands of popular CDs in which plaintiffs held the copyrights, and, without authorization, copied their recordings onto its computer servers so as to be able to replay the recordings for its subscribers.

Specifically, in order to first access such a recording, a subscriber to MP3.com must either "prove" that he already owns the CD version of the recording by inserting his copy of the commercial CD into his computer CD-Rom drive for a few seconds (the "Beam-it Service") or must purchase the CD from one of defendant's cooperating on-line retailers (the "instant Listening Service"). Thereafter, however, the subscriber can access via the Internet from a computer anywhere in the world the copy of plaintiffs' recording made by defendant. Thus, although defendant seeks to portray its service as the "functional equivalent" of storing its subscribers' CDs, in actuality defendant is replaying for the subscribers converted versions of the recordings it copied, without authorization, from plaintiffs' copyrighted CDs. On its face, this makes out a presumptive case of infringement under the Copyright Act of 1976 ("Copyright Act"), 17 U.S.C. § 10, *et seq. See, e.g., Castle Rock Entertainment, Inc. v. Carol Publishing Group, Inc.,* 150 F.3d 132, 137 (2d Cir. 1998*); Hasbro Bradley, Inc. v. Sparkle Toys, Inc.,* 780 F.2d 189, 192 (2d Cir. 1985).[1]

Defendant argues, however, that such copying is protected by the affirmative defense of "fair use." *See* 17 U.S.C. § 107. In analyzing such a defense, the Copyright Act specifies four factors that must be considered: "(1) the purpose and character of the use, including whether such use is of a commercial nature or is for nonprofit educational purposes; (2) the nature of the copyrighted work; (3) the amount and substantiality of the portion used in relation to the copyrighted work as a whole; and (4) the effect of the use upon the potential market for or value of the copyrighted work." *Id.* Other relevant factors may also be considered, since fair use is an "equitable rule of reason" to be applied in light of the overall purposes of the Copyright Act. *Sony Corporation of America v. Universal City Studios, Inc.,* 464 U.S. 417, 448, 454, 104 S.Ct. 774, 78 L.Ed.2d 574 (1984*); see Harper & Row, Publishers, Inc. v. Nation Enterprises,* 471 U.S. 539, 549, 105 S.Ct. 2218, 85 L.Ed.2d 588 (1985).

Regarding the first factor—"the purpose and character of the use"—defendant does not dispute that its purpose is commercial, for while subscribers to My.MP3.com are not currently charged a fee, defendant seeks to attract a sufficiently large subscription base to draw advertising and otherwise make a profit. Consideration of the first factor, however, also involves inquiring into whether the new use essentially repeats the old or whether, in-

---

1. Defendant's only challenge to plaintiffs' *prima facie* case of infringement is the suggestion, buried in a footnote in its opposition papers, that its music computer files are not in fact "reproductions" of plaintiffs' copyrighted works within the meaning of the Copyright Act. *See, e.g.,* 17 U.S.C. § 114(b). Specifically, defendant claims that the simulated sounds on MP3-based music files are not physically identical to the sounds on the original CD recordings. Defendant concedes, however, that the human ear cannot detect a difference between the two. Moreover, defendant admits that a goal of its copying is to create a music file that is sonically as identical to the original CD as possible. In such circumstances, some slight, humanly undetectable difference between the original and the copy does not qualify for exclusion from the coverage of the Act.

stead, it "transforms" it by infusing it with new meaning, new understandings, or the like. *See, e.g., Campbell v. Acuff-Rose Music, Inc.,* 510 U.S. 569, 579, 114 S.Ct. 1164, 127 L.Ed.2d 500 (1994); *Castle Rock,* 150 F.3d at 142; *see also* Pierre N. Leval, *Toward a Fair Use Standard,* 103 Harv. L. Rev. 1105, 111 (1990). Here, although defendant recites that My.MP3.com provides a transformative "space shift" by which subscribers can enjoy the sound recordings contained on their CDs without lugging around the physical discs themselves, this is simply another way of saying that the unauthorized copies are being retransmitted in another medium—an insufficient basis for any legitimate claim of transformation. *See, e.g., Infinity Broadcast Corp. v. Kirkwood,* 150 F.3d 104, 108 (2d Cir. 1998) (rejecting the fair use defense by operator of a service that retransmitted copyrighted radio broadcasts over telephone lines); *Los Angeles News Serv. v. Reuters Television Int'l Ltd.,* 149 F.3d 987 (9th Cir. 1998) (rejecting the fair use defense where television news agencies copied copyrighted news footage and retransmitted it to news organizations), *cert. denied,* 525 U.S. 1141, 119 S.Ct. 1032, 143 L.Ed.2d 41 (1999); *see also American Geophysical Union v. Texaco Inc.,* 60 F.3d 913, 923 (2d Cir.), *cert. dismissed,* 516 U.S. 1005, 116 S.Ct. 592, 133 L.Ed.2d 486 (1995); *Basic Books, Inc. v. Kinko's Graphics Corp.,* 758 F. Supp. 1522, 1530–31 (S.D.N.Y. 1991); *see generally* Leval, *supra,* at 1111 (repetition of copyrighted material that "merely repackages or republishes the original" is unlikely to be deemed a fair use).

Here, defendant adds no new "new aesthetics, new insights and understandings" to the original music recordings it copies, *see Castle Rock,* 150 F.3d at 142 (internal quotation marks omitted), but simply repackages those recordings to facilitate their transmission through another medium. While such services may be innovative, they are not transformative.[2]

Regarding the second factor—"the nature of the copyrighted work"—creative recordings here being copied are "close[ ] to the core of intended copyright protection," *Campbell,* 510 U.S. at 586, 114 S.Ct. 1164, and, conversely, far removed from the more factual or descriptive work more amenable to "fair use," *see Nihon Keizai Shimbun, Inc. v. Comline Business Data, Inc.,* 166 F.3d 65, 72–73 (2d Cir. 1999); *see also Castle Rock,* 150 F.3d at 143–44.

Regarding the third factor—"the amount and substantiality of the portion [of the copyrighted work] used [by the copier] in relation to the copyrighted work as a whole"—it is undisputed that defendant copies, and replays, the entirety of the copyrighted works here in issue, thus again negating any claim of fair use. *See Infinity Broadcast,* 150 F.3d at 109 ("[T]he more of a copyrighted work that is taken, the less likely the use is to be fair...."); *see generally* Leval, *supra,* at 1122 ("[T]he larger the volume...of what is taken, the greater the affront to the interests of the copyright owner, and the less likely that a taking will qualify as a fair use").

Regarding the fourth factor—"the effect of the use upon the potential market for or value of the copyrighted work"—defendant's activities on their face invade plaintiffs' statutory right to license their copyrighted sound recordings to others for reproduction.

---

2. Defendant's reliance on the Ninth Circuit's "reverse engineering" cases, *see Sony Computer Entertainment, Inc. v. Connectix Corp.,* 203 F.3d 596 (9th Cir. 2000); *Sega Enterprises Ltd. v. Accolade, Inc.,* 977 F.2d 1510, 1527 (9th Cir. 1993), is misplaced, because, among other relevant distinctions, those cases involved the copying of software in order to develop a new product, *see Sony Computer Entertainment,* 203 F.3d at 606; *Sega Enterprises,* 977 F.2d at 1522, whereas here defendant copied CDs onto its servers not to create any new form of expression but rather to retransmit the same expression in a different medium.

*See* 17 U.S.C. § 106. Defendant, however, argues that, so far as the derivative market here involves is concerned, plaintiffs have not shown that such licensing is "traditional, reasonable, or likely to be developed." *American Geophysical*, 60 F.3d at 930 & n. 17. Moreover, defendant argues, its activities can only enhance plaintiffs' sales, since subscribers cannot gain access to particular recordings made available by MP3.com unless they have already "purchased" (actually or purportedly), or agreed to purchase, their own CD copies of those recordings.

Such arguments—though dressed in the garb of an expert's "opinion" (that, on inspection, consists almost entirely of speculative and conclusory statements)—are unpersuasive. Any allegedly positive impact of defendant's activities on plaintiffs' prior market in no way frees defendant to usurp a further market that directly derives from reproduction of the plaintiffs' copyrighted works. *See Infinity Broadcast*, 150 F.3d at 111. This would be so even if the copyrightholder had not yet entered the new market in issue, for a copyrighterholder's "exclusive" rights, derived from the Constitution and the Copyright Act, include the right, within broad limits, to curb the development of such a derivative market by refusing to license a copyrighted work or by doing so only on terms the copyright owner finds acceptable. *See Castle Rock*, 150 F.3d at 145–46; *Salinger v. Random House, Inc.*, 811 F.2d 90, 99 (2d Cir.), *cert. denied*, 484 U.S. 890, 108 S.Ct. 213, 98 L.Ed.2d 177 (1987). Here, moreover, plaintiffs have adduced substantial evidence that they have in fact taken steps to enter that market by entering into various licensing agreements.

Finally, regarding defendant's purported reliance on other factors, *see Campbell*, 510 U.S. at 577, 114 S.Ct. 1164, this essentially reduces to the claim that My.MP3.com provides a useful service to consumers that, in its absence, will be served by "pirates." Copyright, however, is not designed to afford consumer protection or convenience but, rather, to protect the copyrightholders' property interests. Moreover, as a practical matter, plaintiffs have indicated no objection in principle to licensing their recordings to companies like MP3.com; they simply want to make sure they get the remuneration the law reserves for them as holders of copyrights on creative works. Stripped to its essence, defendant's "consumer protection" argument amounts to nothing more than a bald claim that defendant should be able to misappropriate plaintiffs' property simply because there is a consumer demand for it. This hardly appeals to the conscience of equity.

In sum, on any view, defendant's "fair use" defense is indefensible and must be denied as a matter of law. Defendant's other affirmative defenses, such as copyright misuse, abandonment, unclean hands, and estoppel, are essentially frivolous and may be disposed of briefly. While defendant contends, under the rubric of copyright misuse, that plaintiffs are misusing their "dominant market position to selectively prosecute only certain online music technology companies," the admissible evidence of records shows only that plaintiffs have reasonably exercised their right to determine which infringers to pursue, and in which order to pursue them, *cf. Broadcast Music, Inc. v. Peppermint Club, Inc.*, 1985 WL 6141, at *4 (N.D. Ohio Dec. 16, 1985). The abandonment defense must also fall since defendant has failed to adduce any competent evidence of an overt act indicating that plaintiffs, who filed suit against MP3.com shortly after MP3.com launched its infringing My.MP3.com service, intentionally abandoned their copyrights. *See Richard Feiner & Co., Inc. v. H.R. Indus., Inc.*, 10 F. Supp. 2d 310, 313 (S.D.N.Y. 1998). Similarly, defendant's estoppel defense must be rejected because defendant has failed to provide any competent evidence that it relied on any action by plaintiffs with respect to defendant's My.MP3.com service. Finally, the Court must reject defendant's unclean hands defense given defendant's failure to come forth with any admissible evidence showing bad faith or misconduct on the part of plaintiffs. *See generally Dunlop-McCullen v. Local 1-S, AFL-CIO-CLC*, 149 F.3d 85, 90 (2d Cir. 1998); *A.H. Emery Co. v. Marcan Prods. Corp.*, 389 F.2d 11, 18 n. 4 (2d Cir.), *cert. denied*, 393 U.S. 835, 89 S.Ct. 109, 21 L.Ed.2d 106 (1968).

...[T]he Court, for the foregoing reasons, has determined that plaintiffs are entitled to partial summary judgment holding defendant to have infringed plaintiffs' copyrights.

---

## Notes and Questions

1. The Ninth Circuit recently considered the fair use doctrine. In *Sony Computer Entertainment, Inc. v. Connectix Corp.*, 203 F.3d 596 (9th Cir. 2000), *petition for cert. filed*, 69 U.S.L.W. 3023 (U.S. June 30, 2000), the plaintiff, a video game system manufacturer, asserted an infringement claim against a developer of emulator software that enabled the manufacturer's games to be played on computers other than the manufacturer's console. The defendant's copying was held necessary to access unprotected functional elements and thus constituted a fair use. In *Sony Computer Entertainment America, Inc. v. Bleem*, No. 99-17137, 2000 WL 959758 (9th Cir. May 4, 2000), the plaintiff, a manufacturer of console video games and game disks, alleged that a developer of software emulator's use of "screen shots" from the plaintiff's games in the defendant's advertising constituted copyright infringement. The use of screen shots in comparative advertising was held likely to be a fair use; the Ninth Circuit vacated the lower court's entry of a preliminary injunction.

2. What societal goals justify legalizing reverse engineering (i.e., the process by which one begins with a known product and works backwards to find the method(s) by which it was developed)? How are the competing interests protected by patent law and by trade secret law?

3. "Transformative" uses are those that add something new to the original creation, with a further purpose or different character, altering the first with new expression, meaning, or message. "Such works...lie a the heart of the fair use doctrine's guarantee of breathing space within the confines of copyright, and the more transformative the new work, the less will be the significance of other factors, like commercialism, that may weigh against a finding of fair use." *Campbell v. Acuff-Rose Music, Inc.*, 510 U.S. at 579.

4. With respect to the viability of fair use as a defense to a claim that technological protection measures have been circumvented in violation of the DMCA, *see Universal City Studios, Inc. v. Reimerdes*, No. 00 Civ. 0277, 2000 U.S. Dist. LEXIS 1169 at *64. There, the court concluded that offering and providing technology designed to circumvent technological measures that control access to copyrighted works fell within the purview of section 1201(a)(2) of the DMCA, which does not provide for a fair use defense. *Id.* at *67. The policies underlying the fair use doctrine were accommodated by exempting reverse engineering, good faith encryption research, security testing, and certain uses by non-profit libraries, archives, and educational institutions. *See* 17 U.S.C.A. §§ 1201(d), (f), (g), (j).

5. In *Sony Corp. v. Universal City Studios, Inc.*, 464 U.S. 417 (1984), manufacturers of videocassette recorders were accused of contributing to infringing home taping of copyrighted television broadcasts. The Supreme Court held that the manufacturers were not liable in view of the substantial numbers of copyright holders who either had authorized or did not object to such taping by viewers. *Id.* at 443, 446. Does the DMCA's prohibition on circumvention alter the analysis of non-infringing fair use by someone who gains access to a protected copyrighted work through circumvention technology? *See* House Comm. on Judiciary, Section-By-Section Analysis of H.R. 2281, as passed by the U.S. House of Rep., Aug. 4, 1998 at 9 (Comm. Print 1998) (stating that "[t]he *Sony* test of 'capability of substantial non-infringing uses,' while still operative in cases claiming contributory infringement of copyright, is not part of this legislation...").

6. To what extent do contributory infringement claims provide a means to advance a single claim to redress the objectionable use, thereby obviating the need to pursue multiple—perhaps numerous—individual infringers?

---

# Trademark

## 1. Fundamental Principles of Trademark

A "trademark" is a word or symbol used to identify the source of goods and distinguish them from the goods emanating from others. A "service" mark is a word or symbol that identifies the source of services and distinguishes them from services rendered by others. Trademarks and service marks are often referred to collectively as "trademarks."

Trademark protection exists as a matter of federal law, state statutory law, and the common law. Trademark rights flow from the use of a mark in commerce. The Lanham Act, 15 U.S.C.A. §§ 1051–72, 1091–96, 111–27 (West 1997 & Supp. 2000), sets forth a comprehensive scheme for federal trademark registrations and provides federal causes of action for infringement of both registered and unregistered trademarks.

Generally, the party that makes first use of a mark in connection with the sale of goods or services enjoys a priority of rights in the mark, and may bring an action against those who subsequently use confusingly similar marks. The more distinctive the trademark, the broader its scope of protection. Distinctiveness is measured on a spectrum, ranging from "generic" terms, to "descriptive" terms, to "suggestive" terms, to "fanciful" and "arbitrary" terms.

Generic marks are names or words used by the general public to describe an item or service; such terms are not distinctive and thus are not entitled to any protection. Descriptive marks refer to the names of people or places, or describe things; such marks generally are not granted protection unless they have acquired distinction in the marketplace by secondary meaning. Suggestive marks suggest, without describing directly, something about the goods or services; such marks are distinctive and are protected when they are used in the marketplace. Fanciful or arbitrary marks do not describe or suggest the item or service; such marks are most distinctive and are entitled to the broadest protection.

Certain benefits may be acquired through registration, either with the U.S. Patent and Trademark Office ("PTO") or with a state government. Trademark applications are examined substantively by the PTO, and thus registration affords *prima facie* evidence of the validity of a trademark. 15 U.S.C. § 1057(b). Federal registration also gives constructive notice of the existence of a mark to all subsequent users.

---

# 2.   Trademark Infringement and Dilution Claims

The trademark owner has the exclusive right to use a mark to identify the source of the relevant goods or services. The owner can therefore prevent the subsequent use of a mark that is likely to cause confusion with the senior user's mark regarding the origin of the goods or services offered, or a mark that is likely to cause confusion as to whether the junior user's goods or services enjoy some form of sponsorship by, or affiliation with, the goods or services offered by the senior user.

Federal trademark infringement actions may be brought by the owner of a valid federal trademark registration. 15 U.S.C.A. § 1114 (West 1997 & Supp. 2000). Owners of unregistered marks also can bring similar actions under federal unfair competition laws against those who use confusingly similar marks. 15 U.S.C.A. § 1125(a) (West 1997 & Supp. 2000). In determining whether confusion is likely, courts generally look to an amalgam of factors, such as the similarity of the marks in sight, sound, and meaning; the similarity of the goods or services; the strength of the prior owner's mark; the similarity of the trade channels; the existence of other similar marks used on similar goods; the defendant's good faith; and whether there has been any actual confusion. *See, e.g., Polaroid Corp. v. Polarad Electronics Corp.*, 287 F.2d 492, 495 (2d Cir.), *cert. denied*, 386 U.S. 36 (1961). Remedies for trademark infringement include injunctive relief, damages, and in some instances, attorneys' fees. 15 U.S.C.A. §§ 1116, 1117 (West 1997 & Supp. 2000).

Trademark "dilution" is actionable under federal law, 15 U.S.C.A. § 1125(c) (West 1997 & Supp. 2000), and under state laws. Dilution can consist of "blurring," which occurs when customers see the mark used to identify goods or services not produced by the trademark owner, or as a result of "tarnishment," which occurs when an unauthorized trademark use taints or degrades the owner's mark. Unlike trademark infringement claims, the dilution plaintiff need not prove a likelihood of confusion. Rather, the dilution plaintiff must show that its mark is famous and that the defendant is engaged in a commercial use that will dilute the mark.

Injunctive relief may be available to prevent conduct that dilutes a famous trademark. In exceptional cases when willful intent is shown, the owner of a famous mark also may be entitled to remedies available to a trademark infringement plaintiff. 15 U.S.C. § 1125. Criminal actions for trademark counterfeiting may be brought by the U.S. Attorney. Many states also have criminal laws designed to address counterfeiting. To prevent importation of infringing or counterfeit goods, the owner of a federal trademark registration can record its mark with the U.S. Customs Service, which is authorized to destroy counterfeit merchandise unless the trademark owner consents to an alternative disposition.

# PLAYBOY ENTERPRISES, INC. v. NETSCAPE COMMUNICATIONS CORP.

United States District Court, Central District of California, Southern Division.
Nos. SA CV 99-320 AHS EEX, SA CV 99-321 AHX EEX, 55 F. Supp. 2d 1070
June 24, 1999

STOTLER, District Judge.

On April 15, 1999, plaintiff Playboy Enterprises, Inc. ("PEI") filed a Motion for Preliminary Injunction against defendant Netscape Communications Corp. and against defendant Excite, Inc....

Defendants operate search engines on the Internet.[1] When a person searches for a particular topic in either search engine, the search engine compiles a list of sites matching or related to the user's search terms, and then posts the list of sites, known as "search results."

Defendants sell advertising space on the search result pages. Known as "banner ads," the advertisements are commonly found at the top of the screen. The ads themselves are often animated and whimsical, and designed to entice the Internet user to "click here." If the user does click on the ad, she is transported to the web site of the advertiser.

As with other media, advertisers seek to maximize the efficacy of their ads by targeting consumers matching a certain demographic profile. Savvy web site operators accommodate the advertisers by "keying" ads to search terms entered by users. That is, instead of posting ads in a random rotation, defendants program their servers to link a pre-selected set of banner ads to certain "key" search terms. Defendants market this context-sensitive advertising ability as a value-added service and charge a premium.

Defendants key various adult entertainment ads to a group of over 450 terms related to adult entertainment, including the terms "playboy" and "playmate." Plaintiff contends that inclusion of those terms violates plaintiff's trademarks rights in those words.

Plaintiff has a trademark on "Playboy(R)" and "Playmate(R)." Plaintiff contends that defendants are infringing and diluting its trademarks (1) by marketing and selling the group of over 450 words, including "playboy" and "playmate," to advertisers, (2) by programming the banner ads to run in response to the search terms "playboy" and "playmate" (i.e., "keying"), and (3) by actually displaying the banner ad on the search results page. As a result, plaintiff contends, Internet users are diverted from plaintiff's official web site and web sites sponsored or approved by plaintiff, which generally will be listed as search results, to other adult entertainment web sites. Plaintiff further argues that defendants intend to divert the users to the non-PEI sites. Plaintiff does not contend, however, that defendants infringe or dilute the marks when defendants' search engines generate a list of Web sites related to "playboy" or "playmate."

Defendants respond that while plaintiff may have a trademark on "Playboy(R)" and "Playmate(R)," defendants do not actually "use" the trademarks qua trademarks. Moreover, even if defendants do use the trademarks, defendants argue that a trademark does not confer an absolute property right on all uses of the protected terms, and that defendants' use of the terms is permitted. Finally, defendants dispute that they have any intent to divert users from clicking on search results (such as PEI's sites) to clicking on banner ads....

---

1. The Court notes that Netscape's search engine is co-branded with Excite, and programmed by Excite, but for purposes of this Motion, the Court treats them both as search engine operators.

## IV. DISCUSSION

Trademark Use

Integral to plaintiff's success on the merits of its case, on either the infringement or dilution theory, is a showing that defendants use plaintiff's trademarks in commerce. Plaintiff does not so show. Rather, plaintiff can only contend that the use of the words "playboy" and "playmate," as keywords or search terms, is equivalent to the use of the trademarks "Playboy(R)" and "Playmate(R)." However, it is undisputed that an Internet user cannot conduct a search using the trademark form of the words, i.e., Playboy(R) and Playmate(R). Rather, the user enters the generic word "playboy" or "playmate." It is also undisputed that the words "playboy" and "playmate" are English words in their own right, and that there exist other trademarks on the words wholly unrelated to PEI. Thus, whether the user is looking for goods and services covered by PEI's trademarks or something altogether unrelated to PEI is anybody's guess. Plaintiff guesses that most users searching the Web for "playboy" and "playmate" are indeed looking for PEI sites, goods and services. Based on that theory, plaintiff argues that since defendants also speculate that users searching for "playboy" and "playmate" are looking for things related to Playboy(R) and Playmate(R), defendants use the trademarks when they key competing adult entertainment goods and services to the generic "playboy" and "playmate."

Plaintiff has not shown that defendants use the terms in their trademark form, i.e., Playboy(R) and Playmate(R), when marketing to advertisers or in the algorithm that effectuates the keying of the ads to the keywords. Thus, plaintiff's argument that defendants "use" plaintiff's trademarks falls short.

Trademark Infringement and Dilution

Even if use of the generic "playboy" and "playmate" were construed to be use of the trademark terms Playboy(R) And Playmate(R), plaintiff still must show that the use violates trademark law. Plaintiff has asserted two theories, trademark infringement and trademark dilution.

### 1. Infringement

"The core element of trademark infringement is the likelihood of confusion, i.e., whether the similarity of the marks is likely to confuse customers about the source of the products." *Official Airline Guides, Inc. v. Goss*, 6 F.3d 1385, 1391 (9th Cir. 1993). Assuming arguendo that defendants' use of "playboy" and "playmate" is use of plaintiff's marks, plaintiff must still show that confusion is likely to result from that use. Plaintiff has not so shown.

Rather, plaintiff relies on the recent case from the Court of Appeals for the Ninth Circuit, *Brookfield Communications, Inc. v. West Coast Entertainment Corp.*, 174 F.3d 1036, 1062–64 (9th Cir. 1999), for the proposition that defendants cause "initial interest confusion" by the use of the words "playboy" and "playmate." Initial interest confusion, as coined by the Ninth Circuit, is a brand of confusion particularly applicable to the Internet. Generally speaking, initial interest confusion may result when a user conducts a search using a trademark term and the results of the search include web sites not sponsored by the holder of the trademark search term, but rather of competitors. *Id.* The Ninth Circuit reasoned that the user may be diverted to an un-sponsored site, and only realize that she has been diverted upon arriving at the competitor's site. Once there, however, even though the user knows she is not in the site initially sought, she may stay.

In that way, the competitor has captured the trademark holder's potential visitors or customers. *Id.*

*Brookfield* is distinguishable from this case, and where applicable, supportive of defendants' position.

First, the trademark at issue in *Brookfield* was not an English word in its own right. In *Brookfield*, the Court compared Brookfield's trademark "MovieBuff" with competitor West Coast's use of the domain name "moviebuff.com," and found them to be "essentially identical" despite the differences in capitalization, which the Court considered "inconsequential in light of the fact that Web addresses are not caps-sensitive..." *Id.* at 1054. However, the Court held that West Coast could use the term "Movie Buff" (or, presumably, "movie buff") with the space, as such is the "proper term for the 'motion picture enthusiast'....It cannot, however, omit the space." *Id.* at 1065. On the other hand, "in light of the fact that it is not a word in the English language, when the term 'MovieBuff' is employed, it is used to refer to Brookfield's products and services, rather than to mean 'motion picture enthusiast.'" *Id.* at 1065.

As English words, "playboy" and "playmate" cannot be said to suggest sponsorship or endorsement of either the web sites that appear as search results (as in *Brookfield*) or the banner ads that adorn the search results page. Although the trademark terms and the English language words are undisputedly identical, which, presumably, leads plaintiff to believe that the use of the English words is akin to use of the trademarks, the holder of a trademark may not remove a word from the English language merely by acquiring trademark rights in it. *Id.*

Second, the use by defendant of plaintiff's trademark in Brookfield was more suspect because the parties compete in the same market—as online providers of film industry information. *See id.* at 1056–57 ("[n]ot only are they not non-competitors, the competitive proximity of their products is actually quite high"). The Ninth Circuit analogized the capture of unsuspecting Internet users by a competitor to highways and billboards:

> Suppose West Coast's competitor puts up a billboard on a highway reading—"West Coast Video: 2 miles ahead at Exit 7"—where West Coast is really located at Exit 8 but Blockbuster is located at Exit 7. Customers looking for West Coast's store will pull off at Exit 7 and drive around looking for it. Unable to locate West, Coast, but seeing the Blockbuster store right by the highway entrance, they may simply rent there.

*Id.* at 1064. Although the customer is not confused as to where she ultimately rents a video, Blockbuster has misappropriated West Coast's goodwill through causing initial consumer confusion. *Id.* The customer has been captured by the competitor in much the same way that defendant in *Brookfield* captures Internet users looking for plaintiff's web site.

Here, the analogy is quite unlike that of a devious placement of a road sign bearing false information. This case presents a scenario more akin to a driver pulling off the freeway in response to a sign that reads "Fast Food Burgers" to find a well-known fast food burger restaurant, next to which stands a billboard that reads: "Better Burgers: 1 Block Further." The driver, previously enticed by the prospect of a burger from the well-known restaurant, now decides she wants to explore other burger options. Assuming that the same entity owns the land on which both the burger restaurant and the competitor's billboard stand, should that entity be liable to the burger restaurant for diverting the driver? That is the rule PEI contends the Court should adopt.

2. Dilution

Trademark dilution is defined as "the lessening of the capacity of a famous mark to identify and distinguish goods or services." 15 U.S.C. § 1127. However, dilution is "not intended to serve as a mere fallback protection for trademark owners unable to prove trademark infringement." *I.P. Lund Trading ApS v. Kohler Co.,* 163 F.3d 27, 48 (1st Cir. 1998).

To establish dilution, plaintiff must show that "(1) [defendants have] made use of a junior mark sufficiently similar to the famous mark to evoke in a relevant universe of consumers a mental association of the two that (2) has caused (3) actual economic harm to the famous mark's economic value by lessening its former selling power as an advertising agent for its goods and services." *Ringling Bros.-Barnum & Bailey Combined Shows, Inc. v. Utah Div'n of Travel Dev.,* 170 F.3d 449, 459 (4th Cir. 1999). Dilution generally occurs through the blurring of a famous mark or tarnishment of the mark, but is not limited to these categories. *See Panavision Int'l, L.P. v. Toeppen,* 141 F.3d 1316, 1326 (9th Cir. 1998). Plaintiff has not shown blurring of its marks, which would occur if defendants used the marks to identify defendants' goods or services. *Id.* at 1326 n. 7. First, as discussed *supra,* plaintiff has not shown that defendant use its marks Playboy(R) and Playmate(R). Further, plaintiff has not presented any evidence that defendants' use of the words "playboy" and "playmate" causes any severance of the association between plaintiff and its marks Playboy(R) and Playmate(R), much less in the minds of Internet users.

Plaintiff has also failed to show tarnishment, which occurs when a famous mark is associated improperly with an inferior or offensive product or service. *Id.* at 1326 n. 7. Plaintiff contends that because the content of the banner ads is more sexually explicit that PEI's content, PEI's marks are being tarnished. Again, plaintiff's argument is based on the incorrect assumption that defendants use plaintiff's marks, rather than the generic words "playboy" and "playmate." But even if the defendant could be said to use plaintiff's marks, plaintiff would still be required to show that associating marks admittedly famous for adult entertainment with other purveyors of adult entertainment somehow harms plaintiff's marks. Whether PEI is a cut above the rest, as it contends, is undercut by the fact that PEI's marks are associated with other purveyors of adult entertainment in other marketing channels, as defendants' exhibits graphically establish. Adoption of plaintiff's tarnishment would secure near-monopoly control of the placement of plaintiff's marks and the associated goods and services on the Internet, where, arguably, "placement" is a nebulous concept. A greater showing of harm is required.

## CONCLUSION

Accordingly, and for the foregoing reasons, the plaintiff's motion is denied....

---

# 3. Defenses

The Lanham Act includes a statutory fair use provision, 15 U.S.C.A. § 1115(b)(4) (West 1997 & Supp. 2000), which addresses common and descriptive uses of language. Under this statutory provision, a party may assert as a defense to a trademark infringement claim that the use of the name, term, or device charged to be an in infringement "is a use, otherwise than as a mark...of a term or device which is descriptive of and used fairly and in good faith only to describe the goods or services of such party, or their geographic origin...." *Id.* The defense may be used in connection with the trademark holder's exclusive right to use a registered mark, but it has also been recognized as a defense to claims of common law trademark infringement and false designation of origin advanced under section 43(a) of the Lanham Act, 15 U.S.C. § 1125(a). The pivotal issue in determining whether the use is within the statutory fair use parameters is not whether the defendant's use identifies or is descriptive of the plaintiff's product, but rather whether the mark in issue is used by the defendant descriptively to identify his own product. *See, e.g., Sunmark, Inc. v. Ocean Spray Cranberries, Inc.,* 64 F.3d 1055, 1058 (7th Cir. 1995) (holding that descriptive use of well known mark for candy called "sweet-tart" to describe the qualities of defendant's cranberry juice product is a fair use).

Another means of defending against a trademark infringement claim also utilizes the "fair use" lexicon but is conceptually different from the statutory defense. "Nominative" fair use, sometimes referred to as "informational," or "referential" fair use, permits the use of a trademark or service mark to identify, describe, or refer to the trademark owner's goods or services. The purpose of the use generally is an important factor in the court's consideration of the defense. Greater latitude is afforded to the use of trademarks in such artistic and critically expressive works than is afforded to uses for commercial exploitation.

In some instances, liability for trademark infringement also may be avoided on general First Amendment grounds. *See, e.g., Girl Scouts of United States v. Bantam Doublday Dell Publ'g Group, Inc.,* 996 F.2d 1477 (2d Cir. 1993) (rejecting contention by Boy Scouts and Girl Scouts of America that the First Amendment did not protect allegedly infringing use of "scouts" in title of books, "Pee Wee Scouts"). In *Bally Total Fitness Holding Corp. v. Faber,* 29 F. Supp. 2d 1161 (C.D. Cal. 1998), the use of "Bally Sucks" on a site criticizing the plaintiff's health clubs was held not to dilute the plaintiff's "Bally" trademark, on the ground that the web-site was using the term for non-commercial expression and in protected expressive speech.

---

## PEOPLE for the ETHICAL TREATMENT of ANIMALS, INC. v. Michael T. DOUGHNEY

United States District Court, Eastern District of Virginia, Alexandria Division
Civil Action No. 99-1336-A, 2000 U.S. Dist. LEXIS 9474
June 12, 2000

OPINION BY: Claude M. Hilton

This matter comes before the Court on Plaintiff's Motion for Partial Summary Judgment and Renewed Motion to Strike, Plaintiff's Motion for Summary Judgment and Defendant's Motion for Summary Judgment. The parties agree that there are no issues of material fact in dispute and this case may be decided on the motions for summary judgment.

This lawsuit arose from a dispute between Plaintiff, People for the Ethical Treatment of Animals ("PETA"), and Defendant, Michael Doughney ("Doughney"), regarding the use of the internet domain name "PETA.ORG." PETA is a non-profit, charitable corporation established in August 1980. PETA has affiliated animal protection organizations in the United Kingdom, Germany, the Netherlands and India who all operate under the name PETA. On August 4, 1992, PETA was given U.S. Trademark Registration Number

1,705,510 duly issued by the United States Patent and Trademark Office for the service mark "PETA" for "educational services; namely providing programs and seminars on the subject of animal rights welfare," and, "promoting the public awareness of the need to prevent cruelty and mistreatment of animals." PETA has used the PETA trademark and trade name continuously in interstate commerce and foreign commerce since 1980.

Defendant, Michael Doughney ("Doughney"), registered many domain names in September 1995, including "PETA.ORG." At that time, PETA had no web sites of its own. Doughney registered "PETA.ORG" with Network Solutions, Inc. for "People Eating Tasty Animals" which he represented to Network Solutions, Inc. was a non-profit organization. No such organization was in existence at the time of the registration of the web site or since that time. Doughney also represented to Network Solutions, Inc. that the name "PETA.ORG" "does not interfere with or infringe upon the rights of any third party."

Doughney's "PETA.ORG" web site contained information and materials antithetical to PETA's purpose. When in operation, "www.peta.org" contained the following description of the web site: "A resource for those who enjoy eating meat, wearing fur and leather, hunting, and the fruits of scientific research." There were over thirty links on the web site to commercial sites promoting among other things the sale of leather goods and meats. Until an internet user actually reached the "PETA.ORG" web site, where the screen read "People Eating Tasty Animals," the user had no way of knowing that the "PETA.ORG" web site was not owned, sponsored or endorsed by PETA.

On January 29, 1996, PETA send Doughney a letter requesting that he relinquish his registration of the "PETA.ORG" name because "it uses and infringes upon the long-standing registered service mark of People for the Ethical Treatment of Animals, whose service mark 'PETA' currently is in full force and effect."

PETA then complained to Network Solutions, Inc. and on or about May 2, 1996, Network Solutions, Inc. placed the "PETA.ORG" domain name on "hold" status. Pursuant to Network Solutions, Inc.'s "hold" status designation, the "PETA.ORG" domain name may not be used by any person or entity. After "PETA.ORG" was put on "hold" status, Doughney transferred the contents of that web site to the internet address "www.mtd.com/tasty."

PETA brought this suit alleging claims for service mark infringement in violation of 15 U.S.C. § 1114..., unfair competition in violation of 15 U.S.C. § 1125(a) and Virginia common law..., service mark dilution and cybersquatting in violation of 15 U.S.C. § 1125(c)....Doughney claims there is no infringement because its web site is a parody. PETA has dropped its claim for damages and seeks the following equitable relief: to enjoin Doughney's unauthorized use of its registered service mark "PETA" in the internet domain name "PETA.ORG," to force Doughney's assignment of the "PETA.ORG" domain name to PETA....

To make out a case for service or trade mark infringement and/or unfair competition, a Plaintiff must prove the following elements: (1) that Plaintiff possesses a Mark; (2) that Defendant uses the Plaintiff's Mark; (3) that such use occurs in commerce; (4) in connection with the sale or offering for sale, distribution, or advertising of goods or services; and (5) in a way that is likely to cause confusion among consumers. 15 U.S.C. §§ 1114, 1125(a). *Lone Star Steakhouse & Saloon v. Alpha of Virginia,* 43 F.3d 922, 930 (4th Cir. 1995).

First, PETA owns the PETA Mark and Defendant admits the PETA Mark's validity and incontestability. The PETA Mark is thus presumed to be distinctive as a matter of law. *Jews for Jesus v. Brodsky,* 993 F. Supp. 282, 295 (D.N.J. 1998), *aff'd* 159 F.3d 1351

(3rd Cir. 1998); *Sporty's Farm. L.L.C. v. Sportsman's Market, Inc.*, 202 F.3d 489, 497 (2d Cir.). Second, Doughney used the identical PETA Mark to register "PETA.ORG" and posting a web site at the internet address "www.peta.org." Third, Doughney admits that his use of the PETA Mark was "in commerce."

The fourth element requires that Defendant's use of the PETA Mark be made in connection with the sale, distribution, or advertising of goods or services. This does not require that Defendant actually caused goods or services to be placed into the stream of commerce. *Jews for Jesus*, 993 F. Supp. at 309. The term "services" has been interpreted broadly to include the dissemination of information, including purely ideological information. *United We Stand America, Inc. v. United We Stand America New York*, 128 F.3d 86, 89–90 (2d Cir. 1997) (citations omitted). Defendant's use of the PETA Mark was "in connection" with goods and services because the use of a misleading domain name has been found to be "in connection with the distribution of services" when it impacts on the Plaintiff's business:

> It is likely to prevent Internet users from reaching [PETA]'s own Internet web site. The prospective users of [PETA]'s services who mistakenly access Defendant's web site may fail to continue to search for [PETA]'s own home page, due to anger, frustration, or the belief that the Plaintiff's home page does not exist.

*Planned Parenthood Federation of America v. Bucci*, 1997 U.S. Dist. LEXIS 3338, 42 U.S.P.Q.2d (BNA) 1430, 1435 (S.D.N.Y.); *Jews for Jesus*, 993 F. Supp. at 309. In addition, the "PETA.ORG" web site contained over thirty separate hyperlinks to commercial operations offering goods and services, including fur, leather, magazines, clothing, equipment and guide services. Under the law, even one such link is sufficient to establish the commercial use requirement of the Lanham Act. *Jews for Jesus*, 993 F. Supp. at 308–09; *Planned Parenthood*, 42 U.S.P.Q.2d (BNA) at 1435.

Last, Defendant's use of PETA's Mark did cause confusion. Doughney copied the Mark identically. This creates a presumption of likelihood of confusion among internet users as a matter of law. *New York State Society of Certified Public Accountants v. Eric Louis Associates. Inc.*, 79 F. Supp. 2d 331, 340 (S.D.N.Y. 1999). In addition, there was evidence of actual confusion by those using the internet who were trying to locate PETA and instead found Doughney's web site.

Doughney's web site certainly dilutes the Mark of PETA. To win on summary judgment for a claim for dilution under 15 U.S.C. § 1125(c)(1), Plaintiff must show that the undisputed facts demonstrate that Defendant's use of "PETA.ORG" diluted the PETA Mark's distinctive quality. Dilution is "the lessening of the capacity of a famous mark to identify and distinguish goods or services, regardless of the presence or absence of (1) competition between the owner of the famous mark and other parties, or (2) likelihood of confusion, mistake or deception." 15 U.S.C. § 1127; *Ringling Bros. v. Utah Division of Travel*, 170 F.3d 449, 452 (4th Cir. 1999). Dilution can occur by "tarnishment" or "blurring." *Jews for Jesus*, 993 F. Supp. at 305; *Ringling Bros.*, 170 F.3d at 452.

Defendant is guilty of "blurring" the famous PETA Mark because (1) Defendant used the identical PETA Mark to mentally associate PETA.ORG to the PETA Mark; and (2) such use caused; (3) actual economic harm to the PETA Mark by lessening its selling power as an advertising agent for PETA's goods and services. *Ringling Bros.*, 170 F.3d at 458. Doughney's site included materials antithetical to the purpose and message of PETA in that "PETA.ORG" included links to commercial enterprises engaged in conduct directly contrary to PETA's animal protection efforts....

Doughney contends there is no infringement in that his web site was a parody. A parody exists when two antithetical ideas appear at the same time. In this instance, an internet user would not realize that they were not on an official PETA web site until after they had used PETA's Mark to access the web page "www.peta.org." Only then would they find Doughney's People Eating Tasty Animals. Doughney knew he was causing confusion by use of the Mark and admitted that it was "possible" that some internet users would be confused when they activated "PETA.ORG" and found the "People Eating Tasty Animals" web site. He also admitted that "many people" would initially assume that they were accessing an authentic PETA web site at "www.peta.org." Only after arriving at the "PETA.ORG" web site could the web site browser determine that this was not a web site owned, controlled or sponsored by PETA. Therefore, the two images: (1) the famous PETA name and (2) the "People Eating Tasty Animals" web site was not a parody because not simultaneous.

The Defendant's affirmative defense of trademark misuse is inapplicable. In 1998, PETA registered the domain names "ringlingbrothers.com," "voguemagazine.com," and "pg.info." Each web site contained messages from PETA criticizing Ringling Bros.-Barnum & Bailey Combined, *Vogue Magazine* and Procter & Gamble Company for mistreatment of animals. In each instance, "ringlingbrothers," "voguemagazine" and "pginfo" were not and are not registered trademarks. PETA received complaints from Conde Nast Publications that owns *Vogue Magazine* and from the Ringling Bros.-Barnum & Bailey Combined Shows regarding PETA's web sites bearing their names. In each case, PETA voluntarily and immediately assigned the domain names to the complaining party. At no time did PETA receive any correspondence of any kind from Procter & Gamble Company complaining about PETA's registration and use of the internet domain name "pginfo.net." Doughney had no relation to any of these web sites and suffered no damages from PETA's operation of any of these web sites.

Defendant's affirmative defense is based in part on a constitutional argument. Doughney contends that this case is an attempt to quash his First Amendment rights to express disagreement with their organization. PETA does not seek to keep Doughney from criticizing PETA. They ask that Doughney not use their mark. When Network Solutions, Inc. placed "PETA.ORG" on "hold" status, Doughney transferred the entire web page to one of his other internet sites, "mtd.com/tasty." PETA has not complained about that web site and even concedes that Doughney has a right to criticize PETA or any organization.

Defendant also raises as a trademark misuse affirmative defense an "unclean hands" argument. However, the doctrine of unclean hands applies only with respect to the right in suit. What is material is not that the plaintiff's hands are dirty, but that he dirtied them in acquiring the right he now asserts. *Estee Lauder, Inc. v. Fragrance Counter*, 189 F.R.D. 269, 272 (S.D.N.Y. 1999); *see also Precision Instrument Mfg. Co. v. Automotive Maintenance Machinery Co.*, 324 U.S. 806, 89 L. Ed. 1381, 65 S. Ct. 993 (1954). The purported grounds for Defendant's "unclean hands"—i.e. PETA's disputes with Ringling Bros. and Vogue, and PETA's web site that is critical of Procter & Gamble—are not at issue in this suit and thus, are not properly the subject of an unclean hands defense.

As PETA has proven its case for its infringement and dilution claims and Doughney can offer no viable defenses to PETA's claims, Summary Judgment should be granted in favor of PETA....

# Issues Relating to Domain Names

## 1.  The Nature of Domain Names

Domain names consist of a top-level domain, such as ".com" (connoting a commercial site); ".edu" (connoting an educational site); ".org" (connoting, among other organizations, non-profit sites); ".gov" (connoting a government site); ".net" (connoting a networking provider); and ".mil" (connoting a military site). Second-level domains consist of a term or series of terms that specify with more particularity the domain name address. Domain names help identify the site and direct visitors to it.

Commercial interests in Internet advertising are significant. Web pages are often used by companies to provide information about their products in a more detailed fashion than can be done through a standard advertisement, especially because the transaction costs for such promotion and for sales of goods and services through electronic media generally are considerably lower than other means that historically have been available.

Consumer access to purchase items or to gather information on the Internet demands an easy way to locate particular companies or brand names. An Internet user often will begin a search by guessing the domain name, especially when information about a well-known organization or product entity is sought, by devising a url that begins with "http://www." or just "www." Web surfers also may utilize trademarks to conduct searches because companies frequently incorporate their marks within their domain names. Because current search engine technology often may produce a lengthy list of web-sites in response to a search, requiring the user to sort through extraneous information to locate the desired company or product, many businesses rely predominantly on their domain names, comprised of the company or brand trademark (and the suffix ".com"), to direct traffic to their sites. *See generally* H.R. Rep. No. 106-412, at 5 (1999).

## 2.  Domain Name Disputes

Disputes relating to the registration and use of domain names have given rise to a disproportionate number of claims relating to trademark issues in cyberspace. Such disputes have been adjudicated through the judicial process. In addition, the Internet Corporation for Assigned Names and Number ("ICANN") has been established to manage the domain name system. In 1999, ICANN established the Uniform Domain Name Dispute Resolution Policy, which is applicable to all registrants through their individual registration agreements with separate registrars. Under the policy, registrants extend warranties that their domain names do not infringe or violate any third-party rights, and that the domain names were not registered for any unlawful purposes. Disputes over such issues as the use of identical or confusingly similar trademarks, and registration or use of domain names in bad faith, are resolved by administrative proceedings. Parties to the dispute may still pursue certain judicial proceedings as well.

Trademark owners have contested the use of certain domain names in several different situations. For example, domain name disputes have arisen when a web-site operator uses a domain name that is identical or similar to a competitor's trade name. In *Washington Speakers Bureau, Inc. v. Leading Authorities, Inc.*, 33 F. Supp. 2d 488, 498 (E.D. Va. 1999), *aff'd*, 217 F.3d 843 (4th Cir. 2000), the Washington Speakers Bureau contested the registrant's domain names "washingtonspeakers.com" and "washingtonspeakers.net." The district court found a likelihood of consumer confusion and that the defendant had registered the names in a bad faith effort to attract its competitor's business. The court ordered the defendant to relinquish its rights to the domain names.

Other challenges based on the use of identical or similar names have been asserted. In one case, *Hasbro, Inc. v. Internet Entertainment Group, Inc.*, 1996 U.S. Dist. LEXIS 11626, 40 U.S.P.Q.2d (BNA) 1479 (W.D. Wash. 1996), the plaintiff, Hasbro, Inc., which manufacturers the board game "Candyland," moved for a preliminary injunction to prohibit the defendants from using the name "candyland" to identify a sexually explicit site and from using "candyland.com" as an Internet domain name. The court granted the injunction.

In *Toys "R" Us, Inc. v. Akkaoui*, No. C 96-3381 CW, 1996 WL 772709 (N.D. Cal. 1996), the defendant registered the domain name "adultsrus.com" for a site used to sell sexual devices and clothing. The name was found to tarnish the " 'R Us" series of marks and a request for injunctive relief was granted. Slight variations in domain names that are similar to trademarks, such as a misspelled word, have met with similar results. Thus, in *PaineWebber, Inc. v. WWWPAINEWEBBER.COM*, No. 9900456, 1999 U.S. Dist. LEXIS 6552 (E.D. Va. Apr. 9, 1999), a preliminary injunction was issued against the link to the address "wwwpainewebber.com" (i.e., with no period between the "www" and "paine") to a pornographic web-site.

Claims also have been advanced when two trademark owners have competing claims to a domain name. In *Hasbro, Inc. v. Clue Computing, Inc.*, 66 F. Supp. 2d 117 (D. Mass. 1999), for instance, the plaintiff, owner of the "Clue" board game, challenged the registration of "clue" by the defendant, who offered computer consulting services. The court ruled that there was no evidence that the defendant had chosen the domain name in order to create consumer confusion. By contrast, in *Planned Parenthood Federation of America, Inc. v. Bucci*, No. 97 Civ. 0659, 1997 WL 133313 (S.D.N.Y. 1997), *aff'd*, 152 F.3d 920 (2d Cir.), *cert. denied*, 525 U.S. 834 (1998), an anti-abortion site's use of the domain name "plannedparenthood.com" was enjoined because of the likelihood of confusion with the "Planned Parenthood" trademark.

Is a domain name a mere address designed to permit access to expressive content, or is it itself speech worthy of protection? "[T]he context in which a symbol is used for purposes of expression is important, for the context may give meaning to the symbol." *Spence v. Washington*, 418 U.S. 405, 410 (1974). In *Name.Space, Inc. v. Network Solutions, Inc.*, 202 F.3d 573, 577 (2d Cir. 2000), the Second Circuit affirmed the district court's determination that three-letter top level domains (".com," ".net," and ".org") were not expressive speech. Recognizing that domain names have a functional purpose, the Second Circuit stated that "whether the mix of functionality is 'sufficiently imbued with the elements of communication' depends on the domain name in question, the intentions of the registrant, the contents of the website, and the technical protocols that govern the [Domain Name System]." *Id.* at 587.

---

# BROOKFIELD COMMUNICATIONS, INC. v. WEST COAST ENTERTAINMENT CORP.

U.S. Court of Appeals, Ninth Circuit
No. 98-56918, 174 F.3d 1036
April 22, 1999

Before CANBY, O'SCANNLAIN, and WARDLAW, Circuit Judges.

O'SCANNLAIN, J.

We must venture into cyberspace to determine whether federal trademark and unfair competition laws prohibit a video rental store chain from using an entertainment-industry information provider's trademark in the domain name of its web site....

Brookfield Communications, Inc. ("Brookfield") appeals the district court's denial of its motion for a preliminary injunction prohibiting West Coast Entertainment Corporation ("West Coast") from using in commerce terms confusingly similar to Brookfield's trademark, "MovieBuff." Brookfield gathers and sells information about the entertainment industry. Founded in 1987 for the purpose of creating and marketing software and services for professionals in the entertainment industry, Brookfield initially offered software applications featuring information such as recent film submissions, industry credits, professional contacts, and future projects. These offerings targeted major Hollywood film studios, independent production companies, agents, actors, directors, and producers.

Brookfield expanded into the broader consumer market with computer software featuring a searchable database containing entertainment-industry related information marketed under the "MovieBuff" mark around December 1993. Brookfield's "MovieBuff" software now targets smaller companies and individual consumers who are not interested in purchasing Brookfield's professional level alternative, The Studio System, and includes comprehensive, searchable, entertainment-industry databases and related software applications containing information such as movie credits, box office receipts, films in development, film release schedules, entertainment news, and listings of executives, agents, actors, and directors. This "MovieBuff" software comes in three versions — (1) the MovieBuff Pro Bundle, (2) the MovieBuff Pro, and (3) MovieBuff — and is sold through various retail stores, such as Borders, Virgin Megastores, Nobody Beats the Wiz, The Writer's Computer Store, Book City, and Samuel French Bookstores.

Sometime in 1996, Brookfield attempted to register the World Wide Web ("the Web") domain name "moviebuff.com" with Network Solutions, Inc. ("Network Solutions"), but was informed that the requested domain name had already been registered by West Coast. Brookfield subsequently registered "brookfieldcomm.com" in May 1996 and "moviebuffonline.com" in September 1996. Sometime in 1996 or 1997, Brookfield began using its web sites to sell its "MovieBuff" computer software and to offer an Internet-based searchable database marketed under the "MovieBuff" mark. Brookfield sells its "MovieBuff" computer software through its "brookfieldcomm.com" and "moviebuffonline.com" web sites and offers subscribers online access to the MovieBuff database itself at its "inhollywood.com" web site.

On August 19, 1997, Brookfield applied to the Patent and Trademark Office (PTO) for federal registration of "MovieBuff" as a mark to designate both goods and services. Its trademark application describes its product as "computer software providing data and information in the field of the motion picture and television industries." Its service mark application describes its service as "providing multiple-user access to an on-line network database offering data and information in the field of the motion picture and television industries." Both federal trademark registrations issued on September 29, 1998. Brookfield had previously obtained a California state trademark registration for the mark "MovieBuff" covering "computer software" in 1994.

In October 1998, Brookfield learned that West Coast—one of the nation's largest video rental store chains with over 500 stores—intended to launch a web site at "moviebuff. com" containing, *inter alia,* a searchable entertainment database similar to "MovieBuff." West Coast had registered "moviebuff.com" with Network Solutions on February 6, 1996 and claims that it chose the domain name because the term "Movie Buff" is part of its service mark, "The Movie Buff's Movie Store," on which a federal registration issued in 1991 covering "retail store services featuring video cassettes and video game cartridges" and "rental of video cassettes and video game cartridges." West Coast notes further that, since at least 1988, it has also used various phrases including the term "Movie Buff" to promote goods and services available at its video stores....

To resolve whether West Coast's use of "moviebuff.com" constitutes trademark infringement or unfair competition, we must first determine whether Brookfield has a valid, protectable trademark interest in the "MovieBuff" mark. Brookfield's registration of the mark on the Principal Register in the Patent and Trademark Office constitutes *prima facie* evidence of the validity of the registered mark and of Brookfield's exclusive right to use the mark on the goods and services specified in the registration. *See* 15 U.S.C. Sections 1057(b); 1115(a).... [We conclude that] Brookfield is the senior user because it marketed "MovieBuff" products well before West Coast began using 'moviebuff.com' in commerce....

Our conclusion comports with the position of the PTO, which effectively announced its finding of no likelihood of confusion between "The Movie Buff's Movie Store " and "MovieBuff" when it placed the latter on the principal register despite West Coast's prior registration of "The Movie Buff's Movie Store." Priority is accordingly to be determined on the basis of whether Brookfield used "MovieBuff" or West Coast used "moviebuff.com" first....

The district court, while recognizing that mere registration of a domain name was not sufficient to constitute commercial use for purposes of the Lanham Act, nevertheless held that registration of a domain name with the intent to use it commercially was sufficient to convey trademark rights. This analysis, however, contradicts both the express statutory language and the case law which firmly establishes that trademark rights are not conveyed through mere intent to use a mark commercially, *see, e.g., Allard Enters. v. Advanced Programming Resources, Inc.,* 146 F.3d 350, 356 [46 USPQ2d 1865] (6th Cir. 1998); *Zazu Designs v. L'Oreal, S.A.,* 979 F.2d 499, 504 [24 USPQ2d 1828] (7th Cir. 1992) ("[A]n intent to use a mark creates no rights a competitor is bound to respect."), nor through mere preparation to use a term as a trademark, *see, e.g., Hydro-Dynamics, Inc. v. George Putnam & Co.,* 811 F.2d 1470, 1473–74 [1 USPQ2d 1772] (Fed. Cir. 1987); *Computer Food Stores, Inc. v. Corner Store Franchises,* 176 U.S.P.Q. 535, 538 (T.T.A.B. 1973).

West Coast no longer disputes that its use—for purposes of the Lanham Act—of "moviebuff.com "did not commence until after February 1996. It instead relies on the alternate argument that its rights vested when it began using "moviebuff.com" in e-mail correspondence with lawyers and customers sometime in mid-1996. West Coast's argument is not without support in our case law—we have indeed held that trademark rights can vest even before any goods or services are actually sold if "the totality of [one's] prior actions, taken together, [can] establish a right to use the trademark." *New West*, 595 F.2d at 1200. Under *New West,* however, West Coast must establish that its e-mail correspondence constituted "'[u]se in a way sufficiently public to identify or distinguish the marked goods in an appropriate segment of the public mind as those of the adopter of the mark.'" *Id.* (quoting *New England Duplicating Co. v. Mendes*, 190 F.2d 415, 418 [90 USPQ 151] (1st Cir. 1951)); *see also Marvel Comics Ltd. v. Defiant,* 837 F. Supp. 546, 550 [28 USPQ2d 1794] (S.D.N.Y. 1993) ("[T]he talismanic test is whether or not the use was sufficiently public to identify or distinguish the marked goods in an appropriate segment of the public mind as those of the adopter of the mark.") (quotation marks and citation omitted).

West Coast fails to meet this standard. Its purported "use" is akin to putting one's mark "on a business office door sign, letterheads, architectural drawings, etc." or on a prototype displayed to a potential buyer, both of which have been held to be insufficient to establish trademark rights. *See Steer Inn Sys., Inc. v. Laughner's Drive-In, Inc.,* 405 F.2d 1401, 1402 [160 USPQ 626] (C.C. P.A. 1969); *Walt Disney Prods. v. Kusan, Inc.,* 204 U.S.P.Q. 284, 288 (C.D. Cal. 1979). Although widespread publicity of a company's mark, such as Marvel Comics's announcement to 13 million comic book readers that "Plasma" would be the title of a new comic book, *see Marvel Comics,* 837 F. Supp. at 550, or the mailing of 430,000 solicitation letters with one's mark to potential subscribers of a magazine, *see New West,* 595 F.2d at 1200, may be sufficient to create an association among the public between the mark and West Coast, mere use in limited e-mail correspondence with lawyers and a few customers is not....

For the foregoing reasons, we conclude that the district court erred in concluding that Brookfield failed to establish a likelihood of success on its claim of being the senior user.

Establishing seniority, however, is only half the battle. Brookfield must also show that the public is likely to be somehow confused about the source or sponsorship of West Coast's "moviebuff.com" web site—and somehow to associate that site with Brookfield. *See* 15 U.S.C. Sections 1114(1); 1125 (a). The Supreme Court has described "the basic objectives of trademark law" as follows: "trademark law, by preventing others from copying a source-identifying mark, 'reduce[s] the customer's costs of shopping and making purchasing decisions,' for it quickly and easily assures a potential customer that this item—the item with this mark—is made by the same producer as other similarly marked items that he or she liked (or disliked) in the past. At the same time, the law helps assure a producer that it (and not an imitating competitor) will reap the financial, reputation-related rewards associated with a desirable product." *Qualitex,* 514 U.S. at 163–64 (internal citations omitted). Where two companies each use a different mark and the simultaneous use of those marks does not cause the consuming public to be confused as to who makes what, granting one company exclusive rights over both marks does nothing to further the objectives of the trademark laws; in fact, prohibiting the use of a mark that the public has come to associate with a company would actually contravene the intended purposes of the trademark law by making it more difficult to identify and to distinguish between different brands of goods.

"The core element of trademark infringement is the likelihood of confusion, i.e., whether the similarity of the marks is likely to confuse customers about the source of the products." *Official Airline Guides,* 6 F.3d at 1391 (quoting *E. & J. Gallo Winery v. Gallo Cattle Co.,* 967 F.2d 1280, 1290 [21 USPQ2d 1824] (9th Cir. 1992)) (quotation marks omitted*); accord International Jensen, Inc. v. Metrosound U.S.A., Inc.,* 4 F.3d 819, 825 [28 USPQ2d 1287] (9th Cir. 1993*); Metro Publ'g, Ltd. v. San Jose Mercury News,* 987 F.2d 637, 640 [25 USPQ2d 2049] (9th Cir. 1993). We look to the following factors for guidance in determining the likelihood of confusion: similarity of the conflicting designations; relatedness or proximity of the two companies' products or services; strength of Brookfield's mark; marketing channels used; degree of care likely to be exercised by purchasers in selecting goods; West Coast's intent in selecting its mark; evidence of actual confusion; and likelihood of expansion in product lines. *See Dr. Seuss Enters. v. Penguin Books USA, Inc.,* 109 F.3d 1394, 1404 [42 USPQ2d 1184] (9th Cir. 1997), *petition for cert. dismissed by,* 118 S. Ct. 27 (1997); *Sleekcraft,*599 F.2d at 348–49; *see also* Restatement (Third) of Unfair Competition Sections 20–23 (1995). These eight factors are often referred to as the *Sleekcraft* factors.

... Where the two marks are entirely dissimilar, there is no likelihood of confusion. "Pepsi" does not infringe Coca-Cola's "Coke." ...

In the present case, the district court found West Coast's domain name "moviebuff.com" to be quite different than Brookfield's domain name "moviebuffonline.com." Comparison of domain names, however, is irrelevant as a matter of law, since the Lanham Act requires that the allegedly infringing mark be compared with the claimant's trademark, *see* 15 U.S.C. Sections 1114(1), 1125(a), which here is "MovieBuff," not " moviebuffonline.com." Properly framed, it is readily apparent that West Coast's allegedly infringing mark is essentially identical to Brookfield's mark "MovieBuff." In terms of appearance, there are differences in capitalization and the addition of ".com" in West Coast's complete domain name, but these differences are inconsequential in light of the fact that Web addresses are not caps-sensitive and that the ".com" top-level domain signifies the site's commercial nature.

Looks aren't everything, so we consider the similarity of sound and meaning. The two marks are pronounced the same way, except that one would say "dot com" at the end of West Coast's mark. Because many companies use domain names comprised of ".com" as the top-level domain with their corporate name or trademark as the second-level domain, *see Beverly,* 1998 WL 320829, at *1, the addition of ".com" is of diminished importance in distinguishing the mark. The irrelevance of the ".com" becomes further apparent once we consider similarity in meaning. The domain name is more than a mere address: like trademarks, second-level domain names communicate information as to source. As we explained in Part II, many Web users are likely to associate "moviebuff. com" with the trademark "MovieBuff," thinking that it is operated by the company that makes "MovieBuff" products and services. Courts, in fact, have routinely concluded that marks were essentially identical in similar contexts. *See, e.g., Public Serv. Co. v. Nexus Energy Software, Inc.,* No. 98-12589, 1999 WL 98973, at *3 (D. Mass. Feb. 24, 1999) (finding "energyplace.com" and "Energy Place" to be virtually identical); *Minnesota Mining & Mfg. Co. v. Taylor,* 21 F. Supp. 2d 1003, 1005 [48 USPQ2d 1701] (D. Minn. 1998) (finding "postit.com" and "Post-It" to be the same*); Interstellar Starship Servs. Ltd. v. Epix, Inc.,* 983 F. Supp. 1331, 1335 [45 USPQ2d 1304] (D. Or. 1997) ("In the context of Internet use, ['epix.com'] is the same mark as ['EPIX']."); *Planned Parenthood Federation of America, Inc. v. Bucci,* No. 97-0629, 1997 WL 133313, at *8 [42 USPQ2d 1430] (S.D.N.Y. Mar. 24, 1997) (concluding that "plannedparenthood.com" and "Planned Parenthood" were essentially identical), *aff'd by,* 152 F.3d 920 (2d Cir. 1998), *cert. denied,* 119 S. Ct. 90 (1998). "MovieBuff" and "moviebuff.com" are, for all intents and purposes, identical in terms of sight, sound, and meaning, we conclude that the similarity factor weighs heavily in favor of Brookfield.

The similarity of marks alone, as we have explained, does not necessarily lead to consumer confusion. Accordingly, we must proceed to consider the relatedness of the products and services offered. Related goods are generally more likely than unrelated goods to confuse the public as to the producers of the goods. *See Official Airline Guides*, 6 F.3d at 1392 (citing *Sleekcraft*, 599 F.2d at 350). In light of the virtual identity of marks, if they were used with identical products or services likelihood of confusion would follow as a matter of course. *See Lindy Pen Co. v. Bic Pen Corp.*, 796 F.2d 254, 256–57 [230 USPQ 791] (9th Cir. 1986) (reversing a district court's finding of no likelihood of confusion even though the six other likelihood of confusion factors all weighed against a finding of likelihood of confusion); *Interpace Corp. v. Lapp, Inc.*, 721 F.2d 460, 462 (3d Cir. 1983). If, on the other hand, Brookfield and West Coast did not compete to any extent whatsoever, the likelihood of confusion would probably be remote. A Web surfer who accessed "moviebuff.com" and reached a web site advertising the services of Schlumberger Ltd. (a large oil drilling company) would be unlikely to think that Brookfield had entered the oil drilling business or was sponsoring the oil driller. *See, e.g., Toys "R" Us, Inc. v. Feinberg*, 26 F. Supp. 2d 639, 643 (S.D.N.Y. 1998) (no likelihood of confusion between "gunsrus.com" firearms web site and "Toys 'R' Us" trademark*); Interstellar Starship*, 983 F. Supp. at 1336 (finding no likelihood of confusion between use of "epix.com" to advertise the Rocky Horror Picture Show and "Epix" trademark registered for use with computer circuit boards)....

Here, both companies offer products and services relating to the entertainment industry generally, and their principal lines of business both relate to movies specifically and are not as different as guns and toys, *see Toys "R" Us*, 26 F. Supp. 2d at 643, or computer circuit boards and the Rocky Horror Picture Show, *see Interstellar Starship*, 983 F. Supp. at 1336. Thus, Brookfield and West Coast are not properly characterized as non-competitors. *See American Int'l Group, Inc. v. American Int'l Bank*, 926 F.2d 829, 832 [17 USPQ2d 1907] (9th Cir. 1991) (concluding that although the parties were not direct competitors, they both provided financial services and that customer confusion could result in light of the similarities between the companies' services).

Not only are they not non-competitors, the competitive proximity of their products is actually quite high. Just as Brookfield's "MovieBuff" is a searchable database with detailed information on films, West Coast's web site features a similar searchable database, which Brookfield points out is licensed from a direct competitor of Brookfield. Undeniably then, the products are used for similar purposes....

In addition to the relatedness of products, West Coast and Brookfield both utilize the Web as a marketing and advertising facility, a factor that courts have consistently recognized as exacerbating the likelihood of confusion. *See, e.g., Public Serv. Co.*, 1999 WL 98973, at *3; *Washington Speakers Bureau, Inc. v. Leading Auths., Inc.*, No. 98-634, 1999 WL 51869, at *9 [49 USPQ2d 1893] (E.D. Va. Feb. 2, 1999); *Jews for Jesus v. Brodsky*, 993 F. Supp. 282, 304–05 [46 USPQ2d 1652] (D.N.J. 1998), *aff'd*, 159 F.3d 1351 (3d Cir. 1998); *Interstellar Starship Servs.*, 983 F. Supp. at 1336; *Planned Parenthood Fed'n of America*, 1997 WL 133313, at *8. Both companies, apparently recognizing the rapidly growing importance of Web commerce, are maneuvering to attract customers via the Web. Not only do they compete for the patronage of an overlapping audience on the Web, both "MovieBuff" and "moviebuff. com" are utilized in conjunction with Web-based products.

Given the virtual identity of "moviebuff.com" and "MovieBuff," the relatedness of the products and services accompanied by those marks, and the companies' simultaneous use of the Web as a marketing and advertising tool, many forms of consumer confusion are likely to result. People surfing the Web for information on "MovieBuff" may confuse "MovieBuff" with the searchable entertainment database at "moviebuff.com" and simply assume that they have reached Brookfield's web site. *See, e.g., Cardservice Int'l*, 950 F. Supp. at 741. In the Internet context, in particular, entering a web site takes little effort—usually one click from a linked site or a search engine's list; thus, Web surfers are more likely to be confused as to the ownership of a web site than traditional patrons of a brick-and-mortar store would be of a store's ownership. Alternatively, they may incorrectly believe that West Coast licensed "MovieBuff" from Brookfield, *see, e.g., Indianapolis Colts, Inc. v. Metropolitan Baltimore Football Club Ltd.*, 34 F.3d 410, 415–16 [31 USPQ2d 1811] (7th Cir. 1994), or that Brookfield otherwise sponsored West Coast's database, *see E. Remy Martin*, 756 F.2d at 1530; *Fuji Photo Film Co. v. Shinohara Shoji Kabushiki Kaisha,*754 F.2d 591, 596 [225 USPQ 540] (5th Cir. 1985). Other consumers may simply believe that West Coast bought out Brookfield or that they are related companies.

Yet other forms of confusion are likely to ensue. Consumers may wrongly assume that the "MovieBuff" database they were searching for is no longer offered, having been replaced by West Coast's entertainment database, and thus simply use the services at West Coast's web site. *See, e.g., Cardservice Int'l*, 950 F. Supp. at 741. And even where people realize, immediately upon accessing "moviebuff.com," that they have reached a site operated by West Coast and wholly unrelated to Brookfield, West Coast will still have gained a customer by appropriating the goodwill that Brookfield has developed in its "MovieBuff" mark. A consumer who was originally looking for Brookfield's products or services may be perfectly content with West Coast's database (especially as it is offered free of charge); but he reached West Coast's site because of its use of Brookfield's mark as its second-level domain name, which is a misappropriation of Brookfield's goodwill by West Coast....

The factors that we have considered so far—the similarity of marks, the relatedness of product offerings, and the overlap in marketing and advertising channels—lead us to the tentative conclusion that Brookfield has made a strong showing of likelihood of confusion....

We [now] turn to intent. "The law has long been established that if an infringer 'adopts his designation with the intent of deriving benefit from the reputation of the trade-mark or trade name, its intent may be sufficient to justify the inference that there are confusing similarities.'" *Pacific Telesis v. International Telesis Comms.*, 994 F.2d 1364, 1369 [26 USPQ2d 1786] (9th Cir. 1993) (quoting Restatement of Torts, Section 729, Comment on Clause (b)f (1938)). An inference of confusion has similarly been deemed appropriate where a mark is adopted with the intent to deceive the public. *See Gallo*, 967 F.2d at 1293 (citing *Sleekcraft*, 599 F.2d at 354)....

This factor favors the plaintiff where the alleged infringer adopted his mark with knowledge, actual or constructive, that it was another's trademark. *See Official Airline Guides*, 6 F.3d at 1394 ("When an alleged infringer knowingly adopts a mark similar to another's, courts will presume an intent to deceive the public."); *Fleischmann Distilling*, 314 F.2d 149 at 157. In the Internet context, in particular, courts have appropriately recognized that the intentional registration of a domain name knowing that the second-level domain is another company's valuable trademark weighs in favor of likelihood of confusion. *See, e.g., Washington Speakers*, 1999 WL 51869, at *10. There is, however, no evidence in the record that West Coast registered "moviebuff.com" with the principal intent of confusing consumers....

Importantly, an intent to confuse consumers is not required for a finding of trademark infringement. *See Dreamwerks,*142 F.3d at 1132 n. 12 ("Absence of malice is no defense to trademark infringement"); *Daddy's Junky Music Stores,* 109 F.3d at 287 ("As noted, the presence of intent can constitute strong evidence of confusion. The converse of this proposition, however, is not true: the lack of intent by a defendant is largely irrelevant in determining if consumers likely will be confused as to source.") (internal quotation marks and citations omitted); *Fleischmann Distilling,* 314 F.2d at 157. Instead, this factor is only relevant to the extent that it bears upon the likelihood that consumers will be confused by the alleged infringer's mark (or to the extent that a court wishes to consider it as an equitable consideration). *See Sleekcraft Boats,* 599 F.2d at 348 n. 10. Here, West Coast's intent does not appear to bear upon the likelihood of confusion because it did not act with such an intent from which it is appropriate to infer consumer confusion.

The final three Sleekcraft factors—evidence of actual confusion, likelihood of expansion in product lines, and purchaser care—do not affect our ultimate conclusion regarding the likelihood of confusion....Actual confusion is not relevant because Brookfield filed suit before West Coast began actively using the "moviebuff.com" mark and thus never had the opportunity to collect information on actual confusion. The likelihood of expansion in product lines factor is relatively unimportant where two companies already compete to a significant extent. *See Official Airline Guides,* 6 F.3d at 1394. In any case, it is neither exceedingly likely nor unlikely that West Coast will enter more directly into Brookfield's principal market, or vice versa.

...Likelihood of confusion is determined on the basis of a "reasonably prudent consumer." *Dreamwerks,* 142 F.3d at 1129; *Sleekcraft,* 599 F.2d at 353. What is expected of this reasonably prudent consumer depends on the circumstances. We expect him to be more discerning—and less easily confused—when he is purchasing expensive items, *see, e.g., Official Airline Guides,* 6 F.3d at 1393 (noting that confusion was unlikely among advertisers when the products in question cost from $2,400 to $16,000), and when the products being sold are marketed primarily to expert buyers, *see, e.g., Accuride Int'l, Inc. v. Accuride Corp.,* 871 F.2d 1531, 1537 [10 USPQ2d 1589] (9th Cir. 1989). We recognize, however, that confusion may often be likely even in the case of expensive goods sold to discerning customers. *See Sleekcraft,* 599 F.3d at 353; *see also, e.g., Daddy's Junky Music Stores,* 109 F.3d at 286; *Banff, Ltd. v. Federated Dep't Stores, Inc.,* 841 F.2d 486, 492 [6 USPQ2d 1187] (2d Cir. 1988). On the other hand, when dealing with inexpensive products, customers are likely to exercise less care, thus making confusion more likely. *See, e.g., Gallo,* 967 F.2d at 1293 (wine and cheese).

The complexity in this case arises because we must consider both entertainment professionals, who probably will take the time and effort to find the specific product they want, and movie devotees, who will be more easily confused as to the source of the database offered at West Coast's web site. In addition, West Coast's site is likely to be visited by many casual movie watchers. The entertainment professional, movie devotee, and casual watcher are likely to exercise high, little, and very little care, respectively. Who is the reasonably prudent consumer?...We need not, however, decide this question now because the purchaser confusion factor, even considered in the light most favorable to West Coast, is not sufficient to overcome the likelihood of confusion strongly established by the other factors we have analyzed....

In light of the foregoing analysis, we conclude that Brookfield has demonstrated a likelihood of success on its claim that West Coast's use of "moviebuff.com" violates the Lanham Act. We are fully aware that although the question of "[w]hether confusion is likely is a factual determination woven into the law," we nevertheless must review only for clear error the district court's conclusion that the evidence of likelihood of confusion in this case was slim. *See Levi Strauss & Co. v. Blue Bell, Inc.*, 778 F.2d 1352, 1356 [228 USPQ 346] (9th Cir. 1985) (en banc). Here, however, we are "left with the definite and firm conviction that a mistake has been made." *Pacific Telesis Group v. International Telesis Comms.*, 994 F.2d 1364, 1367 [26 USPQ2d 1786] (9th Cir. 1993)....

# BIGSTAR ENTERTAINMENT, INC. v. NEXT BIG STAR, INC., *et al.*

Unites States District Court, Southern District of New York
00 Civ. 0911 (VM), 105 F. Supp. 2d 185
April 17, 2000

OPINION BY: Victor Marrero

BigStar Entertainment, Inc. ("BigStar"), plaintiff in this action for a preliminary injunction, seeks to restrain Next Big Star, Inc. and related defendants (collectively, "Next Big Star") from using a name that plaintiff contends infringes on BigStar's prior trademark rights. BigStar's business for over two years has been principally the sale of videos, offered along with free information about the film industry, chat rooms and interviews with movie celebrities, all conducted online through the World Wide Web at "www. bigstar.com." Next Big Star was launched recently to conduct an entertainment talent search. For this purpose, defendants established a website at "www.nextbigstar.com" through which they plan to conduct their talent contest and offer related information, chat rooms and interviews with celebrities.

The case, typical of many trademark disputes, reaches to the fringes of the subtleties that very often enter into what is in a name and manifests the weighty consequences associated with the choice. The parties' legal quarrels here, and the issues they raise, are familiar. But the controversy adds the dimension of cyberspace. It joins the ranks of the exponential number of legal struggles arising out of the use of the Internet—as a mass medium of communication and commerce, and, more and more prolific as consumers and markets expand and competing users clash, as an incubator of lawsuits. Many among this rapidly growing variety of cases raise knotty issues, some of them novel. Do these online collisions pose new, unique difficulties to the law? To what extent do the distinct dimensions of the World Wide Web challenge the established concepts and methods developed to resolve legal conflicts arising from other media? Do the familiar approaches suffice to accommodate analysis of unaccustomed aspects of the new disputes? The case before the Court prompts some of these questions, aspects of which have not been fully addressed in this Circuit.

...For the reasons described below, this Court has concluded that BigStar, though first in time as between these parties to stake out its name, trademark and web domain, has not met the legal burden to establish it is entitled to enjoin Next Big Star at this stage of these proceedings.

## I. FINDINGS OF FACT

...BigStar...has its principal address in cyberspace at "www.bigstar.com." There it operates as an online retailer dedicated exclusively to filmed entertainment products such as videocassettes, digital video discs ("DVDs") and related movie merchandise. Plaintiff's website also provides its visitors with movie industry news, interviews with celebrities, movie previews and periodic online chats in real time with film celebrities.

Plaintiff has used variations of its name as trademarks and in a logo to identify its "Movie Superstore" on the Internet since its incorporation in March 1998 and has used and advertised its name and domain address since the launching of its website in May of 1998. Its website logo contains the words "bigstar.com" and appears in black ("bigstar") and red (".com")....

Plaintiff filed applications for trademark registration protection with the Patent and Trademark Office ("PTO") in October 1998 for "BIGSTAR" and in May 1999 for "BIGSTAR.COM." These applications remain pending. While no opposition to them has been filed to date, at least two parties, including defendants herein, have requested additional time from the PTO within which to consider whether to file a Notice of Opposition to plaintiff's marks.... According to plaintiff, it received over 3 million unique visits to its website in January 2000.

In December 1999, BigStar formed an alliance with Value Vision International Inc. ("Value Vision") and announced a venture into the offline world, where it hopes to produce a weekly television program for Value Vision's cable network. BigStar's show, to be called "THE BIGSTAR SHOW" will consist of human interest stories about film celebrities and their movies and will offer plaintiff's merchandise for sale. Plaintiff has also filed with the PTO an application to register "THE BIGSTAR SHOW" in connection with its television production.

Defendants Next Big Star, Inc. and Next Big Star L.L.C. are...involved with defendant Victory Entertainment Corporation, a multimedia company incorporated in Florida, in the development, sponsorship and production of an online talent competition to be conducted and judged on the Internet and of a related network television program to be produced quarterly in order to introduce the competition winners.... Ed McMahon, a television personality who was previously associated with The Tonight Show and who had hosted a talent competition on national television called Star Search,...joined forces with the defendants and...helped them design the contest, television show and website.

On January 25, 2000, defendants issued a press release promoting their new online talent competition and related television program and the launching of "www.nextbigstar.com" as the site for the competition. Defendants claim that their website received 4.75 million "hits" in the weeks immediately following the announcement of their venture.

Defendants' logo, which was revised shortly after this litigation commenced as a direct result of plaintiff's instant application, now contains the words "ED McMAHON'S nextbigstar.com," the first half of which appears in white or red ("ED McMAHON'S"), with the other words in yellow ("nextbigstar" and "com")....Defendants' website celebrity interviews, along with the information there provided, are intended primarily to promote the talent search and encourage participation. Defendants are also sponsoring a national bus tour to search for talent and, to this end, were scheduled to start visiting some 40 cities in March 2000.... Performances are to be displayed on the Internet for judging by individuals at home who may download, view and vote on them....

Plaintiff, upon learning of defendants' plans...moved on February 7, 2000 for a preliminary injunction under Rule 65 of the Federal Rules of Civil Procedure to restrain defendants from (a) using "Next Big Star" or "nextbigstar.com" as a trademark, trade name, Internet domain name or as part of a logo in connection with their new online talent competition or related television program and (b) taking any other actions designed or intended to infringe and dilute the value of plaintiff's trademarks, logo and domain name....

## II. CONCLUSIONS OF LAW

...BigStar raises an issue that introduces the unique dimensions of the World Wide Web and demands an inquiry regarding the applicability of a legal doctrine developed in other contexts. Plaintiff, as an instance of the likelihood of consumer confusion between the two names here in question, invites the Court to recognize initial interest confusion which may be caused in the Internet context when an initially interested consumer searching for plaintiff's "bigstar.com" website uses a search engine for assistance and is drawn instead to defendants' "nextbigstar.com" site because of the similarity between the web addresses. The concern is that many of those initially interested potential customers of plaintiff's would be diverted and distracted by defendants' site and would either believe that defendants' site is associated with plaintiff's or would not return to plaintiff's domain.

The diversion of initial interest and the resulting relevant confusion under this doctrine relate to what *draws* the consumer to the *other* location in the first place. Even if the customer quickly becomes aware of the competing source's actual identity and can rectify the mistake, the damage to the first user that the courts have identified manifest in three ways: the original diversion of the prospective customers' interest; the potential consequent effect of that diversion on the customer's ultimate decision whether or not to purchase caused by an erroneous impression that two sources of a product may be associated; and the initial credibility which may be accorded by the interested buyer to the junior user's products—customer consideration that otherwise may be unwarranted and that may be built on the strength of the senior user's mark, reputation and goodwill. *See Brookfield Communications, Inc. v. West Coast Entertainment Corp.,* 174 F.3d 1036, 1063–64 (9th Cir. 1999), and cases cited therein.

The initial interest confusion doctrine was developed by the Second Circuit in connection with Lanham Act infringement disputes involving trademarks of products in brick-and-mortar store commerce. *See Mobil Oil Corp.,* 818 F.2d 254; *Grotrian, Helfferich, Schulz, Th. Steinweg Nachf. v. Steinway & Sons,* 523 F.2d 1331 (2d Cir. 1975). The doctrine has not been adopted by this Circuit in the context of alleged infringement arising on the Internet. See *New York State Soc'y of Certified Pub. Accountants v. Eric Louis Associates, Inc.,* 79 F. Supp. 2d 331, 342 n. 5, 1999 WL 1084220, at *26, n.5 (S.D.N.Y. 1999). However, the doctrine as applied by the Second Circuit has made clear that the particular instance of infringement at issue derived from just a particular variety of potential customer confusion and that the analysis to be applied to gauge the likelihood of such confusion rested on the same *Polaroid* factors which guided the appraisal of other recognized forms of trademark infringement confusion. This Court sees no reason why the approach to that assessment would be substantially different were the doctrine to be applied to the facts of this case and an infringement claim arising out of trademarks used for commerce conducted through the Internet....

The *Brookfield* case is distinguishable from the one presently before this Court for several important and mitigating reasons. There, the plaintiff specifically requested injunctive relief against defendants' use of metatags identical to plaintiff's mark. *Id.* at 1061. Here, there is no evidence, or even an allegation by BigStar, that defendants have used "BIGSTAR" or "BIGSTAR.COM" in metatags by which they have diverted to their site the initial interest of potential buyers looking to patronize BigStar. Moreover, plaintiff's argument suggests that potential customers searching for BigStar's domain could be directed by a search engine to defendants' website, that these customers would then assume that defendants' website is somehow associated with the plaintiff's and that they may decide to remain at defendants' site. The core of this argument is that the initial confusion the prospective patrons may encounter by virtue of defendants' mark relates to the *source*. In *Brookfield*, the Court found that there was "no source confusion," in the sense that consumers reaching defendant's web site would know they were patronizing West Coast rather than Brookfield. *Id.* at 1062. The *Brookfield* analysis, in fact, would reject the theory BigStar propounds here. The Ninth Circuit, despite the virtually identical names at issue, noted that "since there is no confusion resulting from the domain address, and since West Coast's initial web page prominently displays its own name, it is difficult to say that a consumer is likely to be confused about whose site he has reached or to think that Brookfield somehow sponsors West Coast's web site." *Id.* at 1062.

Where the *Brookfield* court found wrongful initial interest confusion was in defendants' knowing or intentional use of plaintiff's mark in defendants' metatags, which had the effect of diverting customers looking for Brookfield's products to West Coast's website, thereby enabling defendant to profit from plaintiff's established goodwill and reputation. *Id.* at 1061–65. As stated above, neither the use of metatags by Next Big Star nor evidence of its bad faith in that connection is at issue in the case before this Court.

Second, even if the initial interest confusion through search engine diversion were inadvertent, plaintiff's arguments fail for other reasons that weighed heavily in the *Brookfield* decision. In *Brookfield*, and in other cases bearing on this point, the infringing domain name was masquerading as or was virtually identical to the trademark. *See id.* (domain "moviebuff.com" compared with "MovieBuff" mark). *See also Interstellar Starship Services, Ltd. v. Epix Inc.,* 184 F.3d 1107 (9th Cir. 1999), *cert. denied,* — U.S. — 145 L. Ed. 2d 1073, 120 S. Ct. 1161 (2000) ("epix.com" domain name compared with "EPIX" trematrk); *Eric Louis Associates, Inc.,* 1999 WL 1084220 (domain name "nysscpa.com" caused likelihood of confusion with "NYSSCPA" mark); *SNA, Inc. v. Array,* 51 F. Supp. 2d 542 (E.D. Pa. 1999) (use of plaintiff's exact mark "Seawind" for defendant's "seawind.net" website address highly likely to cause confusion); *Cardservice Int'l, Inc. v. McGee,* 950 F. Supp. 737, 741–42 (E.D. Va. 1997), *aff'd,* 1997 U.S. App. LEXIS 32267 (4th Cir. Nov. 18, 1997) (where companies both provided credit and debit card services, use of defendant's "cardservice.com" domain name "exactly duplicates" and infringes plaintiff's registered "Cardservice" trademark)....

Here, defendants' domain name ("nextbigstar.com") is not "virtually identical" to plaintiff's trademarks or website ("bigstar.com"). Defendants are not using "bigstar. com" as their domain name. Instead, they are using "nextbigstar.com," a domain name which, when examined in the light of the entire context relevant here...is neither identical to the BigStar marks in terms of sight, sound or meaning, nor one the ordinary, reasonably informed relevant purchaser could not regard as exactly the same.

Third, plaintiff's reliance on *Brookfield* and its initial interest analysis fails also because of the identity or close relationship between products involved there and in other cases applying the doctrine. These cases, though stressing that the real test for infringement was the likelihood of confusion rather than direct competition, found strong competitive proximity between the products offered by the rival claimants. Accordingly, as in the case of likelihood of other kinds of confusion, the form associated with the diversion of initial interest presumably would not arise, or would be minimized, in circumstances where the products in question are used for substantially different purposes and therefore the merchants are not in close competitive proximity, even if there may be some similarity between their marks. *Brookfield Communications, Inc.,* 174 F.3d at 1056.

This Court has found that the parties here are not in direct competition with one another,... and their marks and businesses are not sufficiently closely related.... The Court deems it unlikely that an appreciable number of ordinary, reasonably informed potential customers searching for "bigstar.com" to purchase a video or obtain movie star information who mistakenly navigate to the talent search at "nextbigstar.com" would be confused in that they would assume, despite the dissimilarities in the marks, that the two websites are associated. Similarly, we view it as unlikely that numerous such prospective video customers, upon realizing an error in reaching the wrong website, would not resume their endeavor to find the product they originally sought by reason of some attraction to defendants' talent competition. To the extent that the likelihood of some such confusion may nonetheless remain on account of this factor, the Court believes it would not be actionable under the circumstances presented by this case because the operation of the other *Polaroid* factors still weigh heavily against this finding.

Fourth, an essential element present in the facts of the Second Circuit initial interest confusion cases and in *Brookfield* was a strong mark and firmly established product quality, goodwill and reputation developed by the first user. The junior user, offering competing goods, sought knowingly to benefit from public recognition of the senior company's name and credibility by seeking to attract potential customers the infringer ordinarily would not have had. In *Brookfield*, for example, the court determined that plaintiff's mark was suggestive, therefore not requiring a showing of secondary meaning to establish eligibility for protection. Here, as the Court has found, BigStar's marks are descriptive. There is an insufficient record to sustain a finding that plaintiff has established longstanding public recognition of its name, reputation and goodwill or that defendants sought to build their own clientele on the strength of any credibility derived from plaintiff's trademarks.

Fifth, in the initial interest confusion cases arising in the context of the Internet, the similarity of marks at issue involved only two essentially identical names, under circumstances in which either both or only one had established a domain on the World Wide Web. No indication of substantial third party use of the same domain name was involved. Where only two entities are claiming rights to exactly the same or essentially similar mark on the Web, there is a strong likelihood that a prospective customer initially searching for the senior business may be diverted to the junior. But in a case such as here where there is evidence of use by third parties of other "bigstar" web addresses, the likelihood of confusion attributed to initial interest diversion by any one of the users of the mark becomes more speculative and difficult to substantiate, except by strong evidentiary demonstration. In that event, a search engine inquiry originally seeking plaintiff's "bigstar.com" address would produce the sites of the various domains containing other "bigstar.com" addresses as well, to any one of which the prospective purchaser theoretically could be diverted, and not just to defendants' site....

For the foregoing reasons, this Court declines to apply this initial interest confusion doctrine in the context of the Internet in an case involving (1) non-competitors; (2) web addresses not virtually identical; (3) weak marks without sufficient evidence of secondary meaning; (4) substantially different products; (5) similar names and trademarks used by other third parties; (6) no intentional use of plaintiff's marks by defendants in defendants' metatags; and (7) no evidence of bad faith efforts by defendants to divert patronage by trading on any name, goodwill or reputation plaintiff may have established....

# 3. Cybergriping

Numerous web-sites have been formed to criticize particular businesses and products, employing the tactic of registering the domain name "www.[company or product]sucks.com." This developing Internet phenomenon has been characterized as "cybergriping." *See, e.g., Lucent Technologies, Inc. v. Lucentsucks.com,* 95 F. Supp. 2d 528, 535 n. 9 (E.D. Va. 2000) (citing Greg Farrell, *From Sour Grapes to Online Whine,* USA Today (Apr. 6, 2000) at 01B; Thomas E. Anderson, *Emerging Intellectual Property Issues in Cyberspace,* 78 Mich. B. J. 1260, 1263 (1999)).

As mentioned previously, in *Bally Total Fitness Holding Corp. v. Faber,* 29 F. Supp. 2d 1161 (C.D. Cal. 1998), the court held that use of "Bally Sucks" on a site criticizing the plaintiff's health clubs did not dilute the plaintiff's "Bally" trademark. The web-site was found to have used the term for non-commercial expression and in protected expressive speech. An administrative panel of the WIPO Arbitration and Mediation Center reached a different conclusion in *Wal-Mart Stores, Inc. v. Walsucks and Walmart Puerto Rico,* Case No. D2000-0477 (July 20, 2000) <http://www.arbiter.wipo.int/domains/ decisions/html/ d2000-0477.html>. There, the panel determined that the defendant, who registered "walsucks," had engaged in abusive domain name registration.

> When an Internet user enters a word or combination of words into a search engine, the engine identifies websites of potential relevance by canvassing domain names, metatags and (potentially) other web page codes. By using Complainant's "Wal-Mart" mark in its domain name, Respondent makes it likely that Internet users entering "Wal-Mart" into a search engine will find its "wal-martcanadasucks.com" and other "walmart"-formative websites....

> Internet users with search engine results listing Respondent's domains are likely to be puzzled or surprised by the coupling of Complainant's mark with the pejorative verb "sucks." Such users, including potential customers of Complainant, are not likely to conclude that Complainant is the sponsor of the identified websites. However, it is likely (given the relative ease by which web-sites can be entered) that such users will choose to visit the sites, if only to satisfy their curiosity. Respondent will have accomplished his objective of diverting potential customers of Complainant to his websites by the use of domain names that are similar to Complainant's trademark.

*Id.* The panel expressly refrained from making any determination regarding the registrants and users of other "-sucks" formative domain names, and distinguished this case from others using such terminology on the ground that the Respondent did not register the domain names in order to express opinions or seek the expression of others' opinions. Rather, "[t]he record indicates that his intention was to extract money from Complainant," which merited a finding of abusive domain name registration. *Id.*

In another illustration of incorporating "sucks" into the domain name, web-site 2600.com stated that it had tried to register the name "verizonsucks.com," purportedly because "if our past experience with phone companies is any indication, Verizon[, the company formed by the merger of Bell Atlantic and GTE,] will in all probability be thought of this way in the near future." *Verizon Attacks Critical Domain Names,* 2600

(May 8, 2000) <http://www.2600.com/news/2000/0508.html>. According to 2600.com, Verizon sent the site a cease and desist letter, pointing out that the telephone company had registered the domain name itself (presumably to preclude others from creating such a site). *See id.* 2600.com evidently then tried to register the domain name "verizon-REALLYsucks.com," only to be sent another cease and desist letter. *See id.* In response, 2600.com has stated that it registered the domain name "VerizonShouldSpendMore-TimeFixingItsNetworkAndLessMoneyOnLawyers.com." *Id.*

---

# 4. Cybersquatting

The term "cybersquatting" is used colloquially to refer to the act of procuring a domain name of a well-known trademark by a non-trademark holder who then tries to sell the name back to the trademark owner. Because domain name registrars have not checked to see whether a domain name request is related to existing trademarks, it has been simple and inexpensive for any person to register as domain names the marks of established companies. *See generally Sporty's Farm L.L.C. v. Sportsman's Market, Inc.,* 202 F.3d 489 (2d Cir.), *cert. denied,* 120 S.Ct. 2719 (2000).

Cybersquatting can be damaging to businesses in a number of ways. For example, because domain names are exclusive, a cyberpirate's expropriation of a mark as part of a domain name prevents the trademark owner from using that mark as part of its domain name. Moreover, consumers seeking access to a trademark owner's web-site are diverted elsewhere, which may mean lost business opportunities for the trademark owner. A cyberpirate's use may also blur the distinctive quality of the mark, and, when linked to certain types of Internet sites, such as pornographic sites, may tarnish the mark. Additionally, businesses are required to expend resources to police and enforce their trademark rights by preventing unauthorized use, or risk losing or diluting those rights. *See* H.R. Rep. No. 106-412, at 6 (1999). The marks' rightful owners not infrequently have been willing to pay "ransom" funds to reclaim their names that were held "hostage." *See id.* at 5–7; S. Rep. No. 106-140, at 4–7 (1999).

In order to address many of these concerns, on November 29, 1999, Congress enacted the Anticybersquatting Consumer Protection Act, amending section 43 of the federal Trademark Act, 15 U.S.C.A. § 1125 (West 1997 & Supp. 2000). The provision creates a new cause of action for trademark owners to challenge bad faith registration of the owners' trademarks as Internet domain names.

The anticybersquatting legislation is designed to thwart the practice of usurping others' valid trademarks for improper purposes. The statute seeks to "balance[ ] the property interests of trademark owners with the interests of Internet users who would make fair use of others' marks or otherwise engage in protected speech online." 145 Cong. Rec. S9744-01 (daily ed. July 29, 1999) (statement of Sen. Hatch).

What happens when the identity of the cybersquatter cannot readily be ascertained? Under certain circumstances, cybersquatting may be challenged through the assertion of in rem actions against the domain name itself. *See, e.g., Porsche Cars N. Am., Inc. v. Allporsche.com,* No. 99-1804, 2000 U.S. App. LEXIS 12843 (4th Cir. June 9, 2000) (vacating the district court's order of dismissal and remanding the case for reconsideration of the motion to dismiss for lack of in personam jurisdiction in light of the in rem provisions of the Anticybersquatting Act).

# LUCENT TECHNOLOGIES, INC. v.
# LUCENTSUCKS.COM

United States District Court, Eastern District of Virginia, Alexandria Division.
No. Civ. A. 99-1916-A, 95 F. Supp. 2d 528
May 3, 2000

BRINKEMA, District Judge.

Before the Court is the Motion of Defendant lucentsucks.com's [sic] to Dismiss the Complaint, in which defendant argues that plaintiff's failure to comply with the requirements of the recently enacted Anti-Cybersquatting Consumer Protection Act mandates dismissal of the complaint. For the reasons stated below, the motion will be granted.

## I. BACKGROUND

Plaintiff Lucent Technologies, Inc. is a Delaware Corporation with its principal place of business in Murray Hill, New Jersey. It has filed this in rem action against the domain name lucentsucks.com under the Anti-Cybersquatting Consumer Protection Act ("ACPA"), 15 U.S.C. § 1125.

Plaintiff alleges that, on November 30, 1995, its predecessor filed an application with the United States Patent and Trademark Office ("PTO") to register LUCENT as a trademark. Since 1996, plaintiff has manufactured, marketed and sold telecommunications equipment and services under the marks LUCENT and LUCENT TECHNOLOGIES. It has registered and applied to register LUCENT marks with the PTO for a variety of goods and services. Plaintiff alleges that the money and effort it has expended on advertising and promoting its products and services under these marks has created valuable goodwill in the marks.

According to plaintiff, on August 2, 1998, Russell Johnson registered the domain name lucentsucks.com through Network Solutions, Inc. ("NSI"), located in Herndon, Virginia. Plaintiff alleges that the website at this domain name contains pornographic photographs and services for sale.

Plaintiff advances two causes of action: Count I, Trademark Infringement, 15 U.S.C. § 1114(1) and 15 U.S.C. § 1125(a); and Count II, dilution, Section 43(c) of the Lanham Act, 15 U.S.C. § 1125(c). Plaintiff seeks court order directing NSI to transfer registration of lucentsucks.com to Lucent.

## II. DISCUSSION

Lucentsucks.com raises several arguments in support of its argument to dismiss the complaint: plaintiff did not satisfy the in rem jurisdictional requirements of the ACPA; an internet domain name is not "property," for purposes of obtaining in rem jurisdiction; and First Amendment principles would be violated if plaintiff could force forfeiture of defendant domain name. We find for the reasons discussed below that plaintiff failed to satisfy the jurisdictional requirements of the ACPA, and therefore will dismiss the complaint on that basis. Because the ACPA is a new statute, and is still the source of some confusion, we also briefly address some of defendant's other arguments.

## A. The ACPA

On November 29, 1999, the Anticybersquatting Consumer Protection Act ("ACPA"), Pub.L. No. 106-113, 113 Stat. 1501 (codified as amended at 15 U.S.C. §§ 1114, 1116, 1117, 1125, 1127, 1129 (1999)), went into effect as an amendment to the Trademark Act. Congress enacted the ACPA to address the growing phenomenon of "cyberpiracy or cybersquating," which involves "registering, trafficking in, or using domain names (Internet addresses) that are identical or confusingly similar to trademarks with the bad-faith intent to profit from the goodwill of trademarks." H.R. Rep. No. 106-412, at 7 (1999).

Supporters of the ACPA were particularly concerned about anonymous trademark violators on the Internet. That is, they were troubled by the increasing trend of individuals registering domain names in violation of trademark rights and then eluding trademark enforcement because they could not be found. The Senate Judiciary Committee observed:

> A significant problem faced by trademark owners in the fight against cybersquatting is the fact that many cybersquatters register domain names under aliases or otherwise provide false information in their registration applications in order to avoid identification and service of process by the mark owner.

Sen. Rep. No. 106-140, at 4 (1999). The Judiciary Committee believed that including an in rem provision in the ACPA would alleviate the problem of anonymous cybersquatters, by allowing a mark owner to file an action against the domain name itself, provided it satisfied the court that it exercised due diligence in trying to locate the owner of the domain name but could not do so. *Id.*

## B. Plaintiff's Efforts to Comply with the In Rem Provision

Once plaintiff learned of lucentsucks.com, its in-house counsel sought the name and address of the registrant for that domain name from NSI, the registry. NSI's records showed a registrant by the name of Russell Johnson. On November 11, 1999, plaintiff's in-house counsel sent a letter via Federal Express to Johnson at the address listed with NSI. In it, plaintiff demanded that Johnson "immediately cease and desist from engaging in or permitting any further or future use of the Lucent Marks..." The letter was returned by Federal Express as undeliverable.

Plaintiff contacted NSI to determine whether Johnson had changed his address on the lucentsucks.com registration. Although NSI's agreement with registrants requires that they maintain current mail and e-mail addresses, no changes of address were noted for Johnson. Plaintiff then sent another demand letter on December 8, 1999, to the addresses listed with NSI. This letter, however, was sent first class United States Postal Service mail and e-mail. In the letter, plaintiff referred to the in rem provision of the just-enacted ACPA:

> Because we have not been able to reach you, Lucent Technologies Inc. intends to proceed with filing an in rem civil action against your domain name registration Lucentsucks.com pursuant to Section 43(d)(2)(A) of the Lanham Act, 15 U.S.C. § 1125(d)(2)(A).

The e-mail was returned as undeliverable. However, the letter sent via first class mail was successfully delivered to Johnson. The record shows that Johnson had moved after registering the domain name with NSI, and that he left a forwarding address with the United States Postal Service ("U.S.P.S.").

On December 16, 1999, eight days after the second demand letter was mailed and e-mailed, plaintiff filed this action. On December 21, 1999, thirteen days after the second demand letter was sent, Johnson called Lucent's outside counsel. Counsel informed Johnson that an in rem suit had been filed, and Johnson provided counsel a pager number. On December 22, 1999, Johnson called counsel again, allegedly asking for money in exchange for releasing the domain name. Counsel called Johnson later that day to reject the offer. Johnson gave counsel his new address during that call, and counsel sent a copy of the complaint to that address.

Although plaintiff now knew the location of the registrant, it continued to prosecute its in rem action under the ACPA. Plaintiff moved for Entry of Order to Publish Notice of Action on January 7, 2000. The ordered was entered and plaintiff published a notice of the action in *The Washington Post* for two consecutive weeks. It also mailed copies of the Order and the complaint to registrant's address as provided by NSI and as provided by Johnson. Plaintiff filed an affidavit of compliance on February 11, 2000.

## C. Plaintiff Has Not Satisified the Requirements of the In Rem Provision

By the express terms of Section 1125(d)(2)(A)(ii) of the ACPA, a plaintiff may proceed with an in rem action against a domain name if and only if the Court finds either that the plaintiff is unable to obtain in personam jurisdiction over the domain name registrant, or that the plaintiff is unable to find the domain name registrant.[4] Plaintiff does not base in rem jurisdiction on an inability to assert in personam jurisdiction. Instead, it rests its case on Section 1125(d)(2)(A)(ii)(II).…:

> The owner of a mark may file an in rem civil action against a domain name in the judicial district in which the domain name registrar…that registered or assigned the domain name is located if…(ii) the court finds that the owner… (II) through due diligence was not able to find a person who would have been a defendant in a civil action under paragraph (1) by—(aa) sending notice of the alleged violation and intent to proceed under this paragraph to the registrant of the domain name at the postal and e-mail address provided by the registrant to the registrar; and (bb) publishing notice of the action as the court may direct promptly after filing the action.

---

4. The in rem provision, in its entirety, provides:
    The owner of a mark may file an in rem civil action against a domain name in the judicial district in which the domain name registrar, domain name registry, or other domain name authority that registered or assigned the domain name is located if—
    (i)   the domain name violates any right of the owner of a mark registered in the Patent and Trademark Office, or protected under subsection (a) and (c); and
    (ii)  the court finds that the owner—
        (I)   is not able to obtain in personam jurisdiction over a person who would have been a defendant and in a civil action under paragraph (1); or
        (II)  through due diligence was not able to find a person who would have been a defendant in a civil action under paragraph (1) by—
            (aa) sending a notice of the alleged violation and intent to proceed under this paragraph to the registrant of the domain name at the postal and e-mail address provided by the registrant to the registrar; and
            (bb) publishing notice of the action as the court may direct promptly after filing the action.
    15 U.S.C. § 1125(d)(2)(A).

15 U.S.C. § 1125(d)(2)(A).

We find that, based on the allegations in plaintiff's complaint, Russell Johnson, the listed registrant of defendant lucentsucks.com would be "a person who would have been a defendant in a civil action under paragraph (1)." Therefore, proceeding any further in rem is not appropriate. We also find that plaintiff failed to satisfy the due diligence clause, Section 1125(d)(2)(A)(ii)(II)(aa), because it did not allow a reasonable time for Johnson to respond to its December 8, 1999 notice before filing the in rem complaint....

### 3. Congress Prefers In Personam Jurisdiction

Our holding is consistent with the Congressional intent behind the in rem provision of the ACPA. The legislative history clearly shows that Congress enacted the provision to provide a last resort where in personam jurisdiction is impossible, because the domain name registrant is foreign or anonymous. Congress did not intend to provide an easy way for trademark owners to proceed in rem after jumping through a few pro forma hoops.

At least in part, Congressional concern for the Due Process rights of domain name registrants was inspired by this court's decision in *Porsche Cars North America, Inc. v. Porsh.Com*, 51 F. Supp. 2d 707 (E.D. Va. 1999). In *Porsche*, Judge Cacheris highlighted the important constitutional distinction between suing the domain name registrant in personam and not being able to find the registrant, in which case, one may proceed in rem:

> Porsche correctly observes that some of the domain names at issue have registrants whose identities and addresses are unknown and against whom in personam proceedings may be fruitless. But most of the domain names in this case have registrants—whose identities and addresses are known, and who rightly would object to having their interests adjudicated in absentia. The Due Process Clause requires at least some appreciation for the differences between these two groups, and Porsche's pursuit of an in rem remedy that fails to differentiate between them at all is fatal to the Complaint.

*Id.* at 712 (citing *Mullane v. Central Hanover Bank & Trust Co.*, 339 U.S. 306, 317–18, 70 S.Ct. 652, 94 L.Ed. 865 (1950)). Senator Leahy quoted the above language when he introduced the current in rem provisions of ACPA and commented:

> The [*Porsche*] court held that in rem actions against allegedly diluting marks are not constitutionally permitted without regard to whether in personam jurisdiction may be exercised....
>
> This legislation does differentiate between those two different categories of domain name registrants and limits in rem actions to those circumstances where in personam jurisdiction cannot be obtained.

145 Cong. Rec. S14,986–03, S15,026 (daily ed. Nov. 19, 1999) (statement of Sen. Leahy).

In our case, the identity and address of the registrant of the offending domain name, lucentsucks.com, has been found timely and in personam jurisdiction is possible. This is not the scenario envisioned by Congress when it enacted the in rem provision. Therefore, plaintiff is not entitled to proceed with this action.

### D. Defendant's Other Arguments

Besides failure to satisfy the in rem provision, defendant argues that the complaint should be dismissed because a domain name is not "property" justifying in rem jurisdiction, and plaintiff's action is an affront to free speech rights.

### 1. Domain Names are Property

Defendant contends that an Internet domain name is not a "thing," in the same way that a boat or a bridge is a "thing," because it does not occupy space or exist in a particular place. Therefore, according to defendant, a domain name cannot constitute a "res" for purposes of establishing in rem jurisdiction.

This argument has been raised before with regard to the ACPA, and we find Judge Bryan's articulate rejection of it beyond reproach:

> There is no prohibition on a legislative body making something property. Even if a domain name is no more than data, Congress can make data property and assign its place of registration as its situs.

*Ceasars World, Inc. v. Ceasars-Palace.com*, No. 99-550-A, at 5 (E.D. Va. filed Mar. 3, 2000).

### 2. Domain Names Signaling Parody Suggest Absence of Likelihood of Confusion and Bad-Faith Intent

Defendant maintains that dismissal of this complaint is also warranted because, as a matter of law, plaintiff could not make out a violation of trademark rights without infringing the registrant's free speech rights. We need not rule on this argument, because we have found other grounds for dismissal. Nevertheless, we note that defendant's position has some merit.

The likelihood of confusion is a key element when determining whether trademark infringement or dilution has occurred. *Petro Stopping Centers, L.P. v. James River Petroleum, Inc.*, 130 F.3d 88, 91 (4th Cir. 1997) (plaintiff must show that it has a valid trademark and that the defendant's reproduction, counterfeit, copy, or colorable imitation of it creates a likelihood of confusion). The Fourth Circuit has acknowledged that effective parody "diminishes any risk of consumer confusion," and can therefore not give rise to a cause of action under the Trademark Act. *Anheuser-Busch, Inc. v. L & L Wings, Inc.*, 962 F.2d 316, 321 (4th Cir. 1992). Defendant argues persuasively that the average consumer would not confuse lucentsucks.com with a web site sponsored by plaintiff.

Moreover, no civil action for trademark infringement or dilution lies under the ACPA unless the registrant's bad faith intent is demonstrated. 15 U.S.C. § 1125(d)(1)(A)(i). Courts may consider nine factors when determining whether a bad faith intent exists, including "the person's bona fide noncommercial or fair use of the mark in a site accessible under the domain name." 15 U.S.C. § 1125(B)(i)(IV). The House Judiciary Committee explained that this provision is intended to:

> [b]alance the interests of trademark owners with the interests of those who would make the lawful noncommercial or fair uses of others' marks online, such as in comparative advertising, comment, criticism, parody, newsreporting, etc.... The fact that a person may use a mark in a site in such a lawful manner may be an appropriate indication that the person's registration or use of the domain name lacked the required element of bad-faith.

H.R. Rep. No. 106-412, at 9 (1999). As one federal court has explained, "'sucks' has entered the vernacular as a word loaded with criticism." *Bally Total Fitness Holding Corp. v. Faber*, 29 F. Supp. 2d 1161, 1164 (C.D. Cal. 1998) (granting summary judgment to defendant website designer on claims brought pursuant to the Trademark Act, where defendant registered the domain name ballysucks.com). A successful showing that lucentsucks.com is effective parody and/or a cite for critical commentary would seriously undermine the requisite elements for the causes of action at issue in this case.

## III. CONCLUSION

Because we find that plaintiff instituted this in rem action too hastily after mailing and e-mailing the notice of a proposed in rem action to the registrant of lucentsucks.com, we cannot make the necessary prerequisite findings to permit an in rem action to proceed pursuant to Section 1125(d)(2)(A)(ii)(II) of the ACPA. Therefore, defendant's motion will be granted, and plaintiff's in rem action will be dismissed by an appropriate order.

---

What constitutes "bad faith" adoption of the domain name? The anticybersquatting legislation lists several factors for the court's consideration:

- the person's trademark or other intellectual property rights in the domain name;
- the extent to which the domain consists of the person's legal name or a name that is commonly used to identify that person;
- the person's prior use, if any, of the domain name in connection with the *bona fide* offering of goods or services;
- the person's *bona fide* non-commercial or fair use of the mark in a site accessible under the domain name;
- the person's intention to divert consumers from the on-line location of the owner's mark to a site accessible under the domain name that, by creating a likelihood of confusion as to the source, sponsorship, affiliation or endorsement of the site, could harm the goodwill associated with the mark;
- the person's prior pattern of conduct or offer to transfer, sell, or assign the domain name to the mark owner or a third party for financial gain without having used, or intended to use, the domain name in the *bona fide* offering of any goods or services;
- the person's history or provision of material and misleading contact information when registering the domain name or the person's intentional failure to maintain accurate contact information;
- the person's registration or acquisition of multiple domain names that are identical or confusingly similar to the distinctive marks of other parties; and
- the extent to which the mark that is part of the domain name is distinctive or famous.

15 U.S.C.A. § 1125(d)(1)(B)(i) (West 1997). In general, bad faith will not be proven "in any case in which the court determines that the person believed and had reasonable grounds to believe that the use of the domain name was a fair use or otherwise lawful." 15 U.S.C.A. § 1125(d)(1)(c).

The Act is deferential to free speech considerations. *See* 145 Cong. Rec. S9744-01 (daily ed. July 29, 1999). Protection accordingly should be granted to those who make such valid uses of trademarks as for on-line news reporting, comment, criticism, and parody, so as not to affect traditional trademark defenses (such as fair use).

---

# SPORTY'S FARM L.L.C. v.
# SPORTSMAN'S MARKET, INC.

United States Court of Appeals, Second Circuit
Docket Nos. 98-7452, 98-7538, 202 F.3d 489
February 2, 2000

Before: Oakes, Calabresi, and Gibson, Circuit Judges.

Calabresi, Circuit Judge:

This case originally involved the application of the Federal Trademark Dilution Act ("FTDA") to the Internet. *See* Federal Trademark Dilution Act of 1995, Pub.L. No. 104-98, 109 Stat. 985 (codified at 15 U.S.C. §§ 1125, 1127 (Supp. 1996)). While the case was pending on appeal, however, the Anticybersquatting Consumer Protection Act ("ACPA"), Pub. L. No. 106-113 (1999), see H.R. Rep. No. 106-479 (Nov. 18, 1999), was passed and signed into law. That new law applies to this case.

Plaintiff-Counter-Defendant-Appellant-Cross-Appellee Sporty's Farm L.L.C. ("Sporty's Farm") appeals from a judgment, following a bench trial, of the United States District Court for the District of Connecticut (Alfred V. Covello, Chief Judge ) dated March 13, 1998. Defendant-Third-Party-Plaintiff-Counter-Claimant-Appellee-Cross-Appellant Sportsman's Market, Inc. ("Sportsman's") cross-appeals from the same judgment....

Sportsman's is a mail order catalog company that is quite well-known among pilots and aviation enthusiasts for selling products tailored to their needs. In recent years, Sportsman's has expanded its catalog business well beyond the aviation market into that for tools and home accessories. The company annually distributes approximately 18 million catalogs nationwide, and has yearly revenues of about $50 million. Aviation sales account for about 60% of Sportsman's revenue, while non-aviation sales comprise the remaining 40%.

In the 1960s, Sportsman's began using the logo "sporty" to identify its catalogs and products. In 1985, Sportsman's registered the trademark sporty's with the United States Patent and Trademark Office. Since then, Sportsman's has complied with all statutory requirements to preserve its interest in the sporty's mark. Sporty's appears on the cover of all Sportsman's catalogs; Sportsman's international toll free number is 1-800-4sportys; and one of Sportsman's domestic toll free phone numbers is 1-800-Sportys. Sportsman's spends about $10 million per year advertising its sporty's logo.

Omega is a mail order catalog company that sells mainly scientific process measurement and control instruments. In late 1994 or early 1995, the owners of Omega, Arthur and Betty Hollander, decided to enter the aviation catalog business and, for that purpose, formed a wholly-owned subsidiary called Pilot's Depot, LLC ("Pilot's Depot"). Shortly thereafter, Omega registered the domain name sportys.com with NSI. Arthur Hollander was a pilot who received Sportsman's catalogs and thus was aware of the sporty's trademark.

In January 1996, nine months after registering sportys.com, Omega formed another wholly-owned subsidiary called Sporty's Farm and sold it the rights to sportys.com for $16,200. Sporty's Farm grows and sells Christmas trees, and soon began advertising its Christmas trees on a sportys.com web page. When asked how the name Sporty's Farm was selected for Omega's Christmas tree subsidiary, Ralph S. Michael, the CEO of Omega and manager of Sporty's Farm, explained, as summarized by the district court, that in his own mind and among his family, he always thought of and referred to the Pennsylvania land where Sporty's Farm now operates as Spotty's farm. The origin of the name...derived from a childhood memory he had of his uncle's farm in upstate New York. As a youngster, Michael owned a dog named Spotty. Because the dog strayed, his uncle took him to his upstate farm. Michael thereafter referred to the farm as Spotty's farm. The name Sporty's Farm was...a subsequent derivation.

There is, however, no evidence in the record that Hollander was considering starting a Christmas tree business when he registered sportys.com or that Hollander was ever acquainted with Michael's dog Spotty.

In March 1996, Sportsman's discovered that Omega had registered sportys.com as a domain name. Thereafter, and before Sportsman's could take any action, Sporty's Farm brought this declaratory action seeking the right to continue its use of sportys.com. Sportsman's counterclaimed and also sued Omega as a third-party defendant for, *inter alia*, (1) trademark infringement, (2) trademark dilution pursuant to the FTDA, and (3) unfair competition under state law. Both sides sought injunctive relief to force the other to relinquish its claims to sportys.com. While this litigation was ongoing, Sportsman's used "sportys-catalogs.com" as its primary domain name....

As we noted above, while this appeal was pending, Congress passed the ACPA. That law was passed "to protect consumers and American businesses, to promote the growth of online commerce, and to provide clarity in the law for trademark owners by prohibiting the bad-faith and abusive registration of distinctive marks as Internet domain names with the intent to profit from the goodwill associated with such marks—a practice commonly referred to as 'cybersquatting.'" S. Rep. No. 106-140, at 4. In particular, Congress viewed the legal remedies available for victims of cybersquatting before the passage of the ACPA as "expensive and uncertain." H.R. Rep. No. 106-412, at 6. The Senate made clear its view on this point:

> While the [FTDA] has been useful in pursuing cybersquatters, cybersquatters have become increasingly sophisticated as the case law has developed and now take the necessary precautions to insulate themselves from liability. For example, many cybersquatters are now careful to no longer offer the domain name for sale in any manner that could implicate liability under existing trademark dilution case law. And, in cases of warehousing and trafficking in domain names, courts have sometimes declined to provide assistance to trademark holders, leaving them without adequate and effective judicial remedies. This uncertainty as to the trademark law's application to the Internet has produced inconsistent judicial decisions and created extensive monitoring obligations, unnecessary legal costs, and uncertainty for consumers and trademark owners alike.

S. Rep. No. 106-140, at 7.

In short, the ACPA was passed to remedy the perceived shortcomings of applying the FTDA in cybersquatting cases such as this one.

The new act accordingly amends the Trademark Act of 1946, creating a specific federal remedy for cybersquatting. New 15 U.S.C. § 1125(d)(1)(A) reads:

> A person shall be liable in a civil action by the owner of a mark, including a personal name which is protected as a mark under this section, if, without regard to the goods or services of the parties, that person—

   (i)  has a bad faith intent to profit from that mark, including a personal name
        which is protected as a mark under this section; and
  (ii)  registers, traffics in, or uses a domain name that—
        (I)  in the case of a mark that is distinctive at the time of registration of
             the domain name, is identical or confusingly similar to that mark;
        (II) in the case of a famous mark that is famous at the time of registration
             of the domain name, is identical or confusingly similar to or dilutive
             of that mark....

The Act further provides that "a court may order the forfeiture or cancellation of the
domain name or the transfer of the domain name to the owner of the mark," 15 U.S.C.
§ 1125(d)(1)(C), if the domain name was "registered before, on, or after the date of the
enactment of this Act," Pub. L. No. 106-113, § 3010. It also provides that damages can
be awarded for violations of the Act, but that they are not "available with respect to the
registration, trafficking, or use of a domain name that occurs before the date of the enactment of this Act." *Id.*

DISCUSSION...

## "Distinctive" or "Famous"

Under the new Act, we must first determine whether sporty's is a distinctive or famous mark and thus entitled to the ACPA's protection. *See* 15 U.S.C.
§ 1125(d)(1)(A)(ii)(I), (II). The district court concluded that sporty's is both distinctive
and famous. We agree that sporty's is a "distinctive" mark. As a result, and without casting any doubt on the district court's holding in this respect, we need not, and hence do
not, decide whether sporty's is also a "famous" mark.[10]

Distinctiveness refers to inherent qualities of a mark and is a completely different
concept from fame. A mark may be distinctive before it has been used—when its fame
is nonexistent. By the same token, even a famous mark may be so ordinary, or descriptive as to be notable for its lack of distinctiveness. *See Nabisco, Inc. v. PF Brands, Inc.,* 191
F.3d 208, 215–26 (2d Cir. 1999). We have no doubt that sporty's, as used in connection
with Sportsman's catalogue of merchandise and advertising, is inherently distinctive.
Furthermore, Sportsman's filed an affidavit under 15 U.S.C. § 1065 that rendered its
registration of the sporty's mark incontestable, which entitles Sportsman's "to a presumption that its registered trademark is inherently distinctive." *Equine Technologies,*

---

10. In most respects, sporty's meets the rigorous criteria laid out in § 1125(c)(1), requiring both
fame and distinctiveness for protection under the FTDA. *See Nabisco Brands, Inc., v. PF Brands, Inc.,*
191 F.3d 208, 216 (2d Cir. 1999). The mark (1) is sufficiently distinctive (as we discuss in the text),
(2) has been used by Sportsman's for an extended period of time, (3) has had millions of dollars in
advertising spent on it, (4) is used nationwide, and (5) is traded in a wide variety of retail channels.
*See* 15 U.S.C. § 1125(c)(1)(A)–(E). Moreover, the record does not indicate that anyone else besides
Sportsman's uses sporty's, and the mark is, of course, registered with federal authorities. *See id.* at
§ 1125(c)(1)(G)–(H).
   More vexing is the question posed by the criterion that focuses on "the degree of recognition of
the mark in the trading areas and channels of trade used by the marks' owner and the person
against whom the injunction is sought." *Id.* at § 1125(c)(1)(F). Sporty's Farm contends that, although sporty's is a very well-known mark in the pilot and aviation niche market, Sportsman's did
not (and could not) prove that the mark was well-known to Sporty's Farm's customers. We need not
reach this question, as we would have had to do under the FTDA, since the ACPA provides protection not only to famous marks but also to distinctive marks regardless of fame.

*Inc. v. Equitechnology, Inc.,* 68 F.3d 542, 545 (1st Cir. 1995). We therefore conclude that, for the purposes of § 1125(d)(1)(A)(ii)(I), the sporty's mark is distinctive.

### "Identical and Confusingly Similar"

The next question is whether domain name sportys.com is "identical or confusingly similar to" the sporty's mark. 15 U.S.C. § 1125(d)(1)(A)(ii)(I). As we noted above, apostrophes cannot be used in domain names. As a result, the secondary domain name in this case (sportys) is indistinguishable from the Sportsman's trademark (sporty's). *Cf. Brookfield Communications, Inc. v. West Coast Entertainment Corp.,* 174 F.3d 1036, 1055 (9th Cir. 1999) (observing that the differences between the mark "MovieBuff" and the domain name "moviebuff.com" are "inconsequential in light of the fact that Web addresses are not caps-sensitive and that the 'com' top-level domain signifies the site's commercial nature"). We therefore conclude that, although the domain name sportys.com is not precisely identical to the sporty's mark, it is certainly "confusingly similar" to the protected mark under § 1125(d)(1) (A)(ii)(I). *Cf. Wella Corp. v. Wella Graphics, Inc.,* 874 F. Supp. 54, 56 (E.D.N.Y. 1994) (finding the new mark "Wello" confusingly similar to the trademark "Wella").

### "Bad Faith Intent to Profit"

We next turn to the issue of whether Sporty's Farm acted with a "bad faith intent to profit" from the mark sporty's when it registered the domain name sportys.com. 15 U.S.C. § 1125(d)(1)(A)(i). The statute lists nine factors to assist courts in determining when a defendant has acted with a bad faith intent to profit from the use of a mark.[12]

---

12. These factors are:
(I)     the trademark or other intellectual property rights of the person, if any, in the domain name;
(II)    the extent to which the domain name consists of the legal name of the person or a name that is otherwise commonly used to identify that person;
(III)   the person's prior use, if any, of the domain name in connection with the bona fide offering of any goods or services;
(IV)    the person's *bona fide* noncommercial or fair use of the mark in a site accessible under the domain name;
(V)     the person's intent to divert consumers from the mark owner's online location to a site accessible under the domain name that could harm the goodwill represented by the mark, either for commercial gain or with the intent to tarnish or disparage the mark, by creating a likelihood of confusion as to the source, sponsorship, affiliation, or endorsement of the site;
(VI)    the person's offer to transfer, sell, or otherwise assign the domain name to the mark owner or any third party for financial gain without having used, or having an intent to use, the domain name in the *bona fide* offering of any goods or services, or the person's prior conduct indicating a pattern of such conduct;
(VII)   the person's provision of material and misleading false contact information when applying for the registration of the domain name, the person's intentional failure to maintain accurate contact information, or the person's prior conduct indicating a pattern of such conduct;
(VIII)  the person's registration or acquisition of multiple domain names which the person knows are identical or confusingly similar to marks of others that are distinctive at the time of registration of such domain names, or dilutive of famous marks of others that are famous at the time of registration of such domain names, without regard to the goods or services of the parties; and
(IX)    the extent to which the mark incorporated in the person's domain name registration is or is not distinctive and famous within the meaning of subsection(c)(1) of section 43.
15 U.S.C. § 1125(d)(1)(B)(i).

But we are not limited to considering just the listed factors when making our determination of whether the statutory criterion has been met. The factors are, instead, expressly described as indicia that "may" be considered along with other facts. *Id.* § 1125(d)(1)(B)(i).

We hold that there is more than enough evidence in the record below of "bad faith intent to profit" on the part of Sporty's Farm (as that term is defined in the statute), so that "no reasonable factfinder could return a verdict against" Sportsman's. *Norville v. Staten Island Univ. Hosp.,* 196 F.3d 89, 95 (2d Cir. 1999). First, it is clear that neither Sporty's Farm nor Omega had any intellectual property rights in sportys.com at the time Omega registered the domain name. *See id.* § 1125(d)(1) (B)(i)(I). Sporty's Farm was not formed until nine months after the domain name was registered, and it did not begin operations or obtain the domain name from Omega until after this lawsuit was filed. Second, the domain name does not consist of the legal name of the party that registered it, Omega. *See id.* § 1125(d)(1) (B)(i)(II). Moreover, although the domain name does include part of the name of Sporty's Farm, that entity did not exist at the time the domain name was registered.

The third factor, the prior use of the domain name in connection with the bona fide offering of any goods or services, also cuts against Sporty's Farm since it did not use the site until after this litigation began, undermining its claim that the offering of Christmas trees on the site was in good faith. *See id.* § 1125(d)(1)(B)(i)(III). Further weighing in favor of a conclusion that Sporty's Farm had the requisite statutory bad faith intent, as a matter of law, are the following: (1) Sporty's Farm does not claim that its use of the domain name was "noncommercial" or a "fair use of the mark," *see id.* § 1125(d)(1)(B)(i)(IV), (2) Omega sold the mark to Sporty's Farm under suspicious circumstances, *see Sporty's Farm v. Sportsman's Market,* No. 96CV0756 (D. Conn. Mar. 13, 1998), reprinted in Joint Appendix at A277 (describing the circumstances of the transfer of sportys.com); 15 U.S.C. § 1125(d)(1)(B)(i)(VI), and, (3) as we discussed above, the sporty's mark is undoubtedly distinctive, *see id.* § 1125(d)(1)(B)(i)(IX).

The most important grounds for our holding that Sporty's Farm acted with a bad faith intent, however, are the unique circumstances of this case, which do not fit neatly into the specific factors enumerated by Congress but may nevertheless be considered under the statute. We know from the record and from the district court's findings that Omega planned to enter into direct competition with Sportsman's in the pilot and aviation consumer market. As recipients of Sportsman's catalogs, Omega's owners, the Hollanders, were fully aware that sporty's was a very strong mark for consumers of those products. It cannot be doubted, as the court found below, that Omega registered sportys.com for the primary purpose of keeping Sportsman's from using that domain name. Several months later, and after this lawsuit was filed, Omega created another company in an unrelated business that received the name Sporty's Farm so that it could (1) use the sportys.com domain name in some commercial fashion, (2) keep the name away from Sportsman's, and (3) protect itself in the event that Sportsman's brought an infringement claim alleging that a "likelihood of confusion" had been created by Omega's version of cybersquatting. Finally, the explanation given for Sporty's Farm's desire to use the domain name, based on the existence of the dog Spotty, is more amusing than credible. Given these facts and the district court's grant of an equitable injunction under the FTDA, there is ample and overwhelming evidence that, as a matter of law, Sporty's Farm's acted with a "bad faith intent to profit" from the domain name sportys.com as those terms are used in the ACPA.[13] *See Luciano v. Olsten Corp.,* 110 F.3d 210, 214 (2d Cir. 1997) (stating that, as a matter of law, judgment may be granted where "the evidence in favor of the movant is so overwhelming that 'reasonable and fair minded [persons] could not arrive at a verdict against [it].'" (quoting *Cruz v. Local Union No. 3,* 34 F.3d 1148, 1154 (2d Cir. 1994) (alteration in original)).

Remedy

Based on the foregoing, we hold that under §1125(d)(1)(A), Sporty's Farm violated Sportsman's statutory rights by its use of the sportys.com domain name.[14] The question that remains is what remedy is Sportsman's entitled to. The Act permits a court to "order the forfeiture or cancellation of the domain name or the transfer of the domain name to the owner of the mark," §1125(d)(1)(C) for any "domain name [ ] registered before, on, or after the date of the enactment of [the] Act," Pub.L. No. 106-113, §3010. That is precisely what the district court did here, albeit under the pre-existing law, when it directed a) Omega and Sporty's Farm to release their interest in sportys.com and to transfer the name to Sportsman's, and b) permanently enjoined those entities from taking any action to prevent and/or hinder Sportsman's from obtaining the domain name. That relief remains appropriate under the ACPA. We therefore affirm the district court's grant of injunctive relief.

We must also determine, however, if Sportsman's is entitled to damages either under the ACPA or pre-existing law. Under the ACPA, damages are unavailable to Sportsman's since sportys.com was registered and used by Sporty's Farm prior to the passage of the new law. *See id.* (stating that damages can be awarded for violations of the Act but that they are not "available with respect to the registration, trafficking, or use of a domain name that occurs before the date of the enactment of this Act.").

But Sportsman's might, nonetheless, be eligible for damages under the FTDA since there is nothing in the ACPA that precludes, in cybersquatting cases, the award of damages under any pre-existing law. *See* 15 U.S.C §1125(d)(3) (providing that any remedies created by the new act are "in addition to any other civil action or remedy otherwise applicable"). Under the FTDA, "[t]he owner of the famous mark shall be entitled only to injunctive relief unless the person against whom the injunction is sought willfully intended to trade on the owner's reputation or to cause dilution of the famous mark." *Id.* §1125(c)(2). Accordingly, where willful intent to dilute is demonstrated, the owner of the famous mark is—subject to the principles of equity—entitled to recover (1) damages (2) the dilutor's profits, and (3) costs. *See id.; see also id.* §1117(a) (specifying remedies).

We conclude, however, that damages are not available to Sportsman's under the FTDA. The district court found that Sporty's Farm did not act willfully. We review such findings of "willfulness" by a district court for clear error. *See Bambu Sales, Inc. v. Ozak Trading Inc.,* 58 F.3d 849, 854 (2d Cir. 1995). Thus, even assuming the sporty's mark to be famous, we cannot say that the district court clearly erred when it found that Sporty's Farm's actions were not willful. To be sure, that question is a very close one, for

---

13. We expressly note that "bad faith intent to profit" are terms of art in the ACPA and hence should not necessarily be equated with "bad faith" in other contexts.

14. The statute provides that a party "shall be liable in a civil action by the owner of a mark" if it meets the statutory requirements. 15 U.S.C. §1125(d)(1)(A). Although the statute uses the term "liable," it does not follow that damages will be assessed. As we discuss below, damages can be awarded for violations of the Act but they are not "available with respect to the registration, trafficking, or use of a domain name that occurs[, as in this case,] before the date of the enactment of this Act." Pub. L. No. 106-113, §3010.

the facts make clear that, as a Sportsman's customer, Arthur Hollander (Omega's owner) was aware of the significance of the sporty's logo. And the idea of creating a Christmas tree business named Sporty's Farm, allegedly in honor of Spotty the dog, and of giving that business the sportys.com domain name seems to have occurred to Omega only several months after it had registered the name. Nevertheless, given the uncertain state of the law at the time that Sporty's Farm and Omega acted, we cannot say that the district court clearly erred in finding that their behavior did not amount to willful dilution. It follows that Sportsman's is not entitled to damages under the FTDA.

Sportsman's also argues that it is entitled to damages under state law. Because neither the FTDA nor the ACPA preempts state remedies such as CUTPA, damages under Connecticut law are not barred, and hence may be available to Sportsman's. *See* H.R. Rep. No. 104-374, at 4 (1995), *reprinted in* 1996 U.S.C.C.A.N. 1029, 1031; 15 U.S.C. § 1125(d)(3)....

## CONCLUSION

The judgment of the district court is AFFIRMED in all particulars.

---

# PEOPLE for the ETHICAL TREATMENT of ANIMALS, INC. v. Michael T. DOUGHNEY

United States District Court, Eastern District of Virginia, Alexandria Division
Civil Action No. 99-1336-A, 2000 U.S. Dist. LEXIS 9474
June 12, 2000

OPINION BY: Claude M. Hilton

[For the background of this case, *see supra* at 447.]

PETA brought this suit alleging[, among other claims,]...service mark dilution and cybersquatting in violation of 15 U.S.C. § 1125(c)....PETA has dropped its claim for damages and seeks the following equitable relief: to enjoin Doughney's unauthorized use of its registered service mark "PETA" in the internet domain name "PETA.ORG," [and] to force Doughney's assignment of the "PETA.ORG" domain name to PETA....

[For a discussion of the defendant's argument that there is no infringement because its web-site is a parody, *see supra* at 450.]

PETA is...entitled to Summary Judgment under the Anticybersquatting Consumer Protection Act ("ACPA"), 15 U.S.C. § 1125(d)(1)(A). To succeed on Summary Judgment, Plaintiff must show that Defendant (1) has a bad faith intent to profit from using "PETA.ORG;" and (2) the "PETA.ORG" domain name is identical or confusingly similar to, or dilutive of, the distinctive and famous PETA Mark. 15 U.S.C. § 1125(d)(1)(A). The second element has been proved for reasons stated [*supra* at 449]. As to the first element, under the ACPA, there are nine factors a court must consider in making a determination of whether the Defendant had a bad faith intent. 15 U.S.C. § 1125(d)(1)(B). Applying these factors, it appears that Doughney had the requisite bad faith intent.

First, Defendant possessed no intellectual property rights in "PETA.ORG" when he registered the domain name in 1995. Second, the "PETA.ORG" domain name is not the Defendant, Michael T. Doughney's legal name or any name that is otherwise used to identify the Defendant. Third, Defendant had not engaged in prior use of the "PETA.ORG" domain name in connection with the bona fide offering of any goods or services prior to registering "PETA.ORG." Fourth, Defendant used the PETA Mark in a commercial manner. Fifth, Defendant clearly intended to confuse, mislead and divert internet users into accessing his web site which contained information antithetical and therefore harmful to the goodwill represented by the PETA Mark. Sixth, on Doughney's "PETA.ORG" web site, Doughney made reference to seeing what PETA would offer him if PETA did not like his web site. Seventh, Defendant, when registering the domain name "PETA.ORG," falsely stated that "People Eating Tasty Animals" was a non-profit educational organization and that this web site did not infringe any trade mark. Eighth, Defendant has registered other internet domain names which are identical or similar to either marks or names of famous people or organizations he opposes. Ninth, the PETA Mark used in the "PETA.ORG" domain name is distinctive and famous and was so at the time Defendant registered this site in September 1995....

As PETA has proven its case for its infringement and dilution claims and Doughney can offer no viable defenses to PETA's claims, Summary Judgment should be granted in favor of PETA....

---

## Notes and Questions

1.  "Resort to common law theories for protection of developing technologies is not a new phenomenon, but has occurred throughout the twentieth century at times when technology outpaced the development of the law." Bruce P. Keller, *Condemned to Repeat the Past: The Reemergence of Misappropriation and Other Common Law Theories of Protection for Intellectual Property*, 11 Harv. J.L. & Tech. 401, 406 (1998). One cause of action advanced to challenge uses of information has been the tort of misappropriation. *See, e.g., International News Service v. Associated Press*, 248 U.S. 215 (1918) (enjoining defendant from appropriating and selling material that the plaintiff had acquired as a result of organization and the expenditure of labor, skill, and money). The tort is premised on a theory that there is "unauthorized interference... precisely at the point where the profit is to be reaped, in order to divert a material portion of the profit from those who have earned it to those who have not...." *Id.* at 240; *see also National Basketball Association v. Sports Team & Analysis & Tracking Sys., Inc.*, 931 F. Supp. 1124 (S.D.N.Y. 1996), *amended by* 939 F. Supp. 1071 (S.D.N.Y. 1996), *aff'd in part and vacated in part on other grounds sub nom. National Basketball Association v. Motorola, Inc.*, 105 F.3d 841 (2d Cir. 1997) (determining claims of misappropriation, copyright infringement, false advertising, trademark infringement, and unfair competition).

    While misappropriation claims based on the use of material that falls within the subject matter of copyright law may be preempted by the Copyright Act, the claim may remain viable when an "extra element"—such as the time-sensitive value of "hot news"—is present. In order to prevail on a misappropriation claim, the plaintiff must show that he invested substantial time, effort, and money in creating the misappropriated work; the defendant appropriated the work at little or no cost; the defendant used the work in competition with the plaintiff; and the defendant's acts caused the plaintiff injury. *See generally* 2 J. Thomas McCarthy, *Trademarks and Unfair Competiton*, § 10:51 at 10-95 (4th ed. 1999).

    In *DVD Copy Control Association, Inc. v. McLaughlin*, No. CV 786804, 2000 WL 48512 (Cal. Super. Jan. 21, 2000), the plaintiff, the sole licensing entity to grant the scrambling system technology known as "CSS" in DVD format, sought a preliminary injunction. The plaintiff alleged that the defendants had misappropriated the CSS algorithm and master keys. The court granted the relief sought to the extent it required the defendants to remove the trade secret information from their web-sites, stating that "the evidence [was] fairly clear that the trade secret was obtained through reverse engineering." *Id.* at *2. The court refused to enjoin links to other web-sites that contained the protected material, however, "as such an order [would be] overbroad and extremely burdensome." *Id.* at *4.

2. Other claims have been premised on passing off and dilution, *see* discussion *supra* at 442; trespass to chattles theories, *see* discussion *supra* at 314; and unfair competition theories, *see, e.g., Metropolitan Opera Ass'n v. Wagner-Nichols Recorder Corp.,* 199 Misc. 786, 799, 101 N.Y.S.2d 483, 495 (Sup. Ct. 1950), *aff'd,* 279 A.D. 632, 107 N.Y.S.2d 795 (App. Div. 1951) (per curiam) (applying the theory of unfair competition to enjoin piratical conduct; "the doctrine is a broad and flexible one. It has allowed the courts to keep pace with constantly changing technological and economic aspects so as to reach just and realistic results.").

3. Challenges to domain name registration preceded the cybersquatting legislation. *See, e.g., Panavision International, L.P. v. Toeppen,* 141 F.3d 1316 (9th Cir. 1998); *Intermatic Inc. v. Toeppen,* 947 F. Supp. 1227 (N.D. Ill. 1996).

4. Cybersquatting also has been challenged by a class action suit brought against a cybersquatter. *See Omega Protein Corp. v. Flom,* No. H-98-3114 (S.D. Tex. filed Sept. 18, 1999).

5. Note that domain names are registered on an exclusive basis. How does the emerging jurisprudence on domain names affect situations when the term in issue has not been used as a trademark?

6. Some courts have deemed passive holding of a domain name evidence of bad faith by the registrant. *See, e.g., Leland Stanford Junior University v. Zedlar Transcription & Translation,* National Arbitration Forum, Claim No. FA 0006000094970 (July 11, 2000) <http://www.arbitration-forum.com/domains/decisions/94970.htm>; *Telstra Corp. v. Nuclear Marshmallows,* Case No. D2000-0003 (WIPO Feb. 18, 2000) <http://www.arbiter.wipo.int/domains/decisions/html/d2000-003.html>.

---

# Special Applications to Emerging Technologies

## 1. Background

A central feature of the World Wide Web is its ability to link related documents and to facilitate access and navigation by the user. HyperText Markup Language ("HTML") tags describe and create Web documents and display them using browser programs. Use of HyperText Transfer Protocols ("HTTP") enables communication between clients and a server. This helps achieve a seamless interface to additional documents. When such links are made to separate sites, they terminate the connection to the linking site and display the url and contents of the linked-to site.

Links also may be used to create a "deep link," which is a link to a page of the linked-to web-site other than its home page. "In-line links" bring an image contained in a separate file within the text and onto the page the user is viewing. The user typically is not automatically alerted that the image or text called up by the in-line link resides on a separate site. Like in-line links, "framing" technology brings content from one web-site within another, but the framed content appears in a window on the original framing site, allowing two or more web-sites to appear simultaneously on the user's screen. "Metatags" are bits of embedded data which are not visible to the end user, but allow description of web-sites so that search engines can retrieve the site in response to the user's inquiry. Some sites use keyword metatags to achieve favorable positioning in the indices produced by search engines and thereby encourage traffic to their sites.

Proprietary interests increasingly have been the subject of attention in the on-line realm of marketing and commerce. The ease with which information displayed on the World Wide Web may be accessed and referenced through linking, *see* discussion *infra* at 485, and incorporated through framing, *see* discussion *infra* at 506; or with which trademarks may be used as metatags, *see* discussion *infra* at 509, to direct traffic to sites other than those hosted or endorsed by copyright and trademark holders, gives rise to a host of legal issues.

Such controversies are especially prevalent because of the emergence of the Internet as a commercial marketplace. Various business models have been established to generate revenues and attract visitors to sites. In advertising-based models, web-sites charge companies to place advertisements on their sites. Advertisers often measure the efficacy of the advertisement by the number of viewers who have linked to the advertised company's site, which is known as "click-throughs." Cybershopping business models use the World Wide Web as a marketing tool for promoting the company or business, and for the on-line sale of products or services. Businesses engaged in on-line commerce depend on trademarks and keywords to attract visitors interested in their goods and services.

Issues arise when Internet technology is used to divert content, severed from accompanying advertisements, to an independent site. In-line and deep links may bypass advertising because the linked-to site has displayed the advertisement on its home page, which was evaded in favor of interior pages, or because the linking site connected to a page of the linked-to site that did not include advertisements. Because framing technology divides the screen, only portions of the framed sites may be visible at a particular time; framing may thereby disrupt the web-site's advertising by obstructing the site's content with frames. The revenues which would otherwise accrue to the initial site by virtue of users' access to the advertisements are lost. Bypassing advertisements not only results in a diminution of revenue to the site on which the advertisements were displayed, but in practical terms, it also means that the site's owner has ample incentive to seek redress against the owner or operator of the site that thwarted the advertising exposure.

One way site owners have addressed this issue is by implementing technological devices. For example, site operators may restrict linking by requiring users to gain access through passwords or by revising the site's url so as to preclude effective links. More sophisticated tactics, such as "dynamic paging," also are utilized. This approach uses technology to build the Web page only when the user executes a specific program. Because the reference point of dynamic pages is not static, sites endeavoring to link to them lack a fixed site to make a connection. Computer programmers also can require a Web page to recognize specific un-desired links and refuse to process them. "Spiders," which seek to harvest sites in response to a user's search, may be thwarted from indexing the site in the spider's database.

Another protective avenue explored by copyright holders relies on contractual law. Form agreements distributed with software have been referred to as "shrinkwraps." In the non-digital environment, the question of adequate consent arises. In the on-line arena, some web-site operators have tried to manifest consent by the user by condition-ing access to the site on consent.

While technological strategies may ameliorate the effects of diverted traffic, by-passed advertising, and the objectionable usurping of content, they do not necessarily provide complete resolutions. Technical devices may become obsolete or intervening technology may be developed to circumvent the devices' efficacy. Reliance on con-tractual approaches may, among other things, give rise to breaches of the restrictions to which the user purportedly assented. Not surprisingly, resort to litigation to re-dress transgressions of proprietary rights in the digital environment has already oc-curred. Intellectual property law has become a means—either as a supplement to technological mechanisms and contractual arrangements or as an independent av-enue—to protect against objectionable exploitation of copyrighted content.

Pursuit of a lawsuit demands, of course, that a cognizable claim be advanced. To what extent do linking, framing, and metataging practices give rise to tenable claims of copyright infringement, trademark infringement, and dilution? Judicial resolution of disputes relating to such technologies inevitably requires examination of the policies underlying existing law. As one intellectual property specialist remarked, "By frankly as-sessing the conduct at issue, without undue regard for the medium through which it is conducted, one gets to the heart of the policy concerns that led to the creation of the applicable legal rule." Bruce P. Keller, *The Game's the Same: Why Gambling in Cyber-space Violates Federal Law*, 108 Yale L.J. 1569, 1572 (May 1999).

The Supreme Court has endorsed resort to review of basic statutory purposes "when technological change has rendered [the] literal terms ambiguous...." *Sony Corp. v. Uni-versal City Studios, Inc.*, 464 U.S. 417, 432 (1984) (quoting *Twentieth Century Music Corp. v. Aiken*, 422 U.S. 151, 156 (1975)). Copyright law, as discussed previously, *see* discussion *supra* at 389, is designed to promote speech and other creative enterprise by granting exclusive rights to authors whose works satisfy the statutory standards. The vesting of such rights serves as an incentive to create works, because the authors may derive financial or other benefits from having created the work. Ultimately, societal in-terests are advanced by the flow of the resultant works into the market.

> The limited scope of the copyright holder's statutory monopoly, like the lim-ited copyright duration required by the Constitution, reflects a balance of competing claims upon the public interest: Creative work is to be encouraged and rewarded, but private motivation must ultimately serve the cause of pro-moting broad public availability of literature, music, and the other arts. The immediate effect of our copyright law is to secure a fair return for an "author's" creative labor. But the ultimate aim is, by this incentive, to stimulate artistic creativity for the general public good. "The sole interest of the United States and the primary object in conferring the monopoly," [the Supreme] Court has said, "lie in the general benefits derived by the public from the labors of au-thors."

*Id.* at 431–32 (quoting *Fox Film Corp. v. Doyal*, 286 U.S. 123, 127 (1932)).

Trademark law, as discussed previously, *see* discussion *supra* at 441, is premised upon policies designed to protect consumers, safeguard property rights, and promote economic efficiency. Fundamentally, trademark law protects consumers and businesses from confusion as to the origin or source of goods and services. Because goods are associated with particular manufacturers, consumers are able to allocate responsibility for product defects. This practice not only protects consumers, but as well encourages companies to produce quality products. The company's investment in a particular mark also is safeguarded from infringing uses. Economic efficiency is achieved because businesses are encouraged to produce quality products with which they will be identified. Dilution claims likewise protect certain marks from blurring and tarnishment, providing a means to redress poaching on the commercial value of a distinctive mark.

As the following discussion shows, courts have been called upon to apply these rationales in the linking, framing, and metataging contexts. To what extent do the claims asserted under copyright, trademark, and dilution laws exploit the policies underlying the formation of the laws? Professor Maureen O'Rourke has pointed out that from a legal standpoint, neither copyright nor trademark law specifically directly addresses the conduct involved in linking, and she has expressed doubt that the laws consistently address the salient issues. "For example, copyright law generally stands for the proposition that HREF links are permissible. Yet trademark dilution law or section 43(a) [of the Lanham Act] may frustrate HREF linking by making it a violation of the Lanham Act if the linker has not first obtained an agreement allowing it to link. Copyright law also stands for the proposition that the act of framing is not copyright infringement, but it may possibly constitute trademark infringement or unfair competition." Maureen A. O'Rourke, *Fencing Cyberspace: Drawing Borders in a Virtual World*, 82 Minn. L. Rev. 609, 685 (1998). O'Rourke also notes that holding one who facilitates navigation through linking liable under the Lanham Act is at odds with the objectives of trademark law to decrease consumer search costs. *See id.*

As is the case with other aspects of Internet speech, courts must draw upon existing analytical constructs to determine how to apply relevant and analogous principles to disputes arising in the digital realm. Consider the fair use defense, which may, as a doctrine, have adequate analytic elasticity to accommodate application to new technologies. An illustration may be found in *Los Angeles Times v. Free Republic*, No. 98-7840 MMM, 2000 U.S. Dist. LEXIS 5669 (C.D. Cal. Mar. 31, 2000). As discussed previously, in that case, the district court rejected the defendants' First Amendment defense to verbatim copying of the entire text of certain articles published by the *Los Angeles Times* and the *Washington Post*. The defendants had contended that wholesale copying placed visitors to the defendants' site in a better position to express their views concerning the manner in which the media covers current events because they could assess omissions and biases in the articles. The court disagreed that visitors would be unable to comment unless they could read the text of the entire article verbatim, and also noted that visitors' comments more often concerned the underlying news event than the manner in which it was covered. Significantly, even when media coverage was the subject of critique, and wholesale review of the articles was deemed appropriate, the defendants' argument was undermined because of the availability of linking technology. In other words, the defendants could have hyperlinked to the plaintiffs' sites, thereby enabling visitors to the defendants' site to read the full articles of the *Los Angeles Times* and the *Washington Post*.

Thus, the availability of linking practices undermines arguments that blanket copying is necessary to explore legitimate discussion or critique of another's work. This reasoning comports with the economic rationales underlying the fair use doctrine. As a general matter, unauthorized wholesale copying of another's work without permission seems inherently inequitable, in that the fruit of the author's labor is used without compensation.

Linking to content also directs the public to the rightsholder's site, thereby avoiding the risk that attention to the site will be diverted and advertising revenues generated by the traffic will be lost. Hypertext linking consequently provides a technological means to efficiently and expediently make wholesale reference to another's work, without depriving the author of the recognition and ancillary financial rewards attendant to the creation of his publication.*

The practice also fits within the doctrinal underpinnings of the fair use defense. The fair use doctrine is predicated on the author's implied consent to "reasonable and customary" uses when he releases his work for public consumption. *See, e.g., Harper & Row, Publishers, Inc. v. Nation Enterprises*, 471 U.S. 539, 550–51 (1985). Web-site owners who place content on the World Wide Web likewise are effectively presumed to be on notice of normative linking practices, and thus, absent the implementation of restrictions, may be understood to have impliedly acquiesced to links by others. Hence, tacit authorization of reasonable and customary uses parallels the implied license to link to sites to which the Internet provides access.

---

# 2. Linking

## *a. Hypertext Linking*

Linking technology allows web-sites operators to connect their sites to other sites. Each web-site is connected to the Internet by means of certain protocols that permit "the information to become part of a single body of knowledge accessible by all Web visitors." *American Libraries Ass'n v. Pataki*, 969 F. Supp. 160, 166 (S.D.N.Y. 1997). As part of this unified body of knowledge, Web pages are linked together so that the Internet user can move freely from one Web page to another by using his mouse to "click" on a link.

"Links bear a relationship to the information superhighway comparable to the relationship that roadway signs bear to roads but they are more functional. Like roadway signs, they point out the direction. Unlike roadway signs, they take one almost instantaneously to the desired destination with the mere click of an electronic mouse." *Universal City Studios, Inc. v. Reimerdes*, No. Civ. 0277, 2000 U.S. Dist. LEXIS 11696 at *125–26 (S.D.N.Y. Aug. 17, 2000).

A web-site can link to content to which it holds the rights that is located on pages within its site. This presents scant if any legal issues. May web-sites link to content displayed on other sites? Some commentators have analyzed such links as permissible on theories of an implied license and implied consent; web-site owners know that the World Wide Web is navigated by links and should reasonably presume that other sites will link to theirs.

---

\* Used appropriately, linking can confer ancillary benefits. For instance, when the linked-to site is the subject of critical commentary, a link to a site containing additional facts and the subject's viewpoints helps furnish more comprehensive background for the factual support underlying the linking site's opinion and helps indicate countervailing viewpoints to render the portrayal more balanced.

Such links also have been justified by analogy to closing one book and retrieving another that was cross-referenced by the former. Hypertext linking to a third-party web-site requires the user to leave the original web-site and then visit another. Thus the distinction between the perusal of an additional book and the visit to another web-site rests solely with the methodology of the conduct; the former is via physical retrieval of a print publication, and the latter via electronic retrieval of an on-line publication. Because linking generates traffic to the linked-to site (and possibly generates additional advertising revenues as a result), linked-to sites typically do not object to linking practices. *But see Religious Technology Center v. Dataweb B.V.,* No. 96/1048 (Dist. Ct. of the Hague, Civil Law Sector, June 9, 1999) (ruling that Internet service providers commit infringement when they provide Internet access or a hypertext link to sites that display copyrighted work without consent); *see also Bernstein v. JC Penney, Inc.,* 1998 U.S. Dist. LEXIS 19048 (C.D. Cal. Sept. 29, 1998) (claiming that the defendant's web-site linked to other sites, thereby encouraging and directing customers to access sites that displayed copies of the plaintiff's photographs, which were protected by copyright; one of the defendants was dismissed from the suit and the plaintiff withdrew his complaint).

"As a general rule, materials published on the web may be viewed by all Internet users unless affirmative steps are taken to limit access." Brown Raysman Millstein Felder & Steiner LLP, *New Media and the Internet: Staying Interactive in the Hi-Tech Environment* (April–May 2000) at 16. "The prevalent view in the Internet community is that the operator of a Web site is conclusively presumed to have made the site available for linking without any need to obtain prior consent. The entire culture of the Web is based on this notion of free accessibility." Robert L. Tucker, *Information Superhighway Robbery: The Tortious Misuse of Links, Frames, Metatags, and Domain Names,* 4 Va. J.L. & Tech. 8, 25 (1999) (footnotes omitted).

Links are the mainstay of the Internet, and are indispensable to its convenient access to vast bodies of information. In addition to the questions driven by copyright law, questions arise as to the potential liability of the linking site for the substance of the linked-to site. One court has proclaimed that "[a] website owner cannot be held responsible for all of the content of the sites to which it provides links." *DVD Copy Control Association, Inc. v. McLaughlin,* No. CV 786804, 2000 WL 48512 (Cal. 4 Super. Jan. 21, 2000). When a site posted content that had been enjoined, the court deemed a requested injunction precluding linking to web-sites with the prohibited information as unnecessary, because the court had enjoined the posting of the information "in the first instance." *Id.* Thus, the court resolved the issue through direct action against the linking site.

---

# INTELLECTUAL RESERVE, INC. v.
# UTAH LIGHTHOUSE MINISTRY, INC.

United States District Court, District of Utah, Central Division
No. 2:99-CV-808C, 75 F. Supp. 2d 1290
December 6, 1999

Campbell, District Judge.

This matter is before the court on plaintiff's motion for preliminary injunction. Plaintiff claims that unless a preliminary injunction issues, defendants will directly infringe and contribute to the infringement of its copyright in the Church Handbook of

Instructions ("Handbook"). Defendants do not oppose a preliminary injunction, but argue that the scope of the injunction should be restricted to only prohibit direct infringement of plaintiff's copyright.

Having fully considered the arguments of counsel, the submissions of the parties and applicable legal authorities, the court grants plaintiff's motion for a preliminary injunction. However, the scope of the preliminary injunction is limited.

### Discussion

### ...I. Likelihood of Plaintiff Prevailing on the Merits

First, the court considers whether there is a substantial likelihood that plaintiff will eventually prevail on the merits. Plaintiff alleges that the defendants infringed its copyright directly by posting substantial portions of its copyrighted material on defendants' website, and also contributed to infringement of its copyright by inducing, causing or materially contributing to the infringing conduct of another. To determine the proper scope of the preliminary injunction, the court considers the likelihood that plaintiff will prevail on either or both of its claims.

#### A. Direct Infringement

To prevail on its claim of direct copyright infringement, "[p]laintiff must establish both: (1) that it possesses a valid copyright and (2) that [d]efendants 'copied' protectable elements of the copyrighted work." *Country Kids 'N City Slicks, Inc. v. Sheen*, 77 F.3d 1280, 1284 (10th Cir. 1996). Defendants initially conceded in a hearing, for purposes of the temporary restraining order and preliminary injunction, that plaintiff has a valid copyright in the Handbook, and that defendants directly infringed plaintiff's copyright by posting substantial portions of the copyrighted material. Defendants changed their position, in a motion to dismiss, claiming that plaintiff has failed to allege facts necessary to show ownership of a valid copyright. Despite the defendants' newly-raised argument, the court finds, for purpose of this motion, that the plaintiff owns a valid copyright on the material defendants posted on their website. Plaintiff has provided evidence of a copyright registration certificate, and the certificate "constitutes *prima facie* evidence of the validity of the copyright." *Gates Rubber Co. v. Bando Chem. Indus., Ltd.*, 9 F.3d 823, 831 (10th Cir. 1993). Defendants have not advanced any additional affirmative defenses to the claim of direct infringement. Therefore, the court finds that there is a substantial likelihood that plaintiff will prevail on its claim of direct infringement.

#### B. Contributory Infringement

According to plaintiff, after the defendants were ordered to remove the Handbook from their website, the defendants began infringing plaintiff's copyright by inducing, causing, or materially contributing to the infringing conduct of others. It is undisputed that defendants placed a notice on their website that the Handbook was online, and gave three website addresses of websites containing the material defendants were ordered to remove from their website. Defendants also posted e-mails on their website that encouraged browsing those websites, printing copies of the Handbook and sending the Handbook to others.

Although the copyright statute does not expressly impose liability for contributory infringement,

[t]he absence of such express language in the copyright statute does not preclude the imposition of liability for copyright infringements on certain parties
who have not themselves engaged in the infringing activity. For vicarious liability is imposed in virtually all areas of the law, and the concept of contributory infringement is merely a species of the broader problem of identifying
the circumstances in which it is just to hold one accountable for the actions of
another.

*Sony Corp. v. Universal City Studios, Inc.,* 464 U.S. 417, 435, 104 S.Ct. 774, 78 L.Ed.2d
574 (1984) (footnote omitted). Even though "'the lines between direct infringement,
contributory infringement and vicarious liability are not clearly drawn'" distinctions
can be made between them. *Id.* at n. 17 (quoting *Universal City Studios, Inc. v. Sony
Corp.,* 480 F. Supp. 429, 457–58 (C.D. Cal. 1979)). Vicarious liability is grounded in the
tort concept of respondeat superior, and contributory infringement is founded in the
tort concept of enterprise liability. *See Demetriades v. Kaufmann,* 690 F. Supp. 289, 292
(S.D.N.Y. 1988). "[B]enefit and control are the signposts of vicarious liability,
[whereas] knowledge and participation [are] the touchstones of contributory infringement." *Id.* at 293.

Liability for contributory infringement is imposed when "one who, with knowledge
of the infringing activity, induces, causes or materially contributes to the infringing
conduct of another." *Gershwin Publ'g Corp. v. Columbia Artists Mgt., Inc.,* 443 F.2d 1159,
1162 (2d Cir. 1971). Thus, to prevail on its claim of contributory infringement, plaintiff
must first be able to establish that the conduct defendants allegedly aided or encouraged
could amount to infringement. *See Subafilms, Ltd. v. MGM-Pathe Comms. Co.,* 24 F.3d
1088, 1092 (9th Cir. 1994). Defendants argue that they have not contributed to copyright infringement by those who posted the Handbook on websites nor by those who
browsed the websites on their computers.

1. Can the Defendants Be Liable Under a Theory of Contributory Infringement for
the Actions of Those Who Posted the Handbook on the Three Websites?

a. Did those who posted the Handbook on the websites infringe plaintiff's
copyright?

During a hearing on the motion to vacate the temporary restraining order, defendants accepted plaintiff's proffer that the three websites contain the material which
plaintiff alleges is copyrighted. Therefore, plaintiff at trial is likely to establish that those
who have posted the material on the three websites are directly infringing plaintiff's
copyright.

b. Did the defendants induce, cause or materially contribute to the infringement?

The evidence now before the court indicates that there is no direct relationship between the defendants and the people who operate the three websites. The defendants
did not provide the website operators with the plaintiff's copyrighted material, nor
are the defendants receiving any kind of compensation from them. The only connection between the defendants and those who operate the three websites appears to be
the information defendants have posted on their website concerning the infringing
sites. Based on this scant evidence, the court concludes that plaintiff has not shown
that defendants contributed to the infringing action of those who operate the infringing websites.

2. Can the Defendants Be Liable Under a Theory of Contributory Infringement for the Actions of Those Who Browse the Three Infringing Websites?

Defendants make two arguments in support of their position that the activities of those who browse the three websites do not make them liable under a theory of contributory infringement. First, defendants contend that those who browse the infringing websites are not themselves infringing plaintiff's copyright; and second, even if those who browse the websites are infringers, defendants have not materially contributed to the infringing conduct.

### a. Do those who browse the websites infringe plaintiff's copyright?

The first question, then, is whether those who browse any of the three infringing websites are infringing plaintiff's copyright. Central to this inquiry is whether the persons browsing are merely viewing the Handbook (which is not a copyright infringement), or whether they are making a copy of the Handbook (which is a copyright infringement). *See* 17 U.S.C. § 106.

"Copy" is defined in the Copyright Act as: "material objects...in which a work is fixed by any method now known or later developed, and from which the work can be perceived, reproduced, or otherwise communicated, either directly or with the aid of a machine or device." 17 U.S.C. § 101. "A work is 'fixed'...when it's...sufficiently permanent or stable to permit it to be perceived, reproduced, or otherwise communicated for a period of more than transitory duration." *Id.*

When a person browses a website, and by so doing displays the Handbook, a copy of the Handbook is made in the computer's random access memory (RAM), to permit viewing of the material. And in making a copy, even a temporary one, the person who browsed infringes the copyright. *See MAI Systems Corp. v. Peak Computer, Inc.*, 991 F.2d 511, 518 (9th Cir. 1993) (holding that when material is transferred to a computer's RAM, copying has occurred; in the absence of ownership of the copyright or express permission by licence, such an act constitutes copyright infringement); *Marobie-Fl., Inc. v. National Ass'n of Fire Equip. Distrib.*, 983 F. Supp. 1167, 1179 (N.D. Ill. 1997) (noting that liability for copyright infringement is with the persons who cause the display or distribution of the infringing material onto their computer); *see also* Nimmer on Copyright § 8.08(A)(1) (stating that the infringing act of copying may occur from "loading the copyrighted material...into the computer's random access memory (RAM)"). Additionally, a person making a printout or re-posting a copy of the Handbook on another website would infringe plaintiff's copyright.

### b. Did the defendants induce, cause or materially contribute to the infringement?

The court now considers whether the defendants' actions contributed to the infringement of plaintiff's copyright by those who browse the three websites.

The following evidence establishes that defendants have actively encouraged the infringement of plaintiff's copyright after being ordered to remove the Handbook from their website, defendants posted on their website: "Church Handbook of Instructions is back online!" and listed the three website addresses. Defendants also posted e-mail suggesting that the lawsuit against defendants would be affected by people logging onto one of the websites and downloading the complete handbook. One of the e-mails posted by the defendants mentioned sending a copy of the copyrighted material to the media. In response to an e-mail stating that the sender had unsuccessfully tried to browse a website that contained the Handbook, defendants gave further instruction on how to browse the material. At least one of the three websites encourages the copying and post-ing of copies of the allegedly infringing material on other websites.

Based on the above, the court finds that the first element necessary for injunctive re-lief is satisfied.

## II. Irreparable Injury

Because this is a copyright infringement case and plaintiff has demonstrated a likeli-hood of success on the merits, there is a presumption of injury. *See Country Kids 'N City Slicks, Inc. v. Sheen,* 77 F.3d 1280, 1288–89 (10th Cir. 1996). In addition, plaintiff will suffer additional immediate and real irreparable harm if defendants are permitted to post the copyrighted material or to knowingly induce, cause or materially contribute to the infringement of plaintiff's copyright by others.

## III. Harm to Defendants

Defendants argue that their First Amendment rights will be infringed by a prelimi-nary injunction. However, the First Amendment does not give defendants the right to infringe on legally recognized rights under the copyright law. *See Cable/Home Comm. Corp. v. Network Productions, Inc.,* 902 F.2d 829, 849 (11th Cir. 1990). "[C]opyright in-terests [ ] must be guarded under the Constitution, and injunctive relief is a common judicial response to infringement of a valid copyright." *Id.* The court, in fashioning the scope of injunctive relief, is aware of and will protect the defendants' First Amendment rights.

## IV. The Public Interest

Finally, it is in the public's interest to protect the copyright laws and the interests of copyright holders.

### Order

Therefore, for the reasons stated, the court orders the following preliminary injunction:

1. Defendants, their agents and those under their control, shall remove from and not post on defendants' website the material alleged to infringe plaintiff's copyright;

2. Defendants, their agents and those under their control, shall not reproduce or dis-tribute verbatim, in a tangible medium, material alleged to infringe plaintiff's copyright;

3. Defendants, their agents and those under their control, shall remove from and not post on defendants' website, addresses to websites that defendants know, or have reason to know, contain the material alleged to infringe plaintiff's copyright....

---

Can linking practices give rise to a claim of dilution arising out of a perceived associ-ation between the two sites to which the linked-to site objects? Suppose, for example, that a web-site devoted to displays of indecent subject matter hyperlinks to a site that is targeted to children and devoted to animated fairy tale characters. Might the latter site contend that its trademark in the characters has been tarnished by the association with the site related to sexual content?

One example of unwanted association was "Babes on the Web," a controversial site that consisted of an index of women's personal home pages and a collection of links. The web-site linked to pages with photographs of women, and rated each woman on a scale ranging from "Babe-O-Rama" to "Babe-O-Matic." *See* Dwight Silverman, *Battling Over Babes in Cyberland*, Houston Chron. (July 9, 1995) at 6. When several women objected, the site's operator eventually removed the links. *See id.*

---

# PAINEWEBBER INCORPORATED v. WWWPAINEWEBBER.COM, *et al.*

United States District Court, Eastern District of Virginia, Alexandria Division
Civil Action No: 99-0456-A, 1999 U.S. Dist. LEXIS 6552
April 9, 1999

OPINION BY: Claude M. Hilton

This matter came before the Court on plaintiff's motion for a Preliminary Injunction following the Court's entry of a Temporary Restraining Order on April 2, 1999. The Court finds upon consideration of the four factors compromising the Fourth Circuit's "hardship balancing test" for preliminary injunctions, that the plaintiff is entitled to a preliminary injunction.

First, the likelihood of irreparable harm to plaintiff if the preliminary injunction does not issue is very high, in light of the undisputed fact that WWWPAINEWEBBER.COM automatically links with a website offering pornography.

Second, it does not appear that Defendants will suffer any harm if the preliminary junction is granted. To provide security to Defendant, however, the preliminary injunction will be contingent upon the deposit by the plaintiff into this Court of a bond in the amount of $10,000.

Third, the Court finds that "PaineWebber" is a famous mark which will be diluted in violation of 15 U.S.C. § 1115(c) by being linked with pornography. The Court thus finds it likely that the plaintiff will succeed on the merits.

Fourth, the Court finds that the public interest would be served by entry of a preliminary injunction.

THEREFORE, and for the reasons stated from the bench, the Court finds the entry of a Preliminary Injunction to be proper, and it is hereby

ORDERED that upon the posting of a bond in the amount of $10,000 into this Court by the plaintiff:

(1) Defendant Fortuny and his agents, servants and employees and all those acting in concert with him are preliminarily enjoined from operating, maintaining, or sponsoring, or permitting to operate, any web site identified with the domain name WWW-PAINEWEBBER.COM, including but not limited to permitting such site to have any content or to automatically forward or link to any other IP address or domain name whatsoever;

(2) Defendant Fortuny is preliminarily enjoined from selling, disposing or otherwise terminating his rights in and to the WWWPAINEWEBBER.COM domain name; and

(3) Network Solutions, Inc. is ordered to put the domain name WWWPAINEWEBBER.COM on "hold" so that it cannot be used by anyone, until the rights of the parties hereto in and to the domain name can be determined by this Court.

# UNIVERSAL CITY STUDIOS, INC, *et al.* v.
## Shawn C. REIMERDES, *et al.*
### United States District Court, Southern District of New York
No. 00 Civ. 0277(LAK), 55 U.S.P.Q.2d 1873, 2000 U.S. Dist. LEXIS 11696
February 2, 2000

OPINION BY: Lewis A. Kaplan

[For the background of this case, *see supra* at 414.]

Plaintiffs seek...to enjoin defendants from "linking" their 2600.com web site to other sites that make DeCSS available to users. Their request obviously stems in no small part from what defendants themselves have termed their act of "electronic civil disobedience"—their attempt to defeat the purpose of the preliminary injunction by (a) offering the practical equivalent of making DeCSS available on their own web site by electronically linking users to other sites still offering DeCSS, and (b) encouraging other sites that had not been enjoined to offer the program. The dispositive question is whether linking to another web site containing DeCSS constitutes "offering [DeCSS] to the public" or "providing or otherwise trafficking" in it within the meaning of the DMCA. Answering this question requires careful consideration of the nature and types of linking.

Most web pages are written in computer languages, chiefly HTML, which allow the programmer to prescribe the appearance of the web page on the computer screen and, in addition, to instruct the computer to perform an operation if the cursor is placed over a particular point on the screen and the mouse then clicked. Programming a particular point on a screen to transfer the user to another web page when the point, referred to as a hyperlink, is clicked is called linking. Web pages can be designed to link to other web pages on the same site or to web pages maintained by different sites.

As noted earlier, the links that defendants established on their web site are of several types. Some transfer the user to a web page on an outside site that contains a good deal of information of various types, does not itself contain a link to DeCSS, but that links, either directly or via a series of other pages, to another page on the same site that posts the software. It then is up to the user to follow the link or series of links on the linked-to web site in order to arrive at the page with the DeCSS link and commence the download of the software. Others take the user to a page on an outside web site on which there appears a direct link to the DeCSS software and which may or may not contain text or links other than the DeCSS link. The user has only to click on the DeCSS link to commence the download. Still others may directly transfer the user to a file on the linked-to web site such that the download of DeCSS to the user's computer automatically commences without further user intervention.

The statute makes it unlawful to offer, provide or otherwise traffic in described technology. To "traffic" in something is to engage in dealings in it, conduct that necessarily involves awareness of the nature of the subject of the trafficking. To "provide" something, in the sense used in the statute, is to make it available or furnish it. To "offer" is to present or hold it out for consideration. The phrase "or otherwise traffic in" modifies and gives meaning to the words "offer" and "provide." In consequence, the anti-trafficking provision of the DMCA is implicated where one presents, holds out or makes a circumvention technology or device available, knowing its nature, for the purpose of allowing others to acquire it.

To the extent that defendants have linked to sites that automatically commence the process of downloading DeCSS upon a user being transferred by defendants' hyperlinks, there can be no serious question. Defendants are engaged in the functional equivalent of transferring the DeCSS code to the user themselves.

Substantially the same is true of defendants' hyperlinks to web pages that display nothing more than the DeCSS code or present the user only with the choice of commencing a download of DeCSS and no other content. The only distinction is that the entity extending to the user the option of downloading the program is the transferee site rather than defendants, a distinction without a difference.

Potentially more troublesome might be links to pages that offer a good deal of content other than DeCSS but that offer a hyperlink for downloading, or transferring to a page for downloading, DeCSS. If one assumed, for the purposes of argument, that the *Los Angeles Times* web site somewhere contained the DeCSS code, it would be wrong to say that anyone who linked to the *Los Angeles Times* web site, regardless of purpose or the manner in which the link was described, thereby offered, provided or otherwise trafficked in DeCSS merely because DeCSS happened to be available on a site to which one linked. But that is not this case. Defendants urged others to post DeCSS in an effort to disseminate DeCSS and to inform defendants that they were doing so. Defendants then linked their site to those "mirror" sites, after first checking to ensure that the mirror sites in fact were posting DeCSS or something that looked like it, and proclaimed on their own site that DeCSS could be had by clicking on the hyperlinks on defendants' site. By doing so, they offered, provided or otherwise trafficked in DeCSS, and they continue to do so to this day....

Defendants argue...that injunctive relief against dissemination of DeCSS is barred by the prior restraint doctrine. The Court disagrees.

Few phrases are as firmly rooted in our constitutional jurisprudence as the maxim that "any system of prior restraints of expression comes to [a] Court bearing a heavy presumption against its constitutional validity." Yet there is a significant gap between the rhetoric and the reality. Courts often have upheld restrictions on expression that many would describe as prior restraints, sometimes by characterizing the expression as unprotected and on other occasions finding the restraint justified despite its presumed invalidity. Moreover, the prior restraint doctrine, which has expanded far beyond the Blackstonian model that doubtless informed the understanding of the Framers of the First Amendment, has been criticized as filled with "doctrinal ambiguities and inconsistencies resulting from the absence of any detailed judicial analysis of [its] true rationale" and, in one case, even as "fundamentally unintelligible." Nevertheless, the doctrine has a well established core: administrative preclearance requirements for and at least preliminary injunctions against speech as conventionally understood are presumptively unconstitutional. Yet that proposition does not dispose of this case.

The classic prior restraint cases were dramatically different from this one. *Near v. Minnesota* involved a state procedure for abating scandalous and defamatory newspapers as public nuisances. *New York Times Co. v. United States* dealt with an attempt to enjoin a newspaper from publishing an internal government history of the Vietnam War. *Nebraska Press Association v. Stuart* concerned a court order barring the reporting of certain details about a forthcoming murder case. In each case, therefore, the government sought to suppress speech at the very heart of First Amendment concern—expression about public issues of the sort that is indispensable to self government. And while the prior restraint doctrine has been applied well beyond the sphere of political expression, we deal here with something new altogether—computer code, a fundamentally utilitarian construct, albeit one that embodies an expressive element. Hence, it would be a mistake simply to permit its expressive element to drive a characterization of the code as speech no different from the Pentagon Papers, the publication of a newspaper, or the exhibition of a motion picture and then to apply prior restraint rhetoric without a more nuanced consideration of the competing concerns.

In this case, the considerations supporting an injunction are very substantial indeed. Copyright and, more broadly, intellectual property piracy are endemic, as Congress repeatedly has found. The interest served by prohibiting means that facilitate such piracy—the protection of the monopoly granted to copyright owners by the Copyright Act—is of constitutional dimension. There is little room for doubting that broad dissemination of DeCSS threatens ultimately to injure or destroy plaintiffs' ability to distribute their copyrighted products on DVDs and, for that matter, undermine their ability to sell their products to the home video market in other forms. The potential damages probably are incalculable, and these defendants surely would be in no position to compensate plaintiffs for them if plaintiffs were remitted only to *post hoc* damage suits.

On the other side of the coin, the First Amendment interests served by the dissemination of DeCSS on the merits are minimal. The presence of some expressive content in the code should not obscure the fact of its predominant functional character—it is first and foremost a means of causing a machine with which it is used to perform particular tasks.... To be sure, there is much to be said in most circumstances for the usual procedural rationale for the prior restraint doctrine: prior restraints carry with them the risk of erroneously suppressing expression that could not constitutionally be punished after publication. In this context, however, that concern is not persuasive, both because the enjoined expressive element is minimal and because a full trial on the merits has been held. Accordingly, the Court holds that the prior restraint doctrine does not require denial of an injunction in this case....

---

## b. In-Line Linking

In-line linking displays images or text contained in a separate file within the text of the linking site and onto the page being viewed. Thus, this technology makes possible display of images that are visible on screen as part of a web-site's main body, as opposed to being located within a separate window. Such images originate at a source other than the site that is storing the document that is being viewed. Visitors to the linking site are not necessarily aware from the displays on the linking site itself that the images or text had been resident on a separate web-site, because the images or text are visually incorporated into the linking site.

One dispute regarding in-line linking practices centered on "The Dilbert Hack Page," a web-site created by Dan Wallach. The site displayed the Dilbert comic strip via in-line links to United Media, a site where the comic strips are located. United Media objected on behalf of the rightsholder in the comic strip, contending that the in-line links to copyrighted material constituted an unauthorized display of the work. *See* E-mail from John Parker, Legal Counsel for United Feature Syndicate, Inc., to Dan Wallach, Assistant Professor in the Systems Group, Rice University Department of Computer Science

(July 26, 1996) (on file with Rice University <http://www.cs.rice.edu/~dwallach/dilbert/letter2.html>). Wallach contended that he was not infringing because his Web page did not include a copy of the Dilbert comic strip, but instead instructed the user's browser to go to the Dilbert site to retrieve the strip and display it on Wallach's site. In the end, Wallach removed the page, indicating that he wished to avoid litigation.

---

# Link Liability: The Argument for Inline Links and Frames as Infringements of the Copyright Display Right
## Allison Roarty
### 68 Fordham L. Rev. 1011 (1999)

... An inline link automatically imports an image contained in a separate file onto the Web page being viewed. Based on current case law construing the Copyright Act and its theoretical underpinnings, inline linked-to sites have a cause of action for unwanted links under the display right. In addition, if the inline-linked content is time-sensitive, the linked-to site may have a cause of action under misappropriation.

### 1. Inline Linking and the Reproduction Right

The analysis of inline linking and the reproduction right is similar to the deep linking discussion above. It begins with whether the linking site infringes the linked-to site's right to make copies of its work. In analyzing the facts of the Dilbert dispute, the first issue concerns who makes the copy. Wallach, the owner of the inline linking site, does not make a copy of the Dilbert cartoon image. Rather, his code instructs the user's browser to retrieve the image to be displayed on the linking site's Web page. Thus, the linking site does not directly infringe the reproduction right. In order for a court to find Wallach liable for infringement of the reproduction right, the court would have to find contributory infringement.

As with all contributory infringement claims, in the Dilbert dispute the linking site would be held liable for contributory infringement only if there were a finding of direct infringement on the part of the end user.... [C]ourts likely would find that end users merit a fair use defense.

Applying the Copyright Act's four fair use factors to the facts of the Dilbert dispute, the user likely would qualify for a fair use defense for the following reasons:

(1) The purpose and character of the use.

In the scenario of the Dilbert dispute, an end user reading a cartoon is using the material productively because the purpose of her use is entertainment. The end user who is merely browsing is not using the information commercially, because she is not distributing the information, saving it, or printing it out. In scenarios such as the Dilbert dispute, the user does not stand to profit from the use at all, thus weighing in favor of a finding of fair use.

The first factor also looks to whether the use of the Web site in such a scenario is transformative. In the Dilbert dispute, the use does not add anything new to the work. The entire image is linked to Wallach's page. Still, the first factor overall weighs in favor of the user browsing Wallach's Web page.

(2) The nature of the copyrighted work.

The second factor focuses on whether the Dilbert cartoons were published or un-published and whether they are informational or creative. Because the cartoons are al-ready available on the Internet, they have been published. This fact is neutral in the fair use determination because the purpose of the distinction is to allow authors to control the first appearance of their works. In terms of the second component of this factor, the Dilbert cartoons are creative, resulting in a finding against fair use because fair use is expanded for factual works in order to disseminate them to the public, rather than for fictional works such as cartoons. Thus, this fair use factor weighs against the end user.

(3) The amount and substantiality of the portion used in relation to the copy-righted work as a whole.

The end user "uses" the entire cartoon when she browses Wallach's Web site because she copies the cartoon into her computer's RAM when she browses the page. In general, use of a whole work weighs against a finding of fair use. However, the amount of non-infringing copying depends on the purpose and character of the use (the first factor). Hence, regardless of whether the entire work was copied into RAM, the end user had a productive purpose from which she did not stand to profit.

(4) The effect of the use upon the potential market for or value of the copy-righted work.

The fourth factor examines whether the use has harmed the copyright owner's ability to profit from the work and whether such conduct would adversely affect the potential market for the copyrighted work in the future. The fourth factor is the most significant in determining fair use.

Wallach's Web site affects the potential market for the copyrighted work. The inline links cause the end user to evade the United Media home page, depriving the advertiser of possible exposure. This may result in a decrease in advertising revenue. Much like in deep linking cases, the advertising on the United Media site may be seen less frequently because of the inline linking, or its exposure may actually be unaffected because Wal-lach's links provide the site with additional traffic. Nonetheless, those viewing the work via inline links on Wallach's site do not view the advertising on the United Media site at all. The value of the work is therefore harmed.

But because this harm results from the links, and only indirectly from the end user, in a case such as the Dilbert dispute the end user likely would prevail on a fair use de-fense. A plaintiff, therefore, would face difficulty in holding a linking site contributorily liable under current constructions of copyright law. In addition, as in the deep linking situation, for policy reasons a court would likely not find direct infringement on the part of the end user as that would require holding millions of Web users who unknow-ingly view an inlined image liable for copyright infringement.

## 2. Inline Linking and Derivative Works

The Copyright Act requires a transformative use and a resultant original work in order to maintain a derivative-work-right claim. In light of current case law interpret-ing the Act, an unauthorized derivative work was not produced in the Dilbert dispute. Wallach did not make any editorial revision of the Dilbert cartoon—he merely linked to the United Media Web site that contained that day's edition of the cartoon. Whichever cartoon appeared on the United Media Web site then appeared on Wallach's

Web site. An unauthorized derivative work requires originality in order to constitute infringement.

As in the discussion of deep linking and derivative works, the requisite originality was not present because no editorial revisions or modifications were made. Wallach therefore did not somehow alter the original work in order to create a new work. He merely routed the user to the original work, which appeared on his own site.

### 3. Inline Linking and the Display Right

Current case law does, however, indicate that the defendant in the Dilbert dispute infringed the plaintiff's display right. The display right protects the copyright owner against illegal public display of an original work. In the Dilbert dispute, Wallach showed the Dilbert strip on his Web site through the use of a process—inline links. Because the definition of display under the Copyright Act includes showing a copy of a work by any process, Wallach infringed United Media's display right. The House Report concerning the Copyright Act of 1976 states that "[e]ach and every method by which the images or sounds comprising a performance or display are picked up and conveyed is a 'transmission,'" and "[t]he definition of 'transmit'... is broad enough to include all conceivable forms and combinations of wired or wireless communications media." Therefore, when an end user browses a Web site, a transmission has been made and the Web site content is displayed. There is no requirement that Wallach create a copy in order to infringe United Media's display right. He directly infringed by displaying the original work on his own site.

The facts of the Dilbert dispute are analogous to those of the *Webbworld* case.... Much as *Webbworld* displayed images illegally on its adult Web site by allowing its subscribers to view Playboy's images, when Wallach allowed end users who browsed his Web site to view a copyrighted Dilbert cartoon, he in effect displayed the image of the cartoon. To constitute infringement, the display must also be public. *Playboy Enterprises, Inc. v. Frena*,[291] a case in which the defendant displayed copyrighted images on his BBS, provides guidance on this issue. The court in *Frena* looked to the Copyright Act to explain that a public display is "a display 'at a place open to the public or... where a substantial number of persons outside of a normal circle of family and its social acquaintances is gathered.'"[294] Even though the BBS was available only to those users with a password, Frena's unauthorized display of copyrighted images on his BBS was a public display. Wallach's display of the Dilbert comic strip on his Web page was a public display of even greater import, as it was available to all Web browsers.

A linked-to site desirous of fending off unwanted inline linking is most likely to succeed under a display right cause of action. Inline linking has the clear effect of reproducing the work in a public forum without the author's consent, thus depriving the author of the opportunity to gain revenue by controlling the work's display.

### 4. Inline Linking and Misappropriation in Hot News Cases

The facts in the Dilbert dispute do not trigger a cause of action for misappropriation. The online cartoons are within the subject matter of copyright, and the plaintiff seeks to claim a right equivalent to those provided by copyright law. In such a situation, a state-law misappropriation claim would be preempted by federal copyright law. In

---

291. 839 F. Supp. 1552, 1557 (M.D. Fla. 1993)....
294. [*Id.* at 1557.]

order to avoid preemption, one must state a misappropriation claim that features an extra element, putting the claim outside the scope of copyright. The only successful misappropriation claim meeting this requirement has been a hot news claim. However, in the Dilbert scenario, there is no extra element that puts the claim outside the general scope of copyright law, as the cartoons are not informational or highly time-sensitive. If, however, the inline linked-to files or images were time-sensitive, a plaintiff may be able to make out a hot news misappropriation claim.

---

### c. Deep Linking

Questions regarding liability for linking also have arisen when the conduct involves unauthorized "deep linking." This occurs when the original web-site links to a page of another web-site other than its home page. Such practices engender controversy because they may divert visitors from disclaimers and navigation tools located on the home page of the linked-to site. In addition, revenues generated by display of advertising content may be diverted to the linking site, thereby motivating the linked-to site to curtail the practice. One commentator opined, "[s]tores have a right to ask that you enter by the front door, which forces you to pass the impulse-purchase Godiva chocolate counter on your way up to buy undershirts." David M. Mirchin, *Can You Be Held Legally Liable for Hypertext Linking?* Corp. Legal Times (Oct. 1998) at 22. Some sites utilize passwords or other technological devices that require visitors to start at their home page.

In *Ticketmaster Corp. v. Tickets.Com, Inc.*, No. 99-7654, 2000 U.S. Dist. LEXIS 4553 (C.D. Cal. Mar. 27, 2000), the plaintiff alleged that the defendant had, among other things, improperly deep linked to the plaintiff sites. The plaintiff's copyright infringement, passing off, reverse passing off, and the false advertising claims were not dismissed. Significantly, however, the court cautioned that:

> hyperlinking does not itself involve a violation of the Copyright Act (whatever it may do for other claims)[;] since no copying is involved, the customer is automatically transferred to the particular genuine web page of the original author. There is no deception in what is happening. This is analogous to using a library's card index to get reference to particular items, albeit faster and more efficiently.

*Id.* at *6.[3]

In *Shetland Times Limited v. Wills and Another*, 1997 S.L.T. 669 (Sess. Cas. 1996), Lord Hamilton of the Court of Session in Edinburgh, Scotland considered a claim brought by *The Shetland Times*, a newspaper, against Zetnews Ltd. and its managing director. *The Shetland Times* had launched a web-site to make its text and photographs from its print editions available on-line. The newspaper indicated that it expected that once the information service became known to and used by Internet users, the newspaper would be able to sell advertising space on its site's home page. *See id.*

The defendants operated a news reporting service, including a web-site under the name "The Shetland News." The defendants' site included verbatim headlines that had

---

3. In August 2000, the court declined to issue a preliminary injunction. The court observed that since the earlier motion, the plaintiff had devised technical methods to block direct access by deep linking to its interior pages; it was not clear at that time whether these devices would be effective in the future. *See Ticketmaster v. Tickets.com* (C.D. Cal. Aug. 10, 2000) <http://www.gigalaw.com/library/ticketmaster-tickets-2000-08-10-p1.htm>.

appeared in the plaintiff's newspaper on its site, by deep-linking to the plaintiff's site. Accordingly, access to the plaintiff's content, as published both in its print edition and as reproduced on its web-site, could be achieved by the user while by-passing the plaintiff's home page.

The plaintiff asserted that the defendants' practices amounted to copyright infringement. The defendants did not dispute that copyright subsisted in the text of the articles in question, but maintained that no protection extended to the headlines. Lord Hamilton concluded that the plaintiff had made a *prima facie* case that the incorporation by the defendants in the web site of the headlines provided at the plaintiff's web-site constituted an infringement of the English Copyright, Designs and Patents Act of 1988. *Shetland Times v. Wills and Another*, 1997 S.L.T. at 671. Lord Hamilton indicated that there was a question as to whether the headlines were protected by copyright. "However, in light of the concession that a headline could be a literary work and since the headlines at issue (or at least some of them) involve eight or so words designedly together for the purpose of imparting information, it appeared arguable that there was an infringement, at least in some instances, [of the Act]." *Id.*

The court also addressed the argument that any loss was somewhat speculative, stating that it is "fundamental to the setting up by the [plaintiff] of [its] web site that access to [its] material should be gained only by accessing their web site directly. While there has been no loss to date, there is a clear prospect of loss of potential advertising revenue in the foreseeable future." *Id.* at 672. Lord Hamilton granted an interim interdict, which is procedurally analogous to a preliminary injunction.

The parties ultimately settled their dispute by agreeing that each link to articles would include the legend "A Shetland Times Story," that the plaintiff's masthead logo would appear next to each headline, and that the legend on the icon be hyperlinked to the headline page of the plaintiff's web-site. *See* David M. Mirchin, *Can You Be Held Legally Liable for Hypertext Linking?*, Corp. Legal Times (Oct. 1998) at 22.

---

## Link Liability: The Argument for Inline Links and Frames as Infringements of the Copyright Display Right
### Allison Roarty
### 68 Fordham L. Rev. 1011 (1999)

... Based on current case law and theories underpinning copyright law, linked-to sites containing time-sensitive content may have a cause of action for deep linking under the common law doctrine of misappropriation, but do not have a claim in copyright law.

1. Deep Linking and the Reproduction Right

In cases of deep linking, in which one site links to the underlying page of another site, analysis of copyright protection begins by asking whether deep links actually create copies of the work. [In] *Shetland Times*,[218] ... the Shetland News linked to the underlying pages containing the news articles of the Shetland Times. Under United States law, defendant Shetland News does not infringe the reproduction right of the copyright holder because Shetland News does not make copies of the Web page articles. Rather, it

---

218. 1997 S.L.T. 669 (Scot. 1996).

provides links or references to the Shetland Times pages. Technically, it is the user who is making the copy by browsing the page through the link because the page will be stored in the RAM of the user's computer.[221] A copy stored in RAM has been held to meet the fixation requirement of the Copyright Act.[222] In sum, The Shetland News itself likely is not liable for direct infringement of the reproduction right. Most commentators who have addressed the issue agree.

Were *Shetland Times* brought under United States law, in order to hold Shetland News liable for infringement of plaintiff's reproduction right the court would instead have had to find it liable for contributory infringement. Because contributory liability is dependent upon a finding of direct liability, one must identify a direct infringer. In a deep linking scenario, exactly who is making copies of the copyrighted work? In *Shetland Times*, the direct infringer is the end user because the end user is the only party making a copy.

However, it is unlikely that any court would find direct infringement on the part of the end user. This legal issue is not settled, but because the online world facilitates and even requires the infinite creation of copies, courts likely would find that the fair use exception applies to end users browsing the Web. Indeed, one court has indicated in dicta that browsing would be afforded the fair use exception. In addition, at least one commentator has interpreted the Digital Millennium Copyright Act to "confirm[ ] that a temporary copy of a copyrighted work made automatically by a computer when browsing [the Web] is not considered an infringing copy." Some commentators have argued that the end user is not liable for either direct or contributory infringement because the copies that are made while browsing are authorized by an implied license.

To determine whether there is contributory liability in the deep linking that occurred in the *Shetland Times* scenario, it is necessary to examine the fair use exception. The fair use defense is typically unsuccessful when an entire work has been copied. Nonetheless, applying the facts of *Shetland Times* to the four fair use factors

---

221. Computers and file servers use two types of memory: temporary memory, or Random Access Memory (RAM), and permanent memory, which includes hard drives and floppy disks.... When the computer is turned on and used, documents, programs, and other information must be loaded into RAM in order for the computer to work with or display the document or information....But when the user closes a document, the document disappears entirely from RAM....In addition, when the computer is turned off, everything that was in RAM disappears completely....

222. *See Triad Sys. Corp. v. Southeastern Express Co.*, 64 F.3d 1330, 1335 (9th Cir. 1995); *MAI Sys. Corp. v. Peak Computer, Inc.*, 991 F.2d 511, 518–19 (9th Cir. 1993) (upholding a finding of copyright infringement where a repair person who was not authorized to use the computer owner's licensed software turned on the computer, thus loading the operating system into RAM); *Marobie-FL, Inc. v. National Assoc. of Fire Equip. Distribs. and Northwest Nexus, Inc.*, 983 F. Supp. 1167, 1177–78 (N.D. Ill. 1997) (holding that a file in RAM created by a user browsing the Internet was fixed); *Advanced Computer Servs. of Mich., Inc. v. MAI Sys. Corp.*, 845 F. Supp. 356, 362–63 (E.D. Va. 1994); *see also* 2 [Melville B. Nimmer and David Nimmer, *Nimmer on Copyright,*] ... § 8.08[A][1] [(1999)] ("[G]iven that RAM can contain data that may be accessed until the machine is turned off, its fixation would seem to be not merely evanescent."). *But cf.* Digital Millennium Copyright Act of Oct. 28, 1998, Pub. L. No. 105-304, § 302, 112 Stat. (to be codified at 17 U.S.C.) (providing an exception for liability for copies made during the course of computer repairs, and effectively overruling *MAI Sys. Corp.*, 845 F. Supp. at 356. Congress noted in passing the Digital Millennium Copyright Act that "[w]hen a computer is activated, certain software or parts thereof is [sic] automatically copied into the machine's random access memory, or 'RAM.' A clarification in the Copyright Act is necessary in light of judicial decisions holding that such copying is a 'reproduction' under section 106 of the Copyright Act...." H.R. Conf. Rep. No. 105-796, at 76 (1998), reprinted in 1998 U.S.C.C.A.N. 639, 652.

required by the Copyright Act reveals that the end user likely would have a fair use defense.

(1) The purpose and character of the use.

In the case of *Shetland Times*, presumably an end user reading a newspaper article is using the material productively—the purpose of her use is to obtain information. In addition, the end user is not using the information commercially, because presumably she is not sharing the information, storing it, or printing it out. According to the Supreme Court's profit/nonprofit approach to fair use, the importance of this factor is not whether the purpose of the use is monetary gain, but whether the user profits from the copyrighted material without compensating the copyright owner. Under the facts of *Shetland Times*, the user does not stand to profit from the use at all.

The Supreme Court has also explained that the goal of the purpose/character factor is to ascertain whether the new work supersedes the original work, adds something new, or is otherwise transformative.[237] The more transformative the use, the less the other factors, such as commercialism, will weigh. In *Shetland Times*, the use is not transformative, nor does it add anything new at all. Nonetheless, on balance it seems that the first factor weighs in favor of the user reading the Shetland Times. Even the typical browser surfing the Web for recreational purposes other than reading news would likely have a fair use defense. Most browsers search for information and do not derive a profit from what they find.

(2) The nature of the copyrighted work.

The two issues relating to the nature of the copyrighted work are whether the original work was published or unpublished and whether it is informational or creative. In *Shetland Times*, the articles are published because they are already available on the Internet. This does not affect a finding of fair use because the purpose of the inquiry is to provide more protection to unpublished works in order to allow the author control over her own work. The copyrighted work is informational because it is news. This weighs toward a finding of fair use because this aspect of the analysis expands protection for creative or fictional works and decreases protection for factual or informational works so that the latter are more easily disseminated. Thus, a determination of fair use is more probable when the work is factual rather than fictional. Here, because the Shetland Times articles are factual, the balance weighs in favor of the end user.

(3) The amount and substantiality of the portion used in relation to the copyrighted work as a whole.

If browsing the Web site is "using" the material, then a substantial amount of the Web site content is used because the entire article is copied in RAM when the user calls up the corresponding Web page—regardless of whether she actually reads it. The copying of an entire work weighs against a finding of fair use.

The amount of permissible copying varies according to the purpose and character of the use (the first factor). Thus, even though the entire work was copied in RAM, the purpose and character of the use remains productive and non-commercial, thus weighing toward a finding of fair use.

---

237. *See Campbell v. Acuff-Rose Music, Inc.*, 510 U.S. 569, 579 (1994).

(4) The effect of the use upon the potential market for or value of the copyrighted work.

In these cases, there may be an effect on the potential market for the copyrighted work. When users bypass the home page of the Shetland Times, the site owner is deprived of exposure to potential advertisers. This may result in decreased advertising revenue and a consequent decrease in the value of the copyrighted work to site owners. However, it is unclear whether the advertising is viewed less frequently because of the deep linking, or whether exposure to the advertising is unaffected because the links may be providing the site with additional traffic and exposure. Nonetheless, those accessing the site via deep links do not view the advertising at all. The value of the work is harmed. But because this harm results from the links, and only indirectly from the acts of the end user, arguably the end user should be provided a fair use defense. In addition, for policy reasons, it seems unlikely that courts would hold millions of web browsers liable for copyright infringement merely for surfing the Internet.

In sum, under current copyright law, a linked-to site would have difficulty arguing that linking makes unauthorized copies of Web site content. They would have equal difficulty trying to pin contributory liability on linking sites, as end users would likely be provided a fair use defense.

### 2. Deep Linking and Unauthorized Derivative Works

Construed in the context of the case law concerning derivative works, deep linking does not create a derivative work because there is no transformation of the underlying work. For example, in the *Shetland Times* case, the Shetland News has in effect taken a page from the Shetland Times Web site and made it part of the Shetland News site. It has not made editorial revisions by choosing that page from the Shetland Times site and adding it to its own site. Instead, it has merely linked to the entire article. Deep linking, therefore, does not meet the standard of originality required by copyright in order to constitute a derivative work.[251] Hence, the Shetland Times would not be entitled to relief based on an infringement of the derivative work right.

### 3. Deep Linking and the Display Right

Similarly, deep linking does not infringe the copyright owner's display right under current case law. The display right protects the author against unauthorized public displays of a copyrighted work. In *Shetland Times*, the Shetland News does not display the copyrighted work on its Web site. Rather, it links to the Shetland Times site, in effect routing the user to the original work. The end user is, however, unaware that she has left the Shetland News site (the linking site) behind and that the Shetland Times's material is not that of the linking site. In other words, the end user believes she is still on the

---

251. ...Shetland News may have created a "compilation" or "collective work" in the sense that it has selected and arranged the works of *Shetland Times* on the Shetland News Web site. "A 'compilation' is a work formed by the collection and assembling of preexisting materials or of data that are selected, coordinated, or arranged in such a way that the resulting work as a whole constitutes an original work of authorship." 17 U.S.C. § 101; *see Feist Publications Inc. v. Rural Tel. Serv. Co.*, 499 U.S. 340, 348 (1991) ("The compilation author typically chooses which facts to include, in what order to place them, and how to arrange the collected data so that they may be used effectively by readers."). "A 'collective work' is a work, such as a periodical issue, anthology, or encyclopedia, in which a number of contributions, constituting separate and independent works in themselves, are assembled into a collective whole." 17 U.S.C. § 101. However, because the works are not literally a part of the Shetland News Web site, this is likely an unsuccessful argument.

Shetland News site. Such a scenario implicates trademark issues, such as reverse passing off,[254] but it does not implicate copyright law. Thus, under the Copyright Act's definition of display, which calls for an unauthorized public showing, the Shetland Times does not have a claim for infringement of the display right.

### 4. Deep Linking and Misappropriation for Hot News Claims

Under United States law, the facts of the *Shetland Times* case raise the potential for liability for misappropriation, even though the news articles in question are copyrighted content. A misappropriation claim may be preempted when that claim seeks to defend rights commensurate with those provided by copyright law, and when the subject matter of the work itself is copyrightable. However, if in addition to the elements of a copyright claim, an "extra" element exists, then the misappropriation claim is not within the general scope of copyright protection and thus survives preemption.[258] As a result, the legislative history of the Copyright Act indicates, and most courts agree, that a plaintiff is not preempted from making a hot news claim. A hot news claim has been the only type of misappropriation claim to survive preemption when the work is copyrightable and the claim is equivalent to the rights afforded by copyright.

Applying the criteria set forth by the court in *NBA v. Motorola*[260] to the facts of *Shetland Times*, the plaintiff can make out a hot news claim for misappropriation:

(i) as a newspaper, The Shetland Times generates or collects information at some cost or expense;

(ii) because it is a daily newspaper, the value of the information is highly time-sensitive;

(iii) the defendant's use of the information constitutes free-riding on the plaintiff's costly efforts to generate or collect the information because the defendant does nothing but link to the content already existing on the plaintiff's Web site;

(iv) the defendant is a directly competing newspaper who competes with the plaintiff for advertising;

(v) the ability of other parties to free-ride on the efforts of The Shetland Times would so reduce the incentive to produce the product or service that its existence or quality would be substantially threatened. In a competitive situation such as in the *Shetland Times* scenario, misappropriation is an appropriate cause of action for the deep-linked site.

In short, in deep linking cases, a linked-to site may state a cause of action for misappropriation when the site features time-sensitive content. However, based on copyright

---

254. In order to succeed on a claim for reverse passing off under the Lanham Act, a plaintiff must prove: "'(1) that the work at issue originated with plaintiff; (2) that [the] origin of the work was falsely designated by the defendant; (3) that the false designation of origin was likely to cause consumer confusion; and (4) that the plaintiff was harmed by the defendant's false designation of origin.'" *Banff Ltd. v. Express, Inc.*, 921 F. Supp. 1065, 1071 (S.D.N.Y. 1995) (quoting *Lipton v. The Nature Co.*, 71 F.3d 464, 472 (2d Cir. 1995)).

258. *See, e.g.*, *NBA v. Motorola, Inc.*, 105 F.3d 841, 850 (2d Cir. 1997) ("[I]f an 'extra element' is 'required instead of or in addition to the acts of reproduction, [for example], in order to constitute a state-created cause of action, then the right does not lie 'within the general scope of copyright,' and there is no preemption.'" (quoting *Computer Assocs., Int'l v. Altai ,Inc.*, 982 F.2d 693, 716 (2d Cir. 1992)).

260. 105 F.3d 841, 850 (2d Cir. 1997)....

theory and current case law interpreting the protections afforded by copyright law, there is no copyright liability for deep linking....

---

## Notes and Questions

1.  To what extent do courts probe the motivations of litigants' decisions to link to information which they have been enjoined from posting themselves? In *Intellectual Reserve, Inc. v. Utah Lighthouse Ministry, Inc.*, 75 F. Supp. 2d 1290 (D. Utah 1999), the defendants placed a notice on their web-site that the plaintiff's Church Handbook was available on-line, and gave three addresses of web-sites containing the material the defendants had been ordered to remove from their web-site. Defendants also posted e-mails on their web-site that encouraged browsing those web-sites, printing copies of the Handbook and sending the Handbook to others. In granting the preliminary injunction requested by the plaintiff, the court concluded that the defendants had "actively encouraged the infringement of plaintiff's copyright." *Id.* at 1294.

    In *Universal City Studios v. Reimerdes*, No. 00 Civ. 0277, 2000 U.S. Dist. LEXIS 11696 at *73, Judge Kaplan noted that the defendants, who had been enjoined from displaying DeCSS circumvention technology information, termed their act of linking to other sites that made the information available an "act of 'electronic civil disobedience.'" The court characterized the links as an attempt to defeat the purpose of the preliminary injunction by offering the practical equivalent of making DeCSS available on the defendants' site by electronically linking users to other sites still offering DeCSS, and by encouraging other sites that had not been enjoined to offer the program. The court further stated that the defendants had linked to sites posting the circumvention device, "initially tout[ing] it as a way to get free movies, and they later maintained the links to promote the dissemination of the program in an effort to defeat effective judicial relief." *Id.* at *133 (footnote omitted).

2.  Arguments have been made that First Amendment rights are implicated in hyperlinking. In *American Civil Liberties Union v. Miller*, 977 F. Supp. 1228, 1233 n. 5, 1234 (N.D. Ga. 1997), for instance, a state statute that "chill[ed] protected expression" without any "compelling state interest that would be furthered by restricting [certain] linking function[s]...." was questioned.

    In rejecting the defendants' First Amendment defense in *Universal City Studios v. Reimerdes*, No. 00 Civ. 0277, 2000 U.S. Dist. LEXIS 11696, Judge Kaplan stated that while the DeCSS code is expressive, the DMCA as applied is content-neutral and its anti-trafficking provision furthers an important governmental interest; i.e., "the protection of copyrighted works stored on digital media from the vastly expanded risk of piracy in this electronic age. The substantiality of that interest is evident both from the fact that the Constitution specifically empowers Congress to provide for copyright protection and from the significance to our economy of trade in copyrighted materials." *Id.* at *94 (footnotes omitted). The court further noted that this interest is unrelated to the suppression of particular views expressed in copyrighted works and is not broader than necessary to achieve Congressional objectives of preventing infringement and promoting the availability of content in digital form. *Id.*

    Judge Kaplan employed a metaphor to explain infringement in the digital environment, observing that copying decrypted material on-line potentially is exponential rather than linear.

In a common source epidemic, as where members of a population contract a non-contagious disease from a poisoned well, the disease spreads only by exposure to the common source. If one eliminates the source, or closes the contaminated well, the epidemic is stopped. In a propagated outbreak epidemic, on the other hand, the disease spreads from person to person. Hence, finding the initial source of infection accomplishes little, as the disease continues to spread even if the initial source is eliminated. For obvious reasons, then, a propagated outbreak epidemic, all other things being equal, can be far more difficult to control.

... The book infringement hypothetical is analogous to a common source outbreak epidemic. Shut down the printing press (the poisoned well) and one ends the infringement (the disease outbreak). The spread of means of circumventing access to copyrighted works in digital form, however, is analogous to a propagated outbreak epidemic. Finding the original source of infection (e.g., the author of DeCSS or the first person to misuse it) accomplishes nothing, as the disease infringement made possible by DeCSS and the resulting availability of decrypted DVDs) may continue to spread from one person who gains access to the circumvention program or decrypted DVD to another. And each is "infected," i.e., each is capable of making perfect copies of the digital file containing the copyrighted work as the author of the program or the first person to use it for improper purposes. The disease metaphor breaks down principally at the final point. Individuals infected with a real disease become sick, usually are driven by obvious self-interest to seek medical attention, and are cured of the disease if medical science is capable of doing so. Individuals infected with the "disease" of capability of circumventing measures controlling access to copyrighted works in digital form, however, do not suffer from having that ability. They cannot be relied upon to identify themselves to those seeking to control the "disease." And their self-interest will motivate some to misuse the capability, a misuse that, in practical terms, often will be untraceable.

*Id.* at *99–102 (footnotes omitted).

3.  The basis for implying a license to link lies not in affirmative consent by the linked-to site, but rather in the tacit acquiescence by the linked party in placing an unrestricted site on the Web. How does this implied license comport with traditional notions of copyright law, which generally has not required the copyright owner to insulate his material from infringement in order to qualify for protection? To whom should the burdens of implementing technological protective controls in order to safeguard copyright rights be allocated?

4.  Ticketmaster objected to Microsoft's deep links within Ticketmaster's site to direct visitors to tickets available for performances and events referenced on Microsoft's city guides. *See Ticketmaster v. Microsoft*, First Amended Complaint, No. 97-3055 DDP (C.D. Cal. filed May 9, 1997). The case reportedly settled. *See, e.g.,* Bob Tedeschi, *Ticketmaster and Microsoft Settle Suit on Internet Linking*, N.Y. Times (Feb. 15, 1999) at C6.

    To what extent do settlements affect the conduct and expectations about netiquette and other normative conduct, in light of the nascent jurisprudence in this area?

5.  "Technological access control measures have the capacity to prevent fair uses of copyrighted works as well as foul. Hence there is a potential tension between the

use of such access control measures and fair use." *Universal City Studios v. Reimerdes,* No. 00 Civ. 0277, 2000 U.S. Dist. LEXIS 11696 at *3.

6.   Bookmarks allow Web browsers to mark pages of particular sites that they routinely access, in order to permit direct navigation back to the marked paged. Bookmark technology permits marking of a site's interior pages. How does this practice affect the expectation that, absent permission to the contrary, entry to others' sites will be achieved through its home page? Is it incumbent upon the site owner to design the site to limit linking to its home page?

---

# 3.   Framing

Internet technology also permits "framing," which is a practice that allows a web-site to incorporate the content of a remote or third-party site within the original site. The content of the other site is brought into a window that appears on the original framing site. This practice has generated controversy because the framing site continues to display its branding and navigation to the visitor, and because the framing site may alter the framed content within the site.

In *Washington Post v. Total News,* six content providers, The Washington Post Company, Dow Jones & Co., Inc., Times Mirror Company, Time Inc., Cable News Network, Inc., and Reuters New Media Inc., sued an aggregator of Web sources. The defendant had utilized framing technology to display news sites, along with its url, logo, and banner advertisements. By selecting one of the plaintiffs' sites, either by accessing an index on the defendant's home page or a series of icons that appeared in a separate frame at the left margin of the home page, users could access the plaintiffs' content via a hyperlink. The plaintiffs alleged that this practice wrongfully altered views by visitors to their sites. The plaintiffs asserted claims, among others, grounded in misappropriation, trademark infringement, and trademark dilution. The defendant's site had diverted advertising revenue that likely would have inured to the plaintiffs' benefit; the plaintiffs characterized this practice as the operation of a "parasitic website [that is] the Internet equivalent of pirating copyrighted material from a variety of famous newspapers, magazines, or television news programs; packaging those stories to advertisers as part of a competitive publication or program...; and pocketing the advertising revenues generated by their unauthorized use of the material." Complaint, *Washington Post Co. v. Total News, Inc.* (S.D.N.Y. filed Feb. 20, 1997) at ¶¶ 8, 10 (cited in Bruce P. Keller, *Condemned to Repeat the Past: The Reemergence of Misappropriation and Other Common Law Theories of Protection for Intellectual Property,* 11 Harv. J.L. & Tech. 401 (1998)).

The settlement, entered into in June 1997, reportedly required Total News to permanently refrain from framing the plaintiffs' content; using any of the plaintiffs' trademarks or logos on its web site; or intentionally linking to any third-party web-site that engaged in framing practices of the defendants' content. Total News, for its part, was granted a revocable, royalty-free license to link to the plaintiffs' web-sites via non-framing hyperlinks consisting of the sites' names in plain text. *See* Bruce P. Keller, *Condemned to Repeat the Past: Other Common Law Theories of Protection for Intellectual Property,* 11 Harv. J.L. & Tech. at 422–23.

---

# FUTUREDONTICS INC. v. APPLIED ANAGRAMICS INC.

U.S. District Court, Central District of California
No. CV 97-6991 ABC (MANx), 45 U.S.P.Q.2d 2005, 1998 WL 132922
January 30, 1998

Collins, J.

After reviewing the materials submitted by the parties and the case file, it is hereby ORDERED that the Motion to Dismiss of Defendants APPLIED ANAGRAMICS, INC. ("AAI"), ROBERT GOODMAN, NINE TREES DESIGN, and AM.NET (collectively "Defendants") is DENIED....

## Plaintiff's Allegations

Plaintiff... in general alleges that Plaintiff operates a dental referral business utilizing the anagramatic phone number "1-800-DENTIST." AAI owns the registered service mark, "1-800-DENTIST." AAI has granted Plaintiff exclusive use of the telephone number and service mark throughout the United States. "The current 1-800-DENTIST dental referral service has been entirely designed and developed by Futuredontics, which is solely responsible for its success."

In early 1996, Plaintiff decided to establish an Internet site to advertise its dental referral business. Plaintiff's site consists of a number of web pages containing graphics and text, which are copyrightable subject matter.... Plaintiff registered its copyrighted web pages....

AAI established its own site sometime after March 25, 1997.

> The AAI web site includes a "link" through which AAI reproduces web pages from the Futuredontics Site within a "frame" ("AAI Frame Page"). The AAI Frame Page includes a frame around a reproduction of the web page from the Futuredontics Site. The frame includes AAI's logo, information on AAI, and "links to all of AAI's other web pages."... Futuredontics has never authorized AAI to reproduce the Futuredontics Site on the AAI Frame Page.

With respect to the Third Claim for relief, Plaintiff specifically alleges that Futuredontics is the owner of the copyrighted material comprising the web pages on the Futuredontics Site. Plaintiff also alleges that AAI and the other defendants "are willfully infringing Futuredontics' copyright in the material on its web pages by copying that material to the AAI Frame Page and reproducing it there without the permission of Futuredontics."...

## Analysis

To establish copyright infringement, Plaintiff must prove (1) that Plaintiff owned the copyrights, and (2) that Defendants copied Plaintiff's copyrighted work. *Smith v. Jackson*, 84 F.3d 1213, 1218 [39 USPQ2d 1026] (9th Cir. 1996). A copyright is infringed when a person other than the owner violates any of the exclusive rights conferred by copyright. 17 U.S.C. Section 501(a). A copyright owner has several exclusive rights, including the exclusive right to "prepare derivative works based upon the copyrighted works." 17 U.S.C. Section 106(2).

Defendants contend that Plaintiff's copyright infringement claim should be dismissed because the framed link does not create a derivative work.

The Copyright Act defines a "derivative work" as:

a work based upon one or more preexisting works such as...art reproduction, abridgment, condensation, or any other form in which a work may be recast, transformed, or adapted. A work consisting of editorial revisions, annotations, elaborations, or other modifications which, as a whole, represent an original work of authorship, is a "derivative work."

17 U.S.C. Section 101.

The parties sharply dispute what function AAI's framed link serves. Defendants contend that AAI's window or frame provides a "lens" which enables Internet users to view the information that Plaintiff itself placed on the Internet. Plaintiff's complaint, however, alleges that defendants reproduce its copyrighted web page by combining AAI material and Plaintiff's web site. ("The AAI web site includes a 'link' through which AAI reproduces web pages from the Futuredontics Site within [the AAI Frame Page]. The AAI Frame Page includes a frame around a reproduction of the web page from the Futuredontics Site.")

The parties cite to several cases which purportedly support their interpretation of the function AAI's framed link serves. None of these cases, however, is directly on point.

The parties discuss the applicability of *Mirage Editions, Inc. v. Albuquerque A.R.T. Co.*, 856 F.2d 1341, 1343 [8 USPQ2d 1171] (9th Cir. 1988). In *Mirage*, the Ninth Circuit held that transferring and affixing art images with glue to ceramic tiles constituted "the creation of a derivative work in violation of the copyright laws." *Id.* at 1343–44. As this Court noted in its Order denying Plaintiff's request for a preliminary injunction, *Mirage* is distinguishable from the present case. In this case, AAI has not affixed an image to a ceramic tile, rather AAI appears to have placed an electronic frame or border around Plaintiff's web page.

Defendants primarily rely on *Louis Galoob Toys, Inc. v. Nintendo of America, Inc.*, 964 F.2d 965, 968 [22 USPQ2d 1857] (9th Cir. 1992). In that case, the Ninth Circuit held that a Game Genie which merely enhances audiovisual displays which originate in Nintendo game cartridges does not constitute a derivative work because, in part, it does "not incorporate a portion of a copyrighted work in some concrete or permanent form." *Id.* at 968. The Court also noted that the Game Genie could not duplicate or recast a Nintendo game's output. *Galoob* did distinguish *Mirage* and noted that the *Mirage* decision would have been different had the plaintiff "distributed lenses that merely enabled users to view several art works simultaneously." *Id.*

Nevertheless, *Galoob*, like *Mirage*, is distinguishable from the instant case. *Galoob* does not foreclose Plaintiff from establishing that AAI's web page incorporates Futuredontic's web page in some "concrete or permanent form" or that AAI's framed link duplicates or recasts Plaintiff's web page. *Id.*

For these reasons, the Court finds that the cases cited by the parties do not conclusively determine whether Defendants' frame page constitutes a derivative work. Therefore, the Court determines that Plaintiff's Third Claim for Relief sufficiently alleges a claim for copyright infringement.

## Conclusion

For all these reasons, the Court hereby DENIES Defendants' motion to dismiss Plaintiff's copyright infringement claim and DENIES Defendant's alternative motion for judgment on the pleadings with respect to that claim.

———————

# 4. Metatags

"Metatags" are bits of data embedded on a Web page that are not visible to the end user. Keyword metatags allow web-site operators to specify terms that describe their site, so that search engines can index the terms. Metatags are often utilized to achieve favorable positioning in the indices generated by the search engines, as they survey the Web for sites responsive to the search.

Disputes relating to metatags typically occur when web-site creators incorporate trademarks. The search engine that utilizes a "spider" to crawl the Web for responsive sites in effect views the trademark as an indication that the site has information relevant to the search. Consequently, the trademark has been exploited to direct traffic to the site, or at least to attract the attention of the user engaged in the search.

Claims challenging this practice are frequently predicated upon theories of trademark infringement, false advertising, and dilution. In assessing liability, courts have looked to the degree to which the trademark bears a reasonable relationship to the content of the site. In *Playboy Enterprises, Inc. v. Terri Welles, Inc.*, 7 F. Supp. 2d 1098 (S.D. Cal.), *aff'd*, 162 F.3d 1169 (9th Cir. 1998), for example, Playboy challenged the defendant's use of the terms "playmate" and "playboy" in metatags on her web-site. The district court declined to grant the injunctive relief the plaintiff had requested, holding that the defendant's use of the terms was permissible because they referred to her career as a former Playmate of the Year. 7 F. Supp. 2d at 1104. Thereafter, the court granted summary judgment for the defendant on the trademark, dilution, and unfair competition claims. The U.S. District Court for the Southern District of California observed that "Not all web searches using the words 'Playboy,' 'Playmate,' and 'Playboy Playmate of the Year 1981' are intended to find 'Playboy' goods or the official 'Playboy' site.... Ms. Welles' fame and recognition derive from her popularity as a Playboy model and 'Playmate of the Year.' If a consumer cannot remember her name, the logical way to find her site on the web is by using key words that identify her source of recognition to the public...." *Playboy Enterprises, Inc. v. Terri Welles*, 78 F. Supp. 2d 1066, 1095 (S.D. Cal. 1999).

---

# BROOKFIELD COMMUNICATIONS INC. v. WEST COAST ENTERTAINMENT CORP.

U.S. Court of Appeals, Ninth Circuit
No. 98-56918, 174 F.3d 1036
April 22, 1999

Before Canby, O'Scannlain, and Wardlaw, Circuit Judges.

O'Scannlain, J.

[For the background of this case, *see supra* at 453.]

We must venture into cyberspace to determine whether federal trademark and unfair competition laws prohibit a video rental store chain from using an entertainment-industry information provider's trademark...in its metatags....

At first glance, our resolution of the infringement issues in the domain name context would appear to dictate a similar conclusion of likelihood of confusion with respect to West Coast's use of "moviebuff.com: in its metatags. Disposing of the issue so readily, however, would ignore the fact that the likelihood of confusion in the domain name context resulted largely from the associational confusion between West Coast's domain name "moviebuff.com" and Brookfield's trademark "MovieBuff." The question in the metatags context is quite different. Here, we must determine whether West Coast can use "MovieBuff" or "moviebuff.com" in the metatags of its web site at "west-coastvideo.com" or at any other domain address other than"moviebuff.com" (which we have determined that West Coast may not use).

Although entering "MovieBuff" into a search engine is likely to bring up a list including "westcoastvideo.com" if West Coast has included that term in its metatags, the resulting confusion is not as great as where West Coast uses the "moviebuff.com" domain name. First, when the user inputs "MovieBuff" into an Internet search engine, the list produced by the search engine is likely to include both West Coast's and Brookfield's web sites. Thus, in scanning such list, the Web user will often be able to find the particular web site he is seeking. Moreover, even if the Web user chooses the web site belonging to West Coast, he will see that the domain name of the web site he selected is "west-coastvideo.com." Since there is no confusion resulting from the domain address, and since West Coast's initial web page prominently displays its own name, it is difficult to say that a consumer is likely to be confused about whose site he has reached or to think that Brookfield somehow sponsors West Coast's web site.

Nevertheless, West Coast's use of "moviebuff.com" in metatags will still result in what is known as initial interest confusion. Web surfers looking for Brookfield's "MovieBuff" products who are taken by a search engine to "westcoastvideo.com" will find a database similar enough to "MovieBuff" such that a sizeable number of consumers who were originally looking for Brookfield's product will simply decide to utilize West Coast's offerings instead. Although there is no source confusion in the sense that consumers know they are patronizing West Coast rather than Brookfield, there is nevertheless initial interest confusion in the sense that, by using "moviebuff.com" or "MovieBuff" to divert people looking for "MovieBuff" to its web site, West Coast improperly benefits from the goodwill that Brookfield developed in its mark. Recently in *Dr. Seuss*, we explicitly recognized that the use of another's trademark in a manner calculated "to capture initial consumer attention, even though no actual sale is finally completed as a result of the confusion, may be still an infringement." *Dr. Seuss* [*Enters. v. Penguin Books USA, Inc.*, 109 F.3d 1394, 1405 (9th Cir. 1997), *petition for cert. dismissed by* 118 S.Ct. 27 (1997)] (citing *Mobil Oil Corp. v. Pegasus Petroleum Corp.*, 818 F.2d 254, 257–58 [2 USPQ2d 1677] (2d Cir. 1987))....

Both *Dr. Seuss* and the Second Circuit hold that initial interest confusion is actionable under the Lanham Act, which holdings are bolstered by the decisions of many other courts which have similarly recognized that the federal trademark and unfair competition laws do protect against this form of consumer confusion. *See Green Prods.*, 992 F. Supp. 1070, 1076 (N.D. Iowa 1997) ("In essence, ICBP is capitalizing on the strong similarity between Green Products' trademark and ICBP's domain name to lure customers onto its web page."); *Securacomm Consulting, Inc. v. Securacomm Inc.*, 984 F. Supp. 286, 298 [45 USPQ2d 1576] (D.N.J. 1997) ("'Infringement can be based upon confusion that creates initial customer interest, even though no actual sale is finally completed as a result of the confusion.'") (*citing* 3 McCarthy Section 23:6), *rev'd on other grounds*, 166 F.3d 182, 186 [49 USPQ2d 1444] (3d Cir. 1999) ("In this appeal, [appellant] does not challenge the district court's finding of infringement or order of injunctive relief."); *Kompan A.S. v. Park Structures, Inc.*, 890 F. Supp. 1167, 1180 (N.D.N.Y. 1995) ("Kompan argues correctly that it can prevail by showing that confusion between the Kompan and Karavan lines and names will mistakenly lead the consumer to believe there is some connection between the two and therefore develop an interest in the Karavan line that it would not otherwise have had."); *Blockbuster Entertainment Group v. Laylco, Inc.*, 869 F. Supp. 505, 513 [33 USPQ2d 1581] (E.D. Mich. 1994) ("Because the names are so similar and the products sold are identical, some unwitting customers might enter a Video Busters store thinking it is somehow connected to Blockbuster. Those customers probably will realize shortly that Video Busters is not related to Blockbuster, but under [*Ferraria S.P.A. Esercizio v. Roberts*, 944 F.2d 1235 [20 USPQ2d 1001] (6th Cir. 1991)] and *Grotrian* that is irrelevant."); *Jordache Enters., Inc. v. Levi Strauss & Co.*, 841 F. Supp. 506, 514–15 [30 USPQ2d 1721] (S.D.N.Y. 1993) ("Types of confusion that constitute trademark infringement include where...potential consumers initially are attracted to the junior user's mark by virtue of its similarity to the senior user's mark, even though these consumers are not actually confused at the time of purchase."); *Sara Lee Corp. v. Kayser-Roth Corp.*, No. 9200460, 1992 WL 436279, at *24 (W.D.N.C. Dec. 1, 1992) ("That situation offers an opportunity for sale not otherwise available by enabling defendant to interest prospective customers by confusion with the plaintiff's product."); *Television Enter. Network, Inc. v. Entertainment Network, Inc.*, 630 F. Supp. 244, 247 [229 USPQ 47] (D.N.J. 1986) ("Even if the confusion is cured at some intermediate point before the deal is completed, the initial confusion may be damaging and wrongful."*); Koppers Co. v. Krupp-Koppers GmbH*, 517 F. Supp. 836, 844 [210 USPQ 711] (W.D. Pa. 1981) ("[S]ecuring the initial business contact by the defendant because of an assumed association between the parties is wrongful even though the mistake is later rectified."). *See also Forum Corp. of North America v. Forum, Ltd.*, 903 F.2d 434, 442 n. 2 [14 USPQ2d 1950] (7th Cir. 1990) ("We point out that the fact that confusion as to the source of a product or service is eventually dispelled does not eliminate the trademark infringement which has already occurred."). *But see Astra Pharm. Prods., Inc. v. Beckman Instruments, Inc.*, 718 F.2d 1201, 1206–08 [220 USPQ 786] (1st Cir. 1983) (suggesting that only confusion that affects "the ultimate decision of a purchaser whether to buy a particular product" is actionable); *Teletech Customer Care Mgmt. (Cal.), Inc. v. Tele-Tech Co.*, 977 F. Supp. 1407, 1410, 1414 [42 USPQ2d 1913] (C.D. Cal. 1997) (finding likelihood of initial interest confusion but concluding that such "brief confusion is not cognizable under the trademark laws").

Using another's trademark in one's metatags is much like posting a sign with another's trademark in front of one's store. Suppose West Coast's competitor (let's call it "Blockbuster") puts up a billboard on a highway reading—"West Coast Video: 2 miles ahead at Exit 7"—where West Coast is really located at Exit 8 but Blockbuster is located at Exit 7. Customers looking for West Coast's store will pull off at Exit 7 and drive around looking for it. Unable to locate West Coast, but seeing the Blockbuster store right by the highway entrance, they may simply rent there. Even consumers who prefer West Coast may find it not worth the trouble to continue searching for West Coast since there is a Blockbuster right there. Customers are not confused in the narrow sense: they are fully aware that they are purchasing from Blockbuster and they have no reason to believe that Blockbuster is related to, or in any way sponsored by, West Coast. Nevertheless, the fact that there is only initial consumer confusion does not alter the fact that Blockbuster would be misappropriating West Coast's acquired goodwill. *See Blockbuster*, 869 F. Supp. at 513 (finding trademark infringement where the defendant, a video rental store, attracted customers' initial interest by using a sign confusingly to its competitor's even though confusion would end long before the point of sale or rental); *see also Dr. Seuss*, 109 F.3d at 1405; *Mobil Oil*, 818 F.2d at 260; *Green Prods.*, 992 F. Supp. at 1076.

The few courts to consider whether the use of another's trademark in one's metatags constitutes trademark infringement have ruled in the affirmative. For example, in a case in which Playboy Enterprises, Inc. ("Playboy") sued AsiaFocus International, Inc. ("AsiaFocus") for trademark infringement resulting from AsiaFocus's use of the federally registered trademarks "Playboy" and "Playmate" in its HTML code, a district court granted judgment in Playboy's favor, reasoning that AsiaFocus intentionally misled viewers into believing that its Web site was connected with, or sponsored by, Playboy. *See Playboy Enters. v. AsiaFocus Int'l, Inc.*, No. 97-734, 1998 WL 724000, at *3, *6–*7 (E.D. Va. Apr. 10, 1998).

In a similar case also involving Playboy, a district court in California concluded that Playboy had established a likelihood of success on the merits of its claim that defendants' repeated use of "Playboy" within "machine readable code in Defendants' Internet Web pages, so that the PLAYBOY trademark [was] accessible to individuals or Internet search engines which attempt[ed] to access Plaintiff under Plaintiff's PLAYBOY registered trademark" constituted trademark infringement. *See Playboy Enters. v. Calvin Designer Label*, 985 F. Supp. 1220, 1221 [44 USPQ2d 1156] (N.D. Cal. 1997). The court accordingly enjoined the defendants from using Playboy's marks in buried code or metatags. *See id.* at 1221–22.

In a metatags case with an interesting twist, a district court in Massachusetts also enjoined the use of metatags in a manner that resulted in initial interest confusion. *See Niton*, 27 F. Supp. 2d at 102–05. In that case, the defendant Radiation Monitoring Devices ("RMD") did not simply use Niton Corporation's ("Niton") trademark in its metatags. Instead, RMD's web site directly copied Niton's web site's metatags and HTML code. As a result, whenever a search performed on an Internet search engine listed Niton's web site, it also listed RMD's site. Although the opinion did not speak in terms of initial consumer confusion, the court made clear that its issuance of preliminary injunctive relief was based on the fact that RMD was purposefully diverting people looking for Niton to its web site. *See id.* at 104–05.

Consistently with *Dr. Seuss*, the Second Circuit, and the cases which have addressed trademark infringement through metatags use, we conclude that the Lanham Act bars West Coast from including in its metatags any term confusingly similar with Brookfield's mark. West Coast argues that our holding conflicts with Holiday Inns, in which the Sixth Circuit held that there was no trademark infringement where an alleged infringer merely took advantage of a situation in which confusion was likely to exist and did not affirmatively act to create consumer confusion. *See Holiday Inns*, 86 F.3d at 622 (holding that the use of "1-800-405-4329"—which is equivalent to "1-800-H [zero]LIDAY"—did not infringe Holiday Inn's trademark, "1-800-HOLIDAY"). Unlike the defendant in *Holiday Inns*, however, West Coast was not a passive figure; instead, it acted affirmatively in placing Brookfield's trademark in the metatags of its web site, thereby creating the initial interest confusion. Accordingly, our conclusion comports with *Holiday Inns*.

Contrary to West Coast's contentions, we are not in any way restricting West Coast's right to use terms in a manner which would constitute fair use under the Lanham Act. *See New Kids on the Block v. News Amer. Publ'g, Inc.*, 971 F.2d 302, 306–09 [23 USPQ2d 1534] (9th Cir. 1992); *see also August Storck K.G. v. Nabisco, Inc.*, 59 F.3d 616, 617–18 [35 USPQ2d 1211] (7th Cir. 1995). It is well established that the Lanham Act does not prevent one from using a competitor's mark truthfully to identify the competitor's goods, *see, e.g., Smith v. Chanel, Inc.*, 402 F.2d 562, 563 [159 USPQ 388] (9th Cir. 1968) (stating that a copyist may use the originator's mark to identify the product that it has copied), or in comparative advertisements, *see New Kids on the Block*, 971 F.2d at 306–09. This fair use doctrine applies in cyberspace as it does in the real world. *See Radio Channel Networks, Inc. v. Broadcast. Com, Inc.*, No. 98-4799, 1999 WL 124455, at *5–*6 (S.D.N.Y. Mar. 8, 1999); *Bally Total Fitness Holding Corp. v. Faber*, 29 F. Supp. 2d 1161 (C.D. Cal. 1998); *Welles*, 7 F. Supp. 2d at 1103–04; *Patmont Motor Werks, Inc. v. Gateway Marine, Inc.*, No. 96-2703, 1997 WL 811770, at *3–*4 & n.6 (N.D. Cal. Dec. 18, 1997); *see also Universal Tel-A-Talk*, 1998 WL 767440, at *9.

In *Welles*, the case most on point, Playboy sought to enjoin former Playmate of the Year Terri Welles ("Welles") from using "Playmate" or "Playboy" on her web site featuring photographs of herself. *See* 7 F. Supp. 2d at 1100. Welles's web site advertised the fact that she was a former Playmate of the Year, but minimized the use of Playboy's marks; it also contained numerous disclaimers stating that her site was neither endorsed by nor affiliated with Playboy. The district court found that Welles was using "Playboy" and "Playmate" not as trademarks, but rather as descriptive terms fairly and accurately describing her web page, and that her use of "Playboy" and "Playmate" in her web site's metatags was a permissible, good faith attempt to index the content of her web site. It accordingly concluded that her use was permissible under the trademark laws. *See id.* at 1103–04.

We agree that West Coast can legitimately use an appropriate descriptive term in its metatags. But "MovieBuff" is not such a descriptive term. Even though it differs from "Movie Buff" by only a single space, that difference is pivotal. The term "Movie Buff" is a descriptive term, which is routinely used in the English language to describe a movie devotee. "MovieBuff" is not. The term "MovieBuff" is not in the dictionary. *See Merriam-Webster's Collegiate Dictionary* 762 (10th ed. 1998); *American Heritage College Dictionary* 893 (3d ed. 1997*); Webster's New World College Dictionary* 889 (3d ed. 1997); *Webster's Third New Int'l Dictionary* 1480 (unabridged 1993). Nor has that term been used in any published federal or state court opinion. In light of the fact that it is not a word in the English language, when the term "MovieBuff"is employed, it is used to refer to Brookfield's products and services, rather than to mean "motion picture enthusiast." The proper term for the "motion picture enthusiast" is "Movie Buff," which West Coast certainly can use. It cannot, however, omit the space.

Moreover, West Coast is not absolutely barred from using the term "MovieBuff." As we explained above, that term can be legitimately used to describe Brookfield's product. For example, its web page might well include an advertisement banner such as "Why pay for MovieBuff when you can get the same thing here for FREE?" which clearly employs "MovieBuff" to refer to Brookfield's products. West Coast, however, presently uses Brookfield's trademark not to reference Brookfield's products, but instead to describe its own product (in the case of the domain name) and to attract people to its web site (in the case of the metatags). That is not fair use.... As we have seen, registration of a domain name for a Web site does not trump long-established principles of trademark law. When a firm uses a competitor's trademark in the domain name of its web site, users are likely to be confused as to its source or sponsorship. Similarly, using a competitor's trademark in the metatags of such web site is likely to cause what we have described as initial interest confusion. These forms of confusion are exactly what the trademark laws are designed to prevent.

Accordingly, we reverse and remand this case to the district court with instructions to enter a preliminary injunction in favor of Brookfield in accordance with this opinion.

---

## Notes and Questions

1. In *Playboy Enterprises v. AsiaFocus International, Inc.*, No. Civ. A. 97-734-A, 1998 WL 724000 (E.D. Va. Apr. 10, 1998), the defendants had embedded the words "playboy" and "playmate" within their computer source code, which is visible to search engines. The plaintiff, publisher of *Playboy* magazine, owned trademark rights to these words. The Court stated that the defendants had "purposefully employed deceptive tactics to attract consumers to their Web site under the guise that their sites are sponsored by or somehow affiliated with [the plaintiff.]" *Id.* at *3. The court also stated that the defendants' "purposeful tactic of embedding the trademarks PLAYMATE and PLAYBOY in the hidden computer source code [is a] strategy [that] epitomizes the 'blurring' of [the plaintiff's] trademarks." *Id.* at *8.

2. In yet another action brought by Playboy Enterprises, the defendants keyed various "adult entertainment ads to a group of over 450 terms related to adult entertainment, including the terms 'playboy' and 'playmate.'" *See Playboy Enterprises, Inc. v. Netscape Communications Corp.*, 55 F. Supp. 2d 1070, 1072 (C.D. Cal. 1999), aff'd, 202 F.3d 278 (9th Cir. 1999). The court held that the plaintiff did not show that the defendants used the plaintiff's trademarks in commerce or that confusion likely would result from the defendants' use of the marks, and observed that the words "playboy" and "playmate" are "English words in their own right." *Id.* at 1073. The court distinguished the holding in *Brookfield Communications, Inc. v. West Coast Entertainment Corp.*, 174 F.3d 1036, on the ground that the trademark in issue in that case was not an English word "in its own right." *Playboy Enterprises, Inc. v. Netscape Communications Corp.*, 55 F. Supp. 2d at 1074. As well, the use by the defendant of the plaintiff's trademark in *Brookfield* "was more suspect" because there the parties were both on-line providers of film industry information, and thus competed in the same market. *Id.*

3. A United Kingdom court reportedly ordered a company to pay £15,000 damages plus costs on a claim that trademarks belonging to a rival company were improperly included in the defendant's metatags. *See* Linda Harrison, *UK Court Slaps Reseller for Metatag Squatting*, Register (June 2, 2000) <http://www.theregister.co.uk/000602-000023.html>.

4. How does "initial interest confusion" impact on the analysis of the use of linking, framing, and metataging techniques to drive traffic to a web-site? In *Brookfield Communications, Inc. v. West Coast Entertainment Corp.*, 174 F.3d 1036, the Ninth Circuit used the term to connote the confusion that may result when a user conducts a search using a trademark term and the results of the search include web-sites not sponsored by the holder of the trademark search term, but rather of competitors. *Id.* at 1062–64; *see also Playboy Enterprises, Inc. v. Netscape Communications Corp.*, 55 F. Supp. 2d at 1074. The Ninth Circuit reasoned that the user may be diverted to a site that the trademark owner did not sponsor, and only realize the diversion upon arrival at the competitor's site.

5. In *Playboy Enterprises, Inc. v. Netscape Communications Corp.*, 55 F. Supp. 2d at 1075, the district court stated that the defendant's use

is quite unlike that of a devious placement of a road sign bearing false information. This case presents a scenario more akin to a driver pulling off the freeway in response to a sign that reads "Fast Food Burgers" to find a well-known fast food burger restaurant, next to which stands a billboard that reads: "Better Burgers: 1 Block further." The driver, previously enticed by the prospect of a burger from the well-known restaurant, now decides she wants to explore other burger options. Assuming that the same entity owns the land on which both the burger restaurant and the competitor's billboard stand, should that entity be liable to the burger restaurant for diverting the driver?

*Id.*

# Glossary[*]

ACCESS SOFTWARE PROVIDER: a provider of software that screens, allows, or disallows content; selects or analyzes content; or transmits, receives, displays, caches, and searches for content

ADVANCED RESEARCH PROJECTS AGENCY: part of the U.S. Defense Department; began to connect computers in the 1960s

AMERICAN STANDARD CODE FOR INFORMATION INTERCHANGE: a set of 128 alphanumeric and special control characters

APPLET: a program that is downloaded to a user's computer for execution within another application; Java applets, for example, work with Web browser software to enable animated Web presentations

ARPA: *see* ADVANCED RESEARCH PROJECTS AGENCY

ARPANET: ARPA's experimental project of linked computers and computer networks operated by defense contractors and university laboratories conducting defense-related research

ASCII: *see* American Standard Code for Information Interchange

ATTACHMENT: a file appended to an e-mail message

BANDWITH: the amount of data received during a given time period through an Internet connection (the greater the bandwith, the faster the information can be delivered to the computer)

BANNER AD: an advertisement found on the screen of a Web page, commonly located above the displayed text

B2B: refers to business to business transactions

B2C: refers to business to consumer transactions

BBS: *see* BULLETIN BOARD SYSTEM

BITMAP: a common image format (.bmp) defined by a rectangular pattern of pixels

BLURRING: a form of trademark dilution that occurs when customers see a trademark used to identify goods or services that are not produced by the trademark owner

BOOKMARK: a pointer to a particular web-site; within browsers, interesting Web pages can be "bookmarked" or saved for expedient return to the site

BOT: short for "robot;" a computer system that runs automatically

---

[*] This glossary is intended to serve as a guide to assist the reader. Many of the terms referenced herein are susceptible to multiple definitions depending upon the context, custom and usage, and whether they are defined by statute(s) or judicial decisions.

**BROADCAST:** to send the same message simultaneously to multiple recipients

**BROWSE:** to call up, view, or open a web-site onto a computer screen

**BROWSER:** a software program run on a client computer designed to facilitate the locating, viewing, and downloading of Web pages

**BULLETIN BOARD SYSTEM:** a computer-based message center that allows users to access it remotely and to post messages to be accessed by other users

**BYTE:** a bit is the smallest unit of information, indicating the presence or absence of a single feature; a byte is a group of bits processed as one unit of data

**CACHE:** a reserved region of memory where frequently-accessed and/or recently-accessed data can be stored for rapid retrieval

**CACHING:** the process of temporarily storing information in a computer's memory so it can be repeatedly and expeditiously accessed

**CGI:** *see* COMMON GATEWAY INTERFACE

**CGI SCRIPT:** *see* COMMON GATEWAY INTERFACE SCRIPT

**CHAT ROOM:** an on-line forum that enables an individual to communicate with others as a group; messages are exchanged almost immediately

**CLICK:** use of a computer mouse to command a computer function

**CLICK LICENSE:** an on-line license agreement that requires the licensee (i.e., the user) to accept or agree to specific terms and conditions imposed by the licensor before the licensee is provided access to content or software that is being distributed electronically by the licensor

**CLIENT:** a software application (like a Web browser) or computer that connects to and relies on a host server for some of its functionality

**CLOSED DATABASE:** private information services with storehouses of information, typically accessed with an appropriate password and access software, that are not linked together into a single whole

**CLOSED NETWORK:** a network that is not linked to other computers or networks

**CMI:** *see* COPYRIGHT MANAGEMENT INFORMATION

**COMMON GATEWAY INTERFACE:** a server-side specification for how an HTTP server communicates dynamically with users

**COMMON GATEWAY INTERFACE SCRIPT:** a program that processes information transmitted to the Web server; for example, the means by which a web-site can process a fill-in form

**CONTENT PROVIDER:** *see* INFORMATION CONTENT PROVIDER

**COOKIE:** client-side persistent information that allows Web servers to have the Web browser store information about a user's browsing habits, such as which web-sites the user previously visited

**COPYRIGHT MANAGEMENT INFORMATION:** information identifying the work, writer, director, terms and conditions of use, and any other information as the Register of Copyrights may prescribe by regulation (although information concerning users of works is excluded)

**CROSS-MATCHING:** the comparison of data maintained by governmental agencies about the same individual

CYBERSPACE: refers to the digital world constructed by computers, such as the Internet; a decentralized, global medium of communication that links people, institutions, corporations, and governments around the world

CYBERSQUATTING: registration of a domain name in order to deprive the rightful owner of it so as to profit from its sale or from customer confusion as a result of the use

DATABASE: a computerized compilation of information

DECRYPTION: the reverse process of encryption; i.e., decoding the ciphertext message or document into the original plaintext

DEEP LINKING: direction to an interior page of a web-site where visitors are provided with more detailed information on a particular topic; thus, the linking site creates a link to a page located within the linked-to site that is not the latter's home page

DERIVATIVE WORK: a work based upon one or more preexisting works; includes editorial revisions, annotations, translations, adaptations, elaborations, or other modifying details which, as a whole, represents an original work of authorship

DIGITAL ID: electronic codes that provide an Internet user with a means of proving his identity in electronic transactions; authentication of the Digital ID by a Certification Authority (usually the party issuing the Digital ID) allows the receiver of a digital message to be confident as to both the identity of the sender and the integrity of the message

DISPLAY: to present a work or copy thereof, such as by showing a copy of the material on screen

DISTRIBUTED MESSAGE DATABASE: generally user-sponsored newsgroups that are open and discuss particular topics

DOMAIN NAME: the unique name that identifies an Internet site; domain names always have two or more segments, separated by dots (the segment on the left is the most specific, while the part on the right, i.e., the "top level," is the most general); domain names allow a user to reference Internet sites without knowledge of the corresponding IP numeric addresses

DOWNLOAD: the process of copying data, including text and graphics, such as from the Internet onto a computer

E-BOOK: a book that can be downloaded and read on a computer device

E-COMMERCE: conducting business transactions on-line; short for "electronic commerce"

ELECTRONIC BULLETIN BOARD: *see* BULLETIN BOARD SYSTEM

ELECTRONIC MAIL: messages and other files sent from one user to another over a communications network; colloquially known as "e-mail"

E-MAIL: *see* ELECTRONIC MAIL

ENCRYPTION: the process by which the data is transformed into coded text, in order to avoid interception, tampering, and forging of the data

EXTRANET: refers to a company-owned, private portion of the global network that is available to a select group of external parties

F2F: face to face

FAQ: Frequently Asked Questions

**FILE TRANSFER PROTOCOL**: a set of rules for exchanging files between computers via the Internet

**FILTERING**: the process of screening incoming computer content to eliminate certain sites because of their subject matter

**FIREWALL**: acts as security system that prevents unauthorized access to or from an internal network by monitoring traffic between a web-site and the Internet

**FLAME**: an e-mail or chat group message in which the author addresses the reader in an aggressive, often personal manner

**FLAME WAR**: an argument amongst individuals in newsgroups that degenerates into multiple, and often harsh personal attacks

**FRAME**: a feature supported by most modern Web browsers than enables the Web author to divide the browser display area into two or more separate sections; frames provide flexibility in designing and displaying Web pages, but they may not be evenly supported by the installed browser base

**FRAMING**: when one web-site brings content from another web-site into a window that appears on the original framing site so that two or more web-sites appear on the same screen simultaneously

**FREE-NETS**: community networks

**FTP**: *see* FILE TRANSFER PROTOCL

**GATEWAY**: computer hardware and software that allow users to connect from one network to another (dissimilar) network

**GIF**: *see* GRAPHICS INTERCHANGE FORMAT

**GRAPHICS INTERCHANGE FORMAT**: a common image format (many images seen on Web pages are GIF files)

**GRAPHICS USER INTERFACE**: a program interface that uses the computer's graphic capabilities to render the program easier to use

**GUI**: *see* GRAPHIC USER INTERFACE

**HOME PAGE**: the first page of a web-site; a Web document that provides a set of links designed to represent the origin through links, and guides the user directly or indirectly to information about or relevant to that origin, including from one computer to another, from one document to another, and from one page within a particular web-site to another

**HOST**: any computer on a network that is a repository for services available to other computers on the network

**HREF**: *see* HYPERTEXT REFERENCE LINK

**HTML**: *see* HYPERTEXT MARKUP LANGUAGE

**HTTP**: *see* HYPERTEXT TRANSFER PROTOCOL

**HYPERLINK**: a connection between two anchors; clicking on one anchor will take the user to the linked anchor; hyperlinking can be within the same web-site or from one web-site to another

**HYPERTEXT**: generally, any text that contains "links" to other information; thus, words or phrases in the document that can be chosen by a reader and that cause another document to be retrieved and displayed; enables users to link directly from one source of information to another, irrespective of the type or physical location of each computer

**HYPERTEXT MARKUP LANGUAGE:** the coding language used to create hypertext documents for use on the Web; HTML files are meant to be viewed using a browser

**HYPERTEXT REFERENCE LINK:** instructs the browser to go elsewhere; (e.g., to a different page with in the same site, or to a site other than the local web-site)

**HYPERTEXT TRANSFER PROTOCOL:** the protocol for moving hypertext files across the Internet; requires an HTTP client program on one end and an HTTP server program on the other end

**ICAAN:** *See* INTERNET CORPORATION FOR ASSIGNED NAMES AND NUMBERS

**ICON:** a symbol that replaces the need for written instructions and launches an application, program, or performs a hyperlink when clicked

**IMG LINK:** an in-line link that retrieves an image that is located in a separate file into the text and onto the page being viewed

**INFORMATION CONTENT PROVIDER:** any person or entity that is responsible, in whole or part, for the creation or development of information provided through the Internet or any other interactive computer service

**INFORMATION SUPERHIGHWAY:** a term, attributed to Al Gore, used in connection with the Clinton/Gore administration's plan to de-regulate communication services; the term has been commonly used to refer to the Internet

**INFRASTRUCTURE:** the physical architecture of a network

**INTEGRATED SERVICES DIGITAL NETWORK:** a system of all-digital, high bandwidth telephone lines allowing the simultaneous delivery of audio, video, and data

**INTERACTIVE:** refers to participation by the user in or control of what occurs on the computer screen

**INTERACTIVE COMPUTER SERVICE:** any information service, system, or access software provider that provides or enables computer access by multiple users to a computer server

**INTERNET:** a decentralized, complex web of smaller regional networks, designed to be a self-maintaining series of redundant links between computers and computer networks, capable of rapidly transmitting communications without direct human involvement or control, and with the automatic ability to re-route communications if one or more individual links were damaged or otherwise became unavailable; technically, a system comprised of thousands of host computers or servers, all connected to one another via their respective Internet Protocol addresses

**INTERNET CORPORATION FOR ASSIGNED NAMES AND NUMBERS:** established to manage the domain name system; has enacted a Uniform Domain Name Dispute Resolution Policy to govern the resolution of disputes over the use of domain names

**INTERNET PROTOCOL ADDRESS:** an identifier for a computer or device on a TCP/IP network; IP addresses are written as four numbers separated by periods, with the numbers ranging from 0 to 255

**INTERNET RELAY CHAT:** the system that allows Internet users to conduct on-line text-based communication with one or more other users

**INTERNET SERVICE PROVIDER:** a company that provides the user with a connection to the Internet via either a dial-up connection or a direct connection

**INTER-NIC:** the Network Information Center which had registered domain names

**INTRANET:** commonly refers to a company-owned, private portion of the global network which is available to staff but not openly accessible to the company's customers or competitors, or to the public

**IP ADDRESS:** *see* INTERNET PROTOCOL ADDRESS

**IRC:** *see* INTERNET RELAY CHAT

**ISDN:** *see* INTEGRATED SERVICES DIGITAL NETWORK

**ISP:** *see* INTERNET SERVICE PROVIDER

**JAVA:** a programming language developed by Sun Microsystems, similar to C++ but with the flexibility to work with any operating system

**KEYWORD:** a word or group of words used to search for information via a search engine

**LAN:** *see* LOCAL AREA NETWORK

**LINKING:** the use of selected words or graphics on a Web page, typically highlighted, to direct the user to another Web page within or outside the web-site

**LISTSERV:** allows distribution of comments about particular subjects of interest to a group of people; sometimes referred to as a "mail exploder"

**LOCAL AREA NETWORK:** a group of linked computers

**MAIL EXPLODER:** *see* LISTSERV

**MEGABYTE:** one million bytes

**META-DATA:** a framework designed to describe the characteristics of a particular data set, such as how, when, and by whom the data was collected and how it is formatted; meta-data is integral to managing and leveraging corporate data warehouses

**METATAGS:** part of the Web page programming language that is embedded on a Web page, but not visible to the end user; such document information can be extracted by servers and clients for use in identifying, indexing, and cataloging specialized document meta-data

**MIRROR SITE:** an Internet site set up as an alternate to a busy site containing copies of all files stored at the primary location

**MIRRORING:** the act of copying all or substantially all of the contents of a server to a remote server

**MODEM:** refers to "modulator-demodulator;" a device or program that enables a computer to transmit data over telephone lines to a larger computer or computer network that is directly or indirectly connected to the Internet

**MODERATED NEWSGROUP:** a newsgroup that has its messages monitored by an individual who screens the messages, usually for purposes of propriety and relevance

**MOUSETRAPPING:** disabling a browser's "back" and "exit" commands

**MUD:** *see* MULTI-USER DUNGEON

**MULTI-MEDIA:** refers to a variety of products made possible through the integration of sound, graphics, film, and other works in interactive computer systems

**MULTI-USER:** a computer system that supports two or more simultaneous users

**MULTI-USER DUNGEON:** utilizes shared software to create interactive scenarios with animated characters in real-time; textual descriptions furnished by each participant are displayed on screen; also refers to multi-user dimension

**NET:** abbreviation for the Internet

**NETIQUETTE:** unofficial rules and conventions of e-mail and chat room etiquette (e.g., capital letters generally are not used because they indicate SHOUTING)

**NETWORK:** linked group of computers

**NODE:** any single computer connected to a network

**ON-LINE:** refers to the period of time when one is connected to the Internet

**ON-LINE SERVICE PROVIDER:** *see* Internet service provider

**ON-LINE SERVICES:** services that offer access to nationwide computer networks

**ONE-TO-ONE MESSAGING:** an automatic mailing list service, such as a listserv

**ONE-TO-MANY MESSAGING:** addressing and transmitting a message to one or more people, re-routed though a central control point

**PACKET:** a chunk of data; the TCP/IP protocol breaks large data files into smaller packets for transmission; when the data reaches its destination, the protocol ensures that all packets have arrived without error

**PACKET SWITCHING:** communication protocols that allow individual messages to be sub-divided into smaller packets that are sent independently to the destination, and then are automatically reassembled by the receiving computer

**PATENT AND TRADEMARK OFFICE:** the U.S. governmental agency charged with processing and issuing patent and trademark applications and registrations

**PGP:** *see* PRETTY GOOD PRIVACY

**PHREAKING:** the unauthorized use of telephone services

**PICS:** *see* PLATFORM FOR INTERNET CONTENT SELECTION

**PIRATICAL:** copies made without the necessary authorization of the copyright lawful owner

**PLATFORM FOR INTERNET CONTENT SELECTION:** a program launched by the World Wide Web Consortium to develop technical standards that support parents' ability to filter and screen material that their children access on the Web, and for third parties and individual content providers to rate content on the Web

**PLUG-IN:** a small application that extends the built-in capabilities of the Web browser

**PORT:** an interface on a computer to which a device can be connected

**POST:** to place a message in an on-line forum or newsgroup

**POSTING:** a message placed by a user in an on-line forum or newsgroup

**PRETTY GOOD PRIVACY:** an encryption scheme that uses the "public key" approach; messages are encrypted using a publicly available key but can only be deciphered by the intended recipient via a private key

**PROTOCOLS:** standards for the transfer of data between different types of computer networks

**PTO:** *see* PATENT AND TRADEMARK OFFICE

**QBE:** *see* QUERY BY EXAMPLE

**QUERY BY EXAMPLE:** a method of formatting queries to request information from a database management system

**REAL-TIME COMMENT:** engaging in immediate on-line dialogue

**REAL-TIME REMOTE COMPUTER UTILIZATION:** a method of using information by accessing and controlling remote computers in real time using "telnet"

**RE-BOOT:** to re-start the computer

**REMOTE INFORMATION RETRIEVAL:** searching for and retrieving information located on remote computers

**REVERSE CONFUSION:** when a subsequent user selects a trademark that is likely to cause consumers to believe, erroneously, that the goods or services marketed by the prior user are produced by the subsequent user

**REVERSE ENGINEERING:** the process by which one begins with a final product and works backwards to analyze the method(s) by which it was developed

**SEARCH ENGINE:** a program that searches documents for specified keywords and returns a list of the documents where the keywords were found (although search engine is really a general class of programs, the term is often used specifically to describe systems that enable Web users to search for documents); typically, a search engine works by sending out a "spider" to fetch as many documents as possible; another program, called an "indexer," then reads these documents and creates an index based on the words contained in each document; each search engine uses a proprietary algorithm to create its indices so that, ideally, only meaningful results are returned for each query

**SECURE ELECTRONIC TRANSACTION:** a protocol that uses crytography to enable buyers and sellers to exchange credit-card information over the Internet securely

**SECURE SOCKETS LAYER:** a protocol used to transmit encrypted documents via the Internet

**SERVER:** a host computer or a host software application that provides a specified kind of service to client computers; also refers to the software that provides information

**SET:** *see* SECURE ELECTRONIC TRANSACTION

**SITE:** a Web page

**SOFTWARE:** provides instructions that enable a computer to perform tasks that serve the user's needs

**SPAM:** "junk" or unsolicited and unwanted e-mail messages

**SPIDER:** a program that "crawls" the Web to review web-sites to build an index; often gives priority to the terms in the metatags when building the index; sometimes called a "webcrawler"

**SSL:** *see* SECURE SOCKETS LAYER

**SURFING:** browsing or searching the Web

**TACKING:** constructive use theory whereby a trademark holder essentially seeks to "tack" his first use date in the earlier mark onto the subsequent mark

**TAGGING:** labeling content

**TARNISHMENT:** a form of trademark dilution that occurs when the use of a trademark similar to one owned by another presents the danger that consumers will form an unfavorable association with the trademark

**TCP/IP:** *see* TRANSMISSION CONTROL PROTOCOL/INTERNET PROTOCOL

**THREAD:** a sequence of responses to an initial message posting, which enables the user to follow or join an individual discussion in a newsgroup from amongst multiple postings

**TLD:** *see* TOP LEVEL DOMAIN

**TOADING:** unilaterally removing an offender from a list of authorized participants

**TOP LEVEL DOMAIN:** the suffix affixed to an Internet domain name that is part of an Internet site's address (e.g., ".com," ".org.," ".net," ".gov," ".edu")

**TRADE SECRET:** information, including a formula, pattern, compilation, program, device, method, technique, or process that derives independent economic value from not being generally known to or readily ascertainable by others

**TRANSMISSION CONTROL PROTOCOL/INTERNET PROTOCOL:** the suite of protocols that defines the Internet

**UNIFORM RESOURCE LOCATOR:** the standard way to denote the address of any resource on the Internet that is part of the Web; specifies the protocol and identifies the IP address or domain name where the resource is located

**UNMODERATED NEWSGROUP:** a newsgroup that is not monitored; messages are automatically forwarded to adjacent USENET servers that furnish access to the newsgroup

**URL:** *see* UNIFORM RESOURCE LOCATOR

**USER FRIENDLY:** features that facilitate use of a computer

**USER ID:** *see* USER NAME

**USER NAME:** the name by which the computer system identifies the user; also known as a user-id

**VIRUS:** a malicious program that can spread from one computer to others; viruses often can replicate themselves

**WEB CRAWLER:** *see* SPIDER

**WEB PAGE:** a single page of information within a web-site; Web pages are the basic building blocks of web-sites, like the pages in a book

**WEB-SITE:** a single Web page or collection of related Web pages found at a single address

**WEBMASTER:** one who is responsible for managing and administering a web-site, such as by creating Web pages, monitoring traffic, updating the site, and responding to user feedback

**WINSOCK:** an application interface used by programmers for developing Windows applications that can communicate with other computers via the TCP/IP protocol; short for "Windows Socket"

**WWW:** *see* WORLD WIDE WEB

**WORLD WIDE WEB:** a subset of the Internet which uses a combination of text, graphics, audio, and video to provide information to users worldwide; "an abstract (imaginary) space of information" (Tim Berners-Lee, Frequently Asked Questions, *available at* <http://www.w3.org/people/Berners-Lee-Bio.htm/FAQ.html>)

**WORM:** typically refers to a virus; a computer program that can replicate itself

**Y2K:** year 2000, often used in the context of referring to concerns that computer programs and systems would be affected by two-digit date storage programming

# Table of Cases

# Index